Contemporary Labor Economics

Twelfth Edition

Campbell R. McConnell
University of Nebraska

Stanley L. Brue
Pacific Lutheran University

David A. Macpherson
Trinity University

Mc
Graw
Hill

CONTEMPORARY LABOR ECONOMICS

mheducation.com/highered

About the Authors

Campbell R. McConnell earned his PhD from the University of Iowa after receiving degrees from Cornell College and the University of Illinois. He taught at the University of Nebraska–Lincoln from 1953 until his retirement in 1990. He is also the coauthor of the leading introductory economics textbook *Economics,* 21/e (McGraw-Hill/Irwin), as well as *Essentials of Economics,* 3/e, and the brief editions of *Macroeconomics* and *Microeconomics* (all McGraw-Hill/Irwin). He has also edited readers for the principles and labor economics courses. He is a recipient of both the University of Nebraska Distinguished Teaching Award and the James A. Lake Academic Freedom Award and is past president of the Midwest Economics Association. His primary areas of interest are labor economics and economic education. He has an impressive collection of jazz recordings and enjoys reading jazz history.

Stanley L. Brue did his undergraduate work at Augustana College (SD) and received its Distinguished Achievement Award in 1991. He received his PhD from the University of Nebraska–Lincoln. He was a professor at Pacific Lutheran University, where he has been honored as recipient of the Burlington Northern Faculty Achievement Award. He has also received the national Leavey Award for excellence in economic education. Professor Brue has served as national president and chair of the Board of Trustees of Omicron Delta Epsilon International Economics Honorary. He is coauthor of *Economic Scenes,* 5/e (Prentice-Hall); *Economics,* 21/e (McGraw-Hill/Irwin); *The Evolution of Economic Thought,* 8/e (South-Western); *Essentials of Economics,* 3/e (McGraw-Hill/Irwin); and the brief editions of *Macroeconomics* and *Microeconomics* (McGraw-Hill/Irwin). For relaxation, he enjoys international travel, attending sporting events, and skiing with family and friends.

David A. Macpherson received his undergraduate degree and PhD from The Pennsylvania State University. He is the E. M. Stevens Professor of Economics at Trinity University. Professor Macpherson is the author of many articles in leading labor economics and industrial relations journals, including the *Journal of Labor Economics, Industrial and Labor Relations Review,* and the *Journal of Human Resources.* He is coauthor of the annual *Union Membership and Earnings Data Book: Compilations from the Current Population Survey,* published by the Bureau of National Affairs. He is also coauthor of *Pensions and Productivity* and *Economics: Private and Public Choice,* 16/e. His specialty is applied labor economics. Professor Macpherson has served as vice-president of the Southern Economic Association. His current research interests include pensions, discrimination, industry deregulation, labor unions, and the minimum wage. He enjoys listening to classic rock, seeing movies and plays, seeing the world, and going to the seashore with his family.

Preface

THE TWELFTH EDITION

One benefit of authoring a text that has met the test of the market is the opportunity to revise. Revision provides for improvement—to delete the archaic and install the novel, to rectify errors of omission or commission, to rewrite misleading or obscure statements, to introduce more relevant illustrations, to bring more recent data to bear, to upgrade organizational structure, and to enhance pedagogical aids—in short, to build on an accepted framework of ideas. We feel that those who examine this new twelfth edition of *Contemporary Labor Economics* will agree that we have fully exploited this opportunity.

This new edition incorporates many significant changes, several of which were motivated by the comments of colleagues and students. We are especially grateful to the scholars cited in the acknowledgments who provided reviews of the various editions or commented on drafts of the new edition.

New Topics and Expanded Discussions

New, revised, and expanded discussions permeate the twelfth edition. Some of the more important changes are:

- **Economic Trends** This edition includes a number of discussions related to recent economic trends. For example, this edition includes new World of Work boxes on the decline in labor force participation due to the opioid crisis and video gaming (Chapter 3), the increasing importance of social skills (Chapter 8), and the gender wage gap in the shift to a gig economy (Chapter 14). The text also includes new discussions of past and future changes in labor supply (Chapter 3) and legalization of cannabis (Chapter 5). This edition also has updated data throughout the text.

- **Public policy issues** This edition includes a number of new discussions of public policy issues, including politician pay, the opioid crisis, cannabis, health care reform, undocumented immigration, unions, executive compensation, military spending, climate change, and discrimination.

New World of Work Sections

Sixteen of the World of Work boxes are new to this edition. The new titles to this edition are: Labor Supply of Politicians; The Labor Supply Effects of Winning a Lottery Prize; Video Gaming and the Decline in Labor Supply of Young Men; The Opioid Crisis and the Decline in Labor Force Participation; College as Country Club; Ahead of the Pack: Veterinary Occupations are Growing Fast; [Job] Locked and [Un]Loaded; Rising Importance of Social Skills; Labor Supply of Undocumented Workers; *Janus* Decision and Public Sector Unions; Unions and Executive Compensation; The Impact of Military Cutbacks on Civilians; Climate Change and Occupational Health; Does Ban the Box Cause Discrimination?; Evolution of a Family Friendly Occupation; and The Gender Wage Gap in the Gig Economy.

Learning Objectives

At the beginning of every chapter, a learning objective is provided for each heading within the chapter.

DISTINGUISHING FEATURES

At the hazard of immodesty, we feel that this volume embodies a number of features that distinguish it from other books in the field.

Content

In the area of subject matter, the emphasis in Chapter 6 and elsewhere on allocative efficiency is both unique and desirable. The efficiency emphasis makes students realize that *society* has an interest in how labor markets function. Chapter 7 brings together the literature on the principal–agent problem and the "new economics of personnel" in a single, focused chapter. Chapter 8 on the wage structure has been consistently praised by instructors for providing a thorough, systematic treatment of wage differentials and a simplified presentation of the hedonic wage theory. The comprehensive analyses of the impacts of unions and government on labor markets found in Chapters 10–13 also set this book apart.

Chapter 14 provides extensive analysis of labor market discrimination and antidiscrimination policies. Chapter 15 discusses job search within and outside the firm. Chapter 16 confines its focus almost entirely to the distribution of personal *earnings,* rather than the usual discussion of the distribution of *income* and the poverty problem. We believe this approach is more relevant for a textbook on *labor* economics. The critical topic of labor productivity has been largely ignored or treated in a piecemeal fashion in other books. We have upgraded this topic by according it extensive treatment in Chapter 17. Chapter 18 looks at employment and unemployment through a stock–flow perspective and uses the aggregate demand–aggregate supply model to examine natural versus cyclic unemployment. Finally, the appendix provides a comprehensive discussion of information sources that can be used to widen and deepen the reader's understanding of the field.

Organization and Presentation

We have put great stress on the logical organization of subject matter, not only chapter by chapter but within each chapter. We have sought to develop the subject matter logically from micro to macro, from simple theory to real-world complications, and from analysis to policy. Similarly, considerable time has been spent in seeking the optimal arrangement of topics within each chapter. Chapter subheadings have been used liberally; our feeling is that the student should always be aware of the organizational structure and directional flow of the subject matter.

Many key topics of labor economics will be intellectually challenging for most students. We have tried not to impair student understanding with clumsy or oblique exposition. Our purpose is to communicate effectively with students. To this end, we have taken great care that our writing be clear, direct, and uncluttered. It is our goal that the material contained herein be highly accessible to the typical college undergraduate who has limited training in economics.

Pedagogical Features

We have included a variety of pedagogical devices that instructors tell us significantly contribute to student understanding. First, the introduction of each chapter states the goals of the chapter and, in many cases, relates the chapter to prior or future chapters. In addition, the learning objectives for each major head in the chapter are provided. Second, end-of-chapter summaries provide a concise, point-by-point recapitulation of each chapter. Third, key terms and concepts are highlighted at the end of each chapter, and a comprehensive glossary of these and other terms is located at the end of the book. Fourth, ample lists of questions are provided at the end of each chapter. These range from open-ended discussion questions to numerical problems that let students test their understanding of basic analytic concepts. Fifth, each chapter includes one or two Internet exercises and links that help students increase their understanding of the material as well as obtain the most current data available. Sixth, relevant historical statistics that are valuable to both students and instructors are included at the end of the text. Seventh, the within-chapter "Quick Review" summaries and "Your Turn" questions should help students identify key points and study for exams. Furthermore, as indicated previously, the appendix of the book lists and discusses ways the interested reader can update statistical materials found in the book and continue the learning process beyond the course. Finally, we have included 67 short "World of Work" minireadings in this edition.

Supplements

The following ancillaries are available for quick download and convenient access via the Instructor Resource material available through McGraw-Hill Connect®.

Instructor's Manual   *Contemporary Labor Economics* is accompanied by a comprehensive Instructor's Manual by author David Macpherson. Among other features, it contains chapter outlines and learning objectives, and answers to end-of-chapter text questions.

PowerPoint Slides   An extensive set of PowerPoint slides is available for each chapter. These slides, which highlight the main points of each chapter using animation, are available via the instructor resource material available through McGraw-Hill Connect®.

Test Bank

Authored by David Macpherson, the *Test Bank* offers multiple-choice and fill-in-the-blank questions categorized by level of difficulty, AACSB learning categories, Bloom's taxonomy, and topic.

Computerized Test Bank

McGraw-Hill's EZ Test is a flexible and easy-to-use electronic resting program that allows you to create tests from book-specific items. It accommodates a wide range of question types, and you can add your own questions. Multiple versions of the test can be created, and any test can be exported for use with course management systems. EZ Test Online gives you a place to administer your EZ Test-created exams and quizzes online. In addition, you can access the test bank through McGraw-Hill Connect Plus.

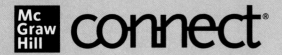

FOR INSTRUCTORS

You're in the driver's seat.

Want to build your own course? No problem. Prefer to use our turnkey, prebuilt course? Easy. Want to make changes throughout the semester? Sure. And you'll save time with Connect's auto-grading too.

65%

Less Time Grading

Laptop: McGraw-Hill; Woman/dog: George Doyle/Getty Images

They'll thank you for it.

Adaptive study resources like SmartBook® 2.0 help your students be better prepared in less time. You can transform your class time from dull definitions to dynamic debates. Find out more about the powerful personalized learning experience available in SmartBook 2.0 at **www.mheducation.com/highered/ connect/smartbook**

Make it simple, make it affordable.

Connect makes it easy with seamless integration using any of the major Learning Management Systems— Blackboard®, Canvas, and D2L, among others—to let you organize your course in one convenient location. Give your students access to digital materials at a discount with our inclusive access program. Ask your McGraw-Hill representative for more information.

Padlock: Jobalou/Getty Images

Solutions for your challenges.

A product isn't a solution. Real solutions are affordable, reliable, and come with training and ongoing support when you need it and how you want it. Our Customer Experience Group can also help you troubleshoot tech problems— although Connect's 99% uptime means you might not need to call them. See for yourself at **status. mheducation.com**

Checkmark: Jobalou/Getty Images

FOR STUDENTS

Effective, efficient studying.

Connect helps you be more productive with your study time and get better grades using tools like SmartBook 2.0, which highlights key concepts and creates a personalized study plan. Connect sets you up for success, so you walk into class with confidence and walk out with better grades.

Study anytime, anywhere.

Download the free ReadAnywhere app and access your online eBook or SmartBook 2.0 assignments when it's convenient, even if you're offline. And since the app automatically syncs with your eBook and SmartBook 2.0 assignments in Connect, all of your work is available every time you open it. Find out more at **www.mheducation.com/readanywhere**

> *"I really liked this app—it made it easy to study when you don't have your textbook in front of you."*
>
> - Jordan Cunningham, Eastern Washington University

No surprises.

The Connect Calendar and Reports tools keep you on track with the work you need to get done and your assignment scores. Life gets busy; Connect tools help you keep learning through it all.

Calendar: owattaphotos/Getty Images

Learning for everyone.

McGraw-Hill works directly with Accessibility Services Departments and faculty to meet the learning needs of all students. Please contact your Accessibility Services office and ask them to email accessibility@mheducation.com, or visit **www.mheducation.com/about/accessibility** for more information.

Top: Jenner Images/Getty Images, Left: Hero Images/Getty Images, Right: Hero Images/Getty Images

Acknowledgments

We would like to express our thanks for the many useful comments and suggestions provided by colleagues who reviewed previous editions of this text during the development stage:

Neil Alper
Northeastern University

John Antel
University of Houston

Martin Asher
Villanova University

Peter S. Barth
University of Connecticut-Storrs

Clare Battista
California Polytechnic State University

Keith A. Bender
University of Wisconsin-Milwaukee

Sherrilyn Billger
Illinois State University

Bruce Brown
University of California-Los Angeles

Don Bruce
University of Tennessee

Clive Bull
New York University

Robert Catlett
Emporia State University

David H. Ciscel
Memphis State University

Vito Colapietro
William Jewell College

John Conant
Indiana State University-Terre Haute

Kelley Cullen
Eastern Washington University

Greg Delemeester
Marietta College

Michael J. Dinoto
University of Idaho

Arthur Dobbelaere
Loyola University

Peter B. Doeringer
Boston University

Paul Engelmann
University of Central Missouri

Abdollah Ferdowsi
Ferris State University

William D. Ferguson
Grinnell College

Roger Frantz
San Diego State University

Scott Fuess, Jr.
University of Nebraska-Lincoln

Robert Gitter
Ohio Wesleyan University

Lonnie M. Golden
University of Wisconsin

Daphne Greenwood
University of Colorado at Colorado Springs

Richard Hansen
Southeast Missouri State University

Michael D. Harsh
Randolph-Macon College

Julia Heath
Memphis State University

Jack Hou
California State University-Long Beach

Yu Hsing
Southeastern Louisiana University

David Huffman
Bridgewater College

Sarah Jackson
Indiana University of Pennsylvania-Indiana

Carl P. Kaiser
Washington and Lee University

Melanie Fox Kean
Austin College

Steven J. Kerno, Jr.
Iowa Wesleyan College

Douglas Kruse
Rutgers University

Julia Lane
University of Louisville

Kevin Lang
Boston University

Laura Leete
Case Western Reserve University

Robert I. Lerman
The Urban Institute

Haizheng Li
Georgia Institute of Technology

Eng Seng Loh
Kent State University

John Marcis
Virginia Commonwealth University

Mindy Marks
University of California-Riverside

Laurence McCulloch
Ohio State University-Columbus

J. Peter Mattila
Iowa State University

Catherine Mulder
Washington College

Eric Nilsson
California State University-San Bernardino

Kelly Noonan
Rider University

Kevin O'Brien
Bradley University

John F. O'Connell
Holy Cross

Mark Pernecky
St. Olaf College

Norris Peterson
Pacific Lutheran University

Jerry Petr
University of Nebraska-Lincoln

Bruce Pietrykowski
University of Michigan-Dearborn

Farahmand Rezvani
Montclair State University

Douglas Romrell
Utah State University

Blair Ruble
Social Sciences Research Council

Timothy Schibik
University of Southern Indiana

Curtis Simon
Clemson University

Robert Simonson
Mankato State University

Patricia Simpson
Loyola University

Larry Singell
University of Oregon

Russell Snyder
Eastern Washington University

Steven Stern
University of Virginia

Chris Swann
SUNY-Stoney Brook

Wade Thomas
Ithaca College

William Torrence
University of Nebraska-Lincoln

Ronald S. Warren, Jr.
University of Georgia

Bill Wilkes
Athens State University

Thomas A. Webb
South-Western College

We are also greatly indebted to the many professionals at McGraw-Hill/Irwin—in particular, Anke Weekes, Kevin White, Marla Sussman, Bobby Pearson, Maria McGreal, David Hash, and Shawntel Schmitt—for their expertise in the production and marketing of this book.

Campbell R. McConnell

Stanley L. Brue

David A. Macpherson

Contents

Preface   iv

Chapter 1
Labor Economics: Introduction and Overview   1

Labor Economics as a Discipline   1
The "Old" and the "New"   3
Economic Perspective   3
World of Work 1.1: Gary Becker: Nobel
    Laureate   5
Overview   6
Payoffs   9

Chapter 2
The Theory of Individual Labor Supply   12

The Work–Leisure Decision: Basic
    Model   12
World of Work 2.1: Work Hours Linked to
    Pollution   26
World of Work 2.2: Labor Supply of
    Politicians   28
Applying and Extending the Model   29
World of Work 2.3: The Labor Supply
    Effects of Winning a Lottery Prize   32
World of Work 2.4: Labor Supply of
    Florida Lobster Fishermen   33
World of Work 2.5: The Labor Supply
    Impact of the Earned Income Tax
    Credit   42

Chapter 3
Population, Participation Rates, and Hours of Work   47

The Population Base   48
Becker's Model: The Allocation of
    Time   49
World of Work 3.1: The Changing Face of
    America   50

World of Work 3.2: Video Gaming and the
    Decline in Labor Supply of Young
    Men   53
Participation Rates: Defined and
    Measured   54
Secular Trend of Participation Rates   55
World of Work 3.3: The Power of the
    Pill   62
World of Work 3.4: Why Do So Few
    Women Work in New York and So
    Many in Minneapolis?   65
World of Work 3.5: The Opioid Crisis and
    the Decline in Labor Force
    Participation   69
Cyclic Changes in Participation
    Rates   69
Hours of Work: Two Trends   72
World of Work 3.6: Time Stress   73

Chapter 4
Labor Quality: Investing in Human Capital   78

Investment in Human Capital: Concept
    and Data   79
The Human Capital Model   79
World of Work 4.1: Recessions and the
    College Enrollment Rate   87
World of Work 4.2: What Is a GED
    Worth?   89
World of Work 4.3: Higher Education:
    Making the Right Choices   92
Human Capital Investment and the
    Distribution of Earnings   96
World of Work 4.4: What You Did in High
    School Matters   100
World of Work 4.5: Reversal of the
    College Gender Gap   102
On-the-Job Training   104
Criticisms of Human Capital
    Theory   110

World of Work 4.6: College as Country
Club   111
World of Work 4.7: Is There More to
College than Money?   114

Chapter 5
The Demand for Labor   119

Derived Demand for Labor   120
A Firm's Short-Run Production
Function   121
Short-Run Demand for Labor: The
Perfectly Competitive Seller   124
Short-Run Demand for Labor: The
Imperfectly Competitive Seller   127
The Long-Run Demand for Labor   129
World of Work 5.1: Has Health Care
Reform Increased Involuntary
Part-Time Work?   131
The Market Demand for Labor   133
World of Work 5.2: Why Has
Manufacturing Employment
Fallen?   134
World of Work 5.3: Comparative
Advantage and the Demand for
Labor   136
Elasticity of Labor Demand   137
Determinants of Demand for Labor   142
World of Work 5.4: Ahead of the Pack:
Veterinary Occupations are Growing
Fast   145
Real-World Applications   146
World of Work 5.5: Occupational
Employment Trends   147
Appendix: Isoquant–Isocost Analysis of
the Long-Run Demand for Labor   152
Isoquant Curves   152
Isocost Curves   153
Least-Cost Combination of Capital and
Labor   154
Deriving the Long-Run Labor Demand
Curve   155

Chapter 6
Wage Determination and the Allocation of Labor   159

Theory of a Perfectly Competitive Labor
Market   160

World of Work 6.1: Hurricanes and Local
Labor Markets   165
World of Work 6.2: China
Syndrome   167
Wage and Employment Determination:
Monopoly in the Product Market   169
Monopsony   171
World of Work 6.3: Pay and Performance
in Professional Baseball   175
Wage Determination: Delayed Supply
Responses   176
World of Work 6.4: Do Medical Students
Know How Much Doctors Earn?   178

Chapter 7
Alternative Pay Schemes and Labor Efficiency   184

Economics of Fringe Benefits   184
Theory of Optimal Fringe Benefits   186
World of Work 7.1: [Job] Locked and
[Un]Loaded   192
The Principal–Agent Problem   193
Pay for Performance   194
World of Work 7.2: End of Teacher
Tenure?   195
World of Work 7.3: Economics of
Tipping   198
Efficiency Wage Payments   203
World of Work 7.4: The Ford Motor
Company's $5 per Day Wage   206
Labor Market Efficiency Revisited   208

Chapter 8
The Wage Structure   212

Perfect Competition: Homogeneous
Workers and Jobs   213
The Wage Structure: Observed
Differentials   214
Wage Differentials: Heterogeneous
Jobs   217
World of Work 8.1: Who Cares and Does
It Matter?   219
Wage Differentials: Heterogeneous
Workers   224
World of Work 8.2: Rising Importance of
Social Skills   225
The Hedonic Theory of Wages   226

World of Work 8.3: Is Exercise Good for
Your Wallet as Well as Your
Heart?   227
World of Work 8.4: Compensating Pay for
Shift Work   231
World of Work 8.5: Placing a Value on
Human Life   232
Wage Differentials: Labor Market
Imperfections   233

Chapter 9
Mobility, Migration, and Efficiency   240

Types of Labor Mobility   241
Migration as an Investment in Human
Capital   242
World of Work 9.1: The Decline in
Geographic Mobility   243
The Determinants of Migration: A Closer
Look   244
The Consequences of Migration   247
Capital and Product Flows   255
U.S. Immigration Policy and Issues   257
World of Work 9.2: Labor Supply of
Undocumented Immigrants   260
World of Work 9.3: What Jobs Do
Undocumented Persons Hold?   262

Chapter 10
Labor Unions and Collective Bargaining   266

Why Unions?   266
Labor Unionism: Facts and Figures   267
World of Work 10.1: *Janus* Decision and
Public Sector Unions   270
Unionism's Decline   276
What Do Unions Want?   282
Unions and Wage Determination   286
World of Work 10.2: The WTO, Trade
Liberalization, and Labor
Standards   288
Strikes and the Bargaining Process   293

Chapter 11
The Economic Impact of Unions   300

The Union Wage Advantage   300
World of Work 11.1: The Cost of a Union
Member   308
Efficiency and Productivity   309

World of Work 11.2: Labor Strife and
Product Quality   315
Firm Profitability   318
World of Work 11.3: Unions and
Investment   319
Distribution of Earnings   320
Other Issues: Inflation, Unemployment,
and Income Shares   323
World of Work 11.4: Unions and Executive
Compensation   324

Chapter 12
**Government and the Labor Market: Employment,
Expenditures, and Taxation   329**

Public Sector Employment and
Wages   329
World of Work 12.1: What Do
Government Workers Do?   331
World of Work 12.2: Beaches, Sunshine,
and Public Sector Pay   334
The Military Sector: The Draft versus the
Voluntary Army   334
World of Work 12.3: The Impact of
Military Cutbacks on Civilians   338
Nonpayroll Spending by Government:
Impact on Labor   338
Labor Market Effects of Publicly Provided
Goods and Services   340
Income Taxation and the Labor
Market   342
World of Work 12.4: Who Pays the Social
Security Payroll Tax?   349

Chapter 13
**Government and the Labor Market: Legislation
and Regulation   353**

Labor Law   353
Minimum Wage Law   357
Occupational Health and Safety
Regulation   364
World of Work 13.1: Climate Change and
Occupational Health   368
World of Work 13.2: The Effect of
Workers' Compensation on Job
Safety   371
Government as a Rent Provider   372
World of Work 13.3: Who Can Whiten
Teeth?   376

Chapter 14
Labor Market Discrimination   381

Gender and Racial Differences   382
World of Work 14.1: The Gender Wage
    Gap among Millennials   384
Discrimination and Its Dimensions   389
Taste for Discrimination Model   391
World of Work 14.2: Competition and
    Discrimination   394
Theory of Statistical Discrimination   396
The Crowding Model: Occupational
    Segregation   397
World of Work 14.3: Does Ban the Box
    Cause Discrimination?   398
World of Work 14.4: Evolution of a Family
    Friendly Occupation   402
Cause and Effect: Nondiscriminatory
    Factors   403
World of Work 14.5: The Gender Gap in
    the Gig Economy   406
Antidiscrimination Policies and
    Issues   407
World of Work 14.6: Orchestrating
    Impartiality   410

Chapter 15
Job Search: External and Internal   415

External Job Search   415
World of Work 15.1: Thinking of Quitting?
    The Boss Knows   418
Internal Labor Markets   422

Chapter 16
The Distribution of Personal Earnings   432

Describing the Distribution of
    Earnings   433
Explaining the Distribution of
    Earnings   437
Mobility within the Earnings
    Distribution   444
World of Work 16.1: Cross-Country
    Differences in Earnings Mobility across
    Generations   445
World of Work 16.2: Government
    Employment and the Earnings
    Distribution   446
Rising Earnings Inequality   447

World of Work 16.3: Rising Leisure Time
    Inequality   451

Chapter 17
**Labor Productivity: Wages, Prices, and
Employment   455**

The Productivity Concept   455
Importance of Productivity
    Increases   458
World of Work 17.1: Growing Gap
    Between Productivity and
    Compensation   460
Long-Run Trend of Labor
    Productivity   463
World of Work 17.2: Is Public Capital
    Productive?   465
Cyclic Changes in Productivity   468
Productivity and Employment   470
A "New Economy" or Not?   475

Chapter 18
Employment and Unemployment   480

Employment and Unemployment
    Statistics   481
World of Work 18.1: Effects of Graduating
    from College in a Bad Economy   486
Macroeconomic Output and Employment
    Determination   488
Frictional Unemployment   490
Structural Unemployment   492
Demand–Deficient Unemployment   493
World of Work 18.2: Why Bad
    Unemployment News Is Usually Good
    for Stocks   496
The Distribution of Unemployment   497
Reducing Unemployment: Public
    Policies   500

Appendix
Information Sources in Labor Economics   506

Sources of Labor Statistics   506
Applications, New Theories, Emerging
    Evidence   513
Textbooks and Research Surveys   518

Glossary   521
Answers to "Your Turn" Questions   540
Name Index   544
Subject Index   553
Data Tables   569

Contemporary
Labor
Economics

Chapter 1

Labor Economics: Introduction and Overview

After reading this chapter, you should be able to:

1. Explain why labor economics is justified as a special field of inquiry.
2. Describe how the economic perspective can be applied to analysis of labor markets.
3. Identify those topics in labor economics that are mainly "microeconomic" and those that are primarily "macroeconomic."
4. Describe several benefits that derive from understanding labor economics.

The core problem of economics permeates all of its specialized branches or subdivisions. This problem is that productive resources are relatively scarce or limited. Society's material wants—the desires of consumers, businesses, and governmental units for goods and services—exceed our productive capacity. That is, our economic system is incapable of providing all the products and services that individuals and institutions would like to have. Because absolute material abundance is impossible, society must choose what goods and services should be produced, how they should be produced, and who should receive them. *Economics* is concerned with the discovery of rules or principles that indicate how such choices can be rationally and efficiently rendered. Because resources are scarce and wants are virtually unlimited, society needs to manage its resources as efficiently as possible to achieve the maximum fulfillment of its wants. Labor, of course, is one of society's scarce productive resources, and this book centers on the problem of its efficient use. *Labor economics examines the organization, functioning, and outcomes of labor markets; the decisions of prospective and present labor market participants; and the public policies relating to the employment and payment of labor resources.*

LABOR ECONOMICS AS A DISCIPLINE

How can a special field of economics concerned solely with labor be justified? What makes labor economics important as an area of inquiry? There are several answers to these questions.

Socioeconomic Issues

First, evidence of the importance of labor economics is all around us. We need to simply glance at the newspaper headlines: "Senator calls for increase in minimum wage"; "General Motors cuts workforce"; "Labor productivity surges"; "Teamsters gain wage hike"; "Growing wage inequality"; "Sexual harassment accusations"; "Free-trade agreement: Boon or bane for employment?"; "Workplace safety improves"; "Gender discrimination charged"; "More single parents in labor force"; "Illegal immigration continues"; "High executive salaries questioned"; "Jobs shipped out to foreigners."

Moreover, labor economics helps us understand causes and outcomes of major socioeconomic trends occurring over the past several decades: the rapid rise in employment in the service industries, the surge in the number of female workers, the precipitous drop in union membership as a percentage of the workforce, the recent increase in immigration to the United States, and the expanding globalization of labor markets.

Quantitative Importance

A second justification for labor economics is quantitative. About 65 percent of U.S. income flows to workers as wages and salaries. Ironically, in the capitalist economies of the world, the bulk of income is received not as capitalist income (profit, rent, and interest) but as wages! The primary source of income for the vast majority of households in the United States is from providing labor services. Quantitatively, labor is our most important economic resource.

Unique Characteristics

Finally, the markets in which labor services are "bought" and "sold" embody special characteristics and peculiarities calling for separate study. Labor market transactions are a far cry from product market transactions. As succinctly stated by the famous British economist Alfred Marshall,

> It matters nothing to the seller of bricks whether they are to be used in building a palace or a sewer; but it matters a great deal to the seller of labor, who undertakes to perform a task of given difficulty, whether or not the place in which it is to be done is a wholesome and pleasant one, and whether or not his associates will be such as he cares to have.[1]

Or as explained by a more recent observer,

> The labor market is a rich and complicated place. When a worker takes a job he expects to earn a wage, but will also care about rates of wage growth, fringe benefits, levels of risk, retirement practices, pensions, promotion and layoff rules, seniority rights, and grievance procedures. In return the worker must give up some time, but he is also asked to upgrade his skills, train other workers, provide effort and ideas, and defer to authority in questions of how his time is spent.[2]

The complexity of labor markets means that the concepts of supply and demand must be substantially revised and reoriented when applied to labor markets. On the supply side, the labor services a worker "rents" to an employer are inseparable from the worker. Because a worker must spend 40 or so hours per week on the job delivering labor services, the nonmonetary facets of a job become extremely significant. Aside from remuneration, the worker is interested in a job's health and safety features, the arduousness of the work, stability of employment, and opportunities for training and advancement. These nonmonetary characteristics may be as important as the direct pay. Indeed a worker's social status, self-esteem, and independence may depend on the availability of labor market work. Thus, the supply decisions of workers are more complex than the supply concept that applies to product markets.

---

[1] Marshall, Alfred. *Principles of Economics*. Cambridge: Ravenio Books, 1936.

[2] Carmichael, H. Lorne. "Self-Enforcing Contracts, Shirking, and Life Cycle Incentives." *The Journal of Economic Perspectives 3*, no. 4 (Autumn, 1989): 65–83. https://DOI:10.1257/jep.3.4.65.

Similarly, whereas the demand for a product is based on the satisfaction or utility it yields, labor is demanded because of its contribution—its productivity—in creating goods and services. The demands for particular kinds of labor are derived from the demands for the products they produce. Society has a demand for automobile workers because there is a demand for automobiles. We have a demand for accountants because we value accounting services. The demand for labor is therefore an indirect or "derived" demand.

The point to be underscored is that an understanding of labor markets presumes an appreciation of the special attributes of labor supply and demand. Unique institutional considerations—such as labor unions and collective bargaining, the minimum wage, occupational licensing, and discrimination—all affect the functioning of labor markets and require special attention.

THE "OLD" AND THE "NEW"

The field of labor economics has long been recognized as an important area of study. But the content or subject matter of the field has changed dramatically in the past few decades. If you were to go to the library and examine a labor text published 40 or 45 years ago, you would find its orientation highly descriptive and historical. Its emphasis would be on the history of the labor movement, a recitation of labor law and salient court cases, the institutional structure of labor unions, and the scope and composition of collective bargaining agreements. In short, the "old" study of labor was descriptive, emphasizing historical developments, facts, institutions, and legal considerations. A primary reason for this approach was that the complexities of labor markets seemed to make them more or less immune to economic analysis. To be sure, labor markets and unemployment were accorded some attention, but the analysis was typically minimal and superficial.

This state of affairs has changed significantly in recent decades. Economists have achieved important analytic breakthroughs in studying labor markets and labor problems. As a result, economic analysis has crowded out historical, institutional, legal, and anecdotal material. Labor economics increasingly has become applied micro and macro theory. The present volume focuses on the techniques and understandings associated with the "new" labor economics. This is not to say, however, that all descriptive aspects of the field have been discarded. As noted earlier, the unique institutional features of labor markets are part of the justification for a special field of economics devoted to labor. Yet the focal point of our approach is the application of economic reasoning to labor markets and labor issues.

ECONOMIC PERSPECTIVE

Contemporary labor economics employs theories of *choice* to analyze and predict the behavior of labor market participants and the economic consequences of labor market activity. It attempts to answer such questions as these: Why do some people decide to work while others do not? Why do some prospective labor market participants choose to delay their labor force entry to attend college? Why do some employers employ few workers and much capital while others use many workers and little capital? Why do firms lay off some workers during recessions but retain others? Labor economists also examine the *outcomes* of the choices made in the labor market: Why do some workers earn $10.00 an hour while others are paid $25 or $60 per hour? Why have women entered the labor force in record numbers during the past few decades? What impact, if any, does immigration have on the wages of native workers?

In short, contemporary labor economics focuses on choices—why they are made and how they generate particular outcomes. It therefore is important to be aware of three implicit assumptions underlying this *economic perspective*.

Relative Scarcity

We know that land, labor, capital, and entrepreneurial resources are scarce, or limited, relative to the many individual and collective wants of society. This relative scarcity dictates that society must choose how and for what purpose labor and other resources should be allocated. Similarly, individuals face a relative scarcity of time and spendable income. They must choose, for example, how much time to devote to jobs, to work in the home, and to leisure. They must choose how much present income (goods and services) to forgo for the prospect of obtaining higher future earnings. They must decide which goods and services to buy and, consequently, which to forgo. Relative scarcity—of time, personal income, and societal resources—is a basic element of the economic perspective.

Purposeful Behavior

Because relative scarcity keeps us from having everything we want, we are forced to choose among alternatives. For every choice, say to work longer hours or to institute a national service program, something is gained and something else is sacrificed. This sacrifice—forgone leisure, forgone private sector output—is an *opportunity cost.*

The economic perspective assumes that people compare costs with expected benefits. A worker will compare the extra utility (income) gained from an added hour of work with the value of the lost leisure. A firm will compare the added revenue from hiring a worker with the extra wage cost, and so forth. Thus, contemporary labor economics looks for purpose, or rationality, in labor market behavior and, for that matter, in many labor market institutions. Relative scarcity necessitates that choices be made; the economic perspective assumes that these choices will be made purposefully rather than randomly or in a chaotic way.

To say that labor market participants behave rationally, however, is not to say that they always achieve their intended goals. Information is imperfect or imperfectly processed; unforeseen events occur; choices made by others positively or adversely affect the outcomes of our own choices. But even choices that in retrospect were "poor" ones are assumed to have been made with the *expectation* of net gain.

Adaptability

Because relative scarcity forces people to make choices, and because choices are made purposefully, labor market participants respond to changes in perceived costs and benefits. Some workers will adjust the number of hours they desire to work when the wage rate they receive changes. Fewer people will decide to obtain a specific skill when the training cost rises or when the wage paid to those already possessing the skill falls. Firms will adjust their hiring when the demand for their product changes. Some workers will migrate from lower-paid regions to areas experiencing a significant rise in labor demand and therefore in wage rates. Union officials will lower their wage demands when the economy encounters recession and unemployment among union workers is high. Restated, the economic perspective assumes that workers, employers, and other labor market participants *adapt, adjust,* or *alter* their behaviors in response to changes in expected costs and expected gains. Contemporary labor economics sorts out these responses, finds predictable patterns, and by so doing, adds to our understanding of the economy.

These three assumptions of the economic perspective—the scarcity of resources relative to wants, purposeful behavior based on comparisons of benefits and costs, and the adaptability of behavior to changing circumstances—underlie all that follows in this text.

1.1 *Quick Review*

- Labor economics examines the organization, functioning, and outcomes of labor markets; the decisions of prospective and present labor market participants; and the public policies relating to the employment and payment of labor resources.

- The new labor economics employs the economic perspective, which assumes that resources are scarce relative to wants, individuals make choices by comparing costs and benefits, and people respond to incentives and disincentives.

Your Turn

Which of these two statements best reflects the economic perspective? "Most workers in America would retire at age 65 even without pensions because this age has long been the customary retirement age." "Most workers in America retire at age 65 because at this age they become eligible for private pensions and full Social Security benefits." (*Answer:* See page 540.)

 ## **World of Work**

Gary Becker: Nobel Laureate

Few economists were surprised when the University of Chicago's Gary Becker was named the winner of the 1992 Nobel Prize in economics. More than any other recent economist, Becker has extended the boundaries of economic analysis.

Becker's theories presume that individuals or households make purposeful choices in attempting to maximize their utility and that these choices depend heavily on incentives. His basic contribution has been to apply this perspective to aspects of human behavior that traditionally were believed to be noneconomic.

Becker's theory of marriage is illustrative. People allegedly seek marriage partners much as they search for jobs or decide which products to buy. Couples stop far short of obtaining complete information about each other before marriage.

At some point the costs of obtaining additional information—the main cost being the benefits of marriage forgone—exceed the extra benefits of more information. After being married for months or years, however, a person learns additional information about his or her spouse's personality and attributes. This new information in some cases places the spouse in a less favorable light, ending the optimality of the original match and causing divorce.

Becker views the household as a little factory, allocating its time between labor market work, household production, and household consumption in producing utility-providing "commodities" (Chapter 3). Households have fewer children—time-intensive "durable goods"—as the "price" of children rises. A major component of this "price" is the forgone earnings associated with having and caring for children.

Becker's theory of human capital (Chapter 4) holds that decisions to invest in education and training are analogous to decisions by firms to purchase physical capital. Applying his approach to crime, Becker concludes that criminals rationally choose between crime and normal labor market work. Also, they respond to changes in costs and benefits, just as noncriminals do. Becker analyzes labor market discrimination (Chapter 14) as a preference or "taste" for which the discriminator is willing to pay.

Because Becker has invaded the traditional territories of sociology, anthropology, demography, and law, he has been called an "intellectual imperialist" (by both supporters and detractors). But as stated by Summers, there can be no doubt that Becker "has profoundly influenced the future of economics by demonstrating the breadth, range, and power of economic reasoning in a context that seemed unimagined a generation ago."[3]

OVERVIEW

Before plunging into the details of specific topics, let's pause for a brief overview of our field of study. This overview is useful for two closely related reasons. First, it provides a sense of direction. More specifically, it reveals the logic underlying the sequence of topics constituting each chapter. Second, the overview shows how the subject matter of any particular chapter relates to other chapters.[4]

Figure 1.1 is helpful in presenting the overview. Reading from left to right, we note that most aspects of labor economics can be fitted without much arbitrariness under the headings of "microeconomics" or "macroeconomics." *Microeconomics* is concerned with the decisions of individual economic units and the functioning of specific markets. On the other hand, *macroeconomics* is concerned with the economy as a whole or with basic aggregates that constitute the economy. The determination of the wage rate and the level of employment in a particular market—carpenters in Oshkosh or retail clerks in Okoboji—are clearly microeconomic matters. In contrast, the average level of real wages, the aggregate levels of employment and unemployment, and the overall price level are issues in macroeconomics. Because some topics straddle micro- and macroeconomics, the subject matter of individual chapters will sometimes pertain to both aspects of economics. However, it is fair to say that Chapters 2 to 15 address topics that are "mainly micro." Similarly, Chapters 16 to 18 are "mainly macro."

Figure 1.1 reemphasizes that microeconomics stresses the working of individual markets. The goal of Chapters 2 to 6 is to develop and bring together the concepts that underlie labor supply and demand. Specifically, in Chapter 2 we examine the simple theory of labor supply. Here we analyze the basic factors that determine whether a person will participate in the labor force and, if so, the number of hours that the individual would prefer to work. We also consider how various pay schemes and income maintenance programs might affect the person's decision to supply labor services.

In Chapter 3 we consider the major determinants of the aggregate amount of labor supplied: population, the labor force participation rates of various demographic groups, and hours of work. In particular, we examine labor supply from a household perspective and explore reasons for the rapid increase in the labor force participation of married women.

Chapter 4 introduces a qualitative dimension to labor supply. Workers can provide more productive effort if they have training. Thus, in Chapter 4 we examine the decision to invest in human capital—that is, in education and training—and explain why it is rational for different individuals to invest in different quantities of human capital.

---

[3] Summers, Lawrence. "An Economist for the Common Man." *BusinessWeek*, October 26, 1992.

[4] This text covers more topics in economics than most instructors will choose to cover in a single course. Also note that chapters and topics can be logically sequenced in numerous ways.

FIGURE 1.1 An Overview of Labor Economics

This diagram shows how the chapters of this volume are divided between microeconomic and macroeconomic topics. Microeconomics focuses on the determinants of labor supply and demand and how supply and demand interact to determine wage rates and employment in various labor markets. In these labor markets, the types and composition of pay are determined, as is the wage structure. Some wage differences persist; others are eroded by mobility and migration. Labor unions, government, and discrimination all affect labor markets through either supply or demand. Macroeconomics stresses the aggregative aspects of labor markets and, in particular, the distribution of earnings, labor productivity, and the overall level of employment.

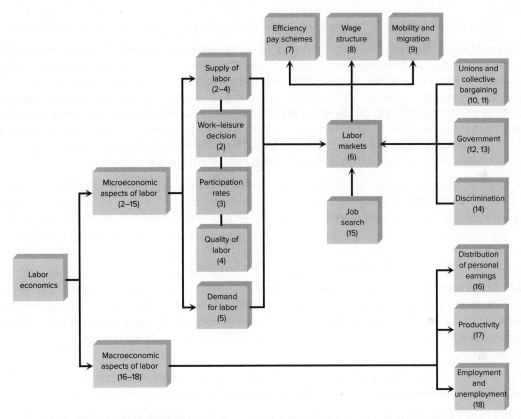

We turn to the demand side of the labor market in Chapter 5. Here we systematically derive the short-run labor demand curve, explaining how the curve varies between a firm that is selling its product competitively and one that is not. The notion of a long-run demand curve is also explored, as is the concept of wage elasticity of demand. Several short applications of demand and elasticity then follow.

Chapter 6 combines labor supply and labor demand to explain how the equilibrium wage rate and level of employment are determined. An array of market models is presented, ranging from a basic perfectly competitive model to relatively complex bilateral monopoly and "cobweb" models. Because of the importance of using scarce resources prudently, the emphasis in Chapter 6 is on the efficiency with which labor is allocated. Is the socially desirable or "right" amount of labor employed in a particular labor market? If not, what is the efficiency loss to society?

Chapters 7 to 9 are important elaborations and modifications of Chapter 6's discussion of the working conditions and outcomes of labor markets. In Chapter 6 worker compensation is treated as a standard hourly wage rate, such as $10 per hour. In Chapter 7 we recognize that worker compensation also involves a whole range of fringe benefits, including health insurance, paid vacations, sick leave, contributions to pensions, and so forth. We discuss why different compensation packages might appeal to different workers. More important, Chapter 7 explains how pay schemes might be designed to promote worker efficiency and productivity.

In Chapter 8 we confront the complex topic of the wage structure. Why do different workers receive different wages? We find that wage differences are traceable to such factors as the varying working conditions and skill requirements of jobs, differences in the human capital and job preferences of workers, and imperfections in labor mobility and the flow of job information.

Chapter 9 continues our elaboration of the labor market, explaining how the movement of labor—from employer to employer, occupation to occupation, and place to place—can contribute to economic efficiency. This mobility is analyzed as an investment in human capital and has a variety of economic ramifications.

As Figure 1.1 suggests, Chapters 10 to 15 focus on a variety of real-world considerations that have a pervasive and profound impact on how wages are determined and how labor markets operate. Specifically, in these chapters we examine how labor unions, government, and discrimination affect labor markets. Chapters 10 and 11 are concerned with unions and collective bargaining. In Chapter 10 we explore the demographics of trade union membership, discuss the size and institutional structure of the labor movement, and present models of the wage bargaining process and strike activity. Chapter 11 is devoted to the effects of unions and collective bargaining on the operation of labor markets. The discussion focuses on the impact of unions on wage rates, efficiency and productivity, firm profitability, and the distribution of earnings.

The direct and subtle ways in which government influences labor markets are the subject matter of Chapters 12 and 13. Chapter 12 considers government as a direct employer of labor and explores how government's fiscal functions affect labor markets. Specifically, we seek to determine how government expenditures and taxes alter wages and employment. In Chapter 13 our attention shifts to the impact of the legislative and regulatory functions of government on labor markets. What are the implications, for example, of minimum wage legislation and regulations concerning worker health and safety?

In addition to labor unions and government, the "institution" of discrimination greatly affects labor markets. Thus, Chapter 14 presents facts and figures about differences in pay by race and gender, introduces several models of race and gender discrimination, and discusses how many of the observed gender and racial wage differences result from discrimination. This chapter also examines antidiscrimination policies and issues in some detail.

Job search behavior has important implications for issues such as unemployment and economic efficiency. Thus, Chapter 15 is devoted to job search within as well as outside a firm.

The next three chapters deal primarily with macroeconomic aspects and outcomes of labor markets. The personal distribution of earnings is the subject of Chapter 16. Here we discuss alternative ways of portraying the overall earnings distribution and measuring the degree of observed inequality. We then offer explanations for the pattern of earnings and discuss related topics such as the degree of mobility within the earnings distribution and the recent trend toward greater earnings inequality.

In Chapter 17 we consider productivity for the important reason that the average levels of real wages—and thus living levels—are intimately related to it. The factors that contribute to the growth of productivity are examined, as are the systematic changes in productivity that occur during the business cycle. The relationships of changes in productivity to the price level and the level of employment are also explained.

Chapter 18 is devoted to the problem of unemployment. Among other things, distinctions are made between frictional, structural, and cyclic unemployment. The distribution of unemployment by occupations and by demographic groups is considered, as are a variety of public policies designed to alleviate unemployment.

The appendix falls outside Figure 1.1's overview, but it is important for staying aware of future developments in labor economics and continuing the study of the field. It lists and discusses sources of labor-related statistics; discusses bibliographic, technical, and nontechnical journals in the field; and cites advanced text-books in labor economics along with books in the closely related fields of labor relations, collective bargaining, and labor law. Students doing term papers or other written assignments in labor economics will want to read this appendix at the outset. Appendix Table 1 lists numerous potential term paper topics that may be of interest.

PAYOFFS

What benefits might you derive from studying labor economics? The payoffs from a basic understanding of the field may be both personal and social. Labor economics yields information and develops analytic tools that may be useful in making personal and managerial decisions relevant to labor markets. Also, a grasp of the field puts you in a better position as a citizen and voter to develop informed positions on labor market issues and policies.

Personal Perspective

At the personal level, the vast majority of readers have already been labor market participants. You have worked summers, in part-time jobs, on your family farm, or perhaps in a school-related internship. Most of you will receive the bulk of your future incomes from the labor market. Thus, many of the topics addressed in this book will have immediate relevance to you. Such topics as job search, unemployment, migration, discrimination, unionism, and labor productivity, to enumerate only a few, will take on new meaning and relevance. For example, if you become a public school-teacher or a state employee, what might you personally expect to gain in terms of salary and fringe benefits by unionization? To what extent does a college education contribute to higher earnings? That is, what rate of return can you expect from investing in higher education? What are the peculiarities of labor markets for college-trained workers? If you are a woman or a member of a minority group, how might discrimination affect your access to specific occupations and your earnings? Similarly, some of you will find yourselves in managerial positions with responsibilities for personnel and labor relations. The background and analytic perspective provided by an understanding of labor economics should be useful in making rational managerial decisions concerning the hiring, firing, promotion, training, and remuneration of workers.

Social Perspective

From a societal viewpoint, a knowledge of labor economics should help make you a more informed citizen and more intelligent voter. The issues here are broad in scope and impact. Should unionization be encouraged or discouraged? Are unions on balance positive or negative forces in our society? Should the government place limits on the salaries of executives, athletes, and entertainers? How might a given change in the tax structure—for example, to a more progressive federal income tax—affect incentives to work? Should the government restrict outsourcing of American jobs to firms or subsidiaries abroad? Should U.S. immigration policies be liberalized or made more restrictive? Should industrially advanced countries use international trade agreements to force developing countries to increase minimum wages, improve working conditions, and meet other labor standards? Should formal education and vocational training be given more or less public support? Is it desirable for employers to pay teenagers wage rates that are lower than the legislated minimum wage? Although detailed and definitive answers to such questions cannot be guaranteed, an understanding of labor economics will provide valuable insights that should help you formulate opinions on these and similar issues.

Chapter Summary

1. The relative scarcity of labor and other productive resources provides an incentive for society to use such resources efficiently.

2. The importance of labor economics is reflected in *(a)* current socioeconomic issues and problems, *(b)* the quantitative dominance of labor as a resource, and *(c)* the unique characteristics of labor supply and demand.

3. In the past two decades, the field of labor economics has put greater emphasis on economic analysis and has deemphasized historical, institutional, and legal aspects.

4. The economic perspective assumes that *(a)* labor and other resources are relatively scarce, *(b)* individuals and institutions make rational or purposeful decisions, and *(c)* decisions are altered or adapted in the light of changing economic circumstances.

5. This volume examines a series of pertinent microeconomic and macroeconomic topics, as outlined in Figure 1.1.

6. An understanding of the content and analytic tools of labor economics contributes to more intelligent personal and social decisions.

Terms and Concepts

labor economics   microeconomics

economic perspective   macroeconomics

Note: To aid you with the terminology, we have included an extensive glossary at the end of this book.

Questions and Study Suggestions

1. Why is economics a science of choices? Explain the kinds of choices confronting workers and employers in labor markets. Distinguish between microeconomics and macroeconomics.

2. In 2019, 163.5 million workers were in the U.S. labor force, of which 6.0 million were unemployed. In view of these facts, how can economists say that labor is a scarce resource?

3. Indicate whether each of the following statements pertains to microeconomics or macroeconomics:

    a. The unemployment rate in the United States was 3.7 percent in 2019.

    b. Workers at the Sleepy Eye grain elevator are paid $10 per hour.

    c. The productivity of American workers as a whole increased by more than 2 percent per year in the last decade.

    d. The money or nominal wages of nursing aides increased by 2 percent in 2019.

    e. The Alpo dog food plant in Bowser, Indiana, laid off 15 workers last month.

4. Why must the concepts of supply and demand as they pertain to product markets be modified when applied to labor markets?

5. What is the relative importance of labor as an economic resource?

6. Briefly compare the "old" and "new" labor economics.

7. What are the major features or assumptions of the economic perspective?

8. Briefly state and justify your position on each of the following proposals:

   a. Women and minorities should be paid the same wage as white males, provided the work is comparable.

   b. The United States should close its boundaries to all immigration.

   c. The federal government should take measures to achieve the 4 percent unemployment rate specified by the Humphrey–Hawkins Act of 1978.

   d. So-called right-to-work laws, which specify that workers who refuse to join unions cannot thereby be deprived of their jobs, should be repealed.

   e. Conditions of worker health and safety should be determined by the labor market, not by government regulation.

9. What benefits might accrue to you from studying labor economics?

Internet Exercise

Economist Magazine

Go to the website for the *Economist* magazine (**http://www.economist.com**). Locate and cite an entry that covers a labor economics issue. In which chapter of this book is the issue discussed?

Internet Links

The Nobel e-Museum website provides information about the Nobel Prize winners in economics (**http://www.nobelprize.org/nobel_prizes/economic-sciences/**).

FRED at the St Louis Federal Reserve website supplies easy to access economic data from many sources (**https://fred.stlouisfed.org/**).

Chapter 2

The Theory of Individual Labor Supply

After reading this chapter, you should be able to:

1. Use the basic income–leisure model to determine an individual's optimal combination of income and leisure.
2. Apply and extend the basic work–leisure model.

In supplying labor, human beings are a curious and diverse lot. Adams moonlights at a second job, while Anderson takes numerous unpaid absences from his only job. College student Brown works full-time while attending school, roommate Bailey works part-time, and classmate Brinkman doesn't work at all. Conway quit her job to raise her young children; Cohen, also with young children, continues to work full-time in the workplace. Downy quickly grabs an opportunity for early retirement; Wong plans to work until she can no longer do so because of old age. Evans welcomes overtime work; Ebert, given an option, routinely rejects it. Fleming supplies more hours of labor when her wage rate rises; Hernandez cuts back on his work hours.

How are these diverse labor supply decisions made? How do individuals decide on the number of hours of labor, if any, to supply in the labor market? Our main goal in this chapter is to develop and apply a basic theory of individual labor supply that will help answer these questions.

THE WORK–LEISURE DECISION: BASIC MODEL

Imagine an individual with a certain amount of education and labor force experience and, therefore, a given level of skills. That individual, having a fixed amount of time available, must decide how that time should be allocated between *work* (labor market activity) and *leisure* (non–labor market activity). In the present context, *work* is time devoted to a paying job. The term *leisure* is used here in a broad sense to include all kinds of activities for which a person does not get paid: work within the household and time spent on consumption, education, commuting, rest, relaxation, and so forth.

Two sets of information are necessary to determine the optimal distribution of an individual's time between work and leisure. First, we require *subjective,* psychological information concerning the individual's work–leisure preferences. This information is embodied in *indifference curves.* Second, we need the *objective* market information that is reflected in a *budget constraint.*

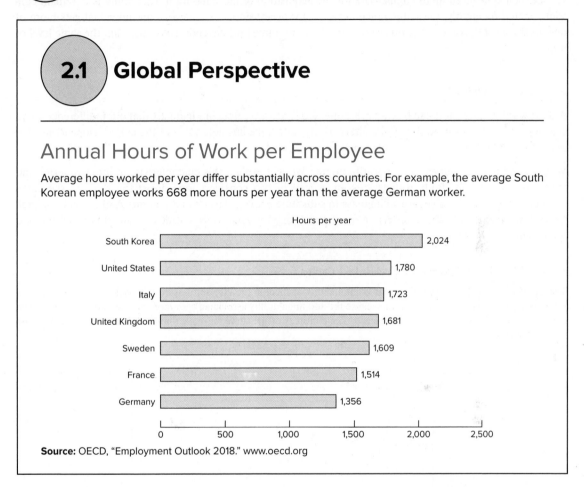

2.1 Global Perspective

Annual Hours of Work per Employee

Average hours worked per year differ substantially across countries. For example, the average South Korean employee works 668 more hours per year than the average German worker.

Hours per year

South Korea	2,024
United States	1,780
Italy	1,723
United Kingdom	1,681
Sweden	1,609
France	1,514
Germany	1,356

0   500   1,000   1,500   2,000   2,500

Source: OECD, "Employment Outlook 2018." www.oecd.org

Indifference Curves

As applied to the work–leisure decision, an *indifference curve shows the various combinations of real income and leisure time that will yield some specific level of utility or satisfaction to the individual.* Curve I_1 in Figure 2.1 is illustrative. Note that we measure daily income on the vertical axis and hours of leisure, or non–labor market activities, from left to right on the horizontal axis. The second horizontal axis reminds us that, given the fixed 24 hours available each day, we may measure the number of hours of work from right to left. According to the definition of indifference curves, each combination of income and leisure designated by any point on I_1 is equally satisfactory; each point on the curve yields the same level of utility to the individual.

Indifference curves embody several salient properties.

1 Negative Slope

The indifference curve slopes downward because leisure and real income from work are both sources of utility or satisfaction. In moving southeast down the curve, some amount of real income—of goods and services—must be given up to compensate for the acquisition of more leisure if total utility is to remain constant. Stated differently, the indifference curve is downward-sloping because as an individual gets more of one good (leisure), some of the other good (real income) must be surrendered to maintain the same level of utility.

2 Convex to Origin

A downward-sloping curve can be concave, convex, or linear. We note in Figure 2.1 that our indifference curve is *convex* (bowed inward) to the origin; alternatively stated, the absolute value of the curve's slope *diminishes* as we move down the curve to the southeast.

Why are indifference curves convex to the origin? We will explain this characteristic in intuitive terms and then more technically. Both explanations are rooted in two considerations. First, the slope of the curve reflects an individual's subjective willingness to substitute between leisure and income. And second, the individual's willingness to substitute leisure for income, or vice versa, varies with the amounts of leisure and income initially possessed.

FIGURE 2.1 An Income–Leisure Indifference Curve

The indifference curve shows the various combinations of income (goods) and leisure that yield some given level of total utility. The curve slopes downward because the additional utility associated with more leisure must be offset by less income so that total utility remains unchanged. The convexity of the curve reflects a diminishing marginal rate of substitution of leisure for income.

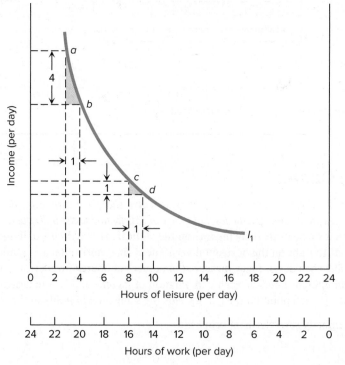

The convexity of an indifference curve reflects the idea that an individual becomes increasingly reluctant to give up any good (in this case income) as it becomes increasingly scarce. Consider the *ab* range of our indifference curve, where the individual has a relatively large amount of income and very little leisure. Here the individual would be willing to give up a relatively large amount of abundant income (four units) in exchange for an additional unit, say an hour, of scarce leisure. The extra utility from the added hour of leisure will perfectly offset the loss of utility from having four fewer units of income. But as we move down the curve to the *cd* range, we find that the individual's circumstances are different in that income is now relatively scarcer and leisure is more abundant. The individual is now willing to trade only a small amount of scarce income (one unit) for an extra hour of leisure. As the individual obtains more leisure, the amount of income the person is willing to give up to gain still more units of leisure becomes smaller and smaller. Thus the indifference curve becomes flatter and flatter. By definition, a curve that flattens out as we move to the southeast is convex to the origin.

In more technical terms, the slope of the indifference curve is measured by the *marginal rate of substitution of leisure for income* (MRS *L, Y*). *The MRS L, Y is the amount of income one must give up to compensate for the gain of one more unit (hour) of leisure.* Although the slope of the indifference curve shown in Figure 2.1 is negative, it is convenient to think of the MRS *L, Y* as an absolute value. In these terms, MRS *L, Y* is large—that is, the slope of the indifference curve is steep—in the northwest or upper range of the curve. You can see this by penciling in a straight line tangent to I_1 at point *a* in Figure 2.1. The slope of your line measures the slope of I_1 at *a*. Observe the steep slope—the high MRS *L, Y*. This high MRS *L, Y* occurs because the person has much income and little leisure. The subjective relative valuation of income is low at the margin, and the subjective relative valuation of leisure is high at the margin. The individual, therefore, is willing to forgo many units of income (four) for an additional unit of leisure.

In moving down the indifference curve to the southeast, the quantities of income and leisure change at each point so that the individual now has less income and more leisure. Relatively more abundant leisure, therefore, has less value at the margin, and increasingly scarce income has more value at the margin. You can see this by penciling in a straight line tangent to *d* on I_1 in Figure 2.1 and comparing the slope to point *a*. This slope (at *d*) is smaller than the slope of the curve at *a*. The basic point is that MRS *L, Y*—the slope of the indifference curve—declines as one moves down the curve. Any curve whose slope or MRS *L, Y* declines as one moves southeast along it is, by definition, convex to the origin.

3 Indifference Map

It is useful to consider an indifference map, which is a whole family or field of indifference curves, as shown in Figure 2.2. Each curve reflects some different level of total utility, much as each contour line on a topographic map reflects a different elevation. Figure 2.2 illustrates only three of a potentially unlimited number of indifference curves. Every possible combination of income and leisure will lie on some indifference curve. Curves farther from the origin indicate higher levels of utility. This can be demonstrated by drawing a 45° diagonal from the origin and noting that its intersection with each successive curve denotes larger amounts of *both* income and leisure. The $y_2 l_2$ combination of income and leisure is preferred to the $y_1 l_1$ combination because the former indicates larger amounts of *both* income and leisure. Similarly, the $y_3 l_3$ combination entails greater total utility than $y_2 l_2$, and so on.[1] It is evident that an individual will maximize total utility by achieving a position on the highest *attainable* indifference curve.

---

[1] Indifference curves cannot intersect. We know that all points on any one curve reflect the same amount of utility, whereas any point above (below) that curve represents a larger (smaller) level of utility. If two indifference curves intersected, the level of utility would be the same at the point of intersection. However, at all other points the levels of utility would differ. Given the definition of an indifference curve, this is logically impossible.

FIGURE 2.2 An Indifference Map for Income and Leisure

An indifference map comprises a number of indifference curves. Each successive curve to the northeast reflects a higher level of total utility.

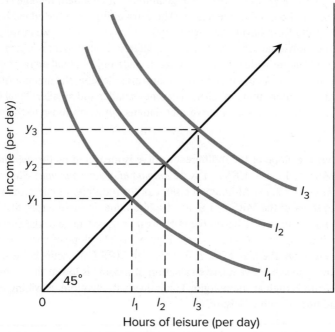

4 Different Work-Leisure Preferences

Just as the tastes of consumers for specific goods and services vary greatly, so do individual preferences for work and leisure. Different preferences for the relative desirability of work and leisure are reflected in the shape of one's indifference curves. In Figure 2.3(a), we present the indifference curves of a "workaholic" who places a low value on leisure and a high value on work (income). Note that the workaholic's curves are relatively flat, indicating that this individual would give up an hour of leisure for a relatively small increase in income. Figure 2.3(b) shows the indifference curves of a "leisure lover" who puts a high value on leisure and a low value on work (income). Observe that this individual's indifference curves are steep, which means that a relatively large increase in income must be realized to sacrifice an hour of leisure. In each case, the indifference curves are convex to the origin, but the rate of decline of MRS L, Y is far greater for the leisure lover than for the workaholic.

Why the differences? First, it may be purely a matter of tastes or preferences rooted in personality. A second and related point is that the occupations of individuals differ. The flat curves of Figure 2.3(a) may pertain to a person who has a creative and challenging occupation—for example, a painter, ceramist, or musician. Such work entails little disutility, and hence it takes only a small increase in income to induce the artist to sacrifice an hour of leisure. Conversely, an unpleasant job in a coal mine or on an assembly line may elicit steep indifference curves. Such work involves substantial disutility, and a large increase in income is required to induce one to give up an hour of leisure. Finally, an individual's personal circumstances may affect his or her relative evaluations of labor market work and leisure. For example, a young mother with two or three preschool children or a college student may have relatively steep indifference curves because "leisure" (non-labor market time) is valuable for child care and studying. Similarly, José may be married and, therefore, may have substantial financial obligations. Consequently, his indifference curves are relatively flat: He is quite willing to give

FIGURE 2.3 **Different Preferences for Work (Income) and Leisure**

The shape of one's indifference curves depends on one's relative preferences for work (income) and leisure. In (a) we portray a "workaholic" who is willing to give up an hour of leisure for only a small increase in income. In comparison the "leisure lover" shown in (b) requires a large increase in income to sacrifice an hour of leisure or non-labor market time.

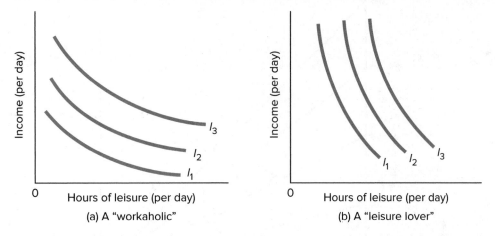

(a) A "workaholic"

(b) A "leisure lover"

up leisure for income. On the other hand, John is single and his financial responsibilities are less compelling. He is less willing to give up leisure for income, and his indifference curves are, therefore, relatively steep. In short, personality, the type of work under consideration, and personal circumstances may influence the shape of a person's indifference curves.

Budget Constraint

Our assertion that the individual maximizes utility by achieving a position on the highest *attainable* indifference curve implies that the choice of curves is constrained. Specifically, the individual is constrained by the amount of monetary income that is available. Let's assume for the moment that an individual's only source of monetary income is from work. In other words, we are assuming that the individual has no nonlabor income, no accumulated savings to draw on, and no possibility of borrowing funds. Let's also suppose that the wage rate confronting this person in the labor market is given in that the individual cannot alter the hourly wage paid for his or her services by varying the number of hours worked.[2] Thus we can draw a *budget (wage) constraint line, which shows all the various combinations of income (goods) and leisure that a worker might realize or obtain, given the wage rate*. If the given wage rate is $1, we can draw a budget line from 24 hours on the horizontal leisure axis to $24 on the vertical income axis in Figure 2.4. Given the $1 wage rate, at the extremes an individual could obtain (*a*) 24 hours of leisure and no income or (*b*) $24 of income and no leisure. The line connecting these two points reveals all other attainable options: $8 of income and 16 hours of leisure, $12 of income and 12 hours of leisure, and so forth. Observe that the absolute value of the slope of this budget line is 1, reflecting the $1 wage rate. In moving northwest along the line, one hour of leisure must be sacrificed to obtain each $1 of income. This is true because the wage rate is $1.

Similarly, if the wage rate is $2, the appropriate budget line would be anchored at 24 hours of leisure and $48 of real income. The slope of this line is 2, again reflecting the wage rate. The budget constraints for wage rates of $3 and $4 are also shown in Figure 2.4. We observe that the budget lines fan out clockwise from the right origin as the wage rate goes up. In each case, the wage rate—the slope of the budget line—reflects the objective

[2] This assumption permits us to use a linear budget constraint.

FIGURE 2.4 Budget Constraints

A budget constraint (line) can be drawn for each possible wage rate. The wage rate determines the slope of each budget line. Specifically, budget lines fan out clockwise from the right origin as the wage rate increases.

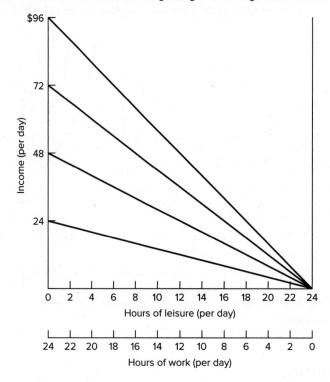

or market rate of exchange between income and leisure. If the wage rate is $1, an individual can exchange one hour of leisure (by working) and obtain $1 worth of income. If the wage rate is $2, one hour of leisure can be exchanged in the labor market for $2 of income, and so forth.[3]

Utility Maximization

The individual's optimal or utility-maximizing position can be determined by bringing together the subjective preferences embodied in the indifference curves and the objective market information contained in each budget line. This is shown in Figure 2.5, where we assume that the wage rate is $2.

Recall that the farther the indifference curve is from the origin, the greater the person's total utility; therefore, an individual will maximize total utility by attaining the highest possible indifference curve. Given the $2 wage rate, no leisure–income combination is attainable outside—to the northeast—of the resulting HW budget constraint. This particular budget constraint allows the individual to realize the highest attainable level of utility at point u_1, where the budget line just touches (is tangent to) indifference curve I_2. Of all the attainable positions on the various indifference curves, point u_1 is clearly on the curve that is farthest from the origin and, therefore, yields the highest achievable level of total utility. We observe that the individual will choose to work 8 hours, earning a daily income of $16 and enjoying 16 hours of leisure.

---

[3] In equation form, the budget constraint is $Y = WH$, where Y = income, W = wage rate, and H = number of hours of work. Hence $Y = W$ $(24 − L) = 24W − WL$, where L = number of hours of leisure and the slope of the budget line is $−W$.

It is important to recognize that at this optimal position, the individual and the market agree about the relative worth of leisure and income at the margin. At u_1 the slope of indifference curve I_2 and the slope of the budget line are equal. The individual's preferences are such that he or she is subjectively willing to substitute leisure for income at precisely the same exchange rate as the objective information of the labor market requires. The *optimal work–leisure position is achieved where MRS L, Y (the slope of the indifference curve) is equal to the wage rate (the slope of the budget line)*. By definition, these slopes are equal only at the point of tangency.

We can reinforce our understanding of the optimal work–leisure position by considering briefly why points *a* and *b* are *not* optimal. Let's start with point *b,* where we note that indifference curve I_1 is steeper than the budget line, or more technically, MRS *L, Y* is greater than the wage rate. For example, the MRS *L, Y* might be 4 while the wage rate is $2. What does this mean? It indicates that an additional hour of leisure is worth $4 to this individual but that she will have to sacrifice only $2 of income to obtain that extra hour of leisure. Acquiring something worth $4 at the cost of something worth only $2 is clearly a beneficial exchange. Thus "trading" income (by working fewer hours) for leisure will benefit her. These trades in effect move her down budget line *HW* and on to successively higher indifference curves. At point u_1, all such trades are exhausted, and this individual and the market agree about the value of work (income) and leisure at the margin. As noted earlier, at u_1 the MRS *L, Y* equals the wage rate. At this point, the individual and the market agree that the marginal hour of leisure is worth $2. Later we will note that at point *b* the individual will feel "overemployed" in that she can increase her total utility by working fewer hours—that is, by moving to a point such as u_1 where she has more leisure and less income.

FIGURE 2.5 **Utility Maximization: The Optimal Choice between Leisure and Income**

The optimal or utility-maximizing combination of leisure and income for the worker is at point u_1, where the budget constraint is tangent to the highest attainable indifference curve I_2.

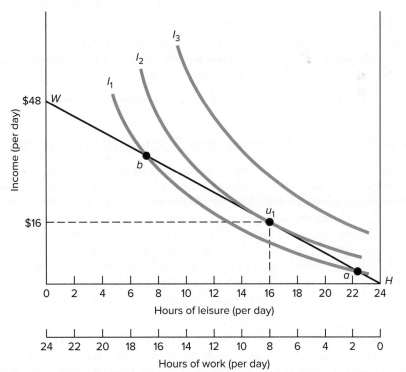

The situation is just the opposite at point a. Here the slope of indifference curve I_1 is less than the budget line; in other words, MRS L, Y is less than the wage rate. To illustrate, the wage rate is $2 and the MRS L, Y might be only $1. This indicates that an hour of leisure is worth only $1 at the margin but that the individual can actually get $2 worth of income by sacrificing an hour of leisure. Getting something worth $2 by giving up something worth only $1 is obviously a beneficial trade. In trading leisure for income (by working more hours), the individual moves up the HW budget line to preferred positions on higher indifference curves. Again, all such beneficial exchanges of leisure for income will be completed when point u_1 is achieved because here the MRS L, Y and the wage rate are equal. At u_1, leisure and income are of equal value at the margin. At point a, the individual would feel "underemployed." She could increase her total utility by working more hours—that is, by moving to a point such as u_1 where she has less leisure and more income.

2.1 *Quick Review*

- An income–leisure indifference curve represents all combinations of income and leisure that provide equal total utility; its slope is called the marginal rate of substitution (MRS).
- Each successive curve to the northeast in an indifference map indicates a greater level of total utility.
- An income–leisure budget line reveals all combinations of income and leisure that a worker can achieve at a specific hourly wage rate.
- The utility-maximizing combination of income and leisure occurs at the point of tangency between the budget line and the highest attainable indifference curve; there MRS L, Y (the slope of the indifference curve) equals the wage rate (the slope of the budget line).

Your Turn

Suppose that at a particular combination of income and leisure, the slope of the budget line is steeper than the slope of the indifference curve it intersects. How should the worker adjust work hours? (*Answer:* See page 540.)

Wage Rate Changes: Income and Substitution Effects

Will an individual choose to work more or fewer hours as the wage rate changes? It depends. Figure 2.6(a) repeats the u_1 utility-maximizing position of Figure 2.5 but adds four more budget lines and indicates the relevant optimal positions associated with each. We observe that for the wage rate increase that moves the budget line from W_1 to W_2, the optimal position moves from u_1 to u_2. On the horizontal axis, we find that the individual chooses fewer hours of leisure and more hours of work. Similarly, the wage rate increase that shifts the budget constraint from W_2 to W_3 also entails more hours of work and fewer hours of leisure at u_3 than is the case at u_2. But the further wage rate boost reflected by the shift of the budget line from W_3 to W_4 produces an optimum at u_4 that involves less work and more leisure than the prior optimum u_3. Similarly, the wage increase depicted by the increase in the budget line from W_4 to W_5 causes a further reduction in hours of work at u_5.

This analysis suggests that *for a specific person, hours of work may for a time increase as wage rates rise, but beyond some point, further wage increases may reduce the hours of labor supplied.* Indeed, we can translate the hours of work–wage rate combinations associated with the five optimal positions of Figure 2.6(a) into a diagram such as that shown in Figure 2.6(b), which has traditional axes measuring wage rates on the vertical axis and hours of labor supplied left to right on the horizontal axis. In so doing, we find that this individual's labor supply curve is forward-rising for a time and then backward-bending. This curve is known as a *backward-bending labor supply curve*, the forward-rising portion being expected or taken for granted. We can envision an individual labor supply curve for each person in the economy. But keep in mind that each individual's preferences for work versus leisure are unique, so the exact location, shape, and point of the backward bend of the curve vary from person to person.

Why is a backward-bending labor supply curve a realistic possibility? This can be explained in terms of the income and substitution effects. When the wage rate changes, these two effects tend to alter one's utility-maximizing position.

Income Effect

The income effect refers to the change in the desired hours of work resulting from a change in income, holding the wage rate constant.[4] We will discover that the income effect of a wage *increase* is found by isolating the increase in work hours resulting solely from the increase in potential income per hour of work, *as if the price of leisure (the wage rate) did not change.* A wage rate increase means that a larger money income is obtainable from a given number of hours of work. We would expect an individual to use a part of this enhanced income to buy goods and services: a new TV, movie tickets, and so on. But if we make the reasonable assumption

FIGURE 2.6 Derivation of the Backward-Bending Labor Supply Curve

In (a) higher wage rates result in a series of increasingly steep budget lines whose tangencies with indifference curves locate a series of utility-maximizing positions. The movement from u_1 to u_2 and u_3 reveals that for a time higher wage rates are associated with longer hours of work, whereas the shifts from u_3 to u_4 and u_5 indicate that still higher wage rates entail fewer hours of work. The overall result is a backward-bending labor supply curve as shown in (b).

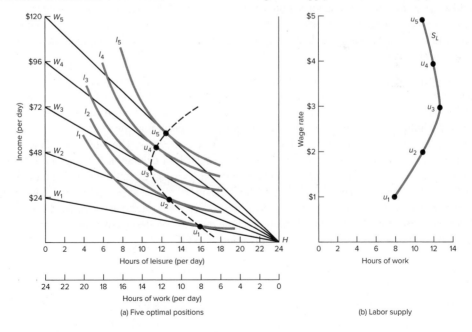

(a) Five optimal positions

(b) Labor supply

---

[4] In mathematical terms, income effect $= \dfrac{\Delta H}{\Delta Y}\bigg|\ \overline{W}\ < 0$, where H = hours of work, Y = income, and $\overline{W}$ = constant wage.

that leisure is a *normal good*–a good of which more is consumed as income rises–then we can expect that a part of one's expanded income might be used to "purchase" leisure. Consumers derive utility not from goods alone but from combinations of goods and nonmarket time (leisure). Movie tickets yield satisfaction only if one has the time to enjoy them. How does one purchase leisure or nonmarket time? In a unique way: by working fewer hours. This means that when wage rates *rise,* and leisure is a normal good, the income effect reduces the desired number of hours of work.

Substitution Effect

The substitution effect indicates the change in the desired hours of work resulting from a change in the wage rate, keeping income constant.[5] In the context of a wage rate increase, it evidences itself in an increase in the desired number of hours of work. When the wage rate increases, the relative price of leisure is altered. Specifically, an increase in the wage rate raises the "price" or opportunity cost of leisure. Because of the higher wage rate, one must now forgo more income (goods) for each hour of leisure consumed (not worked). The basic theory of economic choice implies that an individual will purchase less of any normal good when it becomes relatively more expensive. In brief, the higher price of leisure prompts one to consume less leisure or, in other words, to work more. The substitution effect merely tells us that when wage rates rise and leisure becomes more expensive, it is sensible to substitute work for leisure. For a wage *increase,* the substitution effect makes the person want to work more hours.[6]

Net Effect

The overall effect of an increase in the wage rate on the number of hours an individual wants to work depends on the relative magnitudes of these two effects. Economic theory does not predict the outcome. *If the substitution effect dominates the income effect, the individual will choose to work more hours when the wage rate rises.* Dominance of the substitution effect is reflected in shifts from u_1 to u_2 to u_3 in Figure 2.6(a) and the upward-sloping portion of the labor supply curve in Figure 2.6(b). *But if the income effect is larger than the substitution effect, a wage increase will prompt the individual to work fewer hours.* The movements from u_3 to u_4 and u_5 in Figure 2.6(a) and the backward-bending portion of the labor supply curve in Figure 2.6(b) are relevant in this case.

Table 2.1 provides a useful summary and extension of our discussion of the implications of the relative sizes of the substitution and income effects for the desired hours of work. Columns 1, 2a, and 3 summarize the discussion we have just completed. Note from column 2a that this discussion was couched in terms of a wage rate *increase.* Columns 1, 2b, and 3 are important because they reveal that the impact of the substitution and income effects on hours of work is reversed if we assume a wage *decrease.* The income effect associated with a wage decline is that the desired hours of work increase. That is, a decline in the wage rate will reduce an individual's income from a given number of hours of work, and we can expect the individual to purchase less leisure and, therefore, choose to work more hours. Similarly, in terms of a wage decline, the substitution effect evidences itself as a decline in work hours. A reduction in the wage rate makes leisure cheaper, prompting one to consume more of it. Once again, the final outcome depends on the relative strength of the two effects. Study Table 2.1 carefully to be certain that you fully understand it.

---

[5] In mathematical terms, substitution effect $= \dfrac{\Delta H}{\Delta W}\bigg|\, \overline{Y} > 0$, where H = hours of work, W = wage, and $\overline{Y}$ constant income.

[6] An alternative way to express the substitution effect is to say that a higher wage rate reduces the "price of income" because it now takes a smaller amount of work time to obtain $1 worth of goods. When the wage rate is $2 per hour, the "price" of $1 of income is half an hour of work time. But if the wage rate increases to $4 per hour, the "price" of $1 of income falls to one-quarter of an hour. Now that income is cheaper, it makes sense to purchase more of it. This purchase is made by working more hours and taking less leisure. The classic article is Lionel Robbins, "On the Elasticity of Demand for Income in Terms of Effort," *Economica,* June 1930, pp. 123–129.

TABLE 2.1 Wage Changes and Hours of Work: Substitution and Income Effects

(1) Size of Effects	(2) Impact on Hours of Work		(3) Slope of Labor Supply Curve
	(a) Wage Rate Increase	(b) Wage Rate Decrease	
Substitution effect exceeds income effect.	Increase	Decrease	Positive
Income effect equals substitution effect.	No change	No change	Vertical
Income effect exceeds substitution effect.	Decrease	Increase	Negative

Graphic Portrayal of Income and Substitution Effects

Figure 2.7 permits us to isolate graphically the income and substitution effects associated with a wage rate increase for a specific person. Remember that the substitution effect reflects the change in desired hours of work arising solely because an increase in the wage rate alters the relative prices of income and leisure. Therefore, to isolate the substitution effect, we must control the increase in income created by the increase in the wage rate. Recall, too, that the income effect indicates the change in the hours of work occurring solely because the higher wage rate means a larger total income from any number of hours of work. In portraying the income effect, we must hold constant the relative prices of income and leisure—in other words, the wage rate.

Consider Figure 2.7. As the wage rate increases and shifts the budget line from HW_1 to HW_2, the resulting movement of the utility-maximizing position from u_1 on I_1 to u_2 on I_2 is the consequence of the combined income and substitution effects. We isolate the *income effect* by drawing the budget line nW', which is parallel to HW_1 and tangent to I_2 at point u'_2. The vertical distance Hn measures the amount of *nonlabor* income that would be required to make the individual just as well off (that is, attain the same total utility) at u'_2 as at u_2. But by moving the individual from curve I_1 to curve I_2 with *nonlabor* income, we have left the wage rate (that is, the relative prices of leisure and goods) unchanged.[7] No substitution effect is involved here. The movement from u_1 to u'_2, therefore, measures or isolates the income effect. As noted earlier, this effect results in fewer work hours when analyzed from the vantage point of an increase in wage rates and hence an increase in income. Specifically, the income effect would result in the individual wanting to work $h_1h'_2$ fewer hours.

We isolate the *substitution effect* as follows. The substitution effect occurs solely because the slope of the budget line—the relative prices of income and leisure—has been altered by the assumed increase in the wage rate. We are concerned with budget lines nW' and HW_2 because their comparison involves no change in the individual's well-being; they pertain to the same indifference curve I_2. Line nW', however, reflects the original wage rate (also embodied in HW_1), whereas HW_2 mirrors the new higher wage rate. The movement from u'_2 to u_2 on curve I_2 is the substitution effect. It is solely the result of a change in the relative prices of leisure and goods or, specifically, the fact that goods have become cheaper and leisure more expensive. It is no surprise that this prompts a substitution of work (goods) for leisure. For a wage rate increase, the hours of work rise (the substitution effect). In this case, the individual wishes to work h'_2h_2 more hours.

---

[7] Note that the slopes of HW_1 and nW' are the same; the lines are parallel, meaning the wage rate embodied in both budget lines is the same.

Keep in mind that the individual does not actually "move" to a new optimal position in two distinct steps, but rather goes directly from u_1 to u_2. We have conceptually isolated the income and substitution effects to stress that there are two opposing ways in which a wage increase affects the worker: by increasing monetary income *and* by increasing the relative price of leisure. Both effects are at work, but one effect may dominate the other.[8]

In Figure 2.7, the income and substitution effects can be thought of in terms of a boating analogy. Assume a boat is drifting on the ocean. Suppose the tide moves the boat eastward while the surface wind blows it westward. Both forces are present, but whether the boat actually moves east or west depends on which of these forces is strongest. So it is also with the income and substitution effects of a wage change.

To summarize: In this instance, the income effect is represented by the rightward horizontal movement from u_1 to u'_2–that is, from Hh_1 to Hh'_2 hours of work. The substitution effect is shown by the leftward horizontal movement from u'_2 to u_2–that is, from Hh'_2 to Hh_2 hours of work. In this case, the substitution effect (increased work hours) is larger than the income effect (reduced work hours). The net effect is an increase in hours of work from Hh_1 to Hh_2; at the higher wage rate, the individual wants to work h_1h_2 additional hours.

FIGURE 2.7   The Income and Substitution Effects of a Wage Rate Increase

Assuming leisure is a normal good, the income effect associated with a wage increase will always reduce hours of work. It is shown here as a reduction in work time of $h_1h'_2$ hours. The substitution effect, stemming from a rise in the wage rate, evidences itself in an increase in the hours of work. The increase in hours of work of h'_2h_2 hours shows the substitution effect. In this instance, the substitution effect outweighs the income effect, and the worker chooses to work h_1h_2 additional hours as a result of the higher wage.

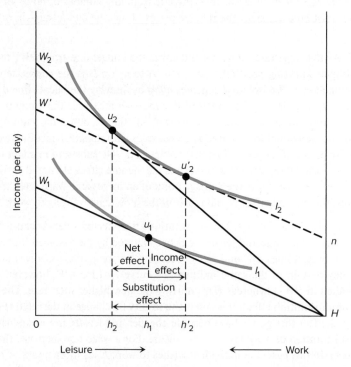

---

[8] We have presented the Hicks decomposition of income and substitution effects, which holds the utility constant when deriving the substitution effect. An alternative approach is the Slutsky decomposition, which holds income level constant when calculating the substitution effect. The decompositions don't differ in the ultimate impact of a wage change on labor supply–just in the intermediate steps.

This individual is clearly on the upward-sloping segment of his or her labor supply curve; the wage rate and the desired hours of work are directly related.

It is a worthwhile exercise for you to diagram and explain the case in which the income effect is larger than the substitution effect, causing the labor supply curve to be backward-bending. Questions 2 and 3 at the end of this chapter also are relevant.

Rationale for the Backward-Bending Supply Curve

From Figure 2.6, we remember that wage rate increases are initially associated with the desire to work more hours. Specifically, for the wage increases that shift the budget line from W_1 through W_3 the absolute value of the substitution effects must be greater than that of the income effects, yielding the forward-rising segment of the labor supply curve. But further increases in the wage rate that shift the budget line from W_3 through W_5 are associated with the choice to work fewer hours. The income effects of these wage rate increases are greater than the substitution effects, yielding the backward-bending segment of the labor supply curve.

What is the rationale for this reversal? The answer is that points u_1 and u_2 are at positions on indifference curves where the amount of leisure is large relative to the amount of income (goods). That is, u_1 and u_2 are located on relatively flat portions of indifference curves, where MRS L, Y is small because the individual is willing to give up substantial amounts of leisure for an additional unit of income or goods. This means that the substitution effect is large—so large that it dominates the income effect. The individual's labor supply curve is forward-rising: Higher wage rates induce more hours of work. But points u_3, u_4, and u_5 are reached only after much leisure has been exchanged in the labor market for income. At these points, the individual has a relatively large amount of income and relatively little leisure. This is reflected in the relative steepness of the indifference curves. In other words, MRS L, Y is large, indicating that the individual is willing to give up only a small amount of leisure for an additional unit of income. This means that the substitution effect is small and in this case is dominated by the income effect. Consequently, the labor supply curve of the individual becomes backward-bending: Rising wage rates are associated with fewer hours of work.

Empirical Evidence

What do empirical studies reveal about labor supply curves? The evidence differs rather sharply between males and females. Specifically, most studies indicate that male labor supply is quite insensitive to changes in wage rates, whereas female labor supply is more responsive to changes in wage rates. In a survey of recent studies, McCelland and Mok report that a 10 percent increase in male and single-women wage rates would change the amount of labor supplied by 1 percent.[9] However, the corresponding figure for married women is 4 percent.[10] Apparently for men the substitution effect very slightly dominates the income effect when wage rates rise. For women, the substitution effect seems to substantially dominate the income effect.

 How might we explain the apparent differences in the labor supply responses of males and females to a wage change? The answer hinges on existing differences in the allocation of time. A high percentage of prime-age adult males—nearly 90 percent—work full-time. Furthermore,

---

[9] Based on the range midpoint in Robert McCelland and Shannon Mom, "A Review of Recent Research on Labor Supply Elasticities," Congressional Budget Office Working Paper 2012-12, October 2012.

[10] For another survey of labor supply elasticities, see Oliver Bargain and Andreas Peichl, "Own-Wage Labor Supply Elasticities: Variation Across Time and Estimation Methods," *IZA Journal of Labor Economics*, October 31, 2016, pp. 1–31. For evidence that the typical estimated labor supply elasticity is too large due to measurement error, seeGarry F. Barrett and Daniel S. Hamermesh, "Labor Supply Elasticities: Overcoming Nonclassical Measurement Error Using More Accurate Hours Data," *Journal of Human Resources*, Winter 2019, pp. 255–265.

men on the average do relatively little housework. Thus, increased hours of work in response to a wage rate increase would have to come at the expense of pure leisure—that is, nonproductive activities or rest and relaxation. Apparently pure leisure and labor market work are not highly substitutable. The result is a small substitution effect for men and a nearly vertical labor supply curve. In comparison, the labor market participation rate for women is significantly less than that for men; many women work part-time, and women assume major responsibility for work within the home. At the risk of oversimplification, this means that while men use their time in basically two ways (market work and pure leisure), women use their time in three ways (market work, work in the home, and pure leisure). For many married women, work in the home and work in the labor market are highly substitutable. That is, household work may be accomplished by doing it oneself *or* by working in the labor market and using a portion of one's earnings for hiring housecleaning and child care help and purchasing prepared meals. Thus, when wage rates increase, many women substitute labor market work for work in the home. They enter the labor force, switch from part-time to full-time jobs, or increase their hours on full-time jobs.[11] In other words, a strong substitution effect occurs, which implies an upward-sloping labor supply curve for married women.

2.1   World of Work

Work Hours Linked to Pollution

Pollution has many effects on the economy. For example, it reduces tourism, lowers property values, and harms the commercial fishing industry and recreational industries. Another possible way pollution may impact the economy is through its effect on work hours.

Pollution has a theoretically ambiguous effect on labor supply. On one hand, greater pollution will tend to decrease work hours since workers will be more likely to get sick and miss work. On the other hand, higher pollution levels may not decrease work hours. The health effects of pollution may not be large enough to impede work. Also, individuals may work more hours if they enjoy leisure less due to poorer health or they consume more health-related goods. Lastly, health-related declines in worker productivity may lower wages, which could lower work hours if the substitution effect outweighs the income effect.

Rema Hanna and Paulina Oliva examine the impact of pollution on work hours by analyzing the effect of the closure of a large oil refinery in Mexico City in March 1991. Pollution, as measured by the levels of sulfur dioxide, fell by 19.7 percent for neighborhoods within a 5-kilometer radius of the oil refinery after the closure. As result, individuals living near the oil refinery increased their average weekly work hours by 1.3 hours (or 3.5 percent) relative to individuals living farther away from the refinery. The distribution of work hours was also affected as well as the level of work hours. Neighborhoods affected by the closure experienced a 6 percentage point increase in the probability of working over 40 hours a week and about a 2.5 percentage point increase in the probability of working more than 10 hours per week.

Source: Based on Rema Hanna and Paulina Oliva, "The Effect of Pollution on Labor Supply: Evidence from a Natural Experiment in Mexico City," *Journal of Public Economics*, February 2015, pp. 68–79.

---

[11] Most of the gender differences in the labor supply result from differences in labor force participation between men and women, not from differences in the hours of work supplied by those working. See James J. Heckman, "What Has Been Learned about Labor Supply in the Past Twenty Years?" *American Economic Review,* May 1993, pp. 116–121.

It is important to note that the sensitivity of married women to wage rates appears to be diminishing over time, and their responsiveness is becoming more like that of men. Blau and Kahn report that the responsiveness of married women to changes in wage rates fell by half between 1980 and 2000.[12] They argue that this finding is the result of women's greater labor market attachment and men and women more equally sharing home and market responsibilities. Bishop, Heim, and Mihaly report a large drop in the responsiveness of single-women to wage rates between 1979 and 2003. They indicate that part of the decline is due to the work requirements instituted in the 1996 welfare reform act.[13]

Elasticity versus Changes in Labor Supply

To this point, we have been discussing the direction in which wage changes cause an individual to alter the hours of work supplied. Implicitly, our discussion has focused on the wage elasticity of individual labor supply. More precisely, *wage elasticity of labor supply* is defined as follows:

$$E_S = \frac{\text{percentage change in quantity of labor supplied}}{\text{percentage change in the wage rate}} \qquad (2.1)$$

Over specific ranges of an individual's labor supply curve, the elasticity coefficient given in Equation (2.1) may be zero (perfectly inelastic), infinite (perfectly elastic), less than 1 (relatively inelastic), greater than 1 (relatively elastic), or negative (backward-bending). The elasticity will depend on the relative strengths of the income and substitution effects generated by a wage rate change. But these movements *along* an existing individual labor supply curve [as in Figure 2.6(b)] should not be confused with *shifts* in the entire supply curve. These shifts—increases or decreases in labor supply—occur in response to changes in either of two factors that we have heretofore held constant. First, changes in *nonlabor income* may shift an individual's labor supply curve. Receiving a large inheritance, winning a lottery, qualifying for a pension, or becoming eligible for welfare benefits may shift one's labor supply curve leftward—that is, cause a decrease in labor supply. Or conversely, the layoff of one's spouse or a significant decline in dividend income may produce an increase (rightward shift) in labor supply.

Second, a change in a person's indifference map—that is, in work–leisure preferences—may shift the labor supply curve. An improvement in working conditions, availability of child care, or large medical bills may change a person's indifference map in ways that increase his or her labor supply. Working in the opposite direction, purchasing a product requiring leisure to enjoy or reaching a culturally acceptable retirement age may alter one's indifference map so that labor supply declines. A more detailed treatment of factors that shift the labor supply curve is provided in Chapter 6.

WW2.2 To summarize: As Figure 2.6 suggests, given work–leisure preferences and nonlabor income, a change in wage rates traces out or locates the individual's labor supply curve. The elasticity of this curve for any particular wage change—that is, the sensitivity of hours one wants to work to a change in wages—depends on the relative sizes of the income and substitution effects. In contrast, changes in work–leisure preferences or in nonlabor income shift the location of one's labor supply curve.

---

[12] Francine D. Blau and Lawrence M. Kahn, "Changes in the Labor Supply of Married Women: 1980–2000," *Journal of Labor Economics,* July 2007, pp. 393–438. For a similar result, see Bradley T. Heim, "The Incredible Shrinking Elasticities: Married Female Labor Supply, 1978–2002," *Journal of Human Resources* 42, No. 4 (2007), pp. 881–918.

[13] Kelly Bishop, Bradley Heim, and Kata Mihaly, "Single Women's Labor Supply Elasticities: Trends and Policy Implications," *Industrial and Labor Relations Review,* October 2009, pp. 146–168.

2.2 World of Work

Labor Supply of Politicians

The labor market for politicians is very different than for most jobs. Politicians compete for a fixed number of positions through an election and can be fired only at election time. The salary of politicians is chosen by legislation rather than through supply and demand forces.

Fisman, Harmon, Kamenica, and Munk examine the labor supply of Members of the European Parliament (MEP) using a sharp change in members' earnings. There are currently 751 MEPs from 28 countries. Before 2009, MEP members received the pay of members of the lower house on the home country parliament. As a result, there was a wide variation in the annual pay of MEPs. In 2004, it ranged from 144,084 Euros for those from Italy to 10,080 for those from Hungary. Starting in 2009, nearly all MEPs were paid about 84,000 Euros per year.

The change in MEP pay affected the willingness of MEPs to run for office. A doubling of MEP pay increases the probability that an MEP runs for reelection by 23 percentage points, and increases the number of parties that run a candidate. A pay increase also significantly reduced the chance that an MEP would quit before the end of her five-year term.

The change in MEP pay affected the quality of MEPs elected candidates. Doubling the MEP salary lowers the probability that an MEP attended ranked in the top 500 in the world by 4.2 percentage points or 14 percent. The researchers suggest that higher pay may be causing less civic-minded or less able individuals to seek office.

MEPs from more corrupt countries have a lower work effort. They are more likely to miss all of the votes in a day and shirk by signing a register so that they could collect their daily allowance and then be absent for all of the votes on that day.

Source: Based on Raymond Fisman, Nikolaj A. Harmon, Emir Kamenica, and Inger Munk, "Labor Supply of Politicians," *Journal of the European Economic Association*, October 2015, pp. 871–905.

2.2 *Quick Review*

- A change in the wage rate produces two simultaneous effects: *(a)* an income effect that, taken alone, changes a worker's desired hours of work in the opposite direction as the wage rate change and *(b)* a substitution effect that, taken alone, changes a worker's desired hours of work in the same direction as the wage rate change.

- As the wage rate rises, the labor supply curve for a typical person first is positively sloped as the substitution effect swamps the income effect; eventually the curve becomes negatively sloped (turns backward) as the income effect of further wage rate hikes exceeds the substitution effect.

- The wage elasticity of supply is the percentage change in the quantity of labor supplied divided by the percentage change in the wage rate.

Your Turn

Suppose an individual's wage rate decreases and the income effect dominates the substitution effect. What will be the impact on the desired hours of work? What is the relevant segment of the person's labor supply curve? (*Answers:* See page 540.)

APPLYING AND EXTENDING THE MODEL

The basic model just developed outlines the logic of the work–leisure decision, provides a rationale for an individual's backward-bending labor supply curve, and helps us understand changes in individual labor supply. Our goal now is to extend, embellish, and apply the basic work–leisure model. Specifically, we want to show that the work–leisure model is useful in delineating reasons for nonparticipation in the labor force, in explaining how a standard workweek might cause certain workers to feel overemployed or underemployed, and in comparing the impact that various pay schemes and income maintenance programs might have on work incentives.

Nonparticipants and the Reservation Wage

Figure 2.8 portrays the case of a nonparticipant: an individual who decides *not* to be in the labor force. Note the following characteristics in Figure 2.8. First, the person's indifference curves are steep, indicating that leisure (nonmarket time) is valued very highly relative to income. The marginal rates of substitution of leisure for income are high, meaning that the individual is quite willing to forgo income for leisure or nonmarket time. This might reflect the preferences of, say, a 20-year-old who deems it important to devote time and effort to attending college. Second, we note the availability of nonlabor income HN. (Ignore all other budget lines but HNW for the moment.) Perhaps this nonlabor income takes the form of an intrahousehold transfer to the young student from the earned income of parents. Finally, the relative flatness of the NW budget line indicates that the wage rate that this individual can earn in the labor market is relatively low. For example, the student may have modest skills and little or no labor market experience and, therefore, is not yet able to command a high wage rate by working.

The optimal position in Figure 2.8 is based on the same principle employed in Figure 2.5: Given budget line HNW, choose the position that puts one on the highest attainable indifference curve. In this case, the highest level of utility is achieved at point N. Here the budget constraint HNW touches I_3. At this point, the individual is *not* participating in the labor market; all of this person's time is devoted to nonmarket activities. The technical reason is that at all points within the axes of the diagram, the person's indifference curves are more steeply sloped than the budget constraint. In other words, at all points within the diagram, the individual values leisure (nonmarket time) more highly at the margin than does the market. Note that in contrast to Figure 2.5, the optimal outcome at N is *not* a tangency position but rather a "corner" solution. At N the wage rate is less than MRS L,Y, which means the individual values nonmarket time more highly than does the market. But given the fact that the individual is a nonparticipant, no further substitution of leisure for work is possible.

The importance of low earning capacity in the labor market and the availability of nonlabor income can be understood if we replace the original budget line HNW in Figure 2.8 with HuW'. This new budget line reduces nonlabor income to zero *and* assumes that a much higher wage rate can be garnered in the labor market. Suppose, for example, that the student is a highly skilled computer programmer who has immediate employment opportunities at a high wage. Or to make the point even more graphic, suppose the student is a premier college basketball player who is sought by the National Basketball Association. We find that under these new conditions the individual would prefer to participate in the labor force. The optimal position will now be at *u*, where the person will want to work six or seven hours per day.

Figure 2.8 also allows us to introduce the concept of the reservation wage, which is useful in understanding why some individuals participate in the labor force and others do not. In simple terms, *the reservation wage is the highest wage rate at which an individual chooses* not *to work or, if you prefer, the lowest wage rate at which one would decide to work.* When nonlabor income is *HN*, as in Figure 2.8, the reservation wage is the market wage rate implicit in the broken budget line that is equal to the slope of indifference curve I_3 at zero hours of work. At this particular wage rate, the value of work and the value of nonmarket time (leisure) are equal. If the market wage is below the reservation wage, the individual will clearly choose to be a nonparticipant. The relatively low market wage rate embodied in the *NW* segment of the *HNW* budget line demonstrates this decision *not* to be in the labor force. In nontechnical terms, at point *N* the value of nonmarket time to this individual exceeds the value of work, and therefore this person's well-being would be reduced by working. Conversely, if the market wage rate were above the reservation wage, the individual would be induced to become a labor market participant. You can demonstrate this by drawing a steeper budget line from point *N* that is tangent to I_4 at some point. With this steeper (higher market wage) budget line, we would find at point *N* that the value of work would be greater than the value of nonmarket time and that the individual's economic welfare would be enhanced by working.

FIGURE 2.8 **Nonparticipation: The College Student**

A high subjective evaluation of nonwork time (reflected in steep indifference curves), the availability of nonlabor income (*HN*), and low earning ability (*NW* is relatively flat) are all factors conducive to not participating in the labor force.

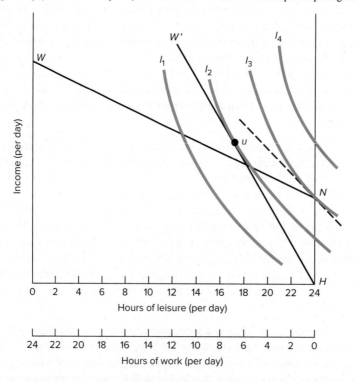

FIGURE 2.9 **Nonparticipation: Pensions and the Elderly**

An elderly worker whose wage rate yields the budget line *HW* will be a labor force participant at *u*. However, when a pension of *HN* becomes available at, say, age 65, the individual will prefer to become a nonparticipant at point *N*.

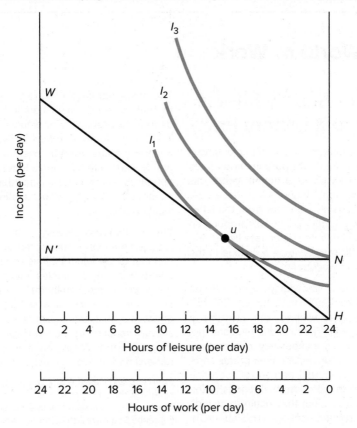

Figure 2.9 illustrates another common instance of nonparticipation in the labor force. Here we assume that an elderly worker is initially participating in the labor force, working about nine hours per day at optimal position *u* on indifference curve I_1. Suppose now that when the worker reaches age 65 a private or public pension of *HN* becomes available, *provided* the individual retires fully from work. In other words, the choice is between budget line *HW* and the associated optimal position at *u* or budget line *NN'* and the corner solution at point *N*. We find that *N* is preferable to *u* because it is associated with the higher indifference curve I_2. In this case, the availability of a pension—for example, Social Security benefits—induces the individual to become a nonparticipant. Stated differently, it shifts the person's labor supply curve [Figure 2.6(b)] leftward so that no labor is supplied at the market wage. Note that the decision to be a nonparticipant entails a *reduction* in money income but a more than compensating *increase* in leisure. The individual is better off at *N* than at *u*, even though income is reduced.

WW2.3   Empirical research confirms several generalizations arising from our discussion of Figures 2.8 and 2.9. First, other things being equal, full-time college attendance *is* a deterrent to labor force participation. This is also true of such things as the desire to care for one's preschool children. Stated alternatively, those who attach great marginal utility to nonmarket time (college attendance, child care) are more likely to be nonparticipants in the labor force. Second, other things being the same, the higher the nonlabor income available to a person from parents, a spouse, Social Security benefits, private pensions, welfare, and other sources, the less likely it is that the person will be a labor force participant. Finally, all else being equal, the greater the opportunity cost of not working—that is, the higher the wage obtainable in the labor market—the more likely it is that a person will be a labor force participant.[14]

2.3   World of Work

The Labor Supply Effects of Winning a Lottery Prize

In the work–leisure model, winning a lottery prize will have a significant pure income effect. We know that if leisure is a normal good, this effect may cause some workers to reduce their work hours or possibly withdraw from the labor force. Graphically, lottery prizes will produce an upward parallel shift in the wage rate line facing an individual. The result will be a decline in the optimal number of work hours.

Cesarini, Lindqvist, Notowidigdo, and Östling examine data from 1991 to 2010 on 247,255 Swedish lottery prize winners age 21 to 64 at the time of the win. Their results indicate that lottery prize winners immediately reduce their labor supply after winning, and their pretax earnings decrease by about 1 percent of the prize amount. The fall in work effort continues in the years following a win, but they diminish as individuals approach retirement age. The labor supply effects are similar by prize amount and the age, education level, and sex of the winner.

The lower earnings of lottery winners are due to both a reduction in hourly earnings and a decreased probability of being employed at all. The fall in hourly earnings is mostly due to a decline in hours worked rather than a drop in the hourly wage rate. Winning a lottery prize doesn't appear to increase the chance that an individual changes her employer, occupation, industry, or location of work.

The spouses of lottery prize winners also reduced their labor supply, but by less than one-half that of the winners. This finding implies that Swedish married couples make labor supply decisions as individuals instead of as a single unit. The existence of a spousal labor supply effect suggests that estimates of the labor supply impacts of government cash transfer programs that focus on only recipients will understate the overall labor supply effects.

Source: David Cesarini, Erik Lindqvist, Matthew J. Notowidigdo, and Robert Östling, "The Effect of Wealth on Individual and Household Labor Supply: Evidence from Swedish Lotteries," *American Economic Review*, December 2017, pp. 3917–3946.

Standard Workday

Our discussion thus far has implicitly assumed that workers can individually determine the number of hours they work. This is typically not the case. In the United States, a standard workday of 8 hours (40 hours per week) has evolved. This is partly due to federal legislation that obligates employers to pay time and a half for hours worked in excess of 40 per week. Furthermore, industries whose technologies involve the continuous processing of goods or components can divide the workday into three 8-hour shifts.

---

[14] Numerous studies confirm these conclusions. For example, for a discussion of the impact of disability insurance on the participation decision, see Eric French and Jae Song, "The Effect of Disability Insurance Receipt on Labor Supply," *American Economic Journal: Economic Policy*, May 2014, pp. 291-337. For a review of the evidence regarding the effect of child care costs on the labor force participation decision, see Taryn W. Morrissey, "Child Care andParent Labor Force Participation: A Review of the Research Literature," *Review of the Economics of the Household*, March 2017, pp. 1-24. For a survey of the effects of taxes, see Michael P. Keane, "Labor Supply and Taxes: A Survey," *Journal of Economic Literature*, December 2011, pp. 961-1075.

2.4 World of Work

Labor Supply of Florida Lobster Fishermen*

Most workers are required by their employer to work a fixed number of hours, which is typically eight hours per day. This restriction makes it more difficult for economists to empirically estimate labor supply curves, which are based on the assumption that individuals can freely choose the number of hours they want to work. As result, researchers have recently focused attention on jobs where workers are free to set the number of hours of work. One such occupation is Florida lobster fishermen.

Florida lobster fishermen have a lot of flexibility to determine their work hours. Fishermen may trap lobster for as many days as they like during the lobster season. A fisherman can work as many or as fewer hours as he or she wants within the daylight hours.

Using daily data on nearly 1,000 lobster fishermen over five fishing seasons, Tess Safford reports that the average fisherman has more than 300 possible days to catch lobsters and

does so about 20 percent of the time. The average fisherman works slightly less than eight hours per day and has hourly earnings of about $150.

One would expect that lobster fishermen would increase their labor supply when the hourly wage rate is higher. Stafford finds support for that conjecture. Lobster fishermen are more likely to work at the beginning of the season when lobsters are more plentiful and thus earnings are higher. They are also more likely to work near new moons when it is easier to catch lobsters.

Most of the responsiveness of labor supply of lobster fishermen comes from the decision to participate rather than hours of work per day. Stafford finds a 10 percent higher hourly wage rate increases the probability of participating by 13 percent to 14 percent. However, the same 10 percent rise in the hourly wage rate increases hours of work by only 0.7 percent.

*Based on Tess M. Stafford, "What Do Fishermen Tell Us That Taxi Drivers Don't? An Empirical Examination of Labor Supply," *Journal of Labor Economics,* July 2015, pp. 683–710.

Overemployment

What may happen when a worker confronts a standard workday of HD hours, as illustrated in Figure 2.10? Consider first the solid indifference curves for Smith shown in the lower right portion of the diagram. Smith's optimal position is at u_s, where he prefers to work only Hh_s hours per day. But this is not a relevant choice; Smith can either work HD hours or not at all. That is, the relevant choice is between working the standard workday at P and being a nonparticipant at N. What to do? In this instance, it is preferable to work the standard workday because it entails a higher indifference curve I_{s2} as opposed to I_{s1}. Note once again that this is not a tangency position. At P the slope of I_{s2} is greater than the slope of the budget line NW. The MRS L, Y exceeds the wage rate, which means that the worker values leisure more highly at the margin than does the market. Clearly Smith would be better off at u_s with more leisure and less work per day.

Simply put, at point P in Figure 2.10 Smith will feel *overemployed.* Faced with a standard workday denying him added leisure, Smith may compensate by engaging in absenteeism; he may more or less habitually miss a day of work every week or so. In fact, the absence rate—the ratio of full-time workers with absences in a typical week to total full-time employment—was 2.9 percent in 2018. In that year, lost work time from absences was 1.5 percent of total hours usually worked. Many of these absent workers are absent without pay. Also, the overemployed worker described in Figure 2.10 may have a relatively high rate of job turnover. The worker obtains more leisure by frequently being "between jobs." Of course, we have purposely ruled out the possibility of part-time employment, which would appeal to this overemployed worker.

Underemployment

The broken indifference curves in the upper left portion of Figure 2.10 portray the position of Jones, an *underemployed* worker. Jones would prefer to be at u_j, where she would work the long workday of Hh_j hours as opposed to the shorter standard workday of HD hours. Note again that P is not a tangency position. At P the slope of Jones' indifference curve I_{j2} is less than the budget line. Jones' MRS L, Y is less than the wage rate. Simply stated, at the margin Jones values leisure less highly than does the market. This means that Jones will feel *underemployed* at P. Jones may realize her desire for more work and less leisure by moonlighting, or taking a second job. You should use Figure 2.10 to demonstrate that Jones might be willing to take a second job even if the wage rate were less than that paid on the primary job. In fact, in 2019 some 8.1 million workers—approximately 5.1 percent of all employees—held multiple jobs.

Survey data suggest that the majority of workers are satisfied with the number of hours they work. In 2001 the Bureau of Labor Statistics surveyed some 30,000 workers, and two-thirds indicated that they would prefer to work their current number of hours at their present rate of pay, rather than work more or fewer hours at proportionately higher or lower earnings. Only 7 percent expressed a preference for shorter hours, with a proportionate decline in earnings. Approximately one-fourth of all surveyed workers wanted to work more

FIGURE 2.10 Overemployment and Underemployment

When confronted with a standard workday of *HD,* Smith (solid indifference curves) will feel overemployed while Jones (broken indifference curves) will feel underemployed.

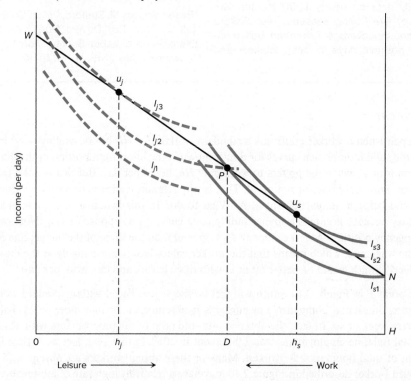

hours, with a proportionate increase in earnings. Not surprisingly, this latter group was dominated by young workers and low-wage earners.[15]

Premium Pay versus Straight Time

Although we ordinarily think of a worker receiving the same wage rate regardless of the number of hours worked, this is not always the case. Indeed, the Fair Labor Standards Act of 1938 specifies that workers covered by the legislation must be paid a premium wage—specifically, time and a half—for hours worked in excess of 40 per week. What impact does this premium pay provision have on the work–leisure decision? And how does it compare with a straight-time equivalent wage rate that provides an identical daily or weekly income from the same number of hours of work? Suppose, for example, that in a given industry a 10-hour workday (50-hour workweek) becomes commonplace. Does it make any difference with respect to work incentives to pay $6 per hour for the first 8 hours of work and $9 per hour for an additional 2 hours of overtime *or* to pay $6.60 per hour for each 10 hours of work? Both payment plans yield the same daily income of $66, so one is inclined to conclude that it makes no difference. But with the aid of Figure 2.11, we find that it *does* make a difference.

FIGURE 2.11   **Premium Wages and Straight-Time Equivalent**

Premium wage rates for overtime work will be more conducive to more hours of work (Hh$_2$) than a straight-time wage rate that would yield an equivalent daily income (Hh$_3$).

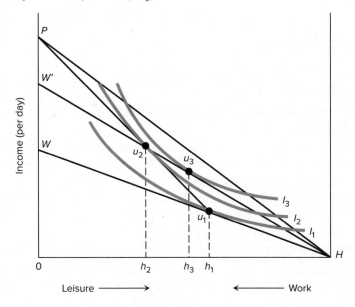

We assume in Figure 2.11 that a worker is initially at the optimal point u_1, where HW is tangent to indifference curve I_1. At u_1 the individual chooses to work Hh_1 hours, which we will presume to be the standard workday. Let us now suppose that the employer offers additional hours of overtime work at premium pay. This renders the u_1W segment of HW irrelevant, and the budget constraint now becomes Hu_1P. We observe that the

[15] Lonnie Golden and Tesfayi Gebreselassie, "Overemployment Mismatches: The Preference for Fewer Work Hours," *Monthly Labor Review,* April 2007, pp. 18–37. For evidence that worker survey responses overstate the extent of hours constraints, see William R. Johnson, "Fixed Costs and Hours Constraints," *Journal of Human Resources,* Winter 2011, pp. 775–799.

optimal position will move to u_2 on the higher indifference curve I_2 and that the worker will choose to work h_1h_2 additional hours. Daily earnings will be u_2h_2.

Consider now the alternative of a straight-line equivalent wage—that is, a standard hourly wage rate that will yield the same daily income of u_2h_2 for the Hh_2 hours of work. We can show the straight-time equivalent wage by drawing a new budget line HW' through u_2. The budget lines Hu_1P and HW' will both yield the same monetary income of u_2h_2 for Hh_2 hours of work. The important point is that if confronted with HW', the worker will want to move from u_2 to a new optimal position at u_3, where fewer hours than Hh_2 are worked. Stated differently, at u_2 indifference curve I_2 cuts HW' from above; that is, MRS L, Y is greater than the wage rate. This means that the worker subjectively values leisure more highly at the margin than does the market, and thus u_2 is no longer the optimal position under a straight-time pay arrangement. Our worker will feel overemployed when working Hh_2 hours on a straight-time pay plan (recall Figure 2.10).

Here is the conclusion: Premium wage rates for overtime work will call forth more hours of work than a straight-time wage rate that yields the same income at the same number of hours as that actually chosen by an individual paid the overtime premium. Why the difference? The use of premium pay will have a relatively small income effect because it applies only to hours worked in excess of Hh_1. In comparison, the straight-time equivalent wage will have a much larger income effect because it applies to *all* hours of work.[16] Figure 2.11 is essentially the labor market analog of price discrimination in the product market. Sellers of some products can obtain more revenue by charging different prices for different quantities of output. In the present analysis, we are observing that an employer can obtain a greater amount of labor for a given outlay by paying different wage rates for different hours of work.[17]

2.3 *Quick Review*

- Steep indifference curves, the availability of nonlabor income, and low earning ability all contribute to nonparticipation in the labor force.
- The reservation wage is the lowest acceptable wage rate; below this wage a person would decide not to participate in the labor force.
- The standard eight-hour workday may leave some workers wanting additional hours of work (underemployed) and others wishing to work fewer hours (overemployed), depending on their indifference maps and earning abilities.
- Premium wage rates for overtime work provide a greater incentive for additional hours of work than a straight-time wage rate yielding an equivalent daily income.

Your Turn

Suppose you have a choice between two otherwise identical jobs, including hourly pay. In one job the employer sets the hours of work each week and in the other you select the number of hours. Which job would you prefer? Why? (*Answer:* See page 540.)

---

[16] Figure 2.11 is drawn so that for the straight-time equivalent wage the substitution effect dominates the income effect, and therefore the individual is on the forward-rising portion of her or his labor supply curve. This is why u_3 entails more hours of work than u_1. Such an outcome is not necessary. The diagram could have been drawn so that u_3 was to the right of u_1, in which case our basic conclusion would be even more evident.

[17] Kenneth E. Boulding, *Economic Analysis*, vol. 1, 4th Edition (New York: Harper and Row, 1966), p. 616. Our conclusion holds only if we restrict the employer from hiring additional workers.

Income Maintenance Programs

The United States has a variety of *income maintenance programs*—also dubbed welfare or public assistance programs—whose purpose is to provide some minimum level of income to all families and individuals.[18] These programs include Supplemental Security Income, Temporary Assistance for Needy Families, food stamps, and Medicaid. Our objective is to examine the possible effects of such programs on work incentives.

Three Basic Features

Although details vary greatly, income maintenance programs have three basic features.

1 The Income Guarantee or Basic Benefit, B   This is the amount of public subsidy an individual or family would be paid if no earned income were received.[19]

2 The Benefit Reduction Rate, t   This refers to the rate at which a family's basic benefit is reduced as earned income increases. For example, if t is .50, then a family's basic benefit will be reduced by $.50 for every $1.00 of wage income earned. This means that if the market wage rate is $5.00, the family's *net* wage rate will be just $2.50 when the benefit reduction provision is taken into account. The critical point is that the benefit reduction rate reduces one's net gain from work. Economists often refer to the benefit reduction rate as an "implicit tax rate" because t has the same impact on the net income of a person participating in an income maintenance program as income tax rates have on the earnings of individuals not in the program.

3 The Break-Even Level of Income, Y_b   The basic benefit and the benefit reduction rate permit the calculation of the *break-even income*. This is the level of earned income at which the actual subsidy payment received by an individual or family becomes zero. It is the level of earned income at which an individual is dropped from an income maintenance program. As we will see in the following illustration, the break-even income depends on the sizes of the basic benefit and the benefit reduction rate.

Illustration

A simple numerical illustration might help relate these concepts to one another. The *actual subsidy payment* S received by an individual can be determined by the following formula:

$$S = B - tY \qquad (2.2)$$

$$\text{where} \quad B \;=\; \text{basic benefit}$$
$$t \;=\; \text{benefit reduction rate}$$
$$Y \;=\; \text{level of earned income}$$

---

[18] Income maintenance programs are not to be confused with various social insurance programs. Income maintenance programs are designed to assist families and individuals who have more or less permanent disabilities or dependent children. These programs are financed out of general tax revenues and are regarded as public charity. To qualify for aid, one must demonstrate economic need. In contrast, social insurance programs (such as Old Age and Survivors Insurance and unemployment compensation) are tailored to replace a portion of the earnings lost due to retirement or temporary unemployment. They are financed by earmarked payroll taxes, and benefits are viewed as earned rights as a consequence of prior financial contributions. For a discussion of a variety of means-tested transfer programs, see Robert A. Moffitt (ed.), *Economics of Means-Tested Transfer Programs in the United States, Vol. 1* (Chicago, IL: University of Chicago Press, 2016).

[19] We simplify by assuming that no nonwage income in the form of, say, interest or dividends is received.

FIGURE 2.12   Income Maintenance and Incentives to Work

An income maintenance program that incorporates both a basic benefit and a benefit reduction rate will change the budget constraint from HW to HBY_bW. This alteration moves the utility-maximizing position from u_1 to u_2 and reduces hours of work.

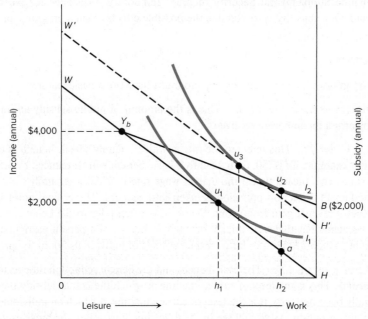

Thus, for example, if B is $2,000, t is 0.50, and Y is $2,000, the actual subsidy payment received will be $1,000:

$$\$1,000 = \$2,000 - 0.50(\$2,000)$$

Furthermore, the break-even level of income can be calculated readily. A glance back at Equation (2.2) suggests that S will become zero—that is, the break-even income will be reached—when earned income Y is equal to B/t.[20] For our illustrative numbers, B is $2,000 and t is 0.50, so B/t—the break-even level of income—is therefore $2,000/0.50, or $4,000. We verify this by substituting the relevant numbers into Equation (2.2):

$$\$0 = \$2,000 - 0.50(\$4,000)$$

Let's incorporate these concepts into Figure 2.12 to examine the impact of an income maintenance program on work incentives. The HW line shows us the budget constraint confronting the individual in the absence of an income maintenance program. The resulting optimal position is at u_1. For simplicity, let's assume that the wage rate is $1.00 per hour and that the individual chooses to work 40 hours per week. Over the 50-week workyear earned income would be $2,000, as shown on the left vertical axis.

Now suppose an income maintenance program with the characteristics just described is enacted. The impact of this program is to change the budget constraint from HW to HBY_bW. Note that HB on the right vertical

---

[20] The algebra is simple. By setting $S = 0$ in Equation (2.2) we get $0 = B - tY$; therefore, $tY = B$ and $Y = B/t$.

axis is the basic benefit; it is the amount of income subsidy the individual would receive if he or she had no earned income. The BY_b segment of the new budget constraint reflects the influence of the benefit reduction rate. Specifically, the slope of the BY_b segment is measured by the *net* wage rate—that is, the market wage rate as it is reduced by the benefit reduction rate. Thus while the absolute value of the slope of HW is 1.00 (reflecting the $1.00 wage rate), the slope of BY_b is only 0.50 (reflecting the $.50 *net* wage rate).[21] The vertical distance between HW and BY_b is equal to S, the actual subsidy received. Point Y_b indicates the break-even level of income because at this point the individual's earned income is sufficiently large ($4,000 in this case) so that the application of the 0.50 benefit reduction rate causes the actual subsidy payment S to become zero [see Equation (2.2)].

We observe in Figure 2.12 that the new optimal position is at u_2, where HBY_bW is tangent to indifference curve I_2. Although the individual's total money income has increased (from h_1u_1 to h_2u_2), *earned* income and the number of hours worked have both declined (from h_1u_1 to h_2a and from Hh_1 to Hh_2, respectively). In our earlier analysis of a wage *increase* (Figure 2.7), we found that the net effect on hours of work (work incentives) depended on the relative sizes of the income effect (reduction in hours of work) and the substitution effect (increase in hours of work). *In the present case, the income and substitution effects both reduce hours of work.* The tendency for the income effect to reduce hours of work is no surprise. The income maintenance program increases monetary income; and assuming leisure is a normal good, some of that income is "spent" on leisure and, therefore, fewer hours are worked. But curiously, the substitution effect also reduces hours of work. The presence of the benefit reduction rate *reduces* the net wage rate; it makes BY_b flatter than HW. Even though the basic benefit raises total monetary income, the benefit reduction feature means there has been an effective decrease in wage rates. Leisure is now cheaper—one sacrifices only $0.50 by not working an hour rather than $1.00—so leisure is substituted for work.

Recalling our earlier diagrammatic separation of the income and substitution effects (Figure 2.7), we can draw the broken line $H'W'$ parallel to HW and tangent to I_2 at u_3. The horizontal distance between u_1 and u_3 is the income effect, and the horizontal distance between u_3 and u_2 is the substitution effect. We observe that both reduce the amount of work supplied.

Controversy

The various income maintenance programs have long been surrounded by controversy. This stems in part from fundamental ideological differences among policy makers. But it also reflects the fact that the accepted goals of income maintenance programs are in conflict with one another and that it is easy to disagree over the proper or optimal trade-offs. In particular, it is generally agreed that income maintenance programs should (*a*) effectively get poor people out of poverty, (*b*) maintain incentives to work, and (*c*) achieve goals 1 and 2 at a reasonable cost.

Figure 2.12 is a useful point of reference in explaining these goal conflicts. The imposition of an income maintenance program triggers income and substitution effects, both of which are negative with respect to work. Furthermore, we might improve the effectiveness of the program in eliminating poverty by increasing the basic benefit—that is, by shifting the BY_b line upward in Figure 2.12. But this will clearly make the program more costly. On one hand, a larger basic benefit would relocate point Y_b to the northwest on line HW and cause additional families to be eligible for subsidies. On the other hand, with a higher basic benefit, people already in the income maintenance program will each receive larger subsidy payments. Goal 1 conflicts with goal 3.

---

[21] As noted, the slope of BY_b reflects the net wage rate wn, which is the wage rate w multiplied by $(1 - t)$; that is, $w_n = (1 - t)w$. In our example, the slope of BY_b is $0.50 = (1 - 0.5)1$. If the benefit reduction rate were 0.25, the net wage rate and slope of BY_b would be $0.75 = (1 - 0.25)1$. If the benefit reduction rate were 1.00, BY_b would be horizontal.

Finally, given the basic benefit, one might want to reduce the benefit reduction rate (increase the slope of the BY_b line) to preserve incentives to work. A reduction in the benefit reduction rate increases the net wage rate, boosting the price of leisure and inducing the substitution of work for leisure. The higher net wage rate may also prompt individuals who are currently not in the labor force to become participants (see Figure 2.8). However, the resulting increase in the slope of the BY_b line will extend point Y_b to the northwest along HW, making more families eligible for subsidies and, therefore, increasing program costs. An increase in the slope of the BY_b line will also boost costs by increasing the actual subsidy received for any given number of hours worked. Goal 2 conflicts with goal 3.[22]

The End of Welfare as an Entitlement

In August 1996, President Clinton signed the Personal Responsibility and Work Opportunity Reconciliation Act (PRWORA), which fundamentally changed the welfare system in the United States. In prior years, the welfare system had been criticized for its inherent work disincentives as well as accused of encouraging dependence among welfare recipients. The welfare reform attempted to correct these perceived deficiencies in several ways and shift more control over welfare to state governments.

A major goal of the law is to make receiving welfare a transition period before returning to work. The law replaced the existing Aid to Families with Dependent Children (AFDC) program with the *Temporary Assistance for Needy Families (TANF)* program. In contrast to AFDC, TANF requires welfare recipients to work after two years of receiving assistance with few exceptions.[23] Welfare recipients may meet the work provision by being employed, attending vocational training, or performing community service. The Act also mandates a five-year lifetime limit on the receipt of cash welfare payments (though states may exempt up to 20 percent of their recipients).[24] It also provides child care and health insurance for families entering the job market. Finally, most forms of public assistance are denied to legal immigrants for five years or until they become citizens.

The PRWORA also tries to encourage responsibility regarding parenthood. It includes provisions to help enforce the collection of child support payments. Teen pregnancy is discouraged with measures such as requiring that unmarried minor parents must live with an adult and stay in school to receive assistance.

As Figure 2.13 shows, since the enactment of welfare reform, there has been a large drop in the number of families receiving welfare. In 1996, 4.6 million families were receiving welfare. By 2019, this figure had fallen by about 80 percent to 0.9 million families.

---

[22] In fact, the effect on work incentives of cutting the benefit reduction rate is more complex than our discussion suggests. On one hand, a decline in the benefit reduction rate will reduce the size of the negative income and substitution effects for those currently receiving benefits; therefore, the hours of work for this group will increase. On the other hand, the lower benefit reduction rate will extend program benefits to additional families that originally had not received benefits. The resultant income and substitution effects will both be negative for this group, causing them to work fewer hours. The overall impact on work incentives will depend on the average response of each group and their relative sizes. See Gary Burtless, "The Economist's Lament: Public Assistance in America," *Journal of Economic Perspectives,* Winter 1990, pp. 68–70.

[23] For an overview of the differences between TANF and AFDC, see Rebecca M. Blank and David T. Ellwood, "The Clinton Legacy for America's Poor," in Jeffrey A. Frankel and Peter R. Orszag (eds.), *American Economic Policy in the 1990s* (Cambridge, MA: MIT Press, 2002).

[24] States are permitted to impose stricter limits if they so choose.

FIGURE 2.13 Welfare Caseloads

Between 1970 and 1994, welfare caseloads under the Aid to Families with Dependent Children (AFDC) program generally expanded. Following enactment of the Temporary Assistance for Needy Families (TANF) program in 1996, welfare caseloads declined by roughly 80 percent.

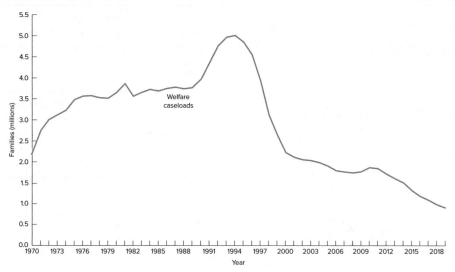

WW2.5 Several factors account for this dramatic drop in caseloads. First, the economic boom during the 1990s improved the labor market conditions facing welfare recipients. The unemployment rate fell over the decade, while inflation-adjusted wages of less skilled workers rose. Wallace and Blank found that the strong economy can explain about one-fifth of the decline in caseloads.[25] Second, the substantial expansion in the early 1990s of the earned income tax credit (EITC) program, which provides a tax subsidy to working low-income families, increased the incentive of welfare recipients to enter the labor market and thus lowered the number of recipients.[26] Third, policy changes such as benefit time limits, welfare benefit reductions, child care expansions, and changes in training programs appear to account for a significant portion of the decline in welfare caseloads. The importance of each factor has yet to be precisely determined.[27] The long-run consequences of welfare reform, including its success in reducing poverty rates, remain to be evaluated.[28]

[25] Geoffrey Wallace and Rebecca M. Blank, "What Goes Up Must Come Down? Explaining the Recent Changes in Public Assistance Caseloads," in Sheldon Danziger (ed.), *Economic Conditions and Welfare Reform* (Kalamazoo, MI: Upjohn Institute, 1999).

[26] One study suggests that the EITC expansion is the most important factor in reducing the welfare caseload. See Bruce D. Meyer and Dan T. Rosenbaum, "Welfare, the Earned Income Tax Credit, and the Labor Supply of Single Mothers," *Quarterly Journal of Economics,* August 2001, pp. 1063–1133. For another study showing a large effect of the EITC, see David T. Ellwood, "The Impact of the Earned Income Tax Credit and Social Policy Reforms on Work, Marriage, and Living Arrangements," *National Tax Journal,* December 2000, pp. 1063–1105.

[27] For a review of the evidence on the impact of welfare reform, see James P. Ziliak, "The Temporary Assistance to Needy Families Program" in Robert F. Moffit (ed.), *The Economics of Means-Tested Transfer Programs in the United States,* vol. 1 (Chicago, IL: University of Chicago, 2016). Also see Jeffrey Grogger and Lynn A. Karoly, *Welfare Reform: Effects of a Decade of Change* (Cambridge, MA: Harvard University Press, 2005).

[28] It is important to note that the reduction in welfare caseloads has increased caseloads in other public assistance programs such as Supplemental Security Income. See Lucie Schmidt and Purvi Sevak, "AFDC, SSI, and Welfare Reform Aggressiveness: Caseload Reductions versus Caseload Shifting," *Journal of Human Resources,* Summer 2004, pp. 792–812.

2.5 World of Work

The Labor Supply Impact of the Earned Income Tax Credit

Since its initiation in 1975, the earned income tax credit (EITC) has grown rapidly and is now the largest antipoverty program in the United States. Currently over 28 million people participate in the program. Spending on the EITC is nearly as much as the combined spending on Temporary Assistance for Needy Families and food stamps.

The EITC supplements the wages of low-income working families by providing a tax credit that reduces their income tax liability. If the tax credit is larger than the amount of income taxes owed, the family receives a check for the difference. The tax credit increases with the number of children and adults in the family, as well as the amount earned, until a plateau is achieved. For example, in 2020 the maximum tax credit was $5,920 for a married couple with two children who earned $14,800. The EITC is phased out as family income level increases. In 2020, families could participate in the program if their income was less than $56,844.

The EITC has two effects on labor supply. First, labor force participation should rise because only employed people may participate in the program. Second, it has an uncertain effect on the hours worked by employed people. Below the plateau level the EITC is the equivalent to a wage increase, and in the phase-out range above the plateau it acts as a wage decrease. Because wage changes have income and substitution effects that work in opposing directions on hours worked, the labor supply effects among those currently working cannot be determined in theory.

There are many studies of the labor supply effects of the EITC. Nichols and Rothstein conclude that the EITC has a positive effect on labor force participation for single mothers, a smaller negative effect for married mothers, and no effect for men. Also, the program appears to slightly increase the hours of those currently working.

Source: Austin Nichols and Jesse Rothstein, "The Earned Income Tax Credit," in Robert A. Moffitt (ed.), *The Economics of Means-Tested Transfer Programs in the United States, vol. 1* (Chicago, IL: University of Chicago Press, 2016).

Chapter Summary

1. In the work–leisure choice model, an indifference curve shows the various combinations of income and leisure that will yield a given level of utility to an individual. Indifference curves are convex to the origin, reflecting a diminishing marginal rate of substitution of leisure for income (MRS L, Y). Curves farther from the origin indicate higher levels of utility.

2. The budget (wage) constraint line shows the various combinations of income and leisure that are obtainable at a given wage rate. The absolute value of the slope of the budget line reflects the wage rate.

3. The individual achieves an optimal or utility-maximizing position by selecting the point that puts him or her on the highest attainable indifference curve.

4. Changing the wage rate and observing predicted changes in one's optimal position suggest the possibility of a backward-bending individual labor supply curve.

5. The impact of a wage change on hours of work depends on the sizes of the income and substitution effects. The income effect measures the portion of a total change in desired hours of work that is due

solely to the change in income caused by the wage change. The substitution effect is the portion of a total change in desired hours of work that is due solely to the wage rate change, the level of income or utility being held constant. For a wage increase (decrease), the income effect decreases (increases) while the substitution effect increases (decreases) desired hours of work.

6. Empirical evidence suggests that women are significantly more responsive to a wage change in their labor supply decisions than are men.

7. The responsiveness of the quantity of labor supplied to a given change in wage rates is measured by the elasticity of labor supply. This is calculated as the percentage change in quantity of labor supplied divided by the percentage change in the wage rate. In contrast, changes in nonlabor income or work-leisure preferences alter the location of an individual's labor supply curve.

8. The case of nonparticipants—individuals who choose not to do labor market work—is portrayed by a corner solution on the right vertical axis of the work-leisure model.

9. The reservation wage is the lowest wage rate at which a person would decide to work.

10. A worker may be overemployed or underemployed when forced to conform to a standard workday. A worker is overemployed (underemployed) when for the standard workday his or her MRS L, Y is greater (less) than the wage rate.

11. A system of premium pay—such as time and a half for overtime work—has a more positive effect on work incentives than the straight-time wage rate that would yield an equivalent income for the same hours of work.

12. Most income maintenance programs entail a basic benefit and a benefit reduction rate from which the break-even level of income can be calculated. Because *(a)* the basic benefit causes only an income effect and *(b)* the benefit reduction rate *reduces* the net wage rate, the income and substitution effects both contribute to a decline in desired hours of work.

13. Welfare is no longer an entitlement, but rather is a temporary assistance program. Between 1996 and 2019, the number of welfare recipients declined by about 80 percent.

Terms and Concepts

indifference curve

marginal rate of substitution of leisure for income

budget (wage) constraint

optimal work-leisure position

backward-bending labor supply curve

income effect

substitution effect

wage elasticity of labor supply

reservation wage

overemployed

underemployed

income maintenance program

income guarantee or basic benefit

benefit reduction rate

break-even level of income

actual subsidy payment

Temporary Assistance for Needy Families (TANF)

Questions and Study Suggestions

1. What information is embodied in *(a)* an indifference curve and *(b)* the budget line in the work–leisure model? Why are indifference curves *(a)* downward-sloping and *(b)* convex to the origin? Draw an indifference map and budget line and locate a worker's optimal position.

2. Indicate in each of the following instances whether the specified circumstances will cause a worker to want to work more or fewer hours:

    a. The wage rate increases and the substitution effect is greater than the income effect.

    b. The wage rate decreases and the income effect is greater than the substitution effect.

    c. The wage rate decreases and the substitution effect is greater than the income effect.

    d. The wage rate increases and the income effect is greater than the substitution effect.

3. Employ a diagram similar to Figure 2.5 to show an individual's leisure–income choices before and after a wage rate *decrease*. Isolate the income and substitution effects, indicate whether each increases or decreases hours of work, and use the two effects to explain the overall impact of the wage decline on hours of work. Is your worker on the forward-rising or backward-bending portion of the labor supply curve?

4. The tax cuts of the Trump administration presumed that income tax cuts would stimulate incentives to work and thereby increase economic growth. Demonstrate this outcome with a work–leisure diagram. What does this outcome assume about the relative sizes of the income and substitution effects? Explain: "The predicted increase in work incentives associated with tax cuts might in fact be more relevant for women than for men."

5. Suppose Lauren is given two options by her employer. *First option:* She may choose her own hours of work and will be paid the relatively low wage rate implied by budget line HW_1 shown in the accompanying diagram. *Second option:* She can work exactly HR hours and will be paid the relatively high wage rate implied by budget line HW_2. Which option will she choose? Justify your answer.

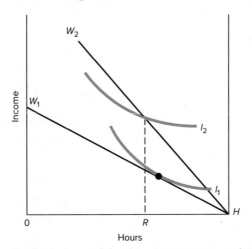

6. Use a work–leisure diagram that includes nonlabor income to portray an individual who is maximizing utility by working, say, eight hours per day. Now compare the labor supply effects of imposing *(a)* a lump-sum tax (a tax that is the same absolute amount at all levels of earned income) and *(b)* a proportional tax of, say, 30 percent on earned income. Do hours of work rise or fall in each case? Can you generalize these outcomes to *all* individuals in the economy? Explain.

7. What set of circumstances will tend to cause an individual to choose not to participate in the labor force? What generalizations can you formulate on the basis of *(a)* education, *(b)* the presence of preschool children, *(c)* level of spouse's income, *(d)* race, and *(e)* location of a household (urban or rural) on the one hand and the probability that a married woman will be a labor force participant on the other?

8. What is the reservation wage? "Other things being equal, one's reservation wage increases as larger amounts of nonlabor income are realized." Do you agree? Explain. Redraw the indifference curves of Figure 2.8 to demonstrate that anything that lowers (raises) the value of nonmarket time will increase (reduce) the probability of labor force participation.

9. Using Figure 2.10, demonstrate that Smith has a stronger "taste" for leisure and a weaker "taste" for work than Jones. What factor(s) might underlie this difference in tastes? Redraw Smith's indifference curves to show the case where she would rather be a nonparticipant than work the standard *HD* workweek.

10. Use Figure 2.11 to explain the following statement: "Although premium wage rates for overtime work will induce workers to work more hours than would a straight-time equivalent wage rate, the latter will entail a higher level of well-being."

11. If an income maintenance program entails a $3,000 basic benefit and a benefit reduction rate of 0.30, what will be the size of the subsidy received by a family that earns $2,000 per year? What will be the family's total income? What break-even level of income does this program imply?

12. In the accompanying diagram, *WH* is the budget line resulting from labor market work. Describe the characteristics of the income maintenance programs implicit in budget lines *HBW′, HBYW,* and *HBW.* Given an individual's work–leisure preferences, which program will entail the strongest disincentives to work? Why? Which entails the weakest disincentives to work? Why? "The higher the basic benefit and the higher the benefit reduction rate, the weaker the work incentive." Do you agree?

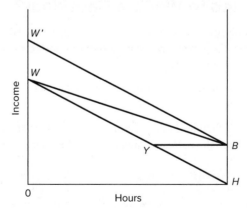

13. In the United States, payments to disabled workers on the average replace about half of their former earnings. In some other countries such as Sweden and the Netherlands, workers with disabilities receive as much as 70 to 90 percent of their average earnings. We also observe that the proportion of workers receiving disability benefits is much lower in the United States than in the latter two nations. Are these findings consistent with the work–leisure model? Explain.

14. Suppose Congress changed our Social Security law to allow recipients to earn as much as they wanted with no reduction in benefits. Use a work–leisure diagram to show the predicted effects on labor supply.

15. One way of aiding low-income families is to increase the minimum wage. An alternative is to provide a direct grant of nonlabor income. Compare the impact of these two options on work incentives.

16. Evaluate the following statements:

   a. "An employer might reduce worker absenteeism by changing from a standard wage rate to premium pay for hours that exceed a fixed minimum."

   b. "A worker who feels underemployed may moonlight even though the wage rate is somewhat lower than the one paid in the worker's first job."

   c. "Given the wage rate, an individual will always prefer a job in which the worker, as opposed to the employer, selects the number of hours worked."

   d. "If at all points within the work–leisure diagram a person's indifference curves are flatter than the budget constraint, then that individual will choose to be a nonparticipant."

   e. "The income effect of any given wage increase is larger for individuals who are currently working many hours than it is for those who are currently working few or no hours."

17. Steve Slacker is age 25, has an MBA degree, but is not working. Instead he is living at a major ski area, using the $3,000 per week he gets from his wealthy family. The family, however, seeing that Steve is becoming a permanent slacker, ends this weekly payment. As a result, Steve chooses to take a job that pays $1,000 a week for 40 hours of work. Construct a single income–leisure choice graph to show Steve's situation before and after his parents' decision. Briefly summarize the outcome for hours of work, total weekly income, and Steve's total utility.

Internet Exercise

What Has Happened to Welfare Caseloads?

Go to the Administration for Children and Families U.S. Welfare Caseloads statistics website (**http://www.acf.hhs.gov/programs/ofa/programs/tanf/data-reports**). Click on the link with the most recent caseload figures.

What was the percentage change in the number of TANF families between 1996 and 2008? What are some possible explanations for this change?

What was the number of TANF families in 2008? For the most recent year shown? What is the percentage change over this period? What are the corresponding numbers for your state?

Internet Links

The Office of Family Assistance in the U.S. Department of Health and Human Services publishes detailed information about the Temporary Assistance for Needy Families program (**www.acf.hhs.gov/programs/ofa**).

The Institute for Research on Poverty website provides academic research, research summaries, and policy briefs on issues related to poverty (**http://www.irp.wisc.edu**).

Chapter 3

Population, Participation Rates, and Hours of Work

After reading this chapter, you should be able to:

1. Describe trends in the population and labor force.
2. Explain Becker's model of the allocation of time.
3. Compute the labor force participation rate.
4. Describe changes in labor force participation rates across demographic groups over the years and explain why these changes have occurred.
5. Describe how the "added-worker effect" and the "discouraged-worker effect" influence labor force participation rates over the business cycle.
6. Cite the reasons for the workweek decline in the early twentieth century and the relative stability of the workweek since World War II.

The 1946–1964 baby boom that added about 76 million people to the labor force gave way to a "baby bust" that will mean much smaller increases in the labor force in the immediate future. During the past decade, immigration added over nine million people to the U.S. population. Disadvantaged groups such as African-Americans and Hispanics constitute a growing percentage of our labor force. Dual-worker families were 9 percent of all families in 1940; today they are 35 percent.

The hustle and bustle of our lives has greatly increased as we juggle education, market work, household activities, and leisure. Divorces are much more common than in earlier periods. The percentage of families with children maintained by single mothers has more than doubled from 10 percent in 1970 to 24 percent today. Since 1950 women have increasingly participated in the labor force; meanwhile the participation rates of older working-age men have declined. The workweek decreased by 20 percent during the first half of the twentieth century, but since then it has remained relatively constant.

These facts all relate to the supply of labor, examined more broadly here than in the previous chapter. For the economy as a whole, the concept of labor supply has many dimensions. As Figure 3.1 indicates, the aggregate of labor services available to a society depends on (*a*) the size and demographic composition of the population, which in turn depend on births, deaths, and net immigration; (*b*) *the labor force participation rate (LFPR)*—that is, the percentage of the working-age population that is actually working or seeking work;

FIGURE 3.1 **Determinants of the Total Labor Services Available**

The total amount of labor services available in an economy depends on the population size, the labor force participation rate, the length of the workweek and workyear, and the quality of the labor force.

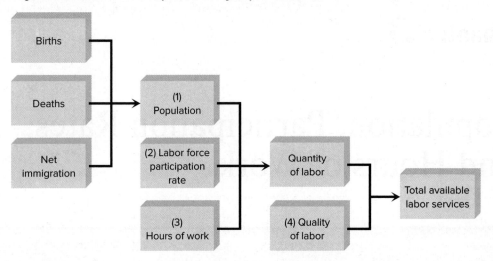

(*c*) the number of hours worked per week or year; and (*d*) the quality of the labor force. In this chapter, we consider the first three of these aspects of labor supply: population, participation rates, and hours of work. Labor quality will be analyzed in Chapter 4.

THE POPULATION BASE

As a broad generalization, the size of a nation's labor force depends on the size of its population and the fraction of its population participating in the labor market. Figure 3.2 portrays the growth of the U.S. population and labor force over the 1950-2018 period. Recalling Figure 3.1, we know that population grows partly as a result of natural increases—that is, the excess of births over deaths—and net immigration. Because death rates are less variable (declining slowly over time), most of the variations in the U.S. population growth have resulted from changes in birthrates and net immigration. For example, the 1946-1964 baby boom added almost 76 million people to the U.S. population who, some 20 years later, entered the labor force in extraordinarily large numbers. Birthrates declined sharply following the baby boom, and this decline has resulted in a slightly lower growth of the population in recent years. But the U.S. population continues to expand. Immigration (considered in detail in Chapter 9) has also fluctuated over time, largely as a consequence of changes in the U.S. immigration policies. In some recent years, immigration has accounted for as much as 20-25 percent of population growth.

WW3.1   With this backdrop of population growth in mind, let's now turn to an economic theory that sheds light on participation rates.

FIGURE 3.2 **Population and Labor Force Growth**

Population and the labor force have both grown significantly in the United States, but rates of growth have varied from one period to another.

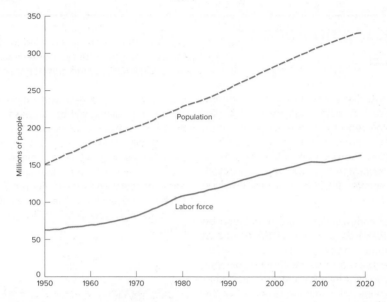

BECKER'S MODEL: THE ALLOCATION OF TIME

In Chapter 2 we introduced a model in which an *individual* was making a choice between labor market work and leisure. While this model proved useful in generating an understanding of the work–leisure decision and a number of its implications, the model has been generalized and expanded by Becker (World of Work 1.1) and others.[1] This generalized *model of the allocation of time* is particularly useful in understanding the main topic at hand: labor force participation.

Two Fundamental Changes

The basic work–leisure choice model can be extended in two fundamental ways.

1 Household Perspective

The first change is that it is frequently more informative to think of the household as the basic decision-making unit rather than the individual. Most people are members of households, and decisions about how they spend their time are strongly influenced by the decisions of other household members. Decision making is interrelated; for example, a wife's decision about whether she should seek labor market work may depend on whether her husband is currently employed, and vice versa.

---

[1] The landmark article is Gary Becker, "A Theory of the Allocation of Time," *Economic Journal,* September 1965, pp. 493–517.

3.1 World of Work

The Changing Face of America

In 2018 the Census Bureau issued a revised population forecast that suggests smaller long-term growth of the U.S. population than did earlier estimates. The report also predicts even more diversity in the population than was projected earlier. By 2050 the U.S. population is expected to rise to 389 million from 323 million in 2016. This new projection for 2050 is down 31 million from earlier projections.

How will the composition of the population be different in 2050 compared to 2016? As shown in the accompanying pie charts, the population in 2050 is expected to be much more diverse. Asians, Hispanics, African-Americans, and other nonwhite groups will comprise over half of the population in 2050.

The population growth will slow in the next several decades due to two main factors. First, the Census Bureau now estimates that 1,068,000 immigrants will arrive each year, down from earlier estimates of 1,712,000. Second, the number of births is expected to slow from 5,001,000 per year to 4,179,000 per year due to a decline in the nation's fertility rate.

If the Census Bureau's predictions are accurate, they have several important implications for the labor force. First, the projected slowdown in labor force growth raises the potential for labor shortages. Second, the lower immigration and smaller fertility rates will accelerate the present aging of the American population. This means, for example, that the ratio of receivers of Social Security benefits to the number of people paying into the system will rise faster than once expected. Third, a renewed emphasis on education and training will be necessary to prepare the growing number of racially diverse youth for high-quality jobs. Finally, workplaces will be transformed, with owners, managers, and workers increasingly being nonwhite. Greater tolerance for racial and ethnic differences will be an absolute necessity if the United States is to retain its high labor productivity and standard of living.

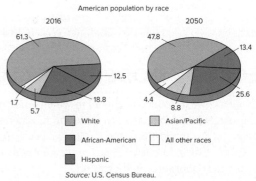

American population by race

Source: U.S. Census Bureau.

Source: U.S. Census Bureau, "Methodology, Assumptions, and Inputs for the 2017 National Population Projections." **www.census.gov**

2 Multiple Uses of Time

In Becker's model of household allocation of time, the traditional work–leisure dichotomy is replaced by a more complex categorization of the uses of time. As Becker sees it, a household should be regarded as an economic unit that is *producing* utility-yielding "commodities." These utility-yielding *commodities* are produced by the household by combining *goods* (goods and services) with *time*. More generally, a household can use the time available to it in at least three basic ways. Time can be (*a*) sold in the labor market to obtain the monetary income required to purchase goods and services (labor market time), (*b*) used in household production (household production time), and (*c*) used in actual consumption of goods and services (consumption time).

Thus, for the typical household, the commodity we call a *meal* is produced by combining certain goods acquired through the provision of labor market time (food bought at the supermarket) with household production time (the time it takes to prepare these goods as a meal) and consumption time (the time it takes to eat the meal). Because the total amount of time available to the household is limited, the alternative uses of time compete with one another. For example, other things being equal, a family in which both spouses engage in labor market work will have less time available for household production and consumption than a family with one nonworking spouse.

Commodity Characteristics

Commodities have two characteristics of considerable significance for any discussion of how a household might allocate its time in general and how it might make labor market participation decisions in particular. First, some commodities are relatively time-intensive, whereas others are relatively goods-intensive. *Time-intensive commodities* are composed of a large amount of time and a small amount of goods. Examples include such "pure" leisure activities as watching the sunset at the beach or dozing in a hammock.[2] *Goods-intensive commodities* require large amounts of goods and little time, such as a meal at a fast-food restaurant. One implication of this distinction is that as time becomes more valuable in the labor market (if wage rates increase), a household may sacrifice time-intensive commodities in favor of goods-intensive commodities to devote more time to labor market work.

The second characteristic of commodities is that, within limits, time and goods are usually substitutable in producing them. Thus, a specific commodity can be produced by the household with much time and a small amount of goods or vice versa. At one extreme, a household can produce a meal with home-grown, home-prepared food. At the other extreme, it can purchase a meal at a restaurant. The former is a highly time-intensive commodity; the latter is a goods-intensive commodity.

Household Choices

In the Becker model, the household has a number of questions to answer as it seeks to maximize its utility. First, what commodities does it want to consume? Second, how does it want to produce these commodities? That is, to what extent should commodities be provided through labor market work as opposed to production in the home? Third, how should individual family members allocate their time among labor market work, home production, consumption, and other possible uses?

The third question is most relevant for the topic at hand.[3] The general principle employed in deciding how each household member should allocate his or her time is that of comparative advantage. The principle of comparative advantage says that an individual should specialize in the productive endeavor that can be

---

[2] In the Becker model, we can think of leisure as the pleasurable consumption of time per se wherein the amount of goods required is zero.

[3] The second question will be treated in the ensuing discussion of the participation rates of the various subaggregates of the population. With regard to the first question, we will assume that the household's preferences for commodities are given, noting that in Becker's model the theory of consumer behavior must be modified to account for the economic value of time. More precisely, a household will be purchasing the utility-maximizing combination of goods $(a, b, \ldots, n)$ when the marginal utility of the last dollar spent on each is the same. Algebraically stated, utility is maximized when $MUa/Pa = MUb/Pb = \cdots = MUn/Pn$, where MU is marginal utility and P is product price. Becker contends that the appropriate prices to be used are *not* simply the market prices of each good but rather the "full price": the market price of a good *plus* the market value of the time used in its consumption. Thus if good a is a two-hour concert whose price is $8 and your time is worth $10 per hour in the labor market, then the full price of the concert is $28 = $8 + (2 × $10). Taking the value of time into account, the full prices of highly time-intensive goods will rise relatively and those of less time-intensive goods will fall relatively, generating a different utility-maximizing combination of goods than if only market prices were used.

performed with the greatest relative efficiency, or in other words, with the least opportunity cost. In apportioning its available time, a household should compare the productivity of each family member in all of the various market and nonmarket activities needing to be performed in producing commodities. The basic rule is that the more productive or proficient one is in a certain activity as compared to other family members, the greater the amount of one's time that should be devoted to that activity. Because family members normally have different characteristics with respect to age, sex, educational attainment, and previous labor market and nonlabor market experience, at any point in time they will differ substantially in the relative efficiency of producing commodities (utility) from market and nonmarket activities. Obviously the wife has a biologically determined comparative advantage in childbearing. Also, through socialization (role definition by society) or because of preferences, or both, many females develop a comparative advantage in other aspects of household production, such as homemaking activities like cleaning, food preparation, and caring for children. Furthermore, we will find evidence in Chapter 14 suggesting that women are often discriminated against in the labor market. Because of such discrimination and assuming that other things (such as education, job training, and labor market experience) are equal, many husbands can obtain more income and therefore more goods for the household from a given amount of labor market work than their wives can. Historically, for many households, the principle of comparative advantage led husbands to devote much of their time to labor market work while their wives engaged in nonmarket work within the home. Similarly, we will find in Chapter 4 that children have a comparative advantage in acquiring education. Education is an investment in human capital, and other things being equal, the rate of return on that investment varies directly with the length of time a person will be in the labor market after his or her education is completed.[4]

Income and Substitution Effects Revisited

It is helpful in understanding Becker's model to reexamine the income and substitution effects within its more general framework.

Becker Income Effect

Assume there is an increase in wage rates. The *income effect* indicates that the household now realizes a larger income for any number of hours of labor market work, and therefore the consumption of most goods will increase.[5] But the consumption of additional goods requires more time. Remember that goods must be combined with time to produce utility-yielding commodities; therefore, with consumption time increasing, hours of work will tend to fall. Although the rationale is different, the income effect reduces hours of work as it did in the simpler model of Chapter 2.

Becker Substitution Effect

There is also a more complex *substitution effect*. A higher market wage rate means that time is more valuable not only in the labor market but also in both the production and consumption activities occurring within the household. On one hand, the household will substitute goods for time in the *production* of commodities as the wage rate rises. This implies that the household will produce commodities in less time-intensive ways. For example, the family may patronize fast-food restaurants with greater frequency and therefore spend less time preparing meals within the home. On the other hand, with respect to *consumption,* the household will alter the mix of commodities it consumes, shifting from time-intensive to goods-intensive commodities as wage

---

[4] For an interesting discussion of the *disadvantages* of intrahousehold specialization, see Francine D. Blau and Anne E. Winkler, *The Economics of Women, Men, and Work,* 8th Edition (Englewood Cliffs, NJ: Prentice-Hall, 2018), Chapter 3 .

[5] The exception, of course, is *inferior goods,* for which purchases decline as incomes increase.

rates increase. Such time-intensive activities as vacations and playing golf may give way to the purchase of a work of art or racquetball. Or alternatively, a week's skiing in Colorado can be made less time-intensive for a Chicagoan by flying to the resort rather than driving. These adjustments in both the production and consumption of commodities release time for paid work in the labor market, therefore, as in our simpler model, this more complex substitution effect increases hours of work when wage rates rise.

WW 3.2
As in our simpler model, the net impact of the income and substitution effects on the hours of labor market work could be either positive or negative, depending on their relative magnitudes. But the alleged superiority of Becker's model is that it embodies a more comprehensive and more realistic portrayal of the uses of time. People do not merely divide their time between the assembly line and the hammock, as a narrow interpretation of Chapter 2's simpler model might imply. As noted earlier, the Becker model is a useful tool for understanding LFPRs, the topic to which we now turn.

3.2 World of Work

Video Gaming and the Decline in Labor Supply of Young Men

In the 2000s, there have been significant changes in the time use of younger men who are in ages 21–30. Between 2004–2007 and 2012–2015, the hours of work for younger men fell by 2.5 hours per week, or more than twice the drop in hours per week for men in ages 31–55. This decline in work hours for younger men was nearly matched by a 2.3 hour per week rise in leisure time.

Increased time in gaming or computer leisure accounted for about 80 percent of the rise in leisure for younger men. By 2015, younger men spent 5.2 hours per week in recreational computer activities, with 3.4 hours devoted specifically to video gaming. The average not-employed younger man devotes 500 hours a year to recreational computer activities, with about 300 hours of that time playing video games. This exceeds the time spent on home production or socializing with friends. Older men and women devote much less time to recreational computer activities and had much smaller growth in these activities during the 2000s.

An analysis of time use data by Mark Aguiar, Mark Bils, Kerwin Kofi Charles, and Erik Hurst suggests that 23–46 percent of the decline in work hours for younger men is due to a significant improvement in computer and video gaming technology. Others suggest, however, that social norms may have changed for younger men. That is, the stigma for not working and playing video games may have fallen.

The researchers also examined how younger men have responded to the decline in their earnings caused by the drop in their work hours. They report the portion of nonemployed younger men living with a parent or close relative rose from 46 percent in 2000 to 67 percent in 2015. They also found little or no decline in the relative consumption of younger men since 2000. They report increased happiness during the 2000s in life satisfaction surveys.

Source: Based on Mark Aguiar, Mark Bils, Kerwin Kofi Charles, and Erik Hurst, "Leisure Luxuries and the Labor Supply of Young Men," Working Paper, August 23, 2018.

3.1 *Quick Review*

- The population base underlying the total supply of labor depends on the birthrate, the death rate, and the rate of net immigration.
- The Becker model of the allocation of time regards households as economic units deciding how best to allocate their time among work, household production, and household consumption to obtain utility-yielding commodities.
- In the Becker income effect, a rise in the wage rate raises income, allowing the household to buy more goods; hours of work fall because these goods require more time to consume.
- In the Becker substitution effect, a rise in the wage rate increases hours of work because households substitute *(a)* goods for time in the production of commodities and *(b)* goods-intensive commodities for time-intensive commodities in consumption.

Your Turn

In general, women's educational levels and real wage rates have increased greatly over the past several decades. Also, women are increasingly participating in the workplace. What do these facts imply about the relative strengths of the Becker income and substitution effects? (*Answer:* See page 540.)

PARTICIPATION RATES: DEFINED AND MEASURED

The LFPR is determined by comparing the actual labor force with the potential labor force or what is sometimes called the "age-eligible population."

In the United States, we consider the *potential labor force* or age-eligible population to be the entire population *less* (*a*) young people under 16 years of age and (*b*) people who are institutionalized. Children under 16 are excluded on the assumption that schooling and child labor laws keep most of them out of the labor force.[6] Furthermore, the segment of the population that is institutionalized—in penal or mental institutions, nursing homes, and so on—is also not available for labor market activities.[7] The *actual labor force* consists of those people who are either (*a*) employed or (*b*) unemployed but actively seeking a job.[8] Thus, in percentage form we can say that the *labor force participation rate* (LFPR) is

$$LFPR = \frac{acutal\ labor\ force}{ptoential\ labor\ force} \times 100 \quad (3.1)$$

or

$$LFPR = \frac{noninstitutionalized\ population\ 16\ years\ of\ age\ or\ over\ in\ the\ labor\ force}{noninstitutionalized\ population} \times 100 \quad (3.2)$$

---

[6] Although excluded from the official definition of the labor force, many people under 16 years of age do engage in labor market activities.

[7] Since 1983, all armed forces personnel stationed in the United States have been considered to be members of the labor force, the rationale being that joining the military is a voluntary decision and therefore represents a viable labor market alternative. Prior to 1983, members of the military were not counted as part of the labor force. The Bureau of Labor Statistics now reports data for both the total labor force and the civilian labor force.

[8] More precise definitions will be introduced in Chapter 18. Note that all part-time workers are included in the labor force.

FIGURE 3.3 **Total, Male, and Female Participation Rates**

The total or aggregate participation rate has slowly drifted upward over time. This is the net consequence of the rapidly rising female participation rate more than compensating for a declining male rate.

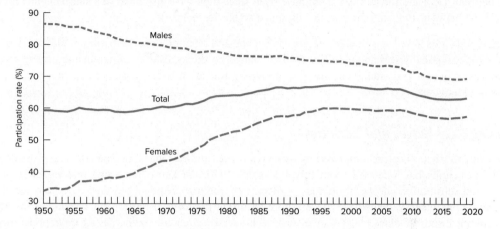

In January 2020, for example, the LFPR was

$$\frac{164,606,000}{259,502,000} \times 100 = 63.4 \text{ \%}$$

Participation rates can be similarly determined for various subaggregates of the population, such as married women, African-American teenage females, and so forth.

SECULAR TREND OF PARTICIPATION RATES

Let's now turn to the long run or secular trend of participation rates in the United States as portrayed in Figure 3.3. You should be forewarned that the factors affecting participation rates are varied and complex; some are economic variables, while others are of an institutional, legal, or attitudinal nature. Thus, although the Becker model is useful in explaining many important changes in participation rates, it cannot be realistically expected to provide a complete understanding of all the forces at work.

Figure 3.3 reveals that the aggregate participation rate has gradually drifted upward since World War II. In 1950, about 60 percent of the age-eligible population were labor force participants. By 2019, that figure had increased to about 63 percent, with most of the rise occurring in the 1970s and 1980s. In Figure 3.3, we also observe that the participation rate of males has declined steadily. Specifically, male participation rates declined from about 86 percent in 1950 to approximately 69 percent in 2019. Until 2000, concomitant increases in female participation rates more than offset this decline. Female participation rates rose from about 34 percent in 1950 to 60 percent in 1999, and have fallen to about 57 percent in 2019. It is important that we understand the major causal factors underlying these trends.

Rebounding Participation Rates of Older Males

Figure 3.4 shows male participation rates by age groups. The message here is that the participation rates of older males have changed markedly. We find a large reduction in the participation rates for males 65 and older between 1950 and the mid-1980s but have risen since then.[9] We also observe a sharp decline for males aged 55–64 between 1950 and the early 1990s, and a small rise since then.

A variety of factors have been cited to explain the decline and rebound in participation of older males. These include (*a*) rising real wages and earnings, (*b*) the changes in the availability of public and private pensions, (*c*) increasing access to disability benefits, (*d*) increasing education levels, and (*e*) rising labor force participation of older wives.

1 Rising Real Wages and Earnings

Economic growth has been accompanied by rising real wages and earnings. For example, real gross domestic product per capita has increased about threefold since 1950. We know that rising real wages entail both income and substitution effects. In the case of older men, the income effect has dominated the substitution effect and, consequently, many have chosen more leisure in the form of retirement. In many instances, the deteriorating health of older males may also have induced retirement by increasing their preferences for leisure or, in terms of Chapter 2, by making their indifference curves steeper.[10] Put in simpler language, as our society has become more affluent over time, the secular increase in real wages and earnings has allowed more workers to accumulate sufficient wealth to retire at an earlier age. The average age of final retirement has fallen by between five and seven years for both men and women since 1950.[11]

FIGURE 3.4 **Male Participation Rates by Age Group**

While the participation rates of males in the 20–24 and 25–54 age groups have remained quite constant, the rates for older males fell significantly and then have risen.

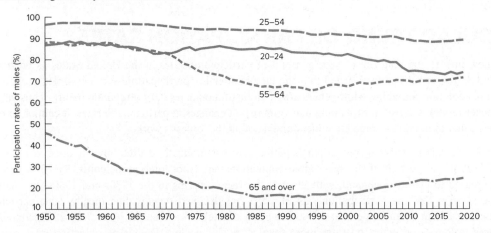

---

[9] Economic incentives don't fully explain the spike in retirement at age 65, see Robin L. Lumsdaine, James H. Stock, and David A. Wise, "Why Are Retirement Rates So High at Age 65?" in David A. Wise (ed.), *Advances in the Economics of Aging* (Chicago, IL: University of Chicago Press, 1996).

[10] Health status played a more important role in the labor force participation decisions of older men early in the 20th century, see Dora L. Costa, "Health and Labor Force Participation of Older Men, 1900–1991," *Journal of Economic History,* March 1996, pp. 62–89.

[11] Murray Gendell, "Older Workers: Increasing Their Labor Force Participation and Hours of Work," *Monthly Labor Review,* January 2008, pp. 41–54.

2 Social Security and Private Pensions

An additional factor in explaining the declining participation rates of older males is the availability of Social Security and private pensions. Established in 1935, the Social Security program now provides retirement benefits for older workers and their survivors in addition to income support in the case of disability or illness. Social Security retirement benefits have been characterized by both expanding coverage and increasingly generous levels, thereby providing an important source of nonlabor income that has induced large numbers of elderly male workers to withdraw from the labor force. In recent years, Social Security benefits have been rising faster than wages in real terms, which enhances the relative attractiveness of retirement. Furthermore, retirement benefits prior to age 65 are subject to a substantial benefit reduction rate—that is, an implicit tax on earned income—which further enhances the incentive for older workers to withdraw from the labor force.[12] Thus, both the income *and* substitution effects associated with Social Security generate disincentives to work.

Although federal legislation prohibits mandatory retirement, the availability of private pensions has been an inducement to early retirement. In 1950 only 16 percent of the labor force was covered by private pension plans; by 2016, 41 percent of all workers were covered. Declining participation rates for the 55–64 age group undoubtedly reflect that many pension plans allow retirement with full or partial benefits on completion of a specified number of years—say, 20 or 30—of employment.

Research by Ippolito[13] suggests that approximately half of the decline in the participation rates of men aged 55–64 in the 1970–1986 period is attributable to two factors: (*a*) changes in the Social Security system that increased retirement benefits by about 50 percent and (*b*) the alteration of private pension rules that encouraged early retirement.

Blau and Goodstein, however, find that changes in Social Security rules that increased the retirement age and increased benefits for retiring past the normal retirement age account for one-quarter to one-half of the rise in the participation rate among males aged 55–69 between 1988–1992 and 2001–2005.[14]

3 Disability Benefits

Evidence also suggests that the disability component of the Social Security program has become increasingly generous and is progressive in the sense that low-wage workers receive relatively larger benefits than high-wage workers. As a result, low-wage workers are more inclined to seek disability benefits as an alternative to labor market participation.[15] Because African-American workers are generally lower income workers, this consideration may explain the larger decline in the participation rates of older African-American workers compared with older white workers.[16]

---

[12] Prior to 2000, the benefit reduction also applied to workers aged 65 to 69. For an analysis of the labor supply impact of this implicit tax, see Steven J. Haider and David S. Loughran, "The Effect of the Social Security Earnings Test on Male Labor Supply: New Evidence from Survey and Administrative Data," *Journal of Human Resources,* Winter 2008, pp. 57–87.

[13] Richard A. Ippolito, "Toward Explaining Earlier Retirement after 1970," *Industrial and Labor Relations Review,* July 1990, pp. 556–569. From a public policy perspective, however, it may be difficult to reverse the increase in early retirement by reducing Social Security benefits, see Alan B. Krueger and Jorn-Steffen Pischke, "The Effect of Social Security on Labor Supply: A Cohort Analysis of the Notch Generation," *Journal of Labor Economics,* October 1992, pp. 412–437.

[14] David M. Blau and Ryan M. Goodstein, "Can Social Security Explain Trends in Labor Force Participation of Older Men in the United States?" *Journal of Human Resources,* Spring 2010, pp. 328–363.

[15] During the 1990s, the labor force participation rate of individuals receiving disability benefits would have been at most 20 percentage points higher had none received benefits, see Susan Chen and Wilbert van der Klaauw, "The Work Disincentive Effects of the Disability Insurance Program in the 1990s," *Journal of Econometrics,* February 2008, pp. 757–784. Also see David H. Autor, Mark Duggan, Kyle Greenberg, and David S. Lyle, "The Impact of Disability Benefits on Labor Supply: Evidence from the VA's Disability Compensation Program," *American Economic Journal: Applied Economics,* July 2016, pp. 31–68

[16] See Donald O. Parsons, "Racial Trends in Male Labor Force Participation," *American Economic Review,* December 1980, pp. 911–920.

4 Rising Educational Levels

Another factor that helps explain the recent rise in the LFPRs of older males is rising educational levels. More educated individuals have higher LFPRs because their wage rates are higher and they have far fewer physical demands than their less-educated counterparts. The proportion of older workers who are high school dropouts has been falling, while the proportion with a college degree has been rising. Blau and Goodstein find that nearly one-fifth of the rise in the labor force participation of males aged 55–69 between 1988–1992 and 2001–2005 was due to increases in educational attainment over the period.[17]

5 Rising Labor Force Participation of Older Wives

Let's consider a fifth and final factor that may account for the recent rise in the participation rates of older males. Tammy Schirle has examined the role of wives in the recent participation rate rise among older married men.[18] She argues that the labor force participation decisions of older married women influence the participation rates of their husbands in two ways. On one hand, the greater family income that results from a working wife causes an income effect that reduces the chance that the husband will work. On the other hand, couples may prefer to spend their leisure time together, particularly at older ages. Husbands may not enjoy their leisure time as much if their wives are working, and thus they prefer to work. If the shared leisure effect dominates the income effect, we would expect that the rising participation rate of older married women will increase the participation rate of older married men. This is exactly what Schirle found. Examining data from 1994 to 2005, she saw that one-quarter of the rise in the U.S. participation rate of married men aged 55–64 was due to increases in the participation rate of their wives.

Rising Female Participation Rates

Figure 3.5 portrays the participation rates of females by age groups. The participation rates of all female age groups have increased over the 69 years shown, with a recent slowing. We observe particularly pronounced increases for the two younger age groups.

Most of the increase in female participation rates shown in Figure 3.5 has been accounted for by married women. For example, the total number of females in the labor force increased by approximately 58 million over the 1950–2019 period. Of this total increase, about two-thirds were married women. In one sense, this is a surprising phenomenon. From the perspective of a household, one might have expected that the participation rate of married women would have declined since World War II as a consequence of the generally rising real wage rates and incomes of married males. And indeed, cross-sectional (point-in-time) studies reveal that the participation rates of married women do in fact vary inversely with their husbands' income. Our analysis in Chapter 2 suggests the reason: If leisure is a normal good, then a household will purchase more leisure as its income rises. Historically, this purchase of leisure was likely to be in the form of the wife's nonparticipation in the labor market. In terms of Figure 2.8, as the husband's income rises, an expanding intrahousehold transfer of income is available to the wife, and the consequent income effect induces her to be a nonparticipant. This line of reasoning suggests that wives in lower income families are likely to work in the labor market because of economic necessity; but as the husband's income increases, more families will enjoy the luxury of having the wife produce commodities at home.

---

[17] Blau and Goodstein, op. cit. For evidence that rising education levels can account for one-third of the rise in participation of married males aged 55 to 64 between 1994 and 2005, see Tammy Schirle, "Why Have the Labor Force Participation Rates of Older Men Increased since the Mid-1990s?" *Journal of Labor Economics,* October 2008, pp. 549–594.

[18] Ibid.

GP3.1

Economists have cited several possible reasons for the rapid rise in women's labor force participation.[19]

How can this reasoning be reconciled with the evidence that the participation rates of married women have actually increased over time? The answer lies partly in the fact that cross-sectional studies do not have a time dimension and therefore ignore or hold constant certain variables other than the husband's income that might have an impact on a wife's decision to participate in the labor force. That is, a number of factors besides husbands' rising incomes have been influencing the participation rates of married women over time. These other factors have so strongly influenced women to enter the labor market that they have overwhelmed the negative effect on labor market work of the generally rising incomes of husbands. Also, during the past three decades, the real income growth of many husbands has slowed or even ceased.

1 Rising Real Wage Rates for Women

There has been a long-run increase in the real wage rates that women can earn in the labor market. This is primarily a consequence of women having acquired more skills through education. As already noted, higher wage rates generate both income and substitution effects within the framework of Becker's model. While the income effect reduces hours of work, the substitution effects related to both production- and consumption-related activities within the home tend to increase them. Goods will be substituted for time in the production of commodities *and* goods-intensive commodities will be substituted for time-intensive goods in the household's mix of consumer commodities. Both adjustments free the wife's time from household activities so that she may spend more time in the labor market. Presumably the substitution effect has dominated the income effect for many women, causing their participation rates to rise. The income effect for married women may be small because its size varies directly with the amount of time they are already devoting to labor market work. In the extreme, the income effect of a rise in wage rates is zero for a married woman who is not currently participating in labor market work. A wage rate increase increases a person's income only if the individual is currently providing hours of labor market work.

FIGURE 3.5 **Female Participation Rates by Age Group**

Aside from the 65 and older group, the participation rates of all women have risen over the past 69 years. The sharpest increases have been for younger women in the 20–24 and 25–54 age groups.

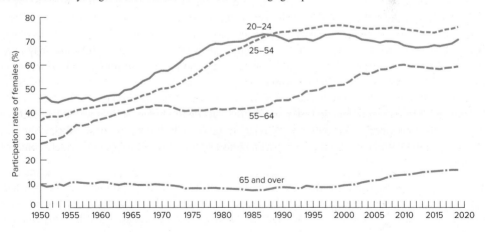

[19] See James P. Smith and Michael P. Ward, "Time Series Growth in the Female Labor Force," *Journal of Labor Economics, Supplement,* January 1985, pp. S59-90; Claudia Goldin, *Understanding the Gender Gap* (New York: Oxford University Press, 1990); Francine D. Blau, "Trends in the Well-Being of American Women, 1970-1995," *Journal of Economic Literature,* March 1998, pp. 112-165; and Francine D. Blau and Anne E. Winkler, op. cit., Chapter 6.

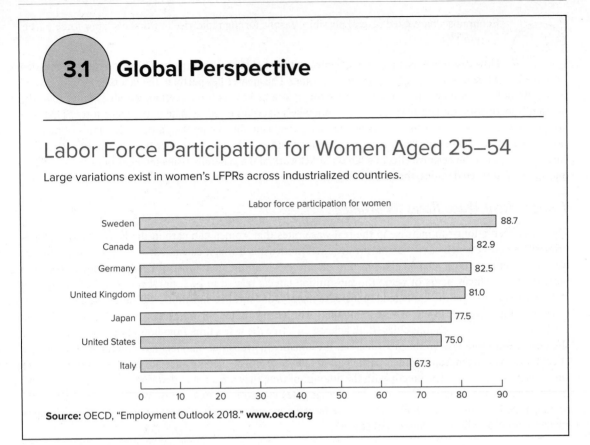

3.1 Global Perspective

Labor Force Participation for Women Aged 25–54

Large variations exist in women's LFPRs across industrialized countries.

Labor force participation for women

Sweden	88.7
Canada	82.9
Germany	82.5
United Kingdom	81.0
Japan	77.5
United States	75.0
Italy	67.3

Source: OECD, "Employment Outlook 2018." **www.oecd.org**

2 Changing Preferences and Attitudes

Rising female participation rates may also result from a fundamental change in female preferences in favor of labor market work. First, the feminist movement of the 1960s may have altered the career objectives of women toward labor market participation. Similarly, antidiscrimination legislation of the 1960s—which specifies equal pay for equal work and presumably has made "men's jobs" more accessible—also may have made labor market work more attractive compared to work in the home. Furthermore, aside from its positive impact on wage rates, greater education for women may have enhanced their tastes or preferences for labor market careers. More generally, society's attitudes about work have changed greatly. In the 1920s and 1930s, there was general disapproval of married women working outside the home. A man would lose status and be regarded as a "poor provider" if his wife was "forced" to take a job. But in the post–World War II period, an attitudinal turnabout emerged: Labor force participation by married women is now widely condoned and encouraged.

Reference to Figure 2.8 is helpful in distinguishing between how higher wage rates on the one hand and changing preferences on the other affect female participation rates. The availability of higher wage rates increases the slope of the budget line, which—given preferences—encourages labor market participation. Similarly, given the wage rates, a change in preferences favorable to market work makes the indifference curves flatter, which is also conducive to participation.

3 Rising Productivity in the Household

The use of more and technologically superior capital goods by businesses over time has been an important factor in increasing the productivity of work time and therefore in raising real wage rates. Larger amounts of improved machinery and equipment permit workers to produce a unit of output with less time. Similarly, the availability of more and better capital goods for household use has permitted households to reduce the amount of time needed to accomplish both production and consumption within the home. For example, supermarkets and the availability of home refrigerators and freezers greatly reduce the amount of time devoted to grocery shopping. The supermarket permits one-stop shopping, and refrigerators and freezers further reduce the number of shopping trips needed per week. Similarly, microwave ovens, vacuum cleaners, automatic clothes washers and dryers, and dishwashers have reduced the amount of time involved in food preparation and housework. Fast-food restaurants circumvent the time-intensive activity of food preparation in the home. By providing direct and convenient transportation, the automobile has reduced the time required to attend a concert, movie, or football game. In terms of Becker's model, the increased availability of such household capital goods has increased productivity in the home, thereby freeing time from household production and consumption and allowing many women to engage in part- and full-time employment in the labor market. Also, a recent study suggests that residential high-speed internet access has increased the labor force participation of married women by making it easier to telework from home as well as reduce time spent on household production tasks such as paying bills.[20]

4 Declining Birthrates

The presence of children (particularly preschool children) is associated with low participation rates for wives. Child care is a highly time-intensive household productive activity that keeps many wives out of the labor force. Although babysitters, nurseries, husbands, and child care centers can substitute for wives in caring for children, the expense and opportunity cost involved often discourage such substitutions. Over time, the widespread availability and use of birth control techniques, coupled with changing lifestyles, have reduced birthrates *and* compacted the span of time over which a family's children are born. Whereas there were about 3.8 lifetime births per woman in 1957 at the peak of the baby boom, that figure has declined to only 1.9 now. Fewer children reduce associated homemaking responsibilities and free married women for labor market work. Moreover, the compression of the time span over which children are born reduces the amount of time during which many women are absent from the labor force for child care responsibilities and is, therefore, more conducive to their pursuit of a labor market career.

Two points must be added. First, higher wage rates are associated with lower fertility rates. More educated women who can command relatively high wage rates in the labor market tend to have fewer children than less-educated women for whom wages are low. Becker's model provides one explanation for this relationship. Child rearing is a highly time-intensive activity, and thus the opportunity cost of children—the income sacrificed by not being in the labor market—is higher for more educated women than for those who are less educated.

The second point is that the presence of young children is currently less of an inhibitor to labor market participation than it has been in the recent past. In fact, the largest increases in labor force participation have been for wives with very young children. In 2017, 62 percent of wives with preschool children participated in the labor force, compared to only 30 percent in 1970. Currently, more than half of all mothers return to work before their youngest children are two years old.

---

[20] Lisa J. Dettling, "Broadband in the Labor Market: The Impact of Residential High-Speed Internet on Married Women's Labor Force Participation," *Industrial and Labor Relations Review,* March 2017, pp. 451–482.

5 Rising Divorce Rates

WW3.3
Marital instability as evidenced in rising divorce rates has undoubtedly motivated many women to establish and maintain labor market ties. Divorce rates rose rapidly in the 1970s and 1980s; and although they have declined slightly since then, they remain much higher than in earlier periods. The economic impact of divorce on women is often disastrous because relatively few women receive substantial alimony or child support payments from their former husbands. All too often the options are poverty, welfare support, or labor market work. In short, more and more married women, not to mention women contemplating marriage, may participate in the labor force as a means of protecting themselves against the financial exigencies of potential divorce. In terms of Figure 2.8, divorced women find themselves with substantially less nonlabor income, and this reduction is an inducement to labor market work.

3.3 World of Work

The Power of the Pill

The first birth control pill was released to the public in 1960. The pill has allowed women to have nearly certain prevention of pregnancy. This invention has caused far-reaching changes to society, including permitting women to plan their careers and childbearing to a much greater degree than before.

The pill was adopted at different rates depending on marital status. Married women quickly adopted the pill as their preferred method of birth control. Within five years, 41 percent of married women under the age of 30 who employed contraception were using it. However, due to legal and social factors, the pill was more slowly adopted by unmarried single women. The age of legal access to the pill was 21 for all but nine states in 1969. The age of legal access was lowered for nearly all states between 1969 and 1974. Thus, by 1976 nearly three-quarters of all single women aged 18 and 19 and using contraception had tried the pill.

Goldin and Katz exploited these interstate differences in the timing of legal access to the pill to examine its impact on the age of first marriage and the proportion of women in professional occupations. Their analysis indicates that access

to the pill can account for about one-third of the rise in the female percentage in professional occupations between 1970 and 1990. Legalized pill access to minors can account for 24–37 percent of the 8.7 percentage point decrease in the proportion of women married before age 23 between the cohorts of women born in the 1940s compared with those born in the early 1950s.

Bailey also utilized interstate differences in timing of legal access to the pill to examine the effects of the pill on female labor supply. Her results show that early access to the pill can account for 3 of the 20 percentage points of increase in LFPRs between 1970 and 1990. It can also account for 67 of the 450 additional annual hours worked on average by women aged 16–30 over that period.

Sources: Claudia Goldin and Lawrence F. Katz, "The Power of the Pill: Oral Contraceptives and Women's Career and Marriage Decisions," *Journal of Political Economy,* August 2002, pp. 730–770; and Martha J. Bailey, "More Power of the Pill: The Impact of Contraceptive Freedom on Women's Life Cycle Labor Supply," *Quarterly Journal of Economics,* February 2006, pp. 289–320.

A word of caution: The cause-and-effect relationships among fertility, divorce rates, and labor force participation are complex and unclear. For example, declines in fertility resulting from more efficient and less-costly birth control techniques undoubtedly encourage labor force participation. On the other hand, the initial choice of a woman to pursue a labor market career may precipitate the decision to have fewer children.

Similarly, the increased likelihood of divorce will tend to reduce fertility because child care is more difficult after a marriage dissolves. Conversely, the presence of few or no children makes divorce less painful and less costly.[21]

6 Expanding Job Accessibility

In addition to a decline in gender discrimination, a variety of other factors have made jobs more accessible to women. First, since World War II there has been a great expansion both absolutely and relatively in the kinds of employment that have traditionally been "women's jobs," such as clerical and secretarial work, retail sales, teaching, and nursing. Second, there has been a long-run shift of the population from farms and rural regions to urban areas, where jobs for women are more abundant and more geographically accessible. Third, the availability of part-time jobs has increased. This development has made it easier for women to reconcile labor market employment with housekeeping tasks.

7 Attempts to Maintain Living Standards

The growth of male earnings during the past two decades has been quite stagnant compared to earlier decades. In fact, for some men—particularly low-wage workers and those in industries hurt by imports—*real* weekly earnings are lower today than a decade, or even two decades, ago. Many households have adjusted to these realities by having both spouses work. That is, they have substituted labor market time for household production time to preserve the family's standard of living (defined either absolutely or relative to other households).[22]

In this view, part of the more recent rise in the female LFPR has been necessitated by the family's desire to make ends meet. In some cases, making ends meet implies paying for basic food, clothing, and shelter. In other instances, it means preserving middle- or upper-class lifestyles, including living in comfortable homes, driving nice cars, enjoying household electronic equipment, and taking family trips. Understandably families look for ways to maintain their standards of living, whatever those levels might be. If spouses had not entered the labor force in record numbers during the past two decades, many households would have suffered absolute or relative declines in real income. Undoubtedly many wives entered the labor force to prevent this from happening. In addition, couples may be concerned about their family income compared to other families; the entry of some women into the labor market may encourage other women to enter in order to maintain their families' relative income levels.[23]

Relative Importance

Fuchs has analyzed the various factors that may have contributed to rising female participation rates, trying to discern their comparative significance.[24] He discounts the importance of such considerations as antidiscrimination legislation and the feminist movement, largely on the basis that their timing is bad. That is, the growth of female participation rates predates both the feminist movement and the passage of

[21] For further discussion, you might consult Blau and Winkler, op. cit., pp. 359–363. For an analysis of the effects of switching from mutual consent to unilateral divorce laws, see Raquel Fernandez and Joyce Wong, "Unilateral Divorce, the Decreasing Gender Gap, and Married Women's Labor Force Participation," *American Economic Review,* May 2014, pp. 342–347.

[22] Some doubt has been cast on the hypothesis that married women are increasing work effort in response to declining wages of husbands, see Chinhui Juhn and Kevin M. Murphy, "Wage Inequality and Family Labor Supply," *Journal of Labor Economics,* January 1997, pp. 72–97.

[23] For some evidence consistent with this hypothesis, see David Neumark and Andrew Postlewaite, "Relative Income Concerns and the Rise in Married Women's Employment," *Journal of Public Economics,* October 1998, pp. 157–183.

[24] Victor R. Fuchs, *How We Live* (Cambridge: Harvard University Press, 1983), pp. 127–133.

antidiscrimination laws (Chapter 14). It also predates the stagnant growth of real earnings experienced by many husbands during recent decades. The problem with attributing rising participation rates for women to the availability of time-saving household goods and related innovations is that cause and effect are unclear. Did innovations such as clothes washers, freezers, fast-food restaurants, and supermarkets simply appear and thereby free up time that married women could devote to labor market work? Or were these innovations made largely in response to needs that arose when women decided for other reasons to enter the labor force? Fuchs believes that their spread in the United States is the *result* of the rising value of time and the rising female participation rates, rather than a causal factor.

More positively, Fuchs feels that rising real wage rates and the expansion of "women's jobs" in the service industries are the most important reasons for rising female participation rates. Better control of fertility is also deemed significant, but once again cause and effect are difficult to unravel. Do women first decide on labor force participation and, as a consequence of this decision, choose to have fewer children? Or does the decision to have smaller families precede the decision to enter the labor force? Fuchs also contends that the growing probability of divorce compels women to achieve and maintain their ties to the labor market. Smith and Ward are in substantial agreement with Fuchs. Their research leads them to conclude that rising real wage rates directly (by creating incentives to work) and indirectly (by inducing lower birthrates) have accounted for almost 60 percent of the increase in the female labor force that has occurred since World War II.[25]

Stalling of Female Labor Supply?

WW3.4   The labor supply of women increased sharply in the 1970s and 1980s. The female participation rate rose eight percentage points in the 1970s, and six percentage points in the 1980s. The next decade was marked by smaller increases in the labor supply of women. Between 2000 and 2015, the participation rate fell for women about three percentage points. Between 2015 and 2018, there was little change in the female participation rate.

A study by Chen Huang examines the participation rate of women between 2000 and 2015.[26] She finds that about two-thirds of the decline is due to the aging of the female labor force. She also reports that about one-third of the decline in overall female participation is due to a drop in the participation rate of women less than age 55. Chen Huang suggests that stagnant or falling real wages for prime-age women can help explain the decline in their participation.

Diane Macunovich has also examined the change in the labor supply of prime-aged women in the 2000s.[27] For women with a college degree, she finds that one-half of their 52-hour drop in hours worked between 1999 and 2009 was due to an increase in the number of children. For other groups of women, she finds that little or none of the changes in the labor supply can be attributed to economic or demographic factors. She speculates that the recent shifts in the labor supply of prime-aged women may be the result of changes in attitudes with regard to spending time in the labor market and at home.

---

[25] Smith and Ward, op. cit., pp. S59–90. For another discussion emphasizing the role of rising wages for women in the rise of female labor force participation as well as declines in the value of their non-market time, see Francine D. Blau and Anne E. Winkler, *The Economics of Women, Men, and Work*, 8th Edition (New York: Oxford University Press, 2018), pp. 136–141.

[26] Chen Huang, "Why Are U.S. Women Decreasing Their Labor Force Participation If Their Wages Are Rising?" *Economic Inquiry*, October 2018, pp. 2010–2026.

[27] See Diane J. Macunovich, "Reversals in the Patterns of Women's Labor Supply in the United States, 1977–2009," *Monthly Labor Review*, November 2010, pp. 16–36.

3.2 Global Perspective

Maximum Duration of Paid Maternity Leave in Weeks

Countries differ greatly in the duration of paid maternity leave that firms are required to give new parents.

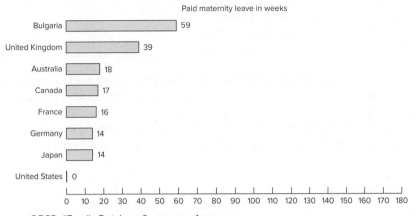

Source: Source: OECD, "Family Database." **www.oecd.org**

3.4 World of Work

Why Do So Few Women Work in New York and So Many in Minneapolis?*

A little noticed fact is that wide variation exists in the labor supply of married women across metropolitan areas. For example, among white non–Hispanic married women aged 25–55 with a high school degree in 2000, 79 percent were employed in Minneapolis, but only 52 percent were employed in New York. This is in sharp contrast to the situations in 1940, when the labor supply of this group of women was lower in

Minneapolis than in New York. Thus, the current high-employment rate in Minneapolis is the result of a much more rapid growth in the labor supply in Minneapolis than in New York.

Using data from the 50 largest metropolitan areas, Dan Black, Natalia Kolesnikova, and Lowell Taylor examine the cross-city variation in the labor supply of married women. They argue that commuting time plays an important role in the labor force participation decisions of married women, particularly those with young children. For a married couple, greater commuting time will increase the fixed cost of working for both partners. This change can cause one partner to leave the labor force (typically the wife) and induce the other partner (typically the husband) to increase work hours.

The evidence is consistent with their hypothesis. Commuting time does vary substantially across metropolitan areas. The daily average in 2000 was 54 minutes for married men and 47 minutes for married women. Commuting time for married women ranged from a low of 38 minutes in Dayton to a high of 63 minutes in New York.

Their results indicate that commuting can explain a large portion of the cross-city variation in the labor supply of married women. They find that each one-minute increase in commuting time will lower the LFPR by 0.3 percentage points for high school educated white non–Hispanic married women. Thus, commuting time can explain about one-third of the differences in the LFPRs between the longest and shortest commuting distance cities. In addition, they find that cities with the largest increases in commuting time between 1980 and 2000, had the smallest growth in the labor supply of married women.

* Based on Dan A. Black, Natalia Kolesnikova, and Lowell J. Taylor, "Why Do So Few Women Work in New York (And So Many in Minneapolis)? Labor Supply of Married Women Across U.S. Cities," *Journal of Urban Economics*, January 2014, pp. 59–71.

Francine Blau and Lawrence Kahn find that the female LFPR in the United States is falling relative to other industrialized countries.[28] In 1990, the labor participation rate of females aged 25–54 ranked 6th out of 22 economically advanced countries. By 2010, that rate dropped to 17th of 22 countries. Their analysis indicates that a significant portion of the relative decline in the U.S. female labor participation rate is due to an expansion of family-friendly policies in other countries such as parental leave programs and part-time work options.

Racial Differences

Important gender differences mark the effect of race on LFPRs.

Females

The participation rates of African-American and white women are nearly identical. This situation was not always the case. In the past, the participation rate of African-American women exceeded that of white women. For example, in the mid-1950s, the difference between the participation rates of African-American and white women was 12–15 percentage points. The gap has been closed because the rise in the participation rate of women (discussed in the previous section) has been concentrated among white women. Relatively little change has occurred in the participation of African-American women because their participation traditionally has been high.

The decline in the racial gap in participation may be a critical factor in explaining why the ratio of African-American incomes to white incomes has increased only modestly in the past two decades or so. The income gains for African-American families, which may have resulted from antidiscrimination legislation and more enlightened attitudes toward minorities, may have been largely offset by the relatively larger numbers of white married women entering the labor force.[29]

---

[28] Francine D. Blau and Lawrence M. Kahn, "Female Labor Supply: Why Is the U.S. Falling Behind?" *American Economic Review*, May 2013, pp. 251–256.

[29] In this section, we have focused on the factors that explain the rise in female labor market employment. For an interesting discussion of the effects of women's labor force participation on marriage, fertility, divorce, and the general well-being of family members, see Blau and Winkler, op. cit., Chapters 13–14.

Males

Since the 1950s, a gap has evolved between the participation rates of African-American males and white males. Thus, for example, in 1955 the participation rates of both groups were approximately 85 percent. But by 2000 the participation rate of white males was 75 percent compared to only 69 percent for African-American males. The gap has stabilized at about 6–7 percent since the mid-1990s.

Why the significantly lower participation rates for African-American men? There is no consensus on this question, but several hypotheses have been offered. First, "a demand-side" hypothesis suggests that the difference may be largely attributable to poorer labor market opportunities for African-American males in general, as reflected in relatively lower wages and weaker prospects for finding jobs. African-American males have lower average levels of educational attainment than white males. Also, on average, the quality of education (as measured by test scores) received by African-American males is lower than that for white males. In this demand-side view, discrimination as embodied in poorer education, lower wages, less-desirable jobs, and the tendency to be the "last hired and first fired" explains why some African-American males remain outside the labor force. A spatial mismatch also may exist between African-American workers and employment opportunities because jobs have moved out of the central cities, where substantial African-American populations are concentrated.[30]

A second view explains the high labor market inactivity of African-Americans as residing primarily on the supply side of the market. Welch[31] has argued that non–labor market opportunities may have improved for African-Americans, affording them more attractive alternatives to labor market work. What are those non–labor market opportunities? One is the receipt of Social Security or public assistance. Indeed, we found in Chapter 2 that the increased availability and enhanced generosity of public income maintenance programs encourage income receivers of all races to withdraw from the labor force (see Figure 2.9 in particular). Because African-Americans are disproportionately represented among the lowest-income groups in our society, we would expect the participation rates of African-Americans to be less than those of whites. Welch notes that in 1980 over 30 percent of African-American men aged 20–24 and almost 22 percent of African-American men aged 35–44 either received Social Security or public assistance or lived with someone who did. Comparable figures for white males were only 13 and 10 percent, respectively. Welch also ponders whether illegal activities are more attractive than labor market work for many African-American men. He points out that young African-American males are six to seven times as likely to be in jail as are whites. Thus, in 1980 some 4.6 percent of African-Americans aged 20–24 were incarcerated as compared to only 0.7 percent for whites. Since 1980, the incarceration rate has risen particularly for African-American males. Patterson and Wildeman estimate that white males spend 6 percent of their work life as a prisoner or as an ex-prisoner, but for African-American males it is 31 percent.[32]

Third, differences in health status may play a role in the different participation rates of older African-American and white males. Bound, Schoenbaum, and Waidmann conclude that racial differences in age, education, and health status can account for 44 percent of the African-American to white difference in

---

[30] For an overview of the spatial mismatch hypothesis, see Laurent Gobillon, Harris Selod, and Yves Zenou, "The Mechanisms of Spatial Mismatch," *Urban Studies,* November 2007, pp. 2401–2427.

[31] Finis Welch, "The Employment of Black Men," *Journal of Labor Economics,* January 1990, pp. S26–74.

[32] Evelyn J. Patterson and Christopher Wildeman, "Mass Imprisonment and the Life Course Revisited: Cumulative Years Spent Imprisoned and Marked for Working-Age Black and White Men," *Social Science Research,* September 2015, pp. 325–337. For evidence indicating that the high incarceration among African-American males has lowered the fertility and increased the school enrollment and early employment rates among young African-American females, see Stéphane Mechoulan, "The External Effects of Black-Male Incarceration on Black Females," *Journal of Labor Economics,* January 2011, pp. 1–35.

participation of males aged 51–61.[33] Evidence exists that some of these health differences may partly be the result of African-American males holding more physically demanding and stressful jobs.

Finally, the relatively lower participation rate for African-American married males may also reflect the relatively high participation rate of African-American wives noted earlier. In terms of Becker's model, African-American women may incur less discrimination in the labor market than African-American men, making it rational for relatively more African-American women and relatively fewer African-American men to participate in labor market work.

Future Fall in the Participation Rate?

As noted earlier, the LFPR reached a peak in 2000 of 67 percent and had fallen to 63 percent by the start of 2019 due to declines in the participation rates of both men and women. The aging of the population and the retirement of the baby boom generation certainly contributed to the fall in participation. Stephanie Aaronson and several other Federal Reserve researchers have examined the causes of the decline in the participation rate between 2007 and 2014.[34] Aging of the population can account for nearly half of the 2.8 percentage point decline by itself.[35] Another important factor is the decline in the participation rate for youths, which is likely due to increasing returns to education and greater competition for low-skill jobs. Increasing video gaming by young males may have also played a role in the decline of their participation (see World of Work Box 3.2).

It is important to note that the participation rate of prime-age males has fallen over the past several decades. The participation rate for males aged 25–54 fell from 94 percent in 1980 to 92 percent in 2000 to 89 percent in 2018. Both labor supply and demand factors have been suggested as responsible for this decline in participation.[36] Reduced demand for workers due to international trade and automation has appeared to play a role in the decline in participation, particularly for less-educated men.[37] Lower labor supply may be due to a variety of causes including a lack of skills or education, higher reservation wages, disability or illness (including the opioid crisis—see World of Work Box 3.5), increased disability benefit receipt, and higher incarceration rates.[38]

WW3.5   Researchers predict that the LFPR will continue to decline over the next decade. The Congressional Budget Office forecasts that the LFPR will fall by another two percentage points between 2019 and 2029 to 61 percent.[39] A large portion of the predicted decline is due to the retirement of baby boomers. Joshua Montes of the Congressional Budget Office predicts that the decline in participation of prime-age workers will stop in the next decade.[40] The increase in participation due to rising educational attainment will exceed future declines in the participation of less-educated, prime-age individuals.

---

[33] John Bound, Michael Schoenbaum, and Timothy Waidmann, "Race and Education Differences in Disability Status and Labor Force Attachment in the Health and Retirement Survey," *Journal of Human Resources,* Suppl. 1995, pp. S227–267.

[34] Stephanie Aaronson, Tomaz Cajner, Bruce Fallick, Felix Galbis-Reig, Christopher Smith, and William Wascher, "Labor Force Participation: Recent Developments and Future Prospects," *Fall 2014 Brookings Papers on Economic Activity,* pp. 197–295.

[35] For an analysis reaching a similar conclusion using 1997 to 2017 data, see Alan B. Krueger, "Where Have All the Workers Gone? An Inquiry into the Decline of the U.S. Labor Force Participation Rate," *Brookings Papers on Economic Activity,* Fall 2017, pp. 1–87.

[36] For a review of the possible causes, see Eleanor Krause and Isabel Sawhill, "What We Know and Don't Know About Declining Labor Force Participation: A Review," Urban Institute Working Paper, May 2017

[37] For a discussion suggesting that reduced labor demand is most responsible for the decline in the related employment to population ratio, see Katharine G. Abraham and Melissa S. Kearney, "Explaining the Decline in the U.S. Employment-to-Population Ratio: A Review of the Evidence," National Bureau of Economic Research Working Paper Number 24333, February 2018. For a similar conclusion, see Didem Tüzemen, "Why Are Prime-Age Men Vanishing from the Labor Force?" Kansas City Federal Reserve *Economic Review,* First Quarter 2018, pp. 5–30.

[38] See "Symposium: The Problems of Men," *Journal of Economic Perspectives,* Spring 2019.

[39] Congressional Budget Office, "The Budget and Economic Outlook: 2019 to 2029," January 2019.

[40] Joshua Montes, "CBO's Projection of Labor Force Participation Rates," Congressional Budget Office Working Paper, March 2018.

3.5 World of Work

The Opioid Crisis and the Decline in Labor Force Participation

The opioid crisis in the United States has exploded since starting in the late 1990s. The first wave of the epidemic started with the abuse of common prescription drugs such as OxyContin and Oxycodone. Between 1999 and 2011, the number of deaths due to prescription opioid overdoses more than quadrupled (with a modest decline since 2011). The next wave, which started about 2012, was a rapid rise in the use of heroin and synthetic opioids such as Fentanyl. The number of deaths due to heroin and synthetic opioids skyrocketed from 8,553 in 2012 to 43,948 in 2017.

The rise in opioid use may also impact work effort. Opioids have a therapeutic use in reducing pain and thus may help individuals continue to work or resume work. However, their sedative effects and high risk of addiction will reduce work effort.

The rapid rise in the use of prescription opioids has had adverse effects on labor force participation. Using county-level data from 2010 to 2015 for 10 states, Harris, Kesslery, Murray, and Glenn find that a 10 percent increase in Schedule II opioid prescriptions causes a 0.56 percentage point decline in labor force participation. Aliprantis, Fee, and Schweitzer using county-level data from 2006 to 2016, find that a 10 percent rise in prescription opioids lowers the prime-age employment rate by 0.50 percentage points and 0.17 for men and women, respectively. The effects are larger for men without a college degree and minority men.

The rise in the use of prescription opioids appears to help explain the recent decline in labor force participation of men. Aliprantis, Fee, and Schweitzer report that prescription opioids can explain 44 percent of the decline in men's labor force participation and 17 percent of the decline in women's labor force participation between 2001 and 2015. Krueger finds prescription opioids can explain 20 percent of the decline in men's labor force participation between 1999–2001 and 2014–2016.

The rise in opioid use could be the result rather than the cause of declining labor force participation. Aliprantis, Fee, and Schweitzer report, however, that short-term unemployment rises do not lead to a greater portion of individuals abusing opioids, and the effects of prescription opioids on participation are similar in both weak and strong labor markets.

Sources: Dionissi Aliprantis, Kyle Fee, and Mark E. Schweitzer, "Opioids and the Labor Market," Federal Reserve Bank of Cleveland Working Paper, 18-07R, March 2019; Matthew C. Harris, Lawrence M. Kesslery, Matthew N. Murray, and M. Elizabeth Glenn, "Prescription Opioids and Labor Market Pains: The Effect of Schedule II Opioids on Labor Force Participation and Unemployment," *Journal of Human Resources*, forthcoming; and Alan B. Krueger, "Where Have All the Workers Gone? An Inquiry into the Decline of the U.S. Labor Force Participation Rate," *Brookings Papers on Economic Activity*, Fall 2017, pp. 1–87.

CYCLIC CHANGES IN PARTICIPATION RATES

Our discussion has concentrated on long-term or secular changes in participation rates. We must now recognize that cyclic changes also occur. Let's consider how cyclic fluctuations might affect a family in which one spouse engages in labor market work while the other performs productive activities within the home. Assume that a recession occurs, causing the employed spouse to lose her or his job. The net effect on overall participation rates depends on the size of the added-worker effect and the discouraged-worker effect.

Added-Worker Effect

The *added-worker effect* is the idea that when the primary breadwinner in a family loses his or her job, other family members will temporarily enter the labor force in the hope of finding employment to offset the decline in the family's income. The rationale involved is reminiscent of Chapter 2's income effect. Specifically, one spouse's earned income may be treated as nonlabor income from the standpoint of the other spouse. In our illustration, the nonemployed family member receives an intrahousehold transfer of some portion of the employed spouse's earnings. From the perspective of the person working in the home, this transfer is nonlabor income. In terms of Figure 2.8, the spouse's job loss will reduce nonlabor income as measured on the right vertical axis. Other things being equal, a decrease in nonlabor (transfer) income tends to cause one to become a labor force participant. This is the underlying rationale of the added-worker effect.[41]

Discouraged-Worker Effect

The *discouraged-worker effect* works in the opposite direction. The discouraged-worker effect suggests that during a recession some unemployed workers (for example, the unemployed spouse in our illustration) become so pessimistic about finding a job with an acceptable wage rate that they cease to actively seek employment and thereby temporarily become nonparticipants. This phenomenon can be explained in terms of the substitution effect. Recessions generally entail declines in the real wages available to unemployed workers and new job seekers, increasing the price of income (that is, increasing the amount of work time that must be expended to earn $1 of goods) and decreasing the price of leisure. This causes some workers to substitute leisure (nonparticipation) for job search. Other things being equal, a decrease in the wage rate will cause some individuals to withdraw from the labor force now that the wage rate available to them is lower. Remember that the substitution effect suggests that a decline in the wage rate available to a worker will decrease the incentive to engage in labor market work.[42]

Procyclic Labor Force Changes

These two effects influence participation rates and labor force size in opposite ways. The added-worker effect increases and the discouraged-worker effect decreases participation rates and labor force size during an economic downturn. Which effect is dominant? What actually happens to participation rates over the business cycle? Empirical research generally indicates that the discouraged-worker effect is dominant, as is evidenced by the fact that the aggregate LFPR rate varies inversely with the unemployment rate. When the unemployment rate increases, the participation rate falls and vice versa.

Why does the discouraged-worker effect apparently outweigh the added-worker effect? Why does the size of the labor force vary in a procyclic fashion? The conventional wisdom is that the discouraged-worker effect applies to many more households than the added-worker effect. For example, if the nation's unemployment rate rises from, say, 5–8 percent, only the 3 percent or so of all families that now contain an additional unemployed member will be subject to the added-worker effect. On the other hand, worsening labor market conditions evidenced by the increase in the unemployment rate and the decline in real wages may discourage actual and potential labor force participants in *all* households. Thus, as the economy moves into a recession,

---

[41] For an examination of the added-worker effect, see J. Melvin Stephens, "Worker Displacement and the Added-Worker Effect," *Journal of Labor Economics,* July 2002, pp. 504–537. For analysis of the added worker effects of the 2007-2009 recession, see Martha A. Starr, "Gender, Added-Worker effects, and the 2007–2009 recession: Looking Within the Household," *Review of Economics of the Household,* June 2014, pp 209–235. For an examination of the added worker effect across 28 European countries, see Julia Bredtmann, Sebastian Otten, and Christian Rulff, "Huband's Unemployment and Wife's Labor Supply: The Added Worker Effect Across Europe," *Industrial and Labor Relations Review,* October 2018, pp. 1201–1231.

[42] For an evaluation of the discouraged-worker effect, see Yolanda K. Kodrzycki, "Discouraged and Other Marginally Attached Workers: Evidence on Their Role in the Labor Market," *New England Economic Review,* May/June 2000, pp. 35–40. Also see Luca Benati, "Some Empirical Evidence on the 'Discouraged Worker' Effect," *Economics Letters,* March 2001, pp. 387–395.

young people who are deciding whether to continue school or drop out to seek employment will note that wage rates are less attractive and jobs more difficult to find. Many of them will decide to stay in school rather than participate in the labor force.

Procyclic changes in the labor force size also have been explained in terms of the *timing* of labor force participation by some individuals. For example, many married women are marginally attached to the labor force in that they plan to engage in labor market work for, say, only half of their adult years. The other half of their time will be spent in household production. Given this planned overall division of time, it is only rational for such women to participate in the labor force in prosperous times when jobs are readily available and real wages are relatively high and, conversely, to be nonparticipants when unemployment is high and available wage rates are low.

The procyclic changes in labor force size are of more than idle academic interest. Such changes have a significant bearing on the magnitude of the official unemployment rate and hence an indirect bearing on macroeconomic policy (Chapter 18). The apparent dominance of the discouraged-worker effect over the added-worker effect means that the labor force shrinks (or at least grows at a below-normal rate) during a recession and the official unemployment rate understates unemployment. During economic expansions, the discouraged-worker effect becomes an "encouraged-worker" effect, and the added-worker effect becomes a "subtracted-worker" effect. The former dominates the latter, and the labor force expands as a result. This means there is a larger-than-normal increase in the labor force during an economic expansion that keeps the official unemployment rate higher than would otherwise be the case. In short, cyclic changes in participation rates cause the official unemployment rate to understate unemployment during a cyclic downswing and to overstate it during an upswing.

3.2 *Quick Review*

- The LFPR measures the percentage of the potential labor force that is either employed or officially unemployed.

- Two pronounced secular trends in LFPRs are the declining rates of older men and the rising rates of working-age women.

- The LFPRs for African-American women have consistently exceeded the rates for white women; the rates for African-American males have dropped far below those of white males.

- The overall LFPR falls as the economy recedes and rises as the economy expands, implying that the discouraged-worker effect (encouraged-worker effect) exceeds the added-worker effect (subtracted-worker effect).

Your Turn

Suppose a hypothetical country has a total population of 100 million, of which 7 million are unemployed (but actively seeking work), 15 million are under 16 or institutionalized, 25 million are eligible to work but not in the labor force, and 53 million are employed. What is the LFPR? (*Answer:* See page 540.)

HOURS OF WORK: TWO TRENDS

Observe in Figure 3.1 that the total amount of labor supplied in the economy depends not only on the number of labor force participants but also on the average number of hours worked per week and per year by those participants; therefore, let's now consider what has happened to hours of work over time.

Figure 3.6 provides an overview of secular changes in the average workweek. The figure shows decade averages of the workweek for production workers in U.S. manufacturing industries. Two important observations are apparent. First, hours of work declined steadily from 1910 to World War II. The average workweek fell by almost 16 percent [(49.4 − 41.5)/49.4] over the 1910-1919 to 1940-1949 period.[43] Second, the average workweek has changed little since the 1940s. Although there is no universally accepted explanation of these trends, interesting and plausible theories have been put forth.

FIGURE 3.6 Average Workweek

The average workweek declined between 1910 and 1940. It has changed little since then.

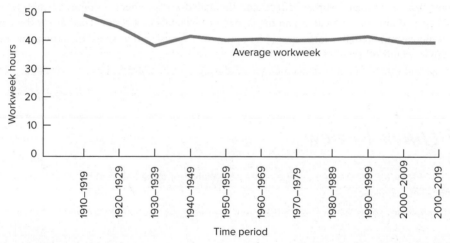

Source: John Wiley & Sons, Inc., "Advertising and Labour Supply: Workweek and Workyear in U.S. Manufacturing Industries, 1919-1976." www.onlinelibrary.wiley.com.

Workweek Decline, 1900–1940

The pre–World War II decline in the workweek is explainable in terms of the basic work-leisure model described in Chapter 2. The essential contention is that the declining workweek is simply a supply response to historically rising real wages and earnings. More precisely, given (*a*) worker income-leisure preferences, (*b*) nonwage incomes, and (*c*) the assumption that leisure is a normal good, rising wage rates over time will reduce the number of hours individuals want to work, provided the income effect exceeds the substitution effect. And, in fact, a substantial amount of empirical evidence indicates that the net effect of wage increases on hours of work has been negative.

---

[43] The shorter hours of the 1930s are largely explainable in terms of the Great Depression; the shorter workweek was widely instituted to spread the smaller demand for labor among more workers.

3.6 | World of Work

Time Stress

Surveys show that many workers face *time stress:* a lack of time to do their desired activities. Among U.S. married couples in which at least one spouse works, 44 percent of men and 55 percent of women say that they are always or often time stressed. Surveys in other countries also indicate that many married couples are time stressed. Australians report a similar amount of time stress as Americans. About one-third of Germans report they are stressed for time, while 70 percent of South Koreans report they suffer this condition.

Using data from these four countries, Hamermesh and Lee examined the factors causing time stress among married couples. Not surprisingly, increases in hours devoted to market work or household production intensify time stress. Holding constant market and household hours worked, they found that increases in earnings lead to greater time stress. They assert that people feel that they are in a time crunch because they don't have enough time to consume the goods they can purchase with their higher income. This does not mean higher income people would be happy if they earned less. They are assumed to be maximizing their utility, but they are unhappy about the time limits they face. Consistent with that assumption, higher income individuals indicate that they are happier with their income and life in general than their lower income counterparts.

Some interesting patterns related to household production also appeared in these data. Household production work appears to generate less time stress than an equivalent amount of market work. Increased efficiency in household production should reduce the amount of time stress. Consistent with that conjecture, an improvement in health status from fair or poor to at least good reduced time stress by the equivalent of at least 10 hours of market work per week.

Source: Daniel S. Hamermesh and Jungmin Lee, "Stressed Out on Four Continents: Time Crunch or Yuppie Kvetch?" *Review of Economics and Statistics,* May 2007, pp. 374–383.

Post–World War II: Workweek Stability

But how does one explain the relative constancy of the workweek in the postwar era? Real wages have continued to rise; but either the substitution effect has somehow offset the income effect, or perhaps some additional factors have been at work in recent decades to offset the tendency of higher wage rates to reduce the workweek.[44]

 Kniesner argues that educational attainment has played an important role in the constancy of the workweek since World War II.[45] He hypothesizes that the supply of labor is positively related to education. Furthermore, he notes that increases in educational attainment have been much greater in the postwar period than the prewar period; in the 1910-1940 period, the increase in the median years of schooling completed was only about 6 percent compared to a 34 percent increase in the 1940-1970 period. Kniesner argues that these differences in educational attainment account for the two trends evidenced in Figure 3.6.

---

[44] Although the average workweek has changed little in the past 50 years, the demographic composition of the workforce has changed dramatically. For more on this point, see Ellen R. McGrattan and Richard Rogerson, "Changes in Hours Worked since 1950," *Quarterly Review* (Federal Reserve Bank of Minneapolis), Winter 1998, pp. 2-19.

[45] Thomas J. Kniesner, "The Full-Time Workweek in the United States, 1900-1970," *Industrial and Labor Relations Review,* October 1976, pp. 3-5, see also Ethel B. Jones, "Comment," and Kniesner, "Reply," *Industrial and Labor Relations Review,* April 1980, pp. 379-389.

Why might more education increase or sustain hours of work? First, a change in preferences may be involved. Education is a means of enhancing one's earning power in the labor market. Decisions to acquire more education may, therefore, reflect a change in tastes favoring a stronger commitment to labor market work. Second, more educated workers generally acquire more pleasant jobs—that is, jobs that are less physically demanding, less structured, more challenging, and so forth. Other things being equal, such job characteristics would make workers less willing to reduce the workweek. Finally, a more educated workforce may increase employer resistance to a declining workweek. The reason for this is that employers incur more fixed costs in recruiting more educated workers and in training them over their job tenures compared to less-educated workers. A shorter workweek will increase these fixed costs per worker hour and thus will increase the overall hourly cost of any given quantity of labor. As their labor forces have become more educated, employers have stiffened their resistance to a shorter workweek.[46]

Three explanations in addition to changes in educational attainment have been suggested for the constancy of the workweek. First, the *Fair Labor Standards Act of 1938* (FLSA) requires employers to pay a wage premium for all hours worked in excess of 40 per week. This legislation tended not only to reduce the length of the workweek but also to standardize it at 40 hours.[47] Second, the rise in the marginal income tax rates since the start of World War II has translated into smaller increases in net (aftertax) wage rates. Thus, the negative supply, or hours of work, response has been much smaller in the postwar era than in earlier decades. Finally, advertising has increased quantitatively and in effectiveness since World War II. This may have increased the desires of workers for more goods and services and therefore induced them to work more hours than otherwise would be the case.

Chapter Summary

1. The aggregate quantity of labor supplied depends on population size, the labor force participation rate, and the number of hours worked weekly and annually.

2. It is fruitful to examine and explain participation rates in terms of Becker's time allocation model. This model views households as producing utility-yielding commodities by combining goods and time. In this context, household members allocate their time to labor market work, household production, and consumption on the basis of comparative advantage.

3. The labor force participation rate is the actual labor force as a percentage of the potential or age-eligible population.

4. In the post–World War II period, the aggregate participation rate has risen from about 59 percent in 1950 to about 63 percent in 2018. This is basically the result of greater participation rates of women (particularly married women), which have more than offset the declining participation rates of males.

5. The participation rate of older males fell and has rebounded in recent years. The changes are attributed to (*a*) rising real wages and earnings, (*b*) the availability of public and private pensions, (*c*) increasing access to disability benefits, (*d*) rising educational levels, and (*e*) increasing labor force participation of older wives.

6. Rising participation rates for women have been caused by (*a*) rising relative wage rates for women, (*b*) stronger female preferences for labor market work, (*c*) rising productivity within the household, (*d*) declining birthrates, (*e*) greater marital instability, (*f*) the greater accessibility of jobs, and (*g*) attempts to maintain family standards of living. In the 2000s, the labor supply of women has stopped increasing.

---

[46] Employer resistance to a shrinking workweek may be reinforced by the growth of fringe benefits that has occurred in the postwar period (Chapter 7). Employer expenditures for such benefits as worker life and health insurance are also fixed costs on a per worker basis, and as with recruitment and training costs, a shortened workweek would entail higher hourly labor costs.

[47] For contrary evidence suggesting the FLSA has had little impact on overtime hours, see Stephen J. Trejo, "Does the Statutory Overtime Premium Discourage Long Workweeks?" *Industrial and Labor Relations Review,* April 2003, pp. 530–551.

7. The participation rates of African-American women and white women are nearly identical today. In the past, the rates of African-American women exceeded those of white women.

8. The participation rates of African-American males have declined over time and are currently 6–7 percentage points lower than for white males. Some analysts stress such demand-side factors as labor market discrimination, inferior educational opportunities, and the geographic inaccessibility of jobs in explaining lower African-American rates. Others focus on such supply-side factors as the availability of public assistance and illegal activities.

9. The overall participation rate has fallen four percentage points since 2000 and is forecast to fall another two percentage points in the next decade. The aging of the labor force has played a significant role in the decline in participation.

10. Procyclic changes in participation rates reflect the net impact of the added-worker and discouraged-worker effects. The added-worker effect suggests that when a family's primary breadwinner loses his or her job, other family members will become labor market participants to sustain the family's income. The discouraged-worker effect indicates that during recession, some unemployed workers will become pessimistic about their prospects for reemployment and will, therefore, withdraw from the labor force. Most empirical studies suggest that the discouraged-worker effect is dominant, with the result that the aggregate labor force participation rate varies inversely with the unemployment rate.

11. The average workweek and workyear declined during the 1910–1940 period, but since World War II both have been quite stable. The earlier workweek and workyear declines have been explained in terms of the income effect's domination of the substitution effect as real wage rates have risen historically. The post–World War II stability of the workweek and workyear has been attributed to increases in education as well as other factors.

Terms and Concepts

Becker's model of the allocation of time

time-intensive and goods-intensive commodities

potential and actual labor forces

labor force participation rate

added-worker and discouraged-worker effects

Fair Labor Standards Act of 1938

Questions and Study Suggestions

1. Briefly discuss the major components of the aggregate labor supply.

2. In what specific ways does Becker's model of the allocation of time differ from the simple work–leisure choice model? Compare the functioning of the income and substitution effects in each of the two models. Do the two effects have the same impact on labor market work in both models?

3. In 2018 the United States had a population of 327 million, of which 68 million were either under 16 years of age or institutionalized. Approximately 162 million people were either employed or unemployed but actively seeking work. What was the participation rate in 2018?

4. What has happened to the aggregate labor force participation rate in the post–World War II period? To the participation rates of males and females?

5. What factors account for the declining participation rates of older males?

6. What factors account for the increase in the participation rates of married women? Use a work–leisure diagram (similar, for example, to Figure 2.8) to explain how *each* of these factors might individually alter either the indifference curves or the budget lines of women and make labor force participation more likely.

7. Compare the participation rates of *(a)* white and African-American women and *(b)* white and African-American men. In each case explain any differences.

8. "The ratio of the incomes of African-American families to the incomes of white families has increased quite slowly in the past two or three decades, despite legislation and a variety of public policies to ameliorate discrimination. One may, therefore, conclude that government programs have failed to lessen racial discrimination." Discuss critically.

9. Use a work–leisure diagram to demonstrate that *(a)* if African-Americans have labor market opportunities that are inferior to those of whites and *(b)* nonlabor income is available in the form of, say, disability benefits, African-Americans will have lower participation rates even though the work–leisure preferences (indifference curves) of African-Americans and whites are identical.

10. "Empirical evidence for the United States suggests that labor force participation varies directly with unemployment." Do you agree? Explain in terms of the discouraged-worker and added-worker effects.

11. "The added-worker effect can be explained in terms of the income effect, while the discouraged-worker effect is based on the substitution effect." Do you agree?

12. What has happened to the length of the workweek and workyear during the past hundred years? Explain any significant trends.

13.

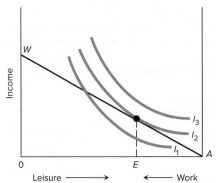

The accompanying diagram restates the basic work–leisure choice model presented in Chapter 2. Use this diagram to explain the declining workweek occurring in the pre–World War II period, making explicit the assumptions underlying your analysis. We noted in the present chapter that the stability of the workweek in the post–World War II era has been attributed by various scholars to such considerations as *(a)* higher taxes on earnings, *(b)* acquisition of more education, and *(c)* advertising. Make alterations in the indifference curves or budget line of the diagram to indicate how *each* of these three factors might contribute to a relatively stable workweek despite rising before-tax real wages.

Internet Exercise

Who Is Participating More in the Labor Force? Who Less?

 Go to the Bureau of Labor Statistics website for the Current Population Survey (**http://www.b ls.gov/cps/cpsdbtabs.htm**) and select "Historical Data for Series in the Monthly Employment Situation News Release" to find information about civilian labor force participation rates (LFPRs) and civilian employment–population ratios (EPRs).

1. What were the LFPRs for men and women in January 1950 and for the most recent month shown? Which rate has increased over this period? Which has declined? What are some possible explanations for these changes?

2. What has been the combined effect of these two trends on the overall labor force participation rate, 1950 to the present? (In your answer, provide the specific overall LFPRs for January 1950 and the most recent month shown.)

3. What were the LFPRs for white women and African-American women in January 1955 and for the most recent month shown? What was the gap in these rates at the beginning of the period and the end of the period? What are some possible explanations for this change?

4. What was the overall civilian employment–population ratio for the most recent month shown? Why are overall EPRs lower than overall LFPRs? (Use this book's glossary definitions for help with this question.)

Internet Links

The Bureau of Labor Statistics website provides many detailed statistics for labor force participation and hours of work (**www.bls.gov**).

Chapter 4

Labor Quality: Investing in Human Capital

After reading this chapter, you should be able to:

1. Explain the meaning of investment in human capital.
2. Use the human capital model to analyze decisions to invest in human capital.
3. Use a supply and demand of human capital to explain the unequal distribution of earnings.
4. Explain general and specific training and their effects on the human capital investment decision, wages, and worker retention.
5. Critically evaluate the human capital model.

Education and training are much in the current news. Today's challenge is being able to compete effectively in the rapidly emerging global marketplace. Experts agree that to maintain our relative standard of living, we must upgrade the education and skill levels of our workforce. They also agree that the dynamic aspects of global technological innovation and product competition have rendered many of our jobs less secure. Continuous education, training, and retraining will be crucial to keeping our workforce fully employed.

In Chapters 2 and 3, we looked primarily at the decisions of whether and to what degree to participate in the labor market. Our emphasis there was on the work–leisure decision and the various participation rates. In this chapter, we turn from the quantitative to the qualitative aspects of labor supply. Workers bring differing levels of formal educational attainment and skills to the labor market. They also acquire substantially different amounts of on-the-job training. A more educated, better trained person is capable of supplying a larger amount of useful productive effort than one with less education and training.

Any activity that increases the quality (productivity) of labor may be considered an investment in human capital. Human capital investments include expenditures not only on formal education and on-the-job training but also on health, migration, job search, and the preschool nurturing of children. Workers can become more productive by improving their physical or mental health and also by moving from locations and jobs where their productivity is relatively low to other locations and jobs where their productivity is relatively high. In fact, in Chapter 9, human capital theory will be the core concept used to analyze labor migration.

INVESTMENT IN HUMAN CAPITAL: CONCEPT AND DATA

When a firm invests in physical capital, it is acquiring some asset that is expected to enhance the firm's flow of net profits over a period of time. For example, a company might purchase new machinery designed to increase output and therefore sales revenues over, say, the ten-year projected useful life of the machinery. The unique characteristic of investment is that *current* expenditures or costs are incurred with the intent that these costs will be more than compensated for by enhanced *future* revenues or returns. Analogously, investments are made in human capital. When a person (or a person's parents or society at large) makes a current expenditure on education or training, it is anticipated that the individual's knowledge and skills and therefore future earnings will be enhanced.[1] The important point is that expenditures on education and training can be fruitfully treated as *investment in human capital* just as expenditures on capital equipment can be understood as investment in physical capital.

Relevant data reveal three things. First, expenditures on education and training are substantial. In the school year 2016–2017, Americans spent some $1,342 billion on elementary, secondary, and higher education. In addition, an estimated 2 percent of payroll is spent each year by employers for on-the-job training.

Second, the educational attainment of the labor force has increased dramatically over the past two decades. For example, in 1992, 13 percent of the civilian labor force aged 25 and older had achieved less than a high school education, while 26 percent had completed four or more years of college. Similar figures for 2018 were 7 and 41 percent, respectively.

Third, investments in education result in an enlarged flow of earnings. This tendency is reflected in the *age–earnings profiles* of Figure 4.1, which show the lifetime earning patterns of male workers who have attained various educational levels. Observe that the average earnings of more educated workers exceed those of less educated workers. Also, the earnings profiles of more educated workers rise more rapidly than those of less educated workers. Differences in the earnings of more and less educated workers tend to widen during workers' prime earning years.

Not shown, the age–earnings profiles of females display similar overall characteristics to those in Figure 4.1 but lie significantly below those of men. Also, the profiles for women are much flatter than those for men. We discuss these gender differences in earnings in detail in Chapter 14.[2]

THE HUMAN CAPITAL MODEL

Let's introduce a simple model to analyze the decision to invest in, say, a college education. Assume you have just graduated from high school and are deciding whether to go to college. From a purely economic standpoint, a rational decision will involve a comparison of the associated costs and benefits. The monetary costs

---

[1] As will be noted later, the payoff from an investment in education may also take nonmonetary forms, such as obtaining a more pleasant job or a greater appreciation of literature and art.

[2] The fact that the age–earnings profiles ultimately decline must be interpreted with some care. Although it is tempting to attribute the declining incomes of older workers to diminished physical vigor and mental alertness, the obsolescence of education and skills, or the decision to work shorter hours, the decline may be largely due to the character of the data. In particular, these data do *not* track the earnings of specific individuals through their lifetimes. Rather, these cross-sectional data show the earnings of different individuals of different ages in some particular year. Longitudinal data that trace the earnings of specific people over time indicate that earnings continue to increase until retirement. The declining segments of the age–earnings profiles in Figure 4.1 may occur because the U.S. economy has been growing, and therefore each succeeding generation has earned more than the preceding one. Thus, the average 45-year-old college-educated worker has higher earnings as shown in the age–earnings profiles simply because he or she is a member of a more recent generation than a 65-year-old college-educated worker.

FIGURE 4.1 **Age–Earnings Profiles by Years of Education**

Age–earnings profiles (in this case for males in 2017) indicate that education "pays" in that more educated workers obtain higher average annual earnings than less educated workers of the same age group.

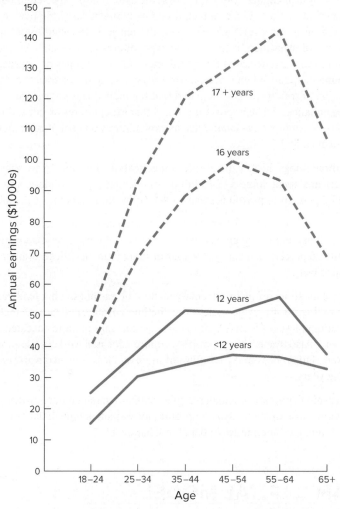

Source: U.S. Census Bureau, "Personal Income Tables, Table PINC-04.2017." www.census.gov

incurred in the purchase of a college education are of two general types. On the one hand, there are *direct* or *out-of-pocket costs* in the form of expenditures for tuition, special fees, and books and supplies. Expenditures for room and board are *not* included as a part of direct costs because you would need food and shelter regardless of whether you attended college or entered the labor market. On the other hand, the *indirect* or *opportunity cost* of going to college is the earnings you give up by not entering the labor market after completing high school. For example, estimates suggest that indirect costs may account for as much as 60–70 percent of the total cost of a college education, at least at public universities. The economic *benefit* of investing in a college education, as we know from Figure 4.1, is an enlarged future flow of earnings.

GP4.1

This conception of a human capital investment decision is portrayed graphically in Figure 4.2. Curve *HH* represents your earnings profile if you decide not to attend college, but rather enter the labor market immediately on the completion of high school at age 18. The *CC* curve is your cost–earnings profile if you decide to undertake a four-year college degree before entering the labor market. We note that area 1 below the horizontal axis represents the direct or out-of-pocket costs (the negative income) incurred in attending college. Area 2 reflects the indirect or opportunity costs; that is, the earnings you forgo while attending college. The sum of areas 1 and 2 shows the total cost (your total investment) in a college education. Area 3—the difference between the *CC* and *HH* curves over ages 22 to 65—shows the gross *incremental* earnings that you will realize by obtaining a college degree; it shows how much *additional* income you will obtain as a college graduate over your work life compared to what you would have earned with just a high school diploma. Your work life in this case is presumed to extend over the 43-year period from age 22 to age 65.

4.1 Global Perspective

College Graduates Worldwide

The percentage of adults aged 25–64 who have a college degree in major industrial countries ranges from 19 percent in Italy to 36 percent in the United Kingdom.

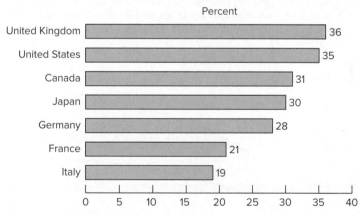

Percent

Country	Percent
United Kingdom	36
United States	35
Canada	31
Japan	30
Germany	28
France	21
Italy	19

Source: OECD, "Education at a Glance 2018." www.oecd.org

Discounting and Net Present Value

We know that to make a rational decision you will want to compare costs (areas 1 and 2) with benefits (area 3). But a complication arises at this point. The costs and benefits associated with investing in a college education accrue at different points in time. This is important because dollars expended and received at different points in time have different value. A meaningful comparison of the costs and benefits associated with a college education requires that these costs and benefits be compared in terms of a common point in time, such as the present. What we seek to determine from the vantage point of an 18-year-old youth is the net present discounted value, or simply the *net present value,* of the present and future costs *and* present and future benefits of a college education.

Time Preference

Why do dollars earned (or expended) have a different value a year, or two or three years, from now than they have today? The immediate answer is that a positive interest rate is paid for borrowing or "renting" money. But this raises an additional question: *Why* is interest paid for the use of money? The answer lies in the notion of *time preference:* the idea that, given the choice, most people prefer the pleasure of indulgence today to the promise of indulgence tomorrow. Most individuals prefer present consumption to future consumption because, given the uncertainties and vagaries of life, the former seems more tangible and therefore more valuable. Time preference, in short, is the idea that people are impatient and subjectively prefer goods in the present over the same goods in the future. It follows that an individual must be compensated by an interest payment to defer present consumption or, alternatively stated, to save a portion of her or his income. If an individual equates $100 worth of goods today with $110 worth of goods a year from now, we can say that his or her time preference rate is 10 percent. The individual must be paid $10 or 10 percent as an inducement to forgo $100 worth of present consumption.

FIGURE 4.2   **Age–Earnings Profiles with and without a College Education**

If an individual decides to enter the labor market after graduation from high school at age 18, the age–earnings profile will be *HH* in comparison with the *CC* profile if she or he had gone to college. Attending college entails both direct costs (tuition, fees, books) and indirect costs (forgone earnings). But on entering the labor market at age 22, the college graduate will enjoy a higher level of annual earnings over her or his working life. To determine whether it is economically rational to invest in a college education, we must find its net present value by discounting costs and benefits back to the present (age 18).

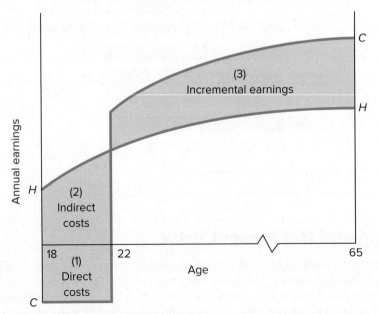

Present Value Formula

Because the preference for present consumption necessitates payment of a positive interest rate, a dollar received a year from now is worth less than a dollar obtained today. A dollar received today can be lent or invested at some positive interest rate and thereby can be worth more than a dollar a year from now. If the interest rate is 10 percent, one can lend $1 today and receive $1.10 at the end of the year; the $1.10 comprises the original $1 plus $0.10 of interest. This can be shown algebraically as follows:

$$V_p(1 + i) = V_1 \quad \textbf{(4.1)}$$

where V_p = present or current value – for example, $1.00 today

V_1 = value(of the $1.00) one year from now

i = interest rate

The $(1 + i)$ term indicates that one receives the original or present value ($1.00) *plus* the interest. Substituting our illustrative numbers, we have

$$\$1.00(1.10) = \$1.10$$

This formulation tells us that, given a 10 percent interest rate, $1.10 received next year is the equivalent of $1.00 in hand today.

Equation (4.1) focuses on determining the *future* value of the $1.00 one has today. As indicated earlier, our goal is to determine the *present* (today's) value of expenditures and revenues incurred and received in the future. We can get at this by restating our original question. Instead of asking how much $1.00 obtained today will be worth a year from now, let's inquire how much $1.10 received a year from now would be worth today. In general terms, the answer is found by solving Equation (4.1) for Vp. Thus,

$$V_p = \frac{V_i}{(1 + i)} \quad \textbf{(4.2)}$$

Equation (4.2) is a *discount formula* for a one-year period. Inserting our illustrative numbers,

$$\$1.00 = \frac{\$1.00}{1.10}$$

That is, $1.10 received a year from now is worth only $1.00 today if the interest rate is 10 percent.

Observing in Figure 4.2 that both costs and benefits are incurred over a number of years, we can extend the discounting formula of Equation (4.2) as follows:

$$V_p = E_0 + \frac{E_i}{(1 + i)^1} + \frac{E_2}{(1 + i)^2} + \frac{E_3}{(1 + i)^3} + \ldots + \frac{E_n}{(1 + i)^n} \quad \textbf{(4.3)}$$

where the E values represent a stream of incremental earnings (E_0 being any additional income received immediately, E_1 the additional income received next year, E_2 the incremental earnings received two years from now, and so forth); n is the duration of the earnings stream or, in other words, the individual's expected working life; and i is the interest rate.[3] Observe that incremental earnings (or costs), E_0, incurred immediately need not be discounted. But the incremental earnings received next year, or one year hence, E_1, must

---

[3] We are sidestepping the troublesome problem of deciding which interest rate is appropriate. A small difference in the rate used can have a substantial impact on the calculation of present value.

be discounted one year. Note further that the denominator of the third term is squared, the fourth is cubed, and so forth. This is so because the values of E_2 and E_3 must be discounted two and three years, respectively, to determine their present value. Dividing E_2–the incremental earnings to be received two years hence–by $(1 + i)$ discounts the value of those earnings for the time elapsed in the first year; but *that* value must be again divided by $(1 + i)$ to find its present value because the time between the first and second year further diminishes the value.

Restating the formula for our high school graduate who enters the labor force at age 18, we have

$$V_p = E_{18} + \frac{E_{19}}{(1+i)} + \frac{E_{20}}{(1+i)^2} + \frac{E_{21}}{(1+i)^3} + \ ... \ + \frac{E_{64}}{(1+i)^{46}} \quad \textbf{(4.4)}$$

which can be more compactly stated as

$$V_p = \sum_{n-18}^{64} \frac{E_n}{(1+i)^{n-18}} \quad \textbf{(4.5)}$$

This formulation tells us that we are calculating the present value (V_p) of the sum (Σ) of the discounted incremental earnings (E_n) over the individual's working life, which runs from age 18 through age 64, after which time he or she retires when attaining age 65. Because n is 64 years of age, the $n = 18$ notation indicates that we are discounting future earnings over 46 (= 64 − 18) years of working life.

Figure 4.2 reminds us that the decision to invest in a college education entails both costs and benefits (enhanced earnings). How can both be accounted for in Equation (4.3) or (4.4)? The answer is to treat costs as negative earnings. Thus, the "earnings" for the four years the individual is in college (E_0, E_1, E_2, *and* E_3) will be the negative sum of the direct and indirect costs incurred in each of those years. For each succeeding year until retirement, incremental earnings will be positive. We therefore are actually calculating the *net* present value of a college education in these two equations.

Decision Rule: $V_p > 0$

The relevant investment criterion or decision rule based on this calculation is that *the individual should make the investment if its net present value is greater than zero.* A positive value tells us that the present discounted value of the benefits exceeds the present discounted value of the costs, and when this is so–when benefits exceed costs–the decision to invest is economically rational. If the net present value is negative, then costs exceed benefits and the investment is not economically justifiable.

Illustration

A truncated example may be helpful at this point. Assume that after graduating from high school, Carl Carlson contemplates enrolling in a one-year intensive course in data processing. The direct costs of the course are $1,000, and the opportunity cost is $5,000. Upon completion of the course, he has been promised employment with the Computex Corporation. Expecting to receive a large inheritance, he plans to work only three years and then retire permanently from the labor force. The incremental income he anticipates earning because of his data-processing training is $2,500, $3,000, and $3,500 for the three years he intends to work. The relevant interest rate at this time is 10 percent. Is the decision to enroll in the data-processing course rational? Substituting these figures in Equation (4.3), we have

$$V_p = E_0 + \frac{E_1}{(1+i)} + \frac{E_2}{(1+i)^2} + \frac{E_3}{(1+i)^3}$$

$$V_p = -\$6,000 + \frac{\$2,500}{(1.10)} + \frac{\$3,000}{(1.10)^2} + \frac{\$3,500}{(1.10)^3}$$

$$V_p = -\$6,000 + \$2,273 + \$2,479 + \$2,630$$

$$V_p = \$1,382$$

Our formula shows that the present value of the benefits (the incremental earnings) totals $7,382 (= $2,273 + $2,479 + $2,630) and exceeds the present value of the costs of $6,000 by $1,382. This positive net present value indicates that it *is* economically rational for Carlson to make this investment in human capital.

Internal Rate of Return

An alternative means of making an investment decision involves calculating the *internal rate of return, r,* on a prospective investment and comparing it with the interest rate *i*. *By definition, the internal rate of return is the rate of discount at which the net present value of a human capital investment will be zero.*

Formula

Instead of using the interest rate *i* in Equation (4.3) to calculate whether the net present value is positive or negative, one determines what particular rate of discount *r* will equate the present values of future costs and benefits so that the net present value is zero. We must modify Equation (4.3) as follows:

$$V_p = E_0 + \frac{E_1}{(1+r)} + \frac{E_2}{(1+r)^2} + \ldots + \frac{E_n}{(1+r)^n} = 0 \quad \textbf{(4.6)}$$

Instead of solving for *Vp* as in Equation (4.3), we solve for *r*, given the *E* values and assuming *Vp* is zero. A moment's reflection makes clear that *r* indicates the maximum rate of interest that one could pay on borrowed funds to finance a human capital investment and still break even.

Decision Rule: r = i

The investment criterion or decision rule appropriate to this approach involves a comparison of the internal rate of return *r* with the interest rate *i*. *If r exceeds the market i, the investment is profitable and should be undertaken.* For example, if one can borrow funds at a 10 percent interest rate and make an investment that yields 15 percent, it is profitable to do so. But *if r is less than i, the investment is unprofitable and should not be undertaken.* If one can borrow money at a 10 percent rate and the prospective investment yields only 5 percent, it is not profitable to invest. As we will discover momentarily, investing in human capital is subject to diminishing returns, so *r* generally declines as the number of years of schooling increases (see Figure 4.4). In this case, given *i, it will be profitable to invest in all human capital investment opportunities up to the point where r = i.*

Generalizations and Implications

The explanatory power of the human capital model is considerable. Let's pause at this point to consider several generalizations that stem from the basic model presented in Figure 4.2 and Equations (4.3) and (4.6).

1 Length of Income Stream

Other things being equal, the longer the stream of postinvestment incremental earnings, the more likely the net present value of an investment in human capital will be positive. Alternatively, the longer the earnings stream, the higher the internal rate of return. A human capital investment made later in life will have a lower net present value (and a lower r) simply because fewer years of work life and, hence, of positive incremental earnings will remain after completion of the investment. This generalization helps explain why it is primarily young people who go to college[4] and why younger people are more likely to migrate (invest in geographic mobility) than older people. It also explains a portion of the earnings differential that has traditionally existed between women and men. In many cases, the participation of women in the labor force has been discontinuous; that is, many women work for a few years after the completion of formal schooling, then marry and stay out of the labor force for a time to bear and raise children. They then reenter the labor force sometime after the last child begins school. In Equations (4.3) and (4.6), this means an abbreviated stream of earnings. This dampens the economic incentive of these particular women to invest in their own human capital by lowering the net present value or the rate of return. Furthermore, their discontinuous labor force participation inhibits employers from investing in their on-the-job training.

2 Costs

Other things being equal, the lower the cost of a human capital investment, the larger the number of people who will find that investment to be profitable. If the direct or indirect costs of attending college were to fall, we would expect enrollment to rise. For example, the guaranteeing of student loans by the government eliminates the risk to the lender and lowers the interest rate charged for borrowing funds to attend college. By reducing the private direct cost[5] of a college education, such loan guarantees increase in college enrollment.[6] Lower direct or indirect costs increase the net present value of a college education, making the investment in education profitable for some who previously found it to be unprofitable.[7]

 A more subtle point ties in with our previous generalization that older individuals are less likely to invest in human capital. Our age–earnings profiles (Figure 4.1) reveal that earnings rise with age. Thus, the opportunity cost of attending college will be greater for the older worker; and other things being equal, the net present value and the internal rate of return associated with human capital investments will be lower. In other words, there are two reasons older people are less likely to invest in a college education: (*a*) The length of their future earnings stream will be relatively short, and (*b*) their opportunity costs of attending college will be high.

---

[4] Although perhaps not rational on investment grounds, the decision of older people to return to college may be justified in terms of consumption (utility) criteria.

[5] Of course, there is no free lunch. Taxpayers (society as a whole) pay the costs associated with loan guarantees. But in calculating the cost of a college education from a *private* (as opposed to a *social*) perspective, loan guarantees reduce the costs to the individual enrollee and increase the private net present value associated with a college education.

[6] Public subsidies appear to have large enrollment effects, particularly for low-income students and those attending community colleges. See Thomas J. Kane and Cecilia Elena Rouse, "The Community College: Educating Students at the Margin between College and Work," *Journal of Economic Perspectives,* Winter 1999, pp. 63–84.

[7] For a series of papers examining the impact of college costs and other factors on college choices, see Caroline M. Hoxby (ed.), *College Choices: The Economics of Where to Go, When to Go, and How to Pay for It* (Chicago, IL: University of Chicago Press, 2004).

4.1 World of Work

Recessions and the College Enrollment Rate

Do recessions increase or decrease the number of college students? The answer, in theory, is uncertain because business downturns yield conflicting effects on college enrollment rates.

Three factors related to the ability to pay for a college education tend to reduce the number of college students during recessions. First, the availability of part-time jobs that may help finance college expenses usually decreases in downturns. Second, the ability of parents to borrow money for college educations (perhaps due to a reduction in income and asset values) may decline. Finally, state and private spending for financial aid may decrease during recessions.

In contrast, recessions tend to lower the cost of attending college because they reduce the earnings of high school graduates or lower the probability of obtaining a job. As a result, the opportunity cost of attending college will fall, and enrollment rates will, therefore, rise.

The empirical evidence indicates that the decreased opportunity cost of college in recessions dominates the reduced ability to pay because college enrollment rates tend to rise significantly during recessions. Dellas and Sakellaris find that a 1 percent increase in the unemployment rate increases the college enrollment rate of 18- to 22-year-olds by 0.8 percentage points. Their models indicate that some recessions may have added more than 400,000 college students. Men and women do not appear to respond differently to recessions. However, the college enrollment rate of nonwhites is less sensitive than that of whites to business downturns.

Source: Harris Dellas and Plutarchos Sakellaris, "On the Cyclicality of Schooling: Theory and Evidence," *Oxford Economic Papers*, January 2003, pp. 148–172. For an analysis of the effects of the 2007–2009 recession, see Bridget Terry Long, "The Financial Crisis and College Enrollment: How Have Students and Their Families Responded," in Jeffrey Brown and Caroline Hoxby (eds.), *How the Financial Crisis and Great Recession Affected Higher Education* (Chicago: University of Chicago Press, 2015).

3 Earnings Differentials

Not only is the *length* of the incremental earnings stream critical in making a human capital investment decision, but so is the *size* of that differential. The generalization is that *other things being equal, the larger the college–high school earnings differential, the larger the number of people who will invest in a college education.* Empirical evidence confirms this generalization. Freeman has argued that in 1970 the labor market for college graduates changed from one characterized by shortages to one of surpluses. One manifestation of this change was that the incremental earnings associated with a college education declined sharply.[8] As a result, the proportion of young people enrolling in colleges declined significantly in the early 1970s. In the 1980s, the earnings advantage for college graduates rebounded. Ge and Yang stated that part of the sharp rise in the rate of college attendance that occurred over the 1980–1996 period was due to the rise in the college premium.[9]

---

[8] Richard B. Freeman, *The Overeducated American* (New York: Academic Press, 1976).
[9] Suqin Ge and Fang Yang, "Accounting for the Gender Gap in College Attainment," *Economic Inquiry,* January 2013, pp. 478–499.

4.2) Global Perspective

College Graduate Earnings Premium

The earnings of college graduates range from 5 percent higher than high school graduates in Sweden to 69 percent higher in the United States.

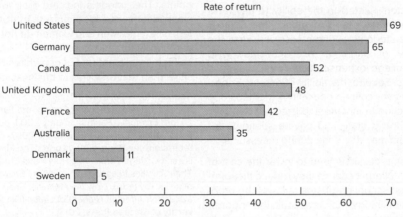

Rate of return

United States	69
Germany	65
Canada	52
United Kingdom	48
France	42
Australia	35
Denmark	11
Sweden	5

0   10   20   30   40   50   60   70

Source: OECD, "Education at a Glance 2018." www.oecd.org

Empirical Data

GP4.2

Numerous empirical studies have estimated the returns of human capital investments at all educational levels. Here we concentrate on those showing private rates of return on investments in a college education.

Rate-of-Return Studies

WW4.2

Speaking very generally, most rate-of-return studies have estimated such rates to be on the order of 10–15 percent.[10] For example, in his classic work Becker estimated the internal rate of return to be 14.5, 13.0, and 14.8 in 1939, 1949, and 1958, respectively.[11] Estimates by Freeman indicate that the private rate of return ranged from 8.5 to 11.0 percent over the 1959–1974 period.[12] The social rate of return for the corresponding period was estimated to range from 7.5 to 11.1 percent. Card finds

---

[10] For surveys of recent studies, see George Psacharopoulos and Anthony Patrinos, "Returns to Investment in Education: A Further Update," *Education Economics,* August 2004, pp. 111–134; and George Psacharopoulos and Harry Anthony Patrinos, "Returns to Investment in Education: A Decennial Review of the Global Literature," World Bank Policy Research Working Paper 8402, 2018.

[11] Gary Becker, *Human Capital,* 2nd Edition (New York: National Bureau of Economic Research, 1975).

[12] Richard B. Freeman, "Overinvestment in College Training?" *Journal of Human Resources,* Summer 1975, p. 296.

a return of 10 percent in 1976.[13] Kane and Rouse report a rate of return of 9 percent to higher education for 1986.[14] Heckman, Lochner, and Todd find a private rate of return of 14 percent for 2000 for white men.[15] Organization for Economic Cooperation and Development report a private rate of return of 18 percent for college education in 2015 for both men and women.[16]

4.2 World of Work

What Is a GED Worth?

The popularity of obtaining high school certification through an equivalency exam has skyrocketed over the past four decades. In 1960, only 2 percent of high school certificates were given through equivalency exams. By 2013, 14 percent of all high school certificates were awarded through equivalency exams.

The General Education Development (GED) program is the main method for achieving high school equivalency through an exam. The program involves dropouts passing a 7½-hour exam covering the areas of writing, social studies, science, reading, and mathematics. The exam is meant to certify that a person has the knowledge and skills of a high school graduate.

Heckman and LaFontaine have examined the economic benefits from obtaining a GED. They found little or no direct benefit to obtaining a GED for those not obtaining postsecondary schooling. The earnings of GED recipients are greater than the earnings of high school dropouts, but this difference is entirely due to the higher ability of GED recipients. This pattern holds for men and women, older and more recent cohorts, and native-born and immigrant workers.

The main avenue for economic benefits from the GED is through greater access to postsecondary education. However, relatively few GED recipients pursue postsecondary education: Only 40 percent attend college at all. Furthermore, only 3 percent of GED recipients complete a four-year college degree, and 5 percent complete an associate degree at a two-year college.

Heckman and LaFontaine conclude that there is no easy shortcut to learning in a classroom.

Source: James J. Heckman and Paul A. LaFontaine, "Bias-Corrected Estimates of GED Returns," *Journal of Labor Economics,* July 2006, pp. 661–700; National Center for Education Statistics, *Digest of Educational Statistics, 2013* (http://www.nces.ed); and GED Testing Service, *2013 Annual Statistical Report on the GED Test* (http://www.gedtestingservice.com). For a summary of research on the GED, see James J. Heckman, John Eric Humphries, and Nicholas S. Mader, "The GED," in Eric. A. Hanushek, Stephen J. Machin, and Ludger Woessmann (eds.), *Handbook of the Economics of Education*, Volume 3 (Amsterdam: North-Holland, 2011), pp. 423–484.

The College Wage Premium

Readers might have a special interest in the trend of the college wage premium in recent decades. We define the *college wage premium* as *the ratio of the earnings of college graduates to the earnings of high school graduates.*

---

[13] David Card, "Using Geographic Variation in College Proximity to Estimate the Return to Schooling," in Louis N. Christofides, E. Kenneth Grant, and Robert Swindisky (eds.), *Labour Market Behavior: Essays in Honour of John Vanderkamp* (Toronto, University of Toronto Press: 1995).

[14] Thomas J. Kane and Cecilia Rouse, "Labor Market Returns to Two- and Four-Year Colleges," *American Economic Review,* June 1995, pp. 600–613.

[15] James J. Heckman, Lance J. Lochner, and Petra E. Todd, "Earnings Functions and Rates of Return," *Journal of Human Capital,* Spring 2008, pp. 1–31. Their internal rate of return estimates differ across demographic groups and estimation techniques.

[16] Organization for Economic Cooperation and Development, *Education at a Glance, 2018* (Paris, France: Organization for Economic Cooperation and Development, 2018). Tables A5.1a and A5.1b.

Figure 4.3 presents this wage premium over the 1973–2018 period for women and men. Data are for workers with exactly a high school or college degree. We observe that in 1973 the ratio was 1.48 for women and 1.38 for men, meaning that college-educated women earned 48 percent and men 38 percent more than high school graduates of the same gender. During the 1970s, the premium dropped moderately for women and fell modestly for men. But since the late 1970s, the wage premiums for women and men have increased sharply, rising from 36 to 80 percent for women and from 34 to 96 percent for men. Studies have found that the most rapid rise in the wage premium has been for young college graduates with one to five years of experience.[17]

Explanations of changes in the college wage premium center on labor supply and demand. It is generally agreed that the declining premium in the 1970s resulted from the large influx of baby boomers completing college, coupled with a relatively stagnant demand for college graduates. There is less consensus about why the college premium soared in the 1980s. Murphy and Welch[18] explain the rapid increase in the wage premium in terms of huge increases in the demand for college-trained workers. In particular, changes in the structure of

FIGURE 4.3   Recent Trends in College Wage Premiums

The college wage premium—measured here as the ratio of earnings of college graduates to the earnings of high school graduates—has varied substantially over time. The premium for women fell moderately in the 1970s. The premium for men drifted downward from 1974 to 1979. Since 1979 the wage premiums for both groups have increased dramatically. Changes in the college premium are generally explained by changes in the supply of and the demand for college- and high school–educated workers.

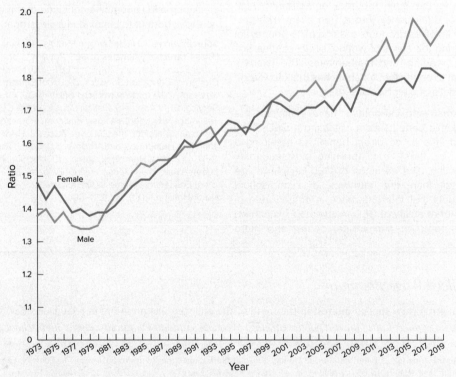

Source: National Bureau of Economic Research, "Current Population Survey (CPS) Basic Monthly Data at the NBER." www.nber.org

---

[17] Kevin Murphy and Finis Welch, "Wage Premiums for College Graduates: Recent Growth and Possible Explanations," *Educational Researcher,* May 1989, pp. 17–26.

[18] Ibid., pp. 13–26.

domestic industry (for example, the shift of employment to high-technology industries) and changes in production techniques (for example, the greater use of computer-aided technologies) may have greatly increased the demand for college-trained workers.[19] Coupled with a relatively slower growth of the college-educated workforce, these demands caused the college premium to rise sharply.

Although the Murphy–Welch interpretation is generally accepted, some economists have pointed out that a growing number of college graduates are working in occupations where college degrees have not traditionally been required. This fact seems to contradict the idea of a growing demand for college graduates relative to their supply. However, Edwin Leuven and Hessel Oosterbeek, in their survey of the research examining whether individuals are overeducated and mismatched for their positions, conclude that is not likely the case.[20]

Caveats

But all such empirical data must be interpreted with some care. First, we have no way of accurately predicting the future. Economists cannot accurately estimate the future earnings of a new college graduate. Data used in research studies to calculate rates of return on human capital investments or the college wage premium are *historical* data. They represent the age–earnings profiles of *past* college graduates who obtained their education as far back as, say, 1970 or even earlier. The observation that college graduates in the labor market in 2017 received on average $29,618 more per year than the typical high school graduate is no guarantee that this difference will persist. By 2027 the amount of incremental income might have widened or diminished.[21]

Also, while incremental earnings affect the decision to invest in a college education, the decision to invest in a college education affects incremental earnings. If college graduates have enjoyed a high earnings differential compared with high school graduates in the recent *past,* an increasing proportion of new high school graduates will invest in a college education. But this investment will increase the supply of college as opposed to high school graduates and will reduce the *future* earnings differential or college premium. A high rate of return in the recent past could contribute to a decreasing rate of return in the future.

Second, the historical data used in human capital studies are in the form of *average* (median) earnings, and the distribution of earnings by educational level around the average is wide. Although a given study may calculate that the average rate of return on a college education is 10 percent, some individuals may earn 30 or 50 percent whereas the return may be negative for others. A significant percentage of those with only high school educations earn more than the median income of college graduates. And some college graduates earn less than the median income of high school graduates.

 Third, the discussion so far has focused on amount of schooling rather than quality of schooling. We have implicitly assumed that the only relevant factor was the number of years students spend in school. However, schooling quality will likely affect the rate of return to schooling. For example, higher quality teachers, better classroom resources, and greater studying by students should increase the rate of return to schooling.

[19] See Daron Acemoglu and David Autor, "Skills, Tasks and Technologies: Implications for Employment and Earnings," in OrleyAshenfelter and DavidCard (eds.) *Handbook of Labor Economics,* Volume 4 (Amsterdam, NL: Elsevier, 2011), pp. 1043–1171.

[20] See Edwin Leuven and Hessel Oosterbeek, "Overeducation and Mismatch in the Labor Market," in Eric A. Hanushek, Stephen Machin, and Ludger Woessmann (eds.), *Handbook of the Economics of Education,* Volume 4, (Amsterdam, Holland: Elsevier, 2011), pp. 283–326. Also see, Paul Beaudry, David A. Green, and Benjamin M. Sand, "The Great Reversal in the Demand for Skill and Cognitive Tasks," in Alexandre Mas and David Card (eds.), *The Labor Market in the Aftermath of the Great Recession* (Chicago: University of Chicago Press, 2015).

[21] For evidence that the college premium changed little between 2010 and 2015, see RobertG. Valletta, "Recent Flattening in the Higher Education Wage Premium: Polarization, Skill Downgrading, or Both?" in Charles Hulten and Valerie Ramey (eds.) *Education, Skills, and Technical Change: Implications for Future U.S. GDP Growth* (Chicago, IL: University of Chicago Press, 2019).

GP4.3

Some evidence exists on how schooling inputs affect the rate of return.[22] A study by Card and Krueger indicates that higher teacher salaries and lower student–teacher ratios raise the return to schooling.[23] They also find that relative improvements in schooling quality among African-Americans account for 20 percent of the decline in the male African-American to white wage gap between 1960 and 1980.[24] However, Heckman, Layne-Farrar, and Todd conclude that schooling inputs have a more modest impact on the return to schooling than estimated by Card and Krueger.[25]

4.3   World of Work

Higher Education: Making the Right Choices

The accompanying table shows the annual salaries of 2014 college graduates by major. Clearly which major one chooses affects one's earnings. These data raise the question of whether other decisions impact a college graduate's earnings. For example, does it matter which college or university one attends?

Dale and Krueger shed light on this and related questions by examining the career earnings of individuals who were accepted and rejected by 27 colleges or universities in 1976 and 1989.* An innovative feature of this study is that the researchers were able to compare the earnings of (a) those who were accepted by a more selective college but decided to attend a less selective college with (b) those who actually attended a more selective college. This technique

enables them to control for the ability problem that plagued previous studies of the impact of college quality on earnings; that is, earlier studies did not sort out whether students who attended elite universities gained higher earnings because they went to a selective school or because the students were smart and ambitious.

The study's results indicate that it does *not* pay to attend a more selective college as measured by the average SAT score of entering freshmen. For example, a student who attended a highly selective school such as Princeton University did not earn more than one who attended a less selective school such as the Pennsylvania State University. An exception to this finding is that minorities and students with poorly educated parents do tend to benefit from attending a highly selective school. This may be the result of these students getting connections they would not be otherwise able to obtain.

However, earnings *are* positively related to the average SAT scores of the schools a student applied to but did not attend. An example is the

---

[22] For a survey, see Eric A. Hanushek, "School Resources," in Eric A. Hanushek and Finis Welch (eds.), *Handbook of the Economics of Education,* Volume 2, (Amsterdam, Holland: Elsevier, 2006), pp. 866–907.

[23] David Card and Alan B. Krueger, "Does School Quality Matter? Returns to Education and the Characteristics of Public Schools in the United States," *Journal of Political Economy,* February 1992, pp. 1–40.

[24] See David Card and Alan B. Krueger, "School Quality and Black/White Relative Earnings: A Direct Assessment," *Quarterly Journal of Economics,* February 1992, pp. 151–200.

[25] James J. Heckman, Anne Layne-Farrar, and Petra Todd, "Does Measured School Quality Really Matter? An Examination of the Earnings–Quality Relationship," in Gary Burtless (ed.), *Does Money Matter? The Effect of School Resources on Student Achievement and Adult Success* (Washington, DC: Brookings Institution, 1996). For a similar conclusion, see Iida Hakkinen, Tanja Kirjavainen, and Roope Uusitalo, "School Resources and Student Achievement Revisited: New Evidence from Panel Data," *Economics of Education Review,* June 2003, pp. 329–335.

acclaimed movie producer and director Steven Spielberg, who applied to the film schools at USC and UCLA and was rejected at both places. He instead attended Cal State Long Beach. This suggests that ambition and a willingness to work hard are more important determinants of earnings than the selectivity of the school one attends.

Estimated Starting Salaries For New College Graduates 2018

Academic Major	Estimated Starting Salary	Academic Major	Estimated Starting Salary
Computer Science	$79,077	Communication and Media Studies	$39,394
Electrical/Electronic Engineering	$72,637	Health and Physical Education/Fitness	$38,859
Chemical Engineering	$68,640	Chemistry	$38,703
Mathematics (incl. Statistics)	$65,349	Sociology	$38,196
Mechanical Engineering	$63,630	Education	$38,092
Management Information Systems	$58,628	Foreign Languages	$38,052
Civil Engineering	$55,933	Criminal Justice and Corrections	$36,319
Finance	$55,811	Psychology	$35,786
Nursing	$55,137	Visual and Performing Arts	$35,569
Economics	$53,402	English	$34,715
Accounting	$52,810	History	$34,597
Business Administration/ Management	$51,208	Journalism	$33,782
Marketing	$46,160	Biology	$32,795
Political Science/ Government	$41,722	Social Work	$31,221

Source: National Association of Colleges and Employers.

* Stacy Dale and Alan B. Krueger. "Estimating the Return to College Selectivity over the Career Using Administrative Earning Data," *Journal of Human Resources,* Spring 2014, pp. 323–358.

4.3 Global Perspective

Average 15-Year-Old Mathematics Score

The mathematics scores on standardized tests for 15-year-olds vary widely across the world.

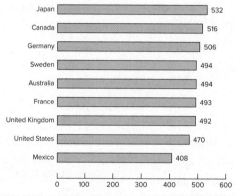

Japan	532
Canada	516
Germany	506
Sweden	494
Australia	494
France	493
United Kingdom	492
United States	470
Mexico	408

Source: OECD, "PISA 2015 Results (Volume I) Excellence and Equity in Education." www.oecd.org

Strayer examines the ways in which school quality affects earnings. He reports that greater high school quality increases the likelihood that a student will attend either a four-year or a two-year college. This increased rate of college attendance in turn raises future earnings. He finds weaker evidence for direct effects of school quality on earnings.[26]

Private versus Social Perspective

To this point, we have viewed the human capital investment decision from a *personal* or *private perspective*; that is, we have viewed benefits and costs strictly from the standpoint of an individual who is contemplating a human capital investment. The investment decision also can be viewed from a *public* or *social perspective*. In changing perspectives, we can retain Equations (4.3) and (4.6); however, we must alter our conceptions of costs and benefits. The private approach includes only costs and benefits accruing to the individual. But from the social perspective, the scope of relevant costs and benefits must be broadened. In particular, the private perspective excludes any public subsidies to education in calculating costs simply because such subsidies are *not* paid by the individual. Similarly, benefits (incremental earnings) should be calculated on an *after-tax* basis from the personal point of view. From the standpoint of society, costs should include any public subsidies to education, and benefits should be in terms of *before-tax* incremental earnings. Presumably the part of incremental earnings taxed away by government will be used to finance public goods and services beneficial to society as a whole.

---

[26] Wayne Strayer, "The Returns to School Quality: College Choice and Earnings," *Journal of Labor Economics,* July 2002, pp. 475–503.

Furthermore, most economists believe that education entails substantial *external* or *social benefits;* that is, benefits accruing to parties other than the individual acquiring the education. From a social perspective, these benefits should clearly be included in estimating the rate of return on human capital investments. What are these social benefits? First, it is well known that more educated workers have lower unemployment rates than less educated workers. Having high unemployment rates, poorly educated workers receive unemployment compensation and welfare benefits with greater frequency and may also find crime a relatively attractive alternative source of income. This means that society might benefit from investing in education by having to pay less in taxes for social welfare programs, crime prevention, and law enforcement. Second, political participation and, presumably, the quality of political decisions might improve with increased literacy and education. More education might mean that society's political processes would function more effectively to the benefit of society at large. Third, there may be intergenerational benefits: The children of better educated parents may grow up in a more desirable home environment and receive better care, guidance, and informal preschool education. Fourth, the research discoveries of highly educated people might yield large and widely dispersed benefits to society. Jonas Salk's discovery of an effective and economic polio vaccine is illustrative.[27]

4.1 *Quick Review*

- Human capital consists of the accumulation of prior investments in education, on-the-job training, health, and other factors that increase productivity.

- The net present value method of computing the return on a human capital investment uses a market interest rate to discount the net earnings of the investment to its present value. If the net present value is positive, the investment should be undertaken.

- The internal rate of return method discovers the unique rate of discount that equates the present value of future earnings and the investment costs. If this internal rate of return exceeds the interest cost of borrowing, the investment should be undertaken.

- Private rates of return on investments in education are on the order of 10–15 percent and seem to be rising; social rates of return are thought to be similar.

Your Turn

Suppose the net present value of an educational investment is highly positive. What can you infer about the investment's internal rate of return relative to the interest cost of borrowing? (*Answer:* See page 540.)

Why is our distinction between private and social rates of return on human capital investments significant? First, the difference between the private and the social perspectives is of potential importance because efficiency demands that the economy's total investment outlay be allocated so that rates of return on human and physical capital should be equal at the margin. If a given amount of investment spending is currently being allocated so that the rate of return on human capital investment is, say, 12 percent, while that on physical

[27] For more detailed discussions of the social and nonmarket benefits from education, see Fabian Lange and Robert Topel, "The Social Value of Education and Human Capital," in Eric A. Hanushek and Finis Welch (eds.), *Handbook of the Economics of Education,* Volume 1, (Amsterdam, Holland: Elsevier, 2006), pp. 459–509; and Lochner Lance, "Nonproduction Benefits of Education: Crime, Health, and Good Citizenship," in Eric A. Hanushek, Stephen Machin and Ludger Woessmann (eds.), *Handbook of the Economics of Education,* Volume 4, (Amsterdam, Holland: Elsevier, 2011), pp. 183–282. Also seeJames J. Heckman, John Eric Humphries, and Gregory Veramendi, "The Nonmarket Benefits of Education and Ability," *Journal of Human Capital,* Summer 2018, pp. 282–304.

capital is only 8 percent, society would benefit by relocating investment from physical to human capital. In making this comparison, it is correct to use the social, rather than the private, rate of return. Thus if we were to find that the *private* rate of return on human capital was equal to the rate of return on physical capital, it would not necessarily be correct to conclude that investment resources were being efficiently divided between human and real capital. If the *social* rate of return was higher (lower) than the private rate, resources would have been underallocated (overallocated) to human capital investments. Incidentally, most studies of social rates of return yield rates that are quite comparable to those found in studies estimating private rates of return.

A second reason that the distinction between the private and social perspectives is important has to do with policy. The social or external benefits associated with education provide the rationale for subsidizing education with public funds. In the interest of allocative efficiency, the size of these public subsidies to education should be determined on the basis of the magnitude of the associated social benefits.

HUMAN CAPITAL INVESTMENT AND THE DISTRIBUTION OF EARNINGS

Why do people vary significantly in the amounts of human capital they acquire? Why is Nguyen a high school dropout, Brooks a high school graduate, and Hassan a PhD? The reasons are many and complex; but by presenting a simple model of the demand for and the supply of human capital, we can gain valuable insights pertinent to this question. In so doing, we will also achieve some understanding of why earnings are quite unequally distributed.

Diminishing Rates of Return

In Figure 4.4, we plot the marginal internal rate of return—the extra return from additional education—for a specific individual for successive years of education. For simplicity, we have assumed that the rate of return falls continuously. In reality, the rate of return on the fourth year of college—the year a student graduates—may yield a higher marginal return than the third year. But in general, it is reasonable to assume that rates of return fall as more investment takes place. Why do these rates of return diminish? The answer is essentially twofold. On the one hand, investment in human capital (education) is subject to the law of diminishing returns. On the other hand, as additional education is undertaken, the attendant benefits fall and the associated costs rise so as to reduce the internal rate of return.

1 Diminishing Returns

Investment in education is subject to the law of diminishing returns. The extra knowledge and skills produced by education or schooling become smaller and smaller as the amount of schooling increases. This means that the incremental earnings from each additional year of schooling will diminish, and therefore so will the rate of return. Think of the individual as analogous to a firm that combines fixed resources with variable inputs to generate a certain output. An individual combines certain physical and mental characteristics with inputs of education or schooling to generate outputs of labor market skills. The individual's physical and mental characteristics—IQ, motor coordination, and so forth—are essentially fixed resources determined by genes and the home environment. To these fixed resources, we add variable inputs in the form of years of schooling. As with any other situation where a variable input is added to some fixed input, the resulting increases in the amount of human capital produced—the new knowledge and skills acquired by the individual—will ultimately

FIGURE 4.4 Rates of Return from Successive Years of Schooling

The rate of return from investing in successive years of schooling diminishes because (*a*) such investment is subject to the law of diminishing returns and (*b*) costs rise and benefits fall as more education is obtained.

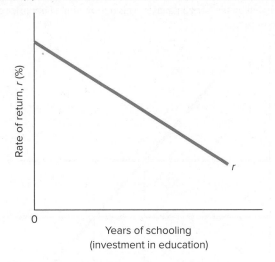

decline. And diminishing returns mean that the rate of return on successive human capital investments will also diminish.

2 Falling Benefits, Rising Costs

We have already touched on the second reason that the internal rate of return will decline as additional education is acquired. Costs tend to rise and benefits tend to fall for successive years of schooling. In addition to having essentially fixed mental and physical characteristics, the individual also possesses a fixed amount of time; that is, a finite work life. It follows that the more years one invests in education, the fewer years one has during which to realize the benefits of incremental income from that investment, hence the lower rate of return. The rate of return also declines because the costs of successive years of schooling tend to rise. On the one hand, the opportunity cost of one's time increases as more education is acquired; that is, an additional year of school has a greater opportunity cost for the holder of a bachelor's degree than for someone who has only a high school diploma. Similarly, the private direct costs of schooling increase. Public subsidies make elementary and high school education essentially free, but a substantial portion of the cost of college and graduate school is borne by the individual student. Studies confirm that the rate of return on schooling diminishes as the amount of schooling increases.

Demand, Supply, and Equilibrium

Why have we identified the curve labeled *r* in Figure 4.5 as a *demand for human capital curve* (D_{hc})? This identification is the result of applying the previously discussed decision rule, which says that investment is profitable if $r > i$ and unprofitable if $r < i$. In the context of Figure 4.5, it is profitable to invest in human capital or schooling up to the point where the marginal rate of return equals the interest rate or, in short, where $r = i$. Thus, in Figure 4.5, we assume that the individual is a "price taker" in borrowing funds for educational purposes and that needed amounts of money capital can be borrowed at a given interest rate. The horizontal line drawn at, say, i_2 indicates that the individual faces a perfectly elastic *supply of investment funds* S_2 at this interest rate. Our $r = i$ rule indicates that e_2 is the most profitable number of years of schooling in which to invest. Similarly, if the market rate of interest were higher at i_3, application of the $r = i$ rule would make

FIGURE 4.5 Deriving the Demand for Human Capital Curve

Application of the $r = i$ rule reveals that the marginal internal rate of return curve is also the demand for human capital curve. Each of the equilibrium points (1, 2, 3) indicates the financial price of investing (i) on the vertical axis and the quantity of human capital demanded on the horizontal axis. This information about price and quantity demanded constitutes the demand curve for human capital.

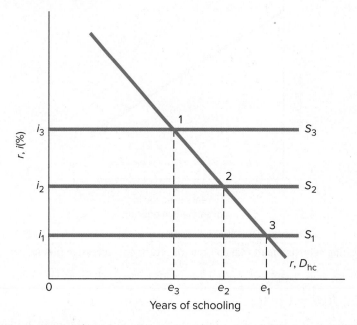

only e_3 years of schooling profitable. If the interest rate were lower at i_1, it would be profitable to invest in e_1 years of schooling. By applying a selection of possible interest rates or money capital prices to the marginal rate of return curve, we locate a number of equilibrium points (1, 2, 3) that indicate the financial price of investing (various possible interest rates) on the vertical axis *and* the corresponding quantities of human capital demanded on the horizontal axis. Any curve containing such information about price and quantity demanded is, by definition, a demand curve—in this case, the demand curve for human capital or schooling.

Differences in Human Capital Investment

The demand and supply curves of Figure 4.5 can explain why different people invest in different amounts of human capital *and,* therefore, realize substantially different earnings. Our emphasis is on three considerations: (*a*) differences in ability, (*b*) differing degrees of uncertainty concerning the capacity to transform skills and knowledge into enhanced earnings due to discrimination, and (*c*) differing access to borrowed funds for human capital investment. The first two factors work through the demand side of the human capital market; the third works through the supply side.

1 Ability Differences

Figure 4.6 embodies two different demand curves for human capital—D_A and D_B for Adams and Bowen, respectively—and a common supply curve. The common supply curve shows that money capital for investment in schooling is available to Adams and Bowen on identical terms. The key question is why Bowen's demand curve for human capital (D_B) is to the right of Adams's (D_A). The answer may be that Bowen has greater abilities—better mental and physical talents and perhaps greater

FIGURE 4.6 **Ability, Discrimination, and Investment in Human Capital**

If Bowen has greater ability to translate schooling into increased labor market productivity and higher earnings than Adams, then Bowen's demand curve for human capital (D_B) will lie farther to the right than Adams's (D_A). Given the interest rate, it will be rational for Bowen to invest in more education than Adams. Similarly, if Adams and Bowen have equal ability but discrimination reduces the amount of incremental income Adams can obtain from additional education, it will be rational for Adams to invest in less education than Bowen.

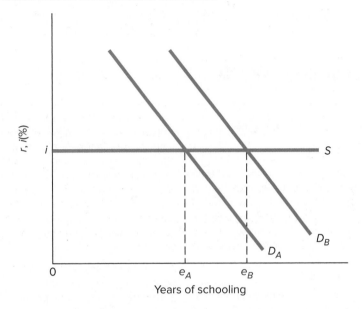

motivation and self-discipline—that cause any given input of schooling to be translated into a larger increase in labor market productivity and earning ability; that is, Bowen is more able than Adams to obtain enhanced earnings for each year of schooling; Bowen is capable of getting more than Adams out of education that is useful in the labor market. Thus, the rate of return on each year of schooling is higher, and Bowen's demand curve for human capital is therefore farther to the right. Given the interest rate and the perfectly elastic supply of financial capital, this means that Bowen will invest in e_B years of schooling, whereas Adams will choose to invest in only e_A years.[28]

Note that because it is rational for more able people to obtain more education than less able people, earnings differentials are compounded. Given the same amount of schooling, we would expect Bowen to earn more than Adams because of the former's greater innate ability. Because it is rational for Bowen to obtain more education than Adams, we would anticipate a further widening of the earnings differential.

2 Discrimination: Uncertainty of Earnings

Let's now assume that Adams and Bowen are identical in terms of ability. But let's suppose that Adams is African-American or female and therefore is more likely to encounter discriminatory barriers to selling in the labor market the higher productivity acquired through education. In other words, Adams may encounter various forms of discrimination that reduce the likelihood of transforming the labor market skills acquired through education into incremental earnings. In Equations (4.3) and (4.6), discrimination creates the

---

[28] Some evidence indicates that less educated people obtain less education mainly because they have a higher discount rate (perhaps they come from a poorer family or have a distaste for education) rather than because they lack ability, see David Card, "Earnings, Schooling, and Ability Revisited," *Research in Labor Economics* 16 (1995), pp. 23–48.

probability that the flow of earnings to African-American (female) Adams will be smaller than those accruing to white (male) Bowen from the same amount of education. This means rates of return on each level of education are lower to Adams than to Bowen. In Figure 4.6, Adams' demand for human capital is less than Bowen's. Given equal access to funds for financing education (the *iS* curve in Figure 4.6), Bowen will again find it rational to invest in more human capital than Adams. Discrimination, which reduces wages and earnings, also has the perverse impact of reducing the incentive for those discriminated against to invest in human capital.

4.4   World of Work

What You Did in High School Matters·

High school students are often told by their teachers that their performance in high school will affect their future. Clearly high school grades affect whether a student is admitted to a college. The effects of high school grades, however, may well extend beyond the college admission decision.

Michael French, Jenny Home, Ioana Popovivic, and Philip Robins examine how high school academic performance impacts future educational attainment and earning in adulthood. Their study uses data from over 10,000 24- to 34-year-olds, and thus are on average about 10 years out of high school. An important advantage of their analysis is that it uses data from high school transcripts rather than less reliable self-reported grades.

High school grades strongly affect future educational attainment and earnings. A one-point increase in high school grade point average (GPA) doubles the probability of completing college, from 21 percent to 42 percent, for both men and women. These estimates control for other factors that may affect future educational attainment, such as family size, school characteristics, innate ability, motivation, and parents' education. Those with higher high school GPAs were also more likely to complete graduate degrees. Similarly, a one-point rise in high school GPA raises annual earnings by 12 percent for males and 14 percent for females.

African-American and Hispanic men obtain more education than whites with the same high school performance and background characteristics. One possible explanation is that minority men are more motivated than their white counterparts.

* Michael T. French, Jenny F. Homer, Ioana Popovicic, and Philip K. Robins, "What You Do in High School Matters: High School GPA, Educational Attainment, and Labor Market Earnings as a Young Adult," *Eastern Economic Journal*, June 2015, pp. 370–386.

---

3 Access to Funds

WW4.5

This brings us to a final consideration. Figure 4.7 portrays the situation where the demand for human capital curves for Adams and Bowen is identical, but Bowen can acquire money capital on more favorable terms than Adams. Why the difference? Bowen may be from a wealthier family that is in a position to pledge certain financial or real assets as collateral and therefore obtain a lower interest rate. Under these conditions, it is rational for Bowen to invest in more years of schooling than Adams.[29]

Interactions

The basic point is that differences in ability, the impact of discrimination, and varying access to financial resources are all reasons various individuals find it rational to obtain different amounts of education. As shown in the age–earnings profiles in Figure 4.1, we note that these differences in educational attainment are important in generating inequality in the distribution of earnings. In fact, the factors that explain educational inequality may interact to generate greater earnings inequality than our discussion would suggest. For example, discrimination not only may influence the demand side of the human capital market to reduce the demands of African-Americans and females for education but may also appear on the supply side. If a lender reasons that discrimination makes it less likely that an African-American or a female will be able to achieve employment in the occupation for which he or she is training, the lender will compensate for this greater risk

FIGURE 4.7   **Access to Funds and Human Capital Investment**

If Bowen has access to financial resources on more favorable terms than Adams, it will be rational for Bowen to invest in a larger amount of education.

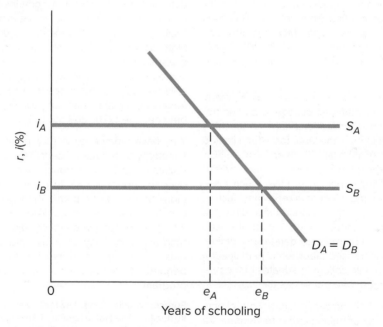

---

[29] A more elusive factor, one's *time preference,* also affects human capital investment. For example, Curt may be highly present-oriented in that he is relatively reluctant to sacrifice current consumption for future benefits. In terms of Equation (4.3), Curt would in effect use a high interest rate in discounting the future flow of earnings. Other things being equal, this would reduce the present value of a human capital investment and decrease the likelihood that it would be undertaken. Conversely, Beth may be highly future-oriented in that she is quite willing to forgo current consumption for future benefits. She would use a low interest rate in discounting Equation (4.3)'s future flow of earnings, tending to increase the present value of a human capital investment and enhancing the likelihood that it will be undertaken. The notion of time preference is helpful in explaining why individuals who are quite homogeneous with respect to ability and access to funds acquire much different amounts of human capital. This matter will be considered further in Chapter 8. For an analysis showing that more educated individuals are more future-oriented, see John T. Warner and Saul Pleeter, "The Personal Discount Rate: Evidence from Military Downsizing Programs," *American Economic Review,* March 2001, pp. 33–53.

by charging a higher rate of interest. This causes the supply of investment funds curve for African-Americans and women to shift upward as in Figure 4.7, and the amount of education acquired will be further diminished. Similarly, individuals with greater ability may also enjoy lower financial costs. Greater ability may stem not simply from one's genetic inheritance but also from the quality of one's home environment. The child fortunate to be born into a high-income family may enjoy more and better preschool education, have greater motivation and self-discipline, and place a higher value on education in general. These considerations mean that the child may have greater ability to absorb education and to increase his or her labor market productivity and earnings. Being born into a high-income family also means a greater ability to finance education on favorable terms.[30]

4.5   World of Work

Reversal of the College Gender Gap

In 1960 there were 0.63 female graduates for every male graduating from college. This ratio has steadily risen over time. More women than men now graduate from college. By 2020 there were 1.35 females for every male graduating from college.

From the late 1950s to the early 1970s, many female students attended college to pursue traditionally female occupations such as teaching and intended to be in the labor force for a limited extent. Starting in the late 1960s and early 1970s, the career expectations of young women started to change: They expected to have much more attachment to the labor market. Many factors played a role in this change, including the women's movement, birth control (see World of Work 3.5), reduced gender discrimination, and an increased labor force participation rate among female college graduates of the previous generation.

As a result of their increased future work expectations, high school girls started to prepare for college in a different manner. They started to take more math and science classes. In 1972 high school boys took 24 percent more math classes and 20 percent more science classes than high school girls. By 1992 virtual parity was achieved between high school boys and girls in math and science class enrollment. High school girls also increased their achievement scores compared to boys. In fact, by 1992 high school girls had an advantage in combined math and reading achievement scores. Goldin, Katz, and Kuziemko find that the increased proportion of high school girls taking math and science classes as well as the rise in the achievement scores of girls relative to boys can account for between 37 and 63 percent of the rise in the female to male ratio of college graduates between the 1970s and the 1990s.

Why have women gone past parity to become a majority of college students? Goldin, Katz, and Kuziemko argue that noncognitive factors may play an important role. In particular, boys have more behavioral problems than girls. Boys are two to three times more likely to suffer from attention deficit hyperactivity disorder (ADHD) than are girls. They are much more likely than girls to engage in criminal activity, get suspended from school, or be in a special education program.

Source: Claudia Goldin, Lawrence Katz, and Ilyana Kuziemko, "The Homecoming of American College Women: The Reversal of the College Gender Gap," *Journal of Economic Perspectives,* Fall 2006, pp. 133–156; and National Center for Education Statistics (http://nces.ed.gov).

[30] For an interesting discussion of how parents affect the earnings of their children, see Paul Taubman, *Income Distribution and Redistribution* (Reading, MA: Addison-Wesley Publishing Company, 1978), Chapter 5.

The comments here correctly imply that public policy may also play a significant role in determining the amounts of human capital various individuals acquire and the consequent distribution of earnings. For example, to the extent that antidiscrimination policies have been effective, variations in individual demand curves for education have been reduced, and so has earnings inequality. Scholarships based on student ability mean that students with the strongest demand curves for human capital would also have the greatest access to funds—a combination that would increase inequality in the distribution of human capital and earnings. Conversely, scholarships on the basis of need or targeted education programs for children from disadvantaged or minority families would reduce inequality in the dispersion of human capital and earnings.

Capital Market Imperfections

The capital market may include certain biases or imperfections causing it to favor investment in physical, rather than human, capital. Such biases are termed *capital market imperfections*. Specifically, funds may be less readily available, or accessible only on less favorable terms, for investment in human capital as compared to real capital or the purchase of consumer durables. Perhaps the primary reason for this is that human capital is embodied in the borrower and therefore is not available as collateral on a loan. If one defaults on a house mortgage or an automobile loan, there is a tangible asset the lender can repossess and sell to recover losses. But in a nation that rejects slavery and indentured servitude, there is no designated asset for the lender to seize if the borrower fails to repay an educational loan. This increases risk to the lender and prompts the inclusion of a risk premium in the interest rate charged. Furthermore, we have noted that other things being equal, it is more rational for young people to make human capital investments than for old people. But young people are less likely to have established credit ratings or collateral assets to allow them to borrow on reasonable terms. Finally, the variation in returns on human capital investments is large. Recall that although college graduates *on the average* earn substantially more than high school graduates, many college graduates earn less than the average high school graduate. This uncertainty of return may inflate the risk premium charged for human capital loans.

The relative unsuitability of the capital market for educational loans has one or two important consequences. First, because of the problems and uncertainties just noted, financial institutions may choose *not* to make human capital loans. This means the amount of human capital investment individuals can undertake will depend on their, or their families', income and wealth. Thus well-to-do families can finance the college educations of their children by the relatively painless process of reducing their volume of saving. But poor families cannot save, and therefore financing a college education implies a possibly severe cut in living standards.[31]

These circumstances may perpetuate a vicious cycle. Individuals and families with little human capital (education) may be poor; being poor, it is extremely difficult for them to finance the acquisition of additional human capital.

Capital market imperfections have a second important implication. If it is in the social interest to achieve a balance or equilibrium between investment in real capital and human capital, then the government may have to offset the imperfections by subsidizing or providing human capital loans. Ideally, an equilibrium between investment in real and human capital would occur when the last dollar spent on human capital contributes the same amount to the domestic output as the last dollar expended on real capital. But the higher interest rates charged for educational loans will restrict expenditures on human capital so that the relative

---

[31] Even publicly supported colleges and universities that feature relatively low tuition and fees may attract fewer students from low-income families simply because their families may not be able to afford the opportunity costs (see Figure 4.2). A very poor family may not be able to forgo the income that a son or daughter can earn by entering the labor market immediately upon graduating from high school. Federal education loan programs have mitigated this problem in recent years. For an analysis of the impact of family finances on college enrollment, see Bhashkar Mazumder, "Family Resources and College Enrollment," *Economic Perspectives* (Federal Reserve Bank of Chicago), 4th Quarter 2003, pp. 30–41.

contribution of the last unit to the national output will exceed that of the last unit of real capital. This indicates that investment resources are being underallocated to human capital. This rationale in part lies behind the loan guarantees and financial resources that government has provided to stimulate educational loans.

4.2 *Quick Review*

- The rate of return from investing in successive units of human capital declines; that is, the investment demand curve is downward-sloping—because opportunity costs rise and marginal benefits fall as more investment occurs.

- The optimal level of investment in human capital occurs when the marginal rate of return, r, equals the interest rate, i (the price of investing).

- It is rational for people having greater ability to obtain more education than others; conversely, those who are discriminated against in the labor market have less incentive to invest in human capital.

- People who have greater access to financial funding for investment on more favorable interest terms will rationally invest more in education than others.

- Imperfections in the capital market may bias investment toward physical capital rather than human capital.

Your Turn

In equilibrium, the marginal rates of return, r, for those with more ability to extract earnings from formal education and those with less ability are equal (see Figure 4.6). So why do people with greater ability get more formal education? (*Answer:* See page 540.)

ON-THE-JOB TRAINING

Many of the usable labor market skills that workers possess are acquired not through formal schooling but rather through *on-the-job training*. Such training may be somewhat formal; that is, workers may undertake a structured trainee program or an apprenticeship program. On the other hand, on-the-job training is often highly informal and therefore difficult to measure or even detect. Less experienced workers often engage in "learning by doing"; they acquire new skills by simply observing more skilled workers, filling in for them when they are ill or on vacation, or engaging in informal conversation during coffee breaks.

Costs and Benefits

Like formal education, on-the-job training entails present sacrifices and future benefits. It, thus, is an investment in human capital and can be analyzed through the net present value and internal rate of return frameworks [Equations (4.3) and (4.6)]. In deciding whether to provide on-the-job training, a firm will weigh the expected added revenues generated by the training against the costs of providing it. If the net present value of the training investment is positive, the firm will invest; if it is negative, it won't. Alternatively, the firm will invest if the internal rate of return of the investment exceeds the interest cost of borrowing.

For employers, providing training may involve such direct costs as classroom instruction or increased worker supervision, along with such indirect costs as reduced worker output during the training period. Workers may have to accept the cost of lower wages during the training period. The potential benefit to firms is that a trained workforce will be more productive and will therefore make greater contributions to the firm's total revenue. Similarly, trained workers can expect higher wages because of their enhanced productivity.

General and Specific Training

To understand how the associated costs and benefits are distributed among workers and employers, we must distinguish between two polar types of on-the-job training. At one extreme, *general training refers to the creation of skills or characteristics that are equally usable in all firms and industries*. Stated differently, general training enhances the productivity of workers of all firms. At the other end of the continuum, *specific training is training that can be used* only *in the particular firm that provides that training*. Specific training increases the worker's productivity only in the firm providing that training. In practice, most on-the-job training contains elements of both general and specific training, and it is therefore difficult to offer unequivocal examples. Nevertheless, we might venture that the abilities to concentrate on a task for a reasonable period, to show up for work regularly and be punctual, to read, to perform simple mathematical manipulations, and to follow instructions all constitute general training. Similarly, gaining word processing, carpentry, or accounting skills would be considered general training. Alternatively, the ability to perform an assembly procedure unique to a firm's product exemplifies specific training. Teaching personnel to answer toll-free telephone questions about a firm's products is another example of specific training.

The distinction between general and specific training is important for at least two reasons. First, it is helpful in explaining whether the worker or the employer is more likely to pay for on-the-job training. Second, it is useful in understanding why employers might be particularly anxious to retain certain of their trained workers.

Distributing Training Costs

Analyzing whether workers or firms pay the costs of on-the-job training gets a bit complex. Let's start by looking at pure cases and then modify our analysis to account for real-world observations. We begin with two broad generalizations, each based on the assumptions that markets are competitive and that workers are perfectly mobile. First, *the worker will pay for general training through lower wages during the training period*. Second, *the firm must bear the cost of specific training*.

General training gives a worker skills and understanding that are transferable; they can be sold to other firms at a higher wage rate. If the employer were to bear the cost, the worker might leave the firm's employment after the training and thus deprive the employer of any return (benefit) on the training investment. Alternatively, in the posttraining period the employer would have to pay a wage rate commensurate with the worker's higher productivity, eliminating any possible return on the training investment to the employer. Therefore, if general on-the-job training is undertaken, it is paid for by the worker in the form of a reduced wage rate during the training period.

On the other hand, a specific skill is not transferable or salable by a worker. Thus, the worker will not pay for such training. If a worker is fired or laid off at the end of a period of specific training, the worker has gained nothing of value to sell in the labor market. The cost is borne by the employer. This typically means that the employer will pay a wage rate in excess of the worker's contribution to the firm's revenue during the training period. Figure 4.8 is useful in elaborating these generalizations.

General Training

Figure 4.8(a) shows the case of general training. Here W_u and MRP_u indicate what the wage rate and marginal revenue product would be for an untrained worker. *Marginal revenue product is the increase in a firm's total revenue associated with the employment of a given worker.*[32] The employment of an additional worker will add to a firm's total output and therefore to its revenue. This addition to its revenue is the MRP.

In Figure 4.8(a), the wage rate and marginal revenue product *during* training are represented by W_t and MRP_t while W_p and MRP_p are the posttraining wage rate and marginal revenue product. MRP_t is below that for an untrained worker because during the training period the worker is diverting time from production to learning. It is important to stress that the higher posttraining marginal revenue product (MRP_p) is relevant *to all firms* because the training is general. Competing firms will therefore bid up the wage rate of this trained worker until it is equal to MRP_p. It is precisely for this reason—that competition will force the posttraining wage rate upward into equality with the posttraining marginal revenue product—that the employer will normally *not* be willing to pay for general training. The employer has no opportunity to obtain a return on its training investment by paying a wage rate less than the worker's marginal revenue product. Why should the employer bear general training costs when the benefits accrue solely to the trained employee in the form of higher wages?

FIGURE 4.8   **Wage Rates and Marginal Revenue Products for General and Specific Training**

(a) *General training.* Because general training is salable to other firms and industries ($W_p = MRP_p$), workers normally must pay for such training that a firm provides. This payment is in the form of a reduced wage ($W < W_u$) during the training period. A possible exception is where the firm faces a legal minimum wage and needs to provide remedial basic education to have a qualified workforce. The firm may conclude that it can pay a wage rate above W_t in the training period and recoup its investment by paying a wage rate slightly below W_p in the posttraining period. Workers facing high costs of job search and relocation may not leave for jobs paying W_p. (b) *Specific training.* Specific training is not transferable to other firms; therefore, the employer must pay for such training. During the training period, the employer pays a wage rate in excess of the worker's marginal revenue product ($W_u > MRP_t$). In the posttraining period, the employer receives a return on specific training because the worker's marginal revenue product will exceed his or her wage rate ($MRP_p > W_u$). Because the employer's return on specific training varies directly with the length of the posttraining period, the employer might voluntarily pay an above-competitive wage (W_p' as compared to W_u) to reduce worker turnover.

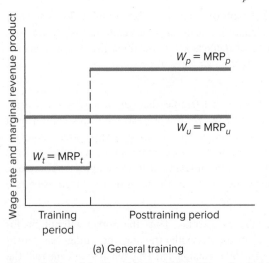

(a) General training

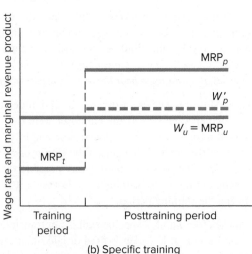

(b) Specific training

Source: Addison, John T., and Stanley Siebert. The market for labor: an analytical treatment. Goodyear Pub. Co., 1979.

---

[32] This concept will be explored in more detail in Chapter 5.

To repeat: The worker pays for general training costs by accepting a wage below that of the untrained worker (W_t as compared to W_u) during the training period. Incidentally, the fact that competition will bid a worker's wage rate up into equality with his or her higher posttraining marginal revenue product (MRP_p), and thereby preclude a return to the employer, explains why general education typically occurs in schools and not on the job.

Global Perspective

Percentage of Workers Receiving Employer-Provided Education and Training

The percentage of workers who receive employer-provided job-related education and training ranges from 12 percent in Ireland to 46 percent in Norway.

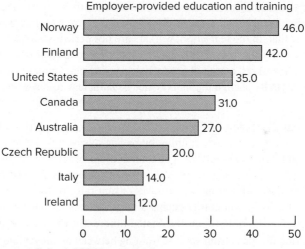

Source: OECD, "Employment Outlook 2003." www.oecd.org

Specific Training

Figure 4.8(b) pertains to specific training. Again, W_u and MRP_u are the wage rate and marginal revenue product of an untrained worker, and MRP_t and MRP_p, respectively, show marginal revenue productivity during and after specific training. In contrast to Figure 4.8(a), the posttraining marginal revenue product applies *only to this firm*. The worker has acquired specific training that will increase productivity in *this* firm; but by definition, specific training is *not* transferable or useful to other firms. Because specific training is not transferable—that is, it will not allow the worker to obtain a higher wage rate as the consequence of labor market competition for his or her services—the worker will refuse to pay for such training and will not accept a lower wage during the training period. Note that during the training period the wage rate will remain at W_u, which means the employer must bear the cost of the training by paying a wage rate that is in excess of the worker's marginal revenue product (MRP_t). However, because specific training is not transferable—that is, it does not increase the worker's marginal revenue product to other firms—the employer need not increase the wage rate above W_u in the posttraining period. Thus, from the employer's standpoint, training imposes a flow of costs (W_u exceeds MRP_t) in the training period that is followed by a flow of benefits or incremental revenues (MRP_p exceeds W_u) in the posttraining period. As shown in Equation (4.3), if the net present value of these flows is positive, the firm will find it profitable to undertake specific training for its workers. Indeed, you have undoubtedly noticed that Figure 4.8(b) resembles Figure 4.2.

Modifications

Our discussion of general and specific training merits modifications in some important ways. First, let's look again at general training [Figure 4.8(a)]. Recently some firms have begun providing new employees with general training—remedial reading, writing, and mathematics—to compensate for a decline in the quality of primary and secondary education. These firms have been forced to provide this general training to ensure themselves a sufficient number of qualified workers. Usually these firms reduce the wage during the training period, as suggested in Figure 4.8. But in other instances, the legal minimum wage precludes this strategy. Thus, some firms may have to pay part of the training costs themselves.

In Figure 4.8(a), we are suggesting that the minimum wage may force some firms offering general training to pay more than W_t during the training period. How is it possible for these firms to recoup these general training expenses? Won't employees take their services elsewhere if they are paid less than W_p after completion of the training? The answer is that, in the real world, workers are not perfectly mobile; it is costly to change jobs and to relocate geographically. Thus, these firms may be able to recoup their investments in general training through paying less than the workers' marginal productivity during part or all of the posttraining period. The extra pay the worker could get by changing jobs may not be sufficient to cover the worker's job search and relocation costs.

We also need to modify our discussion of Figure 4.8(b). We have observed that in the posttraining period the employer realizes a return from specific training by paying a wage (W_u) that is less than each worker's contribution to the firm's total revenue (MRP_p). The total amount of revenue or profit derived from this discrepancy will vary directly with the length of time the worker remains employed by the firm. In short, the employer has a financial interest in lowering the turnover or quit rates of workers with specific training. The employer might accomplish this by voluntarily paying a wage rate somewhat higher than the worker could obtain elsewhere—for example, W_p' rather than W_u. Stated differently, the wage in the posttraining period is likely to be set so as to divide the gains from specific training between employer and employee. Specific training is one of a number of considerations that change labor from a variable input to a *quasi-fixed* factor of production.[33]

A final comment: On the average, individuals who receive the largest amount of formal education also receive more on-the-job specific training. This is not surprising. A person who has demonstrated his or her trainability by completing, say, a college degree is more likely to be selected by an employer for specific on-the-job training than someone with only a high school diploma. Why? Because that individual will be trainable at a lower cost. Indeed, Figure 4.8(b) implies that on-the-job training will have a higher rate of return to employers when workers can absorb training in a short time. A college degree is evidence of the capacity to absorb training quickly. The fact that people with more formal education on the average receive more on-the-job training helps explain why age–earnings profiles of more highly educated workers rise faster than those of less educated workers (see Figure 4.1).

---

[33] The classic study is Walter Oi, "Labor as a Quasi-Fixed Factor," *Journal of Political Economy,* December 1962, pp. 538–555.

4.3 *Quick Review*

- Because general training is salable to other firms, workers must normally pay for it indirectly through reduced pay during the training period.

- Specific training is not transferable to other firms; therefore, the employer normally must pay for it, recouping the investment cost later by paying these workers less than their marginal revenue products (MRPs).

- Faced with a legal minimum wage, some firms needing qualified workers may pay for general training, recouping their expenses by paying workers less than their MRPs during the posttraining period. Because of high job search and relocation costs, many workers will stay at their jobs even though they might be able to earn more elsewhere.

- The employer's return on specific training varies directly with the length of the posttraining period; thus, the employer may pay a higher-than-competitive wage to reduce worker turnover and increase its return on its investment.

Your Turn

Suppose that after graduation you take a job with an employer that offers to pay full tuition for employees wishing to return to school to get an MBA degree during nonwork hours. You are not required to continue working for the firm after getting your MBA. What type of training is this? Who do you think actually pays for it? (*Answer:* See page 540.)

Empirical Evidence

In 2009, 15 percent of employees aged 16–65 reported participating in employer-paid formal training to improve their job skills in the last year. About 25 percent of college-educated workers received training, while 9 percent of those with a high school degree obtained training. Nearly 20 percent of union workers and 14 percent of nonunion workers received training at work. About 17 percent of full-time workers received training, while only 4 percent of part-time workers participated in training.[34]

There has been a kaleidoscope of new research on training.[35] Here are a few recent findings:

- Union workers are more likely to receive training than nonunion workers.[36]

- Positive productivity effects have been found for general but not specific training.[37]

- The likelihood of participating in employer-provided training is greater in larger firms than in smaller ones.[38]

- Most training appears to be general in nature rather than firm-specific.[39]

---

[34] C. Jeffrey Waddoups, "Did Employers in the United States Back Away from Skills Training during the Early 2000s?" *Industrial and Labor Relations Review,* March 2016, pp. 405–434.

[35] For a survey of recent studies on the effects of training, see Harley J. Frazis and James R. Spletzer, "Worker Training: What We've Learned from the NLSY79," *Monthly Labor Review,* February 2005, pp. 48–58.

[36] Christian Dustmann and Uta Schönberg, "Training and Union Wages," *Review of Economics and Statistics,* May 2009, pp. 363–376.

[37] Alan Barrett and Philip J. O'Connell, "Does Training Generally Work? The Returns to In-Company Training," *Industrial and Labor Relations Review,* April 2001, pp. 647–662.

[38] Dan A. Black, Brett J. Noel, and Zheng Wang, "On-the-Job Training, Establishment Size, and Firm Size: Evidence for Economies of Scale in the Production of Human Capital," *Southern Economic Journal,* July 1999, pp. 82–100.

[39] Mark A. Loewenstein and James R. Spletzer, "General and Specific Training: Evidence and Implications," *Journal of Human Resources,* Fall 1999, pp. 710–733.

- The percentage of workers with employer-paid formal training in the last year decreased from 21 percent in 2001 to 15 percent in 2009.[40]
- An analysis of 71 studies reveals that each on-the-job training course raises earnings by 2.6 percent.[41]
- A 10 percentage point increase in the share of trained workers is associated with an increase in productivity of 1.7–3.2 percent and an increase in wages of 1.0–1.7 percent.[42]
- Occupation-specific human capital increases the unemployment rate since it is costly to switch occupations.[43]
- Gender differences in the amount of on-the-job training play only a small role in the gender wage gap.[44]

CRITICISMS OF HUMAN CAPITAL THEORY

A number of criticisms have been made of the human capital model and its applications. The first two criticisms discussed here are concerned with measurement problems and suggest that estimates of the rates of return for investments in education are likely to be biased. Two other criticisms also have implications for measuring the rate of return on human capital investments but are more profound in that they challenge the very concept or theory of investing in human capital.

Investment or Consumption?

WW4.6

One criticism of measuring the rate of return on human capital investment is that it is *not* correct to treat all expenditures for education as investment because, in fact, a portion of such outlays are consumption expenditures. The decision to attend college, for example, is based on broader and more complex considerations than expected increases in labor productivity and enhanced earnings. Some substantial portion of one's expenditures on a college education yields consumption benefits either immediately or in the long run.[45] Expenditures for courses on Shakespeare, ceramics, music appreciation, and so forth yield both immediate and long-run consumption benefits by enlarging an individual's range of interests, tastes, and activities. It is true, of course, that a course in the nineteenth-century English literature not only yields consumption benefits but also enhances the capacity of oral and written expression. And this ability has value in the labor market; it increases productivity and earnings. The problem, however, is that there is no reasonable way to determine what portion of the expense for a literature course is investment and what part is consumption. The main point is that by ignoring the consumption component of educational expenditures and considering *all* such outlays as investment, empirical researchers *understate* the rate of return on educational investments. In other words, by overstating the investment costs we understate the return on that investment.

[40] Waddoups, op. cit.

[41] Carla Haelermans and Lex Borghans, "Wage Effects of On-the-Job Training: A Meta-Analysis," *British Journal of Industrial Relations,* September 2012, pp. 502–528.

[42] Jozef Konings and Stijn Vanormelingen, "The Impact of Training on Productivity and Wages: Firm-Level Evidence," *Review of Economics and Statistics,* May 2015, pp. 485–497.

[43] Benedikt Herz, "Specific Human Capital and Wait Unemployment," *Journal of Labor Economics,* April 2019, pp. 467–508.

[44] Paul Sicilian and Adam J. Grossberg, "Investment in Human Capital and Gender Wage Differences: Evidence from the NLSY," *Applied Economics* 33, no. 4 (March 2001), pp. 463–471.

[45] For an estimate of the consumption value of a college education, see Pedro Carniero, Karsten T. Hansen, and James J. Heckman, "Estimating Distributions of Treatment Effects with an Application to the Returns to Schooling and Measurement of the Effect of Uncertainty on College Choice," *International Economic Review,* May 2003, pp. 361–422.

4.6 World of Work

College as Country Club

Colleges compete for students in terms of consumption amenities such as high-quality residence halls, dining services, and athletic facilities as well as price and academic quality. In 2007, the average four-year college spent $0.51 on consumption amenities for every dollar spent on academic instruction and support. This ratio had wide variability as it ranged from $0.26 at the 10th percentile to $0.80 at the 90th percentile. Clearly, colleges differ in the consumption amenities they provide to their students.

Jacob, McCall, and Stange analyze the effects of student demand for consumption amenities and academic quality by combining student-level data on 1992 and 2004 high school seniors with college-level data on nearly all four-year colleges in the United States. Their analysis indicates that higher ability students have a greater demand for academic quality. Wealthier students are much more willing to pay for consumption amenities.

Schools have strong incentives to respond to these student demands. More selective colleges have an incentive to increase their academic quality since that is the feature most valued by their marginal students. Less selective colleges have a greater incentive to improve consumption amenities since their marginal students value this feature.

Colleges do respond to student preferences for consumption amenities, particularly those facing strong competitive pressures. A one standard deviation increase in enrollment elasticity for consumption amenities is linked to a $0.10 rise in the consumption amenity to academic spending ratio. Student preferences explain 11 percent of the variation in the ratio of consumption amenity spending to academic spending across four-year colleges.

Source: Based on Brian Jacob, Brian McCall, and Kevin Stange, "College as Country Club: Do Colleges Cater to Students' Preferences for Consumption?" *Journal of Labor Economics*, April 2018, pp. 309–348.

Nonwage Benefits

In calculating the internal rate of return, most researchers simply compare the differences in the earnings of high school and college graduates. But the jobs of high school and college graduates differ in other respects. First, the fringe benefits associated with the jobs obtained by college graduates are more generous—both absolutely and as a percentage of earnings—than those received by high school graduates. By ignoring fringe benefits, empirical studies *understate* the rate of return on a college education. Second, the jobs acquired by college graduates are generally more pleasant and interesting than those of high school graduates. This means that a calculated rate of return based on incremental earnings *understates* the total benefits accruing from a college education.

The Ability Problem

Two other related criticisms, labeled the *ability problem* and the *screening hypothesis,* question the very concept of human capital investment. We first consider the *ability problem*.

It is widely recognized that average incomes vary directly with the level of education. But it is less well accepted that a strong, clear-cut cause–effect relationship exists between the two. Critics of human capital theory doubt that the observed income differential is solely—or even primarily—the result of the additional education. To state the problem somewhat differently, the "other things being equal" assumption underlies the simple model of Figure 4.2 and the conclusions derived from it. Critics of human capital theory contend that other things in fact are not likely to be equal. It is widely acknowledged that those who have more intelligence, more self-discipline, and greater motivation—not to mention more family wealth and better job market connections—are more likely to go to college. If we could somehow blot out all of the knowledge and understanding that college graduates acquired in college, we would still expect this group to earn larger incomes than those who decided *not* to attend college. Thus, one can argue that although college graduates earn higher incomes than high school graduates, a substantial portion of that incremental income is *not* traceable to the investment in a college education. In other words, people with high abilities tend to do well in the labor market; the fact that they also attend college may be somewhat incidental to this success. "The only reason that education is correlated with income is that the combination of ability, motivation, and personal habits that it takes to succeed in education happens to be the same combination that it takes to be a productive worker."[46] This criticism implies that if a substantial portion of the incremental earnings enjoyed by college graduates is attributable to their *ability* and not to their *schooling,* then estimated rates of return on investing in a college education will be *overstated*.

Accepting the validity of this criticism, a number of researchers have tried to determine what portion of incremental earnings derives from human capital investment as opposed to differences in ability and other personal characteristics. For example, a study of identical twins concludes that ability bias plays a small role in the measurement of the rate of return to schooling.[47] A more recent study, however, finds that the ability bias accounts for a substantial part of the college wage premium.[48]

It is also worth observing that the causal relationship between education and earnings has important implications for public policy. *If* human capital theorists are correct in arguing that education is the sole or primary cause of higher earnings, then it makes sense to provide more education and training to low-income workers if society chooses to reduce poverty and the degree of income inequality. On the other hand, *if* high incomes are caused primarily by ability, independent of education and training, then a policy of increased spending on the education and training of low-income groups may be of limited success in increasing their incomes and alleviating income inequality.

The Screening Hypothesis

The *screening hypothesis* (or *signaling hypothesis*) is closely related to the ability problem. This hypothesis suggests that education affects earnings not primarily by altering the labor market productivity of students but by grading and labeling students in such a way as to determine their job placement and thereby their earnings.[49] It is argued that employers use educational attainment—for example, the possession of a college degree—as an inexpensive means of identifying workers who are likely to be of high quality. A college degree or other credential thus signals trainability and competence and becomes a ticket of admission to higher level, higher paying jobs where opportunities for further training and promotion are good. Less educated workers are screened from these positions, not necessarily because of their inability to perform the jobs but simply because they do not have the college degrees to give them access to the positions. The incremental income enjoyed by college graduates might be a payment for being credentialed rather than a reward for being more productive.

---

[46] Rivlin, Alice M. "Income Distribution–Can Economists Help?" *The American Economic Review,* 65, no. 2 (May 1975): 1–15.

[47] Orley Ashenfelter and Alan Krueger, "Estimates of the Economic Returns to Schooling from a New Sample of Twins," *American Economic Review,* December 1994, pp. 1157–1173. For similar results using a direct measure of ability, see McKinley Blackburn and David Neumark, "Omitted-Ability Bias and the Increase in the Return to Schooling," *Journal of Labor Economics,* July 1993, pp. 521–544.

[48] James J. Heckman, John Eric Humphries, and Gregory Veramendi, "Returns to Education: The Causal Effects of Education on Earnings, Health, and Smoking," *Journal of Political Economy,* October 2018, pp. S197–246.

[49] Michael Spence, "Job Market Signaling," *Quarterly Journal of Economics,* August 1973, pp. 355–374. For a survey of the screening literature, see Andrew Weiss, "Human Capital vs. Signaling Explanations of Wages," *Journal of Economic Perspectives,* Fall 1996, pp. 133–154.

Viewed from a private perspective, screening should have no effect on the internal rate of return. Whether one is admitted to a higher paying position because of the knowledge and skills acquired in college or because one possesses the necessary credential (a college degree), the fact remains that having attended college typically results in higher earnings. But from a social perspective, the screening hypothesis, if valid, is very important. One might well question the expenditure of $1,342 billion (in 2017) on elementary, secondary, and higher education if the payoff is merely to signal employers that certain workers are above average in terms of intelligence, motivation, and self-discipline. To the extent that a college graduate's incremental earnings stem from screening, the social rate of return of investing in a college education will be *overstated*.

To what extent are the higher earnings of more educated workers due to education augmenting the productivity of workers, as the human capital view suggests? Similarly, to what degree are the higher earnings of such individuals attributable to the screening hypothesis, which indicates that schooling merely flags more productive workers? Does schooling produce skills or merely identify preexistent skills? Empirical evidence is mixed. For example, research by Chatterji and colleagues suggests that as much as 30 percent of the effect of education on earnings might result from screening.[50]

WW4.7

On the other hand, studies by Altonji and Pierret, Wolpin, and Wise question the importance of screening. Altonji and Pierret argue that signaling is likely to be an important part of the return to schooling only to the extent that firms lack good information about the productivity of new workers and that they learn slowly over time.[51] They find evidence that firms do screen young workers on the basis of education, but that employers learn quickly about worker productivity. Altonji and Pierret's calculations suggest that the screening component of the return to schooling is probably only a small part of the difference in wages associated with education. Wolpin has reasoned that if education is a screening device, workers who are to be screened in the process of job acquisition will be prone to purchase more schooling than workers who are not screened. He notes that while salaried workers are screened, self-employed workers are not. Therefore, if schooling is a screening device, salaried workers will tend to purchase more schooling than the self-employed. But he finds that in fact the two groups of workers acquire about the same amount of education, which Wolpin regards as "evidence against a predominant screening interpretation" of the positive association between schooling and earnings.[52] Similarly, Wise has argued that if education does affect worker productivity as the human capital theory suggests, then college degrees of differing quality *and* student performance while attending college should be reflected in salary differentials; that is, if human capital theory is correct, workers with bachelor degrees from high-quality institutions *and* workers who achieved higher grade point averages should be more productive and therefore earn higher salaries. Examining data for some 1,300 college graduates employed by Ford Motor Company, Wise found a "consistent positive relationship between commonly used measures of academic achievement [institutional quality and grade point average] and rates of salary increase." Wise concludes that a "college education is not only a signal of productive ability, but in fact enhances this ability."[53]

[50] Monojit Chatterji, Paul T. Seaman, and Larry D. Singell, Jr., "A Test of the Signaling Hypothesis," *Oxford Economic Papers,* April 2003, pp. 191–215. For further support of the signaling hypothesis, see Harley Frazis, "Human Capital, Signaling, and the Pattern of Returns to Education," *Oxford Economic Papers,* April 2002, pp. 298–320.

[51] Joseph G. Altonji and Charles R. Pierret, "Employer Learning and the Signaling Value of Education," in I. Ohashi and T. Tachibanaki (eds.), *Internal Labour Markets, Incentives, and Employment* (New York: MacMillan Publishing, 1998). For a study individual productivity is more important that employer learning in explaining pay increases, see Lisa B. Kahn and Fabian Lange, "Employer Learning, Productivity, and the Earnings Distribution: Evidence from Performance Measures," *Review of Economic Studies,* October 2014, pp. 1575–1613.

[52] Kenneth Wolpin, "Education and Screening," *American Economic Review,* December 1977, pp. 949–958.

[53] Wise, David A. "Academic Achievement and Job Performance." *The American Economic Review,* 65, no. 3 (1975): 350–366. http://www.jstor.org/stable/1804839.

4.7   World of Work

Is There More to College than Money?*

Over the past few decades, many researchers have examined the economic benefits to individuals of a college degree. Recently more attention has been focused on the noneconomic benefits of college education. College graduates may have better health status than their less educated counterparts for several reasons. First, college graduates, due to additional knowledge, may have a healthier lifestyle through better diets, greater use of seat belts, more exercise, less smoking, and less drug abuse. Second, health insurance coverage rates are higher among college graduates and thus better access to health care. Third, college graduates live and work in safer environments.

The evidence is college graduates are healthier than those with less education. College graduates have healthier behaviors such a lower rate of smoking. Among adults aged 25–64 in 2010, 27 percent of high school graduates were currently smoking, while only 8 percent of college graduates did so. With regard to health outcomes, college graduates are less likely to report that they are in fair or poor health and have lower rates of disability. In addition, they have lower rates of mortality. At age 25, a college graduate can expect to live 9 more years than a person with a less than high school education.

Finally, more educated persons are happier than those with less education. For example, college graduates are more likely to be married and have more stable marriages. They also acquire broader social networks and have more interesting jobs with good working conditions. In addition, college graduates have higher income levels. College graduates have expressed a greater satisfaction with life than those with less education. Among persons aged 25–64, data from 27 countries indicate those with a college education are 18 percentage points more likely to be satisfied with life than those with less than a high school degree. About 10 percentage points of this difference in satisfaction remain after adjusting for age, gender, and income.

* Based on Organization for Economic Cooperation and Development, *Education at a Glance, 2011* (Paris: OECD, 2011), Table A11.3; National Center for Health Statistics, *Health, United States, 2011: With Special Feature on Socioeconomic Status and Health* (Hyattsville, MD: National Center for Health Statistics, 2012); and Lochner Lance, "Nonproduction Benefits of Education: Crime, Health, and Good Citizenship," in Eric A. Hanushek, Stephen Machin, and Ludger Woessmann (eds.), *Handbook of the Economics of Education,* Volume 4 (Amsterdam, Holland: Elsevier, 2011), pp. 183–282.

Recapitulation

There is no question that human capital theory has been the basis for important insights and the cornerstone for myriad revealing empirical studies. But as the ability problem and the screening hypothesis suggest, human capital theory is not universally accepted, and some who accept it do so only with reservations. Although there is almost universal agreement about the positive association between education and earnings, there is disagreement over the *reasons* for this association. Empirical testing is usually indirect in that it is first determined that those with more education and training have higher earnings, and then it is *inferred* that the additional education and training increase worker productivity and thereby cause the enhanced earnings. But the issue remains: Does education increase one's productivity? Or do those who acquire more education earn more simply because they are more able and more motivated? Do educational degrees simply identify productive workers?[54]

Most economists reject the various criticisms of human capital theory, believing that education and training directly increase productivity and earnings. But they also recognize that not all investments in education and training have a positive net present value; some investments are poor ones, and others have sharply diminishing returns. Thus, human capital theory cannot be used uncritically as a basis for public policy. For example, taken alone, massive government investments in human capital to increase economic growth may yield disappointing results. Such policies need to be balanced against alternative policies promoting new technology and greater investment in physical capital.

Chapter Summary

1. Expenditures on education and training that increase one's productivity and future earnings in the labor market can be treated as a human capital investment decision.

2. The decision to invest in a college education entails both direct (out-of-pocket) and indirect (forgone earnings) costs. Benefits take the form of future incremental earnings.

3. There are two basic methods of comparing the benefits and costs associated with a human capital investment. The net present value approach uses a discounting formula to compare the present value of costs and benefits. If the net present value is positive, it is rational to invest. The internal rate of return is the rate of discount at which the net present value of the investment is zero. If the internal rate of return exceeds the interest rate, it is rational to invest.

4. Most empirical studies suggest that the rate of return on investing in a college education has ranged from 10 to 15 percent.

5. The college wage premium—the percentage differential in the earnings of college and high school graduates—has varied significantly over time, rising rapidly since 1979. Changes in the supply of and the demand for college and high school graduates can be used to explain changes in the college wage premium.

6. From a private perspective, the human capital decision excludes public subsidies to education, considers after-tax earnings, and ignores any social or external benefits associated with education. The social perspective includes public subsidies and external benefits and considers before-tax earnings.

7. The demand for human capital curve and the supply of investment funds curve can be combined to explain why various people invest in different amounts of human capital. Ability differences, discrimination, and varying access to financial resources all help explain differences in education and earnings among individuals.

8. The money market may provide funds for human capital investment on less favorable terms than for investment in physical capital, providing some justification for public subsidization of human capital investments.

9. It is useful to distinguish between general and specific on-the-job training. General training generates worker skills that are useful in all firms and industries. Specific training is useful only in the specific firm providing that training. Given competitive markets, workers will normally pay for general training provided by a firm by accepting lower wages during the training period. An exception may occur where firms must pay a legal minimum wage. Employers pay for specific training. Seeking to retain

---

[54] For excellent elaborations of the criticisms of human capital theory, see Bobbie McCrackin, "Education's Contribution to Productivity and Economic Growth," *Economic Review* (Federal Reserve Bank of Atlanta), November 1984, pp. 8–23; and Gian Singh Sahota, "Theories of Personal Income Distribution: A Survey," *Journal of Economic Literature,* March 1978, pp. 11–19.

trained workers, employers may share with workers the increases in total revenue resulting from specific training.

10. Criticisms of human capital theory include the following: *(a)* By failing to recognize that a part of education expenditures is consumption rather than investment, empirical studies understate the rate of return on education; *(b)* empirical studies understate the rate of return on a college education by not taking into account that the jobs of college graduates are more pleasant and entail better fringe benefits than the jobs of high school graduates; *(c)* to the extent that the incremental earnings of college graduates are due to their greater ability and not to schooling per se, the rate of return on a college education will be overstated; *(d)* if a portion of the incremental earnings of college graduates is attributable to screening, the social rate of return on a college education will be overstated.

Terms and Concepts

investment in human capital

age–earnings profiles

net present value

time preference

discount formula

internal rate of return

college wage premium

private perspectives

social perspectives

demand for human capital curve

supply of investment funds

capital market imperfections

on-the-job training

general versus specific training

marginal revenue product

ability problem

screening hypothesis

Questions and Study Suggestions

1. Why might the decision to undertake an educational program be treated as an investment? From a private perspective, what costs and benefits are associated with obtaining a college education? What are the costs and benefits from a social perspective? Explain why it is necessary to determine the present value of costs and benefits in making a rational human capital investment decision.

2. What is the internal rate of return on a human capital investment? Given the internal rate of return, what is the appropriate investment criterion? Compare this to the criterion relevant to the present value approach.

3. Floyd is now working in a job that pays $28,000 per year. He is contemplating a one-year automobile mechanics course that costs $1,000 for books and tuition. Floyd estimates that the course will increase his income to $33,000 in each of the three years following completion of the course. At the end of those three years, Floyd plans to retire to a commune in Boulder, Colorado. The current interest rate is 10 percent. Is it economically rational for Floyd to enroll in the course?

4. Comment on each of the following statements:

   a. Given the work-life cycle of the "traditional" woman, it may be rational for women to invest in less human capital than men.

   b. Older workers are less mobile geographically than younger workers.

   c. An economic recession tends to stimulate college enrollment.

d. One of the disadvantages of Social Security's benefit reduction rate (reducing benefits when earnings exceed a certain level during retirement years) is that it biases investment away from human capital and toward bonds and stocks.

e. The age–earnings profiles of Figure 4.1 clearly indicate that people with more education earn more than people with less education; therefore, personal spending on education is always a good investment.

5. What is the college wage premium? Can you explain why the premium *(a)* declined in the 1970s and *(b)* increased since the 1980s?

6. Assume that a recent high school graduate reads in a magazine that the rate of return on a college education has been estimated to be 15 percent. What advice would you give the graduate in using this information as he or she decides whether to attend college?

7. Why is the internal rate of return from human capital investment subject to diminishing returns? Explain the rationale for identifying the "diminishing rate of returns to education curve" as the "demand for human capital curve." Combine the demand for human capital curve with a "supply of investment funds curve" to explain why various individuals find it rational to invest in different amounts of human capital. What are the implications of your answer for the personal distribution of income? Do you think that the educational system in the United States contributes to more or less equality in the distribution of earnings? Explain. If you wanted to reduce inequality in the distribution of earnings, what policy recommendations would you make?

8. Why might funds be available on less favorable terms for human capital investments than for physical capital investments? In your judgment, does this difference justify public subsidy in the form, say, of federal guarantees of loans to college students? What are some external benefits associated with education? Do you feel that these benefits justify public subsidies to education? Can you provide a rationale for the argument that public subsidies should diminish as students advance to higher and higher educational levels?

9. Describe the expected effects that college scholarships based on *(a)* student ability and *(b)* student need are likely to have on the distribution of earnings.

10. Distinguish between general and specific on-the-job training. Who normally pays for general training? Specific training? Why the difference? Are there any exceptions to these generalizations? Explain.

11. As the following diagram indicates, the distribution of "ability" (here measured by IQ scores) is normal or bell-shaped, but the distribution of earnings is skewed to the right. Can you use human capital theory to reconcile these two distributions?

12. Data show that the age–earnings profiles of women are considerably lower and flatter than those for men. Can you explain these differences?

13. Indicate the implications of each of the following for estimates of the rate of return on a college education: *(a)* the screening hypothesis, *(b)* the possibility that a portion of one's expenditures on college should be considered as consumption rather than investment, *(c)* the fact that people who go to college are generally more able than those who do not, and *(d)* the fact that jobs acquired by college graduates generally entail larger fringe benefits than the jobs of high school graduates. What implications do the ability problem and the screening hypothesis have for public policy toward education?

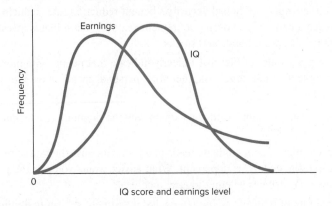

Internet Exercise

What Is a College Degree Worth?

Go to the Census Bureau website web page on educational attainment **(https://www.census.g ov/data/tables/time-series/demo/educational-attainment/cps-historical-time-series.html)** to find information about earnings of workers by education.

What were the annual earnings for high school and college graduates in 1975? For the most recent year shown? What was the ratio of the earnings of college graduates to high school graduates in 1975? In the most recent year? Has the ratio increased or decreased over this period? What factors might help explain this change?

Internet Links

The National Center for Education Statistics website has extensive statistics on primary, secondary, and college education in the United States (**http://nces.ed.gov**). The U.S. Department of Education website gives information regarding the U.S. education system (**www.ed.gov**).

Chapter 5

The Demand for Labor

After reading this chapter, you should be able to:

1. Explain the effects of the demand for labor being a derived demand.
2. Explain how a firm's short-run production function can be used to derive a demand curve for labor.
3. Contrast the labor demand curves of firms that operate in perfectly competitive versus imperfectly competitive output markets.
4. Discusses the differences between short-run and long-run labor demand.
5. Derive the market demand curve for labor from individual firm demands and explain why it is more inelastic than the simple summation of the labor demand curves of all firms in the market.
6. Identify and discuss the determinants of the elasticity of labor demand.
7. Identify and explain the determinants of the demand for labor.
8. Relate the concepts of labor demand to real-world applications.

The previous three chapters have examined the supply of labor. In the present chapter, our attention shifts to the demand side of the labor market. Why do Merck, Microsoft, Micron, and Motorola wish to employ those willing to supply their particular labor services? How is Mattel's demand for labor affected by increases in the demand for the toys it produces? What factors alter Macy's and McDonald's demand for labor? Why might Marriott adjust its level of employment more than Merck when wage rates change for a particular type of labor?

Answers to these and related questions motivate our discussion of labor demand. Then, in Chapter 6, we will combine our understanding of labor demand and labor supply to explain how wage rates are determined.

DERIVED DEMAND FOR LABOR

We should note at the outset that the demand for labor, or for any other productive resource, is a *derived demand*. This means that the demand for labor depends on, or is derived from, the demand for the product or service it is helping to produce or provide. In manufacturing, labor is demanded for the contribution it makes to the production of such products as automobiles, television sets, or loaves of bread. Thus, a decrease in the demand for automobiles will reduce the demand for automobile workers. In the service sector, labor is demanded by firms because it directly provides benefits to consumers. An increase in the demand for child care services, for example, will increase the derived demand for child care workers.

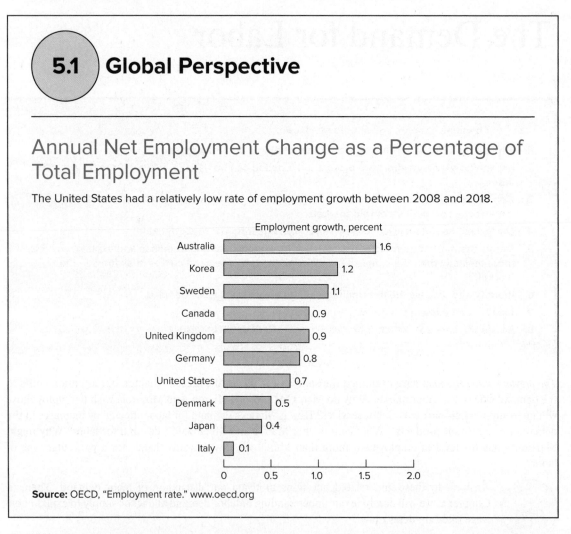

5.1 Global Perspective

Annual Net Employment Change as a Percentage of Total Employment

The United States had a relatively low rate of employment growth between 2008 and 2018.

Employment growth, percent

Australia	1.6
Korea	1.2
Sweden	1.1
Canada	0.9
United Kingdom	0.9
Germany	0.8
United States	0.7
Denmark	0.5
Japan	0.4
Italy	0.1

Source: OECD, "Employment rate." www.oecd.org

The fact that the demand for labor is a derived demand means that the strength of the demand for any particular type of labor will depend on (*a*) how productive that labor is in helping to create some product or service and (*b*) the market value of that item. If type A labor is highly productive in turning out product X, and if product X is highly valued by society, then a strong demand for type A labor will exist. Conversely, the demand will be weak for some kind of labor that is relatively unproductive in producing a good or service that is not of great value to society.

These observations point the way for our discussion. We will find that the immediate determinants of the demand for labor are labor's marginal productivity and the value (price) of its output. Let's begin by examining the short-run production function for a typical firm and then introduce the role of product price. Although our discussion will be cast in terms of a firm producing a particular good, the concepts developed apply equally to firms hiring workers to produce services.

A FIRM'S SHORT-RUN PRODUCTION FUNCTION

A *production function* is a relationship between quantities of resources (inputs) and the corresponding production outcomes (output). We will assume that the production process entails just two inputs—labor L and capital K. To simplify further, let's suppose that a single type of labor is being employed or, in other words, that the firm is hiring homogeneous inputs of labor. Furthermore, initially, we examine the firm as it operates in the short run, *a period in which at least one resource is fixed*. In this case, the fixed resource is the firm's stock of capital—its plant, machinery, and other equipment. As shown in Equation (5.1),

$$\text{TP}_{SR} = f\left(L, \overline{K}\right) \quad (5.1)$$

the firm's total product in the short run (TP_{SR}) is a function of a variable input L (labor) and a fixed input K (capital).

Total, Marginal, and Average Product

What happens to the *total product (TP)* (output) as successive inputs of labor are added to a fixed plant? The answer is provided in Figure 5.1, where the upper graph (a) shows a short-run production function or TP curve and the lower graph (b) displays the corresponding curves for the marginal product (MP) of labor and the average product (AP) of labor.

In the short run, the total product (TP) shown in (a) is *the total output produced by each combination of the variable resource (labor) and the fixed amount of capital*. The *marginal product* (MP) of labor is *the change in TP associated with the addition of one more unit of labor*. It is the absolute change in TP and can be found by drawing a line tangent to the TP curve at any point and then determining the slope of that line. For example, notice line *mm'*, which is drawn tangent to point Z on the TP curve. The slope of *mm'* is zero, and this is the MP as shown at point z on the MP curve in the lower graph. The *average product* (AP) of labor is *the TP divided by the number of labor units*. Geometrically, it is measured as the slope of any straight line drawn from the origin to or through any particular point on the TP curve. For example, observe line $0a$, which radiates from the origin through point Y on TP. The slope ($\Delta \text{TP}/\Delta L$) of $0a$ tells us the AP associated with this particular combination of TP and labor input L. For example, if TP were 20 at point Y, and L were 4, then AP would be 5 ($= 20/4$). This is the value of the slope of line $0a$, which as measured from the origin is the *vertical* rise ($= 20$) divided by the *horizontal* run ($= 4$). If we assume that labor units are labor hours, rather than workers, then this slope measures output per worker hour.

Stages of Production

The relationships between TP, MP, and AP are important. To show these relationships *and* to permit us later to isolate the region in which the firm will operate if it decides to do so, we have divided the TP curve into three stages, but we have also subdivided stage I into two parts. Over segment $0X$ of the TP curve—or stated alternatively, within part IA of stage I—the TP curve is increasing at an *increasing* rate. As observed in the lower graph, this implies that MP($= \Delta TP/\Delta L$) necessarily is rising. For example, suppose the TPs associated with the first three workers were 3, 8, and 15, respectively. The corresponding MPs would be 3 (= 3 − 0), 5 (= 8 − 3), 5 (= 15 − 8), and 7 (= 15 − 8). Note, too, from the lower graph that because MP exceeds AP, the latter also is rising. This is a matter of arithmetic necessity: Whenever a number that is greater than the average of some total is added to that total, the average must rise. In the present context, MP is the addition to TP while AP is the average of TP. Hence, when MP exceeds AP, AP must rise.[1]

FIGURE 5.1   A Firm's Short-Run Production Function

As labor is added to a fixed amount of capital, TP will eventually increase by diminishing amounts, reach a maximum, and then decline as shown in (a). MPs in (b) reflect the changes in TP associated with each additional input of labor. The relationship between MP and AP is such that MP intersects AP where AP is at its maximum. The *yz* segment of the MP curve in stage II is the basis for the short-run labor demand curve.

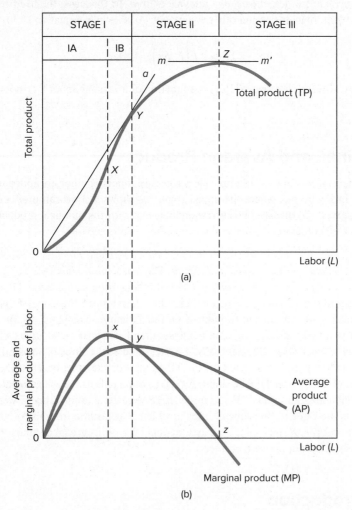

---

[1] You raise your cumulative grade point average by earning grades in the most recent (marginal) semester that are higher than your current average.

Next observe segment *XY*—or stage IB—of the production function in Figure 5.1(a). The TP curve is now such that TP is still increasing as more workers are hired, but at a *decreasing* rate, and therefore MP [graph (b)] is declining. Notice that MP reached its maximum at point *x* in the lower graph and that this point corresponds to point *X* on the production function. But beyond points *X* and *x*, MP falls. We see, however, that even though MP is now falling, it still is above AP, and hence AP continues to rise. Finally, observe that the end of range IB of stage I is marked by the point at which AP is at its maximum and just equals MP (point *y*). The fact that AP is at a maximum at point *Y* on the TP curve is confirmed by ray 0*a*. The slope of 0*a*—which, remember, measures AP—is greater than would be the slope of any other straight line drawn between the origin and a specific point on the TP curve.

In stage II, later referred to as the *zone of production,* TP continues to rise at a diminishing rate. Consequently, MP continues to decline. But now AP also falls because MP finally is less than AP. Again, simple arithmetic tells us that when a number (MP) that is less than the current average of a total is added to that total (TP), the average (AP) must fall.

At the dividing line between stages II and III, TP reaches its maximum point *Z* and MP becomes zero (point *z*), indicating that beyond this point additional workers detract from TP. In stage III, TP falls and MP is therefore negative, the latter causing AP to continue to decline.

Law of Diminishing Marginal Returns

Why do TP, MP, and AP behave in the manner shown in Figure 5.1? Let's focus on marginal product, keeping in mind that changes in MP are related to changes in TP and AP. Why does MP rise, then fall, and eventually become negative? It is *not* because the quality of labor declines as more of it is hired; remember that all workers are assumed to be identical. Rather, the reason is that the fixed capital at first gets used increasingly productively as more workers are employed but eventually becomes more and more burdened. Imagine a firm that possesses a fixed amount of machinery and equipment. As this firm hires its initial workers, each worker will contribute more to output than the previous worker because the firm will be better able to use its machinery and equipment. Time will be saved because each worker can specialize in a task and will no longer have to scramble from one job operation to another. Successively greater increases in output will occur because the new workers will permit capital equipment to be used more intensively during the day. Thus, for a time the added, or marginal, product of extra workers will rise.

These increases in MP cannot be realized indefinitely. As still more labor is added to the fixed machinery and equipment, the *law of diminishing marginal returns* will take hold. This law states that *as successive units of a variable resource (labor) are added to a fixed resource (capital), beyond some point the MP attributable to each additional unit of the variable resource will decline.* At some point, labor will become so abundant relative to the fixed capital that additional workers cannot add as much to output as did previous workers. For example, an added worker may have to wait in line to use the machines. At the extreme, the continuous addition of labor will so overcrowd the plant that the MP of still more labor will become negative, reducing TP (stage III).

Zone of Production

The characteristics of TP, MP, and AP discussed in Figure 5.1 are summarized in Table 5.1. In reviewing this table, notice that stage II of the production function is designated as the *zone of production*. To see why, let's establish that the left boundary of stage II in Figure 5.1 is where the efficiency of labor—as measured by its AP—is at a maximum. Similarly, the right boundary is where the efficiency of the fixed resource capital is maximized. Notice first that at point *Y* on TP and *y* on AP and MP, total product *per unit of labor* is at its maximum. This is shown both by ray 0*a*, which is the steepest line that can be drawn from the origin to any point on TP, and by the AP curve, because AP *is* TP/*L*. Next, note that at point *Z* on TP and *z* on MP, TP is at a maximum. Because capital (*K*) is fixed, this implies that the AP of *K* is also at a maximum. That is, TP *per unit of capital* is greater at the right boundary of stage II than at any other point. The generalization here is that if a firm chooses to operate, *it will want to produce at a level of output where changes in labor contribute to increasing efficiency of either labor or capital.*[2]

TABLE 5.1 Production Function Variables: A Summary

			Total Product, TP_L	Marginal Product, MP_L	Average Product, AP_L
	Stage I	IA	Increasing at an increasing rate	Increasing and greater than AP	Increasing
		IB	Increasing at a decreasing rate	Declining but greater than AP	Increasing
Zone of Production	Stage II		Increasing at a decreasing rate	Declining and less than AP	Declining
	Stage III		Declining	Negative and less than AP	Declining

This is *not* the case in either stage I or III. In stage I, additions to labor *increase* both the efficiency of labor *and* the efficiency of capital. The former can easily be seen by the rising AP curve; the latter is true because capital is constant and TP is rising, thereby increasing the AP of capital (= *TP*/*K*). The firm, therefore, will desire to move at least to the left boundary of stage II.

What about stage III? Inspection of Figure 5.1(a) and (b) shows that the addition of labor *reduces* the efficiency of *both* labor and capital. Notice that the AP of labor is falling. Also, because there is less TP than before, the TP/*K* ratio is declining. Stated differently, the firm will not operate in stage III because it can *add* to the efficiency of labor and capital and to its TP by *reducing* employment.

Conclusion? The profit-maximizing or loss-minimizing firm that chooses to operate will face an MP curve indicated by line segment *yz* in Figure 5.1(b). *This MP curve is the underlying basis for the firm's short-run demand for labor curve.*

SHORT-RUN DEMAND FOR LABOR: THE PERFECTLY COMPETITIVE SELLER

To see how segment *yz* in Figure 5.1(b) relates to labor demand, let's next (*a*) transform the TP and MP information in that figure to hypothetical numbers via a table and (*b*) convert our analysis from output to monetary terms. Employers, after all, decide how many workers to hire in terms of *revenues* and *costs* rather than in output terms.

---

[2] This generalization applies only to a competitive firm. For an imperfectly competitive firm such as a monopoly, *only* stage III is necessarily a non-profit-maximizing area. In maximizing profits, a monopolist may restrict output and therefore employment to some point in stage I.

Consider Table 5.2. Columns 1–3 are merely numerical illustrations of the relationships within the zone of production, showing TP and MP but omitting AP. To simplify, we have identified only the range of labor inputs over which diminishing marginal productivity sets in. Recalling our earlier discussion of the demand for labor as a derived demand, note that column 4 shows the price of the product that is being produced. The fact that this $2 price does not decline as more output is produced and sold indicates that the firm is selling its output in a perfectly competitive market. In technical terms, the firm's *product* demand curve is perfectly elastic; the firm is a "price taker." For example, this firm may be selling standardized products such as grain or fresh fish.

TABLE 5.2 **Demand for Labor: Firm Selling in a Perfectly Competitive Product Market (Hypothetical Data)**

(1)Units of Labor, L	(2)TP	(3)MP	(4)Product Price, P	(5)Total Revenue, TR	(6)MRP ($\Delta TR/\Delta L$)	(7)VMP (MP × P)
4	15		$2	$30		
5	27	12	2	54	$24	$24
6	36	9	2	72	18	18
7	42	6	2	84	12	12
8	45	3	2	90	6	6
9	46	1	2	92	2	2

Multiplying column 2 by column 4, we obtain total revenue (sometimes called *total revenue product*) in column 5. From these total revenue data, we can easily compute *marginal revenue product* (MRP), which is *the increase (change) in total revenue resulting from the employment of each additional labor unit*. These figures are shown in column 6. The MRP schedule shown by columns 1 and 6 is strictly proportional to the MP schedule, shown by columns 1 and 3. In this case, MRP is *twice* as large as MP because price is $2.

Columns 1 and 6–the MRP schedule–constitute the firm's *short-run labor demand curve*. To justify and explain this assertion, we must first understand the rule that a profit-maximizing firm will apply in determining the number of workers to employ. *A profit-maximizing employer should hire workers so long as each successive worker adds more to the firm's total revenue than to its total cost*. We have just noted that the amount that each successive unit of labor adds to total revenue is measured by MRP. The amount that a worker adds to total costs is measured by *marginal wage cost* (MWC), defined as *the change in total wage cost resulting from the employment of one more labor unit*. Thus, we can abbreviate our rule by saying that the profit-maximizing firm should hire units of labor up to the point at which MRP = MWC.[3] If at some level of employment MRP exceeds MWC, it will be profitable to employ more labor. If for some level of employment MWC exceeds MRP, the firm will increase its profits by hiring less labor.

Let's now assume that the employer for whom Table 5.2 is relevant is hiring labor under purely competitive conditions. This means the firm is a "wage taker" in that it employs a negligible portion of the total labor supply and therefore exerts no perceptible influence on the wage rate. Perhaps this is a fish-processing firm that is hiring people to clean fish. The market wage rate is "given" to the employer, and it follows that the total wage cost (the wage bill) increases by the amount of the wage rate W for each additional unit of labor hired. In other words, the wage rate and the MWC are equal. We can thus modify our MRP = MWC rule for the

---

[3] The rationale for this rule is the same as that for the marginal revenue equals marginal cost (MR = MC) rule, which identifies the profit-maximizing output in the product market. The difference is that the MRP = MWC rule is in terms of *inputs* of labor, whereas the MR = MC rule is in terms of *outputs* of product.

firm hiring competitively and restate it as the MRP = *W* rule. The profit-maximizing firm that is a perfectly competitive employer of labor should employ units of labor up to the point at which MRP equals the wage rate *W*.

We now can apply the MRP = *W* rule to demonstrate our earlier assertion: The MRP schedule shown in columns 1 and 6, derived directly from the MRP data from the zone of production, *is* the firm's short-run labor demand curve. The MRP data from columns 1 and 6 are graphed in Figure 5.2 to demonstrate this point. This schedule and curve indicate the amount of labor this firm would demand at several separate competitively determined wage rates. First let's suppose that the wage rate is $23.99, an amount infinitesimally less than $24. This firm will decide to employ five units of labor because it either adds to profits or subtracts from losses by hiring these units of labor. But the firm will not employ the sixth, seventh, and further units because MRP < *W* for each of them.

Next, suppose that the wage rate falls to $11.99. The MRP = *W* rule indicates that the firm will now also hire the sixth and seventh units of labor. If the wage rate falls further to, say, $1.99, it will employ nine units of labor. We conclude then that *the MRP curve in Figure 5.2 is the firm's short-run labor demand curve* because each point on it indicates the quantity of labor that a firm will demand at each possible wage rate. Any curve that embodies this information on wage rate and quantity of labor demanded is, by definition, the firm's labor demand curve.

One further point needs to be made: Where there is perfect competition in the product market, a firm's MRP or labor demand curve is also the *value of marginal product* (VMP) curve. *The VMP is the extra output in dollar terms that accrues to society when an extra unit of labor is employed.* Columns 1 and 7 in Table 5.2 show the VMP schedule in our example. Notice that VMP is determined by multiplying MP (column 3) by the product price (column 4). We observe in this case that VMP, the value of the marginal product, is identical to MRP, the extra revenue accruing to the firm when it adds a unit of labor (column 6). For this reason, we label the demand for labor curve in Figure 5.2 as VMP, as well as MRP.

FIGURE 5.2 The Labor Demand Curve of a Perfectly Competitive Seller

Application of the MRP = *W* rule reveals that the MRP curve is the firm's short-run labor demand curve. Under perfect competition in the product market, MRP = VMP (value of MP) and the labor demand curve slopes downward solely because of diminishing marginal productivity.

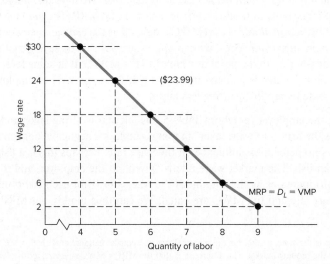

What is the logic underlying the equality of VMP and MRP when perfect competition prevails in the product market? Because the competitive firm is a price taker, it can sell as many units of output as it desires at the market price (= $2). The sale of *each* additional unit of the product adds the product price (= $2) to the firm's total revenue; therefore, the seller's *marginal revenue* (MR) is constant and is equal to the product price. In this situation, the extra *revenue* to the firm from employing an additional labor unit (= MR × MP) equals the social *value* of the extra output (= P × MP) contributed by that unit of labor.

SHORT-RUN DEMAND FOR LABOR: THE IMPERFECTLY COMPETITIVE SELLER

Most firms in our economy do *not* sell their products in purely competitive markets; rather, they sell under imperfectly competitive conditions. That is, the firms are monopolies, oligopolies, or monopolistically competitive sellers. When a firm can set its price—rather than being forced to accept a market-determined price—it has some monopoly power.

The change in assumptions about product market conditions from pure competition to imperfect competition alters our analysis in an important way. Because of product uniqueness or differentiation, the imperfectly competitive seller's product demand curve is downward-sloping rather than perfectly elastic. This means the firm must lower its price to sell the output contributed by each successive worker. Furthermore, because we assume that the firm cannot engage in price discrimination, it must lower the price not only on the last unit produced but also on all other units, which otherwise would have commanded a higher price. The sale of an extra unit of output, therefore, does *not* add its full price to the firm's MR, as it does in perfect competition. To obtain the MR for the imperfectly competitive seller, one must subtract the potential revenue lost on the other units from the new revenue gained from the last unit. Because MR is less than the product price, the imperfectly competitive seller's MRP (= MR × MP) is less than that of the perfectly competitive seller (= P × MP). Recall that the perfectly competitive firm suffers no decline in MR as it sells the extra output of added workers.

Thus, the MRP or labor demand curve of the purely competitive seller falls for a *single* reason—MP diminishes as more units of labor are employed. But the MRP or labor demand curve of the imperfectly competitive seller declines for *two* reasons—MP falls as more units of labor are employed *and* product price declines as output increases. Table 5.3 takes this second consideration into account. The production data of columns 1 to 3 are precisely the same as in Table 5.2, but in column 4, we recognize that product price must drop to sell the MP of each successive worker.

TABLE 5.3 Demand for Labor: Firm Selling in an Imperfectly Competitive Product Market (Hypothetical Data)

(1)Units of Labor, L	(2)TP	(3)MP	(4)Product Price, P	(5)Total Revenue, TR	(6)MRP ($\Delta TR / \Delta L$)	(7)VMP (MP × P)
4	15		$2.60	$39.00		
5	27	12	2.40	64.80	$25.80	$28.80
6	36	9	2.20	79.20	14.40	19.80
7	42	6	2.10	88.20	9.00	12.60
8	45	3	2.00	90.00	1.80	6.00
9	46	1	1.90	87.40	−2.60	1.90

It is worth reemphasizing that the lower price accompanying each increase in output applies not only to the output produced by each additional worker but also to all prior units that otherwise could have been sold at a higher price. For example, the fifth worker's MP is 12 units, and these 12 units can be sold for $2.40 each or, as a group, for $28.80. This is the VMP of labor—that is, the value of the added output from society's perspective (column 7). But the MRP of the fifth worker is only $25.80. Why the $3.00 difference? To sell the 12 units associated with the fifth worker, the firm must accept a $0.20 price cut on *each* of the 15 units produced by the previous workers—units that could have been sold for $2.60 each. Thus, the MRP of the fifth worker is only $25.80 [= $28.80 − (15 × $0.20)]. Similarly, the sixth worker's MRP is only $14.40. Although the 9 units produced are worth $2.20 each in the market and therefore their VMP is $19.80, the worker does *not* add $19.80 to the firm's total revenue when account is taken of the $0.20 price cut on the 27 units produced by the previous workers. Specifically, the sixth worker's MRP is $14.40 [= $19.80 − (27 × $0.20)]. The other MRP figures in column 6 of Table 5.3 are similarly explained. Comparison of columns 6 and 7 reveals that at each level of employment, VMP (the value of the extra product to buyers) exceeds MRP (the extra revenue to the firm). The efficiency implications of this difference will be examined in Chapter 6.

As in the case of the purely competitive seller, application of the MRP = W rule to the MRP curve will yield the conclusion that the MRP curve *is* the firm's labor demand curve. However, by plotting the imperfectly competitive seller's MRP or labor demand curve D_L in Figure 5.3 and comparing it with the demand curve in Figure 5.2, we find visual support for an important generalization: *All else being equal, the imperfectly competitive seller's labor demand curve is less elastic than that of the purely competitive seller.* It is not surprising that a firm that possesses monopoly power is less responsive to wage rate changes than a purely competitive seller. The tendency for the imperfectly competitive seller to add fewer workers as the wage rate declines is merely the labor market reflection of the firm's restriction of output in the product market. Other things being equal, the seller possessing monopoly power will find it profitable to produce less output than it would in a purely competitive industry. In producing this smaller output, the seller with monopoly power will employ fewer workers.

5.1 *Quick Review*

- The demand for labor is derived from the demand for the product or service that it helps produce.

- As labor is added to a fixed amount of capital, the TP of labor first increases at an increasing rate, then increases at a diminishing rate, and then declines; this implies that the MP of labor first rises, then falls, and finally becomes negative.

- Because a perfectly competitive firm will hire employees up to where WR = MRP, the MRP curve is the firm's labor demand curve.

- The labor demand curve for an imperfectly competitive seller will not be as strong as for a perfectly competitive seller because the former must lower its product price on all units of output as more output is produced (MR < P).

Your Turn

Assume labor is the only variable input and that an additional unit of labor increases total output from 65 to 73 units. If the product sells for $4 per unit in a perfectly competitive market, what is the MRP of this additional worker? Would the MRP be higher or lower than this amount if the firm were a monopolist and had to lower its price to sell all 73 units? (*Answer:* See page 540.)

Finally, notice that the VMP schedule that is also plotted in Figure 5.3 lies to the right of the firm's $D_L =$ MRP curve. This visually depicts our previous conclusion: The MR accruing to an imperfectly competitive seller from hiring an additional unit of labor is less than the market value of the extra output the unit of labor helps produce [(MRP = MR × MP) < (VMP = $P × MP$)].

THE LONG-RUN DEMAND FOR LABOR[4]

Thus far, we have derived and discussed the firm's short-run production function [Equation (5.1)] and demand for labor, which presuppose that labor is a variable input and that the amount of capital is fixed. We now turn to the long-run production relationship shown in Equation (5.2), where we find that *both* labor and capital are variable. Once again, we assume that L and K are the only two inputs and that labor is homogeneous.

$$TP_{LR} = f(L, K) \quad (5.2)$$

The *long-run demand for labor* is *a schedule or curve indicating the amount of labor that firms will employ at each possible wage rate when both labor and capital are variable.* The long-run labor demand curve declines because

FIGURE 5.3 The Labor Demand for an Imperfectly Competitive Seller

Under imperfect competition in the product market, the firm's demand curve will slope downward because MP diminishes as more units of labor are employed *and* because the firm must reduce the product price on all units of output as more output is produced. Also, the *MRP* (= *MR* × *MP*) for the imperfect competitor is less than the VMP (= *P* × MP) at all levels of employment beyond the first unit.

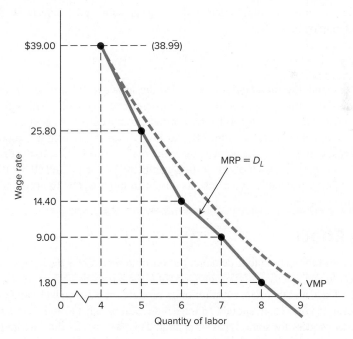

---

[4] We provide a more advanced derivation of the long-run demand for labor curve in the appendix of this chapter. There, and in the discussion that follows, we ignore the long-run "profit-maximizing effect" of a wage rate change. For simplicity, we focus on the short-run output effect and the long-run substitution effect.

FIGURE 5.4   **The Output Effect of a Wage Rate Decline**

All else being equal, a decline in the wage rate will reduce marginal cost (from MC_1 to MC_2) and increase the profit-maximizing level (MR = MC) of output (from Q_1 to Q_2). To produce the extra output, the firm will wish to employ more labor.

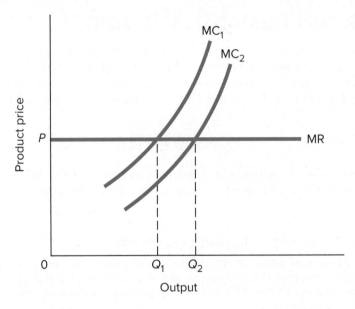

a wage change produces a short-run output effect and a long-run substitution effect, which together alter the firm's optimal level of employment.

Output Effect

As it relates to labor demand, the *output effect* (also called the *scale effect*) is *the change in employment resulting solely from the effect of a wage change on the employer's costs of production*. This effect is present in the short run and is demonstrated in Figure 5.4. Under normal circumstances, a decline in the wage rate shifts a firm's marginal cost curve downward, as from MC_1 to MC_2. That is, the firm can produce any additional unit of output at less cost than before. The reduced marginal cost (MC_2) relative to the firm's MR means that MR now exceeds marginal costs for each of the Q_1 to Q_2 units. Adhering to the MR = MC profit-maximizing rule, the firm will now find it profitable to increase its output from Q_1 to Q_2. To accomplish this, it will wish to expand its employment of labor.

Substitution Effect

WW5.1

As it relates to long-run labor demand, the *substitution effect* is *the change in employment resulting solely from a change in the relative price of labor, output being held constant*. In the short run, capital is fixed, and therefore substitution in production between labor and capital *cannot* occur. In the long run, however, the firm can respond to a wage reduction by substituting the relatively less expensive labor in the production process for some types of capital. This fact means that the long-run response to a wage change will be greater than the short-run response. In other words, the long-run demand for labor will be more elastic than the short-run demand curve.

5.1 World of Work

Has Health Care Reform Increased Involuntary Part-Time Work?[*]

When enacted in 2010, the Patient Protection and Affordable Care Act (PPACA) required that firms with 50 or more employees provide health insurance for their full-time workers or be subjected to penalties beginning in 2014. Although the implementation date was later delayed until 2015 or 2016 depending on firm size, there is evidence that employers were making adjustments to the costs associated with the PPACA as early as 2012.

One way firms can avoid the penalties contained in the PPACA is to provide health insurance to their full-time workers. However, providing health insurance coverage is costly and employers have an incentive to shift this cost to their employees by requiring worker contributions or reducing wages. These approaches are less effective for low-wage workers since the PPACA limits how much low-wage workers can be required to contribute to the cost of health insurance and the minimum wage may prevent firms to completely passing on the cost to workers through wage reductions. Thus, employers have an incentive to find an alternative method to avoid the insurance coverage requirement, particularly for low-wage employees. One such way to avoid the penalty and the cost of providing health coverage is to shift from full-time to part-time (<30 hours per week) workers. A failure to provide part-time workers with coverage does not result in a penalty.

Even and Macpherson examine the impact of the PPACA on the share of workers who are involuntarily part-time. They define affected workers as those who worked 30 or more hours per week without employer-provided health insurance at a firm with 100 or more workers. They report that as the share of those affected by the PPACA increased in an occupation, the share of workers who are part-time as well as involuntary part-time also rose after 2010. Their estimates indicate that in 2015 about 700,000 additional workers without a college degree were involuntarily employed part-time instead of full-time as a result of the PPACA. Nearly one-third of involuntary part-time employment in 2015 among workers without a college degree was due to the PPACA mandate.

* William E. Even and David A. Macpherson, "The Affordable Care Act and the Growth of Involuntary Part-Time Employment," *Industrial and Labor Relations Review*, August 2019, pp. 955–980.

The Combined Effects

In Figure 5.5, we use these ideas to depict a long-run labor demand curve D_{LR}. Initially, suppose that the firm faces the short-run labor demand curve D_{SR} and also that the initial equilibrium wage rate and equilibrium quantity of labor are W_1 and Q as shown by point a. Now suppose that the wage rate declines from W_1 to W_2, resulting in an *output effect* that increases employment to Q_1 at b. In the long run, however, capital is variable, and therefore, a *substitution effect* also occurs that further increases the quantity of labor employed to Q_2 at point c. Although the short-run adjustment is from a to b, the additional long-run adjustment is from b to c. The locus of the long-run adjustment points a and c determines the location of the *long-run* demand for labor curve. As observed in Figure 5.5, the long-run curve D_{LR} is more elastic than the short-run labor demand curve.

FIGURE 5.5 The Long-Run Labor Demand Curve

A wage reduction from W_1 to W_2 increases the equilibrium short-run quantity of labor from Q to Q_1 *(output effect)*. In the long run, however, the firm also substitutes labor for capital, resulting in a *substitution effect* of $Q_1 Q_2$. The long-run labor demand curve, therefore, results from both effects and is found by connecting points such as *a* and *c*.

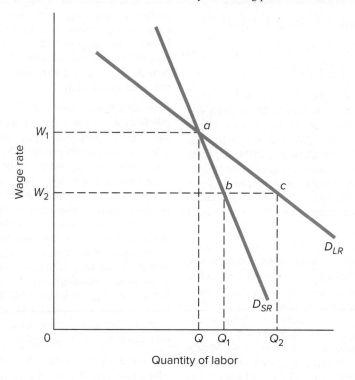

Other Factors

Several other factors tend to make a firm's long-run labor demand curve more elastic than its short-run curve. Three such factors in particular deserve mention.

1 Product Demand

As we will explain shortly in our discussion of the determinants of the elasticity of labor demand, *product demand* is more elastic in the long run than in the short run, making the demand for labor more elastic over longer periods. Other things being equal, the greater the consumer response to a product price change, the greater the firm's employment response to a wage rate change.

2 Labor–Capital Interactions

Under production conditions described as "normal," a change in the quantity of one factor causes the MP of another factor to change in the same direction. This idea relates to the demand for labor as follows. Let's again assume that the wage rate for a particular type of labor falls, causing the quantity of labor demanded in the short run to rise. This increase in the quantity of labor itself becomes important to the long-run adjustment process: It increases the MP and hence the MRP of capital. Just as the MRP of labor *is* the firm's short-run demand for labor, the MRP of capital *is* the firm's short-run demand for capital (labor being constant).

Given the price of capital, we would therefore expect more capital to be employed, which in turn will increase the MP and demand for labor. Thus, the long-run employment response resulting from the wage decrease will be greater than the short-run response.

3 Technology

In the long run, the technology implicitly assumed constant when we constructed our short-run production function can be expected to change in response to major, permanent movements in relative factor prices. Investors and entrepreneurs direct their greatest effort toward discovering and implementing new technologies that reduce the need for relatively higher priced inputs. When the price of labor falls relative to the price of capital, these efforts get channeled toward technologies that economize on the use of capital and that increase the use of labor. The long-run response to the wage rate decline, therefore, exceeds the short-run response.

WW5.2   Here's an important point: We have cast our entire discussion of the downward-sloping long-run labor demand curve in terms of a wage *decline*. You are urged to reinforce the conclusion that labor demand is more elastic in the long run than in the short run by analyzing the short-versus long-run effects of an *increase* in the wage rate.

THE MARKET DEMAND FOR LABOR

We have now demonstrated that the MRP curve derives from the MP curve in the firm's zone of production and *is* the firm's short-run demand curve for labor. We also have established that a firm's long-run demand for labor is more elastic than its short-run demand. Let's next turn our attention to the market demand for labor. At first thought, we might reason that the total or *market demand for labor* of a particular type can be determined by simply summing (horizontally on a graph) the labor demand curves of all firms that employ this kind of labor. Thus if there were, say, 200 firms with labor demand curves identical to the firm portrayed in Table 5.2, we would simply multiply the amounts of labor demanded at the various wage rates by 200 and thereby determine the market demand curve. However, this simple process ignores an important aggregation problem. The problem arises because certain magnitudes (such as product price), which are correctly viewed as constant from the vantage point of the *individual firm*, must be treated as variable from the standpoint of the *entire market*.

To illustrate, let's suppose there are, say, 200 competitive firms, each with a labor demand curve identical to that shown earlier in Figure 5.2. Assume also that these firms are all producing a given product that they are selling in competition with one another. From the perspective of the *individual firm*, when the wage rate declines, the use of more labor will result in a *negligible* increase in the market supply of the product and, therefore, no change in product price. But because *all firms* experience the lower wage rate and respond by hiring more workers and increasing their outputs, there will be a *substantial* increase in the supply of the product. This change in supply will reduce the product price. This point is critical because, as we showed earlier in Table 5.2, product price is a determinant of each firm's labor demand curve. Specifically, a lower product price will reduce MRP and shift the labor demand curve of each firm to the left. This implies that the market demand for labor is in fact *less elastic* than that yielded by a simple summation of each firm's labor demand curve.[5]

---

[5] If *all* employers are monopolists in their distinct product markets, our conclusion does not hold. As pointed out in the discussion of Figure 5.3, the monopolist's labor demand curve already incorporates the declines in product price that accompany output increases. Thus to get the market labor demand curve, one can sum the labor demand curves of the monopolists.

5.2 World of Work

Why Has Manufacturing Employment Fallen?

Recently there has been increasing concern about the dramatic drop in U.S. manufacturing employment. In 2018, 8 percent of workers were employed in manufacturing, down from 31 percent in 1950. The number of manufacturing workers declined from 18.7 million in 1980 to 12.7 million in 2018.

There are five reasons for the decrease in manufacturing employment. First, consumer spending, in the United States as well as other industrialized countries, has shifted away from manufactured goods. In 2018, 31 percent of U.S. consumer spending was on goods. The corresponding figures for 1979 and 1950 were 53 percent and 67 percent. The likely reasons behind this shift are the rise in real wages and labor force participation of married women, which caused households to substitute purchased services for tasks previously done at home.

Second, U.S. manufacturing firms have been investing in more and higher quality capital equipment to be competitive in global markets. This investment has permitted them to increase their output while using fewer workers. Since 1987, the productivity of manufacturing workers has been rising at an annual rate of 2.6 percent, which is greater than the 1.9 percent annual increase for overall nonfarm labor productivity.

Third, the expansion of international trade has changed the mix of goods produced in the United States. Gains from trade occur when countries specialize in goods they can produce more efficiently relative to other nations. The United States has specialized in goods that are produced using relatively more capital and skilled workers than other countries. As a result, employment has fallen in industries, such as apparel, that are labor-intensive and use less skilled workers.

Fourth, U.S. trade policy changed in 2001 so that tariffs on Chinese imports were permanently, rather than temporarily, set at a low level. This change encouraged U.S. firms to shift operations to China or work with a Chinese exporter. Also, it encouraged Chinese firms to invest in entering or expanding into the U.S. market. U.S. manufacturing industries more exposed to Chinese competition experienced a greater employment loss.

Finally, U.S. manufacturers have increasingly used workers from temporary help agencies to handle short-term fluctuations in demand rather than hire permanent workers. These temporary workers are counted as service workers, not manufacturing workers. Also, manufacturing firms have hired service companies to provide support functions such as janitorial and payroll processing.

Sources: Congressional Budget Office, "What Accounts for the Decline in Manufacturing Employment?" Economic and Budget Issue Brief, February 18, 2004; and Congressional Budget Office, "Factors Underlying the Decline in Manufacturing Employment Since 2000" Economic and Budget Issue Brief, December 23, 2008. Justin R. Pierce and Peter K. Schott, "The Surprisingly Swift Decline of U.S. Manufacturing Employment," *American Economic Review*, July 2016, pp. 1632–1662. Updated statistics from **http://www.bls.gov** and **http://www.bea.gov.**

Consider Figure 5.6, in which the diagram on the left (a) shows labor demand for one of the 200 firms and the diagram on the right (b) shows the market demand for labor. The individual firm is initially in equilibrium at point c, where the wage rate is W_1 and employment is Q_1. The labor demand curve D_{L1} is based on a product price of $2.00, as shown in column 4 of Table 5.2. If the wage rate falls to W_2, ceteris paribus (other things being equal), the firm would now find it profitable to move to a new equilibrium at e', where it would hire Q'_2, workers. But our ceteris paribus assumption does *not* hold in the context of a number of firms that are hiring this kind of labor to produce the same product. The lower wage induces *all* of the firms to hire more labor. This increases output or product supply, which then reduces product price. This lower price—say $1.60

FIGURE 5.6   The Market Demand Curve for Labor

The market demand curve for labor is less elastic than the simple horizontal summation of the labor demand curves of the individual employers. A lower wage induces all firms to hire more labor and produce more output, causing the supply of the product to increase. The resulting decline in product price shifts the firms' labor demand curves to the left. Consequently, total employment rises from C to E in graph (b), rather than from C to E'.

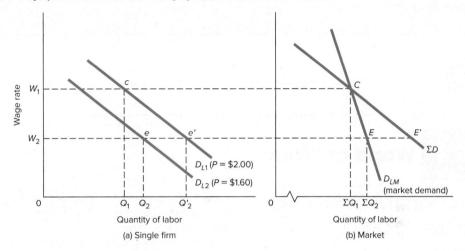

(a) Single firm

(b) Market

as compared to the original $2.00—feeds back to the labor demand curve for each firm, shifting those curves leftward as indicated by the move from D_{L1} to D_{L2} in Figure 5.6(a). In effect, each firm then recalculates its MRP or labor demand using the new lower price. Thus, each firm achieves equilibrium at point e by hiring only Q_2, as opposed to Q'_2, workers at the wage rate W_2. The market labor demand curve in Figure 5.6(b) is therefore *not* curve CE', the simple horizontal summation of the demand for labor curves for all 200 firms. Rather, it is the horizontal summation of all quantities, such as Q_1 at wage rate W_1 on D_{L1}, *and* the summation of all quantities, such as Q_2 at wage rate W_2, that fall on the "price-adjusted" market demand curve that cuts through points CE in Figure 5.6(b). As shown there, the correct price-adjusted market demand curve CE is less elastic than the incorrect "simple summation" CE' curve.

5.2 *Quick Review*

- The long-run demand curve for labor is more elastic than the short-run curve because in the long run there are both output and substitution effects; only an output effect occurs in the short run.

- The output effect of a wage rate change is the change in employment resulting from a change in the employer's costs of production; the substitution effect is the employment change caused by the altered price of labor relative to the price of capital.

- The market demand curve for labor is less elastic than the simple summation of the labor demand curves of individual employers; by inducing all firms to hire more labor and produce more output, the lower wage increases product supply, reduces product price, and lowers each firm's MRP.

Your Turn

In 2009, the United Automobile Workers reduced wage rates in the American auto industry. Referring to the output and substitution effects, explain how these lower wages might have contributed to the rebound in auto employment experienced by General Motors, Ford, and Chrysler since 2010. (*Answer:* See page 540–541.)

WW5.3

5.3   World of Work

Comparative Advantage and the Demand for Labor

As it applies to international trade, the principle of comparative advantage states that total output will be greatest when each good is produced by the nation with the lower opportunity cost. For example, suppose that in the United States 15 units of chemicals must be sacrificed to produce 1 unit of raincoats, whereas in South Korea 10 units of chemicals must be sacrificed for each unit of raincoats. The opportunity cost of a unit of raincoats in South Korea thus is lower (= 10 units of chemicals) than it is in the United States (= 15 units of chemicals). South Korea, therefore, should specialize in raincoats. Similarly, the United States should specialize in producing chemicals because it has lower opportunity costs (= 1/15 raincoat) than South Korea (= 1/10 raincoat). South Korea will specialize in raincoats and trade them for chemicals; the United States will specialize in chemicals and trade them for raincoats.

How will this specialization and trade affect labor demand in the United States and South Korea? Most obviously, the demand for workers employed in chemical production will rise in the United States, and the demand for workers who produce raincoats will fall. The opposite outcomes will occur in South Korea. Because international trade causes both positive and negative shifts in the demand for labor, the impact on the total demand for labor in each country is uncertain. It is clear, however, that specialization will increase the total output available in the two nations. Specialization promotes the expansion of relatively efficient industries that have a comparative advantage and indirectly causes the contraction of relatively inefficient industries. This means that specialization shifts resources—including labor—toward more productive uses. If the total number of workers remains constant in each nation, each worker on average will be able to buy more output. That is, either wages will rise or the prices of goods will fall so that real earnings (= nominal earnings/price level) will increase.

It is important to note that comparative advantage, not differences in wage rates between two nations, drives international trade. Low wage rates in South Korea do *not* give it a special international advantage. High American wage rates do *not* condemn the United States to be a net importer of goods. Even if low wages in South Korea would have permitted it to produce chemicals more cheaply in dollar terms than the United States, South Korea would still benefit by specializing in raincoats and buying chemicals from the United States. By so doing, South Korea could reduce its true costs of obtaining chemicals (raincoats forgone), just as trade permits the United States to get raincoats at a lower true cost (chemicals forgone) than if it had to use domestic resources for this purpose.

ELASTICITY OF LABOR DEMAND

We have concluded that the long-run demand curve is more elastic than the short-run curve and that the market demand for labor is less elastic than a curve derived by a simple summation of labor demand curves of individual firms. These references to elasticity raise an important unanswered question: What determines the *sensitivity* of employment to a change in the wage rate? That is, what determines the *elasticity of labor demand?* Let's examine this topic in more detail.

The Elasticity Coefficient

The sensitivity of the quantity of labor demanded to wage rate changes is measured by the *wage elasticity coefficient* E_d, as shown in Equation (5.3):

$$E_d = \frac{\text{percentage change in quantity of labor demanded}}{\text{percentage change in the wage rate}} \quad (5.3)$$

Because the wage rate and the quantity of labor demanded are inversely related, the elasticity coefficient will always be negative. By convention, the minus sign is taken as understood and therefore is ignored. Also, you should be aware that percentage calculations present a "reversibility" problem. For example, a wage rate increase from $5 to $10 is a *100 percent* increase, whereas a wage decrease from $10 to $5 is only a *50 percent* decline. Economists, therefore, use the *averages* of the two wages and the *averages* of the two quantities as the bases when computing wage elasticity coefficients. In terms of our previous example, a wage change from $10 to $5 and one from $5 to $10 are each considered to be 67 percent changes [= 5 / [($10 + $5) / 2]].

The equation that incorporates the averaging technique when computing wage elasticity is known as a *midpoints formula* and is shown as Equation (5.4):

$$E_d = \frac{\text{change in quantity}}{\text{sum of quantities} / 2} \div \frac{\text{change in wage}}{\text{sum of wages} / 2} \quad (5.4)$$

Demand is *elastic*–meaning that employers are quite responsive to a change in wage rates–if a given percentage change in the wage rate results in a larger percentage change in the quantity of labor demanded. In this case, the absolute value of the elasticity coefficient will be greater than 1. Conversely, demand is *inelastic* when a given percentage change in the wage rate causes a smaller percentage change in the amount of labor demanded. In this instance, E_d will be less than 1, indicating that employers are relatively insensitive to changes in wage rates. Finally, demand is *unit elastic*–meaning that the coefficient is 1–when a given percentage in the wage rate causes an equal percentage change in the amount of labor demanded.

The Total Wage Bill Rules

You may recall from basic economics that we can determine the price elasticity of demand for a product by observing what happens to total revenue when product price changes. Similar rules, called the *total wage bill rules,* are used to assess the wage elasticity of demand.

Consider Figure 5.7, which displays two separate labor demand curves D_{L1} and D_{L2}. Suppose initially that the wage rate is $8, at which the firm hires five units of labor. The *total wage bill,* defined as $W \times Q$, in this case is $40 (= $8 × 5). This amount also happens to be the *total wage income* as viewed by the five workers. Now let's suppose the wage rate rises to $12. This increase produces two opposing effects on the wage bill. The higher wage rate increases the wage bill, but the decrease in employment reduces it. With D_{L1}, the

FIGURE 5.7 The Total Wage Bill Rules

If a change in the wage rate causes the total wage bill ($W \times Q$) to change in the opposite direction, then labor demand is elastic. This is the case along the $8 to $12 segment of D_{L1}, where the total wage bill falls from $40 (= $8 × 5) to $24 (= $12 × 2) when the wage rate rises from $8 to $12. In the case of labor demand D_{L2}, however, this same wage increase causes the total wage bill to rise from $40 to $48 (= $12 × 4). This second situation supports the generalization that when demand is inelastic, the wage rate and the total wage bill change in the same direction.

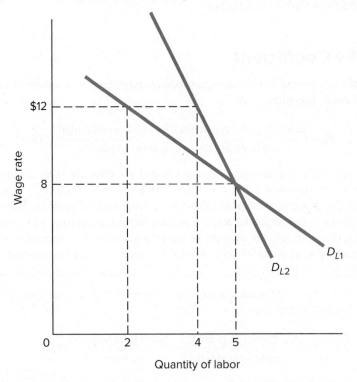

firm responds to the $4 higher wage rate by reducing the amount of labor employed from five to two units. The wage increase boosts the wage bill by $8 (= $4 × 2), while the decline in employment lowers it by $24 (= $8 × 3). The net effect is that the wage bill falls by $16 from $40 (= $8 × 5) to $24 (= $12 × 2). *When labor demand is elastic, a change in the wage rate causes the total wage bill to move in the opposite direction.*

On the other hand, notice that for labor demand D_{L2}, the $4 higher wage adds more to the wage bill ($4 × 4 = $16) than the one-unit decline in employment subtracts ($8 × 1 = $8), causing the total wage bill to rise from $40 (= $8 × 5) to $48 (= $12 × 4). *When labor demand is inelastic, a change in the wage rate causes the total wage bill to move in the same direction.* Finally, *where labor demand is unit elastic (= 1), a change in the wage rate leaves the total wage bill unchanged.*

We can confirm the results of the total wage bill tests by using the midpoints formula [Equation (5.4)] to compute elasticity coefficients for the appropriate segments of D_{L1} and D_{L2} in Figure 5.7. The $8 to $12 wage change is a 40 percent increase [= $4 / [($8 + $12) / 2]], whereas we see from D_{L1} that the three-unit change in quantity is an 86 percent decline [= 4 / [(5 + 2) / 2]]. Because the percentage decrease in quantity exceeds the percentage increase in the wage, labor demand is elastic (the wage bill falls as the wage increases). In the case of D_{L2}, the same 40 percent rise in the wage produces only a 22 percent employment decline [= 1 / [(5 + 4) / 2]]; hence, demand is inelastic (the wage bill increases as the wage rises).

Determinants of Elasticity

What determines the elasticity of the market demand for labor? The theoretical generalizations are as follows.[6]

1 Elasticity of Product Demand

Because the demand for labor is a derived demand, the elasticity of demand for labor's output will influence the elasticity of demand for labor. Other things being equal, *the greater the price elasticity of product demand, the greater the elasticity of labor demand.* It is simple to see why this is so. If the wage rate falls, the cost of producing the product will decline. This cuts the price of the product and increases the quantity demanded. If the elasticity of product demand is great, that increase in the quantity of the product demanded will be large and thus necessitate a large increase in the quantity of labor to produce that additional output. This implies an elastic demand for labor. But if the demand for the product is inelastic, the increase in the amount of the product demanded will be small, as will be the increase in the quantity of labor demanded. This suggests that the demand for labor would be inelastic.

This generalization has two noteworthy implications. First, other things being equal, the greater the monopoly power an individual firm possesses in the product market, the less elastic is its demand for labor. This is confirmed by Figures 5.2 and 5.3, discussed previously. Recall that in Figure 5.2, the firm is selling its product in a perfectly competitive market, implying that it is a price taker facing a perfectly elastic product demand curve. The resulting demand for labor curve slopes downward solely because of diminishing returns. Contrast that curve to the one for the imperfectly competitive seller shown in Figure 5.3. This firm's product demand curve is less elastic, as evidenced by MR being less than price (Table 5.3). Thus, the labor demand curve in Figure 5.3 also is less elastic; it slopes downward not only because of diminishing marginal productivity but also because of the less than perfectly elastic product demand, meaning that product price falls with increased output.

A second implication is that labor demand will be more elastic in the long run than in the short run. Wage elasticity tends to be greater in the long run because price elasticity of product demand is greater in the long run. Consumers are often creatures of habit and only slowly change their buying behavior in response to a price change. Coffee drinkers may not immediately reduce their consumption when the price of coffee rises; but given sufficient time, some may acquire a taste for tea. Another factor at work here is that some products are used mainly in conjunction with costly durable goods. For example, when the price of electricity rises, people who have electric furnaces and other appliances do not respond by greatly reducing their consumption of electricity. But as time transpires, the elasticity of the demand for electricity—*and the elasticity of the derived demand for workers in that industry*—becomes greater. People eventually replace their electric furnaces and water heaters with devices that use natural gas, solar energy, wood, or even coal.

2 Ratio of Labor Costs to Total Costs

In general, all other things being the same, *the larger the proportion of total production costs accounted for by labor, the greater will be the elasticity of demand for labor.*[7] The rationale here is straightforward. Compare these two cases. *Case one:* If labor costs were the only production cost—that is, if the ratio of labor to total

---

[6] These generalizations were developed in 1890 by Alfred Marshall in his *Principles of Economics* (London: Macmillan Publishing Company, 1890) and refined by John R. Hicks, *The Theory of Wages,* 2nd Edition (New York: St. Martin's Press, 1966), pp. 241–247. For this reason, they are often referred to as the "Hicks–Marshall rules of derived demand."

[7] *Technical note:* This proposition assumes that the product demand elasticity is greater than the elasticity of substitution between capital and labor, see Hicks, op. cit., pp. 241–247.

costs were 100 percent—then a 20 percent increase in the wage rate would increase unit costs by 20 percent. Given product demand, this large cost increase eventually would cause a considerable increase in product price, a sizable reduction in sales of output, and therefore a large decline in the employment of labor. *Case two:* If labor costs were only 10 percent of total cost, then the same 20 percent increase in the wage rate would increase total unit costs by only 2 percent. Assuming the same product demand as in case one, this relatively small cost increase will generate a more modest decline in employment. Case one implies a more elastic demand for labor than case two. The same 20 percent wage increase caused a larger percentage decline in employment in case one than in case two.

Service industries such as education, temporary workers, and building maintenance exemplify situations in which firms' labor costs are a large percentage of total costs. In these industries, wage increases translate into large cost increases, resulting in relatively elastic labor demand curves. Conversely, highly capital-intensive industries such as electricity generation and brewing are examples of markets in which labor costs are small relative to total costs. Labor demand curves in these industries are relatively inelastic.

3 Substitutability of Other Inputs

Other things being equal, *the greater the substitutability of other inputs for labor, the greater will be the elasticity of demand for labor.* If technology is such that capital is readily substitutable for labor, then a small increase in the wage rate will elicit a substantial increase in the amount of machinery used and a large decline in the amount of labor employed. Conversely, a small drop in the wage rate will induce a large substitution of labor for capital. The demand for labor will tend to be elastic in this case. In other instances, technology may dictate that a certain amount of labor is more or less indispensable to the production process; that is, the substitution of capital for labor is highly constrained. In the extreme, the production process may involve fixed proportions; for example, two airline pilots—no more and no fewer—may be required to fly a commercial airliner. In this case, a change in the wage rate will have little short-run effect on the number of pilots employed, and this implies an inelastic demand for labor.

It is worth noting that *time* plays an important role in the input substitution process, just as it does in the previously discussed process through which consumer goods are substituted for one another. The longer the period of elapsed time since a wage rate was changed, the more elastic are labor demand curves. For example, a firm's truck drivers may obtain a substantial wage increase with little or no immediate decline in employment. But over time, as the firm's trucks wear out and are replaced, the company may purchase larger trucks and thereby be able to deliver the same total output with significantly fewer drivers. Alternatively, as the firm's trucks depreciate, it might turn to entirely different means of transportation for delivery.

4 Supply Elasticity of Other Inputs

The fourth determinant of the elasticity of demand for labor is simply an extension of the third determinant. The generalization is that other things being equal, *the greater the elasticity of the supply of other inputs, the greater the elasticity of demand for labor.* In discussing our third generalization, we implicitly assumed that the prices of nonlabor inputs—such as capital—are unaffected by a change in the demand for them. But this may not be realistic.

To illustrate, assume once again that an increase in the wage rate prompts the firm to substitute capital for labor. This increase in the demand for capital will leave the price of capital unchanged only in the special case where the supply of capital is perfectly elastic. But let's suppose the supply of capital curve slopes upward, so that an increase in demand would increase its price. Furthermore, the less elastic the supply of capital, the greater the increase in the price of capital in response to any given increase in demand. Any resulting change in the price of capital is important because it will retard or dampen the substitution of capital for labor and reduce the elasticity of demand for labor. More specifically, if the supply of capital is inelastic, a given increase in the demand for capital will cause a large increase in the price of capital, greatly retarding the substitution process. This implies that the demand for labor will be inelastic. Conversely, if the supply of capital is highly elastic, the same increase in demand will cause only a small increase in the price of capital, dampening the substitution process only slightly. This suggests that the demand for labor will be elastic.

Estimates of Wage Elasticity

Hamermesh has summarized and compared more than 100 studies of labor demand and has concluded that the overall long-run labor demand elasticity in the United States is 1.0.[8] This coefficient implies a unitary elastic labor demand curve, which means that for every 10 percent change in the wage rate, employment changes in the opposite direction by 10 percent. Hamermesh concludes that about two-thirds of the long-run elasticity response takes the form of the output effect, with the other third consisting of the substitution effect. Other studies generally support Hamermesh's estimates, although problems of statistical design and incomplete data make research in this area difficult.

Studies also reveal that labor demand elasticities vary greatly by industry, type of labor, and occupational group. For example, Clark and Freeman estimate that the wage elasticity for all U.S. manufacturing is about 1.[9] Ashenfelter and Ehrenberg find that the wage elasticity in public education is 1.06.[10] Other studies show that the elasticity of labor demand is higher for teenagers than for adults, is greater for production workers than for nonproduction workers, is higher for low-skilled workers than for high-skilled workers, and is larger in nondurable goods industries than in durable goods industries.

Significance of Wage Elasticity

Of what practical significance are such estimates of labor demand elasticity? The answer is that private and public policies might be greatly affected by the size of the wage rate–employment trade-off suggested by the elasticity estimates.

In the private sphere, a union's bargaining strategy might be influenced by the elasticity of labor demand for its workers. We might expect a union of higher skilled engineers in the aerospace industry (where the demand for labor is inelastic) to bargain more aggressively for higher wages than a union of restaurant workers (where the demand for labor is elastic). The reason? A given percentage increase in wage rates will generate a smaller decline in employment for the higher skilled engineers than for the lower skilled restaurant workers.

Similarly, a union will wish to know something about its employer's wage elasticity before agreeing to a wage reduction purportedly necessary to save jobs threatened by intense import competition. The more elastic the employer's demand for labor, the greater the likelihood that the union will agree to a wage concession. Under conditions of elastic labor demand, the wage cut will be more effective in preserving jobs than when demand is inelastic.

The effectiveness and impact of government policies often depend on the elasticity of labor demand. The employment consequences of a rise in the minimum wage rate, for example, will depend on the elasticity of demand for workers affected by the change. Similarly, the effectiveness of a program providing wage subsidies to employers who hire disadvantaged workers will depend on the elasticity of labor demand in the industries employing low-skilled labor. The more elastic the labor demand, the greater will be the increase in employment resulting from the wage subsidies.

---

[8] Daniel S. Hamermesh, *Labor Demand* (Princeton, NJ: Princeton University Press, 1993), Chapter 3.
[9] Kim B. Clark and Richard B. Freeman, "How Elastic Is the Demand for Labor?" *Review of Economics and Statistics,* November 1980, pp. 509–520.
[10] Orley Ashenfelter and Ronald G. Ehrenberg, "The Demand for Labor in the Public Sector," in Daniel Hamermesh (ed.), *Labor in the Public and Nonprofit Sectors* (Princeton, NJ: Princeton University Press, 1975), p. 71.

DETERMINANTS OF DEMAND FOR LABOR

The movement along a labor demand curve implied by the concept of elasticity is quite distinct from an increase or decrease in labor demand. The latter implies shifts of the demand for labor curve either rightward or leftward. What factors cause such shifts? The major *determinants of labor demand* are product demand, productivity, the number of employers, and the prices of other resources.

Product Demand

A change in the demand for the product that a particular type of labor is producing, all else being equal, will shift the labor demand curve in the same direction. For example, suppose that in Table 5.2 and Figure 5.2 an increase in product demand occurs, causing the product price to rise from $2 to $3. If we plotted the *new* MRP data onto Figure 5.2, we would observe that the demand for labor curve shifted rightward. A decline in the demand for the product would likewise shift the labor demand curve leftward.

Productivity

Assuming that it does not cause a fully offsetting change in product price, a change in the MP of labor will shift the labor demand curve in the same direction. Again return to Table 5.2 and Figure 5.2. Suppose technology improves, shifting the entire production function (column 2 in relationship to column 1 in Table 5.2) upward. More concretely, let's assume a doubling of the TP produced by each worker in combination with the fixed capital. Clearly MP in column 3 and consequently MRP in column 6 would increase. If the new MRP data were plotted in Figure 5.2, we would observe that labor demand had shifted rightward. Conversely, a decline in productivity would shift the labor demand curve leftward.

Number of Employers

Recall that we found the market demand for labor in Figure 5.6 by summing horizontally the "price-adjusted" labor demand curves of individual employers. *Assuming no change in employment by other firms, a change in the number of firms employing a particular type of labor will change the demand for labor in the same direction.* In terms of Figure 5.6, D_{LR} will shift rightward if additional firms enter this labor market to hire workers; it will shift leftward if firms leave, all else being equal.

Prices of Other Resources

Changes in the prices of other inputs such as capital, land, and raw materials can shift the demand curve for labor. To illustrate this idea, we focus solely on changes in the price of capital. Normally labor and capital are *substitutes in production,* meaning that a given quantity of output can be produced with much capital and little labor *or* much labor and little capital. Now suppose the price of capital falls. Our task is to determine the impact of this price decline on the demand for labor.

Gross Substitutes[11]

If labor and capital are *gross substitutes,* the decline in the price of capital will *decrease* the demand for labor. *Gross substitutes are inputs such that when the price of one changes, the demand for the other changes in the same direction.* This correctly implies that here the substitution effect outweighs the output effect. The decline in

---

[11] The term *gross* as a modifier of *substitutes* and *complements* in this discussion is in keeping with terminology used in advanced economics. As used here, the concepts are *gross* because they encompass both substitution and output effects. So-called *net* substitutes and complements, on the other hand, focus only on substitution effects, holding output constant.

the price of capital lowers the marginal cost of producing the output, which taken alone would result in an expansion of output and an *increase* in the demand for labor (the output effect). But the lower priced capital is substituted for labor, which taken alone would *reduce* the demand for labor (the substitution effect). Where labor and capital are gross substitutes, this latter substitution effect swamps the output effect, and labor demand falls. For example, the decline in the price of security equipment used by businesses to protect against illegal entries has reduced the demand for night guards.

5.3 *Quick Review*

- Wage elasticity measures the sensitivity of the amount of labor demanded to wage rate changes; it is the percentage change in quantity of labor demanded divided by the percentage change in price.

- When changes in the wage rate cause the wage bill *(W × Q)* to move in the opposite direction, labor demand is elastic; when the wage bill remains constant, labor demand is unit elastic; and when the wage bill moves in the same direction, labor demand is inelastic.

- The major determinants of wage elasticity are the *(a)* elasticity of product demand, *(b)* ratio of labor costs to total costs, *(c)* substitutability of other inputs, and *(d)* supply elasticity of other inputs.

- The factors that shift the labor demand curve include *(a)* changes in product demand, *(b)* changes in labor productivity, *(c)* changes in the number of employers, and *(d)* changes in the prices of other inputs.

Your Turn

Suppose the price of capital falls relative to the wage rate and, as a result, the demand for labor increases. Are these inputs gross substitutes, or are they gross complements? What can you infer about the relative strengths of the output and substitution effects? (*Answers:* See page 541.)

Gross Complements

GP5.2

If, on the other hand, labor and capital are *gross complements*, a decline in the price of capital will *increase* the demand for labor. *Gross complements are inputs such that when the price of one changes, the demand for the other changes in the opposite direction.* In this case of a decline in the price of capital, the output effect outweighs the substitution effect, and the demand for labor increases. Restated, the fall in the price of capital reduces production costs and increases sales so much that the resulting increased demand for labor overwhelms the substitution of capital for labor occurring in the production process. When labor and capital are gross complements, a decrease (increase) in the price of capital increases (decreases) the demand for labor. For example, the decline in the price of computers over the past three decades increased the demand for computer programmers.

5.2   Global Perspective

Self-Employment as a Percentage of Total Employment

The percentage of workers who are self-employed in the United States is the lowest among the major industrialized countries.

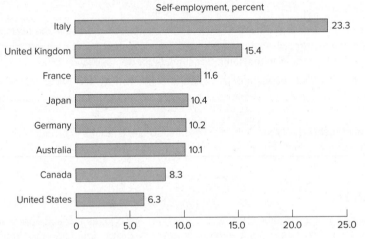

Self-employment, percent

Italy	23.3
United Kingdom	15.4
France	11.6
Japan	10.4
Germany	10.2
Australia	10.1
Canada	8.3
United States	6.3

0   5.0   10.0   15.0   20.0   25.0

Source: OECD, "Self-employment rate." www.oecd.org

GP5.3

Thus far, we have assumed that labor and capital are substitutes in production. What can we conclude about the impact of a change in the price of capital on the demand for labor in the extreme case in which labor and capital are *not* substitutable in the production process? Suppose instead that labor and capital are *pure complements in production,* meaning they are used in direct proportion to one another in producing the output. An example would be crane operators and cranes; more cranes require more operators on a one-for-one basis. The decline in the price of capital in this instance will unambiguously increase the demand for labor. Pure complements in production are always gross complements because there is no substitution effect. The lower price of capital will reduce the firm's marginal cost and cause it to increase its output, bolstering its demand for labor.

WW5.4

Remember these generalizations: *(a) A change in the price of a resource that is a substitute in production for labor may change the demand for labor either in the same or in the opposite direction, depending on whether the resources are gross substitutes or gross complements, respectively;* *(b) a change in the price of a resource that is a pure complement in production (used in a fixed proportion with labor) will change the demand for labor in the opposite direction—it will always be a gross complement.*

5.3 Global Perspective

Temporary Employment as a Percentage of Total Employment

The United States has a low rate of employment in jobs with time-limited contracts relative to other countries.

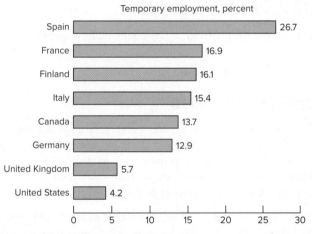

Temporary employment, percent

Country	Percent
Spain	26.7
France	16.9
Finland	16.1
Italy	15.4
Canada	13.7
Germany	12.9
United Kingdom	5.7
United States	4.2

Source: OECD, "Temporary employment." www.oecd.org

5.4 World of Work

Ahead of the Pack: Veterinary Occupations are Growing Fast·

Employment in veterinary occupations such as veterinarians, veterinary technicians, and veterinary assistants is expected to grow by 51,700 or 19 percent between 2016 and 2026. This growth rate is almost three times faster than that for the average occupation over this period.

Three factors are increasing pet care spending and thus employment in veterinary occupations. First, the pet population has grown over the past three decades. The portion of households with a pet rose from half in 1988 to nearly two-thirds in 2018. The number of dogs rose 50 percent between 1988 and 2017. The increasing number of pets is increasing spending on veterinary service.

Second, the average lifespan of both cats and dogs has been rising. The average life expectancy for dogs rose from 10.5 years in 2002 to 11.8 years in 2016. The average life expectancy for cats rose from 11.9 years in 2002 to 12.9 years in 2016. Older pets require more spending on veterinary services including diagnostic exams and treatments.

Third, the availability of diagnostic tests and treatment options for pets has increased over time. Improvements in technology for human healthcare, such as computed tomography (CT) and magnetic resonance imaging (MRI), have migrated to animal care. As a result, veterinar-

ians are now able to provide more and better care for sick and injured pets. Pet owners have willing to spend more to have their pets live longer. Spending on veterinary services rose from one-quarter to one-third of spending by households on pets between 2007 and 2016.

* Based on Stanislava Ilic-Godfrey, "Ahead of the Pack: Why are Veterinary Occupations Growing Much Faster Than Average?" *Beyond The Numbers,* March 2019, pp. 1–7.

REAL-WORLD APPLICATIONS

The concepts of labor demand and the elasticity of labor demand have great practical significance, as seen in the following examples.

Textile and Apparel Industries

In 1973, there were 2.4 million U.S. textile and apparel workers; by 2016 this figure had dropped to 245,000 workers. An additional 61,000 workers are expected to lose their jobs by 2026. Several factors help explain this dramatic decline in jobs. First, foreign competition, due to decreased trade barriers, has reduced the demand for American textiles and apparel. The share of total American textile and apparel sales accounted for by domestic producers has fallen from 95 percent in 1970 to less than 60 percent today.

Another factor has been the spread of automation in textile and apparel manufacturing. Industrial robots and assembly-line labor are gross substitutes, meaning that lower prices for robots have produced substitution effects exceeding output effects. The net effect has been a decline in the demand for textile and apparel workers. Coupled with the reduced demand for the product, the substitution of robots for workers has sharply reduced employment in these industries.[12]

Cannabis

Even though the use of cannabis was illegal at the federal level in 2019, in at least 33 states medical use of cannabis was legal.[13] In ten of these states, the recreational use of cannabis was legal. Employment in the cannabis industry has been expanding very rapidly as its use has become legal in more states. The U.S. government does not provide separate data on the cannabis industry. Zip Recruiters, however, estimated there were 200,000 to 300,000 workers in the cannabis industry in 2019. Most employment in the industry is in lower paid jobs such as agricultural workers and "budtenders" who help customers purchase cannabis. As the industry has expanded, the demand has increased for higher paid positions such as chemists., software engineers, and nurses who consult with patients.

---

[12] For more about employment trends in the textile and apparel industries, see Mark Mittelhauser, "Employment Trends in Textiles and Apparel, 1973–2005," *Monthly Labor Review,* August 1997, pp. 24–35.

[13] These and the other statistics in this section are based on Conor Dougherty, "Cannabis Industry Produces Sweet Fruit: Jobs," *New York Times*, April 28, 2019

Personal Computers

The last three decades have seen a remarkable drop in the average price of personal computers and an equally amazing rise in the computing power of the typical machine. The effects of these developments on labor demand have been pervasive. For example, the demand for workers in some segments of the computer industry has significantly increased. Between 1990 and 2014, employment in the computer systems design industry (programming and software) expanded at an annual 6.0 percent growth rate. Apple Corporation, which was founded in 1976, boasted 132,000 workers in 2018. Microsoft, a major producer of software, employed 135,000 people in 2018, up from 476 workers in 1983.

In some offices, personal computers have been gross substitutes for labor, thus reducing the demand for labor and allowing these firms to use fewer workers to produce their outputs. But in other instances, computers and labor have proven to be gross complements. The decline in computer prices has reduced production costs to the extent that product prices have dropped, product sales have increased, and the derived demand for workers has risen. Also, keyboard personnel and computers are pure complements. Thus, there is no substitution effect; a keyboard worker is needed for each computer.

Today about two-thirds of workers use a personal computer at work at least sometime during the day. Krueger has estimated that workers who use computers earn 10–15 percent more than otherwise similar workers who do not use this technology.[14]

5.5   World of Work

Occupational Employment Trends

Labor demand shifts are important because they alter wage rates and employment in specific occupations. An increase in labor demand for a particular occupation will raise employment in the occupation, and declines in labor demand will lower it. For example, let's examine occupations that are facing increases in labor demand (wage rates are discussed in the next chapter).

The table below lists the ten fastest-growing occupations, in percentage terms, for 2016–2026. Not surprisingly, service and construction occupations dominate the list. Overall, the demand for service and construction workers is growing faster than the demand for manufacturing and mining workers.

Five of the top ten fastest-growing occupations are linked to health care. The reasons for rising demand for home health aides, personal care aides, physician assistants, nurse practitioners, and physical therapy assistants are: (a) the aging of the U.S. population with its increased extended illnesses; (b) rising income, which has led to greater spending on health care; and (c) the rising rate of health insurance, which enables more people to be able to buy health care.

Three of the fastest-growing occupations are related to "big data." The rapid improvements in technology have made much more data available about consumers. As a result, there has been a rise in the demand for workers who can analyze these data.

---

[14] Alan B. Krueger, "How Computers Have Changed the Wage Structure: Evidence from Microdata, 1984–1989," *Quarterly Journal of Economics,* February 1993, pp. 33–60. For additional evidence regarding the impact of computers on wages, see Harry A. Krashinsky, "Do Marital Status and Computer Usage Really Change the Wage Structure?," *Journal of Human Resources,* Summer 2004, pp. 774–791; and Peter Dolton and Panu Pelkonen, "The Wage Effects of Computer Use: Evidence from WERS 2004," *British Journal of Industrial Relations,* December 2008, pp. 587–630.

Two of the most rapidly growing occupations are related to renewable energy. Increasing concern about climate change has increased the demand for renewable energy sources such as solar and wind power interpretation and translation services.

The Ten Fastest-Growing Occupations in Percentage Terms, 2016–2026

Occupation	Employment (Thousands of Jobs)		Percentage Increase
	2016	2026	
Solar photovoltaic installers	11	23	105
Wind turbine service technicians	6	11	96
Home health aides	912	1,343	47
Personal care aides	2,016	2,794	39
Physician assistants	106	146	37
Nurse practitioners	156	212	36
Statisticians	37	50	34
Physical therapist assistants	88	116	31
Software developers, applications	831	1,087	31
Mathematicians	3	4	30

Source: Bureau of Labor Statistics, "Employment Projections." www.bls.gov

Minimum Wage

As we detail in Chapter 13, federal law requires that covered workers earn an hourly wage rate of at least $7.25. Critics contend that an above-equilibrium minimum wage moves employers upward along their downward-sloping labor demand curves and causes unemployment, particularly among teenage workers. Workers who remain employed at the minimum wage will receive higher incomes than otherwise. The amount of income lost by job losers and the income gained by those who keep their jobs will depend on the elasticity of demand for minimum-wage labor. Studies have generally found that a 10 percent increase in the minimum wage reduces employment from 1 to 3 percent, meaning that demand is inelastic. Thus, the minimum wage increases the wage income of minimum-wage workers as a group (increases the wage bill). The case made by critics of the minimum wage would be stronger if the demand for low-wage labor were elastic.

Contingent Workers

A dramatic labor market change of recent years has been that many employers have reduced the size of their core workforce. Simultaneously, they have increased the use of contingent workers (temporary help, independent contractors, and on-call workers). Between 1990 and 2018, employment in the temporary help industry grew at the rapid rate of 3.5 percent per year, which was more than three times the growth rate of nonfarm employment. The number of workers in the industry rose from 1,156,000 to 3,008,000 over this period.

Why has the demand for contingent workers increased so rapidly? Several factors have been at work. These workers are usually paid less than permanent workers. Also, increasingly expensive fringe benefits are minimal or nonexistent for many contingent workers.

A second and closely related reason for the growing demand for contingent workers is that these workers give firms more flexibility in responding to changing economic conditions. As product demand shifts, firms can readily increase or decrease the sizes of their workforces through altering their temporary, on-call, and subcontracted employment. This flexibility enhances the competitive positions of firms and improves their ability to succeed in international markets.

Chapter Summary

1. The demand for labor is a derived demand and therefore depends on the marginal productivity of labor and the price or market value of the product.

2. The segment of the MP curve that is positive and lies below the AP curve is the basis for the short-run labor demand curve. More specifically, the short-run demand curve for labor is determined by applying the MRP = W rule to the firm's MRP data.

3. Other things being equal, the demand for labor curve of a perfectly competitive seller is more elastic than that of an imperfectly competitive seller. This difference occurs because the imperfectly competitive seller needs to reduce product price to sell additional units of output, whereas the purely competitive seller does not. This also means that the imperfectly competitive seller's MRP curve lies to the left of the corresponding VMP curve, whereas MRP and the value of the MP are identical for the perfectly competitive seller.

4. A firm's long-run labor demand curve is more elastic than its short-run curve because in the long run, the firm has sufficient time to adjust nonlabor inputs such as capital. In the short run, a wage change produces only an output effect; in the long run, it also creates a substitution effect. In addition, such factors as product demand elasticity, labor–capital interactions, and technology contribute to the greater long-run wage elasticity.

5. The market demand for a given type of labor is less elastic than a simple horizontal summation of the short- or long-run demand curves of individual employers. The reason for this is that as employers as a group hire more workers and produce more output, product supply will increase significantly and product price will therefore decline.

6. The elasticity of labor demand is measured by comparing the percentage change in the quantity of labor demanded with a given percentage change in the wage rate. If the elasticity coefficient is greater than 1, demand is relatively elastic. If it is less than 1, demand is relatively inelastic. When demand is elastic, changes in the wage rate cause the total wage bill to change in the *opposite* direction. When demand is inelastic, changes in the wage rate cause the total wage bill to move in the *same* direction.

7. The demand for labor generally is more elastic *(a)* the greater the elasticity of product demand, *(b)* the larger the ratio of labor cost to total cost, *(c)* the greater the substitutability of other inputs for labor, and *(d)* the greater the elasticity of supply of other inputs.

8. The location of the labor demand curve depends on *(a)* product demand, *(b)* the marginal productivity of labor, *(c)* the number of employers, and *(d)* the prices of other inputs. When any of these determinants of demand change, the labor demand curve shifts to a new location.

9. Labor and capital can be either substitutes or pure complements in production. If they are substitutes in production, they can be either gross substitutes or gross complements. When the price of a gross substitute changes, the demand for the other resource changes in the same direction. When the price of gross complement changes, the demand for the other resource changes in the opposite direction.

10. The concepts of labor demand, changes in labor demand, and the elasticity of labor demand have great applicability to real-world situations.

Terms and Concepts

derived demand

production function

total product

marginal product

average product

law of diminishing marginal returns

zone of production

marginal revenue product

short-run labor demand curve

marginal wage cost

value of marginal product

long-run demand for labor

output effect

substitution effect

market demand for labor

elasticity of labor demand

wage elasticity coefficient

total wage bill rules

determinants of labor demand

gross substitutes

gross complements

Questions and Study Suggestions

1. Graph a short-run production function (one variable resource) showing the correct relationships between total product, average product, and marginal product.

2. "Only that portion of the MP curve that lies below AP constitutes the basis for the firm's short-run demand curve for labor." Explain.

3. Explain how marginal revenue product is derived. Why is the MRP curve the firm's short-run labor demand curve? Explain how and why the labor demand curves of a perfectly competitive seller and an imperfectly competitive seller differ.

4. Given the data in Table A, complete the labor demand schedule shown in Table B. Contrast this schedule to the value of marginal product schedule that would exist given these data. Explain why the labor demand and VMP schedules differ.

Table A

Inputs of Labor	Total Product	Product Price
0	0	$1.10
1	17	1.00
2	32	0.90
3	45	0.80
4	55	0.70
5	62	0.65
6	68	0.60

Table B

Labor Demand Schedule	
Wage Rate	Quantity Demanded
$18	
14	
11	
6	
2	
1	

5. Explain how each of the following would affect the demand schedule you derived in Question 4: *(a)* an increase in the price of a gross substitute for labor, *(b)* a decrease in the price of a pure complement in production with labor, and *(c)* a decrease in the demand for the product that the labor helps produce.

6. Referring to the output and substitution effects, explain why an increase in the wage rate for autoworkers will generate more of a negative employment response in the long run than in the short run. Assume there is no productivity increase and no change in the price of nonlabor resources.

7. "It would be incorrect to say that an industry's labor demand curve is simply the horizontal sum of the demand curves of the individual firms." Do you agree? Explain.

8. Suppose marginal productivity tripled while product price fell by half in Table 5.2. What would be the net impact on the location of the short-run labor demand curve in Figure 5.2?

9. Use the concepts of *(a)* substitutes in production versus pure complements in production and *(b)* gross substitutes versus gross complements to assess the likely impact of the rapid decline in the price of computers and related office equipment on the labor demand for secretaries.

10. Use the total wage bill rules and the labor demand schedule in Question 4 to determine whether demand is elastic or inelastic over the $6–$11 wage rate range. Compute the elasticity coefficient using Equation (5.4).

11. The productivity of farm labor has increased substantially since World War II. How can this be reconciled with the fact that labor has moved from agricultural to nonagricultural occupations over this period?

12. Contrast and explain changes in the demand for textile workers and fast-food workers over the past two decades. Why is the elasticity of labor demand crucial to the debate about the effects of increasing the minimum wage?

Internet Exercise

Which Industries Are Growing and Which Are Declining?

Go to the Bureau of Labor Statistics Current Employment Statistics website **(www.bls.gov/ces/home.htm)** and in sequence select "CES Databases" and "Top Picks" to find information about employment by industry. Click on "reformat" to change the years of data extracted.

What was the amount for total nonfarm employment in January 1980 and for the most recent month shown? What is the percentage change in employment over this period?

What was the employment level for manufacturing and services in January 1980 and for the most recent month shown? In which industry has employment increased over this period? In which has it declined? What has been the percentage change in employment for both sectors? Suggest a possible explanation for the difference in employment growth between these sectors.

Provide *one* other specific statistic of your choice from the data on employment levels. For example, "In January 2019, the employment level for the mining and logging industry was *xxx.x* thousand workers."

Internet Links

The Bureau of Labor Statistics Employment and Unemployment website provides information about layoffs and job turnover, as well as employment by state, occupation, and industry (**www.bls.gov/bls/employment.htm**).

Appendix

Isoquant–Isocost Analysis of the Long-Run Demand for Labor

A more advanced derivation of the firm's long-run downward-sloping labor demand curve is based on (*a*) isoquant and (*b*) isocost curves.

ISOQUANT CURVES

An *isoquant curve shows the various possible combinations of two inputs that are capable of producing a specific quantity of physical output.* By definition, then, output is the same at all points on a *single* isoquant. For example, total output is 100 units of some product or service on curve Q_{100} in Figure 5.8 when 20 units of capital are combined with 7 units of labor *or* when 10 units of capital and 15 units of labor are employed.[15] Isoquants—or equal output curves—possess several other characteristics.

FIGURE 5.8   Isoquant Curves

Every point on a specific isoquant represents some combination of inputs (in this case, capital and labor) that produces a given level of total output. Isoquants, or "equal output curves," farther to the northeast indicate higher levels of total output.

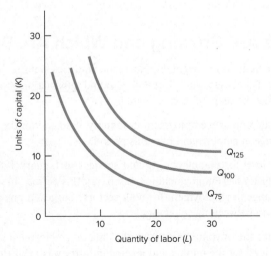

---

[15] For simplicity, we will assume that the only two resources are capital and labor, disregarding all combinations of capital and labor that are not within a firm's zone of production.

1 Downward Slope

Assuming that capital and labor are substitutes in production, if a firm employs less capital (K), then to maintain a specific level of output, it must employ more labor (L). Conversely, to hold total output constant, using less of L will require it to employ more of K. There is thus an *inverse* relationship between K and L at each output level, implying a downward-sloping isoquant curve.

2 Convexity to the Origin

Isoquants are convex to the origin because capital and labor are not perfect substitutes for one another. For example, an excavating company can substitute labor and capital to produce a specific level of output—perhaps clearing 1,000 acres of wooded land in a fixed amount of time. But labor and capital are not perfectly substitutable for this purpose. To understand this and see why the firm's isoquant curve is convex to the origin, compare the following circumstances. First suppose the firm is using a single bulldozer and hundreds of workers. Clearly an extra bulldozer would compensate, or substitute, for many workers in producing this output. Contrast that to a second situation in which the firm has 100 bulldozers but relatively fewer workers. The addition of still another machine would have a relatively low substitution value; for example, it might compensate for only one or two workers. Why? The firm already has numerous bulldozers; it needs people to operate them, supervise the operation, and cut down the trees that cannot be bulldozed.

This same concept can be viewed in the opposite way. When the firm is employing only a small amount of labor and a large amount of equipment, an extra worker will possess a relatively high substitution value—that is, compensate for the reduction of a large amount of capital. As more labor is added, however, the decrease in capital permitted by an added unit of labor will decline. Stated in technical terms, the absolute value of the *marginal rate of technical substitution* of labor for capital will fall as more labor is added. This MRTS L, K, shown symbolically in Equation (5.5) is the absolute value of the slope of the isoquant at a given point.

$$\text{MRTS } L, \ K = \frac{\Delta K}{\Delta L} \quad (5.5)$$

Returning to Figure 5.8, we see that each isoquant is convex to the origin. As one moves along Q_{75} from left to right, the absolute value of the slope of the curve declines; in other words, the curve gets flatter. A curve that gets flatter (whose absolute slope declines) as one moves southeast is convex to the origin.

3 Higher Output to the Northeast

Each isoquant farther to the northeast reflects combinations of K and L that produce a greater level of total output than the previous curve. Isoquant Q_{125} represents greater output than Q_{100}, which in turn reflects more output than Q_{75}. Two other points are relevant here. First, we have drawn only three of the many possible isoquant curves. Second, just as equal elevation lines on a contour map never intersect, neither do these equal output lines.

ISOCOST CURVES

A profit-maximizing firm will seek to minimize the costs of producing a given output. To accomplish this task, it will need to know the prices of K and L. These prices let the firm determine the various combinations of K and L that are available to it for a specific expenditure. For example, if the prices of K and L are \$6 and \$4 per unit, respectively, the input combinations that can be obtained from a given outlay, say \$120, would be \$6 times the quantity of K plus \$4 times the quantity of L. One possibility would be to use 20 units of K (= \$120 = \$6 × 20) and no labor. At the other extreme, this firm could use zero units of capital and 30 units

FIGURE 5.9   An Isocost Curve

An isocost (equal expenditure) curve shows the various combinations of two inputs—in this case, capital and labor—that can be purchased with a specific dollar outlay, given the prices of the two inputs. The slope of an isocost line measures the price of one input divided by the price of the other.

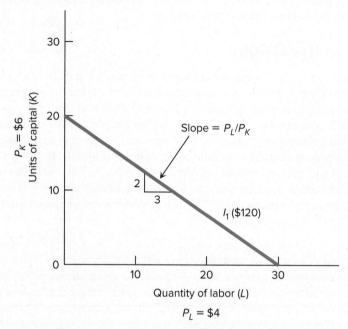

$P_L = \$4$

of labor (= $120 = 30 \times \$4$). Another such combination would be $10K$ and $15L$. In Figure 5.9, we plot these three points and connect them with a straight line. This line is an *isocost curve*; it shows all the various combinations of capital and labor that can be purchased by a particular outlay, given the prices of K and L. Note that the absolute value of the slope of this "equal expenditure" line is the ratio of the price of labor to the price of capital; that is, the slope is $\frac{2}{3}\left(= \frac{\$4}{\$6}\right)$.

The location of a particular isocost curve depends on (*a*) the total expenditure and (*b*) the relative prices of *L* and *K*. Given the prices of *K* and *L*, the greater the total expenditure, the farther the isocost curve will lie outward from the origin. If the total outlay were enlarged from $120 to $150, and the prices of *K* and *L* remained unchanged, the isocost curve shown in Figure 5.9 would shift outward in a parallel fashion. Similarly, a smaller outlay would shift it inward. Second, the location of an isocost curve depends on the relative prices of *L* and *K*. Given the total expenditure, the higher the price of *L* relative to the price of *K*, the *steeper* the isocost curve; the lower the price of *L* relative to the price of *K*, the *flatter* the curve.

LEAST-COST COMBINATION OF CAPITAL AND LABOR

By overlaying the isocost curve in Figure 5.9 onto Figure 5.8's isoquant map, we can determine the firm's cost-minimizing combination of *K* and *L* for a given quantity of total output. Stated somewhat differently, this allows us to determine the lowest cost *per unit of output*. This *least-cost combination of resources* occurs at the *tangency point* of the isoquant curve Q_{100} and the isocost curve I_1 (point *a*) in Figure 5.10. At point *a* the slope of the isoquant, the MRTS *L, K,* just equals the ratio of the prices of labor and capital—the slope of the isocost curve. The firm will use 10 units of capital and employ 15 units of labor. This expenditure of $120

FIGURE 5.10 The Least-Cost Combination of Capital and Labor

The least-cost combination of capital and labor used to produce 100 units of output is at point *a,* where the isocost line is tangent to isoquant Q_{100}. At *a*, the marginal rate of technical substitution of labor for capital (MRTS L, K) equals the ratio of the price of labor to the price of capital. In this case, the firm will use 10 units of capital, employ 15 units of labor, and in the process expend $120.

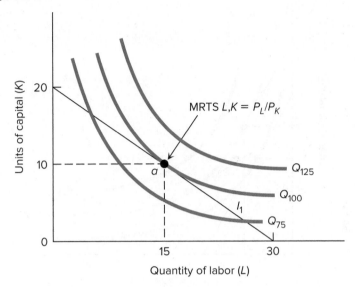

is the minimum outlay possible in achieving this level of output. To reinforce this proposition, you should determine why combinations of K and L represented by other points on Q_{100} are *not* optimal.

DERIVING THE LONG-RUN LABOR DEMAND CURVE

Earlier in this chapter, we derived a *short-run* labor demand curve by holding capital constant, adding units of labor to generate an MP schedule, multiplying MP with the extra revenue gained from the sale of additional product, and graphing the resulting marginal revenue product schedule. By applying the W = MRP rule, we demonstrated that the MRP curve *is* the short-run labor demand curve. Now we derive a *long-run* labor demand curve directly from our isoquant–isocost analysis. In Figure 5.11(a), we reproduce our $120 isocost line I_1 and the isoquant Q_{100}, which is tangent to it at point *a*. We then drop a perpendicular dashed line down to the horizontal axis of graph (b), which also measures units of labor, but measures the price of labor, or wage rate, vertically. Recall that the price of L is assumed to be $4, at which the optimal level of employment is 15 units of labor. This gives us point A in the lower graph.

Now suppose some factor (perhaps emigration) reduces the labor supply and increases the price of labor from $4 to $12. We need to ascertain graphically the effect of this increase of the wage rate on the quantity of labor demanded. To accomplish this, let's proceed in several steps. First, we must draw a new isocost curve, reflecting the new ratio of the price of L to K. Inasmuch as the price of labor is now $12 while the price of K is assumed to remain constant at $6, the new isocost curve will have a slope of 2 (= $12 / $6). Because we wish initially to hold the level of output constant at Q_{100}, we construct isocost curve I_2, which has a slope of 2 and is tangent to Q_{100} at point *b* in Figure 5.11(a).

Our next step is to determine the new combination of K and L that would be used *if* output were to be held constant. This is shown at point *b*, where the marginal rate of technical substitution on isoquant curve Q_{100}

FIGURE 5.11   Deriving the Long-Run Labor Demand Curve

When the price of labor rises from \$4 to \$12, the substitution effect causes the firm to use more capital and less labor, while the output effect reduces the use of both. The labor demand curve is determined in (b) by plotting the quantity of labor demanded before and after the increase in the wage rate from \$4 to \$12.

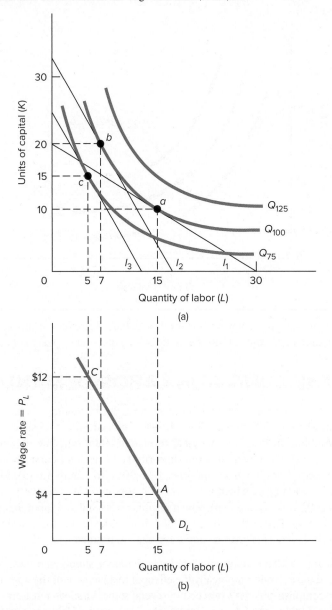

equals the slope of isocost curve I_2 ($20K$ and $7L$). Notice what has happened thus far: In response to the higher wage rate, the firm has substituted more capital (+10) for less labor (−8). This is the *substitution effect* of the wage increase. It is defined as *the change in the quantity of an input demanded resulting from a change in the price of the input, with the output remaining constant.*

The final step is to acknowledge that the increase of the price of labor from $4 to $12 will cause the firm to reassess its profit-maximizing level of output. In particular, production costs are now higher and, given product demand, the firm will find it profitable to produce less output. Let's assume that this reevaluation results in the firm's decision to reduce its output from Q_{100} to Q_{75}. Given the new $12 to $6 price ratio of L and K, we simply push the I_2 line inward in a parallel fashion until it is tangent with this lower isoquant. The new tangency position is at c, where the firm is using $15K$ and $5L$. This *output effect* further reduces the cost-minimizing quantity of labor: Not as much labor is needed to produce the smaller quantity of output. This effect is defined as *the change in employment of an input resulting from the cost change associated with the change in the input's price.* Dropping a dashed perpendicular line downward from point c, we derive point C in the lower graph. At the new wage rate of $12, the firm desires to hire only 5 units of labor. By finding a series of points such as a and c in the upper graph and A and C in the lower one, and then by determining the locus of these latter points, we derive a long-run labor demand curve such as D_L in graph (b). This curve slopes downward because of both a *substitution effect* (-8 labor units) and an *output effect* (-2 units).

Appendix Summary

1. An isoquant curve shows the various possible combinations of two inputs that are capable of producing a specific quantity of physical output.

2. An isocost curve shows the various combinations of two inputs that a firm can purchase with a given outlay or expenditure.

3. The firm's cost-minimizing combination of inputs in achieving a given output is found at the tangency point between the isocost and isoquant curves, where the marginal rate of technical substitution of labor for capital (slope of the isoquant curve) equals the ratio of the input prices (slope of the isocost curve).

4. Changing the price of either input while holding the price of the other resource and the level of output constant produces a new isocost curve that has a new tangency position on the given isoquant curve. This generates a *substitution effect* that results in the use of less of the resource that rose in price and more of the resource that did not experience a price change.

5. An increase in the price of a resource also increases the cost per unit of the product. This creates an *output effect* tending to reduce the employment of both labor and capital.

6. A downward-sloping long-run labor demand curve can be derived by plotting the wage rate–quantity combinations associated with changing the price of labor (wage rate).

Appendix Terms and Concepts

isoquant curve

marginal rate of technical substitution

isocost curve

least-cost combination of resources

substitution effect

output effect

Appendix Questions and Study Suggestions

1. Explain why isoquant curves for inputs that are substitutes in production *(a)* are negatively sloped, *(b)* are convex to the origin, and *(c)* never intersect.

2. Suppose the quantity of capital is fixed at 10 units in Figure 5.8. Explain, by drawing a horizontal line rightward from $10K$, the short-run law of diminishing marginal returns discussed in the body of this chapter. *Hint:* Observe the distance between the isoquants along your horizontal line.

3. Explain how each of the following, other things being equal, would shift the isocost curve shown in Figure 5.9: *(a)* a decrease in the price of *L*, *(b)* a simultaneous and proportional increase in the prices of both *K* and *L*, and *(c)* an increase in the total outlay, or expenditure, from $120 to $150.

4. Explain graphically how isoquant–isocost analysis can be used to derive a long-run labor demand curve. Distinguish between the substitution and output effects.

5. By referring to Figure 5.11(a), explain the impact of the increase of the price of labor on the cost-minimizing quantity of capital. What can you conclude about the relative strengths of the substitution and output effects as they relate to the demand for capital in this specific situation?

6. Is labor demand *(a)* elastic, *(b)* unit elastic, or *(c)* inelastic over the $4–$12 wage rate range of D_L in Figure 5.11(b)? Explain by referring to the total wage bill rules (Figure 5.7) and the midpoint formula for elasticity [Equation (5.4)].

Chapter 6

Wage Determination and the Allocation of Labor

After reading this chapter, you should be able to:

1. Explain the supply and demand of labor in a perfectly competitive labor market.
2. Discuss the effects on wage and employment if an employer is a monopolist in the product market.
3. Explain the effects on wage and employment if an employer is a monopsonist in the labor market.
4. Explain why labor markets characterized by delayed supply responses may exhibit a cobweb-shaped adjustment path to equilibrium.

Something quite remarkable happens in the United States every workday. Over 156 million of us go to work sometime, somewhere, during the day. We work at an amazing array of jobs: We are carpenters, secretaries, executives, professional athletes, lawyers, dockworkers, farmhands, geologists, hairstylists, nurses, managers, truck drivers, and professors. And the list goes on. Equally remarkable are the pay differences among us. Professional baseball players make, on average, $1,947 per hour; restaurant employees, $12 per hour.

Who or what determines the occupational composition of the total jobs in the economy? What mechanisms allocate us to our various occupations and specific workplaces? How are occupational and individual wage rates determined? In this chapter, we combine labor supply and labor demand into basic models that help us answer these important questions.

In reading this chapter, note that we are assuming for simplicity that all compensation is paid in the form of the wage rate. In Chapter 7, we will relax this assumption, specifically looking at the composition of pay and the economics of fringe benefits.

THEORY OF A PERFECTLY COMPETITIVE LABOR MARKET

A *perfectly competitive labor market* has the following characteristics that contrast it with other labor markets: (*a*) a large number of firms competing with one another to hire a specific type of labor to fill identical jobs; (*b*) numerous qualified people who have identical skills and independently supply their labor services; (*c*) "wage-taking" behavior—that is, neither workers nor firms exert control over the market wage; and (*d*) perfect, costless information and labor mobility.

Let's examine the components, operation, and outcomes of this stylized labor market in some detail. Specifically, we will divide our discussion into three subsections: the labor market, the hiring decision by an individual firm, and allocative efficiency.

The Labor Market

We can best analyze the competitive market for a specific type of labor by separating it into two parts: labor demand that reflects the behavior of employers and labor supply, deriving from the decisions of workers.

Labor Demand and Supply

Recall from the previous chapter (Figure 5.6) that we find the market demand for a particular type of labor by summing over a range of wage rates, the price-adjusted amounts of labor that employers desire to hire at each of the various wage rates. Also remember that *individual* labor supply curves are normally backward-bending. Can we then conclude that the *market* supply of a particular grade of labor is also backward-bending? In most labor markets, this is not the case; market supply curves generally slope upward and to the right, indicating that collectively workers will offer more labor hours at higher relative wage rates. Why is this so?

Figure 6.1 helps explain the positive relationship between the wage rate and the quantity of labor hours supplied in most labor markets. Graph (a) displays five separate backward-bending *individual* labor supply curves in a specific labor market, while graph (b) sums the curves horizontally to produce a *market* labor supply curve.[1] Notice from their respective labor supply curves S_A and S_B that at wage W_1, Adams will offer 4 hours of labor and Bates 6 hours. We simply sum these outcomes ($4 + 6$) to get point x at wage W_1 on the market labor supply curve shown in graph (b). Now let's suppose the wage rate rises from W_1 to W_2 in this labor market while all other wage rates remain constant. Adams will increase her hours from 4 to 5 and Bates will work 10 hours rather than 6. We know from previous analysis that this implies that for these two workers, substitution effects exceed income effects over the W_1 to W_2 wage range. But also notice that at W_2, a third worker—Choy (S_C)—chooses to participate in this labor market, deciding to offer 5 hours of labor. Presumably he is attracted away from another labor market, household production, or leisure by the W_2 wage rate. Thus, the total quantity of hours supplied is 20 ($= 5 + 10 + 5$), as shown by point y in the right graph. Finally, observe wage rate W_3, at which Adams and Bates choose to work fewer hours than previously, but Choy decides to offer 6 hours, and two new workers—Davis (S_D) and Egan (S_E)—now enter this labor market. The total number of hours, as observed at point z on the market labor supply curve, is now 30 ($= 2 + 7 + 6 + 7 + 8$).

Conclusion? Even though specific people may reduce their hours of work as the market wage rises, labor supply curves of specific labor markets generally are positively sloped over realistic wage ranges. *Higher relative wages attract workers away from household production, leisure, or other labor markets and toward the labor market in which the wage increased.*

---

[1] We are assuming that while all these workers have identical skills, they have differing preferences for leisure, differing levels of nonwage income, and so forth. Thus, their reservation wages and individual labor supply curves differ.

FIGURE 6.1 The Market Supply of Labor

Even though specific individuals normally have backward-bending labor supply curves, labor supply curves generally are positively sloped over realistic wage ranges. Higher relative wages attract workers away from household production, leisure, or their previous jobs. The height of the market labor supply measures the opportunity cost of using the marginal labor hour in this employment. The shorter the time period, the less elastic is this curve.

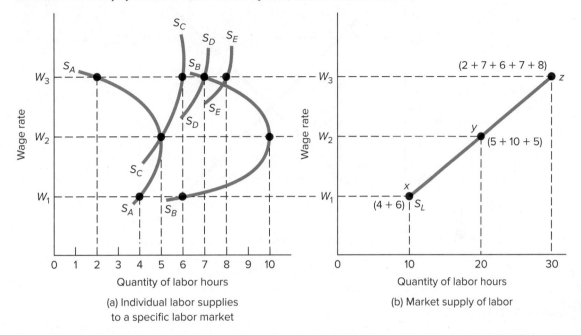

(a) Individual labor supplies to a specific labor market

(b) Market supply of labor

The vertical height of the market labor supply curve xyz measures the opportunity cost of employing the last labor hour in this occupation. For example, point y on S_L in Figure 6.1(b) indicates that wage rate W_2 is necessary to entice the 20th hour of labor. Where there is competition in product and labor markets, perfect information, and costless migration, the value of the alternative activity which that hour previously produced—either as utility from leisure or as output from work in a different occupation—is equivalent to W_2. To attract 30 hours of labor compared to 20, the wage must rise to W_3 (point z) because the 21st through 30th hours generate more than W_2 worth of value to workers and society in their alternative uses. To attract these hours to this labor market, these opportunity costs must be compensated for via a higher wage rate. *In perfectly competitive product and labor markets, labor supply curves measure marginal opportunity costs.*

One final point needs to be emphasized concerning market labor supply. The shorter the time period and the more specialized the variety of labor, the less elastic the labor supply curve. In the short run, increases in the wage may not result in significant increases in the number of workers in a market; but in the long run, human capital investments can be undertaken that will allow greater responsiveness to the higher relative wage.

Equilibrium

Figure 6.2 combines the market labor demand and supply curves for a specific type of labor and shows the equilibrium wage W_0 and the equilibrium quantity of labor Q_0. If the wage were W_{es}, an *excess supply* or surplus of labor $(b - a)$ would occur, driving the wage down to W_0. If instead the wage rate were W_{ed}, an *excess demand* or shortage $(e - c)$ of workers would develop, and the wage would increase to W_0. Wage W_0 and employment level Q_0 is the only wage–employment combination at which the market clears. At W_0, the number of hours offered by labor suppliers just matches the number of hours that firms desire to employ.

FIGURE 6.2 Wage and Employment Determination

The equilibrium wage rate W_0 and level of employment Q_0 occur at the intersection of labor supply and demand. A surplus, or excess supply, of ba would occur at wage rate W_{es}; a shortage, or excess demand, of ec would result if the wage were W_{ed}.

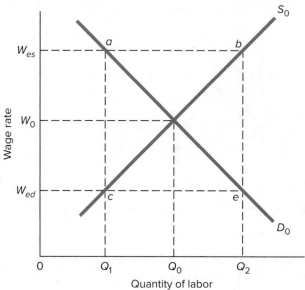

Determinants

The supply and demand curves in Figure 6.2 are drawn holding constant all factors other than the wage rate for this variety of labor. But a number of other factors—or **determinants of labor supply and demand**—can change and cause either rightward or leftward shifts in the curves. We discussed many of these factors in Chapters 2 and 5; they are simply formalized here in Table 6.1. The distinctions between "changes in demand" versus "changes in quantity demanded" *and* "changes in supply" versus "changes in quantity supplied" apply to the labor market as well as the product market. Changes in the determinants of labor demand and supply shown in the table shift the entire curves; these curve shifts are designated as "changes in labor demand" and "changes in labor supply." Changes in the wage rate, on the other hand, cause movements *along* demand and supply curves; that is, the quantity of labor demanded or supplied changes. But in the short run, changes in the wage rate normally do not cause shifts of the curves themselves.

To demonstrate how a competitive market for a particular type of labor operates and to emphasize the role of the determinants of supply and demand, let's suppose that the labor market in Figure 6.3 is characterized by labor demand D_0 and labor supply S_0, which together produce equilibrium wage and employment levels W_0 and Q_0 (point c). Next assume that demand declines for the product produced by firms hiring this labor, reducing the price of the product and thus the **marginal revenue product** (MRP) of labor (demand determinant 1, Table 6.1). Also, let's suppose that simultaneously the federal government releases findings of a definitive research study that concludes that the considerable health and safety risks that were heretofore associated with this occupation are in fact minimal. Taken alone, this information will increase the relative nonwage attractiveness of this labor and shift the labor supply curve rightward—say from S_0 to S_1 (supply determinant 4, Table 6.1).

TABLE 6.1 The Determinants of Labor Supply and Demand

Determinants of Labor Supply

1. **Other wage rates**

   An increase (decrease) in the wages paid in other occupations for which workers in a particular labor market are qualified will decrease (increase) labor supply.

2. **Nonwage income**

   An increase (decrease) in income other than from employment will decrease (increase) labor supply.

3. **Preferences for work versus leisure**

   A net increase (decrease) in people's preferences for work relative to leisure will increase (decrease) labor supply.

4. **Nonwage aspects of the job**

   An improvement (worsening) of the nonwage aspects of the job will increase (reduce) labor supply.

5. **Number of qualified suppliers**

   An increase (decrease) in the number of qualified suppliers of a specific grade of labor will increase (decrease) labor supply.

Determinants of Labor Demand

1. **Product demand**

   Changes in product demand that increase (decrease) the product price will raise (lower) the marginal revenue product (MRP) of labor and therefore increase (decrease) the demand for labor.

2. **Productivity**

   Assuming that it does not cause an offsetting decline in product price, an increase (decrease) in productivity will increase (decrease) the demand for labor.

3. **Prices of other resources**

   Where resources are *gross complements* (output effect > substitution effect), an increase (decrease) in the price of a substitute in production will decrease (increase) the demand for labor; where resources are *gross substitutes* (substitution effect > output effect), an increase (decrease) in the price of a substitute in production will increase (decrease) the demand for labor. An increase (decrease) in the price of a pure complement in production will decrease (increase) labor demand (no substitution effect; therefore a gross complement).

4. **Number of employers**

   Assuming no change in employment by other firms hiring a specific grade of labor, an increase (decrease) in the number of employers will increase (decrease) the demand for labor.

FIGURE 6.3 Changes in Demand, Supply, and Market Equilibrium

Changes in labor supply and demand create initial shortages or surpluses in labor markets, followed by adjustments to new equilibrium wage rates and employment. Here the decline in demand from D_0 to D_1 and increase in supply from S_0 to S_1 produce an initial excess supply of ab at wage W_0. Consequently, the wage rate falls to W_1; and because the decline in demand is large relative to the increase in supply, the equilibrium quantity falls from Q_0 to Q_1.

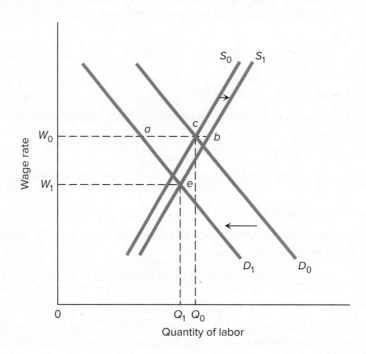

WW6.1   Now observe that at the initial wage rate W_0 the number of workers seeking jobs in this occupation (point b) exceeds the number of workers that firms wish to hire (point a). How will the market adjust to this surplus? Because wages are assumed to be perfectly flexible, the wage rate will drop to W_1, where the labor market will once again clear (point e). Figure 6.3 illustrates two generalizations. First, taken alone, a decline in labor demand reduces *both* the wage rate and quantity of labor employed. Second, an increase in labor supply—also viewed separately—reduces the wage rate and increases equilibrium quantity. In this case, the net outcome of the simultaneous changes in supply and demand is a decline in the wage rate from W_0 to W_1 and a fall in the quantity of labor offered and employed from Q_0 to Q_1. The latter occurred because the decrease in demand was greater than the increase in labor supply. At W_1, the Q_1Q_0 workers formerly employed in this market were not sufficiently compensated for their opportunity costs, and they left this occupation for leisure, household production, or other jobs.

WW6.2

6.1 World of Work

Hurricanes and Local Labor Markets

Hurricanes are very destructive: They can kill thousands of people and destroy property worth billions of dollars. These powerful storms occur each year between June 1 and November 30 when the water temperature is 80 degrees or more. However, we can't forecast exactly where or when a hurricane will hit.

In afflicted locations, hurricanes affect both labor supply and demand. Hurricanes decrease labor supply because people flee stricken areas. Hurricanes also have an uncertain, but likely positive, effect on labor demand. If a hurricane destroys a lot of property and capital, employers will leave and reduce labor demand. If a hurricane hits mostly residential areas, labor demand may rise as employers try to fill vacant positions. In addition, labor demand may rise if firms substitute labor for destroyed physical capital. If labor supply falls and labor demand rises, wages will rise with an uncertain effect on employment.

Ariel Belasen and Solomon Polachek have examined the impact of hurricanes on wages and employment in Florida over the 1988–2005 period using quarterly data. It is useful to study Florida because all of its 67 counties were hit by at least 1 of the 19 hurricanes that landed in Florida over this period. In fact, five of the six most destructive Atlantic hurricanes during this period landed in Florida.

Belasen and Polachek's results indicate that the impact of a hurricane in a county directly struck depends on the severity of the storm. High-intensity storms raise earnings by 4.4 percent and decrease employment by 4.8 percent relative to a typical county. Low-intensity storms increase earnings by 1.3 percent and decrease employment by 1.5 percent relative to a typical county. The employment and earnings effects diminish over time but linger for as long as two years after a hurricane hits.

Source: Ariel R. Belasen and Solomon W. Polachek, "How Disasters Affect Local Labor Markets: The Effects of Hurricanes in Florida," *Journal of Human Resources,* Winter 2009, pp. 251–276.

The Hiring Decision by an Individual Firm

Given the presence of market wage W_0 or W_1 in Figure 6.3, how will a firm operating in a perfectly competitive labor and product market decide on the quantity of labor to employ? The answer can be found in Figure 6.4. Graph (a) portrays the labor market for a specific occupational group, and graph (b) shows the labor supply and demand curves for an individual firm hiring this labor. Because this particular employer is just one of many firms in this labor market, its decision on how many workers to employ will not affect the market wage. Instead, this firm is a wage taker in the same sense that a perfectly competitive seller is a price taker in the product market. The single employer in (b) has no incentive to pay more than the equilibrium wage W_0 because at the W_0 wage, it can attract as many labor units as it wants. On the other hand, if it offers a wage below W_0, it will attract *no* units of labor. All workers who possess this skill have marginal opportunity costs of at least W_0; they can get a minimum of W_0 in alternative employment. Consequently, the horizontal wage line W_0 in Figure 6.4(b) *is* this firm's labor supply curve (S_L). You will observe that it is perfectly elastic.

Curve S_L in graph (b) also indicates this firm's average wage cost and marginal wage cost. *Average wage cost* (AWC) is *the total wage cost (TWC) divided by the number of units of labor employed. Marginal wage cost* (MWC), on the other hand, is *the absolute change in TWC resulting from the employment of an additional unit of labor.* To see why AWC and MWC are equal in this case, suppose the firm hires 100 labor hours at $8 per hour. The total hourly wage bill will be $800 (= $8 × 100). What will be the AWC and MWC?

FIGURE 6.4 Perfect Competition: The Labor Market (a) and the Individual Firm (b)

In a perfectly competitive labor market, the equilibrium wage rate W_0 and quantity of labor Q_0 are determined by supply and demand, as shown in (a). The individual firm (b) hiring in this market is a wage taker; its labor supply curve, S_L = MWC = AWC, is perfectly elastic at W_0. The firm maximizes its profits by hiring Q_0 units of labor (MRP = MWC). Assuming competition in the product market, this employment level constitutes an efficient allocation of resources (VMP = P_L).

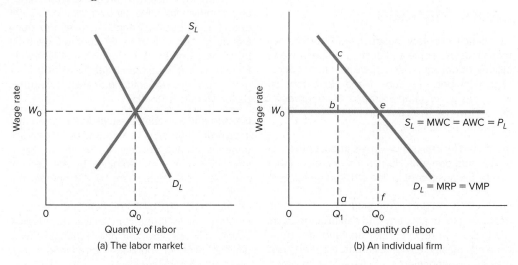

(a) The labor market

(b) An individual firm

Answers: AWC = $8 (= $800 / 100); MWC (extra cost of the last worker hour) = $8 (= $800 − $792). And if the firm hires 200 labor hours? Answers: TWC = $1,600; AWC = $8 (= $1,600 / 200); MWC = $8 (= $1,600 − $1,592). For all levels of employment, W = $8 = MWC = AWC = S_L in this labor market.

Recall from Chapter 5 that in the short run a firm's demand for labor curve *is* its MRP curve. Thus, this firm can compare the additional revenue (MRP) obtained by hiring one more unit of labor with the added cost (MWC) or, in this case, the wage rate (W = MWC). If MRP > W, it will employ the particular hour of labor; on the other hand, if MRP < W, it will not. To generalize: *The profit-maximizing employer will obtain its optimal level of employment where MRP = MWC.* We label this equality the **MRP = MWC rule**.

The profit-maximizing quantity is Q_0 in Figure 6.4(b). To confirm this, observe level Q_1, where MRP, as shown by the vertical distance *ac,* exceeds MWC (distance *ab*). Clearly this firm will gain profits if it hires this unit of labor because it can sell the added product produced by this worker for more than the wage W_0 (= MWC). This is true for all units of labor up to Q_0, where MRP and MWC are equal (distance *fe*). Beyond Q_0 diminishing returns finally reduce marginal product (MP) to the extent that MRP (= MP × P) lies below the market wage W_0 (= MWC). Thus, this firm's total profit will fall if it hires more than Q_0 worker hours.

Allocative Efficiency

We stressed at the outset of Chapter 1 that labor is a scarce resource, and it therefore behooves society to use it efficiently. How do we define an efficient allocation of labor? Is labor efficiently allocated in the perfectly competitive labor market just discussed? And what about the noncompetitive labor market models to follow?

6.2 | World of Work

China Syndrome*

The U.S. volume of imports from China skyrocketed over the past two decades, while exports have not risen as much. Spending on Chinese imports rose from 0.6 percent of all U.S. spending in 1990 to 4.6 percent in 2007. Chinese imports now account for over 30 percent of all imports in the apparel, textiles, furniture, electrical appliances, and jewelry industries. This rapid rise in imports from China has raised concerns about its impact on the U.S. economy.

David Autor, David Dorn, and Gordon Hanson have examined the impact of changes in exposure to Chinese import competition on 722 U.S. labor markets between 1990 and 2007. Rising import competition from China will lower the demand for U.S. manufactured products and thus the demand for manufacturing workers. They find that labor markets with more exposure to Chinese imports had greater declines in manufacturing employment than those with less exposure. The employment declines were concentrated among those without a college degree. Their study reports that increases in Chinese import competition account for 21 percent of the decline in U.S. manufacturing employment over the 1990 to 2007 period.

The increase in Chinese import competition also affected wages. The layoffs in manufacturing lowered the demand for nonmanufactured products and raised labor supply in the nonmanufacturing sector. Because of these shifts, the wages of nonmanufacturing workers declined. Wages in the manufacturing sector did not decline, possibly because the most productive workers kept their jobs.

The declines in wages and employment due to increases in Chinese import competition also increased the demand for government transfer payments. Not surprisingly, the largest increases were for unemployment, disability, retirement, and health care benefit payments. However, the increase in government transfer payments offset only a small part of the decline in household income caused by the decline in worker earnings.

* Based on David H. Autor, David Dorn, and Gordon H. Hanson, "The China Syndrome: Local Labor Market Effects of Import Competition in the United States," *American Economic Review*, December 2013, pp. 2121–2168.

Labor Market Efficiency

Let's first bring the notion of allocative efficiency into focus. An *efficient allocation of labor* is realized when workers are being directed to their highest-valued uses. Labor is being allocated efficiently when society obtains the largest amount of domestic output from the given amount of labor available. Stated technically, available labor is efficiently allocated when its value of MP or VMP—the dollar value to society of its MP—is the same in all alternative employments.

This assertion can be demonstrated through a simple example. Suppose that type A labor (for example, assembly-line labor) is capable of producing both product x (autos) and product y (refrigerators). Suppose the available amount of type A labor is currently allocated so that the VMP of labor in producing autos is $12 and its VMP in producing refrigerators is $8. In short, VMP_{Ax} (= $12) > VMP_{Ay} (= $8). This is *not* an efficient allocation of type A labor because it is not making the maximum contribution to domestic output. It is clear that by shifting a worker from producing y (refrigerators) to making x (autos), the domestic output can be increased by $4 (= $12 − $8). This reallocation will cause a movement down the VMP curve for x and up the VMP curve for y. That is, VMP_{Ax} will fall and VMP_{Ay} will rise. The indicated reallocation from y to x should continue until the VMP of type A labor is the same for both products, or $VMP_{Ax} = VMP_{Ay}$. In our example, this might occur where, say, $\text{VMP}_{Ax} = \text{VMP}_{Ay} = \$10$. When this equality is achieved, no further reallocation of labor will cause a net increase in the domestic output.

If we expand our example from just two products to any number of products (that is, n products), we can state the condition for allocative efficiency for any given type of labor by the following equation:

$$VMP_{Ax} = VMP_{Ay} = \quad \ldots \quad = VMP_{An} = P_{LA} \quad (6.1)$$

where A is the given type of labor; $x, y, \ldots, n$ represent all possible products that labor might produce; and VMP is the value of labor's MP in producing the various products.

Observe that in Equation (6.1) we have made the VMPs of labor equal not only to one another but also to the *price of labor* P_L. Why so? The reason is that we take into consideration that type A labor will be made available in this labor market only if the price of labor is sufficiently high to cover the opportunity costs of those supplying their labor services. Type A labor may be used in non-type A work, household production (child care, meal preparation, and the like), or pure leisure. Indeed, the optimal position in Chapter 2's work–leisure model (specifically point u_1 in Figure 2.5) defines an efficient allocation of labor (time) between labor market and non-labor market activities. In Figure 6.1, we found that such individual work–leisure allocations—along with wage opportunities in other labor markets—are reflected in the labor supply curve within a competitive labor market. Thus, Equation (6.1) tells us that human resources are efficiently allocated when the values of the last units of labor in various labor market uses (producing goods $x, y, \ldots, n$) are all equal and these values in turn are equal to the opportunity cost of labor P_L (the marginal value of alternative work, non-labor market production, and leisure). Alternatively, an *underallocation* of a particular type of labor to labor market production occurs when its VMP in any employment exceeds P_L; an *overallocation* occurs when its VMP in any labor market employment is less than P_L.

Perfect Competition and Allocative Efficiency

Having defined allocative efficiency, let's consider our second question: Do perfectly competitive labor markets result in an efficient allocation of labor? Figure 6.5 is simply an expansion of Figure 6.4 to show the equilibrium positions of representative firms from several competitive industries—that is, industries producing x, y, and n with type A labor. Note that equilibrium for the three representative firms occurs at employment levels Q_{Ax}, Q_{Ay}, and Q_{An}, respectively. The equilibrium positions are the result of each firm's desire to maximize profits by equating the MRPs of A with the MWC of A. But perfect competition in the hiring of labor means that P_{LA} equals the MWC of A. Similarly, perfect competition in the sale of the three products means that the MRP of A equals its VMP for all three products. Thus, each firm maximizes profits where MWC = MRP. But because $P_{LA} = \text{MWC}$ *and* MRP = VMP for all competitive firms using type A labor, we find that Equation (6.1) is fulfilled. In short, competitive labor markets *do* result in an efficient allocation of labor. This is an example of Adam Smith's famous concept of the "invisible hand." In competitive labor and product markets, pursuit of private self-interest (profit maximization) furthers society's interest (an efficient allocation of scarce resources). It is as if there is an unseen coordinator moving resources to where they are most beneficial to society.

With this understanding of allocative efficiency and its realization when perfect competition prevails, let's now seek to determine whether noncompetitive labor markets are consistent with an efficient allocation of labor.

FIGURE 6.5 Perfect Competition and an Efficient Allocation of Labor

Representative firms producing goods such as x, y, and n maximize profits by employing type A labor where the marginal revenue product of labor (MRP) equals the marginal wage cost (MWC). Perfect competition in the product market ensures that MRP equals the value of marginal product (VMP), and perfect competition in the labor market means that MWC equals the price of labor (P_L). Thus, VMP matches P_L in each use, satisfying the condition for efficiency in the allocation of type A labor: $VMP_{Ax} = VMP_{Ay} = \ldots = VMP_{An} = P_L$.

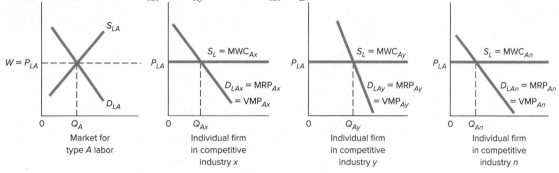

WAGE AND EMPLOYMENT DETERMINATION: MONOPOLY IN THE PRODUCT MARKET

To this point, we have assumed that the employers hiring labor in a perfectly competitive labor market are price takers in the product market; that is, they do not possess monopoly power. But recall from Chapter 5, specifically Table 5.3 and Figure 5.3, that if a firm is a monopolist in the sale of its product, it will face a downward-sloping product demand curve. This means that increases in its output will require price reductions, and because the lower prices will apply to all the firm's output, its marginal revenue (MR) will be less than its price. Consequently, MRP_L (= $MP \times MR$) will fall for two reasons: (a) MP will decline because of diminishing returns (also true for perfect product market competition), *and* (b) MR will decline more rapidly than price as more workers are hired (in perfect competition, MR is constant and equals product price P).

The labor market consequences of product market monopoly are shown in Figure 6.6. Here we assume that the labor market is perfectly competitive but that one particular firm hiring this type of labor is a monopolist in the sale of its product. Restated, this type of labor is used by thousands of firms, not just this monopolist, and thus there is competition in the labor market.

Figure 6.6 indicates that this monopolist is a wage taker and therefore faces the perfectly elastic labor supply curve shown as S_L. This supply curve coincides with the firm's MWC and its average wage cost AWC, just as it did in our previous model.

Labor demand curve D_c is the MRP curve that would have existed had there been competition rather than monopoly and therefore no decline in MR as the firm increased its employment and output. This MRP curve would be equal to VMP; the firm's revenue gain from hiring one more worker would equal society's gain in output. On the other hand, demand curve D_m is the *monopolist's* MRP curve. In this case, MRP *does not equal* VMP. The value of the extra output of each worker to the monopolist is less than the value to society. The reason again: The monopolist's sale of an additional unit of output does not add the full amount of the product's price to its MR. Thus, MRP (= $MR \times MP$)–the value to the firm–is less than VMP (= $P \times MP$)–the value to society.[2]

---

[2] If you are not clear on this point, review Table 5.3 and Figure 5.3.

FIGURE 6.6   Wage Rate and Employment Determination: Monopoly in the Product Market

Because a product market monopolist faces a downward-sloping demand curve, increased hiring of labor and the resulting larger output force the firm to lower its price. And because it must lower its price on all units, its marginal revenue (MR) is less than the price. Thus, the firm's MRP curve (MP × MR) lies below the VMP curve (MP × P), and this employer hires Q_m rather than Q_c units of labor. An efficiency loss to society of bce results.

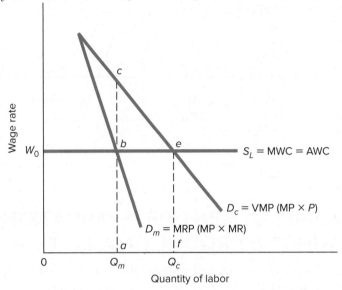

Several noteworthy outcomes of monopoly in the product market are evident in Figure 6.6. First, the monopolist's labor demand curve D_m is *less elastic* than the competitive curve D_c. Second, the monopolist behaves in the same way as the competitor by determining its profit-maximizing level of employment where MRP = MWC. Nevertheless, this equality produces a lower level of employment—Q_m in this case—than would occur under competitive product market conditions (Q_c). Third, the wage paid by the monopolist is the same as that paid by competitive firms. Without unions, both are wage takers.[3] Fourth, labor resources are misallocated. To understand why recall that in a perfectly competitive labor market the price of labor ($P_L = W$) reflects the marginal opportunity cost to society of using a resource in a particular employment. Also, remember that the VMP of labor is a measure of the added contribution to output of a worker in a specific employment. Notice in the figure VMP > P_L (W_0) for the Q_m through Q_c workers. This implies that too few labor resources are being allocated to this employment and therefore too many are allocated somewhere else. An efficiency loss of area bce occurs. Assuming costless labor mobility, if Q_mQ_c (or be) workers were reallocated from alternative activities to work in this industry, the *net* value of society's output would rise by area bce. These workers would contribute output valued at $acef$ in this employment—the value of the total product added—whereas they previously contributed output valued at area $abef$—the opportunity cost to society of using them here.[4]

---

[3] For evidence supporting this theoretical prediction, see Leonard W. Weiss, "Concentration and Labor Earnings," *American Economic Review,* March 1966, pp. 96–117.

The less elastic labor demand curve possessed by the monopolist, however, may increase the collective bargaining power of unions and result in a higher wage for workers in monopolized product markets. For evidence of a positive impact of monopoly power on wages, see Stephen Nickell, "Product Markets and Labour Markets," *Labour Economics,* March 1999, pp. 1–20.

[4] We are assuming that the monopoly firm cannot "price discriminate." If it could charge purchasers the exact price they would be willing to pay rather than do without the product, MRP would coincide with VMP in Figure 6.6. The firm would now find it profitable to hire Q_c (rather than Q_m) workers, and labor resources would be allocated efficiently (Q_c).

6.1 *Quick Review*

- Changes in the determinants of labor supply and demand (Table 6.1) shift the labor supply and demand curves and produce new equilibrium wage and employment levels.

- The perfectly competitive firm is a wage taker whose labor supply curve is perfectly elastic (WR = MWC = AWC); it maximizes profit at the level of employment where MWC equals MRP (MWC = MRP).

- By equating the value of the MP of labor (= VMP_L) and the opportunity cost of labor (= P_L), perfect competition in product and labor markets creates allocative efficiency.

- Because a product market monopolist's MRP (= MP × MR) curve lies below the VMP (= MP × P) curve, employment is less in the monopolized industry than it would be if the industry were competitive. So an efficiency loss occurs.

Your Turn

Assume that perfectly competitive firms are employing labor in profit-maximizing amounts. Now suppose that, all else being equal, the market supply of this labor increases. How will the firms respond? How will they know when to stop responding? Explain, referring to MRP and MWC. (*Answers:* See page 541.)

MONOPSONY

Thus far, we have assumed that the labor market is perfectly competitive. Now we wish to analyze a labor market where either a single firm is the sole hirer of a particular type of labor or two or more employers collude to fix a below-competitive wage. These market circumstances are called *pure monopsony* and *joint monopsony*, respectively. For simplicity, our discussion will be confined to pure forms of monopsony, but keep in mind that monopsony power, much the same as monopoly power, extends beyond the *pure* model to include weaker forms of market power.

We will again assume that (*a*) there are numerous qualified, homogeneous workers who act independently to secure employment in the monopsonized labor market, and (*b*) information is perfect and mobility is costless. But unlike the perfect competitor, the monopsonist is a wage setter; it can control the wage rate it pays by adjusting the amount of labor it hires, much as a product market monopolist can control its price by adjusting its output.

Table 6.2 contains the elements needed to examine labor supply and demand, wage and employment determination, and allocative outcomes in the monopsony model. Comprehension of the table will greatly clarify the graphic analysis that follows.

TABLE 6.2 Wage and Employment Determination: Monopsony (Hypothetical Data)

(1) Units of Labor	(2) (AWC) Wage	(3) TWC	(4) MWC	(5) (VMP) MRP
1	$1	$1	$1	$7
2	2	4	3	6
3	3	9	5	5
4	4	16	7	4
5	5	25	9	3
6	6	36	11	2

Notice in Table 6.2 that columns 1 and 2 indicate that the firm must increase the wage rate it pays to attract more units of labor toward this market and away from alternative employment opportunities. We assume that this firm cannot "wage discriminate" when hiring additional workers; it must pay the higher wage *to all workers,* including those who could have been attracted at a lower wage. This fact is reflected in column 3, where TWC is shown. We find the values for TWC by multiplying the units of labor by the wage rate, rather than by summing the wage column. For example, if the monopsonist hires five units of labor, it will have to pay $5 for each, for a total of $25. Next notice the MWC shown in column 4. The extra cost of hiring, say, the fifth unit of labor ($9) is more than the wage paid for that unit ($5). Each of the four labor units that could have been attracted at $4 must now also be paid $5. The $1 extra wage paid for each of these workers (= $4 total) plus the $5 paid for the fifth worker yield the $9 MWC in column 4. To generalize: *The monopsonist's MWC exceeds the wage rate because it must pay a higher wage to attract more workers, and it must pay this higher wage to all workers.*

Finally, note column 5 in Table 6.2, which shows the MRP of labor. We know that the MRP schedule is the firm's short-run demand for labor curve. In this case, we can avoid unnecessary complexity by assuming that the monopsonist is selling its product in a perfectly competitive market, and therefore MRP = VMP. We will soon discover, however, that the monopsonist will disregard this MRP schedule once it selects its profit-maximizing level of employment.

Figure 6.7 shows the monopsony model graphically. The labor supply curve slopes upward because the monopsonist is the only firm hiring this labor and hence faces the market labor supply curve. Notice that S_L is also the firm's AWC curve (TWC/quantity of labor). MWC lies above and rises more rapidly than S_L because the higher wage rate paid to attract an additional worker must also be paid to all workers already employed. As we previously indicated, the MR curve MRP is the competitive labor demand curve and also measures the value of the MP of labor, VMP.

What quantity of labor will this monopsonistic firm hire, and what wage will it pay? To maximize profits, the firm will equate MWC with MRP, as shown at point *a,* and employ Q_1 units of labor. To understand this, suppose the firm employed Q_c units of labor rather than Q_1. The MWC of the Q_c unit is shown by point *b* on the MWC curve, but the MRP of the extra labor is only *c*; thus, the firm would lose profits equal to area *abc* by its action. To repeat: *The monopsonist, like the perfect competitor, finds its profit-maximizing employment level where MRP equals MWC.*

Having decided to hire Q_1 units of labor, the monopsonist's effective labor demand becomes a single point *e* rather than the entire curve D_L. This point lies along the market labor supply curve S_L, allowing the firm to

FIGURE 6.7   Wage Rate and Employment Determination Monopsony

The firm's MWC lies above the S_L = AWC curve in a monopsonistic labor market. The monopsonist equates MRP with its MWC at point a and chooses to hire Q_1 units of labor. To attract these workers, it need only pay W_1 an hour, as shown by point e. The firm thus pays a lower wage rate (W_1 rather than W_c) and hires fewer units of labor (Q_1 as compared to Q_c) than firms in a competitive labor market. Society loses area eac because of allocative inefficiency.

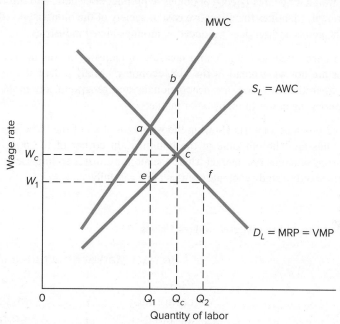

set the wage at W_1. The market clears at this wage; the quantity of labor demanded by the firm, Q_1, equals the amount of labor that suppliers are willing to offer. This equilibrium wage corresponds to that in Table 6.2 (circled row of data). Notice from point f on the MRP = VMP curve in Figure 6.7, however, that this monopsonist would prefer to hire Q_2 units of labor *if* it could hire each unit at a W_1 wage. Thus, the monopsonist may perceive a shortage of this type of labor. It would like more units of labor at the W_1 wage than it can get, but its self-interest keeps it from raising the wage above W_1. This may explain why monopsony markets, such as the one for nurses, are characterized by chronically unfilled job vacancies.[5] If we transformed this labor market into a perfectly competitive one, the equilibrium wage and quantity of labor would be W_c and Q_c units, respectively (point c). But as previously indicated, it simply is not profitable for this monopsonist to hire the Q_c units of labor and pay W_c to all Q_c workers. Instead, it restricts the quantity of labor hired and pays (a) a lower-than-competitive wage (W_1 compared to W_c) and (b) a wage below the MRP of the last unit of labor employed (e as opposed to a).

It is easy to see the basic divergence between the monopsonist's profit-maximizing goal and society's desire to maximize the total value of its output. Indeed, MRP equals MWC at Q_1 units of labor, but VMP is greater than the supply price of labor, W_1 (= Q_1e). Remember that the market labor supply curve reflects the price

[5] The traditional view is that the labor market for nurses is monopsonistic. Hospitals are relatively few, particularly in small-and medium-size cities, see Richard Hurd, "Equilibrium Vacancies in a Labor Market Dominated by Non-Profit Firms: The 'Shortage' of Nurses," *Review of Economics and Statistics,* May 1973, pp. 234–240. Other research, however, questions whether monopsony exists in the market for nurses, see Barry T. Hirsch and Edward J. Schumacher, "Classic or New Monopsony? Searching for Evidence in Nursing Labor Markets," *Journal of Health Economics,* September 2005, pp. 969–989. There appears to be evidence that monopsony power does increase during downturns, see Boris Hirsch, Elke J. Jahn, Claus Schnabel, "Do Employers Have More Monopsony Power in Slack Labor Markets?" *Industrial and Labor Relations Review,* May 2018, pp. 676–704.

of labor in terms of the value of the output that the labor can produce in the next best employment opportunity. We observe that along segment *ac* of the VMP curve, the VMP of the Q_1Q_c labor units exceeds the opportunity cost to society of using that labor in this specific employment (shown by *ec* on the supply of labor curve). Therefore, if society reallocated this labor from alternative employments to this market, it would gain output of more value than it would forgo. The labor would contribute total output shown by area Q_1acQ_c in Figure 6.7. Society would forgo area Q_1ecQ_c of domestic product elsewhere, and thus the net gain would be area *eac*. This latter triangle identifies the allocative cost to society of the monopsonized labor market. Labor is underallocated to the goods and services produced in monopsonized industries.

Several attempts have been made to identify and measure monopsony power in real-world labor markets. Monopsony outcomes are not widespread in the U.S. economy.[6] Many potential employers exist for most workers, particularly when these workers are occupationally and geographically mobile. Also, strong labor unions counteract monopsony power in many labor markets.

WW6.3   Table 6.3 provides a matrix showing the wage outcomes of the three labor market models discussed thus far. The outcome in the bottom right corner of the matrix simply extends the monopsony outcome to a market where the monopsonist is an imperfect competitor in the sale of the product. You are urged to study each part of this table carefully.

TABLE 6.3 Wage Outcomes of Labor Markets without Unions

		Product Market Structure (Firm)	
		Perfect competitor in sale of product (MR = P)	Monopolist in sale of product (MR < P)
Labor Market Structure (Firm)	Perfect competitor in hire of labor (MWC = W)	W = MRP = VMP (Figure 6.4)	W = MRP W < VMP (Figure 6.6)
	Monopsonist in hire of labor (MWC > W)	W < MRP (= VMP) (Figure 6.7)	W < MRP (< VMP)

[6] For a survey of theoretical and empirical studies of monopsony, see William M. Boal and Michael R. Ransom, "Monopsony in the Labor Market," *Journal of Economic Literature,* March 1997, pp. 86–112, see also Alan Manning, *Monopsony in Motion: Imperfect Competition in Labor Markets* (Princeton, NJ: Princeton University Press, 2003).

6.3 World of Work

Pay and Performance in Professional Baseball

Professional baseball has provided an interesting laboratory in which the predictions of orthodox wage theory have been empirically tested. Until 1976 professional baseball players were bound to a single team through the so-called reserve clause that prevented players from selling their talents on the open (competitive) market. Stated differently, the reserve clause conferred monopsony power on the team that originally drafted the player. Labor market theory (Figure 6.7) would lead us to predict that this monopsony power would let teams pay wages less than a player's MRP. However, since 1976 major league players have been able to become "free agents" at the end of their sixth season of play; at that time, they can sell their services to any team. Theory suggests that free agents should be able to increase their salaries and bring them more closely into accord with their MRPs. Research tends to confirm both predictions.

Scully[*] found that before baseball players could become free agents, their salaries were substantially below their MRPs. He estimated a player's MRP as follows. First, he determined the relationship between a team's winning percentage and its revenue. Then he estimated the relationship between various possible measures of player productivity and a team's winning percentage. He found the ratio of strikeouts to walks for pitchers and the slugging averages for hitters (all nonpitchers) to be the best indicators of a player's contribution to the winning percentage. These two estimates were combined to calculate the contribution of a player to a team's total revenue.

Scully discovered that prior to free agency the estimated MRPs of both pitchers and hitters were substantially greater than player salaries. Even the lowest quality pitchers received on the average salaries amounting to only about 54 percent of their MRPs. "Star" players were exploited more than other players. The best pitchers received salaries that were only about 21 percent of their MRPs, according to Scully. The same general results applied to hitters. For example, the least productive hitters on the average received a salary equal to about 37 percent of their MRPs.

Several researchers have examined the impact of free agency on baseball players' salaries.[†] In accordance with the predictions of labor market theory, their studies indicate that the competitive bidding of free agency brought the salaries of free agents more closely into accord with their MRPs. The overturning of the monopsonistic reserve clause forced owners to pay players more closely in relation to their contribution to team revenues.

Thanks largely to free agency, the average salary in major league baseball had soared to $4.05 million for the 2020 season.

* Gerald W. Scully, "Pay and Performance in Major League Baseball," *American Economic Review,* December 1974, pp. 915–930.

† For surveys of such studies, see Andrew Zimbalist, *Baseball and Billions* (New York: Basic Books, 1992); and Lawrence M. Kahn, "The Sports Business as a Labor Market Laboratory," *Journal of Economic Perspectives,* Summer 2000, pp. 75–94.

WAGE DETERMINATION: DELAYED SUPPLY RESPONSES

The standard supply and demand model of the labor market (Figures 6.2 and 6.3) assumes that suppliers of labor respond quickly to changes in the market wage rate brought about by changes in labor demand. When the market wage rate rises in relative terms, more workers offer their labor services in that market. When the market wage falls, fewer workers supply their labor services there. Movements of this sort along a market supply of labor curve bring the quantity of labor supplied into equality with the quantity of labor demanded at the equilibrium wage rate. In brief, the labor market immediately clears.

Although rapid supply responses are indeed characteristic of some labor markets, in other situations labor supply adjustments are less rapid than the standard model suggests. In fact, in some cases, supply adjustments may take several years. Our attention now turns to a model of one of these slowly adjusting labor markets.

Cobweb Model

Consider Figure 6.8, where we depict the market for new engineers who are recent college graduates. Suppose labor demand and supply initially are D and S, respectively. Also assume that the market is presently in equilibrium at a, where the wage rate is W_0 and the level of employment is Q_0.

Now suppose an unexpected increase in the demand for engineers occurs, perhaps because of the emergence of new technologies. In the standard labor market model, the market would quickly clear at the intersection

FIGURE 6.8   Cobweb Model

The market for highly trained professionals such as engineers is characterized by delayed supply responses to changes in demand and wage rates. Because the quantity of labor supplied is temporarily fixed at Q_0, the wage rate rises to W_1 when demand changes from D to D_1. At wage rate W_1, Q_1 engineers eventually are attracted to this profession. With supply fixed at Q_1, however, the wage rate falls to W_2. Given this wage rate, the quantity of engineers available eventually falls to Q_2. This cycle repeats until equilibrium is achieved—in this case at the intersection of S and D_1.

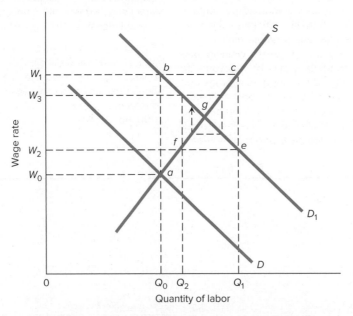

of supply S and demand D_1. But the market for new engineers and other highly trained professionals is atypical. It is not unusual in these markets to observe four- or five-year delays in the supply response to new labor market conditions. Students currently enrolling in engineering schools will not graduate and enter the labor force for several years.

In the immediate market period, the number of new engineers available remains temporarily fixed at Q_0. The immediate market period is so short that there is no quantity-supplied response to a change in the wage rate. We might therefore envision a vertical *immediate-market-period labor supply curve* emanating upward from Q_0 through a and b. Supply curve S, on the other hand, may be thought of as the *long-run supply curve;* it indicates the *eventual* response of labor suppliers to changes in wage rates. Here, the long run entails a four- to five-year period.

Given that Q_0 engineers are now in the labor force and that demand now is D_1, a *shortage* of workers will occur at W_0 and the market wage rate will shoot upward to W_1. This wage rate will eliminate the shortage because at point b, demand curve D_1 intersects the vertical immediate-market-period labor supply curve comprising Q_0ab.

This is only the beginning of the story. Because of the high wage rate W_1, numerous new students will flock to the field of engineering. When they graduate some five years hence, Q_1 engineers will be available in the labor market. This supply response is determined at c on the long-run supply curve S and results from the previous wage rate W_1. In effect, the vertical immediate-market-period labor supply curve shifts rightward in a parallel fashion from Q_0 to Q_1.

Now that the quantity of labor supplied is again temporarily fixed—this time at Q_1—a *surplus* of bc engineers occurs at W_1. The wage rate consequently drops to W_2 (point e on D_1). Here the new immediate-market-period labor supply curve going upward from Q_1 through e and c cuts the demand curve D_1 at e, and the surplus is eliminated.

This scenario continues. Although the new starting wage rate W_2 is considerably lower than W_1, it will not immediately elicit a decline in the number of new engineers offering their labor services. Recent graduates holding engineering degrees are not likely to abandon their careers in response to lower relative salaries. Moreover, wage rate W_2 in all likelihood is higher than wage rates available to engineers in nonengineering jobs. The relatively low-wage rate W_2, however, *does* affect the decisions of beginning college students who are planning their academic programs. The poor starting pay will discourage these students from opting to become engineers. In four or five years, colleges will confer fewer engineering diplomas during their graduation ceremonies. The number of new engineers in this labor market will fall from Q_1 to Q_2, the latter being determined at f on long-run supply curve S. Given demand D_1, a shortage of fe engineers occurs, and the wage rate responds by rising from W_2 to W_3.

The cycle just described repeats itself. The quantity of labor *demanded* in each period depends on the wage rate at that time; the quantity of labor *supplied* in each period results from the wage rate during the previous period when education and career decisions were originally made. In this instance, equilibrium eventually is achieved at the intersection of the long-run labor supply curve S and demand curve D_1. You are urged to carry the analysis forward through another cycle to test your understanding of this unusual model. The adjustment path toward equilibrium at g results in a cobweb pattern; for that reason, this model is called a *cobweb model.*

Two further observations merit comment. It is entirely possible for still another shift in labor demand to occur before the cobweb path is completed to g. Thus, a new set of cobweb adjustments may be necessitated. Also, the elasticities of the demand and supply curves might be such that the market does not move to the ultimate equilibrium at g, but rather continues to oscillate between periodic shortages and surpluses.[7]

---

[7] For the cobweb model to converge toward equilibrium, the supply curve must be steeper than the demand curve.

Evidence and Controversy

Cobweb models help explain adjustments in several labor markets having long training periods and highly specialized labor. For example, historical cobweb adjustments have been found in the markets for new engineers, lawyers, and physicists.[8] Recent evidence, however, indicates demand shocks are now causing a greater change in employment and a smaller adjustment of wages for information technology workers than in the past due to increased immigration of skilled workers.[9]

But not all economists find the cobweb model persuasive. Some critics question the relevance of the model to the majority of today's labor markets for the college-trained workforce. You will note that in the model labor market participants are assumed to adjust their career decisions to changes in *starting salaries*. Some economists suggest that the more likely scenario is that college students look to the present value of *lifetime earnings streams* in making education and career decisions.[10] Other critics assert that today's students are highly attuned to the possible boom–bust potential in some labor markets; therefore, they form *rational*

6.4   World of Work

Do Medical Students Know How Much Doctors Earn?

Usually, labor economists assume that individuals make unbiased predictions about their future income prospects. That is, people make income forecasts that are not systematically high or low. Economists also assume that people have access to the same information and use this information in the same manner to generate their income forecasts.

Nicholson tested these assumptions by examining how much medical students know about the current earnings of physicians. To conduct his study, Nicholson used data from an annual survey, conducted between 1974 and 1998, of medical students at a large medical school in Philadelphia. The survey asks first- and fourth-

year medical school students how much physicians currently receive in six specialties and which specialty they prefer.

The results indicate that medical students have a significant amount of error in their estimates of current earnings of physicians. The average medical student overestimated physician earnings in the 1970s, but now she underestimates earnings by 25 percent. Although the average error rate is substantial, students are more accurate in estimating earnings for their preferred specialties. Also, students learn over time: The forecast error is 35 percent lower for students in the fourth year than those in the first year. The error rate varies by demographic group: Students who are female, older, or have a higher medical entrance exam score tend to underestimate earnings more than their peers.

Source: Sean Nicholson, "How Much Do Medical Students Know about Physician Income?" *Journal of Human Resources,* Winter 2005, pp. 100–114.

---

[8] Richard B. Freeman, "A Cobweb Model of the Starting Salary of New Engineers," *Industrial and Labor Relations Review,* January 1976, pp. 236–248; Freeman, "Legal Cobwebs: A Recursive Model of the Market for New Lawyers," *Review of Economics and Statistics,* May 1975, pp. 171–180; Freeman, "Supply and Salary Adjustments to the Changing Science Manpower Markets: Physics, 1948–1973," *American Economic Review,* March 1975, pp. 27–39.

[9] John Bound, Breno Bragal, Joseph M. Golden, and Sarah Turner, "Pathways to Adjustment: The Case of Information Technology Workers," *American Economic Review,* May 2013, pp. 203–207.

[10] See Joel W. Hay, "Physicians' Specialty Choice and Specialty Income," in G. Duru and J. H. P. Paelinck (eds.), *Econometrics of Health Care* (Netherlands: Kluwer Academic, 1991); and Sean Nicholson, "Physician Specialty Choice under Uncertainty," *Journal of Labor Economics,* October 2002, pp. 816–847.

expectations about the end result of any sudden change in the demand for labor and adjust their supply responses accordingly. If either of these two related criticisms is correct, the abrupt changes in immediate-market-period labor supply in the cobweb model and the resulting oscillating path to equilibrium are less likely to occur. That is, equilibrium is more likely to be achieved without the cobweb effects.

In any event, the cobweb model is important because it reminds us that labor supply adjustments are not always as immediate or as certain as our basic labor market model predicts. The upshot is that many labor markets may better be characterized as moving toward allocative efficiency (VMP $=$ P_L) than as having actually achieved it.

6.2 *Quick Review*

- A monopsonist pays a lower wage rate and employs fewer workers than firms hiring in a competitive labor market; this outcome is allocatively inefficient.

- In the cobweb model, the equilibrium wage rate is achieved only after a period of oscillating wage rate changes caused by recurring labor shortages and surpluses.

Your Turn

Why does the monopsonist's MWC curve lie above the market labor supply curve? Isn't this a disadvantage to the monopsonist? (*Answers:* See page 541.)

Chapter Summary

1. In a competitive labor market, the demand for labor is a price-adjusted summation of labor demand by independently acting individual employers, and the supply of labor is a summation of the responses of individual workers to various wage rates. Market supply and demand determine an equilibrium wage rate and level of employment.

2. The vertical height of the market labor supply curve measures the opportunity cost to society of employing the last worker in some specific use (P_L). The vertical height of the labor demand curve indicates the extra revenue the employer gains by hiring that unit of labor (MRP) and, given perfectly competitive markets, the value of that output to society (VMP).

3. The locations of the supply and demand curves in the labor market depend on the determinants of each (Table 6.1). When one of these determinants changes, the affected curve shifts either rightward or leftward, altering the equilibrium wage and employment levels.

4. The individual firm operating in a perfectly competitive labor market is a wage taker. This implies that its MWC equals the wage rate W; that is, the supply of labor is perfectly elastic. This firm maximizes its profits by hiring the quantity of labor at which MRP = MWC, or MRP = W.

5. An efficient allocation of labor occurs when the VMPs of a particular type of labor are equal in various uses and these VMPs also equal the opportunity cost P_L of that labor. Perfectly competitive product and resource markets result in allocative efficiency. By maximizing profits where MRP = MWC, firms also equate VMP and P_L because MRP = VMP and MWC = P_L.

6. Monopoly in the product market causes MR to fall faster than product price as more workers are hired and output is expanded. Because product price P exceeds MR, it follows that MRP (= MP × MR) is less than VMP (= MP × P). The result is less employment and an underallocation of labor resources relative to the case of perfect competition in the product market.

7. Under monopsony MWC > S_L (or P_L) because the employer must bid up wages to attract a greater quantity of labor and pay the higher wage to all workers. Consequently, it will employ fewer workers than under competitive conditions and pay a wage rate below the MRP of labor. This underallocation of labor resources (VMP > P_L) reduces the total value of output in the economy.

8. The cobweb model traces labor supply adjustments to changes in labor demand and wage rates in markets characterized by long training periods. The equilibrium wage rate is achieved only after a period of oscillating wage rate changes caused by recurring labor shortages and surpluses.

Terms and Concepts

perfectly competitive labor market

determinants of labor supply and demand

marginal revenue product

average wage cost

marginal wage cost

MRP = MWC rule

efficient allocation of labor

price of labor

pure monopsony

joint monopsony

cobweb model

Questions and Study Suggestions

1. List the distinct characteristics of a perfectly competitive labor market and compare them to the characteristics of monopsony.

2. Explain why most market labor supply curves slope upward and to the right, even though individual labor supply curves are presumed to be backward-bending. How does the height of a market labor supply curve relate to the concept of opportunity costs?

3. What effect will each of the following have on the market labor demand for a specific type of labor?

    a. An increase in product demand that increases product price.

    b. A decline in the productivity of this type of labor.

    c. An increase in the price of a gross substitute for labor.

    d. A decline in the price of a gross complement for labor.

    e. The demise of several firms that hire this labor.

    f. A decline in the market wage rate for this labor.

    g. A series of mergers that transforms the product market into a monopoly.

4. Predict the impact of each of the following on the equilibrium wage rate and level of employment in labor market A:

    a. An increase in labor demand and supply in labor market A.

    b. The transformation of labor market A from a competitive to a monopsonistic market.

5. Assume a surplus of doctors exists. Use labor market supply and demand graphics to depict this outcome. How would the market remedy this situation in the short run and the long run?

Q_B	VMP_{Bx}	VMP_{By}
1	$18	$23
2	15	19
3	12	15
4	9	11
5	6	9
6	3	5

6. Answer the following questions on the basis of the table shown here. Q_B is type B labor, and VMP_{Bx} and VMP_{By} are the industry values of the MPs of this labor in producing x and y, the only two goods in the economy.

   a. Explain why the VMPs in the table decline as more units of labor are employed.

   b. If the supply price or opportunity cost of labor P_L is $9, how many units of type B labor need to be used in producing x and y to achieve an efficient allocation of labor? What will be the combined total value of the two outputs?

   c. Suppose P_L is $15 and that presently five units of labor are being allocated to producing x while two units are being allocated to y. Is this an efficient allocation of labor? Why or why not? If not, what is the efficient allocation of type B labor?

   d. Suppose P_L is $25 and three units of labor are being allocated to producing x, while six units are being allocated to producing y. Explain why this is not an efficient allocation of labor. What *is* the efficient allocation of this type of labor? What gain in the total value of leisure, alternative outputs, or home production results from this reallocation of labor?

   e. Suppose product x is sold in a perfectly competitive product market. Also ignore the VMP_{By} column and assume that the VMP_{Bx} schedule is representative of each firm hiring workers in a perfectly competitive labor market. If the market wage rate is $12, what will be each firm's MWC? What will be their MRPs at their profit-maximizing level of employment? Explain why an efficient allocation of labor will occur in this industry.

7. Complete the following table for a single firm operating in labor market A and product market AA:

Units of Labor	Wage Rate (W)	Total Wage Cost	MWC	MRP	VMP
1	$10			$16	$16
2	10			14	15
3	10			12	14
4	10			10	12
5	10			8	10
6	10			6	8

a. What, if anything, can one conclude about the degree of competition in labor market *A* and product market *AA?*

b. What is the profit-maximizing level of employment? Explain.

c. Does this profit-maximizing level of employment yield allocative efficiency? Explain.

8. Use the production data shown here on the left and the labor supply data on the right for a single firm to answer the following questions. Assume that this firm is selling its product for $1 per unit in a perfectly competitive product market.

Units of Labor	Total Product
0	0
1	13
2	25
3	34
4	42
5	46
6	48

Units of Labor	Wage Rate
0	–
1	$1
2	2
3	3
4	4
5	5
6	6

a. How many workers will this firm choose to employ?

b. What will be its profit-maximizing wage rate?

c. What labor market model do these data best describe?

9. Assume a firm *(a)* is a monopsonist in hiring labor and *(b)* is selling its product as a monopolist. Portray this market graphically. Correctly label all relevant curves, show the equilibrium wage rate and level of employment, and indicate the efficiency loss (if any).

10. Use graphical analysis to show how an unexpected decline in labor demand may set off a cobweb adjustment cycle in a labor market for highly trained professionals. In explaining your graph, distinguish between the immediate-period supply curve and the long-run supply curve.

Internet Exercise

Who Is Getting Pay Raises and Who Is Getting Pay Cuts?

 Go to the Bureau of Labor Statistics Data website **(https://www.bls.gov/data/home.htm)** and select "Series Report." Enter the following ID series numbers: CES1000000001, CES1000000032, CES4200000001, and CES4200000032. Then click on "All Years." This will retrieve average hourly earnings (in 1982–1984 dollars) and employment for mining and logging and retail trade.

What were the average real hourly wage and employment rates in 1979 and 1995 in the retail trade and mining and logging industries? What were the percentage changes in the wage rate and employment for both industries? On the basis of the changes in wages and employment, what can you infer about the relative size of the changes in labor demand and labor supply?

What are the average real hourly wages and employment rates for the most recent month shown in the retail trade and mining and logging industries? What were the percentage changes between 1995 and the most recent month for the wage rate and employment for both industries? On the basis of the changes in wages and employment, what can you infer about the relative size of the changes in labor demand and labor supply?

Internet Links

 The Bureau of Labor Statistics Wages, Earnings, and Benefits website contains detailed statistics about wages by state, occupation, and industry **(https://www.bls.gov/bls/blswage.htm)**.

Chapter 7

Alternative Pay Schemes and Labor Efficiency

After reading this chapter, you should be able to:

1. Describe the types and growth in fringe benefits.
2. Explain the wage-fringe model.
3. Describe the principal-agent problem as it applies to the employer–employee relationship.
4. Explain how incentive pay plans solve the principal-agent problem.
5. Explain the efficiency wage model.
6. Refine the definition of efficiency to include compensation issues.

Most of you will be seeking full-time employment when you graduate from college. Let's suppose you are offered a job relating to your college major. Before accepting this particular job offer, what information about the compensation package would you want to know? Our surmise is that first you would want to know about the annual salary or the hourly wage. What else? No doubt you would seek information about the fringe benefit package. How good are the medical benefits? Is there disability insurance? Are there paid vacations? Does the firm contribute to a pension plan?

In Chapter 6, we identified and explained several basic models of wage determination. Our assumption in those models was that all compensation was in the form of an hourly wage rate, such as $20 per hour. But as the previous paragraph suggests, in reality, fringe benefits constitute an important element of our compensation. In addition, firms are not indifferent about the composition of the total compensation they pay; for example, they may wish to structure their pay package in special ways to enhance work effort and reduce turnover. The goal of this chapter is to examine pay packages that are more complex in composition and purpose than the standard hourly wage rate.

ECONOMICS OF FRINGE BENEFITS

We begin by analyzing the economics of the fringe benefit portion of total compensation. *Total compensation* comprises wage earnings and the costs of fringe benefits. *Fringe benefits* include public (legally mandated) programs such as Social Security, unemployment compensation, and workers' compensation. They also include many private nonmandatory programs such as private pensions, medical and dental insurance, paid vacations, and sick leave. We will find that fringe benefits can increase the utility workers receive from a given amount of total compensation. Fringe benefits also can benefit the firm by permitting it to retain and attract high-quality workers.

Fringe Benefits: Facts

Fringe benefits constitute a significant portion of total compensation, and they have grown rapidly as a percentage of total compensation during the past several decades.

1 Fringe Benefits as a Proportion of Total Compensation

The Bureau of Labor Statistics (BLS) has broken down employee compensation among wage and salary workers.[1] As shown in Figure 7.1, *wages and salaries* constitute about 69 percent of total compensation among wage and salary workers, while *employee fringe benefits* account for about 31 percent.

It is instructive to examine the various fringe benefit components of the compensation pie. Observe from Figure 7.1 that *legally required benefits* comprise 7.3 percent of total compensation. These benefits include Social Security, railroad retirement and supplemental retirement, federal and state unemployment insurance, workers' compensation, and state temporary disability insurance benefits. *Paid leaves,* which include paid vacations, paid holidays, paid sick leave, and the like, account for 7.2 percent of total employee compensation. Note that *insurance benefits*–for life, health, and sickness and accident insurance–comprise an 8.7 percent share.

The remaining slices of the employee compensation pie are *retirement and savings benefits* (5.4 percent), which include retirement plans and saving thrift plans; and *supplemental pay* (2.8 percent), comprising premium pay for overtime and work on holidays, shift differentials, nonproduction bonuses, and lump-sum payments.

FIGURE 7.1   **Components of Total Compensation (Wage and Salary Workers, in Percent)**

Fringe benefits account for 31 percent of the total compensation among wage and salary workers.

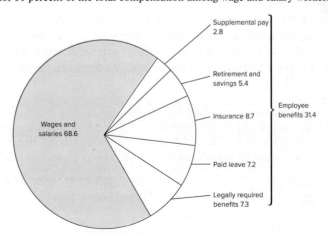

Source: Bureau of Labor Statistics, "Employer Costs for Employee Compensation–March 2018." www.bls.gov

---

[1] U.S. Bureau of Labor Statistics, *Employer Costs for Employee Compensation,* U.S. Department of Labor. News Release 14-2208, December 2014.

FIGURE 7.2 **Relative Growth of Fringe Benefits**

Fringe benefits have increased dramatically as a percentage of total compensation since 1929.

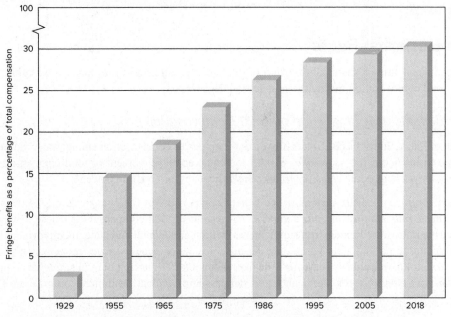

Source: Bureau of Labor Statistics, "Employee Benefits in a Changing Economy: A BLS Chartbook." www.bls.gov

The composition of total compensation varies greatly by industry. For example, the fringe benefits proportion of employee compensation is larger (*a*) in high-paying industries than in low-paying ones and (*b*) in goods-producing industries compared to service industries. The proportion and specific types of benefits also vary by industry. For example, paid leaves comprise about 9 percent of total compensation in information, whereas they are only about 3 percent in leisure and hospitality.

Finally, the BLS data reveal that the composition of total compensation also differs by occupational group. For example, because of legally mandated fringe benefits, the fringe benefit share of total compensation is greater for blue-collar workers than for white-collar workers. As another example, legally required benefits are a significantly higher percentage of total pay for transportation workers than for executives.

2 Fringe Benefit Growth

Fringe benefits have grown significantly as a component of total employee compensation during the past several decades. This growth is shown in Figure 7.2, where we see that fringe benefits for all workers have expanded from less than 3 percent of total compensation in 1929 to 31 percent of total pay in 2018.

Why are fringe benefits a significant component of total compensation? What explains their rapid growth? A model of optimal fringe benefits will help us answer these questions.

THEORY OF OPTIMAL FRINGE BENEFITS

The theory of optimal fringe benefits is a variation of the income–leisure choice problem encountered in Chapter 2. There we saw that a budget constraint (wage rate line) limited the worker to specific combinations

FIGURE 7.3 **A Worker's Indifference Map for Wages and Fringe Benefits**

Each indifference curve shows the combinations of wages and fringe benefits that yield a specific level of total utility. Indifference curves farther to the northeast in the indifference map represent higher levels of total utility; therefore, they are preferred by the worker.

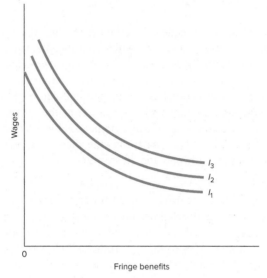

of earnings and leisure (Figure 2.5). The worker chose the single combination of these two "goods" that provided the highest utility. This choice was made on the basis of the worker's subjective evaluation of the trade-off between earnings and leisure in relationship to the objectively determined budget constraint.

In a similar way, we might think of a worker facing a choice between wages and fringe benefits. The worker's preferences for these two "goods" are reflected in an *indifference map.* The budget constraint takes the form of the employer's total compensation line, or an *isoprofit curve.*[2]

Worker's Indifference Map

Each indifference curve shown in Figure 7.3 displays combinations of wages and fringe benefits yielding the same level of satisfaction or utility to the worker. Thus, a single indifference curve such as I_1 reflects a constant level of total utility. As we move northeast from the origin, each successive indifference curve entails a higher level of total utility.

The downward slope of each indifference curve indicates that workers view wages and fringes as each yielding utility and therefore being somewhat substitutable. At first thought, this may seem surprising because most fringes are *in-kind benefits—benefits in the form of a specific kind of good or service.* Would not a worker (consumer) always be better off with—and therefore prefer—an additional dollar's worth of (cash) wages rather than an additional dollar's worth of some specific fringe benefit? One dollar in cash wages represents generalized purchasing power that can be spent on $1 worth of whatever good or service is most preferred by (yields the most marginal utility to) the consumer. An in-kind fringe benefit, on the other hand, ties the

[2] The analysis that follows was developed by Ronald G. Ehrenberg and Robert S. Smith. See Smith and Ehrenberg, "Estimating Wage-Fringe Trade-Offs: Some Data Problems," in Jack E. Triplett (ed.), *The Measurement of Labor Cost* (Chicago: University of Chicago Press, 1983), pp. 347–367; and Ehrenberg and Smith, *Modern Labor Economics,* 11th Edition (Boston, MA: Pearson, 2012), pp. 262–269.

individual to the particular good or service. In fact, that good or service may provide little or no marginal utility, or satisfaction, to a particular worker. An on-the-job daycare center yields little satisfaction to a worker who does not have children or to an older worker whose children are grown. Nevertheless, there are two major reasons that workers are in fact willing to sacrifice some of their wages to obtain a package of fringe benefits.

First, and undoubtedly of the greatest consequence, certain fringe benefits entail a large tax advantage to workers. For example, workers do not pay taxes on the deferred income benefits embodied in private pension plans until those benefits are actually received. Pensions allow principal, interest, and dividends to accumulate at a pretax growth rate rather than a posttax pace. Also, because the worker's earned income will likely fall to zero at retirement, the income provided by the pension plan might be taxed at a lower marginal tax rate (say, 15 percent) than the same amount paid as wages during the worker's active work life (e.g., 28 or 35 percent). In short, pensions are a means of deferring income to achieve lower tax rates. The after-tax value of $1 of pension contribution is perceived to be greater than the after-tax value of $1 of current wage income. Similarly, premiums paid by employers for health and life insurance are subject to neither the Social Security tax nor the personal income tax.[3]

Second, workers may be willing to substitute fringe benefits for part of their wages to guard against their own tendency to purchase goods that provide more immediate gratification than, say, health insurance or pension annuities. People may realize that their cash earnings tend to get spent on other items such as cars, boats, clothing, and vacations; thus, they are willing to sacrifice some of their earnings to "lock in" health and pension benefits that they know are important for their future. By accepting pay packages that contain fringe benefits, workers ensure that insurance, pension, and other benefits are available when needed.

Observe that the indifference curves not only slope downward but are convex to the origin (as was the case in our income–leisure diagrams in Chapter 2). Stated technically, the marginal rate of substitution of fringe benefits for wages falls as more benefits are added. When a person has few fringe benefits, he or she is willing to trade off a large amount of wages for an additional unit of fringe benefits. But as the amount of fringe benefits rises, the marginal utility of still more fringe benefits falls, and the person is less willing to sacrifice wage payments to attain still more units of them.

Employer's Isoprofit Curve

For a given level of output, a firm will wish to minimize its total compensation per hour of work to help maximize its profits. In Figure 7.4 we show a firm's *isoprofit curve, WF,* which *indicates the various combinations of wages and fringe benefits providing a given profit.* We assume for simplicity that competition in the product market has resulted in a *normal profit.* We also suppose that competition in the labor market has forced this firm to pay the total compensation indicated by the combinations of wages and fringes demonstrated by curve *WF.* That is, *WF* shows the combinations of wages and fringe benefits that allow the firm to maintain a normal profit, given the "prices" of wages and fringe benefits.

Close inspection of this isoprofit line in Figure 7.4 reveals that its slope is −1. In this example, a $1 reduction in wages accompanied by a $1 increase in fringe benefits leaves the total compensation to the worker—and thus the total profits to the firm—unchanged. The firm's total compensation and profits are the same if it pays $0W$ wages and no fringe benefits or no wages and $0F$ fringe benefits. Similarly, total compensation is the same for all other combinations of wages and fringe benefits indicated by line *WF.*

---

[3] For studies examining the role of taxes in employee demand for fringe benefits, see Bradley T. Heim and Ithai Z. Lurie, "The Effect of Recent Tax Changes on Tax-Preferred Saving Behavior," *National Tax Journal,* June 2012, pp. 283–312; andJohn Beshears, James J. Choi, David Laibson, and Brigitte C. Madrian, "Does Front-Loading Taxation Increase Savings? Evidence from Roth 401(k) Introductions," *Journal of Public Economics,* July 2017, pp. 84–95.

FIGURE 7.4 An Employer's Isoprofit Curve (Normal Profit)

An isoprofit curve portrays the various combinations of wages and fringe benefits that yield a specific level of profits. We assume that competition will result in a normal profit. Thus, *WF* shows the various combinations of wages and fringes the firm can afford to provide, given the "prices" of the alternative forms of compensation.

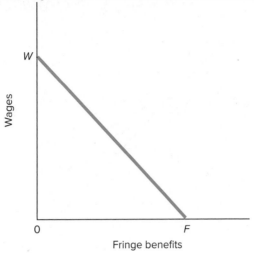

Wage–Fringe Optimum

Noting that the axes of Figures 7.3 and 7.4 are the same, we can now determine the worker's utility-maximizing combination of wages and fringe benefits. Of all the attainable combinations of wages and fringe benefits along line *WF* in Figure 7.5, combination W_0 and F_0 yields the worker's greatest satisfaction, or utility. Specifically, the utility-maximizing combination is the one tangent to the highest attainable indifference curve (I_2 at *b*). To test this proposition, note that points *a* (all wage payments and no fringes) and *c* (relatively low-wage payments and high fringes) are inferior to point *b*. That is, at these points the worker is on lower-than-attainable indifference curve I_1. This person can attain the higher indifference curve I_2 if the wages–fringes combination is appropriately adjusted from point *a* or *c* toward *b*.

Although indifference maps vary among individual workers, we will suppose for simplicity that this worker's preferences for wage payments and fringe benefits are representative of the average worker. Differing indifference maps among workers—and therefore differing wage–fringe optima—are discussed in Chapter 8.

Causes of Fringe Benefit Growth

Let's next consider the implications of a lower "price" for fringe benefits. In Figure 7.6, we have drawn a new normal-profit isoprofit line *WF'* that has a flatter slope than line *WF*. The shift from *WF* to *WF'* tells us that the relative per-unit cost or "price" of fringe benefits has fallen. Restated, the firm can now supply more fringe benefits at all but the highest wage without increasing its total compensation; thus, it can provide more fringe benefits without reducing its profits. The firm can now exchange a dollar's worth of wages for more than a dollar's worth of benefits, even though these benefits cost only a dollar. It will want to offer its workers this better trade-off between wages and fringe benefits to attract and retain the highest-quality employees. In fact, a competitive labor market will dictate that the firm pay compensation to workers as indicated by line *WF'* because other firms will bid up the level of total compensation to this level.

This new normal-profit isoprofit line results in a new tangency position at point *d* on a higher indifference curve, I_3. Observe that this representative worker now selects a combination of wages and fringes more

FIGURE 7.5   Wage–Fringe Optimum

The optimal combination of wages and fringe benefits is at b, where the isoprofit curve is tangent to the highest attainable indifference curve I_2. Here the firm will provide W_0 wages and F_0 fringe benefits. Points a and c are also attainable combinations of wages and fringes but yield less total utility, as is evidenced by their locations on the lower indifference curve I_1.

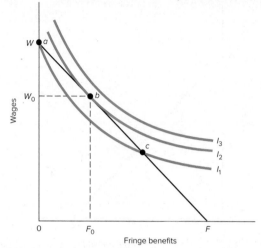

heavily weighted in favor of fringe benefits. The decline in the price of fringe benefits has both enabled and enticed the worker to "buy" more fringe benefits. He or she now has more real income (wages plus fringes) and views fringe benefits as being a relatively "better buy" than they were before. Consequently, this worker opts for more fringe benefits and achieves a higher level of utility (I_3 at d rather than I_2 at b).

The obvious question is what might cause the normal-profit isoprofit line to fan outward as indicated in Figure 7.6. What might lower the price of fringe benefits and enable the firm to offer more of them and still retain the same levels of total compensation and normal profits? The answers to these questions provide the basis for a list of reasons why fringe benefits have grown historically.

Tax Advantages to the Employer

We have observed that fringe benefits confer tax advantages to the worker. These fringe benefits also reduce taxes owed by the employer. The employer must pay half of the 15.3 percent Social Security payroll tax on worker earnings up to $118,500 (2015) for each employee. For workers earning less than this amount, the firm reduces its payroll tax burden by tilting the pay package away from wage earnings and toward fringe benefits. Suppose a worker earns $30,000 a year. At the 2015 payroll tax rate of 7.65 percent, the employer would have to pay $2,295 of tax. But if the employer instead pays the worker $20,000 in earnings and $10,000 of fringe benefits, the tax burden for the firm falls to $1,530 (= $20,000 × 0.0765). Multiplied by thousands of workers, the tax savings to a large firm can be considerable. The upshot is that the firm can offer fringe benefits worth more than a dollar for a dollar reduction in direct pay. In Figure 7.6, the normal-profit isoprofit line fans outward as indicated by the shift from WF to WF'. Because the Social Security tax base and rate have both increased historically, the optimal level of fringe benefits has risen.[4]

---

[4] For a study examining the impact of taxes on the probability that a worker is eligible for health insurance, see Anne Beeson Royalty, "Tax Preferences for Fringe Benefits and Workers' Eligibility for Employer Health Insurance," *Journal of Public Economics,* February 2000, pp. 209–227. Also see Thomas L. Selden, "The Impact of Increased Tax Subsidies on the Insurance Coverage of Self-Employed Families: Evidence from the 1996–2003 Medical Expenditure Panel Survey," *Journal of Human Resources,* Winter 2009, pp. 115–139.

Economies of Scale

Significant economies of scale usually exist in the collective purchase of fringe benefits that lower their prices to buyers. In particular, the average administrative costs and agent fees are much less in purchasing medical, life, disability, or dental insurance for a group than for an individual.[5] In addition, group policies eliminate the *adverse selection problem*—the tendency for individuals who are most likely to draw large benefits to sign up for insurance. As with tax advantages, the "discount prices" on insurance reduce the per-unit cost of fringes and rotate the normal-profit isoprofit line outward, as in Figure 7.6. The result is that a worker is enticed to accept more fringe benefits than previously. To the extent that cost savings have increased historically as the size of firms has grown, the optimal amount of fringe benefits has also grown.

Efficiency Considerations

WW7.1   Employers are interested in protecting their training investments and reducing their recruiting and training costs. They may see fringe benefits as a way to tie workers to jobs and hence to reduce quits. Pension benefits, in particular, are effective in reducing employee turnover.[6] Lower turnover means that a higher proportion of the firm's workers are experienced workers who are well past the training stage. Consequently, the average productivity of a firm's workforce rises.

FIGURE 7.6 **Fringe Benefit Growth**

A decrease in the price of fringe benefits due to tax advantages, scale economies, and efficiency considerations fans the normal-profit isoprofit line outward. This allows the worker to attain a higher indifference curve (I_3 rather than I_2). In the process, fringe benefits expand from F_0 to F_1.

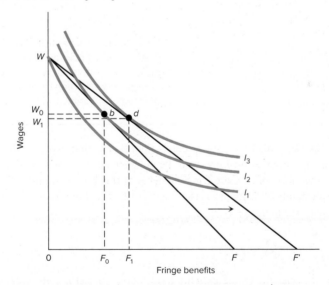

[5] For studies documenting economies of scale in the administration of pension plans, see Jacob A. Bikker and Jan De Freu, "Operating Costs of Pension Funds: The Impact of Scale, Governance, and Pension Design," *Journal of Pension Economics and Finance,* January 2009, pp. 63–89; and Gosse A. G. Alserda, Jacob A. Bikker, and Fieke S. G. Van Der Lecq, "X-Efficiency and Economies of Scale in Pension Fund Administration and Investment," *Applied Economics,* Issue 48 2018, pp. 5164–5188.

[6] For example, see William E. Even and David A. Macpherson, "Employer Size and Labor Turnover: The Role of Pensions," *Industrial and Labor Relations Review,* July 1996, pp. 707–728; and Harley Frazis and Mark A. Loewenstein, "How Responsive Are Quits to Benefits?" *Journal of Human Resources,* Fall 2013, pp. 969–997. For a recent analysis of the effect of pension type on employee turnover, see Dan Goldhaber, Cyrus Grout, Kristian L. Holden, "Pension Structure and Employee Turnover: Evidence from a Large Public Pension System," *Industrial and Labor Relations Review,* August 2017, pp. 976–1007.

7.1 World of Work

[Job] Locked and [Un]Loaded*

Health insurance coverage may cause some workers to stay on a job they would prefer to leave. Access to affordable health insurance is usually tied to being employed at a firm that offers health insurance. Firms that provide health insurance often require waiting periods before covering new workers or completely exclude a new worker's preexisting medical conditions. As a consequence, some workers may be reluctant to change jobs because of concerns about losing health insurance coverage. This reduced job mobility is known as "job lock."

The Patient Protection and Affordable Care Act (PPACA), enacted in 2010, reduces "job lock" by increasing health insurance portability. One of the ways it does so is through its dependent insurance mandate, which permits adults under the age of 26 to be covered by their parent's health insurance plan. This reduces job lock since young adults can change jobs without losing health insurance coverage,

Kofoed and Frasier examine the effects of the PPACA dependent health insurance mandate on the reenlistment in the U.S. Army. They compared the change in the reenlistment rates of soldiers aged 23–25 who gained access to dependent health insurance to soldiers aged 27–30 who did not get such access. Their analysis indicates that the reenlistment rate of the younger soldiers fell 5 percent relative to the older soldier reenlistment rates after the policy change. Furthermore, the decrease in the reenlistment rate was largest among the talented soldiers as measured by test scores.

The reduced job lock is having adverse effects for the military since it is losing some of its most able soldiers. However, the affected individuals and overall labor market benefit from the reduced labor market frictions. Younger soldiers with dependent health insurance coverage were more likely to attend college, which will improve their future job opportunities.

* Based on Michael S. Kofoed and Wyatt J. Frasier, "[Job] Locked and [Un]loaded: The Effect of the Affordable Care Act Dependency Mandate on Reenlistment in the U.S. Army," *Journal of Health Economics,* May 2019, pp. 103–116.

Viewed by the firm, pension benefits thus are less costly than their dollar expense. From a dollar outlay, the firm must subtract the added revenue resulting from the enhanced productivity arising from the fringe benefit package. A firm can, therefore, offer more fringe benefits of this kind without suffering a loss of profits.[7] Because the training investments of firms have risen historically, firms increasingly have had an incentive to use fringe benefits to reduce turnover.

Other Factors

There are several other reasons why fringe benefits have increased historically. Certain fringe benefits are quite *income elastic.* They involve pension coverage and such services as medical and dental care, purchases of which are quite sensitive to increases in income. Thus, as worker incomes have grown historically, it is not

---

[7] Although the overall productivity-enhancing aspects of fringe benefits are thought to dominate, some fringe benefits may reduce productivity. For example, paid sick leave may encourage absenteeism. Also, certain fringe benefits may attract employees who are most likely to draw upon the particular benefits, thus increasing the cost of the fringe benefit program to the employer. For example, a firm that offers parental leave may attract a disproportionate number of employees who have children. For a discussion of the public policy implications of this problem, see Lawrence H. Summers, "Some Simple Economics of Mandated Benefits," *American Economic Review,* May 1989, pp. 177–183.

surprising that the "purchase" of such fringes has also expanded.[8] Also, the federal government has raised mandated fringe benefits such as Social Security and unemployment compensation. Finally, we will find in Chapter 11 that unionization historically has been a factor in the rise in fringe benefits. On average, union workers receive more generous fringe benefits than nonunion workers. Also, nonunion firms often emulate union contracts as a way to deter unionism.

7.1 *Quick Review*

- Fringe benefits account for 31 percent of the total compensation among wage and salary workers.
- In the wage–fringe benefit model, the optimal combination of wages and fringe benefits occurs where the isoprofit curve is tangent to the highest attainable indifference curve.
- Favorable tax treatment, economies of scale, and efficiency considerations have reduced the "price" of fringe benefits, expanding their availability and enhancing worker utility.

Your Turn

Suppose the government decides to tax fringe benefits as ordinary income. What would happen to the slopes of the typical worker's indifference curves? How would this affect the optimal amount of fringe benefits? (*Answer:* See page 541.)

THE PRINCIPAL–AGENT PROBLEM

We next turn to a discussion of the relationship between pay and performance. This pay may take the form of either direct cash or fringe benefits. But as a prelude to this topic, we need to explore the nature of the relationship between firms and workers.

We know from our discussion in previous chapters that firms hire employees because workers help produce goods and services that firms can sell for a profit in the marketplace. In this respect, workers might be thought of as the firms' *agents—parties who are hired to advance the interests of others.* Alternatively, firms can be conceived of as *principals—parties who hire others to help them achieve their objectives.* In this case, the firms' or principals' objective is profits. Employees are willing to help firms earn profits in return for payments of wage income. This income enables workers to buy goods and services that yield utility; thus, the relationship between principals (firms) and agents (workers) is based on mutual self-interest; the employment relationship benefits both firms and workers. But to say that principals and agents share common interests is not to say that all their interests are identical. In situations where interests between firms and workers diverge, a so-called principal–agent problem might arise.

The *principal-agent problem occurs when agents (workers) pursue some of their own objectives in conflict with achieving the goals of the principals (firms).* Firms desire to maximize profits; workers wish to maximize utility. Profit maximization requires that employees work all agreed-upon hours at agreed-upon levels of effort. Otherwise, output will be reduced, and average and marginal costs of production will be higher. But under many employment circumstances, workers can enhance their own utility by engaging in *opportunistic behavior* that directly conflicts with profit maximization. Specifically, workers can increase their leisure by *shirking—*that is, by either *taking unauthorized work breaks or giving less than agreed-upon effort during work*

---

[8] Stephen Woodbury, "Substitution Between Wage and Nonwage Benefits," *American Economic Review,* March 1983, pp. 166–182.

hours. If undetected by firms, this shirking permits workers to increase their leisure—through reduced work time and effort—without forfeiting income. In terms of our earlier income-leisure model (Figure 2.5), workers who neglect or evade work can attain greater total utility than that available along their wage rate lines. In effect, undetected shirking allows workers to attain indifference curves like I_3 in Figure 2.5.

An important proposition derives from the principal–agent perspective. *Quite simply, firms (principals) have a profit incentive to find ways to reduce or eliminate principal-agent problems.* The remainder of this chapter explores various facets of this proposition.

PAY FOR PERFORMANCE

One way that firms might attempt to solve the principal-agent problem is to tie pay directly to output or performance. Some so-called *incentive pay plans* have become increasingly popular throughout the economy. These pay schemes include piece rates, commissions and royalties, raises and promotions, bonuses, profit and equity sharing, and tournament pay.[9]

Piece Rates

Piece rates are compensation paid in proportion to the number of units of personal output. This compensation is often found in situations where workers control the pace of work, and firms find it expensive to monitor worker effort. For example, apple pickers are paid by the bushel, apparel workers are paid by the piece, and typists are paid by the page. Although piece rates are normally associated with low-paying jobs, this type of pay is more ordinary than commonly thought. Surgeons in private practice set fees on a per-operation basis, tax preparers charge fixed amounts for each simple tax return, and lawyers charge set amounts for the various types of wills they draw up.

Evidence indicates that workers who are paid piece rates earn 10–15 percent more pay than comparable hourly paid workers in the same industry.[10] Nevertheless, piece rates have several drawbacks that have collectively resulted in their declining importance in the American industry. First, in industries where technological change is rapid, it can be very difficult for employers to find the profit-maximizing piece rates. Workers can artificially boost the piece rate by agreeing among themselves to make the job seem more difficult and time-consuming than is actually the case.[11] Second, piece rates increase the likelihood of weekly, monthly, and even yearly income variability for workers. Thus to attract workers to piece-rate jobs, firms may have to pay wage premiums (Chapter 8) to compensate workers for this risk of earnings variation. Employers could save the cost of this premium pay by paying a straight hourly wage. Third, where production is complex and team-oriented, it is difficult to ascribe units of output directly to the performance of individuals. Who produces each tube of Colgate toothpaste, can of Campbell's soup, or bottle of Coca-Cola? Fourth, close cooperation among workers is required for successful team performance. Piece rates reward independent work effort and therefore do little to promote this needed cooperation. Finally, piece rates suffer from their own advantage:

---

[9] For an analysis of the determinants of method of pay, see Charles Brown, "Firms' Choice of Method of Pay," *Industrial and Labor Relations Review,* February 1990, pp. S165–S182.

[10] Charles Brown, "Wage Levels and Method of Pay," *Rand Journal of Economics,* Autumn 1992, pp. 366–375. For a study reporting 20 to 22 percent higher productivity among piece-rate workers, see Bruce Shearer, "Piece Rates, Fixed Wages, and Incentives: Evidence from a Field Experiment," *Review of Economic Studies,* April 2004, pp. 513–534. For evidence that piece rates increase the probability of workplace injury by 5 percentage points, see Keith A. Bender, Colin P. Green, and John S. Heywood, "Piece Rates and Workplace Injury: Does Survey Evidence Support Adam Smith?" *Journal of Population Economics,* April 2012, pp. 569–590. The authors suggest this evidence indicates that the piece rate earnings premium could be partly a compensating wage differential for job injury.

[11] Stephen Jones, *The Economics of Conformism* (New York: Basil Blackwell, 1984).

The rapid production pace they elicit often results in poor product quality. For these reasons, piece rates have increasingly given way to *time rates—pay based on units of time such as hours, months, or years.*

Commissions and Royalties

Unlike piece rates, which link pay to units of output, commissions and royalties tie pay to the value of sales. *Commissions* are commonly received by realtors, insurance agents, stockbrokers, and sales personnel. A glance at the classified sections of big-city newspapers will reveal several columns of help-wanted ad for commissioned workers. *Royalties* also are set as a percentage of sales revenue. They typically are paid to authors, film producers, recording artists, and similar professionals. For instance, about $10 of the price of this textbook—if it is new—accrues to the authors (and we thank you).

7.2 World of Work

End of Teacher Tenure?*

Tenure is a unique employment system in which school teachers can gain almost complete future job security. After a probationary period as few as two years in some states, a teachers' school decides either to grant tenure or to end the person's employment at the school.

The historical purpose of tenure has been to protect teachers against arbitrary discharge for nonwork reasons (such as political views) or teaching controversial topics. But tenure also has some potential drawbacks. The job security it provides may prevent the termination of incompetent teachers. The presence of under-performing teachers in schools has led to attempts to eliminate teacher tenure. In June 2014, Rolf Treu, a Los Angeles County trial judge, ruled in *Vergara v. California* that teacher tenure violated the California state constitution. His ruling stated that teacher tenure denies a student's right to "equality of educational opportunity" since tenure makes it difficult to fire bad teachers and such poor teachers "substantially undermine" student's education. A similar suit has been filed in New York State as well.

Academic research indicates that improving teacher quality can have positive long-lasting impacts on students. Raj Chetty, John Freidman, and Jonah Rockoff use data on test scores, school records, and tax return forms to examine the long-term effects of teacher quality. Their

research finds that students who had higher quality teachers are more likely to attend college, have higher earnings, and are more likely to not have children as a teenager. They report that replacing a teacher in the bottom 5 percent of teacher quality with one of average quality would raise student's lifetime earnings by $250,000 per classroom.

However, other research indicates that eliminating teacher tenure may not yield the gains that its proponents expect to occur. Using data on new teachers in North Carolina, Matthew Chingos examined the early career paths of high- and low-quality teachers. He reports that principals are not terminating ineffective teachers at higher rate when the tenure decision is made after the fourth year. He also reports that less than two-fifths of teachers in the top quartile of teacher quality remained employed by the fifth year, which makes it more difficult for schools to dismiss their worst teachers.

* Based on Haley Sweetland Edwards, "Taking on Teacher Tenure," *TIME,* November 3, 2014, pp. 35–39; Raj Chetty, John N. Freidman, and Jonah E. Rockoff, "The Long-Term Impacts of Teachers II: Teacher Value-Added and Student Outcomes in Adulthood," *American Economic Review,* September 2014, pp. 2633–2679; and Matthew M. Chingos, "Ending Teacher Tenure Would Have Little Impact on Its Own," Brown Center on Education Policy, Brookings Institution, September 2014.

Commissions and royalties are efficient where work effort and work hours are difficult to observe. Time rates in these situations would bring forth attendant shirking problems for the firm because observing the worker would be very expensive. By aligning the interests of the firms and the workers, commissions and royalties help overcome the principal–agent problem.

Raises and Promotions

A sizable proportion of American workers receive time payments as fixed annual salaries. These workers are typically engaged in team production; thus, it is not easy to monitor their efforts or measure their output. Time payments, rather than piece rates, commissions, or royalties, therefore, are optimal. But why fixed annual salaries and not fixed hourly pay? The reason is that managers and professionals are *quasi-fixed resources,* at least for a one-year period.[12] A firm's use of salaried workers is largely independent of its level of production. Salaried workers thus are akin to fixed resources such as capital and land (*quasi-* means "as if"). For example, enterprises need accountants, lawyers, managers, and marketing personnel when production and sales are brisk and also when they are slack. In addition, firms incur high search, hiring, and training costs in employing salaried workers. Laying them off would risk quits that would end the firms' opportunities to gain returns on prior expensive investments in specific training [Figure 4.8(b)]. On a more mundane level, high-skilled workers may simply be in a position to demand and receive the greater income security associated with fixed annual salaries.

But for all their benefits, annual salaries present a potential shirking problem. Let's describe this problem and then explore its solution.

Salaries and Work Incentives

In Figure 7.7, we demonstrate the principal–agent problem associated with salaries. Our methodology will be to compare the optimal hours of work under conditions of hourly pay and an annual salary.

1 Hourly Pay   First observe wage rate line *WH,* the slope of which indicates a particular level of hourly pay. Given this hourly wage, the worker characterized by the indifference map shown will choose to work h_1 hours and earn an annual income Y_1. This $h_1 Y_1$ combination of work and income permits the worker to attain indifference curve I_1 at *a,* which represents the highest level of total utility possible along the wage rate line. For illustrative purposes, let's suppose that h_1 hours of work symbolize annual hours of work resulting from the normal 40-hour week.

2 Annual Salary   Now let's convert the Y_1 income earned by working h_1 hours to an annual salary of the same amount (= Y_1). The new budget constraint in Figure 7.7 becomes HSY_1 and indicates this person will receive Y_1 income irrespective of hours of work. Presumably, because of the nature of the job, the number of hours the person actually works while on the job is not easily observed. The worker now can achieve a higher level of utility by shirking. That is, the worker has an incentive to reduce work hours from h_1 to, say, h_2, allowing the worker to reach higher indifference curve I_2 at *b.* At the extreme, the worker can achieve a still higher level of utility by working zero hours (*c* on I_3). In both cases, the annual salary ensures that the income level remains at Y_1.

Solution: Raises and Promotions

One solution to the salary problem posed in Figure 7.7 is for the firm to establish performance-based raises and promotions. The prospect of future raises and promotions means that the worker's decision about hours

[12] Walter Oi, "Labor as a Quasi-Fixed Factor," *Journal of Political Economy,* December 1962, pp. 538–555.

FIGURE 7.7 Salaries and Work Incentives

Wage rate line *WH* indicates a specific level of hourly pay that will provide an annual income equal to Y_1 at h_1 hours of work. An equivalent annual salary of Y_1 will allow the worker to obtain higher indifference curve I_2 or I_3 by reducing the actual number of hours worked to h_2 or H. The firm can overcome this incentive problem by offering future raises and promotions to those who work h_1 or more hours.

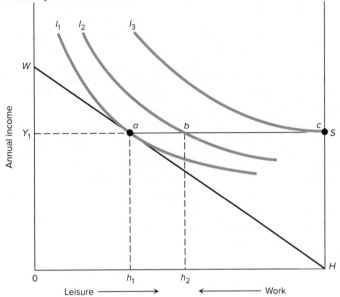

of work versus leisure in any given year is *not* based on that year's salary alone. Rather, the salaried worker chooses the optimal hours with a view toward maximizing lifetime utility. Desiring to obtain raises and earn promotions, the worker may decide to work more than h_1 hours this year. In fact, salaried employees work more hours weekly than hourly paid workers. One reason may be the importance of raises and promotions to salaried workers. If the worker gains the reputation of being a low producer, advancement within the firm's job hierarchy is unlikely.[13]

Bonuses

Bonuses are an increasingly popular form of incentive pay. *Bonuses are payments beyond the annual salary based on some factor such as personal or firm performance.* Their advantage to the firm is that they may elicit extra work effort. Another advantage is that they do not permanently raise base salaries or hourly wages, as do raises, promotions, or other forms of merit pay. Therefore, during an economic slump, bonuses can be readily forgone while higher wages or salaries are not readily reduced.

Personal Performance

Some bonuses are geared to personal performance that is formally assessed by superiors. If the superior rates the worker highly, the person receives a bonus. In other instances, bonuses are based on some quantifiable output. Professional football players, for example, may receive bonuses for passing for more than a

---

[13] A competing explanation for the long hours of salaried workers is that these people may gain direct utility from the work they do, independent of compensation. At the extreme, the total utility of some professional workers would decline if they cut back their hours.

7.3 World of Work

Economics of Tipping

Although tips are generally small amounts of money, they are a very important income source for workers in some occupations. Tips total $42 billion per year in restaurants alone. According to a 2015 study at **www.payscale.com,** waiters and waitresses get $8.20, or 62 percent of their total hourly income, as a result of tips; bartenders receive $9.60, or 59 percent of their total hourly income, in gratuities; and banquet captains obtain $8.70, or 42 percent of their total hourly income, from tips.

Two main reasons have been proposed for why people tip. One reason is the desire to conform to social norms. Surveys indicate that people feel guilty and are embarrassed if they don't tip. A second potential reason is to encourage the waiter to provide high-quality service in the future. However, this can't be the only reason for

tipping: People tip even when they do not plan to visit a restaurant again.

Several patterns have emerged from research on tips, which has focused on restaurant workers. The average tip is close to the perceived norm of 15 percent of the bill amount. Not surprisingly, the most important factor that affects tip size is the size of the bill. Better service quality does increase the size of tips. However, the difference between poor and good service often results in tip differences of only about 0.5–2.5 percent of the bill size. A server's friendliness and connection with the customer more significantly impact tips.

Sources: www.payscale.com; Ofer H. Azar, "The Social Norm of Tipping: A Review," *Journal of Applied Social Psychology,* February 2007, pp. 380–402; and Ofer H. Azar, "Strategic Behavior and Social Norms in Tipped Service Industries," *The B.E. Journal of Economic Analysis & Policy,* no. 1 (2008), article 7.

certain number of touchdowns or getting more than a specified number of quarterback sacks. Such "piece-rate" bonuses are less common in industries where individual performance is less directly measurable.

 Bonuses based on individual performance may solve one form of the principal–agent problem, but they may create other kinds. Although this pay system may increase individual effort, it may channel the effort toward behavior that is counter to the employer's overall goals. For example, a basketball player who receives bonuses for assists may tend to pass the ball rather than take wide-open shots. Or a worker whose bonus depends on an evaluation from a superior may spend excessive time pleasing the superior. As a result, the worker may spend less time on, say, developing original product ideas that later might produce higher profits. To repeat: It is relatively easy to structure bonuses to eliminate the shirking problem. But it is difficult to structure bonuses, so they do not create other principal–agent problems.

Team Performance

One solution to the problem just discussed is to base individual bonuses on the performance of the team. The team, in this case, might be an actual team—as in professional sports—or teams such as departments, divisions, or entire enterprises. Once team goals are established, the bonus for each team member depends only on whether the team goals are met. Most formal bonus programs in U.S. enterprises are based on group, rather than personal, contributions to output or profits. Group bonus schemes based on physical output or costs are referred to as *gainsharing schemes.*

Team bonuses have a major drawback in that they create a potential *free-rider problem.* As the size of the unit or team increases, the effect of each worker's efforts on achieving the goals of the firm diminishes. Where the number of workers is large, individual workers are tempted to shirk. They realize that their personal shirking will not appreciably reduce the firm's output and profits. Thus if others work hard, the shirker can still obtain a team bonus. It is unclear how workers who work energetically will respond to free riders. One possibility is that they may "punish" the free riders by reducing their own efforts, in which case the bonus plan will surely fail. Alternatively, it is possible that workers may eventually develop a strategy of cooperation—all agreeing to work hard and all monitoring each other to realize the optimal bonuses for all. The point is that depending on the severity of the free-rider problem, team bonuses *may* or *may not* increase team productivity.[14]

Team bonuses are more likely to succeed when they are targeted at a relatively small group of top executives whose decisions directly affect profits. In fact, bonuses based on profitability account for about half of the total pay for senior executives. Do these large bonuses improve corporate performance? Past research tentatively suggests that the answer is yes. But these studies also indicate that the profit increases attributable to bonuses tend to be relatively small.[15]

Profit Sharing

Profit sharing is *a pay system that allocates a specified portion of a firm's profits to employees.* This form of pay increased during the 1980s when workers in basic industries such as autos and primary metals accepted profit sharing in lieu of wage increases. Profit sharing also has become increasingly common for senior executives in large corporations. According to the National Center for Employee Ownership, 14.2 million workers participated in profit-sharing plans in 2016.[16] Most participants are in deferred plans, in which profits are credited to employees for distribution at some future date such as retirement.[17]

At first thought, the link between profit sharing and productivity seems straightforward. Proponents of profit sharing contend that it transforms workers into minicapitalists who work harder to reap a share of the firm's profits. The extra effort creates extra output and profits, thus making the plan self-financing. Profit sharing therefore aligns the interests of firms and their workforces. That is, profit sharing supposedly overcomes the principal–agent problem.

But in reality, the theoretical link between profit sharing and improved efficiency is not so clear-cut.[18] The main reason is that profit sharing is tied to *group* performance. This tie creates the free-rider problem that we identified in our discussion of bonuses. The larger the organization, the greater the possibility that the free-rider problem will short-circuit the profit sharing–productivity link. The success of a profit-sharing plan depends crucially on how well the free-rider problem is resolved.

The effectiveness of profit-sharing plans therefore is an empirical question. O'Boyle, Patel, and Gonzalez-Mulé conducted a meta-analysis of 102 studies representing 56,984 firms across the world. They found a 4 percent

---

[14] For analysis indicating that organizing a large firm into autonomous work groups can induce mutual monitoring among employees and thus overcome the free-riding problems associated with bonuses, see Marc Knez and Duncan Simester, "Firm-Wide Incentives and Mutual Monitoring at Continental Airlines," *Journal of Labor Economics,* October 2001, pp. 743–772.

[15] A representative set of these studies is found in the symposium "Do Compensation Policies Matter?" *Industrial and Labor Relations Review,* special issue, February 1990.

[16] www.nceo.org.

[17] Edward M. Coates III, "Profit Sharing Today: Plans and Provisions," *Monthly Labor Review,* April 1991, pp. 19–25. This source lists and discusses the pros and cons of profit-sharing plans.

[18] Martin L. Weitzman and Douglas L. Kruse provide an excellent discussion of the issues surrounding profit sharing. See their "Profit Sharing and Productivity," in Alan S. Blinder (ed.), *Paying for Productivity* (Washington, DC: Brookings Institution, 1990), pp. 95–141. Our previous discussion of the free-rider problem associated with bonuses drew on this source.

effect of employee ownership on firm performance.[19] Their results suggest that workers under profit-sharing plans are able to overcome the free-rider problem.

Equity Compensation

Equity compensation is *a pay scheme where part of the worker's compensation is given or invested in the firm's stock.* An increasingly popular form of equity compensation is *stock options,* which *give an employee the right to purchase a fixed number of shares of stock at a set price for a given time period.*[20] The price at which the option is given is called the *grant price* and is typically set at the market price when the stock option is given to the worker. Workers with stock options can make a profit if the market price rises above the grant price; that is, they can *exercise their option* to purchase the stock from the firm at the grant price and sell it at the market price.

In 2014, 8 percent of all private workers had a stock option.[21] There is substantial variation in the incidence of stock options. The proportion of workers with stock options was 2 percent among workers earning in the bottom 10 percent of wages and 16 percent among workers in the top 10 percent of wages. The percentage of employees with stock options was highest in management, business, and financial occupations (16 percent) and lowest in construction, extraction, farming, fishing, and forestry occupations (2 percent).

Stock options have a similar incentive effect to profit-sharing plans. That is, stock options mesh the interests of the firm's shareholders with those of the employees. Workers have the incentive to work hard and increase the firm's profits. Greater profits will raise the market price of the firm's stock and thus raise the value of the workers' stock options. However, stock options suffer from the free-rider problem because the value of the stock options is tied to group rather than individual performance.

Tournament Pay

Some incentive pay schemes base compensation on relative performance. Such pay plans are known as *tournament pay*. For example, tennis or golf tournaments structure pay on the basis of where participants finish in the tournament. Typically the first prize is extremely high, with pay dropping a bit but still remaining high for the next few places. Rewards then sink rapidly for rankings well below the top spots. One purpose of this pay scheme is to promote greater performance by *all* participants throughout the rankings. Everyone aspires to the top prize; therefore, everyone works hard to achieve it. Lower pay is tolerated by many because of their opportunity to win one of the few big prizes.[22]

[19] Ernest H. O'Boyle, Pankaj C. Patel, and Erik Gonzalez-Mulé , "Employee Ownership and Firm Performance: A Meta-Analysis," *Human Resource Management Journal,* November 2016, pp. 425–448. For evidence that ESOPs increase the probability of firm survival, see Joseph Blasi, Douglas Kruse, and Dan Weltmann, "Firm Survival and Performance in Privately-held ESOP Companies," in Douglas Kruse (ed.), *Sharing Ownership, Profits, and Decision-Making in the 21st Century* (Bingley, UK: Emerald Publishing, 2013), pp. 109–124.
[20] For information about stock options and less common types of equity compensation, see William J. Wiatrowski, "Putting Stock in Benefits: How Prevalent Is It?" *Compensation and Working Conditions,* Fall 2000, pp. 2–7. Also see James Sesil, Maya Kroumova, Douglas Kruse, and Joseph Blasi. "Broad-based Employee Stock Options in the United States: Company Performance and Characteristics," *Management Revue,* Issue 2, 2007, pp. 5–22.
[21] U.S. Bureau of Labor Statistics, *National Compensation Survey: Employee Benefits in the United States, March 2018* (Washington, D.C: U.S. Bureau of Labor Statistics, 2018), Table 41.
[22] Edward Lazear and Sherwin Rosen, "Rank Order Tournaments as an Optimum Labor Contract," *Journal of Political Economy,* October 1981, pp. 841–864. The interested reader may also wish to refer to Ronald G. Ehrenberg and Michael L. Bognanno, "Do Tournaments Have Incentive Effects?" *Journal of Political Economy,* December 1990, pp. 1307–1324; and Jed DeVaro, "Internal Promotion Competitions in Firms," *RAND Journal of Economics,* Autumn 2006, pp. 521–542.

GP7.1

Tournament pay may have applications beyond sporting events.[23] Some observers speculate that the multimillion-dollar salaries paid to chief executive officers of large corporations may be equivalent to first-place prizes in a tournament. Indeed, compensation received by CEOs may exceed their personal marginal revenue products. The "excessive" pay (Table 7.1) may be efficient because it increases the Marginal Revenue Products of younger corporate managers, who aspire to one day become the CEO.

TABLE 7.1 The 10 Highest-Paid Chief Executive Officers, 2018

Name	Company	Total Pay (millions)
Elon Musk	Tesla	$2,284.0
David M. Zaslav	Discovery	$129.0
Nikesh Arora	Palo Alto Networks	$125.0
Mark V. Hurd	Oracle	$108.0
Safra A. Catz	Oracle	$108.0
John J. Legre	T-Mobile	$67.0
Robert A. Iger	Walt Disney	$66.0
James Heppelmann	PTC	$50.0
Fabrizio Freda	Estee Lauder	$48.0
Vivek Shah	J2 Global	$45.0

Source: *New York Times,* "The Highest-Paid C.E.O.s of 2018: A Year So Lucrative, We Had to Redraw Our Chart." www.nytimes.com

This view of CEO pay is controversial, as we will soon detail; but let's first look at some of its possible implications. First, managers who seek the top spot in the corporation but fall somewhat short will also be paid more than their MRPs. The firm may even tolerate deadwood at the senior level. Firms that gain reputations for arbitrarily firing older, less effective executives may not be able to attract a sufficient number of young workers to the tournament pay scheme. These younger workers may be unwilling to incur the risk of falling short of the top spots after expending years of effort to achieve them. The assurances that other high-paying jobs exist in the hierarchy and that employment is relatively secure may be important to the continuing success of this pay scheme.

Second, tournament pay may help rationalize "golden parachute" provisions in executive compensation contracts. These provisions provide for large lump-sum compensation to executives who lose their jobs as a result of corporate takeovers. Golden parachutes—often worth millions of dollars—allow the executives to float comfortably to their next jobs.

Several explanations for these provisions have been offered. Perhaps these large sums deter hostile takeovers by making them more expensive. Or perhaps the corporate owners (shareholders) believe these large awards will discourage CEOs from fending off takeovers that bid up stock prices and increase the shareholders' wealth.

Tournament pay provides a complementary explanation. Perhaps golden parachutes are partly insurance against losing the full amount of the CEO prize once it is won. People ascending to CEO positions expect

---

[23] For example, see Michael L. Bognanno, "Corporate Tournaments," *Journal of Labor Economics,* April 2001, pp. 290–315; and Margaret Brehm, Scott A. Imberman, Michael F. Lovenheim, "Achievement Effects of Individual Performance Incentives in a Teacher Merit Pay Tournament," *Labour Economics,* January 2017, pp. 133–150.

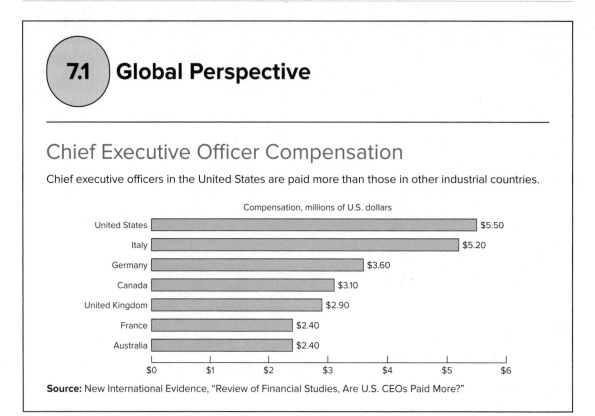

7.1 Global Perspective

Chief Executive Officer Compensation

Chief executive officers in the United States are paid more than those in other industrial countries.

Compensation, millions of U.S. dollars

Country	Compensation
United States	$5.50
Italy	$5.20
Germany	$3.60
Canada	$3.10
United Kingdom	$2.90
France	$2.40
Australia	$2.40

Source: New International Evidence, "Review of Financial Studies, Are U.S. CEOs Paid More?"

to receive high compensation for several years. But an unforeseen corporate takeover that results in the discharge of the present CEO will wipe out part of the compensation prize. This possibility may undermine the desired incentive effects of the compensation scheme. The solution: golden parachutes that insure against at least part of the lost pay resulting from a takeover.

Finally, tournament pay may help explain why many CEOs have relatively short tenures prior to their retirements. Turnover at the top at relatively frequent intervals is important to open up opportunities for those lower in the corporate hierarchy; thus, CEOs normally are given generous retirement incentives, usually at age 65. In this way, the top-to-bottom work incentives created by the pay scheme are maintained.

Critics of the tournament explanation of high CEO pay dismiss the relevance of the theory to executive pay. They assert that such pay schemes are not optimal in corporations, where participants have opportunities to sabotage one another's performance. In this view, a tournament pay scheme within a corporate setting is more likely to promote detrimental strategic behavior by executives. Teamwork allegedly would erode, and overall productivity would decline.

If CEO compensation is not part of a tournament pay scheme, why is this pay so high? Perhaps high CEO pay simply reflects supply-and-demand realities. Because the decisions of CEOs affect entire corporations, their productivity is extremely high. Meanwhile, the supply of experienced, top corporate decision makers is low. The labor market result is very high pay, as is true for other superstars, such as those in sports and entertainment.

Critics of high CEO pay dismiss this view, arguing that CEO pay tends to be "excessive" mainly because of the "mutual admiration society" that often develops among CEOs and corporate board members. Many members of corporate boards, themselves CEOs of other corporations, overrate the CEO's importance and worth. In this view, some of the profits rightfully belonging to stockholders are instead diverted to extraordinarily high CEO pay. Between 1989 and 2000, chief executive pay rose from 53 to 383 times the average production worker pay. Relative CEO compensation fell between 2000 and 2009 and has rebounded up since then. In 2017, CEO compensation was 312 times the average production worker pay.[24]

This high CEO compensation has drawn considerable complaint from unions, stockholders, and politicians. In response, the Securities and Exchange Commission (SEC) in 1992 established new rules requiring that corporations clearly spell out directly to their stockholders the compensation of their five highest-paid executives. The SEC believes that this informational approach will help stockholders identify and ferret out excessive CEO pay. Also, in 1993 Congress eliminated corporate tax deductions for executive salaries exceeding $1 million annually (with an exception for pay directly tied to the firm's earnings performance).[25]

In 2017, the SEC required that all publicly traded companies must disclose the ratio of their CEO pay to the median pay of their employees. It is clear that "excessive" CEO pay is highly controversial and will continue to be debated.[26]

EFFICIENCY WAGE PAYMENTS

Pay-for-performance plans are most capable of solving the principal–agent problem in circumstances where individual output can be readily measured. But in many jobs measuring or assessing individual output is at best difficult and at worst impossible. One solution to the principal–agent problem in these circumstances is direct observation of the agents' actions on the job. Firms can reduce shirking by *monitoring* the *efforts* of workers (e.g., by hiring supervisors). Fearing the loss of their jobs, most workers will not shirk when they are being observed because presumably those who do will be identified and replaced. Supervision, therefore, may be an effective way to reduce the principal–agent problem in some circumstances. For this reason, many jobs in the economy are supervisory.

Monitoring workers, however, is costly in some employment circumstances. It makes little economic sense, for example, to hire someone to monitor the effort of a security guard, a babysitter, a house painter, or a manager. Also, it may be prohibitively costly to hire enough supervisors to monitor the quality of each worker's performance in assembly-line work. As a result, some economists suggest that firms search for approaches other than monitoring or pay for performance to synchronize the interests of the workers with those of the firm.

How might firms deal with the principal–agent problem when supervision is costly and individual output is difficult to measure? One such approach may be to pay workers a wage that is above the market-clearing level.

Wage–Productivity Dependence

In the models discussed in Chapter 6, we explicitly assumed that labor was homogeneous and implicitly assumed that a change in wage rates did not alter the marginal product of labor and hence the location of the labor demand curve. Any change in the wage rate, therefore, altered the quantity of labor demanded; it did *not* change the location of the demand curve itself. However, under some conditions a wage rise may positively affect labor efficiency, causing a rightward shift of the labor demand curve.

Theories that incorporate the aforementioned possibility—that wage increases may increase productivity—are called *efficiency wage theories.* An *efficiency wage* is one that minimizes an employer's wage cost per effective unit

---

[24] Lawrence Mishel and Jessica Schieder, "CEO Compensation Surged in 2017," *Economic Policy Institute Report,* August 16, 2018.

[25] For evidence suggesting that the law made little impact on CEO pay, see Nancy L. Rose and Catherine Wolfram, "Regulating Executive Pay: Using the Tax Code to Influence Chief Executive Compensation," *Journal of Labor Economics,* April 2002, part 2, pp. S138–175.

[26] For a survey of research on executive compensation, see Alex Edmans, Xavier Gabaix, and Dirk Jente, "Executive Compensation: A Survey of Theory and Evidence," in Benjamin Hermalin and Michael Weisbach (eds.), *The Handbook of the Economics of Corporate Governance, Volume 1* (Amsterdam, NL: North-Holland , 2017), pp. 383–539.

of labor service employed. The key phrase is "per *effective* unit of labor service." Under the customary assumptions of competitive labor markets and homogeneous labor inputs, the market-clearing wage (determined where labor supply and demand intersect) *is* the wage that minimizes a firm's wage cost per effective unit of labor service employed. All workers are assumed to be equally and fully effective in the production process. If a firm pays a below-market-clearing wage, the company will not attract the desired number of workers. If it pays an above-market-clearing wage, its wage cost per effective unit of labor will rise because equally efficient units could have been hired at the lower market wage. We will discover, however, that under assumptions of heterogeneous labor and wage–productivity dependence, a firm may find that it can *lower* its wage cost per effective unit of labor service by paying a *higher* wage rate.

A simple numerical example will help demonstrate this general principle. Suppose workers who are fully effective at some task can each produce 10 units of a particular output per hour. Next suppose that the market wage rate is $5 an hour and that for reasons we will discuss shortly, workers each produce only 5 units of output per hour at the $5 wage. In this circumstance, we find that each *effective* unit of labor service costs an employer $10 per hour. The firm needs two hours of labor services to obtain 10 units of output (= 2×5), and each hour costs $5 in wages.

What if the firm discovers that it can obtain fully effective units of labor—those that produce 10 units of hourly output—by paying $8 an hour? This implies that the hourly wage cost per effective unit of labor declines by $2 (= $10 - $8) as the wage rate rises by $3 (= $8 - $5).

The unusual outcome illustrated by our simple example is possible where a higher wage more than proportionally induces greater employee work effort, improves the workers' capabilities, or increases the proportion of highly skilled workers in a particular workforce.

Shirking Model of Efficiency Wages

The shirking model of efficiency wages theorizes that some enterprises pay more than the market-clearing wage to reduce employee shirking. In some situations, employers have little information about how diligently workers are performing their duties (e.g., night security workers at an office building). Moreover, full supervision and monitoring of such workers may be too costly (hiring other security workers to watch security workers). Under these conditions, the possibility arises that all employees will choose to shirk. To counter this possibility, firms may opt to pay workers more than the market-clearing wage. This higher pay increases the relative value of the job as viewed by each worker. It also raises the cost of being terminated for shirking, should it be detected. In familiar economic wording, the higher opportunity cost (price) of shirking reduces the amount of shirking occurring. Worker productivity improves more than proportionally to the higher wage, the labor demand curve is located farther rightward, and wage costs per effective unit of labor decline.[27]

Other Efficiency Wage Theories

Although less relevant to the principal–agent problem, there are other variations of the efficiency wage idea, two of which are the *nutritional* and the *labor turnover* models.

1 Nutritional Model   In a relatively poor nation, an increase in the real wage might elevate the nutritional and health levels of workers. This will positively affect their physical vigor, mental alertness, and therefore

---

[27] The reader interested in a more advanced treatment of efficiency wage theories should consult George A. Akerlof and Janet L. Yellen (eds.), *Efficiency Wage Models of the Labor Market* (Cambridge: Cambridge University Press, 1986); Andrew Weiss, *Efficiency Wages: Models of Unemployment, Layoffs, and Wage Dispersions* (Princeton, NJ: Princeton University Press, 1991); and Kevin M. Murphy and Robert H. Topel, "Efficiency Wages Reconsidered: Theory and Evidence," in Yoram Weiss and Gideon Fishelson (eds.), *Advances in Theory and Measurement of Unemployment* (London: MacMillan, 1990).

their productivity. Thus, real wage increases could shift labor demand curves rightward, benefiting employers as well as employees.[28]

2 Labor Turnover Model   Employers may increase wages to reduce costly *labor turnover, the rate at which workers quit their jobs, necessitating their replacement by new workers.* We have seen that employers bear the costs of providing firm-specific training to new workers. Also, because workers normally "learn by doing," new workers are not initially as proficient as the people they replace.

An above-market-clearing wage raises the workers' costs of quitting their jobs and thus lowers the likelihood that they will quit. Lower labor turnover, in turn, increases worker productivity *on the average* because it increases the proportion of experienced workers relative to those being trained and still "learning by doing." The result is that the higher wage rate shifts the labor demand curve rightward.

Implication: Nonclearing Labor Markets

Efficiency wage theories produce several interesting implications, one of which is that permanent unemployment may exist under conditions of equilibrium in labor markets.[29] We demonstrate this possibility in Figure 7.8, where the initial equilibrium wage rate and level of employment are W_1 and Q_1. Suppose the firm discovers it can reduce its wage cost per effective unit of labor by increasing the wage to W_2 (from *a* to *b*). This decline in the wage cost per effective unit of labor results from the rightward shift of the labor demand curve from D_{L1} to D_{L2}—that is, from an increase in the marginal product of labor. The wage cost per effective unit of labor declines because the extra output of workers presumably rises more than the firm's wage expense. Observe that we have drawn the demand increase such that the firm continues to employ Q_1 workers

FIGURE 7.8   Efficiency Wage Model

Under some conditions, an increase in the wage may increase worker efficiency and labor demand. In this situation, we suppose that the firm increases the wage from W_1 to W_2, which shifts labor demand from D_{L1} to D_{L2} and minimizes the firm's wage cost per effective unit of labor. Although W_2 is an equilibrium wage, it is not a market-clearing wage, as shown by the surplus of labor *bc*.

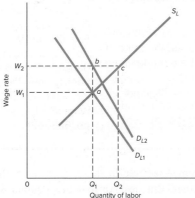

[28] Harvey Leibenstein, "The Theory of Underemployment in Densely Populated Backward Areas," in Harvey Leibenstein (ed.), *Economic Backwardness and Economic Growth* (New York: John Wiley & Sons, 1963), Chapter 6. For a critical review of the empirical evidence on the nutritional model, see John Strauss and Duncan Thomas, "Health, Nutrition, and Economic Development," *Journal of Economic Literature,* June 1998, pp. 766–817.

[29] We explore other implications of the efficiency wage models in later discussions of wage differentials (Chapter 8) and frictional unemployment (Chapter 18).

(at *b*) as before, but the efficiency wage just as reasonably could have shifted the curve to a greater or lesser extent than that shown.[30]

7.4   World of Work

The Ford Motor Company's $5 per Day Wage*

In 1914 Ford Motor Company made headlines by offering autoworkers the grand sum of $5 per day, up from $2.50 per day. This wage offer was newsworthy because at that time the typical market wage in manufacturing was just $2–$3 per day.

What was Ford's rationale for offering a higher-than-competitive wage? Statistics indicate that the company was suffering from unusually high quit rates and absenteeism. Ford apparently reasoned that a high wage rate would increase worker productivity by increasing morale and reducing employee turnover. Only workers who had been at Ford for at least six months were eligible for the $5 per day wage. Nevertheless, 10,000 workers applied for employment with Ford in the immediate period following the announcement of the wage hike.

According to historians of this era, the Ford strategy succeeded. The $5 wage raised the value of the job to Ford workers, who therefore became loyal to the company and worked hard to retain their high-paying jobs. The quit and absenteeism rates both plummeted, and in 1914 labor productivity at Ford rose by an estimated 51 percent.

How does this increase in productivity relate to economic theory? We know from Chapter 5 that normally a change in the wage rate does not affect labor productivity and therefore does not affect labor demand. Instead the firm responds to a change in the wage rate by altering the quantity of labor it "purchases." This adjustment is shown graphically as a point-to-point movement along the firm's existing labor demand curve. But in the 1914 Ford situation, the $2.50 boost in the daily wage increased labor productivity. Stated in economic terms, the $5 wage was an *efficiency wage*. The wage increase to $5 per day raised the marginal product of Ford workers. This translated into an increase in Ford's marginal revenue product schedule, which we know is its demand for labor curve.

In brief, Ford's experience with its $5 daily wage is consistent with the theory that efficiency wages may in some situations be optimal for reducing principal–agent problems.

* This discussion is based in part on Daniel M. G. Raff and Lawrence Summers, "Did Henry Ford Pay Efficiency Wages?" *Journal of Labor Economics,* pt. 2, October 1987, pp. S57–86. For evidence indicating that Henry Ford did *not* intentionally pay efficiency wages, see Jason E. Taylor, "Did Henry Ford Mean to Pay Efficiency Wages?" *Journal of Labor Research,* Fall 2003, pp. 683–694.

Wage rate W_2 is the new equilibrium wage rate in this market; at *b,* the firm has no incentive to reduce the wage rate or to increase it further. But observe that this equilibrium wage is *not* the market-clearing wage. At W_2 the firm employs Q_1 workers, whereas we see from point *c* on the supply curve that Q_2 workers seek employment. Assuming that workers do not find jobs elsewhere, permanent unemployment of *bc* occurs in this particular labor market. The more elastic the labor demand and supply curves, the greater

---

[30] A technical note is required here. Each demand curve in Figure 7.8 is a separate "pseudo-demand curve," which holds worker quality and effort constant and assumes that the firm is hiring labor competitively. In fact, this is a wage-setting firm and as such does not have a labor demand curve (just as a monopolist does not have a supply curve). Demand in this case is actually the single point *b* on D_{L2}.

the unemployment. The closer to c that the efficiency demand curve intersects the labor supply curve, the less equilibrium unemployment.

An additional important point: In the shirking efficiency wage model, the bc unemployment is partly the reason for the wage–productivity dependence in the first place. The threat of losing a relatively high-paying job and of becoming part of the bc unemployed workers serves as a disciplining device to discourage shirking and to encourage full effort. In the absence of the resulting equilibrium unemployment, the labor demand curve might not shift from D_{L1} to D_{L2} in response to the higher wage.

Criticisms

Detractors of efficiency wage theories question whether these models add greatly to our understanding of labor markets in advanced economies. Critics of the shirking model, in particular, point out that several of the pay-for-performance plans discussed earlier in this chapter could serve as alternatives to efficiency wages as ways to guard against poor worker performance. As examples, where monitoring workers is costly, the firm can pay on a piece rate or a commission basis. Where individual performance is difficult to measure, bonus pay based on team performance can be implemented.

Second, critics point out that a firm could require employees to post a bond that they would forfeit if they were found to have been negligent in performing their job duties.

Finally, detractors of the efficiency wage theory note that firms can reduce shirking by establishing pay plans in which part of the workers' pay is deferred until later years or until employees qualify for pensions. Encouraged by the deferred income, workers will work hard to maintain employment within the firm.

7.2 *Quick Review*

- The principal–agent problem is the conflict of interest that occurs when agents pursue their own objectives to the detriment of meeting the principal's objectives.
- Pay-for-performance plans such as piece rates, commissions and royalties, raises and promotions, bonuses, profit sharing, and tournament pay are designed to minimize principal–agent problems.
- Efficiency wages are above-market-clearing wages designed to reduce employee shirking and labor turnover; they are equilibrium wages because, given labor supply and demand, employers have no incentive to change them.
- Because they are set higher than market-clearing wages, efficiency wages may contribute to permanent unemployment.

Your Turn

What is the major difficulty with profit sharing as a means of overcoming the principal–agent problem? (*Answer:* See page 541.)

Each of these devices, argue the critics, can reduce the principal–agent problem at less expense than paying above-market-clearing wages.[31]

LABOR MARKET EFFICIENCY REVISITED

The basic supply and demand models in Chapter 6 provide meaningful insights into wages and the efficient allocation of labor. But in this chapter, we have seen that the decisions of workers and firms are substantially more complex than our earlier models suggest. A variety of compensation schemes are available, each potentially optimal for a particular type of job and worker. Workers therefore must make choices not only about hours and pay but also about a variety of types of pay. Similarly, firms must not only make hiring and total pay decisions; they must also weigh the costs and benefits of a full range of possible compensation schemes. Some schemes may reduce worker productivity; others may greatly enhance it.

In this chapter, our previous definition of labor market efficiency has been extended. In Chapter 6, we found that efficiency occurred when no worker could be switched from one *job* to another to produce more economic well-being. Now we must append to that definition the following phrase: "Neither can any worker be switched from one *compensation scheme* to another to increase economic well-being." Labor market efficiency requires that workers be allocated to optimal work. It also demands that optimal compensation packages be implemented. Privately optimal compensation choices normally are also socially optimal, the exception being where efficiency wages are paid. Recall that these payments may create unemployment.

Chapter Summary

1. Total compensation consists of wage and fringe benefits. Fringe benefits include *legally required benefits,* such as Social Security contributions, and *voluntary benefits,* such as paid leaves, insurance benefits, and private pensions. About 30 percent of total pay takes the form of fringe benefits, broadly defined.

2. An employee's preferences for wages and fringe benefits can be set forth in an indifference map. Each indifference curve shows the various combinations of wages and fringe benefits that yield a given level of utility. An employer's normal-profit isoprofit curve displays the various combinations of wages and fringe benefits that yield a normal profit. The worker achieves an optimal or utility-maximizing combination of wages and fringe benefits by selecting the wage–fringe mix that enables the worker to attain the highest possible indifference curve.

3. Several factors explain the historical growth of fringe benefits. These include (*a*) the tax advantages they confer; (*b*) the scale economies resulting from their collective purchase; (*c*) their ability to reduce job turnover and motivate workers; (*d*) the sensitivity of fringe benefits, such as medical and dental care, to increases in income; (*e*) legal mandates by the federal government; and (*f*) the historical growth of union contracts, in which fringe benefits are relatively large.

4. The relationship between firms and workers is one of principals (firms) and agents (workers). Firms attempt to reduce the so-called principal–agent problem, which occurs when agents pursue their own goals rather than the objectives of the principals.

5. Piece rates, commissions, and royalties are pay schemes designed to tie pay directly to productivity.

---

[31] For empirical evidence on the efficiency wage idea, see Adriana D. Kugler, "Employee Referrals and Efficiency Wages," *Labour Economics,* October 2003, pp. 531–561; Darin Lee and Nicholas G. Rupp, "Retracting a Gift: How Does Employee Effort Respond to Wage Reductions?" *Journal of Labor Economics,* October 2007, pp. 725–762; and David A. Macpherson, Kislaya Prasad, and Timothy C. Salmon, "Deferred Compensation vs. Efficiency Wages: An Experimental Test of Effort Provision and Self-Selection," *Journal of Economic Behavior and Organization,* June 2014, pp. 90–107.

6. Workers receiving annual salaries may have an incentive to reduce work hours below levels that they would work if they were paid by the hour. The prospect of raises and promotions reduces this principal–agent problem.

7. Bonuses can elicit greater work effort and thereby increase productivity. But bonuses attached to personal performance may direct behavior away from team goals. Bonuses based on team or firm performance help solve this problem but create a potential free-rider problem when the team is large. Research indicates that executive bonuses have some positive effect on corporate performance.

8. Assuming minimal free-rider problems, profit-sharing plans and stock options synchronize the interests of firms and their workers. Recent research points toward a positive link between profit sharing and productivity.

9. Tournament pay assigns an extraordinarily high reward to the top performer and is designed to maximize performance by all who are striving to achieve the top spot. Some observers view high CEO pay as an efficient aspect of such pay schemes. Critics dismiss this idea as being a rationalization of excessive CEO pay, arguing instead that high CEO pay has resulted from improper corporate board oversight of stockholders' interests.

10. In situations where supervision of workers is minimal, a dependence between the wage paid and productivity may occur. The firm may find that it can increase its profits by paying an efficiency wage—a wage above the market-clearing wage. An interesting implication of efficiency wage theories is that persistent unemployment may be consistent with equilibrium in the labor market.

Terms and Concepts

fringe benefits	royalties
in-kind benefits	quasi-fixed resources
isoprofit curve	bonuses
agents	free-rider problem
principals	profit sharing
principal–agent problem	equity compensation
shirking	stock options
incentive pay plans	tournament pay
piece rates	monitoring
time rates	efficiency wage
commissions	labor turnover

Questions and Study Suggestions

1. What is an isoprofit curve as it relates to wages and fringe benefits? What is a normal-profit isoprofit curve? In what respect is a normal-profit isoprofit curve a *budget constraint* as viewed by a worker? At which point on the employer's isoprofit curve will a rational worker choose to locate? Explain.

2. In Figure 7.6 the reduction in the cost of fringe benefits resulted in an increase in the amount of fringe benefits and a *reduction* in the wage income received. Redraw the worker's indifference map to demonstrate a circumstance in which fringe benefits would not go up by as much, but wage income would *increase*. Explain the difference between the two situations.

3. The U.S. Office of Management and Budget has estimated that the tax-exempt status of fringe benefits such as pensions and group insurance reduced tax revenue to the Treasury by about $460 billion in 2018. Some economists have suggested that the federal government recover this tax revenue by taxing fringe benefits as ordinary income. Use Figure 7.5 to explain how this proposal would affect (a) the slope of the indifference curves and (b) the slope of the isoprofit curve. What would be the likely effect on the optimal level of fringe benefits?

4. Explain what is meant by the term *principal–agent problem.* Have you ever worked in a setting where this problem has arisen? If so, do you think that increased monitoring would have eliminated the problem? Why don't firms simply hire more supervisors to eliminate shirking problems?

5. Identify and explain a separate common problem associated with each of the following pairs of compensation plans:

   a. Piece rates; bonuses tied to individual performance.

   b. Bonuses applied to team performance; profit-sharing plans.

6. Demonstrate graphically why someone guaranteed an annual salary might choose to work fewer hours than someone who could earn that same amount through hourly pay. Reconcile your answer with the fact that salaried workers in general work more hours weekly than people receiving hourly pay.

7. Speculate on what actions workers might take to resolve a free-rider problem arising from a profit-sharing plan.

8. People often sell goods (or raffle tickets) as part of a fund-raising project. These projects typically offer valuable prizes to those who sell over a fixed number of units. Often a grand prize, like a trip to Hawaii, is offered to the person who sells the most units. Why are these prizes offered? Relate this example to the high pay received by chief executive officers of large corporations.

9. Discuss the following statement in relationship to (a) the tournament theory of executive pay and (b) the "World of Work" 7.2 on faculty tenure: "The new economics of personnel rationalizes whatever exists. If a compensation structure prevails, so goes this view, it *must* be efficient. The policy implication therefore is to "let it be" *(laissez faire).* Thus what poses as economic analysis is actually political conservatism."

10. How might payment of an efficiency wage (a) reduce shirking by employees and (b) reduce employee turnover? What is the implication of the efficiency wage theory for unemployment? In what way are piece rates, commissions, royalties, profit sharing, and stock options substitutes for efficiency wages?

11. What are stock options? How do they relate to the principal–agent problem?

12. As an employer, suppose you find it costly to monitor employee effort 100 percent of the time. What compensation options are available to ensure that you get appropriate levels of employee effort? What factors would you consider in choosing among these options?

Internet Exercise

What Is Happening to Health Insurance?

WWW...   Go to the Bureau of Labor Statistics National Compensation Survey–Benefits website (**https://www.bls.gov/ncs/ebs/home.htm**) and select "Top Picks" under EBS Databases. Then click on "Percent of All Workers Participating in Medical Care," "Percent of Participating Employees with Single Coverage Medical Care and Employee Contribution Required," and "All Years." This will retrieve the percentage of workers with health insurance coverage at private establishments as well as the percentage of covered workers required to help pay for their own coverage.

What was the percentage of workers with health insurance coverage in 2010? What is the figure for the most recent year shown?

What was the percentage of workers with health insurance coverage who were required to help contribute toward the cost of single coverage in 2010? What is the figure for the most recent year shown? What is a possible explanation for the trends in health insurance coverage and the fraction of workers required to help pay for their own coverage?

Provide *one* other specific statistic of your choice from the data on fringe benefits. For example: "In 2019, the percentage of all workers at private establishments with access to employer assistance to child care was xx percent."

Internet Links

 The website of *Forbes* contains an annual special report on the compensation of chief executive officers **(https://www.forbes.com)**.

The National Center for Employee Ownership website gives information on employee stock ownership plans and stock options **(https://www.nceo.org)**.

The U.S. Census Bureau website provides detailed statistics regarding health insurance coverage **(https://www.census.gov/topics/health/health-insurance.html)**.

The Employee Benefits Research Institute website provides summaries of research related to employee benefits **(https://www.ebri.org)**.

Chapter 8

The Wage Structure

After reading this chapter, you should be able to:

1. Explain the effects if all workers and jobs are homogeneous and all labor markets are perfectly competitive.
2. Describe patterns of wage differentials by industry, occupation, and location.
3. Identify sources of wage differentials arising from differences in job or employer characteristics.
4. Identify sources of wage differentials arising from differences in worker characteristics.
5. Explain the hedonic theory of wages.
6. Describe the role of labor immobilities and costly or imperfect information in observed wage differentials.

As evidence all around us suggests, there are large variations in wages and salaries in the United States. An elite fashion model may earn $2 million annually; her photographer, $100,000; and her makeup artist, $50,000. Meanwhile, a teacher's aide glancing at the model in a magazine ad may earn $15,000. A union tile layer may make $58,000 a year, while the secretary at the tile firm earns $26,000. A lawyer charging $300 per hour may pay her babysitter $7.00 per hour. A chemist may earn $90,000 each year; a mixologist (bartender), $25,000. An entertainer from San Diego dressed as a chicken may make $250,000 a year; a deli worker making chicken sandwiches, $25,000.

Many of these wage differences in the economy are *equilibrium wage differentials*—they do not elicit the movement of labor from the lower-paying to the higher-paying jobs. Other wage variations are *transitional wage differentials*—they promote worker mobility that eventually reduces the wage disparities. In this chapter, we examine the wage structure resulting from the working of labor markets and explain why wage differentials occur and persist. In Chapter 9, we look at labor mobility and migration induced by transitional wage differentials and examine the wage narrowing that eventually results.

PERFECT COMPETITION: HOMOGENEOUS WORKERS AND JOBS

In Chapter 6, we analyzed a perfectly competitive labor market for a *specific type of labor*. Let's now extend the assumption of *homogeneous workers and jobs* to *all* employees and firms in the economy. If information is perfect and job searches and migration are costless, labor resources will flow among various employments and regions of the economy until all workers have the same real wage.

The process whereby wages equalize is demonstrated in Figure 8.1. Initially assume that labor demand and supply are D_a and S_a, respectively, in submarket A and D_b and S_b in submarket B. These supply and demand conditions produce a $15 hourly wage in submarket A compared to a $10 wage in B. In each instance, the wage rate equals the VMP of labor, but note that the VMP of the Q_b worker in submarket B is less than the wage rate and VMP of the Q_a employee in submarket A. The consequence? Workers will exit submarket B and take jobs in higher-paying submarket A. The decline in labor supply in B from S_b to S_b' and the increase in A from S_a to S_a' will reduce the equilibrium wage in A from $15 to $12.50. The market-clearing wage in submarket B will rise from $10 to $12.50. Following the movement of workers between the two submarkets, the wage rates will be equal ($12.50) and in turn will be equal to the opportunity cost or supply price P_L of the last unit of labor ($12.50) in each market.

FIGURE 8.1   Wage Equalization in Perfect Competition

If labor supply and demand are S_a and D_a in labor submarket A and S_b and D_b in submarket B, a $5 wage differential (= $15 in A minus $10 in B) will emerge. Assuming that jobs and workers are homogeneous and information and mobility are costless, workers will leave submarket B for the higher-paying submarket A. The decline of labor supply in B from S_b to S_b' and the increase in submarket A from S_a to S_a' will cause the wage rates in each submarket to equalize at $12.50.

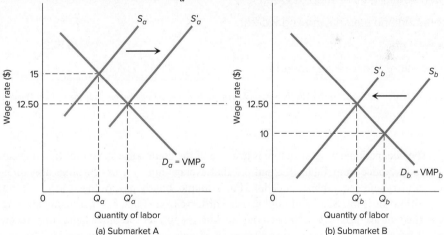

We may thus summarize as follows: If all jobs and workers are homogeneous and there is perfect mobility and competition, the *wage structure*—defined as *the array of wage rates paid to workers*—will evidence no variability. The average wage rate will be the *only* wage rate in the economy.

THE WAGE STRUCTURE: OBSERVED DIFFERENTIALS

Casual observation of the economy reveals that in fact, wage differentials *do* exist and that many of them persist over time. Table 8.1 shows an overview of occupational wage differentials. Observe that the average hourly pay of management, business, and financial workers in 2018 was $39.13, while production workers received $19.69 and service employees $15.67. Hourly earnings also vary within occupational categories such as those shown in Table 8.1. For example, under the category of "service workers," one would discover a difference in hourly earnings between people providing private household services and those providing protective services to corporations. Also, the highest-paid service workers earn more than the lowest-paid workers who are classified as sales workers, even though the average hourly salary is higher for the latter occupational group.

TABLE 8.1 Hourly Earnings by Occupational Group, 2018

Occupational Group	Average Hourly Earnings
Management, business, and financial workers	$39.13
Professional and related workers	$33.70
Installation, maintenance, and repair workers	$24.37
Construction and extraction workers	$23.16
Sales workers	$22.76
Production workers	$19.69
Office and administrative support workers	$19.15
Transportation and material moving workers	$18.51
Service workers	$15.67
Farming, fishing, and forestry workers	$14.45

Source: Bureau of National Affairs, *"Union Membership and Earnings Data Book: Compilations from the Current Population Survey."*

GP8.1

The occupational wage structure is just one of the many wage structures that one can isolate for study. Notice from Tables 8.2 and 8.3 that average hourly gross earnings also differ greatly by industry and geographical location. For example, hourly pay averaged $18.15 in retail trade in 2018 while it was $35.38 in mining. Also observe from Table 8.3 that manufacturing workers in New Jersey earned an average of $41.20 per hour; in Mississippi, on the other hand, they received $20.98. Finally, as of 2018 female earnings were about 80 percent of male earnings, and the pay for African–Americans was 78 percent of that paid to whites.

TABLE 8.2 **Average Hourly Earnings by Industry Group, 2018**

Industry Group	Average Hourly Earnings
Mining	$35.38
Finance, insurance, real estate, rental, and leasing	$34.43
Public administration	$31.39
Manufacturing	$28.77
Transportation, warehousing, information, and utilities	$28.76
Wholesale trade	$27.92
Construction	$25.60
Services	$25.02
Retail trade	$18.15
Agriculture, forestry, and fisheries	$16.41

Source: Bureau of National Affairs, "*Union Membership and Earnings Data Book: Compilations from the Current Population Survey.*"

TABLE 8.3 **Average Hourly Earnings of Private Workers in Manufacturing Industries by Selected States, 2018**

State	Average Hourly Earnings
New Jersey	$41.20
Massachusetts	$39.60
California	$34.29
Connecticut	$32.28
Colorado	$30.75
Texas	$29.25
Pennsylvania	$28.47
New York	$28.37
Iowa	$26.24
Florida	$25.61
Wisconsin	$25.11
South Carolina	$24.54
Alabama	$22.16
Mississippi	$20.98

Source: Bureau of National Affairs, "*Union Membership and Earnings Data Book: Compilations from the Current Population Survey.*"

8.1   Global Perspective

Hourly Pay around the World

Hourly Pay in U.S. Dollars, 2016

Switzerland	60.36
Norway	48.62
Belgium	47.26
Denmark	45.32
Germany	43.18
Sweden	41.68
Austria	39.54
United States	39.03
Finland	38.72
Australia	38.19
France	37.72
Ireland	36.23
Netherlands	34.60
Italy	32.49
Canada	30.08
United Kingdom	28.41
Singapore	26.75
Japan	26.46
New Zealand	23.67
Spain	23.44
South Korea	22.98
Israel	22.63
Argentina	16.77
Greece	15.70
Estonia	11.60
Slovakia	11.57
Portugal	10.96
Czech Republic	10.71
Taiwan	9.82
Hungary	8.60
Poland	8.53
Brazil	7.98
Turkey	6.09
Mexico	3.91
Philippines	2.06

Wage differentials are quite pronounced worldwide. The accompanying chart shows the average hourly pay for manufacturing workers in U.S. dollars for various nations for 2016. As defined here, hourly pay comprises all payments made directly to the worker, including pay for time worked; pay for vacations, holidays, and other special payments; and in-kind payments. Also included in the figures are employer expenditures for legally required insurance programs and private benefit plans. All wages are before-tax amounts and are converted to U.S. dollars through appropriate exchange rate adjustments.

Several facts stand out from this chart. First, hourly compensation varies greatly around the world. Second, pay for production workers in the United States is not as high as it is in a number of European nations. Finally, hourly wage rates in nations such as Brazil, Turkey, Mexico, and the Philippines are exceptionally low relative to pay in the more mature industrial nations. *Caution:* Prices of goods and services vary widely among these nations. Because exchange rates do not perfectly reflect this fact, these figures are only rough approximations of actual differences in purchasing power and living standards.

Source: The Conference Board, "International Comparisons of Hourly Compensation Costs in Manufacturing, 2016 - Summary Tables." www.conference-board.org

What are the sources of these wage differentials, and how can they persist? Why do some wage differences narrow over time while others remain the same or increase? To answer these and related questions, we need to abandon several assumptions made in the previous section of this chapter. More specifically, wage differentials occur because (*a*) jobs are heterogeneous, (*b*) workers are heterogeneous, and (*c*) labor markets are imperfect.

WAGE DIFFERENTIALS: HETEROGENEOUS JOBS

In Figure 8.1, we assumed that jobs were identical to one another in all respects. Utility-maximizing employees thus needed to consider only the wage rate itself in deciding where to work. Higher wages in one submarket would attract workers there. But in reality, jobs are heterogeneous rather than homogeneous. In particular, *heterogeneous jobs* have differing nonwage attributes, require different types and degrees of skill, or vary in the efficacy of paying efficiency wages to increase productivity. Employers also vary with respect to such things as union status, firm size, and discriminatory attitudes.

Compensating Differentials

Nonwage aspects of jobs vary greatly and are the source of *compensating wage differentials*. *These differentials consist of the extra pay that an employer must provide to compensate a worker for some undesirable job characteristic that does not exist in an alternative employment.* Compensating wage differentials are thus equilibrium wage differentials because they do *not* cause workers to shift to the higher-paying jobs and thereby cause wage rates to move toward equality.

Figure 8.1 is useful in showing this concept. In our previous discussion of this figure, we assumed that the jobs shown in labor submarkets A and B were homogeneous. Now let's suppose instead that the jobs in submarket A are performed outdoors in freezing weather throughout the year while the work in B occurs indoors in pleasant surroundings. Recall from Table 6.1 that one category of determinants of labor supply consists of the nonwage attributes of employment. Because of the indicated differences in nonwage amenities between submarkets A and B, labor supply will be less in A relative to B. If, for example, S_a is the labor supply curve in submarket A while S_b portrays supply in B, the *equilibrium* wage rate in A will be $10 as contrasted to $5 in submarket B.

The extra $5 paid in A is called a *wage premium, compensating wage differential,* or *equalizing difference.* No movement of workers from B to A will occur, as happened when jobs were assumed to be homogeneous. This $5 wage differential will *persist;* it will change only in response to changes in the other determinants of supply and demand in either of the two labor markets.

Several additional points need to be highlighted here. First, the observed wage disparity—$5—does *not* reflect an actual difference in net advantage or net utility between the two jobs. Taking the nonwage characteristics of the two jobs into account, workers Q_a and Q_b are equally paid; they both *net* $5 of utility from an hour of work. In A, $10 of wage minus $5 of extra disutility equals $5 net; in B, $5 of wage minus $0 of extra disutility equals $5 net.

Second, assuming demand is the same in both markets, employment will be lower where the compensating wage differential must be paid. Notice in Figure 8.1 that only Q_a workers are employed in A as contrasted to Q_b in B.

Finally, it is clear that the compensating wage differential performs the socially useful function of allocating labor resources to a productive task that is not as pleasant as others.

Having established the basic principle of compensating wage differentials, we next examine the types of non-wage aspects of jobs that cause differing labor supply curves and therefore compensating payments. Specifically, let's examine each of the following sources of compensating differentials: (*a*) risk of job injury and death, (*b*) fringe benefits, (*c*) job status, (*d*) job location, (*e*) the regularity of earnings, and (*f*) the prospect for wage advancement.

1 Risk of Job Injury or Death

The greater the risk of being injured or killed on the job, the less the labor supply to a particular occupation. For this reason, jobs that have high risks of accidents relative to others requiring similar skill will command compensating wage differentials. Viscusi has estimated that the average earnings premium for risk of injury and death in the American economy is about 5 percent. Although other studies have produced mixed findings, collectively they confirm the existence of compensating differentials, particularly those associated with higher probabilities of *fatal* injury on the job.[1]

2 Fringe Benefits

Fringe benefits vary greatly among employers who hire similar workers and pay similar wage rates. How might this fact relate to wage differentials? Suppose some firms hiring specific labor pay only $18 an hour while others pay the $18 and provide such fringe benefits as sick leave, paid vacations, and medical and dental insurance. Other things being equal, workers will choose to offer their services to these latter employers. To attract qualified workers, the firms that do not provide fringe benefits will have to pay a compensating wage differential that in effect will equalize the gross hourly compensation between the two groups.[2]

3 Job Status

Some jobs offer high status and prestige and hence attract many willing suppliers; other employment carries with it the social stigma of being mundane, uninspiring, and dirty. As an extreme example, there is more status in being a semiskilled worker in the burgeoning electronics industry than in being a similarly skilled worker in, say, a sewage disposal plant. To the extent that labor supply behavior is affected by status seeking, compensating wage differentials may emerge between low- and high-prestige work.

| WW8.1 | Status, of course, is defined culturally, and thus the degree of esteem society places on various jobs is subject to change. For example, in the early 1970s working for the U.S. military commanded limited status, reflecting widespread disapproval of the Vietnam War. On the other |

hand, the successful U.S. military action in the Persian Gulf in 1991 boosted public esteem for those in the military. One result was that the supply of labor to the military increased, enabling the military to meet recruitment goals more easily.

---

[1] W. Kip Viscusi, *Employment Hazards: An Investigation of Market Performance* (Cambridge, MA: Harvard University Press, 1979). In a review he reaches a similar conclusion; see W. Kip Viscusi, "The Value of Risks to Life and Health," *Journal of Economic Literature,* December 1993, pp. 1912–1946. Also see Keith A. Bender and Hosne Mridha, "The Effect of Local Area Unemployment on Compensating Wage Differentials for Injury Risk," *Southern Economic Journal,* October 2011, pp. 287–307. For evidence that workers get less risk as risk levels increase for commercial fishing deckhands, see Kurt Lavetti, "The Estimation of Compensating Wage Differentials: Lessons from the *Deadliest Catch,*" *Journal of Business and Economic Statistics,* Issue 1 (2020), pp. 165–182.

[2] Although the evidence is far from conclusive, several studies support the idea of a trade-off between wages and fringe benefits. See Craig A. Olson, "Do Workers Accept Lower Wages in Exchange for Health Benefits?" *Journal of Labor Economics,* April 2002, part 2, pp. S91–114. For evidence that a trade-off exists between wages and firm-provided worker's compensation insurance coverage, see Price V. Fishback and Shawn Everett Kantor, "Did Workers Pay for the Passage of Workers' Compensation Laws?" *Quarterly Journal of Economics,* August 1995, pp. 713–742. For weak evidence a trade-off exists between wages and employer health insurance costs in the public sector, see Paige Qina and Michael Chernew, "Compensating Wage Differentials and the Impact of Health Insurance in the Public Sector on Wages and Hours," *Journal of Health Economics,* December 2014, pp. 77–87.

8.1 World of Work

Who Cares and Does It Matter?*

Caring jobs are those that involve helping others develop their human capabilities. Caring positions are disproportionately held by women and are in fields such as child care, education (teachers), and health care (doctors, nurses, physical therapists). It is widely perceived that workers in jobs with more caring have lower wages.

Caring work could result in either a positive or a negative compensating wage differential. On one hand, a negative compensating wage differential will exist if the marginal worker prefers to be performing caring work. On the other hand, a positive compensating wage differential will exist if the marginal worker dislikes caring work.

A wage differential for caring jobs could be the result of other factors. A negative wage differential may occur if employer discrimination against women in noncaring jobs results in women being "crowded" into caring jobs and thus lowering wages in caring jobs. A positive wage premium may occur if caring jobs pay efficiency wages as it is difficult to monitor workers in such jobs.

Hirsch and Manzella empirically examine the effect of caring work on wages. They use data on 334,769 workers matched to two occupational-level indexes of caring work, which are measured on a 0 to 1 scale. One index, "assisting and caring for others," specifies the level of caring required for the job. The other index, "concern for others," indicates the type of worker needed in the job. As expected, on both measures women are more likely to be in caring jobs. For women, the average values are 0.45 for the "assisting and caring for others" index and 0.78 for the "concern for others" index. The corresponding figures for men are 0.39 and 0.69, respectively.

Caring work does result in modestly lower wages. Hirsch and Manzella find that wages are 1.4 percent lower for women and 2 percent lower for men with a one standard deviation rise in caring work, with "assisting and caring for others" and "concern for others" contributing similarly. The magnitude of estimated caring wage differentials is modest as compared to other wage differentials, such as union wage premiums, gender pay gaps, and firm size premiums. Eliminating the caring wage differential would result in little change in the gender wage gap since it is so small.

* Based on Barry T. Hirsch and Julia Manzella, "Who Cares—and Does It Matter? Measuring Wage Penalties for Caring Work," *Research in Labor Economics: Why Are Women Becoming More Like Men (and Men More Like Women) in the Labor Market,* 2015, pp. 213–275.

4 Job Location

Similar jobs also differ greatly with respect to their locations, which in turn vary in amenities and living costs. Cities noted for their "livability" may attract a larger supply of workers in a specific occupation than cities mainly noted for their smokestack industries. Consequently, compensating differentials may arise in locations lacking amenities.[3]

Differences in price levels between areas of the country may also result in the need to pay compensating money, or *nominal* wage payments. New York City is a good example. Because the cost of living is so high

---

[3] For evidence on how locational factors such as crime rates and air pollution affect wage differentials, see Jennifer Roback, "Wages, Rents, and the Quality of Life," *Journal of Political Economy,* December 1982, pp. 1257-1278. Also see Lucie Schmidt and Paul N. Courant, "Sometimes Close Is Good Enough: The Value of Nearby Environmental Amenities," *Journal of Regional Science,* December 2006, pp. 931-951.

there, a given nominal wage rate is not equal in purchasing power to the same wage rate in, say, Kansas City. Therefore, relative to labor demand, the number of workers who are willing to supply a particular type of labor at *each nominal wage* is less in New York City than in Kansas City. The labor market result is that the equilibrium nominal wage is higher in New York City. Differentials in nominal wage rates are needed to more closely align *real* wage rates among the two geographical labor markets.

5 Job Security: Regularity of Earnings

Some jobs provide employment security for long periods and explicit or implicit assurances that one will work full weeks throughout the year. Other positions—for example, construction, consulting, and commissioned sales—are characterized by variability of employment, the variability of earnings, or both. Because a specific paycheck is not ensured each week of the year, fewer workers may find these occupations attractive and, all else being equal, people who work in these jobs may receive a compensating wage differential. Restated, the hourly wage may be relatively high as compensation for the low probability that it will be earned 40 hours a week for the entire year.

Empirical evidence supports the theoretical conclusion that compensating wage differentials will arise for jobs in which unemployment is more likely. Magnani finds that a one standard deviation increase in the risk of unemployment results in a compensating wage premium between 8.5 and 19 percent.[4] Moretti reports a similar wage differential resulting from unemployment risk.[5] A study by Topel concluded that unemployment insurance greatly reduces compensating wage differentials. In the absence of insurance, an added percentage point of expected unemployment increases a worker's wage rate by about 2.5 percent.[6] Finally, Hamermesh and Wolfe have decomposed the compensating wage differential for unemployment into two parts: that paid for a higher probability of job loss and that resulting from a longer duration of job loss, should it occur. They conclude that nearly all the compensating differential results from the longer duration of job loss, rather than from the higher probability of losing one's job.[7]

6 Prospect of Wage Advancement

Jobs are also heterogeneous with respect to the amount of firm-financed investment in human capital provided over the years. For example, someone entering the banking profession at age 22 might reasonably expect to receive rather continuous on-the-job training leading to promotions to successively higher-paying positions over time. A person that same age who decides to be a carpenter is not likely to experience as large an overall increase in earnings over the years. Assuming that people's time preferences for earnings are the same, at any given wage people will opt for jobs with greater prospects for earnings increases. Thus, labor supply will be greater to these jobs and less to employment with flat lifetime earnings streams. This will necessitate a compensating wage differential for *entry-level* pay in the latter type of occupation. In our example, we would expect the beginning pay of the bank employee to be less than that of the carpenter. This type of compensating differential is confirmed by research finding that lower starting salaries for inexperienced workers are systematically related to higher rates of wage growth as the length of time on the job increases.[8]

---

[4] Elisabetta Magnani, "Product Market Volatility and the Adjustment of Earnings to Risk," *Industrial Relations,* April 2002, pp. 304–328.

[5] Enrich Moretti, "Do Wages Compensate for Risk of Unemployment? Parametric and Semiparametric Evidence from Seasonal Jobs," *Journal of Risk and Uncertainty,* January 2000, pp. 45–66.

[6] Robert H. Topel, "Equilibrium Earnings, Turnover, and Unemployment: New Evidence," *Journal of Labor Economics,* October 1984, pp. 500–522.

[7] Daniel S. Hamermesh and John R. Wolfe, "Compensating Wage Differentials and the Duration of Job Loss," *Journal of Labor Economics,* January 1990, pp. S175–197.

[8] David Neumark and Paul Taubman, "Why Do Wage Profiles Slope Upward? Tests of the General Human Capital Model," *Journal of Labor Economics,* October 1995, pp. 736–761.

Differing Skill Requirements

We have established that one reason for wage differentials in a market economy is differing nonwage aspects of jobs. But jobs are clearly heterogeneous in a second major way: They have widely different skill requirements. To illustrate, let's compare two hypothetical occupations. Suppose these two jobs have identical nonwage attributes and all workers have similar preferences for current versus future earnings. But suppose job X requires five years of education beyond high school while job Y demands only a high school diploma. If these two occupations paid an identical wage rate, people would have *no* incentive for making occupational choices to select employment X. Why? The unsurprising answer is that occupation X is more costly to enter than Y. Occupation X necessitates much more investment in human capital to meet the skill requirement, and therefore if the hourly pay is the same in both occupations, the return on the investment for the extra five years of education is negative. That is, the present value of the gained earnings is zero (one receives the same wage after investment as before investment), whereas the present value of the costs is positive and substantial (tuition, books, sacrificed earnings for five years).

The point is that wage equality between occupations X and Y is not sustainable; wage equality would create a disequilibrium. To attract enough people to occupation X, employers must pay these workers more than they pay people in occupation Y. An equilibrium wage differential, therefore, will persist between the two occupations. The earnings difference created by this wage gap must be just sufficient to produce an internal rate of return r on the investment in five years of education equal to the cost of borrowing i, as discussed in Chapter 4. If the wage differential and therefore r were greater than this i, more people would enter college and pursue the advanced degree. This eventually would expand labor supply, reduce the market wage in occupation X, lower the rate of return, and reduce the wage differential between the two occupations to a sustainable level. On the other hand, if the wage differential were insufficient between occupations X and Y, fewer people would enter occupation X, and eventually, the wage differential would rise to the equilibrium one.

To reiterate: Other things being equal, jobs that require large amounts of education and training will pay a higher wage rate than those that do not. The wide variety of skill requirements for various jobs constitutes a major source of wage disparity in the economy. The difference in pay between skilled and unskilled workers is called the *skill differential*.

Wage differentials created by differing skill requirements can either *increase, lessen,* or *reverse* wage variances produced by differences in nonwage aspects of jobs. For example, suppose job A is characterized by a high risk of injury and hence pays a $3 hourly compensating wage premium relative to safe job B. Now let's make two alternative assumptions about the skill differentials between the two jobs. First, suppose the skills necessary to perform dangerous job A are greater than those needed in safe job B. Obviously the actual wage differential will *exceed* the $3 hourly wage premium paid for the risk of injury. Alternatively, suppose the risky job A requires little skill while job B demands costly investment in human capital. In this second case, the actual wage differential between A and B will be *less than* $3 hourly and, depending on the size of the skill differential, may even reverse the pay so that safe job B pays more than dangerous job A. Real-world example: Certified public accountants on average earn more than loggers, even though loggers have a much greater risk of being injured on the job.

Conclusion? The frequent observation that higher-paid workers also seem to have more desirable working conditions does not refute the theory of compensating wage differentials. Rather, this observation simply indicates that in many cases the wage gap created by differences in skills *offsets* the compensating differential working in the opposite direction. Without the compensating differential, the actual wage gap would be even greater. Furthermore, if pleasant working conditions are a normal good ("purchases" of them rise with increases in income), then we would expect to find better working conditions and higher wages positively correlated. Workers who are more highly skilled can afford to "buy" better working conditions as part of their overall compensation package; they can afford to give up some of the relatively high direct wage for more nonwage job amenities. Competition in hiring these highly skilled workers will force employers to offer compensation packages that reflect this greater demand for nonwage amenities.

Differences Based on Efficiency Wage Payments

We found in Chapter 7 that under some circumstances employers may find it profitable to pay wages above market-clearing levels. Because these circumstances vary *within* and *among* industries, efficiency wages may help explain wage differentials among workers possessing similar qualifications. Pay differentials resulting from efficiency wage payments will be *equilibrium differentials* because the firms will have no incentive to reduce their wages even though qualified people offer to work for lower wages.

Shirking Model and Wage Differentials

The shirking model suggests that firms will pay efficiency wages either where it is costly to monitor the performance of employees or where the employer's cost of poor performance is high. Recall that the above-market wage raises the cost of job loss to workers, which elicits conscientious efforts and reduces the employer's cost per effective unit of labor. On the other hand, where monitoring workers is inexpensive or where the cost of malfeasance by individual workers is low, the cost per effective unit of labor will be minimized at the lower market-clearing wage. These differing circumstances will create wage differentials that are unrelated to skill differentials or to differences in nonwage amenities.

Turnover Model and Wage Differentials

Recall that the turnover version of the efficiency wage model suggested that firms pay above-market-clearing wages where hiring and training costs are large. The above-market-clearing wage increases the value of the job to the worker, thus reducing the turnover rate (quit rate). Consequently, the average level of job experience and the productivity of the firm's labor both rise. The point is that wages may vary across and within industries depending on the efficiency gains, if any, arising from pay strategies that purposely increase the value of the job from the standpoint of the worker.

Other Job or Employer Heterogeneities

Although differences in nonwage amenities and disamenities, variations in skill requirements of alternative employment, and efficiency wage payments appear to be the major heterogeneities of jobs that create wage differentials, several other job or employer differences may contribute to this phenomenon. For instance, employers or jobs differ in such things as (*a*) union status, (*b*) tendency to discriminate, and (*c*) absolute and relative firm size.

1 Union Status

We will find in Chapter 11 that empirical evidence suggests that, on the average, unions generate a substantial wage advantage for their members. Part of this differential may be a compensating wage premium for the structured work setting, inflexible hours, and employer-set overtime that are characteristic of unionized firms. Another part may reflect the higher productivity that some economists attribute to unionized labor. But most economists conclude that the union–nonunion wage differential also includes a separate component of economic rent deriving from the ability of unions to exert market power. In this latter respect, the existence of both union and nonunion jobs creates a distinct job heterogeneity that helps explain wage disparities.

2 Tendency to Discriminate

We will discover in Chapter 14 that employers may possess varying tendencies to discriminate; that is, some employers are biased toward or against hiring certain classes of workers, say, African–Americans, females, or specific ethnic minorities. Thus, direct wage discrimination may occur in some labor markets. The demand for those whom firms prefer will increase; the demand for those whom firms discriminate against will decline; and an observable wage differential will emerge between whites and African–Americans, males and females, and other groups. Much disagreement exists about whether these observed differentials will persist or be eroded by competitive market forces.

3 Absolute and Relative Firm Size

Several studies indicate that large firms or those with major market shares pay higher wages and salaries in general than smaller firms. There are various possible explanations for this, some involving the previously discussed job heterogeneities. First, large firms are more likely than small firms to be unionized. Second, workers in large firms may be more productive than otherwise comparable workers in small enterprises. This higher productivity may be due to (a) greater amounts and better quality of capital per worker, (b) more on-the-job training necessitated by skill specialization, or (c) the possibility that workers in large firms are "superior" employees who require less supervision than average workers.[9]

A third possibility is that the higher pay observed in large firms is a compensating wage premium. Larger firms may be more bureaucratic and less pleasant places to work than smaller companies. Also, larger firms are more likely to be located in major metropolitan areas, where overall living costs, in addition to commuting and parking expenses, are high.

Finally, firms possessing large market shares often make significant economic profits. This may increase workers' bargaining power and consequently enable them to secure higher wage rates.[10]

The firm size premium has fallen steadily since the early 1980s. Bloom et al. report that the earnings advantage for the average worker in a firm with 10,000 workers relative to the average worker in 100 workers fell from 47 percent in 1980–1984 to 20 percent in 2010–2013.[11] They find that most of the decline is due to a drop in the firm size-wage premium within industries. Even and Macpherson find that the large firm wage premium fell the most for the least educated and one-third of the decline was due to workers becoming more similar across firm sizes.[12] Expanding the compensation measure from the wage rate to include employer contributions to health insurance and pensions shrinks the decline of the size premium by nearly one-quarter.

[9] For more about this topic, see Charles Brown and James Medoff, "The Employer-Size Wage Effect," *Journal of Political Economy,* October 1989, pp. 1027–1059; Todd L. Idson and Walter Y. Oi, "Firm Size and Wages," in Orley Ashenfelter and David Card (eds.), *Handbook of Labor Economics,* vol. 3B (Amsterdam: North-Holland, 1999), pp. 2165–2214; Thierry Lallemand, Robert Plasman, and Francois Rycx, "Why Do Large Firms Pay Higher Wages? Evidence from Matched Worker-Firm Data," *International Journal of Manpower,* no. 7/8(2005), pp. 705–723; and Ana Ferrer and Stephanie Lluis, "Should Workers Care about Firm Size?" *Industrial and Labor Relations Review,* October 2008, pp. 104–125.

[10] David Blachflower, Andrew Oswald, and Mario Garrett, "Insider Power in Wage Determination," *Economica,* May 1990, pp. 143–170; and S. Nickell, J. Vainiomaki, and Sushil Wadhwani, "Wages and Product Market Power," *Economica,* November 1994, pp. 457–473.

[11] Nicholas Bloom, Fatih Guvenen, Benjamin S. Smith, Jae Song, and Till von Wachter, "The Disappearing Large-Firm Wage Premium," *American Economic Review,* May 2018, pp. 317–322.

[12] William E. Even and David A. Macpherson, "Is Bigger Still Better? The Decline of the Wage Premium at Large Firms," *Southern Economic Journal,* April 2012, pp. 1181–1201.

WAGE DIFFERENTIALS: HETEROGENEOUS WORKERS

Having observed that heterogeneities among jobs and employers constitute a major source of wage disparities, we now turn to an equally important factor influencing the wage structure: *heterogeneous workers*. The wage equality initially predicted in Figure 8.1 relied on our assumption not only that all *jobs* were identical but also that all *workers* in the labor force were equally productive. In reality, people have greatly differing stocks of human capital as well as differing preferences for nonwage aspects of jobs.

Differing Human Capital: Noncompeting Groups

In Chapter 16, we will discuss the personal distribution of earnings as it relates to such characteristics as age, years of education, quality of education, native ability, and family background. That approach points out an important reality: People are not homogeneous. Of particular significance to our discussion of the wage structure is the fact that people possess differing stocks of human capital. At any point in time, the labor force consists of numerous *noncompeting groups,* each of which represents one or several occupations for which the members of the group qualify.

Differences in stocks of human capital may result from differing innate abilities to learn and perform. Relatively few people possess the required intellectual or physical endowments to be a nuclear physicist, a professional football quarterback, a petroleum engineer, an opera singer, or a professional model. There is no effective competition in the labor market between these groups and larger groups of skilled and unskilled workers. Nor is there substitutability between nuclear physicists and professional athletes. In fact, even within occupational groups, workers are not always perfectly substitutable. For example, some professional football players command salaries far above the average pay for that occupation. The reason: Other players are only imperfect substitutes because of differences in innate abilities.

More significantly, noncompeting groups result from differences in the type, amount, and quality of education and training that people possess. For instance, the employment options for recent high school graduates include being a farmworker, a gasoline station attendant, a member of the armed forces, an unskilled construction worker, or a fast-food employee. Each of these categories of workers can be classified into one broad group because each is capable of doing the other jobs. But none of the workers in this group currently offer direct competition to, say, lawyers or accountants, who find themselves in other, more exclusive groups.

Workers can and do move from one noncompeting group to another by investing in human capital. The gasoline attendant may decide to attend college to obtain a degree in accounting. But this presupposes that the person has the financial means and innate intelligence to pursue this degree successfully. To the extent that income, creditworthiness, and native learning skills are unequally distributed, wage differentials between noncompeting groups can persist. Also, bear in mind that the *quality* of education varies. A degree in accounting from a relatively unknown college may not generate the same postinvestment earnings as a degree from a more prestigious university.

WW8.2   To summarize: People have differing stocks of human capital according to native endowments and the type, amount, and quality of education and training they possess. Unsurprisingly, the result is a wide variety of groups, subgroups, or even individuals who are not readily substitutable for one another in the labor market. In the short run, these human capital heterogeneities produce wage differentials due to the varying productivity of workers. People can move toward the higher-paying positions in the long run, but the extent of such movements is limited by differing abilities to finance human capital investments and differing inherent abilities to absorb and apply education and training. Therefore, wage differentials remain.

8.2 World of Work

Rising Importance of Social Skills

Computers have become much more powerful and are now very good at performing routine tasks. However, they still are unable to simulate human interaction well. Human interaction requires the ability to understand subtleties in language as well as grasp nonverbal signals. Team production requires human interaction so that workers can take advantage of their co-worker's strengths and respond to unanticipated changes.

David Deming finds that positions requiring high levels of social interaction increased grew by 11.8 percentage points, between 1980 and 2012, as a share of employment. In contrast, the share of jobs that require high math skills but less social skills such as engineers, drafters, and architects fell by 3.3 percentage points over the same period. Employment grew most rapidly for jobs requiring high levels of both math skill and social skills such as managers, teachers, nurses and therapists, physicians, lawyers, and economists.

To examine whether social skills have become more important over time in determining wages, Deming uses data from two surveys following individuals aged 25–33. He finds that a one standard deviation increase in social skills increased wages by 3.7 percent in the mid-2000s as compared to only 2.0 percent in the mid-1980s and 1990s. He also reports workers with higher social skills are more likely to work in occupations requiring greater social skills and that they earn higher wages if they enter these occupations.

Source: Based on David J. Deming, "The Growing Importance of Social Skills in the Labor Market," *Quarterly Journal of Economics,* November 2017, pp. 1593–1640.

Differing Individual Preferences

In addition to possessing differing stocks of human capital, people also are heterogeneous with respect to their preferences for such things as (*a*) present versus future income and (*b*) various nonwage aspects of work.

Differences in Time Preferences

Some people are highly present-oriented: They discount the future heavily or ignore it entirely. Other people have a great willingness or ability to sacrifice present satisfaction to obtain greater future rewards. In terms of Chapter 4's investment in human capital framework, we are saying that people have differing discount rates—or "i's" in Equation (4.3). People who are highly present-oriented will have high discount rates, or i's. They will not be willing to sacrifice consumption today unless as a result they can obtain substantially more dollars in the future. The higher the i in Equation (4.3), the lower the net present value of the prospective investment and the less the likelihood that people will undertake a given investment in human capital. On the other hand, people who are more future-oriented will be willing to forgo current consumption for the expectation of obtaining relatively small additions to earnings later. In technical terms, such people will have low discount rates (i's) and will perceive a given investment in human capital to have a higher net present value. Consequently, they will obtain more human capital than the more present-oriented individuals.

These differences in time preferences have a significant implication for the theory of noncompeting groups. Specifically, they help explain why people who possess similar innate abilities and access to financing often choose to obtain differing levels of human capital. We have seen that these disparities in amounts of human

8.1 *Quick Review*

- A single wage rate would exist if all workers and jobs were homogeneous, markets were perfectly competitive, and mobility and migration were unimpeded.
- Heterogeneous jobs (differing nonwage attributes, skill requirements, and other features) are a major source of wage differentials.
- Sources of compensating wage differentials include differing risks of injury and death, fringe benefits, job status, job location, regularity of earnings, prospects for wage advancement, and control over the pace of work.
- Wage differentials also arise because workers are heterogeneous; their human capital, time preferences, and tastes for nonwage aspects of jobs differ.

Your Turn

Generally, salaries of state governors are far below those of similarly qualified top executives in the private sector. How can these wage differentials persist? (*Answer:* See page 541.)

capital are a major source of wage differentials. Restated, differences in time preferences, which in themselves represent a worker heterogeneity, help explain an even more significant heterogeneity: differing stocks of human capital.[13]

Tastes for Nonwage Aspects of Jobs

We noted earlier that jobs are heterogeneous with respect to such nonwage features as probability of job accidents, fringe benefits, job status, location, regularity of earnings, prospects for wage advance, and control over the work pace. People also differ in their preferences for these nonwage amenities and disamenities: Workers as well as jobs are heterogeneous in this regard. As examples, some workers value job safety highly, while others are far less averse to risks; some people desire positions having paid vacations, while others find vacations boring and would gladly forgo paid absences for higher hourly pay; and some individuals seek status, while others do not care what people think of their occupations.

THE HEDONIC THEORY OF WAGES

The fact that both jobs *and* workers are heterogeneous is contained in the *hedonic theory of wages*.[14] The term *hedonic* derives from the philosophical concept of hedonism, which hypothesizes that people pursue utility (pleasure), such as wage income, and avoid disutility (pain), such as jobs having unpleasant working

---

[13] For an analysis of differences in time preferences, see John T. Warner and Saul Pleeter, "The Personal Discount Rate: Evidence from Military Downsizing Programs," *American Economic Review,* March 2001, pp. 33–53.

[14] Sherwin Rosen, "Hedonic Prices and Implicit Markets," *Journal of Political Economy,* January–February 1974, pp. 34–55.

conditions. According to the hedonic theory, workers are interested in maximizing *net* utility and therefore are willing to "exchange" that which produces utility to get reductions in something that yields disutility.

8.3   World of Work

Is Exercise Good for Your Wallet as Well as Your Heart?*

Research has consistently shown that regular exercise leads to beneficial effects on an individual's health including improved heart health and less obesity. Exercise has also been demonstrated to lead to improved mental function, increased psychological well-being, and raised energy levels. These three factors can directly raise an individual's productivity and thus wages. Exercise can indirectly raise an individual's wages by demonstrating to an employer that he or she is disciplined or through social networking effects.

Exercise may also impact earnings through its effects on obesity. Heavier people have lower wages, and this wage penalty increases with age. The lower earnings may be the result of discrimination, employers passing on higher health costs, or lower self-esteem.

Vasilios Kosteas examines the impact of exercise by using data on 6,190 individuals aged 33–41. There is a wide range of exercise behavior in the sample. Nearly 32 percent never exercise and 39 percent regularly exercise (at least once a week). Men are more likely to regularly exercise than women, as 46 percent of men regularly exercise versus 31 percent of women.

The analysis, which controls for obesity, reveals that regular exercise raises earnings 7 percent for men and 9 percent for women. More frequent exercise (at least three times a week) raises earnings even more, particularly for women. Their earnings are nearly 12 percent higher than those who never exercise. These earnings effects may encourage additional exercise.

* Based on Vasilios D. Kosteas, "The Effect of Exercise on Earnings: Evidence from the NLSY," *Journal of Labor Research,* Spring 2012, pp. 225–250.

The Worker's Indifference Map

The hedonic wage theory often is portrayed in terms of a trade-off between a "good" (the wage) and a work-related "bad" (e.g., the probability of injury). However, the *absence* of a "bad" (the probability that an injury will not occur) is indeed a "good"; therefore, the theory can also be presented in terms of trading off wages and nonwage amenities. This allows the use of standard indifference curve analysis.

It is reasonable to assume that the typical worker places a positive value on the wage rate being paid and the nonwage amenities that a job offers. In a manner similar to the wage–fringe benefit analysis in Chapter 7, a worker faces a subjective trade-off between two things yielding utility.

Figure 8.2 is illustrative, where the wage rate is measured on the vertical axis and a single nonwage amenity is shown on the horizontal axis. This nonwage amenity may be any one of several positive job attributes—for example, the probability of *not* being injured on the job, the advantages associated with the job's location, or the expenses saved and leisure gained as commuting time declines.

FIGURE 8.2   **An Indifference Map for Wages and Nonwage Amenities**

The hedonic indifference map is composed of a number of indifference curves. Each individual curve shows the various combinations of wage rates and a particular nonwage amenity (e.g., job safety) that yield a specific level of total utility. Each successive curve to the northeast reflects a higher level of total utility.

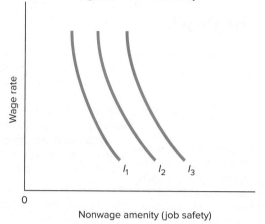

Let's suppose the particular nonwage amenity measured left to right on the horizontal axis is the degree of job safety (the probability of not being injured on the job). Each indifference curve shows the various combinations of wages and degrees of job safety that will yield some given level of utility or satisfaction to this worker. Recall that each point on a specific indifference curve is equally satisfactory, but total utility can be increased by getting to a higher indifference curve—that is, by moving northeast from I_1 to I_2 to I_3.

The indifference curves in Figure 8.2 are steep, implying that this individual is highly averse to risks. To understand this conclusion, observe curve I_1 and notice that this person places a high substitution value on extra degrees of job safety. A very large increase in the wage rate is necessary to compensate him or her for a small reduction in safety (a small increase in the probability of job injury). But indifference maps vary from person to person; another worker may be far less averse to risk and therefore will have relatively flat indifference curves compared to those in Figure 8.2. Succinctly stated, workers are heterogeneous with respect to their preferences for nonwage amenities.

The Employer's Normal-Profit Isoprofit Curve

It is reasonable to assume that an employer can reduce the probability of job injury or, alternatively stated, increase the safety of the workplace. For example, the employer might provide education programs about job safety, purchase safer machinery, provide protective work gear, or slow the pace of work. But because these steps are costly, the employer faces a trade-off between the wages offered and the degree of job safety provided to workers. To maintain any given level of profits, the firm can either (*a*) pay lower wages and provide a high degree of job safety or (*b*) pay higher wages and take fewer actions to reduce the risk of job-related accidents.

Figure 8.3 shows a normal-profit isoprofit curve, which in this case indicates the various combinations of wage rates and degrees of job safety yielding a given normal profit. Observe that this curve is concave; it is not a straight line as was the isoprofit curve for wage rates and fringe benefits in Figure 7.4. Why the difference? In Chapter 7, we assumed that the trade-off between wage rates and fringe benefits was constant. But the concave shape of the isoprofit curve in Figure 8.3 derives from the realistic assumption that each unit of added job safety comes at increasing expense and therefore results in a successively larger wage reduction.

FIGURE 8.3 Isoprofit Curve

The employer's isoprofit curve portrays the various combinations of wage rates and job amenities (e.g., job safety) that yield a given level of profit. Competition among firms will result in only normal profits (zero economic profit) in the long run; therefore, firms will be forced to make their "wage rate–job amenity" decisions along a curve such as P.

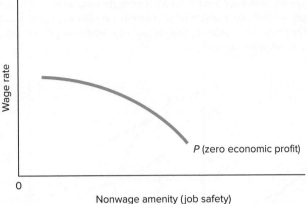

Successive units of expense (wage reduction) yield diminishing returns to job safety. Marginal costs typically rise as more job safety is produced; therefore, as one moves rightward on P, the curve becomes increasingly steep.

But not all employers have identical isoprofit curves; they too are heterogeneous. The isoprofit curve in Figure 8.3 is relatively flat, indicating that this firm can "purchase" job safety at a low marginal cost. Note from P that large increments of job safety are associated with only small reductions in the wage. But other firms may not be so fortunate. Their technological constraints may make it extremely difficult to reduce the risk of accidents and therefore very costly to produce a safe work environment. These firms would face steep normal-profit isoprofit curves.

Matching Workers with Jobs

Figure 8.4 portrays the optimal combination of wage rate and job safety for two distinct sets of employers and workers. Workers A and B possess identical stocks of human capital, but have greatly different tastes for the nonwage amenity for job safety. The isoprofit curves P_A in graph (a) and P_B in (b) show the highest profit levels attainable for firms A and B, given the competitive nature of their respective industries. The general slope of isoprofit curve P_A is less steep than that of P_B. This indicates that for technological reasons, the marginal cost of producing job safety is more in firm B than in A. Restated, a specific increase in job safety reduces the wage rate more for firm B than for A.

WW8.4   Now observe the indifference curves I_A and I_B in graphs (a) and (b). These are the highest attainable indifference curves for each worker. Curve I_A is relatively steep, implying that person A is quite averse to the risk of job injury (he values job safety highly). On the other hand, the curve for person B is relatively flat, indicating that B is less concerned about job injury or death than A. Obviously workers A and B have differing tastes for this particular job disamenity.

Each worker maximizes total utility where her or his highest indifference curve is tangent to the employer's zero-economic profit isoprofit curve. Worker A will choose to work for employer A and, as indicated by point a in the left graph, will receive wage rate W_A. Along with this low wage, the person will obtain a large

FIGURE 8.4 Matching Heterogeneous Workers and Jobs

Graph (a) portrays an optimal job match between worker A, who places a high value on job safety at the margin, and firm A, which can produce job safety at relatively low marginal cost. Graph (b) shows the utility-maximizing and profit-maximizing wage rate–nonwage amenity combination (point b) for a worker who is less averse to risk and a firm that has high marginal costs of making the workplace safer. Graph (c) plots the optimal wage–job safety combinations shown in (a) and (b). Line WS in graph (c) indicates the general relationship between wage rates and job safety in a labor market characterized by many—not just two—heterogeneous workers and jobs. Higher wage rates are associated with lower levels of nonwage amenities, other things being the same.

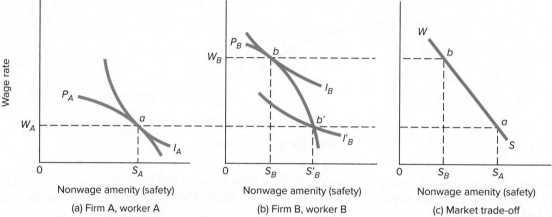

(a) Firm A, worker A   (b) Firm B, worker B   (c) Market trade-off

quantity of the amenity job safety. Job and worker heterogeneity therefore produce an optimal match between an individual who is highly averse to risk and an employer who has relatively low marginal costs of producing job safety. Similarly, worker B will match up with employer B and receive a higher wage rate W_B but will be employed in a more dangerous work setting. The matching of laborer B and firm B maximizes the interests of both: Employer B has a high marginal cost of producing job safety, and this worker is willing to trade off much of that amenity for a higher wage rate.

Labor Market Implications

The hedonic wage model has some interesting—and in some cases controversial—implications. Let's sample a few.

First, the labor market will generate wage differentials among people who possess identical amounts of human capital. Other things being equal, higher wages will tend to be associated with fewer nonwage amenities. This is shown in graph (c) in Figure 8.4. Line WS, which connects points such as a and b in the two left graphs, indicates the general inverse relationships between wage rates and job safety in a labor market characterized by many—not just two—heterogeneous workers and jobs. The wage differentials possible along this line are persistent, or equilibrium, differentials; they will not create movements of workers among the jobs.

Second, laws that set a minimum standard for nonwage job amenities may actually reduce the utility of some workers. This is shown through reference again to Figure 8.4. If the government forces firm B (graph b) to increase its job safety from S_B to, say, S'_B, it will move from point b downward on P_B to b', and worker B will be forced to indifference curve I'_B, which clearly is below I_B.

8.4 World of Work

Compensating Pay for Shift Work

In the hedonic theory of wages, compensating wage differentials arise for jobs with onerous working conditions. The market wage in these occupations must increase sufficiently to compensate the last worker employed for the disutility that person associates with the poor working conditions. These compensating wage premiums, however, enable some workers to increase their net utility. Specifically, people who are less averse to the poor working conditions or who are comparatively less productive in normal jobs may enhance their net utility by accepting work under inferior conditions. For these individuals, the utility gain from the extra pay may exceed the utility loss from the poor conditions. In this regard, economists say that some workers "self-select" into occupations having poorer working conditions but paying compensating wage premiums.

Kostiuk has found precisely this outcome for work done at night, commonly called "shift work." Shift work is more prevalent than generally supposed, with about 15 percent of full-time wage and salary workers not working a regular daytime schedule. Using data from supplements to the Census Bureau's *Current Population Survey,* Kostiuk found an 8.2 percent wage premium

associated with shift work in manufacturing. Union shift workers received an 18.1 percent wage premium; nonunion shift workers, a 4.3 percent differential.

Kostiuk's findings partly reflect the self-selection mentioned earlier. He discovered that workers with less education had a larger wage premium for shift work than did more educated workers doing similar shift work. This higher relative wage premium for less educated workers enticed more of them to take shift-work jobs. Thought of differently, if the typical night-work employee had instead worked during the day, his or her pay would be less than the pay of typical day-shift workers. On average, night-shift workers are less educated than day-shift workers doing similar work.

The upshot is that the shift-work sector, with its compensating wage differentials, raises the wage of less educated workers and reduces overall wage inequality. Shift work narrows the distribution of earnings on two counts: (*a*) It provides a compensating wage differential for adverse working conditions, and (*b*) it attracts workers who have a below-average potential for daytime earnings.

Source: P. F. Kostiuk, "Compensating Differentials for Shift Work," *Journal of Political Economy,* part 1, October 1990, pp. 1054–1075.

Third, part of the observed male–female earnings differential may reflect differing tastes for positive job amenities such as pleasant working conditions, a short commuting distance, and a low probability of job injury. In terms of Figure 8.4, *if* indifference curves for females as a group tend to be more on the order of I_A rather than I_B, women will match up to a greater extent than men with jobs that have lower pay but also better nonwage amenities. Filer finds evidence to support this possibility. Apparently a portion of the observed male–female earnings differential among similarly trained workers results from compensating differentials.[15]

Finally, the hedonic model extends our earlier discussion of optimal fringe benefits (Figure 7.5) both in terms of worker indifference maps and employer isoprofit curves. Indifference maps of the utility trade-off between wages and fringe benefits vary from worker to worker. Workers who place a high marginal valuation on fringe benefits—that is, have relatively steep indifference curves—will therefore match up with firms offering

[15] Randall K. Filer, "Male–Female Wage Differences: The Importance of Compensating Differentials," *Industrial and Labor Relations Review,* April 1985, pp. 426–437.

pay packages containing significant fringe benefits. Conversely, workers whose valuations of cash wages are higher at the margin than valuations of fringe benefits are more likely to opt to work for firms with relatively fewer fringe benefits but higher cash wages.

In addition, variations in indifference maps among workers help to explain the existence of so-called *cafeteria plans,* which permit workers to choose among a wide range of fringe benefits. These plans allow heterogeneous workers to individually attain higher indifference curves than they could if they had to accept a fixed package of fringe benefits determined by the firm. Examples: A female worker with young children may select child care benefits; an older male worker may opt to have his pension fund enhanced. By increasing the total utility workers receive from any given dollar amount of compensation, cafeteria plans may enable firms to attract and retain higher-quality workers.

> **WW8.5** The composition of fringe benefits may vary among firms, depending on the marginal cost of providing each fringe benefit. For example, a university may provide free tuition for children of employees, whereas a retail firm may give its workers discounts on merchandise. In each situation, the firm shapes the fringe benefit package in a particular way because of the relatively low marginal cost of providing a specific fringe benefit.

8.5   World of Work

Placing a Value on Human Life

Agencies such as the Environmental Protection Agency, Federal Aviation Administration, and Occupational Safety and Health Administration are required by law to determine the expected monetary costs and benefits of any new regulations. Because lives saved are an important benefit of many of the regulations, these federal agencies need to estimate the economic value of human life.

The traditional approach to placing an economic value on human life relies on the concept of human capital. A so-called wrongful death from, say, an airline crash eliminates earnings over the remaining years of the person's expected work life. Economists use earnings data for similar individuals in the same occupation to estimate the present value of the amount of wages and fringe benefits lost over these years. Although estimates vary by age and occupation, this method places the value of life on average at between $700,000 and $1 million.

A more recent, controversial approach to attaching a value to human life relies on the hedonic wage theory (Figure 8.4). We know that employers must pay compensating wage differentials to induce people to work at dangerous jobs. The size of these differentials reveals information about the amount of money that firms must pay per job-related death. Suppose, for example, that risk-averse behavior of labor suppliers forces firms to pay compensating wages of $1,000 annually for every 0.1 percent (=0.001) increase in the probability of death on the job. On average, every job-related death therefore costs firms $1 million (= $1,000/0.001), a sum that could be thought of as the economic value of each life.

The hedonic method typically yields higher estimates of the value of human life than does the human capital approach. For example, hedonic estimates developed by the federal regulatory agencies range upward to $9.2 million per life saved.

8.2 *Quick Review*

- In the hedonic wage model, indifference curves show the various combinations of wage rates and levels of a particular nonwage amenity that yield specific levels of total utility.

- The employer's normal-profit isoprofit curve depicts the various combinations of wage rates and specific nonwage amenities that yield a normal profit.

- The optimal job match occurs where the worker's highest attainable indifference curve is tangent to the employer's normal-profit isoprofit curve.

- Workers who have a strong preference for a particular nonwage amenity will tend to match up with employers who can provide the amenity at a relatively low marginal cost. Other things being equal, these workers will receive lower pay than workers who have weak preferences for the nonwage amenity and match up with employers who provide less of it due to its high marginal cost.

Your Turn

How might a person who actually enjoys working outdoors in extremely cold temperatures benefit from the more general worker preference for employment in climate-controlled buildings or in mild outdoor temperatures? (*Answer:* See page 541.)

WAGE DIFFERENTIALS: LABOR MARKET IMPERFECTIONS

Wage differences can be explained largely—but not fully—on the basis of heterogeneous jobs, employers, and workers. They also occur because of labor market imperfections that impede labor mobility. Such factors as imperfect information, costly migration, and various other barriers to mobility interact to create and maintain wage differentials.

Imperfect Labor Market Information

We assumed that labor market information was perfect in Figure 8.1, but in reality it is imperfect and costly to obtain. Recognizing that workers are heterogeneous, firms search the labor market to find workers who are best suited for employment. Similarly, workers gather information about prospective job opportunities by scanning help-wanted ads, writing letters, inquiring at business establishments, and so forth. These search efforts by firms and prospective employees involve direct costs and opportunity costs of time. Furthermore, the activity of gaining information eventually will yield diminishing returns. Translated into costs, this implies that the marginal cost of obtaining information will increase as more of it is sought. The fact that information is imperfect and increasingly costly to obtain has important implications for labor market activity and the wage structure.[16] Specifically, it implies that (*a*) a range of wage rates may exist for any given occupation, independently of compensating differentials, and (*b*) when changes in demand cause wage differentials, long-run supply adjustments are likely to be slow.

---

[16] It also has important implications for job search (Chapter 15) and unemployment (Chapter 18).

1 Wage Rate Distributions

Once we introduce costly information, job searches, and heterogeneous workers and employers into our analysis, the likelihood there will be a single equilibrium wage (as in Figure 6.1) for each type of labor greatly diminishes. Rather, we can expect to find a *range* of equilibrium wages for each type of labor. This range may be very narrow or quite broad, depending on the individual circumstances within each occupational labor market.

Figure 8.5 portrays one of the many possible wage rate distributions. This particular distribution is symmetrical, but other types of distributions are entirely possible. The horizontal axis shows a range of wages, $18.00 through $19.80, and the vertical axis measures the relative frequency of the occurrence of each subrange of wages in the distribution. The area covered by the wage distribution equals 1; there is a 100 percent probability that the wage will fall within the $18.00-$19.80 range. Likewise, 0.05 or 5 percent of all wages will be between $18.00 and $18.19, 8 percent will lie between $18.20 and $18.39, and so forth.

FIGURE 8.5 A Wage Rate Distribution

Under conditions of costly information and job searches, competitive labor markets generate an equilibrium distribution of wage rates within a single occupation, rather than an equilibrium hourly wage. In this example, 20 percent of the workers receive a wage rate between $18.80 and $18.99 an hour; but some workers (5 percent) earn as little as $18.00-$18.19, while another percent makes $19.60-$19.79 an hour. The area under the frequency distribution sums to 1 (100 percent).

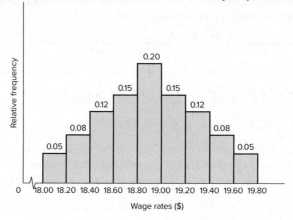

How can a wage rate distribution such as that depicted in Figure 8.5 persist? Won't workers move from lower-paying to higher-paying jobs, with a single equilibrium wage rate eventually resulting? The ideas of costly information and costly job searches provide the answers to these questions. Employers will set wages according to their individual circumstances and their estimates of the market wage rate. Some employers may pay slightly more—others slightly less—than the average wage. But because information is imperfect and costly to obtain, some workers and firms will be unaware that greater or lesser wages are being paid to similar workers. Other employees may recognize that there is a variance in pay but also realize that it is costly to discover which employers of this labor are paying the higher amounts. In technical terms, many workers will judge the marginal cost of obtaining the necessary information to exceed the expected marginal gain from the higher wage. Thus, they will remain in their present places of employment, and the wage differentials will persist. *Under conditions of imperfect, costly information, it is entirely possible for wage differences within occupations to be equilibrium differentials—that is, differentials that do not evoke job switching.*[17]

---

[17] The classic article on this point is George J. Stigler, "Information in the Labor Market," *Journal of Political Economy,* October 1962, pp. S94-105.

2 Lengthy Adjustment Periods

A second implication of imperfect, costly information is that long-run supply adjustments to wage differentials created by changes in demand may take months or even years to occur. Suppose, for example, that the demand for labor in occupation X rises sharply. Given an upward-sloping short-run labor supply curve, a wage increase in occupation X will result. But information concerning this new wage is likely to be incompletely disseminated. People choosing the types and amounts of human capital to obtain will learn *gradually* of the higher wage in occupation X. Of course as more time transpires, more information will become known. But even then some potential labor suppliers to X will wonder if this is indeed a permanent wage differential relative to other occupations or one that will quickly evaporate by the time they become qualified.

Once people *do* begin to recognize that the wage rate in occupation X is permanent, some will respond and eventually create a flow of labor into X and away from, say, Y and Z. This will cause the wage narrowing predicted by the pure theory. But recall from our discussion of the cobweb model in Chapter 6 (Figure 6.8) that in some occupations requiring long training periods—such as law and engineering—the supply response may be so great that the wage differential not only is eliminated but also turns in the opposite direction. Then, in the next period, still another overadjustment may occur, reducing labor supply so dramatically that a positive wage differential again arises. Thus, as shown by the wage rate adjustment path in Figure 8.6, some wage rates may for a time oscillate above and below the long-run equilibrium wage W_e. Note from the diagram that the wage rate shifts from W_0 to W_1 to W_2, and so forth, as units of time transpire. To summarize: Labor markets in which information is imperfect and costly will be characterized by many transitional wage differentials, which exist because of lengthy and occasionally oscillating adjustment paths to final equilibrium.[18]

Immobilities

Labor immobilities, defined simply as *impediments to the movement of labor,* constitute another major reason that wage differentials occur and sometimes persist. For convenience, we will classify these barriers to labor mobility as geographic, institutional, and sociological.

1 Geographic Immobilities

We will discover in Chapter 9 that wage differences between geographic areas provide an incentive for workers to migrate. By moving to a high-wage location, a worker can enhance lifetime earnings. But moving also involves costs, such as transportation expenses, forgone earnings during the move, the inconvenience of adjusting to a new job and community, the negative aspects of leaving family and friends, and the possible loss of seniority and pension benefits. If these costs deter migration to the extent that an insufficient number of migrants are attracted to the higher-paying locale, geographic wage differentials will persist.

2 Institutional Immobilities

Restrictions on mobility imposed by such institutions as government and unions may reinforce geographic immobilities. As we will discuss in Chapter 13, government licensing of occupations can restrict the movement of qualified workers among jobs. Also, differing licensing requirements in various states can limit worker mobility geographically. Craft unions also are a factor here; they impede mobility by limiting the access

---

[18] For a discussion of alternative wage rate adjustment paths, see Belton M. Fleisher and Thomas J. Kniesner, *Labor Economics: Theory, Evidence, and Policy,* 3rd Edition (Englewood Cliffs, NJ: Prentice-Hall, Inc., 1984), pp. 186–191. Also of interest is Jean Helwege, "Sectoral Shifts and Interindustry Wage Differentials," *Journal of Labor Economics,* January 1992, pp. 55–84.

of nonunion workers to union-controlled apprenticeship programs and union-filled jobs. Other institutional immobilities involve pension plans and seniority rights, which reduce people's incentives to move from one job to another.

3 Sociological Immobilities

Finally, there are numerous sociological barriers to labor mobility. In Chapter 14, we examine theories of labor market discrimination by race and gender. For example, females appear to be crowded into certain occupations. This drives down the equilibrium wage in these occupations and raises it elsewhere. To the extent that barriers keep qualified women from moving from these lower-paying positions to higher-paying occupations, wage differentials between the sexes can persist. In the same vein, African–Americans historically were excluded from certain higher-paying occupations either through informal understandings by employers or through formal prohibitions by unions. As an example of the latter, over 20 national unions had constitutional provisions barring African–Americans from membership in 1930. In fact, some unions such as the Locomotive Engineers and the Railway Conductors still excluded African–Americans from membership in 1964, when the Civil Rights Act was passed.[19]

Figure 8.7 provides a schematic overview of the major contributing factors to wage differentials. This diagram merits your careful consideration.

FIGURE 8.6 **Wage Rate Adjustment Path**

An increase in labor demand initially may cause a substantial wage increase to, say, W_0 in occupations that require long training periods. But the supply response to the higher wage may create a surplus of labor to the occupation in the subsequent period, driving the wage rate lower, say, to W_1. For a time the wage rate may oscillate above and below the long-run equilibrium wage rate W_e before equilibrium in the market is finally restored. During the transition periods, wage differentials between this occupation and others paying W_e will be observed.

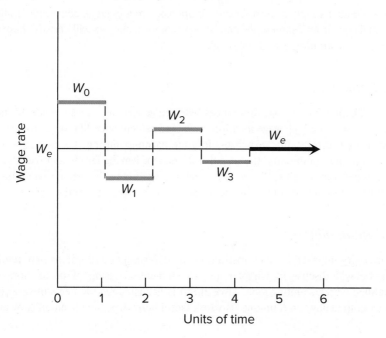

[19] F. Ray Marshall, Vernon M. Briggs, Jr., and Allan King, *Labor Economics,* 5th Edition (Homewood, IL: R. D. Irwin, Inc., 1984), p. 567.

FIGURE 8.7 Sources of Wage Differentials: A Review

Wage differentials arise because jobs are heterogeneous, workers are heterogeneous, and markets are imperfect. Heterogeneous jobs *and* heterogeneous workers are the underpinning of the hedonic wage, or job-matching, model.

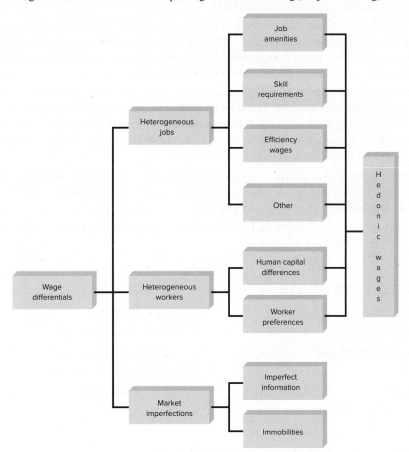

Chapter Summary

1. Theoretically, if *all* workers and jobs were homogeneous and all labor markets were perfectly competitive, then workers would move among the various jobs until the wages paid in all markets were identical.

2. Casual and empirical examinations of wage rates and weekly earnings reveal that a variety of wage differentials exist and that many of them persist over time.

3. Several nonwage aspects of jobs influence supply decisions in ways that generate compensating wage differentials. These nonwage factors include *(a)* risk of job injury and death, *(b)* fringe benefits, *(c)* job status, *(d)* job location, *(e)* the regularity of earnings, and *(f)* the prospect for wage advancement.

4. Differences in skill requirements also produce wage differences. Other things being equal, to attract enough laborers to an occupation requiring considerable prior investment in human capital, employers must pay these workers more than they pay less skilled employees.

5. Efficiency wage theories have been advanced to explain pay differences within and among industries. These theories predict that wages will be higher where it is difficult to monitor the performance of workers, where the costs to employers of mistakes by individual workers are large, and where high labor turnover significantly reduces productivity.

6. Another major source of wage disparities is heterogeneous workers. Specifically, workers possess greatly varying stocks of human capital and differing preferences for various nonwage aspects of work. Consequently, the overall labor market is composed of numerous submarkets consisting of groups of workers who offer little competition to other groups.

7. The hedonic theory of wages hypothesizes that workers who possess differing subjective preferences for wages compared to nonwage job amenities seek optimal matches with employers who differ in their costs of providing those nonwage attributes. Among a wide variety of implications that flow from this model is the basic one that labor markets will generate sustained wage differentials, even among people who have similar stocks of human capital.

8. Imperfect and costly market information is another reason that wage differentials exist. Imperfect and costly information creates ranges of wage rates, independent of other factors, and explains why transitional wage differentials often are long-lasting.

9. Labor market immobilities—geographic, institutional, and sociological—also help explain persistent earnings differences among workers.

Terms and Concepts

equilibrium wage differentials	skill differential
transitional wage differentials	heterogeneous workers
homogeneous workers and jobs	noncompeting groups
wage structure	hedonic theory of wages
heterogeneous jobs	labor immobilities
compensating wage differentials	

Questions and Study Suggestions

1. Suppose all workers and jobs in a hypothetical economy are homogeneous. Explain why no wage differentials would exist if this economy were perfectly competitive and information and mobility were costless. Explain why wage differentials would arise if, on the other hand, information and mobility were imperfect and costly.

2. Analyze why college professors generally earn less than their professional PhD counterparts who are employed by corporations.

3. Discuss: "Many of the lowest-paid people in society—for example, short-order cooks—also have relatively poor working conditions. Hence the theory of compensating wage differentials is disproved."

4. Explain why it may be in a worker's *short-term* best interest to have job titles restated to add status: say, becoming a mixologist rather than a bartender or being referred to as a sanitation engineer rather than a garbage worker. Why may such title changes not be in the *long-term* best interest of these workers, however?

5. Explain how the theory of investment in human capital relates to the notion of noncompeting groups and how the latter relates to the presence of equilibrium wage differentials.

6. Referring back to Figure 7.8, explain why wage differentials resulting exclusively from efficiency wage payments (shirking model *and* turnover model) will persist rather than erode over time.

7. What is the hedonic theory of wage differentials? Discuss the characteristics of a normal-profit isoprofit curve. Combine isoprofit curves with worker indifference curves to explain how two workers with identical stocks of human capital might be paid different wage rates.

8. Speculate about why the average hourly wage rate paid by manufacturing firms to production workers is so much lower in Mississippi than in Michigan (Table 8.3).

9. Explain how each of the following relates to wage differentials: *(a)* seniority provisions, *(b)* varying state licensing requirements for occupations, *(c)* racial segregation, and *(d)* regional cost-of-living differences.

10. Explain why "pay comparability" legislation requiring that the public sector remunerate government employees at wages equal to private sector counterparts might create excess supplies of labor in public sector labor markets.

11. Suppose that *(a)* employers must pay higher wages to attract workers from wider geographic areas and hence higher wages are associated with longer commuting distances (less of the amenity "closeness of job to home") and *(b)* females have greater tastes for having jobs close to their homes than do males. Use the hedonic wage model to show graphically why a male–female wage differential might emerge, independent of skill differences or gender discrimination.

Internet Exercise

Who Earns the Big Bucks? Who Doesn't?

 Go to the Bureau of Labor Statistics Occupational Employment Statistics website (**http://www.bls.gov/oes/home.htm**) and select "OES Data" and "National Cross-Industry" for the most recent year shown. Provide the mean (average) wage for one relatively high-paying and one relatively low-paying occupation in 10 of the broad occupational categories ("Management Occupation," "Business and Financial Operations Occupations," and so on). What general factors explain the differences you observe within broad occupational categories and among the categories? (Answer in a one-paragraph essay.)

Select the OES Code to view the employment distribution of annual pay for "Real Estate Brokers" in "Sales and Related Occupations." What is the minimum salary required to be in the top 25 percent of brokers? What is the highest salary a broker can earn and be in the bottom 10 percent of brokers? What might explain these striking differences in pay?

Go to ESPN's Sportszone at **http://espn.go.com/golf/moneylist** to identify the top five leading money winners and their earnings on the men's PGA tour, women's PGA tour (LPGA), Champions tour, Nationwide tour, and European tour. This information can be found by selecting each tour under "Money Leaders" (use either the current earnings or the earnings for the previous year, whichever are listed). What, in general, explains the differences you observe among the top earnings on the five professional tours?

Internet Links

 The *Forbes* magazine website reports the salaries of celebrities, executives, and others (**http://www.forbes.com/lists**).

Chapter 9

Mobility, Migration, and Efficiency

After reading this chapter, you should be able to:

1. **Distinguish between the various types of labor mobility and explain the relative importance of each.**
2. **Use the analytic framework of human capital investment to explain the migration decision of a household.**
3. **Discuss the determinants of migration.**
4. **Discuss the economic consequences of labor migration.**
5. **Explain how capital and product flows affect wage differentials and labor mobility.**
6. **Summarize the history of U.S. immigration policy and critically evaluate the economic impact of illegal immigration.**

You most likely know someone who has recently changed employers, occupations, or job locations. Indeed, the movement of workers—*labor mobility*—is one of the striking features of labor markets. Alvarez, an auto mechanic, moves from Arizona to Arkansas. Pearson, a public schoolteacher, quits to become a private detective. Kioski, an executive of a North Carolina firm, gets transferred to New Mexico.

In the real world, changes are common in such things as product demand, labor productivity, levels of human capital, family circumstances, and personal attitudes toward nonwage amenities. These changes induce some workers to switch employers, occupations, geographical locations, or some combination of all three. Also, employers respond to changing economic circumstances by hiring, transferring, or discharging workers; closing or expanding present facilities; or moving operations to new locations.

Combined, these actions of workers and employers produce much movement of labor from employer to employer, occupation to occupation, and place to place. Careful observation often reveals that this mobility arises in response to transitional wage differentials, which tend to erode as markets move toward equilibrium. Mobility is central to the operation of labor markets; it promotes allocative efficiency by shuffling workers to society's highest-valued employments.

TYPES OF LABOR MOBILITY

The boxes in Figure 9.1 categorize several important kinds of labor mobility. The columns of the boxes identify locational characteristics of the employment change, and the rows indicate occupational characteristics. Let's describe the kind of labor mobility associated with each box.

Box I: Job Change/No Change in Occupation or Residence

Box I indicates mobility in which neither the worker's occupation nor residence changes. This form of mobility occurs frequently—for example, when electrical engineers switch employers within California's Silicon Valley or when automobile salespeople quit one dealership to work for another. This category also includes transfers of employees from one of a firm's units to another in the same local area—for example, when a bank employee is reassigned from one branch of a local bank to another.

Box II: Occupational Change/No Change in Residence

This box identifies changes in occupation not accompanied by changes in residence. Much of this *occupational mobility* involves moves to closely related occupations, such as when a carpenter takes a job in a lumberyard or when a production worker is promoted to a supervisory position within a firm. But in other cases, this mobility is characterized by a significant occupational change: For example, a part-time warehouse employee who completes college might accept a job as a securities broker in the same town. Approximately 1 out of 10 workers in the United States is employed in a different occupation than he or she was in the previous year. A vast majority of these changes in occupation are accounted for by people who are less than 35 years old. Many of these changes also involve geographic mobility (box IV).

FIGURE 9.1 **Types of Mobility**

Mobility can take several forms, four of which are summarized by boxes I through IV. Specifically, it can involve a job change, but no change in occupation or residence (box I); an occupational change, but no change in residence (box II); a geographic move to a job in the same occupation (box III); or geographic migration accompanied by a change in occupation (box IV).

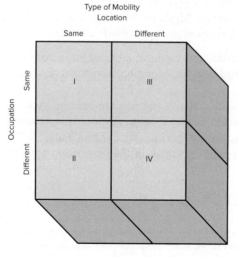

Box III: Geographic Change/No Change in Occupation

Geographic mobility pertains to movements of workers from a job in one city, state, or nation to another. About 10 percent of the total U.S. population changes residences each year. Moves from one county or state to another are involved in 36 percent of these residency changes. Transfers of employees by companies range between 400,000 and 500,000 annually. In recent years, net immigration to the United States has been about 1 million people per year.

In many cases, geographic moves cause changes in jobs but not changes in occupations. Examples: An executive for an aerospace firm gets transferred from Wichita to Seattle; a farmworker moves from Mexico to the United States; a corporate lawyer leaves a New York City law firm to join one in Boston; a professional football player gets traded from New Orleans to Chicago.

Box IV: Geographic Change/Change in Occupation

Approximately 30 percent of geographic job-related moves are accompanied by changes in occupations; thus, these changes represent both geographic and occupational mobility. For example, a discharged steelworker might leave Pennsylvania to take a job as a construction worker in Arizona. Or perhaps a high schoolteacher might move from a small town to take a position as an insurance claims adjuster in a distant urban area.

To limit our focus and retain clarity, we will confine our attention to *geographic* mobility (boxes III and IV) in the remainder of the chapter. But much of the analysis that follows can also be directly applied to the other forms of labor mobility.

MIGRATION AS AN INVESTMENT IN HUMAN CAPITAL

Labor migration has been extensively studied by economists, sociologists, demographers, and geographers. One important way economists have contributed to the understanding of geographic mobility is through the development and testing of the human capital model of migration. We know that human capital consists of the income-producing skill, knowledge, and experience embodied within individuals. This stock of capital can be increased by specific actions—investments in human capital—that require *present* sacrifices but increase the stream of *future* earnings over one's lifetime. Such actions include obtaining more education, gaining added training, and maintaining one's health. Migration to a higher-paying job is also a human capital investment because it entails present sacrifices to obtain higher future earnings.

Will migration occur in all situations where a potential exists for increased lifetime earnings? The answer is no because there are costs associated with the migration investment that must be weighed against the expected gains. The main costs are transportation expenses, forgone income during the move, psychic costs of leaving family and friends, and the loss of seniority and pension benefits. According to our analysis in Chapter 4, if the present value of the expected increased earnings exceeds the present value of these investment costs, the person will choose to move. If the opposite is true, the individual will conclude that it is not worthwhile to migrate, even though the earnings potential in the destination area may be higher than in the present location.[1]

---

[1] The classic article about this topic is by Larry A. Sjaastad, "The Costs and Returns of Human Migration," *Journal of Political Economy,* suppl., October 1962, pp. 80–93. For a survey of labor mobility models, Orn B. Bodvarsson, Nicole B. Simpson, Chad Sparber, "Migration Theory" in Barry R. Chiswick and Paul W. Miller (eds.), *Handbook of the Economics of International Migration* (Amsterdam: Elsevier, 2015), pp. 3–47. Also see Michael J. White and David P. Lindstrom, "Internal Migration" in Dudley L. Poston, Jr. (ed.), *Handbook of Population* (New York, NY: Springer 2019), pp. 383–419.

9.1 World of Work

The Decline in Geographic Mobility*

Migration rates within the United States rose gradually from 1900 to 1980, but since then they have steadily dropped. In the 1981–1990 period, the annual interstate migration rate was 2.9 percent. By the 2011–2018 period, it had dropped to 1.6 percent. Migration rates have fallen for both short- and long-distance moves and for nearly all subgroups of the population.

Molloy, Smith, and Wozniak examine the causes of the post–1980 decline in migration rates. They find that shifts across demographic and socioeconomic groups can do little to explain the decline. They offer four other possible explanations of the fall in migration. First, the rise of two-career couples may have made such couples less willing to move. Second, the rise in telecommuting has reduced the need for workers to move for a job but is unlikely to play a major role as the share of workers working at home rose from 2.1 percent in 1980 to only 4.1 percent in 2009. Third, locations may become less specialized in the goods and services produced, and so the available jobs are more similar across the country. There is some evidence to support this hypothesis as the share of the population in densely populated cities has fallen, while the share in less dense metropolitan areas has risen. Lastly, amenities have become more similar across areas and so there is less of a need to move.

Molloy, Smith, and Wozniak also examine the role of the decline in the housing market and the economy since the drop in migration since 2005. They argue that the economy did not play a large role since migration dropped before the start of the recession. The housing market is a more likely candidate since the timing of the decline in the housing market more closely matches the drop in migration. The housing market decline may affect migration since those homeowners with negative equity (their mortgage exceeds the value of their home) may be less willing to move. However, Molloy, Smith, and Wozniak discount the role of the housing market decline since the drop in migration rates was similar for renters and homeowners, and states with a higher portion of homes with negative equity did not have a larger drop in migration.

*Based on Raven Molloy, Christopher L. Smith, and Abigail Wozniak, "Internal Migration in the United States," *Journal of Economic Perspectives,* Summer 2011, pp. 173–196. Updated statistics from https://www.census.gov/topics/population/migration.html

Equation (9.1)—a modification of Equation (4.3) in Chapter 4—gives the net present value of migration:

$$V_p = \sum_{n=1}^{N} \frac{E_2 - E_1}{(1+i)^n} - \sum_{n=1}^{N} \frac{C}{(1+i)^n} - Z \quad (9.1)$$

where V_p = present value of net benefits

E_2 = earnings from new job in year n

E_1 = earnings from existing job in year n

N = length of time expected on new job

i = interest rate (discount rate)

n = year in which benefits and costs accrue

C = direct and indirect monetary costs resulting from move in the year n

Z = net psychic costs of move (psychic costs minus psychic gains)

In Equation (9.1), if $V_p > 0$, implying that the expected earnings gain exceeds the combined monetary and net psychic investment costs, the person will migrate. If, conversely, $V_p < 0$, the person will remain in his or her present job and location. All else being equal, the greater the annual earnings differential $(E_2 - E_1)$ between the two jobs, the higher will be the present value of the net benefits (V_p), and the more likely it will be that an individual will migrate.

THE DETERMINANTS OF MIGRATION: A CLOSER LOOK

Various factors besides the annual earnings differential $(E_2 - E_1)$ influence the discounted present value of the total earnings and costs streams in Equation (9.1) and thereby affect the present value of the net benefits and the decision to migrate. These factors or *determinants of migration* include age, family circumstances, education, distance, and unemployment.

Age

Migration studies consistently find that age is a major factor determining the probability of migration. *All else being equal, the older that a person is, the less likely he or she is to migrate.* There are several reasons for this, each having to do with reducing the gain in net earnings from migrating or increasing the costs of moving.

First, older migrants have fewer years to recoup their investment costs. Given a specific cost of migrating, the shorter the time period one has to gain the annual earnings advantage, the smaller the V_p term in Equation (9.1). A young person may view a relatively small wage differential as significant over his or her lifetime; a person who is two or three years away from retirement is not likely to incur migration costs to achieve this same short-lived annual differential.

Second, older people tend to have higher levels of human capital that are specific to their present employers. Age, length of time on a job (job tenure), and annual wages are all positively correlated. The longer a person's job tenure, the greater the amount of on-the-job training and employer-financed investment of a specific variety he or she is likely to have. This human capital, by definition, is *not* transferable to other jobs; thus, the wage one receives after several years of job tenure partially reflects a return on a specific investment in human capital and is likely to be higher than the wage obtainable elsewhere. Regardless of the length of time available to recoup the investment costs, older people may, therefore, be less likely to migrate.[2]

The cost of moving is a third age-related consideration affecting migration. Older people often have higher migration costs than do younger people. For example, a young person may be able to transport possessions across the country in a 4-by-8-foot U-Haul trailer, whereas an older person may need to hire a professional mover who uses a moving van. Or as another example, a younger person who migrates may lose little seniority or future pension benefits, whereas an older person may incur very large costs of this type.[3] Also, the psychic costs of migration may rise with age. Older people are more likely than younger workers to have roots in their present communities, children in the local school systems, and an extensive network of workplace friends. The higher these net psychic costs—Z in Equation (9.1)—the lower the value of V_p and the less likely one is to migrate.

Finally, the inverse relationship between age and migration exists partially because people are most mobile after completing lengthy investments in human capital. Many people begin "job shopping" at the end of high

---

[2] Jacob Mincer and Boyan Jovanovic, "Labor Mobility and Wages," in Sherwin Rosen (ed.), *Studies in Labor Markets* (Chicago: University of Chicago Press, 1981), pp. 21–63.

[3] For evidence that the prospect of leaving behind an employer-provided pension constitutes a high cost of changing jobs, see Steven Allen, Robert Clark, and Ann McDermed, "Pensions, Bonding, and Lifetime Jobs," *Journal of Human Resources,* Summer 1993, pp. 463–481.

school—ages 18-19—which may result in geographic moves.[4] Migration is even more pronounced for college graduates who enter regional and national labor markets. It, therefore, is not surprising that the peak age for labor migration in the United States is 23.

Family Factors

The potential costs of migrating multiply as family size increases; therefore, we would expect married workers to have less tendency to migrate than single people, other factors such as age and education being constant. Furthermore, it seems logical to expect higher migration rates for married workers whose spouses either do not work or work at low pay. If both spouses earn a high wage, the family's cost in forgoing income during the move will be high; and when combined with the possibility that one spouse will not find a job in the destination location, this cost reduces the net present value to the family from migration. Finally, the presence of school-age children can be expected to reduce the likelihood of migration. The parents and children may conclude that the psychic costs associated with the move are too great relative to the expected monetary gain.

These particular predictions from the human capital model are supported by empirical evidence. Mincer has found that (*a*) unmarried people are more likely to move; (*b*) the wife's employment inhibits family migration; (*c*) the longer the wife's tenure, the less likely a family will migrate; and (*d*) the presence of school-age children in the family reduces migration.[5]

Education

Within age groupings, the level of educational attainment beyond high school is a major predictor of how likely one is to migrate within the United States. *The higher one's educational attainment, all else being equal, the more likely it is that one will migrate.*[6] Several reasons have been offered for this relationship. College graduates and those with postgraduate training—MBAs, PhDs, lawyers, CPAs—search for employment in regional and national labor markets in which employers seek qualified employees. These markets often have substantial job information and participants who possess excellent ability to analyze and assess the available information. The potential for economic gain from migration also may be increased by the heterogeneity of many of the workers and positions.[7] Union wage scales and minimum wage rates reduce wage differentials within occupations not requiring college training. On the other hand, the wide disparities of pay for professional and managerial employees provide more opportunity to move to jobs entailing greater responsibility and pay. Less specialized workers may have a greater opportunity to increase their earnings through *occupational* mobility within their present locale (box II in Figure 9.1). That route may not be open to highly specialized workers, who, therefore, may use *geographic* migration to achieve gains in earnings.

---

[4] William Johnson, "A Theory of Job Shopping," *Quarterly Journal of Economics,* May 1978, pp. 261-278.

[5] Jacob Mincer, "Family Migration Decisions," *Journal of Political Economy,* October 1978, pp. 749-774. Where both the husband and the wife have a college degree, the probability of migration is 4 percent lower when the wife works, see Dora L. Costa and Matthew E. Kahn, "Power Couples: Changes in the Locational Choice of the College Educated, 1940-1990," *Quarterly Journal of Economics,* November 2000, pp. 1287-1315. Also see Janice Compton and Robert A. Pollak, "Why Are Power Couples Increasingly Concentrated in Large Metropolitan Areas?" *Journal of Labor Economics,* July 2007, pp. 475-512.

[6] Larry H. Long, "Migration Differentials by Education and Occupation: Trends and Variations," *Demography,* May 1973, p. 245. Also see Michael A. Quinn and Stephen Rubb "The Importance of Education-Occupation Matching in Migration Decisions," *Demography,* February 2005, pp. 153-167; and Aude Bernard and Martin Bell, "Educational Selectivity of Internal Migrants: A Global Assessment," *Demographic Research,* July-December 2018, pp. 835-854.

[7] For evidence that highly educated workers are more likely to migrate in response to positive labor demand changes, see Abigail Wozniak, "Are College Graduates More Responsive to Distant Labor Market Opportunities?" *Journal of Human Resources,* Fall 2010, pp. 944-970.

Other factors are also at work here. College-educated workers are more apt to get transferred to new geographic locations and, if not transferred, are more likely than those with fewer years of schooling to have new jobs already in place upon migrating. Thus, the probability of their failure to find a job once they move to the new area is zero, and the expected earnings gain over their lifetimes is increased. Finally, people who have college degrees may attach fewer psychic costs Z to leaving their hometowns. Many college students initially migrate to new areas to attend school in the first place, and this experience may make it easier for them to move again when new economic opportunities are present. Or perhaps the fact that these people moved geographically to attend college indicates that they have lower innate psychic costs of or stronger preferences for migration than those who did not make that same choice initially. For whatever reasons, studies show that people who move once are more inclined to migrate again.

Distance

The probability of migrating varies inversely with the distance a person must move. The greater the distance, the less information a potential migrant is likely to possess about the job opportunities available. Also, transportation costs usually increase with distance. Finally, the longer the physical distance of the move, the more probable it is that psychic costs will be substantial. With respect to such costs, it is one matter to move across town, another to move to a nearby state, and still another to migrate across the country or to another nation. Psychic costs may be partially reduced, but not necessarily eliminated, by following "beaten paths" and congregating in specific neighborhoods within the destination area. Migrants often follow the routes previously taken by family, friends, and relatives. These earlier migrants ease the transition for those who follow by providing job information, employment contacts, temporary living quarters, and cultural continuity. But the longer the distance of the move, the less available the information about wage disparities and the greater the psychic cost; thus, the likelihood is less that one will migrate.[8]

Unemployment Rates

On the basis of the human capital model, high unemployment rates in an origin location should increase the net benefits from migrating and *push* workers away. That is, an unemployed person must assess the probability of gaining employment in the *origin* location relative to the probability of gaining employment at the potential *destination*. Although evidence on this matter is surprisingly mixed, studies support the following generalizations: (*a*) *Families headed by unemployed people are more likely to migrate than others,* and (*b*) *the rate of unemployment at the origin positively affects out-migration.*[9] Such out-migration may not always be as great as we might expect, however, when the decision makers are mainly older and less educated workers or when unemployment compensation and other income transfers are relatively high.

Does the unemployment rate at the possible destination influence the migration decision by affecting the probability of getting employment and therefore increasing the *expected value* of discounted net benefits? No definitive conclusion can be reached for this question. For one thing, the general unemployment rate does not always reflect the probability that a specific *individual* will find employment. Also, in-migration itself can

[8] See Henry Herzog, Jr., and Alan M. Schlottmann, "Labor Force Migration and Allocative Efficiency," *Economic Inquiry,* July 1981, pp. 459–475; and Paul S. Davies, Michael J. Greenwood, and Haizheng Li, "A Conditional Logic Approach to U.S. State-to-State Migration," *Journal of Regional Science,* May 2001, pp. 337–360.

[9] See Julie DaVanzo, "Does Unemployment Affect Migration? Evidence from Micro Data," *Review of Economics and Statistics,* November 1978, pp. 32–37; and Davies, Greenwood, and Li, ibid. Also see Raven E. Saks and Abigail Wozniak, "Labor Reallocation over the Business Cycle: New Evidence from Internal Migration," *Journal of Labor Economics,* October 2011, pp. 697–739; and Kristiina Huttunen, Jarle Møen, and Kjell G. Salvanes, "Job Loss and Regional Mobility," *Journal of Labor Economics,* April 2018, pp. 479–509.

increase unemployment rates at the destination. Nevertheless, one generalization is possible: Currently unemployed workers tend to migrate to destinations with lower-than-average unemployment rates.

Other Factors

Many other factors may influence migration, and we list only a few of them here. First, studies show that home ownership deters migration.[10] Second, a higher rate of international immigration into an area tends to reduce in-migration rates and raise out-migration rates among native-born workers.[11] This appears to be the result of depressed wages associated with increased international immigration. Third, state and local government policies may influence labor migration. Examples: (*a*) High personal tax rates that reduce disposable income may impede migration to the high-tax area, (*b*) high levels of per capita government spending on services may increase in-migration, and (*c*) government policies that attract new industries are likely to cause greater migration to a particular locale. Fourth, location characteristics have differing impacts on the migration decisions across age cohorts. The business environment has a larger impact than consumer amenities on the decisions of younger, well-educated workers. The reverse is true for workers near retirement age.[12] Fifth, in the case of international migration, the language spoken at the destination is a prime factor affecting mobility. Immigration quotas and emigration prohibitions also greatly influence international migration. In addition, many international migrants are pushed from their present places of residence by political repression and war. Sixth, union membership may be a determining factor. By providing workers with a voice with which to change undesirable working conditions, unions may reduce voluntary "exits" and reduce mobility and migration (Chapter 11). Or from a different perspective, perhaps the wage gains that unions secure for workers reduce the incentive for members to migrate to new jobs. Seventh, some scholars suggest that people increasingly have placed a high priority on crime and climate in their migration decisions.[13] Although extremely diverse, these factors share a common feature: They all influence V_p in Equation (9.1) by affecting the expected gains from migrating, the expected costs, or some combination of each.[14]

THE CONSEQUENCES OF MIGRATION

The consequences of domestic and international migration have several dimensions. Initially, we will examine the individual gains from migration by asking: What is the return on this form of investment in human capital? We then will analyze the increased output accruing to society from migration. There we will also attempt to sort out the distribution of net gains. Who benefits? Who loses?

Personal Gains

People expect to increase their lifetime utility when they *voluntarily* decide to migrate from one area to another. One interesting way to conceptualize this expected gain is to ask: What amount of money would we have to pay to entice the migrant to reject the job opportunity? This dollar amount is an estimate of the migrant's expected gain from moving to the new location.

---

[10] Alicia Sasser Modestino and Julia Dennett, "Are American Homeowners Locked into their Houses? The Impact of Housing Market Conditions on State-to-State Migration," *Regional Science and Urban Economics,* March 2013, pp. 322–337.

[11] George J. Borjas, "Native Internal Migration and the Labor Market Impact of Immigration," *Journal of Human Resources,* Spring 2006, pp. 221–258.

[12] Yong Chen and Stuart S. Rosenthal, "Local Amenities and Life-Cycle Migration: Do People Move for Jobs or Fun?" *Journal of Urban Economics,* November 2008, pp. 519–537.

[13] Richard J. Cebula, "Migration and the Tiebout–Tullock Hypothesis Revisited," *Review of Regional Studies,* Winter–Spring 2002, pp. 87–96.

[14] For a very readable summary of the various factors affecting migration, see Raven Molloy, Christopher L. Smith, and Abigail Wozniak, "Internal Migration in the United States," *Journal of Economic Perspectives,* Summer 2011, pp. 173–196.

Empirical Evidence

Empirical studies confirm that migration increases the lifetime earnings of the average mover.[15] The estimated rate of return is similar to that on other forms of investment in human capital, meaning it generally lies in the 10–15 percent range.

Caveats

At least five cautions or complications must be mentioned when generalizing about rates of return to migration.

1 Uncertainty and Imperfect Information   Migration decisions are based on *expected* net benefits, and most are made under circumstances of uncertainty and imperfect information. High *average* rates of return do not imply positive returns for *all* migrants. In many instances, the expected gain from migration simply does not materialize—the anticipated job is not found at the destination, the living costs are higher in the new area than anticipated, the psychic costs of being away from family and friends are greater than expected, and the anticipated raises and promotions are not forthcoming. Thus, there are major *backflows* in migration patterns.[16] Although this return migration is costly to those involved, it does perform a useful economic function: It increases the availability of information about the destination to other potential migrants, enabling them to assess better the benefits and costs of moving. This makes subsequent migration more efficient.

Also, not all return migration indicates an unprofitable investment in human capital. Some people temporarily migrate to accumulate wealth or enhance their stock of human capital via on-the-job training or after-work education. Most return to their original locations after reaching their financial or human capital goals. For example, most of those who built the Alaskan pipeline returned to the lower 48 states after completion of their task. Also, many undocumented persons who cross the U.S.–Mexican border return to Mexico.[17]

2 Timing of Earnings Gains   Lifetime income gains from migration do not necessarily mean that migrants receive gains from earnings during the first few postmigration years. Studies show that some migrants experience reduced earnings in the first few years after moving. These reductions, however, tend to be followed by more than commensurate increases in earnings in later years. Stated differently, some migrants accept a short-term postmigration reduction in earnings as an investment cost for faster-growing future earnings.

3 Earnings Disparities   Increases in lifetime earnings do not imply that migrants necessarily will receive annual earnings equal to those received by people already at the destination. The skills that migrants possess are not always perfectly transferable between regions (because of occupational licensure), between employers (because of specific training), or between nations (because of language and other factors). This lack of *skill transferability* may mean that migrants—although perhaps improving their own wage—may be paid less than similarly trained, educated, and employed workers at the destination. For example, Chiswick and Miller in their survey of empirical studies conclude that immigrants who are fluent in English earn about 10–20 percent more than their nonfluent counterparts.[18] There is also evidence that the effect of English fluency on earnings was stronger for the 2005–2009 period than for earlier periods.[19]

---

[15] For example, see Kristen Keith and Abagail McWilliams, "The Returns to Job Mobility and Job Search by Gender," *Industrial and Labor Relations Review,* April 1999, pp. 460–477.

[16] For a survey of the evidence regarding out-migration of foreign-born immigrants, see Christian Dustmann and Joseph-Simon Gorlach, "Selective Out-Migration and the Estimation of Immigrants' Earnings Profiles," in Barry R. Chiswick and Paul W. Miller (eds.), *Handbook of the Economics of International Migration* (Amsterdam: Elsevier, 2015), pp. 489–532.

[17] Michael J. Piore, *Birds of Passage: Migrant Labor and Industrial Societies* (Cambridge: Cambridge University Press, 1979), pp. 149–154.

[18] Barry R. Chiswick and Paul R. Miller, "International Migration and the Economics of Language," in Barry R. Chiswick and Paul R. Miller (eds.), *Handbook of the Economics of International Migration* (Amsterdam: Elsevier, 2015), pp. 212–269.

[19] Ibid.

On the other hand, migration tends to be characterized by *self-selection*. Because some migrants choose to move while others with similar skills do not, it is possible that the former have greater motivation for personal economic achievement and greater willingness to sacrifice current consumption for higher levels of later consumption. As Chiswick has pointed out:

> Such self-selected immigrants would tend to have higher earnings than the native born in the destination, if it were not for the disadvantage of being foreign born. Combining the [negative] effects of skill transferability and favorable self-selection suggests that the earnings of the foreign born may eventually equal and then surpass those of the native born.[20]

Do the earnings of immigrants in fact eventually exceed those of native-born Americans? For earlier immigrants, Chiswick found that, given equal amounts of education and premigration labor experience, male immigrants on average achieved earnings parity with their native-born cohorts after 11–15 years and after that had higher earnings by as much as 5 percent.[21] However, more recent studies have discovered that immigrants arriving in the United States since the second half of the 1970s are on average less skilled than previous immigrants. In addition, the skill disadvantage of new immigrants was larger in the last four decades than in the 1970s. The earnings of these more recent immigrants remain 12–20 percent below those of comparable native-born workers.[22]

Internal migrants within the United States—as distinct from immigrants from abroad—rather quickly assimilate in their new locales. A recent study indicates that young internal migrants initially earn less than similar natives in the area to which they migrate, but this wage differential disappears within a few years. The initial wage disadvantage is greater the longer the distance moved and the poorer the economic conditions in the destination locale.[23]

4 Earnings of Spouses   A gain in family earnings from migration does not necessarily mean a gain in earnings for both working spouses. On average, migration increases the earnings of husbands but tends to reduce the earnings for wives, at least over the following five-year period.[24] Apparently, the higher average earnings and stronger labor force attachment of husbands relative to that of wives entice families to migrate in response to improved earnings for the husband. These moves, on the average, increase the family's income; but they also reduce either the wife's incentive to work (income effect), her market opportunities, or some combination of the two. It is important to note that husbands now are as likely to be the trailing spouse as wives.[25]

5 Wage Reductions from Job Losses   A positive rate of return to migration does not necessarily imply higher earnings than would have accrued had past wage rates continued to be earned. Some migrants are pushed into moving by job loss or political repression. For these people, job mobility is not totally voluntary. For example, suppose that Smith, a 50-year-old Ohio steelworker, earns $18 an hour in wages and fringe benefits, has children in college, and has lived all of his life in the same locale. If Smith is displaced from his job

---

[20] Chiswick, Barry R. "Immigrant earnings patterns by sex, race, and ethnic groupings." *Monthly Labor Review* 103, no. 10 (October 1980), 22–25.

[21] Ibid., p. 23. Also see Chiswick's "The Effect of Americanization of Foreign-Born Men," *Journal of Political Economy,* October 1978, pp. 897–921; and James Long, "The Effect of Americanization on Earnings: Some Evidence for Women," *Journal of Political Economy,* June 1980, pp. 620–629.

[22] George J. Borjas, "The Economic Analysis of Immigration," in Orley C. Ashenfelter and David Card (eds.), *Handbook of Labor Economics,* Volume 3A (Amsterdam: Elsevier, 1999), pp. 1697–1760; Harriet Orcutt Duleep, "The Adjustment of Immigrants in the Labor Market," in Barry R. Chiswick and Paul W. Miller (eds.), *Handbook of the Economics of International Migration* (Amsterdam: Elsevier, 2015), pp. 108–182.

[23] George J. Borjas, Stephen G. Bonars, and Stephen J. Trejo, "Assimilation and the Earnings of Young Internal Migrants," *Review of Economics and Statistics,* February 1992, pp. 170–175.

[24] For example, see Solomon Polachek and Francis Horvath, "A Life Cycle Approach to Migration," in Ronald G. Ehrenberg (ed.), *Research in Labor Economics* (Greenwich, CT: JAI Press, 1971), pp. 103–149; and Terra McKinnish, "Spousal Mobility and Earnings," *Demography,* November 2008, pp. 829–849.

[25] Thomas J. Cooke, "All Tied Up: Tied Staying and Tied Migration within the United States, 1997 to 2007," *SDemograohic Research,* July-December 2013, pp. 817–836.

because of a factory shutdown, exhausts his unemployment benefits, and eventually finds a job at $12 an hour in a new occupation in the Southwest, can we conclude that migration enhanced his well-being? Considerable misunderstanding exists about this point. The job loss and its consequences for Smith and his family are indeed severe in that income from work falls to zero. But once this event occurs, Smith faces a new set of prospective earnings streams over the remainder of his work life. For illustrative purposes, let's assume that the highest-paying job he can find in his present locale is at $8 an hour. By migrating to the Southwest where he can earn $12 an hour, Smith does increase his lifetime earnings, other things being equal, even though these earnings are considerably lower than those that would have accrued in the absence of the job loss. Migration increases lifetime earnings for most movers; it does not always increase earnings above levels that existed prior to a job loss.

Wage Narrowing and Efficiency Gains

Economic efficiency exists when a nation achieves the greatest possible real domestic output or income from its available land, labor, capital, and entrepreneurial resources. Labor mobility is crucial in approaching this goal. To illustrate, let's suppose, first, that there are only two labor markets, each perfectly competitive and each situated in a different geographic location. Second, suppose that each labor market contains a fixed number of workers and there is no unemployment in either market. Third, we assume that nonwage job amenities and locational attributes are the same in both areas. A fourth assumption is that capital is immobile. Finally, we assume that workers possess perfect information about wages and working conditions in both markets and that migration between the two markets is costless.

Numerical Illustration

Columns 1_A and 2_A in Table 9.1 display the demand for labor in market A, while columns 1_B and 2_B show it for B. Notice that the wages are given in *annual* terms and that, because of our assumption of perfect competition in the product and labor markets, these wages equal the value of the marginal product (VMP) of labor.[26] Columns 3_A and 3_B cumulate the VMP data to show the value of the total product (VTP) associated with each level of employment. Also, notice that the VMP is greater for each labor input in labor market A than in B. This difference in the strength of labor demand is not crucial to our analysis but presumably arises from a greater capital and technological endowment in A than in B, so that the marginal product of labor is higher in market A.

Now suppose that initially two workers are employed in market A and each earns $23,000 annually (boxed figure), while eight workers, earning $7,000 apiece, are working in B (boxed figure). Next we relax the assumption that these are separate markets and observe that given our other assumptions, workers in B will migrate to labor market A in pursuit of higher earnings.

What will happen to annual earnings in the respective markets as this migration occurs? The number of workers in A will increase, causing the market wage there to fall. In region B, the corresponding decline in the quantity of labor will increase the equilibrium wage. Migration will continue until the wage advantage in A is totally eliminated. This occurs in Table 9.1 at $15,000 (circled data). At this annual wage, employers in the highly capital-endowed region A will hire six workers, while those in the less endowed area B will hire four workers. To generalize: *Assuming perfect competition, costless information, and costless migration, market wages will equal the VMP of labor (W = VMP), and labor will relocate until VMPs are equal in all labor markets* ($VMP_A = VMP_B$).

---

[26] If this is not clear, you may want to review the discussion pertinent to Table 5.2.

TABLE 9.1 Allocative Efficiency: The Role of Labor Mobility

Labor Market A			Labor Market B		
(1A) Workers	(2A) VMP$_A$ Annual Wage	(3A) VTP$_A$	(1B) Workers	(2B) VMP$_B$ Annual Wage	(3B) VTP$_B$
1	$25,000	$25,000	1	$21,000	$21,000
2	23,000	48,000	2	19,000	40,000
3	21,000	69,000	3	17,000	57,000
4	19,000	88,000	4	15,000	72,000
5	17,000	105,000	5	13,000	85,000
6	15,000	120,000	6	11,000	96,000
7	13,000	133,000	7	9,000	105,000
8	11,000	144,000	8	7,000	112,000
9	9,000	153,000	9	5,000	117,000
10	7,000	160,000	10	3,000	120,000

Does this migration of labor enhance the total value of output in our hypothetical nation? To determine the answer, again note columns 3$_A$ and 3$_B$ in Table 9.1. Before migration, the VTP was $48,000 in labor market A and $112,000 in B. Thus, the combined premigration VTP was $160,000 (= $48,000 + $112,000). And after migration? A glance at the table shows it to be $192,000. The six workers in A produce a combined output valued at $120,000, while the four workers in B produce $72,000. In this simple model, then, we observe that wage differentials create an incentive for labor to move from one market to another. This mobility, or migration, equalizes wages and results in allocative efficiency [Equation (6.1)]; it generates the highest possible value of total output from the available resources.

Graphic Portrayal

We can easily show graphically both the wage narrowing and the *efficiency gains from migration* that arise. For variety and to extend our focus, let's now employ an international, rather than an interregional, example. Figure 9.2(a) shows the demand for labor in the United States, and graph (b) portrays the labor demand curve for Mexico.

Suppose the employment and wage levels in the United States and Mexico are $0e$, W_u, and $0l$, W_m, respectively. Because information is assumed to be perfect and migration is assumed to be costless, labor will flow from Mexico to the United States until the equilibrium wage of W_e is achieved in each nation. Notice the positive efficiency gains accruing from this migration. The United States *gains* domestic output equal to the area *ebcf* in graph (a), and Mexico *loses* domestic output equivalent to the area *kijl* in graph (b). Because the U.S. gain exceeds the Mexican loss, the total value of the combined output produced by the two nations rises. Stated differently, the sum of the areas *0acf* in graph (a) and *0hik* in (b) exceeds the premigration areas *0abe* plus *0hjl*. Conclusion? Given our assumptions, wage-induced labor migration—whether internal or international—increases the total income and output in the *combined* origin and destination. Quite simply, migration enables a larger total real output to be achieved from a given available amount of resources.

FIGURE 9.2   The Efficiency Gains from Migration

The migration of labor from low-wage Mexico (b) to high-wage United States (a) will increase the domestic output and reduce the average wage rate in the United States and produce the opposite effects in Mexico. The output gain of *ebcf* in the United States exceeds the loss of *kijl* in Mexico; therefore, the net value of the combined outputs from the two nations rises.

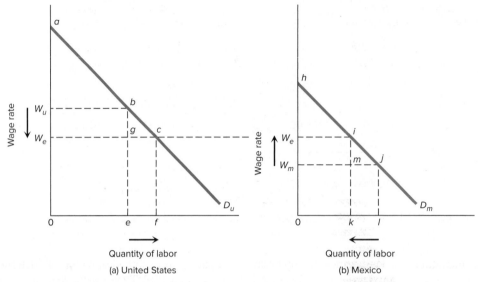

External Effects

The generalization drawn from Table 9.1 and Figure 9.2 raises an important question: If the efficiency gains from migration are so direct and evident, why do so many people in origin and destination locales view migration negatively? Although numerous noneconomic factors are also at work, much of the explanation is economic in character and can be understood by analyzing *migration externalities,* or the third-party effects. These externalities can be *real* or *pecuniary* and either positive or negative.

1 Real Negative Externalities

Real negative externalities are effects of private actions spilling over to the third parties and creating misallocations of resources (economic inefficiency). An example is water pollution. If a firm produces a product and in the process pollutes a river used by downstream municipalities, recreational enthusiasts, and industries, then the firm fails to cover all the costs of its actions. The price of the firm's product is too low, more resources are devoted to producing this output than is socially optimal, and downstream users incur costs that absorb further resources. In some circumstances, mass migration generates similar negative spillovers. As Thurow points out,

> Private incomes may increase enough to more than make up for the costs of moving, but the social costs of accommodating people in a crowded urban area may exceed the net private gain. More public services must be provided, and congestion may increase. Excess capacity, and hence waste, may develop in the production of social services (schools, etc.) in areas from which people are moving, and new investment in social services may be needed in areas to which they are moving.[27]

---

[27] Thurow, Lester C. Investment in human capital, Belmont, CA: Wadsworth Publishing Company, 1970.

Put simply, where negative externalities from migration are substantial and diffuse, the private gains to migrants and employers will overstate the net gain to society. Under these circumstances, more migration will occur than is consistent with an optimal allocation of society's resources. For example, this outcome occurs when substantial migration to a rapidly growing area increases congestion, crime, and other external costs.

2 Pecuniary Externalities: Income Redistribution

Most of the expressed opposition to emigration and immigration, however, arises not from these potential real externalities but rather from numerous pecuniary (financial) ones. *Pecuniary externalities may be defined as acts that redistribute income among individuals and groups.* Such redistributive effects typically give rise to active resistance on the part of adversely affected groups and engender heated political debate. Careful analysis of Figure 9.2 reveals several redistributive impacts of migration.

Losses in the Origin Nation   Although immigration from Mexico to the United States *increases* the total product in the United States, it *reduces* it in Mexico. Stated more generally, migration increases the VTP produced in the combined economies of the origin and destination; but under most conditions, these gains accrue to the destination. There are exceptions, of course. As an extreme example, if the *kl* workers who migrate to the United States are unemployable (value of marginal product = 0), then no increased output is forthcoming, and the destination nation will be the loser by virtue of having to support the migrants. Conversely, the origin nation will gain because its fixed domestic output will be shared among fewer people. Also, many migrants save a large portion of their wages and send these funds home or bring them back as a lump sum at the end of their temporary stay. In these cases, the origin nation captures a share of the efficiency gains. But when migration is permanent, is in response to higher wages in the destination nation, and involves migrants who leave jobs in the origin nation, the destination nation experiences an increase in national income while the origin nation loses. These distributional impacts partially explain why "brain drains"—the emigration of highly skilled workers—are a source of economic concern for some nations.[28]

Reduced Wage Income to Native Workers   The second consequence of migration for income distribution is also evident from Figure 9.2. Immigration increases the supply of labor in the United States from $0e$ to $0f$, driving down the average wage rate from W_u to W_e and reducing the wage income to native U.S. workers from $0W_ube$ to $0W_ege$. Notice that immigration may or may not increase the total wage income in the United States: That depends on the elasticity of labor demand (Figure 5.7). It is clear, however, that the influx of the *ef* workers reduces the wage income accruing to the $0e$ native U.S. workers. In Mexico, the reduction in labor supply *increases* the wage rate (W_e rather than W_m) for those who remain. Another generalization thus emerges: Immigration is likely to be opposed by laborers in the destination region or nation, whereas workers in the place of origin are likely to support emigration.

This generalization, however, must be accompanied by an important caution relating to our distinction made in Chapter 5 between gross substitutes and gross complements. Immigrants to the United States are *gross substitutes* (substitution effect > output effect) for some labor market groups, reducing the labor demand and wages for these groups. On the other hand, the immigrants are *gross complements* (output effect > substitution effect) for other domestic workers, causing labor demand and wages for these groups to rise. Therefore, not all groups of workers are equally affected by immigration. Overall, a recent survey of empirical studies concludes that immigration has a small effect on the wages of native workers, but new immigrants reduce the earnings

---

[28] Brain drains also are viewed negatively because the origin nation loses the return on investments in human capital that it may have either paid for in full or partially subsidized. For a theoretical discussion of brain drains, see Viem Kevok and Hayne Leland, "An Economic Model of the Brain Drain," *American Economic Review,* March 1982, pp. 91–100. For a discussion of the empirical evidence regarding the effects of brain drains, see John Gibson and David McKenzie, "Eight Questions about Brain Drain," *Journal of Economic Perspectives,* Summer 2011, pp. 107–128.

of previous immigrants.[29] However, the measured effects of immigration on native workers are sensitive to the research approach.[30] The negative effect of low-skilled immigration on native wages in an area may be, at least partially, mitigated by the migration causing native individuals to perform better in school, obtain more education, and take communication-intensive jobs for which they have a comparative advantage.[31]

It is important to note that low-skilled immigrants tend to migrate toward areas with smaller labor supply increases among native-born workers, thus reducing geographic earnings differentials.[32]

Gains to Owners of Capital   A third potential for opposition to migration by some groups in origin and destination locales arises from the impact of migration on labor income relative to capital income. We again return to Figure 9.2, graph (a). Immigration increases the total nonimmigrant national income in the United States by the triangle *gbc*. To see why, note that the VTP rises from 0*abe* to 0*acf* in the United States. Of the total gain (*ebcf*), migrants receive *egcf*. This leaves triangle *gbc* as the increase in total nonimmigrant income. Now recall that in the previous paragraph we concluded that the wage bill to native U.S. workers falls. So who receives the gain that native workers lose? The answer, of course, is U.S. businesses. They gain area $W_e W_u bg$ at the expense of native U.S. workers and also obtain the added product shown by the triangle *gbc*; thus, this simple model suggests that business interests gain added income from immigration—at least in the short run—and conversely actually lose income when substantial out-migration occurs. This helps explain why some U.S. businesses historically have recruited foreign workers to come to the United States. For example, Chinese workers were recruited to help build the railroads, and migrant agricultural workers presently are recruited to help harvest U.S. crops and produce.

The conclusion that businesses gain from migration at the expense of domestic workers must be tempered by the fact that this is a short-run, partial-equilibrium model. The theoretical possibilities become more complicated when a long-run, general-equilibrium approach is used and when various assumptions are relaxed. For example, the new migrants are likely to spend portions of their earnings in the United States. This will increase the demand for many types of labor and may increase wages for workers who are not close substitutes in production for the specific immigrant labor. In addition, the gain in business income relative to the stock of U.S. capital increases the rate of return on capital. This increase tends to raise domestic investment spending and consequently enlarges the stock of U.S. capital. Under normal production conditions, the marginal product of labor therefore will rise and labor demand will increase; thus, in the long run, part of the negative impact of immigration on the wage rate may be lessened or eliminated. But the basic point is clear: Differing views of the desirability of open migration policies, undocumented persons, and brain drains can partially be understood in the context of the actual and perceived redistributional effects of migration.

Fiscal Impacts   One final distributional outcome merits discussion. An inflow of immigrants can affect the distribution of disposable income in a destination nation or area through its effect on transfer payments and tax collections. If the immigrants to the United States in Figure 9.2 are highly educated and skilled professionals, for example, we would expect little opposition from the general U.S. public. These workers most probably will be net taxpayers and not major recipients of cash and in-kind transfer payments. However, if the immigrants are illiterate, low-skilled individuals who are not likely to find permanent employment in the United States, then this influx may necessitate increased government spending on transfer payments and social

---

[29] Francine D. Blau and Lawrence M. Kahn, "Immigration and the Distribution of Incomes," in Barry R.Chiswick and Paul W.Miller (eds.), *Handbook of the Economics of International Migration* (Amsterdam: Elsevier, 2015), pp. 793–843. for a similar conclusion, see Brian C. Cadena, Brian Duncan, and Stephen J. Trejo, "The Labor Market Integration and Impacts of US Immigrants," in Barry R.Chiswick and Paul W.Miller (eds.), *Handbook of the Economics of International Migration* (Amsterdam: Elsevier, 2015), pp. 1197–1259.

[30] Christian Dustmann, Uta Schönberg, and Jan Stuhler, "The Impact of Immigration: Why Do Studies Reach Such Different Results?" *Journal of Economic Perspectives,* Fall 2016, pp. 31–56. Also see, Joan Llull, "The Effect of Immigration on Wages: Exploiting Exogenous Variation at the National Level," *Journal of Human Resources,* Summer 2018, pp 608–662.

[31] Peter McHenry, "Immigration and the Human Capital of Natives," *Journal of Human Resources,* Winter 2015, pp. 34–71.

[32] Brian C. Cadena, "Native Competition and Low-Skilled Immigrant Inflows," *Journal of Human Resources,* Fall 2013, pp. 910–944.

9.1 *Quick Review*

- Occupational mobility involves workers changing occupations; geographic mobility involves workers moving to jobs in another city, state, or nation.

- The decision to move geographically can be viewed through the investment in human capital framework; a worker will move when the net present value of migration, V_p, is positive.

- Along with the annual earnings differential, important determinants of migration include age, family factors, education, distance, and unemployment rates.

- Migration produces earnings gains for movers, wage narrowing among regions, and real output gains for society. Generally, migration reduces wage income to native workers with skills similar to those of the immigrants and increases the income of owners of capital.

Your Turn

Suppose the E_2 and N values in the net present value equation [Equation (9.1)] fall while the Z value rises. What will happen to V_p and the likelihood of migration? (*Answer:* See page 541.)

service programs. As a consequence, this specific immigration may produce higher taxes for U.S. citizens, lower average transfer payments to native low-income residents, or some combination of each; thus, taxpayers and low-income residents in the United States may oppose the migration. A real externality might even result from the increased taxes and transfers through a disincentive impact on labor supply. This rests on the assumption, of course, that the immigrants are eligible for the transfer programs and extensively use them.

Historically, the immigrant population in the United States was less likely than the native population to receive welfare benefits.[33] But welfare participation by immigrants increased after the late 1970s and by the mid-1990s was greater for immigrants than for natives. In 1996 Congress enacted the Personal Responsibility and Work Opportunity Reconciliation Act, which drastically reduced the availability of welfare and food stamps to noncitizen legal immigrants. As a result, welfare and food stamp participation among immigrants is now below that of natives.[34]

CAPITAL AND PRODUCT FLOWS

Table 9.1 and Figure 9.2 overstate the probable extent of labor migration between two regions or nations for reasons other than those associated with the costs of obtaining information and migrating. Through differing rates of investment, capital itself is mobile in the long run. Also, products made in one locale are sold in many others. These facts have considerable significance for labor migration.

---

[33] Francine Blau, "The Use of Transfer Payments for Immigrants," *Industrial and Labor Relations Review,* January 1984, pp. 222–239; and Julian L. Simon, "Immigrants, Taxes, and Welfare in the United States," *Population Development Review,* March 1984, pp. 55–69.

[34] See George J. Borjas, "Welfare Reform and Immigrant Participation in Welfare Programs," *International Migration Review,* Winter 2002, pp. 1093–1123; and Christopher R. Bollinger and Paul Hagstrom, "Food Stamp Program Participation of Refugees and Immigrants," *Southern Economic Journal,* January 2008, pp. 665–692.

Capital Flows

The impacts of *capital mobility* and interregional or international trade on wage differentials and therefore on labor migration are illustrated in Figure 9.3. Here we use the United States and South Korea in a simplified example. Notice initially that given the labor demand curves D in each nation, wages in the United States W_u exceed those in South Korea W_k. Our previous analysis implied that this wage differential would induce Korean workers to migrate to the United States. But other forces are also at work. The lower Korean wage rate might cause some U.S. producers to abandon production facilities in the United States and construct new facilities in Korea. We would expect this increase in capital in Korea to increase the marginal product and value of marginal product of labor there. The labor demand curve, therefore, would shift outward, say to D_1 as shown in graph (b) of Figure 9.3. Conversely, the lower stock of capital in the United States would reduce labor demand from D to D_1 (graph a).

The increase in labor demand from D to D_1 in South Korea raises the market wage from W_k to W_e. In the United States, the decline in demand from D to D_1 lowers the wage from W_u to W_e. Capital mobility thus has removed the wage disparity in our model and eliminated the incentive for labor to migrate. But as is true with labor mobility, migration of capital is very costly and is impeded by many real-world economic, political, and legal obstacles. For example, U.S. meat producers would not likely find it profitable to move to South Korea to realize savings in labor costs. Other costs such as transporting livestock to Korean facilities and shipping meat products back to U.S. markets would be too high. Thus, although significant flows of capital *have* occurred (e.g., from the northeast United States to the South and Southwest and from the United States to South Korea, Mexico, and elsewhere), their role in narrowing wage differentials has been somewhat limited. But to the extent that capital is mobile, wage differentials between areas are smaller; and thus less labor migration will occur than if investment is confined to the domestic economy.

FIGURE 9.3 **The Impact of Capital and Product Flows on Wage Differentials**

A high wage rate in the United States W_u and a low-wage rate in South Korea W_k may cause either (*a*) flows of capital from the United States toward South Korea or (*b*) a price advantage for Korean-produced goods. In either case, the demand for labor is likely to increase in South Korea and decline in the United States. Thus, the wage rate differential will narrow, and consequently no labor migration will occur.

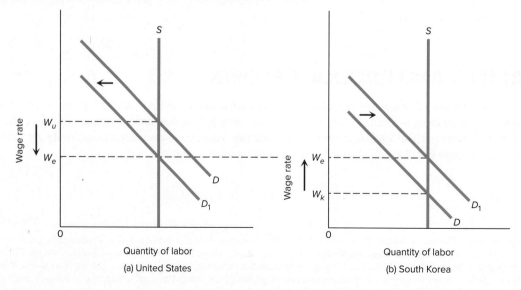

(a) United States   (b) South Korea

Product Flows

Interregional and international trade has a similar potential effect on wage differences and labor mobility. Again return to Figure 9.3. Now suppose that capital and labor are immobile, U.S. and South Korean workers are homogeneous, and the costs of transporting goods between the two nations are zero. What effect will the low Korean wage W_k compared to the high U.S. wage W_u have on the relative competitiveness of Korean versus U.S. goods? Assuming that competition forces product prices down to marginal costs in both nations, U.S. consumers would reallocate their expenditures toward the lower-priced Korean goods. This would increase the total demand for these imports and eventually raise the derived demand for Korean labor. As shown by the outward shift of the labor demand curve from D to D_1 in Figure 9.3(b), this would increase the Korean wage rate. The opposite chain of events would occur in the United States, where reduced product demand would shift the derived demand for U.S. labor leftward from D to D_1 and reduce the wage to W_e. This wage narrowing via product flows diminishes the extent of labor migration if we relax the assumption that labor is immobile. But in reality, transportation costs are so high for many goods and services that shipping them long distances is not economical; thus, trade can be expected to narrow, but not equalize, wages in the long run.

Conclusion: *Labor migration, capital mobility, and trade between regions and nations all complement one another in promoting an efficient allocation of resources.* Labor mobility simply is one aspect of the broader mobility of resources and commodities in the economy. In fact, the U.S. government has at times promoted investment in less developed nations and has reduced trade barriers to slow immigration from those nations into the United States.

U.S. IMMIGRATION POLICY AND ISSUES

Our analysis of the motivations for migration, the efficiency gains produced by this mobility, and the problem of gainers versus losers provides the tools necessary for understanding some of the controversies surrounding U.S. immigration patterns and policies.

History and Scope

Before World War I, immigration to the United States was virtually unimpeded. The great influx of foreign labor occurring in the 19th century contributed to economic growth and to rising levels of per capita income. The flow of immigrants was slowed by World War I and the restrictive Immigration Acts of 1921 and 1924. These acts established immigration quotas for various nationalities based on the number of foreign-born people of that nationality in the United States in specific census years. In addition, the laws allowed several categories of nonquota immigrants to enter the United States. Between 1921 and 1965, only 10 million people entered the United States, and over half were nonquota immigrants, including 900,000 Canadians, 500,000 Mexicans, and thousands of spouses and children of U.S. citizens.

In 1965 amendments to the 1952 Immigration and Nationality Act shifted the preferences of the quota system away from northern and western European immigrants and toward a more evenly balanced set of nationalities. Further amendments established a worldwide annual ceiling of 270,000 immigrants, set an annual limit of 20,000 individuals per nation, and developed a six-point preference system giving priority to people who have specific job skills. Immediate relatives of U.S. citizens, refugees, and people seeking political asylum, however, were exempt from these provisions and ceilings.

Figure 9.4 shows the number of legal immigrants to the United States in selected years. During the 1980s, legal immigration ranged from a low of 531,000 in 1980 to a high of 1,091,000 in 1989, but generally was 550,000–600,000 each year. The number of legal immigrants jumped considerably in 1989, 1990, and 1991–three years when many former undocumented immigrants were granted permanent residence under the amnesty provisions of the Immigration Reform and Control Act of 1986.

To the numbers in Figure 9.4 we must add the undocumented persons who arrived mainly from Mexico, the Caribbean, and Central and South America. The U.S. Census Bureau estimates that the net inflow of undocumented persons averaged about 200,000 annually between 1980 and 1990; therefore, it was not uncommon for total immigration (legal and illegal) to exceed 750,000 annually during that period.

Immigration increased further during the 1990s. In late 1990 Congress passed an immigration law raising the legal immigration cap from about 500,000 to 700,000 people annually, not counting refugees. This law reserves 140,000 permanent residency visas each year for high-skilled professional workers. It also grants 10,000 residency slots to immigrants who either invest at least $1 million in the U.S. economy and create 10 or more full-time jobs or who invest $500,000 in targeted depressed areas in the United States.

Meanwhile, despite the passage of the Immigration Reform and Control Act, the flow of undocumented immigrants has continued. This law granted amnesty and legal status to undocumented individuals who had lived in the United States since 1982. It also made it illegal for employers to hire undocumented workers.[35] The idea behind the employer sanctions was to diminish or eliminate the demand for the services of undocumented workers, thereby reducing their incentive to enter the country. But illegal immigrants have skirted this law by obtaining counterfeit documents; thus, studies indicate that the law has had no long-term impact on undocumented immigration.

FIGURE 9.4 Legal Immigration to the United States

Legal immigration increased gradually during the 1970s and 1980s until 1988. The number of legal immigrants rose dramatically from 1989 to 1991 as many former undocumented immigrants were permitted to become legal immigrants by the Immigration Reform and Control Act of 1986. Since the 1990s, legal immigration has remained relatively high. Currently, about 1 million people become legal immigrants each year.

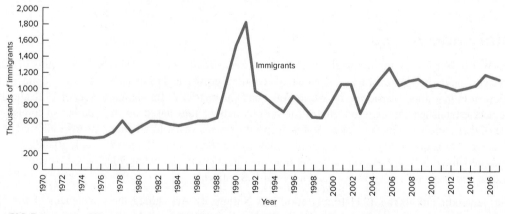

Source: U.S. Department of Homeland Security, "2017 Yearbook of Immigration Statistics." www.dhs.gov

---

[35] For a study examining the wage effects of the Immigration Reform and Control Act, see Julie A. Phillips and Douglas S. Massey, "The New Labor Market: Immigrants and Wages after IRCA," *Demography,* May 1999, pp. 233–246. For evidence regarding the Act's impact on illegal immigration, see Pia M. Orrenius and Madeline Zavodny, "Do Amnesty Programs Reduce Undocumented Immigration? Evidence from IRCA," *Demography,* August 2003, pp. 437–450. One study indicates that the Act increased discrimination against Latinos. See Cynthia Bansak and Steven Raphael, "Immigration Reform and the Earnings of Latino Workers: Do Employer Sanctions Cause Discrimination?" *Industrial and Labor Relations Review,* January 2001, pp. 275–295.

GP9.1 Coupled with the liberalized provisions of the 1990 immigration law, the continued flow of illegal immigrants means that on average about 1,200,000 immigrants have entered the United States each year since 2000.

9.1 Global Perspective

Immigrants as a Percentage of the Population*

Among advanced industrial nations, the percentage of the population who are immigrants ranges from 6.1 in Finland to 29.0 in Switzerland.

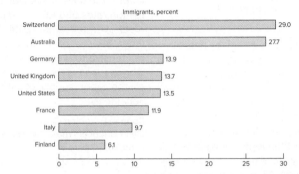

Immigrants, percent

Country	Percent
Switzerland	29.0
Australia	27.7
Germany	13.9
United Kingdom	13.7
United States	13.5
France	11.9
Italy	9.7
Finland	6.1

Source: Organization for Economic Cooperation and Development. www.oecd.org

* Data are for 2016. All data are for the total population.

Effects of Undocumented Immigration

The inflow of *undocumented persons* into the United States over the past few decades has made immigration and immigration policy a major public issue in the United States. The main reason for the general concern is that most undocumented immigrants are unskilled workers. People fear that these individuals and their families reduce employment opportunities for the existing workforce, depress wage rates in already low-wage labor markets, and financially strain U.S. taxpayers via their receipt of transfer payments and use of social service programs. Are these concerns justified? Unfortunately, a simple yes or no answer cannot be provided.

1 Employment Effects

WW9.2 Some observers contend that the employment of undocumented persons decreases the employment of domestic workers on a one-for-one basis. They argue that a given number of jobs exist in the economy and that if one of these positions is taken by an illegal worker, that job is no longer available for a legal resident. At the other extreme is the claim that undocumented persons accept only work that resident workers are unwilling to perform and thus take no jobs from native workers. As we will demonstrate, both views are somewhat simplistic.

9.2 World of Work

Labor Supply of Undocumented Immigrants

More than 11 million undocumented immigrants are living in the United States. In recent years multiple proposals have been suggested to provide a path to citizenship for at least some of these individuals. Due to the large number of undocumented persons, any change in their legal status could have significant effects on the labor market and government programs such as Social Security.

Using data from individual-level survey data from 1994 to 2014, George Borjas analyzes the labor supply of undocumented immigrants. Among U.S. residents aged 20–64, he estimates that 5.4 percent of those aged 20–64 are undocumented immigrants and 12.5 percent are legal immigrants. Undocumented immigrants are four to five years younger than legal immigrants and native residents. They are also much more likely to be less educated as 42 percent are a high dropout as compared to 7 percent of native residents and 19 percent of legal immigrants.

Goerge Borjas reaches four conclusions in his analysis. First, undocumented men are much more likely to be in the labor force (92 percent) than legal immigrant men (85 percent) who are more likely to be in the labor force than native men (81 percent). The wide gap in the participation rates between undocumented men and native men is even wider after accounting in differences in skills and other characteristics. Second, undocumented women are much less likely to participate in the labor force than legal immigrant women, who are less likely to be in the labor force than native women. Third, the participation rates of undocumented men and women rose over the 1994–2014 period. Fourth, the labor supply of undocumented men is less responsive to wages than legal immigrant men, who are less responsive than native men. Overall the labor supply of undocumented men is very inelastic.

Source: Based on George J. Borjas, "The Labor Supply of Undocumented Immigrants," *Labour Economics*, June 2017, pp. 1–13.

Figure 9.5 illustrates a market for unskilled agricultural workers. The curve D is the typical labor demand curve with which we are familiar. Supply curve S_d portrays the labor supply of domestic workers, while curve S_t reflects the total supply of domestic *and* undocumented immigrant workers; thus, the horizontal distance between S_t and S_d is the number of undocumented workers who will offer their labor services at each wage rate.

Given the presence of the undocumented immigrant workers, the market wage and level of employment are W_t and Q_t. At this low wage, *no* domestic workers are willing to work. In this case, the reservation wage of domestic workers is simply too high. Perhaps this results from the availability of nonwage income, a high marginal value or opportunity cost associated with leisure, or a perceived lack of possibilities for advancement in the job. Can we, therefore, conclude that undocumented persons take work that U.S. workers do not want? In Figure 9.5 the answer is yes, *but* only if we add "at the low wage W_t." If all the undocumented persons were deported, the wage would rise to W_d in this market, and *some* U.S. workers, specifically $0Q_d$, would indeed be willing to do this work. The point is this: So-called undesirable work will attract U.S. workers if the compensating wage premium is sufficiently high (Chapter 8). If the undocumented persons were deported and if employers continued to offer wage rate W_t, there would be a shortage $0Q_t$. But this shortage would occur because the wage rate would not have been allowed to rise to its equilibrium, not because U.S. workers are unwilling to do work that undocumented persons are willing to perform. The willingness to work at any given job depends partly on the wage rate being paid.[36]

WW9.3   The opposite argument, that undocumented persons reduce domestic employment by an amount equal to the employment of undocumented persons, is also misleading. As shown in Figure 9.5, the presence of the undocumented laborers *increases* the total number of jobs in this low-skilled labor market. With the undocumented migration, the number of jobs is Q_t; without the inflow, it is only Q_d. It is erroneous to contend that deportation of the Q_t undocumented migrants would cause an increase in domestic employment of Q_t. But it is correct to say that native employment would increase by the amount Q_d in this labor market. We conclude that undocumented immigration does cause some substitution of undocumented persons for domestic workers but that the amount of displacement most likely is less than the total employment of the undocumented persons.[37]

FIGURE 9.5   **The Impact of Undocumented Persons on Domestic Jobs and Wages**

The presence of undocumented persons in this low-wage labor market shifts the labor supply curve to S_t and reduces the market wage from W_d to W_t. At W_t, all workers hired are undocumented persons. If the undocumented persons were deported, however, Q_d domestic workers would be employed; thus, it is misleading to conclude that undocumented persons accept jobs that domestic workers will not take. It is also misleading to conclude that the deportation of undocumented persons would create employment for native workers on a one-for-one basis.

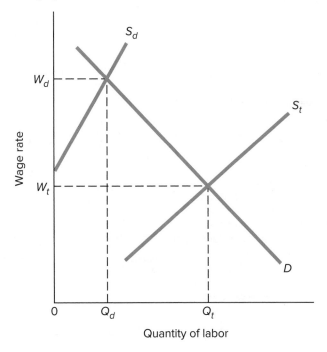

---

[36] Attempted illegal immigration is sensitive to changes in Mexican wages. Higher wages in Mexico reduce illegal immigration; lower wages increase it. See Gordon Hanson and Antonio Spilimbergo, "Illegal Immigration, Border Enforcement, and Relative Wages: Evidence from Apprehensions at U.S.–Mexico Border," *American Economic Review,* December 1999, pp. 1337–1357.

[37] For a survey indicating that immigration flows have only small effects on the employment of less skilled workers, see David Card, "Is the New Immigration Really So Bad?" *Economic Journal,* November 2005, pp. F300–F323.

2 Wage Effects

There is little doubt that large inflows of migrants—be they legal or undocumented—can depress some wage rates. Note in Figure 9.5 that the increase in labor supply reduces the U.S. market wage from W_d to W_t. However, the impact of undocumented immigration on wages appears to be minimal at current levels of undocumented immigration.[38] The only measurable impact occurs in U.S. border cities.[39]

The overall effect of undocumented immigration on the average wage rate in the economy is less clear. Some native workers and undocumented immigrants are gross complements. This means that the reduced wage rate associated with the illegal immigration lowers production costs, creating an output effect that increases labor demand for certain native workers. As one example, it is possible that undocumented immigration raises the demand for native workers who help transport and merchandise fruit. Also, spending by undocumented persons in the United States adds to the demand for products and therefore increases the derived demand for labor. For example, the demand for many workers in the barrios of Los Angeles may be greater because of the presence of undocumented immigrant workers. On the other hand, this impact is reduced because many undocumented persons remit large portions of their pay to their families living abroad.[40]

9.3 World of Work

What Jobs Do Undocumented Workers Hold?

Undocumented immigrant workers play an important role in the U.S. economy. There are estimated to be 7 million such workers in the United States, making up 5 percent of the total workforce.

Undocumented persons are concentrated in different occupations than are native workers. About three-fifths of native workers are in white-collar occupations, but only one-quarter of undocumented persons workers are in such occupations. Undocumented persons workers are much more likely to work in occupations that have low education requirements or do not require a license. Undocumented persons are about three times more likely than native workers to be employed in agricultural occupations (4 percent) and construction and extractive occupations (19 percent). The proportion of service occupations (31 percent) is about double that of native workers (16 percent).

An alternative way to view the employment of undocumented persons is to measure how much of an occupation is filled by undocumented persons. In a few occupations, undocumented persons compose a large proportion of all workers employed. For example, undocumented persons make up 24 percent of all workers employed in agricultural occupations. Undocumented persons comprise 17 percent of employment in cleaning occupations, 14 percent in construction industries, and 12 percent in food preparation industries.

Source: Jeffrey S. Passel, "The Size and Characteristics of the Unauthorized Migrant Population in the U.S.: Estimates Based on the March 2005 Current Population Survey," Pew Hispanic Center Research Report, March 2006.

---

[38] For a survey of the evidence, see Pia Orrenius and Madeline Zavodny, "Undocumented Immigration and Human Trafficking" in Barry R.Chiswick and Paul W.Miller (eds.), *Handbook of the Economics of International Migration* (Amsterdam: Elsevier, 2015), pp. 660–716.

[39] Gordon H. Hanson, Raymond Roberston, and Antonio Spilimbergo, "Does Border Enforcement Protect U.S. Workers from Illegal Immigration?" *Review of Economics and Statistics,* February 2002, pp. 73–92.

[40] For evidence that these large remittances are an important source of funds for less developed countries, see Bilin Neyapti, "Trends in Workers' Remittances: A Worldwide Overview," *Emerging Markets Finance and Trade,* March–April 2004, pp. 83–90.

So what can we conclude concerning the impact of undocumented immigration on wage rates? The safest conclusion—given real-world complexities—is that *large-scale* undocumented immigration does reduce the wage rate for substitutable low-skilled domestic workers. But undocumented immigration probably has little *net* impact on the average level of wages in the United States.

3 Fiscal Effects

Finally, what are the effects of undocumented immigrants on tax revenues, transfer expenditures, and public services? Undocumented immigrants do not qualify legally for public assistance from such programs as Medicaid and food stamps. Nevertheless, the easy availability of forged documents has recently increased their participation in these programs. Also, if immigrants displace low-paid native workers, then immigrants may impose an indirect cost on the U.S. welfare and income maintenance programs.[41]

On the other hand, we must remember that most undocumented immigrants are young workers without families, whereas eligibility for the major transfer programs depends on such characteristics as old age, illness, disability, or position as the female head of a household. And although undocumented immigrants do use many local public services such as schools, roads, and parks, and most also pay Social Security taxes, user fees, and sales taxes. Most scholars of undocumented immigration conclude that these immigrants remain net taxpayers.

Chapter Summary

1. Mobility takes numerous forms, including occupational mobility and geographic mobility.

2. The decision to migrate can be viewed from a human capital perspective, by which the present value of expected gains in lifetime earnings is compared to investment costs (transportation expenses, forgone income during the move, and psychic costs).

3. Various factors can influence the decision to migrate. Age is inversely related to the probability of migrating, family status influences the migration decision in several ways, educational attainment and mobility are positively related, the likelihood of migration and the distance of the move are negatively related, unemployed people are more likely to move than those who have jobs, and a high unemployment rate in a destination area reduces the probability that an unemployed worker will migrate there.

4. The average lifetime rate of return on migration is positive and is estimated to be in the 10–15 percent range.

5. Labor mobility contributes to allocative efficiency by relocating labor resources away from lower-valued and toward higher-valued employment. Under conditions of perfect competition and costless migration, workers of a given type will relocate until the value of the marginal product (VMP) of labor is the same in all similar employments ($VMP_a = VMP_b = \cdots = VMP_n$), at which point labor is being allocated efficiently.

6. Along with the positive outcomes, migration may generate negative externalities, which if real may reduce the efficiency gains of migration and if pecuniary may alter the distribution of income among various individuals and groups in origin and destination areas.

7. Wage differentials may generate capital and product flows that tend to equalize wages in the long run and reduce the extent of labor migration.

---

[41] Evidence suggests, however, that illegal immigration has had little impact on the unemployment of youth and minority groups, see C. R. Winegarden and Lay B. Khors, "Undocumented Immigration and Unemployment of U.S. Youth and Minority Workers: Econometric Evidence," *Review of Economics and Statistics,* February 1991, pp. 105–112.

8. Total annual immigration to the United States has averaged about 650,000 during the 1980s and about 970,000 since 1992.

9. Undocumented persons in the United States do not reduce native employment by the full extent of the employment of the illegals, but they do depress wage rates in some labor markets. The overall wage effect of undocumented immigration is thought to be slight.

Terms and Concepts

labor mobility

occupational mobility

geographic mobility

determinants of migration

skill transferability

self-selection

efficiency gains from migration

migration externalities (real versus pecuniary)

capital mobility

undocumented persons (employment, wage rate, and fiscal impacts)

Questions and Study Suggestions

1. Use Equation (9.1) to explain the likely effect of each of the following on the present value of net benefits from migration: *(a)* age, *(b)* distance, *(c)* education, *(d)* marital status, and *(e)* the discount rate (interest rate).

2. What is meant by the term *beaten paths?* How do such paths increase V_p in Equation (9.1) and thereby increase the likelihood of migration?

3. Why are people who possess *specific* human capital less likely to change jobs, other things being equal, than those who possess *general* human capital? Does this imply that people who possess large amounts of specific human capital will never migrate? Explain.

4. Use Table 9.1 to determine the impact of wage-induced labor migration on

   a. The combined output of the two regions.

   b. Capital versus wage income in the destination region.

   c. The average wage rate in the origin region.

   d. The total wage bill for the native workers in the destination region.

5. Use the variables in Equation (9.1) to cite at least two reasons why it may be rational for a family to migrate from one part of the country to another, even though the hypothetical move produces a decline in family earnings in the first year of work following the move.

6. How might a wage differential between two regions be reduced via movements of capital to the low-wage area?

7. Comment on this statement: "If we deported all undocumented persons who are now in the United States, our total national unemployment would decline by the same number of people."

8. How might labor mobility and migration affect the degree of monopsony power (Chapter 6) in labor markets?

9. Is it consistent to favor the free movement of labor *within* the United States and be opposed to immigration *into* the United States?

10. If one believes in free international trade, then to be consistent, must one also advocate unrestricted international migration of labor?

11. Analyze this statement: "U.S. tariffs on imported products from low-wage foreign nations create an incentive for migration of low-skilled immigrants into the United States."

Internet Exercise

Where Are the Immigrants Coming From?

Go to the Department of Homeland Security Publications website **(http://www.dhs.gov/profiles-legal-permanent-residents)** to find information about legal immigrants.

For the year shown, from which country did the largest number of legal immigrants come from? From which country is the number of legal immigrants growing fastest? Offer an explanation for why this country or these countries have such high emigration rates.

Internet Links

The U.S. Census Bureau reports internal migration rates for U.S. residents **(http://www.census.gov/topics/population/migration.html)**.

Chapter 10

Labor Unions and Collective Bargaining

After reading this chapter, you should be able to:

1. Describe the historical background to the development of labor unions.
2. Describe the distribution of union membership and the basic structure of American labor unionism.
3. Summarize recent trends in private sector unionism and evaluate the various explanations for the relative decline in union membership.
4. Explain the monopoly union and efficient contract models of unions and summarize the empirical evidence.
5. Summarize the techniques that unions use to raise the wages of their members.
6. Explain the accident and asymmetric information models of strikes.

Experts on etiquette agree that it is unwise to bring up certain topics—politics and religion, for example—in social conversations with new acquaintances. These topics often evoke strong emotions, differing opinions, and the potential for unwanted debate. Unionism is another such topic. A strongly expressed opinion on this subject stated in a social setting may generate unwanted verbal fireworks.

Opinion, of course, is not fact; nor is opinion always based on sound analysis. The main objective in this chapter and Chapter 11 is to deepen our understanding of unions, their goals, and their activities. Our approach will be factual and analytic; thus, these two chapters provide useful information that will help you develop an informed opinion about unionism in America.

WHY UNIONS?

Myriad theories have been designed to explain the origins and evolution of labor unions.[1] We will settle for the straightforward historical view that unions are essentially the offspring of industrialization. Most

---

[1] See, for example, Simeon Larson and Bruce Nissen (eds.), *Theories of the Labor Movement* (Detroit Wayne State University Press, 1987). Ray Marshall and Brian Rungeling, *The Role of Unions in the American Economy,* 2nd Edition (New York: Joint Council on Economic Education, 1985), present an excellent elaboration of the theory discussed here and a succinct history of the American labor movement.

preindustrial workers were self-sufficient, self-employed artisans, craftspeople, or farmers who worked in their own homes and on their own land. These workers were simultaneously employers and employees. Industrialization, however, undermined this system of self-employment and made many workers dependent on factory owners for employment and income. Industrialization also separated the functions of management and labor.

Although employers may not have purposely mistreated labor, competitive pressures in the product market often forced them to pay meager wages, to make their employees work long and hard, to provide minimal on-the-job amenities, and to terminate workers when lagging product demand made them redundant. In short, industrialization forced workers into a position of dependence where their earnings, working conditions, and security were largely beyond their control as individuals. To represent, protect, and enhance their interests, workers formed unions to bargain collectively with employers.

LABOR UNIONISM: FACTS AND FIGURES

Before analyzing the collective bargaining process and its economic implications, it is important that we gain a basic understanding of the scope and character of unionization in the United States. Specifically, let's discuss (*a*) the distribution of unionized labor by industry, occupation, gender, race, age, and location; (*b*) the structure of organized labor; and (*c*) the decline in the relative size of the unionized sector that has occurred over the past several decades.

Who Belongs to Unions?

In 2018 approximately 14.7 million of the 153 million civilian nonagricultural workers belonged to unions. In other words, about 10 percent of American workers were union members. But the likelihood that any given worker will be a union member depends on the occupation and industry with which the worker is associated, personal characteristics (gender, race, and age), and geographic location.

1 Industry and Occupation

Table 10.1 shows the percentage of wage and salary workers who are unionized by industry and occupational classification. Union membership is heavily concentrated in goods-producing industries (mining, construction, and manufacturing) and is relatively low in most service-oriented industries (wholesale and retail trade; finance, insurance, and real estate; and services). The exceptions are the low level of unionization in goods-producing agriculture and the high level in the service-providing transportation, information, and public utilities industries. The high union density in transportation, information, and public utilities partially results because these industries "are typically publicly regulated, highly concentrated within individual labor markets, and capital intensive—all of which lead to low labor demand elasticities, large expected benefits from union representation, and low organizing costs."[2] Also notable is the high level of unionization in public administration, which reflects the fact that almost three-fourths of all postal workers are organized and also the vigorous growth of public sector unionism at the state and local levels during the past few decades.

Table 10.1 also makes clear that blue-collar workers are much more heavily unionized than white-collar workers. The reasons for this difference include the following: First, some white-collar workers are managers, and under existing labor law, employers are not obligated to bargain with supervisory employees. Second, many white-collar workers identify with management and aspire to move upward from worker to

---

[2] Hirsch, Barry T., and John T. Addison, *The Economic Analysis of Unions* (Boston: Allen & Unwin, 1986).

management status. They feel that union membership is "unprofessional" and a potential obstacle to their ambitions. Finally, on the average, white-collar workers enjoy higher wages and better working conditions than blue-collar workers, so the former may feel they have less need for unions.

With some important exceptions, the industrial–occupational pattern of unionization was established by the late 1940s. Industries that were heavily unionized by that time remain so now. Today most workers do *not* become union members by organizing their employers, but rather join a union because they take a job with an already unionized employer.

The previously noted high level of unionization in the public sector merits additional attention. Prior to the 1960s, government workers were weakly organized and seemed destined to remain so because most public sector employment entailed white-collar service jobs *and* a high proportion of government workers were women. Nevertheless, between the mid-1960s and the early 1970s, public sector union membership more than quadrupled, and today we find union density in the public sector to be more than twice as great as for the economy as a whole. This expansion is quite remarkable in view of the fact that private sector unionism has been declining significantly.

10.1 Global Perspective

Union Membership as a Percentage of Wage and Salary Workers

Union membership varies widely across countries—ranging from 11 percent in the United States to 67 percent in Sweden.

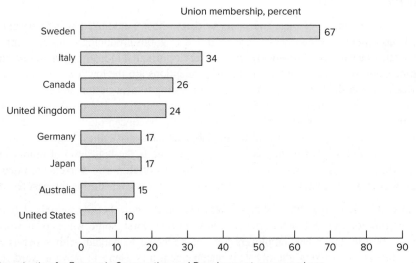

Union membership, percent

Country	Percent
Sweden	67
Italy	34
Canada	26
United Kingdom	24
Germany	17
Japan	17
Australia	15
United States	10

Source: Organization for Economic Cooperation and Development. www.oecd.org

TABLE 10.1 Union Membership by Industry and Occupation

Industry	Percent Union
Agriculture	2
Mining	5
Construction	14
Manufacturing	9
Transportation, information, and public utilities	20
Wholesale and retail trade	4
Finance, insurance, and real estate	2
Services	10
Public Administration	29
Occupation	
Professional	16
Managers, business, and financial	4
Clerical workers	9
Sales workers	3
Construction and Extraction	17
Installers and repair	15
Production	14
Transportation	16
Service	10

*Percentage of employed wage and salary workers who belong to unions.

Source: Bureau of National Affairs, *"Union Membership and Earnings Data Book: Compilations from the Current Population Survey."* http://unionstats.gsu.edu

What caused this striking spurt of union growth among government workers? Most important, in the 1960s and 1970s a variety of state and local laws were passed that established mechanisms for government employees to vote for or against unionism and required government employers to bargain with unionized workers. Executive orders at the federal level accomplished much the same for federal employees. In short, a new legislative climate gave public sector workers in the 1960s and 1970s the opportunity to join unions—an opportunity private sector workers had enjoyed since the 1930s.

Despite this new legal environment, why did public sector unionism experience such rapid growth while private sector unionism was on the wane? On the one hand, a pent-up demand for unionization may have existed that the favorable legal environment simply unleashed. On the other hand, private employers have typically

10.1 World of Work

Janus Decision and Public Sector Unions

On June 27, 2018, the U.S. Supreme Court overturned 40 years of precedent with a 5-4 controversial decision in *Janus v. American Federation of State, County, and Municipal Employees, Council 31.* The *Janus* decision orders that the 5.9 million state and local government workers who are not union members but are covered by union contracts cannot be required to pay "agency fees." Previously, public sector unions were allowed to compel the payment of agency fees for union activities related to "collective bargaining" but not "political and ideological activities" from covered workers who declined to join the union. These fees were typically 75–85 percent of union member dues.

Within two weeks of the *Janus* ruling, about one-third of the 22 affected states took steps to protect public sector unions from bearing the full impact of the decision. New York Andrew Cuomo issued an executive order preventing the sharing of contact information of public workers with groups attempting to inform workers about their ability to stop paying agency fees. In New York, California, Maryland, and Washington, unions were provided the contact information of new hires so their representatives could meet with new employees to encourage them to join the union. In California, Washington, and New Jersey, public employers were not allowed to discourage union membership. Some new state-laws allow unions to provide services such as representation during grievance and arbitration cases exclusively to members.

Much of the new state legislation makes it more difficult to drop union membership. These laws limit the period in which union members can revoke their union membership and increasing the steps they must do to drop membership. For example, New Jersey allows public sector workers only 10 days per year to drop union membership.

In addition to legislation, legal cases were also filed after the *Janus decision*. Multiple lawsuits attempt to stop deductions for agency fees after the *Janus* decision for reasons such as having short windows of 10 or 15 days to the stop deduction of agency fees. Lawsuits were also filed in Ohio, California, New Jersey, Connecticut, Pennsylvania, and Minnesota to obtain refunds of agency fees deducted from paychecks before the *Janus* decision.

The full effect of the *Janus* decision will be not observed for a while since it will take time for workers to be aware of their rights. However, some effects were seen quickly. The number of agency fee payers dropped by 210,000 in 2018 for two major public-employee unions. Agency fee payers fell by 98 percent for the American Federation of State, County and Municipal Employees (AFSCME) and 94 percent for the Service Employees International Union. Overall, AFSCME reported a 6 percent loss in members, agency fee payers and retirees in 2018.

Source: Based on Daniel DiSalvo, "Public-Sector Unions after Janus: An Update," Manhattan Institute Issue Brief, February 2019; Heather Gies, "A Blow But Not Fatal: 9 Months after Janus, AFSCME reports 94% Retention," Salon, April 6, 2019, https://www.salon.com/2019/04/06/a-blow-but-not-fatal-9-months-after-janus-afscme-reports-94-retention_partner/; and Robert Iafolla, "Mass Exodus of Public Union Fee Payers After High Court Ruling," Bloomberg Law *Daily Labor Report*, April 5, 2019.

demonstrated considerable resistance to unionization to the extent that they have frequently broken both the spirit and the letter of labor law. In contrast, public sector employers have not fought the unionization of their workers until recently.[3]

---

[3] This paragraph is based on Richard B. Freeman, "Unionism Comes to the Public Sector," *Journal of Economic Literature,* March 1986, pp. 41–86.

The rapid growth of public sector unionism occurred largely in the 1960–1976 period. Since 1976 there has been little or no growth as membership has leveled off at about 36 percent of all public sector employees. It is probably correct to say that the era of dramatic public sector union growth is now behind us.[4]

Starting in 2011, however, public sector unions faced strong challenges to their bargaining power in New Jersey and Wisconsin. The newly elected governors of these two states facing budget shortfalls attempted to reduce the collective bargaining rights of public sector workers in their states. Scott Walker, the governor of Wisconsin, promoted a bill that eliminated the ability of nonpublic safety public sector workers to bargain over health and pension benefits, limited wage increases to inflation, required most unions to hold annual votes of whether workers want to remain union members, and ended the collection of union dues from worker paychecks. This bill led to bitter protests in the state, but it was ultimately enacted into law.

WW10.1 Chris Christie, the governor of New Jersey, was successful in his attempt to reduce the compensation of state and local government workers. At his urging, the legislature passed a bill that increased the amounts that state and local government workers must contribute toward their pension and health benefits, suspended cost of living increases for retirees until the pension fund for state and local government workers is fully funded, and increased retirement ages. The legislation also reduced the collective bargaining rights of public workers by allowing the state to decide health care terms unilaterally if contract talks reach an impasse.

2 Personal Characteristics: Gender, Race, and Age

Table 10.2 indicates that personal characteristics are associated with the likelihood of union membership. We observe that men are much more likely than women to be union members. This difference is *not* attributable to any fundamental attitude differences based on gender; rather, it occurs because women are disproportionately represented in less unionized industries and occupations. For example, many women are employed in retail sales, food service, and office work, where the levels of unionization are low. Furthermore, women on average have a less permanent attachment than men to the labor force; thus, the present value of the *lifetime* wage gains from unionization will be lower for women than for men, making union membership relatively less attractive to women.[5]

We also see from Table 10.2 that a larger proportion of African–Americans than whites belong to unions. This difference reflects the industrial distribution of workers. Specifically, a disproportionately larger number of African–Americans have blue-collar jobs. Another explanatory factor is that unionization results in larger relative wage gains for African–American workers than for white workers.[6] African–Americans stand to benefit relatively more than whites by belonging to unions.

Table 10.2 also reveals that young workers (under 25 years of age) are less likely than older workers to have union cards. Once again, this is largely explainable in terms of the kinds of jobs young workers acquire. Specifically, as we will see momentarily, the traditional blue-collar, goods-producing, unionized sectors of the economy have not been expanding rapidly in recent years and, therefore, have not been a major source of jobs to youths entering the labor force. Rather, the largely nonunion service sectors have been growing and providing more jobs. Today high school graduates are more likely to take jobs with nonunion fast-food chains; 30 years ago many high school graduates found work in unionized automobile or steel manufacturing plants.

[4] Linda N. Edwards, "The Future of Public Sector Unions: Stagnation or Growth?" *American Economic Review,* May 1989, pp. 161–165.
[5] Two articles addressing the topic of this paragraph are William E. Even and David A. Macpherson, "The Decline of Private-Sector Unionism and the Gender Wage Gap," *Journal of Human Resources,* Spring 1993, pp. 279–296; and Diane S. Sinclair, "The Importance of Sex for the Propensity to Unionize," *British Journal of Industrial Relations,* June 1995, pp. 173–190.
[6] For evidence that African-Americans have a stronger demand for unionization than other groups, see Gregory Defreitas, "Unionization among Racial and Ethnic Minorities," *Industrial and Labor Relations Review,* January 1993, pp. 284–301.

TABLE 10.2 Union Membership by Gender, Race, and Age

Personal Characteristic	Percentage Union
Male	11
Female	10
White	10
African–American	13
Under 25	4
25 and over	11

*Percentage of employed wage and salary workers who belong to unions.

Source: Bureau of National Affairs, *"Union Membership and Earnings Data Book: Compilations from the Current Population Survey."* http://unionstats.gsu.edu

3 Location

To a considerable degree the labor movement in the United States is an urban phenomenon. Six heavily urbanized, heavily industrialized states—New York, California, Pennsylvania, Illinois, Ohio, and Michigan—account for approximately half of all union members.[7] Furthermore, the percentage of workers who are unionized in the South is only about two-thirds that of the rest of the country. This may stem in part from the occupational and industrial makeup of jobs in the South, but it is also claimed that employers and the general populace there simply are more inclined to be antiunion.

Structure of Organized Labor[8]

Figure 10.1 provides a thumbnail sketch of the structure of American labor organizations. There are three major levels of union organizations: the federation, national unions,[9] and local unions.

AFL-CIO

The *American Federation of Labor and Congress of Industrial Organizations,* better known as the *AFL-CIO,* is a loose and voluntary federation of independent and autonomous national unions. We note in Figure 10.1 that 55 national unions with a combined membership of about 12 million workers belonged to the AFL–CIO in 2018, while approximately 60 national unions possessing an aggregate membership of about 4 million were independent of the AFL–CIO. The AFL–CIO does *not* engage in collective bargaining but is the primary political organ of organized labor. The AFL–CIO formulates labor's views on a spectrum of political issues ranging from the minimum wage to foreign policy, publicizes labor's positions, and engages in political lobbying.[10] The AFL–CIO is also responsible for settling jurisdictional disputes among affiliated national unions; that is, it determines which union has the right to organize a particular group of nonunion workers.

---

[7] Barry T. Hirsch and David A. Macpherson, *Union Membership and Earnings Data Book: Compilations from Current Population Survey* (2019 Edition) (Washington, DC: Bureau of National Affairs, 2019).

[8] The ensuing discussion draws on Marten Estey, *The Unions: Structure, Development and Management,* 3rd Edition (New York: Harcourt Brace Jovanovich, 1981), Chapter 3. For a discussion of the labor movement and a detailed consideration of its structure, see John W. Budd, *Labor Relations: Striking a Balance,* 4th Edition (New York: McGraw-Hill, 2013), Chapters 4–6.

[9] Some national unions call themselves "international" unions—for example, the International Brotherhood of Electrical Workers (IBEW)—which usually means that there are some affiliated locals in Canada or Puerto Rico.

[10] For an analysis of organized labor's effectiveness in the political sphere, see Richard B. Freeman and James L. Medoff, *What Do Unions Do?* (New York: Basic Books, Inc., 1984), Chapter 13. Also see Roland Zullo, "Union Membership and Political Inclusion," *Industrial and Labor Relations Review,* October 2008, pp. 22–38.

Change to Win

The *Change to Win federation* is a loose federation of three independent national unions, which was started in 2005. As shown in Figure 10.1, two national unions, which represent a total of 3 million workers, belong to the Change to Win federation. The federation focuses on organizing new union members.

National Unions

The *national unions* are federations of local unions that are typically in either the same industry ("industrial unions" such as those made up of autoworkers or steelworkers) or the same skilled occupation ("craft unions" such as those representing carpenters and electricians). Table 10.3 lists the largest national unions, most of which are affiliated with either the AFL–CIO or the Change to Win federation. The largest union that is not affiliated with the AFL–CIO is the National Education Association, which has about three million members.

A national union has two primary functions: (*a*) organizing the unorganized workers in its craft or industry and (*b*) negotiating collective bargaining agreements. Responsibility for the latter function, however, may be shared in some cases with local unions, depending on the size of the local and the industry involved. For example, if the relevant product market is local (such as housing construction), the local carpenters, bricklayers, and other craft unions are likely to negotiate their own bargaining contracts. But where the product market is regional or national in scope (e.g., textiles or automobiles), contract negotiation is usually performed by the national union rather than its locals. The reasons for this are twofold. Most importantly, the national union wants to standardize wages—to "take wages out of competition"—so that employers who would pay high union wages would not be penalized by losing sales to other firms paying low union wages. Furthermore, collective bargaining has become very complex and legalistic, requiring skilled negotiators, lawyers, and so forth. Consequently, it is likely that economies of scale are to be gained by relying on national negotiators.

FIGURE 10.1   The Institutional Organization of American Unionism

Organized labor in the United States consists of the AFL–CIO, Change to Win federation, and numerous independent unions. The AFL–CIO's basic function is to formulate and promote labor's views on a wide range of economic, social, and political issues. The Change to Win federation is focused on organizing new union members. The national unions generally have responsibility for negotiating collective bargaining agreements, whereas the locals are concerned with administering those agreements.

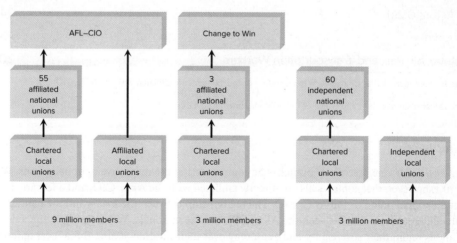

TABLE 10.3 Labor Organizations Reporting 200,000 Members or More (in Thousands)

Labor Organization	Members
National Education Association (Independent)	3,003
Service Employees (Change to Win)	1,918
Teachers	1,678
Teamsters (Change to Win)	1,389
State & County Government Workers	1,327
Food and Commercial Workers	1,248
Transportation Trades	708
Electrical Workers	673
Communication Workers	627
United Steel Workers	582
Machinists	573
Laborers	561
Carpenters (Independent)	435
Aerospace and Autoworkers	396
Operating Engineers	394
Plumbers	348
Police Fraternal Order (Independent)	340
Federal Government Employees	333
Firefighters	315
Unite Hire	302
Letter Carriers	288
Screen Actors Guild	242
Postal Workers	235
Sheet Metal, Air, Rail, and Transportation Workers	203

*All organizations not identified as Change to Win federation or Independent are affiliated with the AFL−CIO.

Sources: U.S. Department of Labor; and Office of Labor Management Standards.

Local Unions

Generally, *local unions* are essentially branches or components of the respective national unions. We observe in Figure 10.1, however, that some locals are directly affiliated with the AFL−CIO, and a few are not affiliated with either a national union or the AFL−CIO. The relationship between the locals and the national unions is significantly different from that between the AFL−CIO and the nationals. When they join the federation, the national unions retain their sovereignty and autonomy over their internal affairs. But a local union is usually subservient to its national union. For example, locals are often required to clear a decision to strike with the national before undertaking such action. Furthermore, the national union has the power to suspend or to disband one of its locals.

This is not to downgrade the role of the local union. Locals perform the important functions of administering or policing the bargaining contract and seeking the resolution of worker grievances that may arise in interpreting the contract.

Active, interested, and effective local leadership tends to produce a favorable reaction from the members, and vice versa. In short, the local union *is* the union to the members. Its performance is the basis for many opinions about unions.[11]

Diversity of Bargaining Structures

The term *bargaining structure* refers to *the scope of the employees and employers covered by a collective bargaining agreement;* the bargaining structure tells us who bargains with whom. In the United States, a great diversity of bargaining structures exists. The diversity is implicit in Figure 10.1 and in the fact that about 2,000 major collective bargaining contracts (those involving 1,000 or more workers) are currently in force. Thousands of other collective bargaining agreements cover smaller employers.

Many unions negotiate with a single-plant employer. Others bargain on a more centralized basis with multiplant employers. In this case, firms with many plants negotiate a "master agreement" with one or more unions, which then applies to workers in all of the firm's plants.[12] Greater centralization is involved in *pattern bargaining,* where the union negotiates a contract with a particular firm in an industry, and this contract—or a slightly modified version—comprises the demands the union seeks to impose on all other employers in that industry. In still other instances, multiemployer bargaining occurs: Employers in a given industry will form an employers' association (e.g., the Bituminous Coal Owners Association) and bargain as a group with the union.

Although the determinants of a bargaining structure are manifold and complex,[13] pragmatic considerations and perceived effects on each party's bargaining power are important. For example, where employers are numerous and small and their markets are highly localized, unions are likely to bargain a citywide agreement with an employers' association. Both employers and the union may see advantages in such a bargaining structure. First, there may be some economies of scale in negotiations; it would be costly for the union to have to negotiate separate agreements with a larger number of employers. Second, employers may feel that they can enhance their bargaining power by negotiating as a group rather than individually. Finally—and perhaps most important—by standardizing wage rates through a citywide agreement, each employer avoids the risk of incurring a competitive disadvantage vis-à-vis other firms because of higher-wage costs. Similarly, the union "takes wages out of competition" and avoids the problem of job loss in higher-wage union firms.[14] Thus in building construction, hotels and motels, retail trade, and local trucking, citywide agreements are quite common. Regional multiemployer bargaining has also been practiced in trucking, bituminous coal, and the basic steel industry, among others.

---

[11] Estey, op. cit., pp. 50–51.

[12] The master agreement is often supplemented by a local agreement that addresses issues and conditions unique to particular plants.

[13] For a systematic discussion of the determination of bargaining structure, see Harry C. Katz, Thomas A. Kochan, and Alexander J. S. Colvin, *Introduction to Collective Bargaining and Industrial Relations,* 4th Edition (New York: Irwin/McGraw-Hill, 2008), Chapter 7.

[14] By lessening the ability of consumers to substitute nonunion products for union products, increased union coverage in an industry will lower the elasticity of demand for the products sold by the unionized firms. We know from Chapter 5 that reduced elasticity of product demand reduces the elasticity of labor demand, enabling the union to increase wage rates without experiencing large losses of employment.

10.1 *Quick Review*

- Unions are a by-product of industrialization, through which workers' earnings, working conditions, and security became dependent on decisions of business owners. Unions arose to represent, protect, and enhance the interests of workers.
- In 2018 approximately 14.7 million of the 153 million members of the American nonagricultural workforce belonged to unions.
- Unionization varies greatly by industry, occupation, gender, race, age, and location.
- Organized labor in the United States consists of the AFL–CIO (a federation of 55 affiliated national unions), Change to Win federation (a federation of three affiliated national unions), and about 60 independent national unions.

Your Turn

Based on national statistics, who would most likely be a union member: Susan, a white female, age 23, who is a sales worker in Iowa, or Isaiah, an African–American male, age 53, who is a transportation worker in Ohio? (*Answer:* See page 541.)

Single-company bargaining is common in many basic manufacturing industries where large oligopolistic corporations feel sufficiently strong to "go it alone" in negotiating with the union. But frequently the negotiation of a contract with one firm will establish a pattern for other firms in the same industry. The automobile industry is the most publicized example of pattern bargaining. When contracts terminate every three years, the United Auto Workers selects one of the "Big Three" manufacturers for contract renegotiation. The negotiated contract serves as the standard for dealing with the other automakers. This bargaining structure is advantageous to the union because lost wages during a possible strike will be less if only one firm is struck rather than the entire industry. Furthermore, the firm experiencing the work stoppage will lose sales to its nonstruck competitors, creating pressure on the former to accept the union's demands. The basic point is that there is no such thing as a typical bargaining structure in the United States.

UNIONISM'S DECLINE

We have just noted that some 14.7 million workers—about 10 percent of civilian nonagricultural workers—belonged to unions in 2018. Figure 10.2 provides a historical overview of trends in union membership. Two points stand out. First, the unionized sector is clearly the minority component of the labor force. Union membership has never exceeded 34 percent of the total labor force. The United States, incidentally, is relatively nonunion compared to most other industrially advanced Western economies. For example, estimates indicate that 68 percent of all wage and salary workers are organized in Sweden. Comparable figures for Australia, Canada, and Japan are 18, 28, and 18 percent, respectively.

The second point is that unionism in the United States is on the decline. In the mid-1940s, the percentage of workers belonging to a labor union peaked at 34 percent. The unionized proportion of the workforce has been steadily falling since then.[15] This decline resulted from union membership's failing to grow as fast as the labor force. Since 1980 the *absolute* number of active union members has also been falling.

---

[15] Although the overall rate of union membership has been falling, it was rising in the public sector during this period.

FIGURE 10.2 **Union Membership in the United States among Nonagricultural Workers**

The rate of U.S. union membership has never exceeded 34 percent of the total labor force. It has been declining since the mid-1940s.

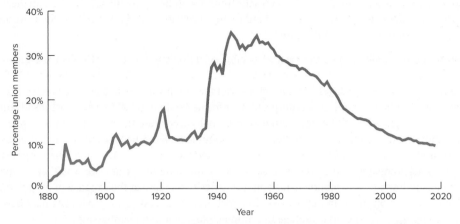

Sources: National Bureau of Economic Research, "Spurts in Union Growth: Defining Moments and Social Processes" www.nber.org; University of Chicago Press, "*The Defining Moment: The Great Depression and the American Economy in the Twentieth Century;*" and Bureau of National Affairs, "*Union Membership and Earnings Data Book: Compilations from the Current Population Survey.*"

Why has this happened? A variety of explanations have been put forth. We will examine the three most widely discussed hypotheses and briefly note several other potential contributors to the wane of unionism.[16]

The Structural Change Hypothesis

The most publicized view, the *structural change hypothesis,* is that a variety of structural changes occurring both in our economy and in the labor force have been unfavorable to the expansion of union membership. This view embraces a number of interrelated observations.

First, consumer demand and, therefore, employment patterns have shifted away from traditional union strongholds. Generally speaking, domestic output has been shifting away from blue-collar manufactured goods (where unions have been strong) to white-collar services (where unions have been weak). This change in the mix of industrial output may be reinforced by increased competition from imports in highly union-ized sectors such as automobiles and steel. Growing import competition in these industries has curtailed domestic employment and, therefore, union membership. As our economy has become increasingly open to low-labor-cost foreign competition, American unionized firms have found themselves at a serious competitive disadvantage.

Second, a disproportionate share of employment growth in recent years has been provided by small firms, which are less likely to be unionized than large firms.

---

[16] The reader who seeks more detail about this topic should consult Henry S. Farber and Alan B. Krueger, "Union Membership in the United States: The Decline Continues," in Bruce E. Kaufman and Morris M. Kleiner (eds.), *Employee Representation: Alternatives and Future Directions* (Madison, WI: Industrial Relations Research Association, 1993), pp. 105–134; "Symposium on the Future of Private Sector Unions in the United States: Part 1," *Journal of Labor Research,* Spring 2001, pp. 226–354; and Henry S. Farber, "Union Membership in the United States: The Divergence between the Public and Private Sectors," in Jane Hannaway and Andrew J. Rother-ham (eds.), *Collective Bargaining in Education: Negotiating Change in Today's Schools* (Cambridge, MA: Harvard Education Press, 2006), pp. 27–51.

Third, an unusually large proportion of the increase in employment in recent years has been concentrated among women, youths, and part-time workers—groups that have allegedly been difficult to organize because of their less firm attachment to the labor force.

Fourth, spurred by rising energy costs, the long-run trend for industry to shift from the Northeast and the Midwest where unionism is a "way of life" to "hard-to-organize" areas of the South and Southwest may have impeded the expansion of union membership.

A final and ironic possibility is that the relative decline of unionism may in part reflect the greater success unions apparently have had in gaining a wage advantage over nonunion workers. As we will find in the next chapter, there is evidence suggesting that on the average union workers in the 1970s realized an enlarged wage advantage over their nonunion counterparts. Confronted with a growing wage cost disadvantage vis-à-vis nonunion employers, we would expect union employers to accelerate the substitution of capital for labor, subcontract more work to nonunion suppliers, open nonunion plants in less industrialized areas, or have components produced in low-wage nations. These actions reduce the growth of employment opportunities in the union sector as compared to the nonunion sector. Perhaps more important, we would also expect output and employment in lower-cost nonunion firms and industries to increase at the expense of output and employment in higher-cost union firms and industries. In short, union success in raising wages may have changed the industry composition to the disadvantage of union employment and membership.[17]

Several potential flaws in the structural change hypothesis have been noted.[18] First, other advanced capitalist countries have experienced structural changes similar to those that have occurred in the United States, and their labor movements continue to grow both absolutely and relatively. Canada is perhaps the most relevant example. Second, historically union growth has been realized in good measure by the unionization of groups of workers who were once regarded as traditionally nonunion. The unionization of blue-collar workers in the mass-production industries such as automobiles and steel in the 1930s and the organizing of public sector workers more recently are cases in point. Given this history, why can't women workers, young workers, immigrants, and southern workers be brought into the labor movement to spur its continued growth? Finally, surveys indicate that young and female workers—who, we found in Table 10.2, are now less unionized—are in fact as much, or more, prounion as more heavily unionized older and male workers. Yet unions are losing an increasing proportion of National Labor Relations Board (NLRB) elections when workers vote to determine whether they want to be unionized.

Managerial Opposition Hypothesis

Such criticisms have led Freeman and Medoff to question the adequacy of the structural change explanation, arguing that intensified *managerial opposition* to unions has also been a major deterrent to union growth. Freeman and Medoff contend that beginning in the 1970s unions have increased the union wage advantage they enjoy vis-à-vis nonunion workers, and as a result, union firms have become less profitable than nonunion firms.[19] As a reaction, managerial opposition to unions has crystallized and become more aggressive. This opposition takes a variety of forms, both legal and illegal. Legal antiunion tactics include written and verbal

---

[17] For a discussion and empirical evidence on this point, see Peter D. Linneman, Michael L. Wachter, and William H. Carter, "Evaluating the Evidence on Union Employment and Wages," *Industrial and Labor Relations Review,* October 1990, pp. 34–53. For contrary evidence for the construction industry, see Dale Belman and Paula B. Voos, "Union Wages and Union Decline: Evidence from the Construction Industry," *Industrial and Labor Relations Review,* October 2006, pp. 67–87.

[18] Freeman and Medoff, op. cit., Chapter 15.

[19] Although substantial union wage differentials induce workers to join unions, the same union wage differentials reduce profits and increase managerial opposition to unionization. Freeman contends that the latter effect outweighs the former and that "as much as one-quarter of the decline in the proportion [of workers] organized through NLRB elections may be attributed to the increased union wage premium of the 1970s and its adverse effects on firm profitability which raised management opposition," see Richard B. Freeman, "The Effect of the Union Wage Differential on Management Opposition and Union Organizing Success," *American Economic Review,* May 1986, pp. 92–96.

communications with workers indicating that unionism will create an adversarial relationship between labor and management that will be generally detrimental to workers. Similarly, management may suggest that with unionization, strikes will be frequent and costly to workers. Also, firms may hire permanent strikebreakers to replace striking workers. Or management may use various tactics to delay the NLRB union certification election, reasoning correctly that an extension of the election period tends to reduce worker enthusiasm for unionization. It is increasingly common for employers to hire labor–management consultants who specialize in mounting aggressive antiunion drives to dissuade workers from unionizing or, alternatively, to persuade union workers to decertify their union.[20]

Freeman and Medoff contend that the use of illegal antiunion tactics has risen dramatically. In particular, they argue that it has become increasingly common for management to identify and dismiss leading pro-union workers, even though this is prohibited by the Wagner Act. The increasing popularity of this tactic stems from the fact that when proven guilty, the employers receive only light penalties. Given these antiunion strategies, the labor movement has gone into relative eclipse.

Freeman cites 13 studies of the impact of management antiunion activities on the outcomes of union organizational drives and representation elections. He observes that in 12 of the 13 studies such management activity was found to be effective. He concludes that managerial opposition is critical in determining the success or failure of union organizational campaigns and is a major factor in explaining the deunionization of the American economy.[21] In contrast, Flanagan concludes that managerial opposition played in the decline of union membership, but the opposition leveled off in the mid-1980s by most measures and that the union membership decline since then is not due to increasing management opposition.[22]

The Substitution Hypothesis

The *substitution hypothesis* is the notion that other institutions—specifically government and employers—have come to provide the services, benefits, and employment conditions that were historically available to workers only through unionization. This substitution of employer- and government-provided services to workers has allegedly reduced the need for and attractiveness of union membership. Thus, Neumann and Rissman note that many of today's public programs that relate to the labor market—such as unemployment insurance, workers' compensation, Social Security, and health and safety laws—were once important goals of labor unions. Their empirical analysis leads them to conclude that historically government has been responsible for providing more and more "unionlike" services, and this has simply lessened the need for workers to join unions.[23]

Similarly, some employers have attempted to install "progressive" labor policies to usurp worker demand for union representation. Such employers establish two-way communication channels with workers, provide for orderly handling of worker grievances, create worker participation schemes, offer seniority protection, pay attractive wages and fringe benefits, and so forth. By averting the major source of pro-union sentiments—job dissatisfaction—employers remain union-free. Here employers are substituting their own benefits for those ordinarily sought through unions and thereby beat unions at their own game.

---

[20] An organization called Executive Enterprises Institute claims that 80 percent of the *Fortune* 500 companies send representatives to attend its seminars such as "How to Stay Union Free in the 21st Century." For an analysis of such firms, see John Logan, "The Union Avoidance Industry in the United States," *British Journal of Industrial Relations,* December 2006, pp. 651–675.

[21] Richard B. Freeman, "Contraction and Expansion: The Divergence of Private Sector and Public Unionism in the United States," *Journal of Economic Perspectives,* Spring 1988, pp. 82–83.

[22] Robert J. Flanagan, "Has Management Strangled Unions?" *Journal of Labor Research,* Winter 2005, pp. 33–66.

[23] George R. Neumann and Ellen R. Rissman, "Where Have All the Union Members Gone?" *Journal of Labor Economics,* April 1984, pp. 175–192. The results from the small number of empirical studies of the Neumann and Rissman hypothesis have been mixed, see Christopher K. Coombs, "The Decline in American Trade Union Membership and the 'Government Substitution' Hypothesis: A Review of the Econometric Literature," *Journal of Labor Research,* June 2008, pp. 99–113.

Examining data on worker attitudes toward unions, Farber observes that workers who are satisfied with their jobs are much less likely to vote for union representation than are dissatisfied workers. His data indicate that the reported levels of satisfaction of nonunion workers with their pay and job security rose dramatically over the 1977–1984 period he examined. Furthermore, nonunion workers' perception of the effectiveness of unions in improving wages and working conditions has diminished. Farber's conclusion is that there has been a significant decline in the demand for union representation among nonunion workers that is independent of structural changes in the labor force and in industry.[24] Farber further supports his view with additional evidence in a controversial paper co-authored with Krueger.[25] The two find that virtually all of the decline in union membership between 1977 and 1991 was caused by a decline in worker demand for union representation, as compared to a decline in the availability of traditionally unionized jobs.

Other Factors

Our three hypotheses do not exhaust the factors that might be contributing to the decline of unionism. For example, evidence suggests that union efforts to organize the unorganized have been insufficient.[26] It has also been argued that the basic values of American society, which stress the free market and competitive individualism, do not provide a fertile environment for a strong labor movement. Finally, the public policy environment became increasingly promanagement during the Reagan–Bush era. In particular, NLRB rulings became increasingly antilabor, creating an administrative and legal environment hostile to union growth.

Relative Importance

Interesting attempts have been made to quantify the significance of the various factors that may have contributed to unionism's decline. How important are structural changes—as compared to, say, enhanced managerial opposition or a diminished effort by unions to organize workers—in explaining the labor movement's eclipse? Although quantification is difficult and estimates must be treated with some caution, some reasonable measures are available. For example, Farber has confirmed that structural changes in the economy have been of some significance. He estimates that about 40 percent of the decline in organized labor's relative share of the labor force over the 1956–1978 period resulted from shifts toward more workers in nonmanufacturing jobs, more white-collar workers, more female workers, and the South.[27]

Similarly, Farber and Western conclude that most of the decline in private sector union membership over the 1973–1998 period was due to a greater employment growth rate in the nonunion sector than the union sector.[28] They also find that the fall in union organizing activity over the period accounted for only a small part of the decline in unionism. In fact, they report that even if the organizing rate had been *five* times the current rate, the unionization rate would have still fallen between 1973 and 1985 and stabilized since then at about 18 percent.

---

[24] Henry S. Farber, "Trends in Worker Demand for Union Representation," *American Economic Review,* May 1989, pp. 166–171.

[25] Henry S. Farber and Alan B. Krueger, "Union Membership in the United States: The Decline Continues," in Bruce E. Kaufman and Morris M. Kleiner (eds.), *Employee Representation: Alternatives and Future Directions* (Madison, WI: Industrial Relations Research Association, 1993), pp. 105–134.

[26] Gary N. Chaison and Dileep G. Dahvale, "A Note on the Severity of the Decline in Union Organizing Activity," *Industrial and Labor Relations Review,* April 1990, pp. 366–373. For evidence that the Change to Win Federation has not increased organizing success, see Rachel Aleks, "Estimating the Effect of 'Change to Win' on Organizing," *Industrial and Labor Relations Review,* May 2015, pp. 584–605.

[27] Henry S. Farber, "The Extent of Unionization in the United States," in Thomas A. Kochan (ed.), *Challenges and Choices Facing American Labor* (Cambridge, MA: MIT Press, 1985), pp. 15–43. For a study reaching a similar conclusion, see C. Timothy Koeller, "Union Activity and the Decline in American Trade Union Membership," *Journal of Labor Research,* Winter 1994, pp. 19–32.

[28] Henry S. Farber and Bruce Western, "Accounting for the Decline of Unions in the Private Sector, 1973–1998," *Journal of Labor Research,* Summer 2001, pp. 459–485.

Freeman[29] has studied the declining success of unions in winning NLRB certification elections and estimates that over one-fourth to almost one-half of the decline in union success in organizing workers through NLRB elections is attributable to managerial opposition. Freeman's overall rough assessment is that about 40 percent of the total decline in unionism is attributable to increased managerial opposition, another 20 percent is the result of reduced efforts by unions to organize nonunion workers, and the remaining 40 percent is due to structural changes in the economy and unknown forces.

Union Responses

How have unions reacted to their declines?

Mergers

A basic response of unions to the relative decline of organized labor has been for unions with similar jurisdictions to merge with one another. Of the more than 164 labor organization mergers that have occurred between 1956 and 2007, about 50 percent took place between 1977 and 1994. While it is true that trade union ideology stresses unity, practical considerations have clearly been paramount in recent mergers. Shrinking membership, declining income from dues, and the desire to achieve a strong and united voice in collective bargaining negotiations have all contributed to the recent impetus for mergers.[30]

Changes in Strategies

Another response by unions to declining membership has been changes in union organizing and negotiation strategies.

Unions have increased their efforts to train union organizers and have attempted to define bargaining demands that appeal to white-collar professionals and to an increasingly female labor force. For example, some unions are giving a lower priority to wages and working conditions and putting more emphasis on such objectives as parental leave, child care, and flexible work schedules. Many unions have formulated positions on issues such as worker drug testing and AIDS protection that are of concern to potential members. Moreover, unions have begun to offer several nontraditional services, such as low-interest credit cards and job counseling, to both union and nonunion members. The idea is to create union allegiance and associate membership even though a worker may not presently hold a job in a union bargaining unit.

On the negotiation front, unions increasingly have chosen to avoid strikes, which employers frequently countered by hiring permanent strikebreakers who later voted to decertify the union. One alternative to the strike that has gained prominence and some success is the union-sponsored *work slowdown* or "working sitdown." Rather than proceeding with their work as usual, union members "go by the book," which implies working to the very minimum of their job requirements. The decline in production reduces the firm's profitability, much as a strike would; but the employees do not lose their pay or risk replacement by strikebreakers. The goal is to convince management that it is in the firm's interest to negotiate seriously with the union.

[29] Richard B. Freeman, "Why Are Unions Faring Poorly in NLRB Representation Elections?" in Thomas A. Kochan (ed.), *Challenges and Choices Facing American Labor* (Cambridge, MA: MIT Press, 1985), pp. 45-64.

[30] Elizabeth A. Ashack, "Major Union Mergers, Alliances, and Disaffiliations, 1995-2007," *Compensation and Working Conditions,* September 2008, pp. 1-5. Also see Gary Chaison, "Union Mergers in the U.S. and Abroad," *Journal of Labor Research,* Winter 2004, pp. 97-115; Kim Moody, "The Direction of Union Mergers in the United States: The Rise of Conglomerate Unionism," *British Journal of Industrial Relations,* December 2009, pp. 676-700; and John Pencavel, "The Changing Size Distribution of U.S. Trade Unions and Its Description by Pareto's Distribution," *Industrial and Labor Relations Review,* January 2014, pp. 138-170.

10.2 *Quick Review*

- Union membership as a percentage of the labor force has fallen steadily over recent decades; also, the absolute number of union members is lower today than in 1980.

- Three hypotheses—perhaps complementary—have been offered to explain the decline in unionism: *(a)* structural changes in industry composition and location, *(b)* renewed managerial opposition to unions, and *(c)* substitution by government and employers of services formerly provided by unions.

- Unions have responded to their decline by merging and developing creative strategies to serve members' needs.

Your Turn

Which of the following would most likely *increase* union membership as a percentage of the labor force: *(a)* the movement of manufacturing firms from the Northeast to the Southwest, *(b)* a decline in imports, *(c)* expansion of high-technology industries such as computer chips and software, or *(d)* a relative decline in employment in the public sector? (*Answer:* See page 541.)

WHAT DO UNIONS WANT?

With some understanding of the size of the labor movement, the kinds of workers who are most likely to belong to unions, the structure of organized labor, and the possible causes of the relative decline in union membership, let's now turn to the thorny question of union objectives.

Monopoly Union Model

Samuel Gompers, founder of the American Federation of Labor (AFL), is reported to have answered "more, more, more!" when asked what unions wanted. Economists typically believe that the goal of a union is to increase both the wages and employment of its members.[31] As a result, economists usually assume that a union's total utility is positively related to the union wage rate W and the union employment level E. Potential levels of a union's total utility are represented by the union indifference curves I_1, I_2, I_3, and I_4 in Figure 10.3. Each curve shows the combinations of wages and employment at which the union is indifferent. The curves are negatively sloped because if the wage rate increases, the employment level must decrease for total utility to remain constant. The opposite is true for employment increases. The curves are convex to the origin because the union is less willing to trade off additional wages for more employment at low-wage levels and is more willing to trade off wages for more employment at high wages. Finally, higher indifference curves (those farther outward from the origin) indicate greater levels of union utility; they represent higher wages *and* greater employment.

Given these indifference curves, what will be the impact of a union on the wage and employment level? Assume that without a union, competitive forces would produce wage rate W_c and employment level Q_c (point c in Figure 10.3). The *monopoly union* model assumes that the union sets the wage rate and the firm determines the level of union employment based on this wage rate. Because the firm is maximizing its profits, it

---

[31] For a survey of models of union objectives, see Bruce E. Kaufman, "Models of Union Wage Determination: What Have We Learned since Dunlop and Ross?" *Industrial Relations*, January 2002, pp. 110–158. Also see, Nicholas P. Lawson, "Is Collective Bargaining Pareto Efficient? A Survey of the Literature," *Journal Labor Research*, September 2011, pp. 282–304.

FIGURE 10.3 Monopoly Union Model

In the monopoly union model, the utility-maximizing wage and employment combination for the union is point *u,* where the union indifference curve I_3 is just tangent to the labor demand curve D_L. The union raises the wage rate from W_c to W_u, the firm decreases employment from Q_c to Q_u, and the union increases its total utility from I_1 to I_3.

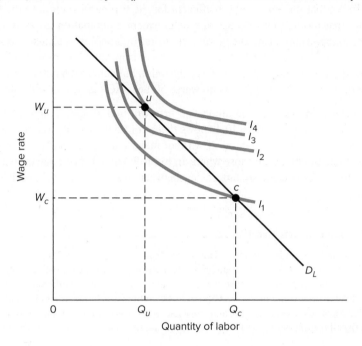

will choose an employment level on its labor demand curve. As a result, the wage and employment combinations available to the union are those on the firm's labor demand curve. In Figure 10.3, the utility-maximizing wage and employment combination for the union is point *u,* where the union indifference curve I_3 is just tangent to the labor demand curve D_L. The corresponding wage rate is W_u and employment level is Q_u. No other combination of wages and employment provides as much utility to the union as this one. Compared to the nonunion outcome, this combination represents a rise in the wage rate from W_c to W_u, a decrease in employment from Q_c to Q_u, and an increase in the union's total utility from I_1 to I_3.

Efficient Contracts Model

Economists have pointed out that the wage and employment combination under monopoly unionism is not efficient for the two parties. A contract is not efficient if some other wage and employment combination can make at least one party better off without making the other party worse off. If instead of the union setting the wage rate and the firm determining the employment level, the union and firm bargain over the wage rate and employment, then an efficient outcome can occur. The combinations of wage and employment where at least one party can be made better off without the other party being made worse off are called *efficient contracts*. These contracts are efficient in terms of the interests of the two parties. They are not necessarily efficient in terms of the economy's allocation of labor resources.

Figure 10.4 illustrates the efficient contracts model. The figure replicates the union indifference curves I_3 and I_4 and the labor demand curve D_L from Figure 10.3. It also introduces a new family of curves called *isoprofit* curves, π_1 and π_2. The isoprofit curves show combinations of wage rates and employment that yield identical profits for the firm. The maximum profit for a given wage rate is a point on the labor demand curve. Lower isoprofit curves represent *higher* profit levels because wages are lower at each level of employment. Thus, a profit-maximizing firm desires to be on the lowest possible isoprofit curve.

Under the monopoly union model, the wage and employment combination would be at point u on the labor demand curve D_L. To see that this outcome is inefficient for the two parties, suppose the firm and the union negotiated a contract that resulted in the wage and employment combination at point x. Compared to the point u result under monopoly unionism, the union is no worse off at point x because it is still on indifference curve I_3, but the firm earns higher profits by being on the lower isoprofit curve π_2 instead of π_1. Alternatively, suppose the negotiated outcome was at point y. Then the union has achieved a higher utility level by being on the higher indifference curve I_4, and the firm is no worse off because it is still on isoprofit curve π_1.

There are a whole set of contracts that the union and firm will find at least as appealing as the monopoly union contract. The shaded area in Figure 10.4 shows these contracts. Among them, the efficient contracts are those where no party can be made better off without making the other party worse off. These efficient wage and employment combinations are those where an isoprofit curve is just tangent to a union indifference curve. The line xy that connects these tangencies between points x and y is called a *contract curve* (or *bargaining curve*).

FIGURE 10.4   Efficient Contracts Model

The outcome of the monopoly union is at point u. This wage (W_u) and employment (Q_u) combination is not efficient for the two parties because at least one of them could be made better off by moving off the labor demand curve. At point x, the union is no worse off than at point u because the union remains on the same indifference curve, but the firm earns higher profits by moving to a lower isoprofit curve. At point y, the union has achieved a higher utility level than at point u by being on a higher indifference curve, and the firm is no worse off because it stays on the same isoprofit curve. The line xy is a contract curve that shows the series of efficient contracts that the union and firm will bargain over.

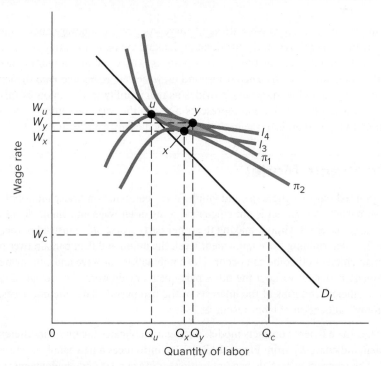

Although each point on the contract curve *xy* leaves each party at least as well off as at point *u,* the parties are not indifferent to where on the curve an agreement is reached. The union would prefer to be closer to point *y* because it will achieve a higher indifference curve and thus greater total utility. The firm would rather be closer to point *x* because it gains higher profits (a lower isoprofit curve). The relative bargaining power of the firm and the union will determine where on the contract curve the settlement occurs.

Although the contract curve shown on the line *xy* has a positive slope, the contract curve can be negatively sloped, positively sloped, or vertical. The slope of the contract curve depends on the shapes of the firm's isoprofit curves and the union's indifference curves.

An interesting shape for a potential contract curve is one that is vertical at the competitive employment level. Economists call this type of contract curve a *strongly efficient contract* curve. In this case, the union and firm agree to set the employment at the level that would occur without a union. The total profit level will be maximized at this employment level, and the union and firm bargain over each party's share of the fixed pie of profits. In this context, if the union gets an additional dollar of income through a higher wage, then the firm must get a dollar less of income. The union can raise wages above the competitive level only in industries that earn economic profits. Otherwise the firm would go out of business.

In general, the efficient contract outcome will result in a lower wage and more employment than the monopoly union outcome. Economists have suggested this helps explain the requirements for excess labor in union contracts. These stipulations or "featherbedding" take the form of work rules specifying minimum work crew sizes or narrow job descriptions.

Empirical Evidence

A direct test of the efficient contracts model is whether unions bargain over employment as well as wages. Contrary to the predictions of the efficient contracts model, a survey of the largest U.S. and British labor unions reveals that union contracts almost always allow firms to unilaterally set the employment level.[32] Although unions do not appear to bargain over employment directly, some researchers have suggested they may indirectly affect employment by bargaining over capital–labor ratios.[33] For example, contracts for public school teachers often mandate minimum teacher–student ratios or maximum class sizes. However, this is inconclusive support for the efficient contract model because the firms are allowed to change the level of capital, which would affect the level of employment.

Some studies have attempted indirect tests of the efficient contracts model.[34] These studies rely on the fact that efficient contracts and monopoly union models have different predictions regarding which factors affect the level of union employment. For example, the monopoly union model assumes that the union sets the wage and the firm determines the employment level based on this wage. As a result, the union employment level should be related to the union wage, but it should have no relationship to the competitive wage. The strongly efficient contract model assumes that the level of union employment is fixed at the level that would occur without a union; therefore, the union wage should have no effect on the union employment level. Instead, the union employment level should be solely determined by the competitive wage.

---

[32] Andrew J. Oswald, "Efficient Contracts Are on the Labour Demand Curve: Theory and Facts," *Labour Economics,* June 1993, pp. 85–113.

[33] For example, see George E. Johnson, "Work Rules, Featherbedding, and Pareto Optimal Union-Management Bargaining," *Journal of Labor Economics,* January 1990, pp. S237–259; and Andrew Clark, "Efficient Bargains and the McDonald–Solow Conjecture," *Journal of Labor Economics,* October 1990, pp. 502–528.

[34] For a critical review of these indirect tests, see Alison Booth, *The Economics of Trade Unions* (Cambridge: Cambridge University Press, 1995), pp. 134–141.

The findings from these indirect tests yield mixed support for the efficient contracts model. Two studies, using 27 years of data from the printing industry, find that union employment levels are related to the competitive wage rate.[35] This result is consistent with the efficient contracts model. On the other hand, a study using construction data from Sweden finds support for both the monopoly union and the efficient contract models.[36] The study's findings vary with the different statistical techniques employed. There is also inconclusive evidence regarding the existence of a vertical contract curve.[37] It is unlikely that a single model can apply to all unions at all points in time.[38]

UNIONS AND WAGE DETERMINATION

GP10.2

Unions can increase the wage rate paid to their members who have jobs by (*a*) increasing the demand for labor, (*b*) restricting the supply of labor, and (*c*) bargaining for an above-equilibrium wage.

Increasing the Demand for Labor

To the limited extent that a union can increase the demand for labor, it can raise *both* the market wage rate and the quantity of labor hired. This is shown in Figure 10.5, where an increase in labor demand from D_0 to D_1 results in a rise in the wage rate from W_0 to W_1 and an increase in employment from Q_0 to Q_1. The more elastic the supply of labor, the less the increase in the wage rate relative to the rise in employment.

A union can increase labor demand through actions that alter one or more determinants of labor demand. Specifically, it can try to (*a*) increase product demand, (*b*) enhance labor productivity, (*c*) influence the price of related resources, and (*d*) increase the number of buyers of its specific labor services. Let's analyze these actions and cite examples of each.

1 Increasing Product Demand

Unions do not have direct control over the demand for the product they help produce, but they can influence it through political lobbying. For example, unions often actively support proposed legislation that would increase government purchases of the products they make. It is not surprising to see a construction union lobbying for new highway projects, urban mass-transit proposals, plans to revitalize urban areas, or flood control and related water projects. Nor is it unusual to discover teachers' organizations pushing for legislation to increase government spending on education.

For similar reasons, unions also lobby for legislation that bolsters private sector demand for union-made products. For example, unions in the aerospace industry strongly supported legislation granting interest rate subsidies to foreign purchasers of commercial airplanes produced in the United States.

---

[35] See Thomas E. MaCurdy and John H. Pencavel, "Testing between Competing Models of Wage and Employment Determination in Unionized Markets," *Journal of Political Economy,* June 1986, pp. S3–39; and James N. Brown and Orley Ashenfelter, "Testing the Efficiency of Labor Contracts," *Journal of Political Economy,* June 1986, pp. S40–87. For a study reporting a similar finding, see David Card, "The Efficient Contracts with Costly Adjustment: Short-Run Employment Determination for Airline Mechanics," *American Economic Review,* December 1986, pp. 1045–1071.

[36] Thomas Aronsson, Karl-Gustaf Lofgren, and Magnus Wikstrom, "Monopoly Union and Efficient Bargaining: Wage and Employment Determination in the Swedish Construction Sector," *European Journal of Political Economy,* August 1993, pp. 357–370.

[37] For an analysis finding evidence of a strong efficient contract curve, see John M. Abowd, "The Effect of Wage Bargains on the Stock Market Value of the Firm," *American Economic Review,* September 1989, pp. 774–800. For contrary evidence, see MaCurdy and Pencavel, op. cit.

[38] MaCurdy and Pencavel, op. cit.

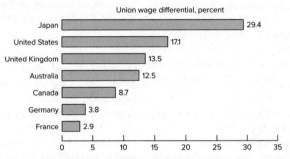

10.2 Global Perspective

Percentage of Union Wage Differential, Controlling for Worker Characteristics

Japan has the highest union wage differential (the percentage by which union pay exceeds nonunion pay) among major industrial countries.

Union wage differential, percent

Japan	29.4
United States	17.1
United Kingdom	13.5
Australia	12.5
Canada	8.7
Germany	3.8
France	2.9

Source: David G. Blachflower and Alex Bryson, "Changes over Time in Union Relative Wage Effects in the UK and US Revisited," in John T. Addison and Claus Schnabel (eds.), *International Handbook of Trade Unions* (Cheltenham, England, and Northhampton, MA: Edward Elgar 2003), Chapter 7. The wage differential estimates cover the period 1994–1999.

FIGURE 10.5 Union Techniques: Increasing the Demand for Labor

To the extent that unions can increase the demand for union labor (D_0 to D_1), they can realize higher-wage rates (W_0 to W_1) and increased employment (Q_0 to Q_1).

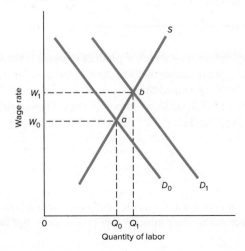

10.2 World of Work

The WTO, Trade Liberalization, and Labor Standards

In November 1999, tens of thousands of people took part in sometimes violent demonstrations in Seattle. The protestors were expressing their opposition to the policies of the World Trade Organization (WTO), which was meeting to reach an agreement on a plan for trade liberalization. The WTO has continued to face protestors at its more recent meetings. The activists are concerned that the over 164-nation WTO is not addressing issues involving worker rights and the environment.

The objective of the WTO, which was formed in 1995, is to lessen trade barriers. Its main principle is that each country must treat all other member countries equally with regard to trade barriers. For example, if the United States decides to lower the tariff on foreign cars, then it must lower this tariff for *all* imported cars. There are exceptions for regional trade pacts and developing countries. If a country violates the rules, the WTO may levy sanctions against it.

Labor unions, which were heavily involved in the Seattle protests, want the WTO to have labor and environmental standards. For example, they want the WTO to include in international trade rules a minimum age for child labor, the right to organize and collectively bargain for wages, a minimum wage, and working condition standards.

Union members would clearly benefit if these labor standards were adopted. The cost of manufacturing foreign goods would rise and increase the relative price of foreign goods. As a result, the demand for the products that unions help produce would shift rightward. This in turn would raise the demand for union workers.

However, most WTO member nations believe that making such labor and environmental standards part of international trade agreements would simply benefit union workers in the highly developed nations at the broader expense of consumers in the industrially advanced nations as well as consumers and workers in the developing nations. By increasing labor and production costs in the developing nations, such standards would give an advantage to industrially advanced nations that already meet the standards. That would reduce imports and raise prices to consumers worldwide. It would also do great harm to the developing nations by impeding their economic growth. Such growth enables them eventually to afford and implement stricter labor and environmental standards.

Source: Compiled from news reports.

WW10.2

Still another way unions may increase product demand is through political support for laws that increase the price of goods that are close substitutes for those made by union members. For instance, in 2009 the United Steel Workers of America (USWA), which represents rubber workers in the tire industry, obtained U.S. tariffs on imported tires. These tariffs increased the price of a substitute good (imported tires), raising the demand for domestic tires and strengthening the demand for USWA members.

2 Enhancing Productivity

We know that the strength of labor demand in a specific occupation depends partly on productivity (Marginal Product). Firms control most factors that determine worker productivity. But two possible ways unions might be able to influence output per worker-hour are participation in joint labor–management committees on productivity (sometimes called *quality circles*) and *codetermination,* which consists of direct worker participation in the decision processes of the firms. The latter also is sometimes called *worker democracy.* The purpose of both approaches is to improve internal communication within the firm and increase productivity through an emphasis on teamwork and profit incentives.

3 Influencing the Prices of Related Inputs

Where labor and some other resource are gross substitutes (substitution effect > output effect), unions can bolster the demand for their own labor by raising the relative price of the other resource. Unions do not have direct control over prices of alternative resources, but there are examples of political actions by unions that might influence such prices. First, unions—generally being populated by higher-paid, skilled workers—may support increases in the minimum wage as a way to raise the relative price of substitutable less skilled, nonunionized labor. As a simple example, suppose two less skilled workers can produce the same amount of output in an hour as one skilled union laborer, but that the hourly pay for the unskilled workers is $10 while the union scale is $25. Obviously, firms would hire unskilled workers (per-unit wage cost of output = $20). Now assume that unions successfully lobby for a $15 per hour minimum wage for all workers. Assuming that skilled and unskilled workers are substitutes in production and also gross substitutes, this increase in the price of unskilled workers will increase the demand for skilled union workers. The reason is that now each unit of the product can be produced at less cost by hiring one union worker at $25 an hour rather than employing two unskilled workers at $30 (= 2 × $15).

The *Davis-Bacon Act* (1931) and its amendments provide another example of how unions might be able to increase the price of a resource that is a substitute in production with labor—in this case the price of *skilled nonunion* labor. The Act, which has strong union support, requires contractors engaged in federally financed projects to pay "prevailing wages." The latter, in effect, are union wages because the formula for determining prevailing wages mandates that the wage rate that occurs with the greatest frequency be observed. Because nonunion firms normally pay their workers less than the union scale, the Act has the effect of raising the price of nonunion labor. Where union and nonunion labor are gross substitutes, the demand for union labor rises, enabling unions to bargain for higher wages without fear of losing federal work to nonunion firms.[39]

4 Increasing the Number of Employers

Unions can increase the demand for their labor by lobbying for government programs that encourage new employers to establish operations in a local area. For example, unions might favor the issuing of industrial revenue bonds to build industrial parks and property tax breaks to attract domestic or foreign manufacturers.

Restricting the Supply of Labor

Unions also can boost wages by reducing the supply of labor. However, the union must accept a decrease in employment in achieving this wage hike. Fortunately for the union, the restriction of labor supply is more likely to occur in a dynamic context wherein the effect is merely to restrict the growth of job opportunities.

In Figure 10.6 we depict a dynamic labor market in which both labor demand and supply are increasing. Let's suppose that demand is rising because of increases in product demand and productivity; supply is increasing

---

[39] For empirical evidence in support of the hypothesis that the Davis–Bacon Act increases union wages by increasing union bargaining power, the reader should consult Daniel P. Kessler and Lawrence F. Katz, "Prevailing Wage Laws and Construction Labor Markets," *Industrial and Labor Relations Review,* January 2001, pp. 259–274. Also see Mike Clark, "The Effects of Prevailing Wage Laws: A Comparison of Individual Workers' Wages Earned on and off Prevailing Wage Construction Projects," *Journal of Labor Research,* Fall 2005, pp. 725–738.

because of population growth, which is expanding the number of people qualified to supply this labor. In the absence of the union, the increases in demand (D_0 to D_1) and supply (S_0 to the broken line S_1) would raise the wage rate and level of employment from W_0 to W_1 and Q_0 to Q_1, respectively (point a to b).

Now let's introduce the union and suppose that it takes actions that keep labor supply from expanding to S_1. The result? The market wage will rise to W_u, not W_1, and the quantity of labor hired will be Q_u as opposed to Q_1. This union has increased the wage rate by restricting the growth of labor supply. In this case, the action also slows the growth rate of employment: $(Q_u - Q_0) / Q_0$ compared to $(Q_1 - Q_0) / Q_0$. The greater the elasticity of labor demand, of course, the greater the negative employment impact of a given supply restriction.

Unions can restrict labor supply by taking actions or supporting government policies that alter one or more determinants of labor supply. One of these factors in particular (reducing the number of qualified suppliers) is most easily influenced by unions. One other (influencing nonwage income) is also of some significance.

1 Reducing the Number of Qualified Suppliers of Labor

One way that unions, in general, can limit the supply of qualified workers in a specific labor market is to restrict the overall "stock" of qualified workers in the nation. This partially explains why organized labor has strongly supported (a) limited immigration, (b) child labor laws, (c) compulsory retirement, and (d) shorter workweeks.

FIGURE 10.6 **Union Techniques: Restricting the Supply of Labor**

In a dynamic labor market characterized by normal expansion of labor demand and supply, such as D_0 to D_1 and S_0 to S_1, a union or professional organization may be able to increase wage rates (W_1 to W_u) through actions that restrict normal increases in labor supply (S_0 rather than S_1). However, these actions also slow the rate of growth of union employment $[(Q_u - Q_0)/Q_0$ compared to $(Q_1 - Q_0)/Q_0]$.

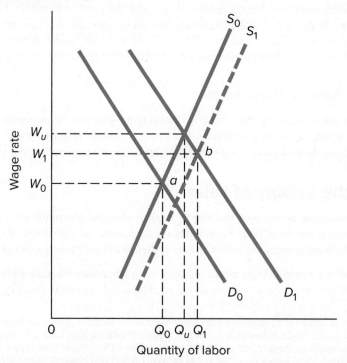

Unions also can restrict labor supply for particular jobs by limiting entry into the occupation itself. For example, craft unions composed of workers of a specific skill—such as plumbers, carpenters, or bricklayers—and some professional groups such as the American Medical Association allegedly have controlled access to training and established extraordinarily long apprenticeship programs to limit labor supply. Thus, this type of unionism is sometimes referred to as *exclusive unionism;* the supply restriction derives from actions that exclude potential workers from participating in the trade or profession.

Of perhaps greater importance, unions and professional groups have been able to limit entry to certain jobs through *occupational licensure, which is the enactment of laws by government to force practitioners of a trade to meet certain requirements.* These requirements may specify the level of educational attainment or amount of work experience needed and may also include the passing of an examination to obtain a license. State licensing boards have wide discretion in establishing the tests and standards needed to qualify for a license. In fact, there is evidence suggesting that some boards adjust the "pass rate" as a way to control the rate of entry into the licensed occupation.[40] Furthermore, the licensing requirements may include a minimum residency stipulation that inhibits the flow of qualified workers between states. Hence occupational licensure restricts labor supply and increases the wage rate as shown in Figure 10.6.[41]

A final means by which unions may limit labor supply to an occupation is through discrimination by race or gender. Some predominantly male craft unions and professional organizations have explicitly or implicitly argued that their particular type of work is "too physical" or "too stressful" to be performed by females and then have taken such actions as instituting overly rigorous physical requirements to make it difficult for women to enter the trade or occupation. Some craft unions also have engaged in racial segregation, perhaps resulting from the direct economic self-interest evident in Figure 10.6.[42]

2 Influencing Nonwage Income

Unions and professional organizations may also improve their wages by affecting the nonwage income determinant of labor supply. They may be able to accomplish this through legislation that provides income to unemployed workers, partially disabled workers, and older citizens. Stated differently, among the several reasons why labor unions generally support increased unemployment compensation, workers' compensation, and Social Security retirement benefits is the fact that these sources of nonwage income reduce labor force participation and, therefore, raise the before-tax wages to those employed. This is *not* to suggest that this is a primary reason for such support; after all, union members must join others in paying for government transfers through higher taxes (lower after-tax wages). Rather, such support is consistent with Figure 10.6.

Bargaining for an Above-Equilibrium Wage

In addition to restricting the supply of labor to an occupation (shifting the labor supply curve leftward), some unions succeed in enlisting as union members a large percentage of the available workers in an industry or occupation. Through the recruitment of union members, an *industrial union* can gain control over a firm's labor supply. During negotiations the union, therefore, can credibly threaten to withhold labor—to strike—unless the employer increases its wage offer. Because these unions attempt to attract or "include" all

---

[40] Alex Maurizi, "Occupational Licensing and the Public Interest," *Journal of Political Economy,* March/April 1974, pp. 399–413.

[41] For evidence consistent with this point, see Morris Kliener, "Occupational Licensing," *Journal of Economic Perspectives,* Fall 2000, pp. 189–202. Also see Morris M. Kleiner, *Licensing Occupations: Ensuring Quality or Restricting Competition?* (Kalamazoo, MI: W.E. Upjohn Institute, 2006).

[42] For evidence of discrimination by unions, see Orley Ashenfelter, "Discrimination and Trade Unions," in Orley Ashenfelter and Albert Rees (eds.), *Discrimination in Labor Markets* (Princeton, NJ: Princeton University Press, 1973), see also Larry D. Singell, Jr., "Racial Differences in the Employment Policy of State and Local Governments: The Case of Male Workers," *Southern Economic Journal,* October 1991, pp. 430–444. The economic aspects of labor market discrimination will be examined in detail in Chapter 14.

potential industry workers into the union, this form of unionism is called *inclusive unionism*. Examples of industrial unions that control high percentages of industry labor supply within the domestic economy include the United Auto Workers and the United Steelworkers of America (USA).

The impact of control over labor supply by a union is shown graphically in Figure 10.7. Suppose employers in this labor market act independently, and in the absence of the union the competitive equilibrium wage rate and level of employment are W_c and Q_c. Now suppose a union forms and successfully bargains for the higher, above-equilibrium wage rate W_u. This in effect makes the labor supply curve perfectly elastic over the $W_u a$ range. If employers hire any number of workers within this range, they must pay the union scale W_u or the union will withdraw *all* labor via a strike. If the employers desire more than a workers, however, say because of a major expansion of labor demand during the life of the union contract, they will need to pay wages above the union's scale to attract workers away from alternative jobs paying more than W_u.

This model enables us to understand several observed labor market phenomena and union actions. First, it explains why some unionized labor markets are characterized by chronic waiting lists for jobs. Second, and closely related, it clarifies why labor organizations place great emphasis on gaining *union security* provisions in labor contracts. The union's bargaining power relies to a great extent on the credibility of its threat to call for a strike and on its ability to withhold the firm's entire labor supply once a work stoppage occurs. A *union shop clause* permits the firm to hire nonunion workers but requires that workers join the union following a probationary period. These clauses typically increase the percentage of workers who are union members; thus, a strike occurring when the existing contract expires is likely to deprive the firm of such a substantial portion

FIGURE 10.7 Union Techniques: Bargaining for a Higher Wage

By organizing all available workers and securing union shops, inclusive unions may successfully bargain for a wage rate, such as W_u, that is above the competitive wage rate W_c. The effects are to make the labor supply curve perfectly elastic between W_u and point a (MWC = AWC = S_L) to reduce employment from Q_c to Q_u. The more elastic the labor demand, the greater the employment impact.

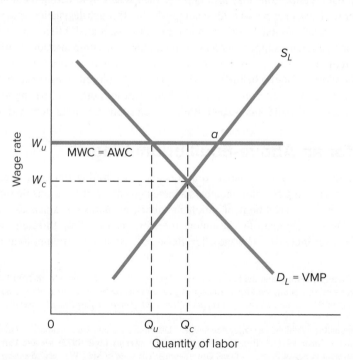

of its labor supply that the firm will be forced to curtail or cease production. The potential or actual loss of profit from a threatened or actual strike increases the union's bargaining power and improves the union's chances of getting an above-equilibrium wage, such as W_u in Figure 10.7.

Third, the distance $Q_u\,Q_c$ in Figure 10.7 sheds light on why unions are interested in securing contract provisions that reduce the elasticity of labor demand. The lower this elasticity, the smaller the number of displaced workers from any given wage increase. Recall that one major determinant of the elasticity of labor demand is the substitutability of other inputs. What contract provisions might reduce the substitution of capital for union labor? What provisions might limit the substitution of nonunion labor for union workers? Examples of the first include provisions limiting new technology, requiring redundant labor ("featherbedding"), and providing supplementary unemployment benefits (SUBs). By dictating the pace of the introduction of new technology and engaging in featherbedding, the union can temporarily reduce the elasticity of labor demand—that is, slow the substitution of capital for labor in response to wage increases. SUBs and severance pay provisions perform a similar function; if high enough, they raise the effective price of any capital used to replace union labor. Examples of contract provisions that reduce the substitutability of nonunion and union labor include clauses preventing subcontracting and plant relocation. Both are sometimes used to economize on the use of union labor following union-imposed wage increases. But by preventing such actions, the union at least temporarily reduces the elasticity of labor demand.

The employment impact of the union-imposed above-equilibrium wage in Figure 10.7 will be greater as time transpires. For example, the firm may resist continuing the contract provisions that keep the short-run demand curve inelastic. Alternatively, foreign or nonunion competition may arise in response to the high product prices in unionized industries. On the other hand, in a growing economy, the demand curves for most types of labor gradually shift rightward over time. Instead of an absolute decline in the number of jobs in the unionized labor market, the outcome may simply be slower growth of job opportunities. In this respect, no specific layoff of existing union workers is observed. This may explain why some union leaders have in the past erroneously concluded that demand for labor curves is highly inelastic.

STRIKES AND THE BARGAINING PROCESS[43]

The threat of a strike is a critical source of bargaining power for a union. A strike imposes costs on both the firm and the union. The firm suffers reduced profits due to the work stoppage, while the union members lose earnings. The party with the greater ability to sustain these costs will have greater bargaining power in contract negotiations. Because the *potential* cost of a strike is large for both the union and the firm, nearly all contract negotiations are settled without a strike.

Accident Model

The existence of strikes has been a problem for economists because strikes appear to be an inefficient result of the collective bargaining process. A strike imposes costs, so both the union and the firm could be better off if they agreed to the poststrike settlement before the strike occurred; thus, economists have often viewed strikes as accidents or errors in the negotiating process.

Sir John Hicks developed the most famous *accident model* of strikes.[44] Consider Figure 10.8, which illustrates his model. The Hicks model assumes that the willingness of an employer to make wage concessions rises with the expected length of a strike. The employer concession curve EC shows the *maximum* wage the firm would be willing to pay to avoid a strike of a given length. On the other hand, the model assumes the wage demands

---

[43] This section draws on Hirsch and Addison, op. cit., Chapter 4.

[44] John R. Hicks, *The Theory of Wages,* 2nd Edition (New York: Macmillan, 1963).

of the union fall with the expected length of a strike. The union resistance curve UR shows the *minimum* wage a union would be willing to accept to avoid a strike of a given length. If both the union and firm are well informed about the other party's concession curve, the wage settlement will occur at W^* where the EC and UR curves intersect, and no strike will occur.

The shape and position of the firm concession and union resistance curves will determine the wage settlement and the expected strike length. A higher or flatter UR curve, which indicates greater union resistance, will increase both the wage settlement and the expected strike length. Union resistance is likely to be greater when the expected costs of a strike for a union are lower. For example, if a strong labor market enables union members to be temporarily employed elsewhere or striking union members can obtain unemployment benefits, their wage demands are likely to be greater. A lower or flatter EC curve, which indicates greater employer resistance, will lower the wage settlement and increase the expected strike length. Employer resistance will be greater when the demand for union labor is elastic. The elasticity of union labor will be greater when it is easy to substitute away from union labor in the production process, product demand is more elastic, and union labor costs are a large share of total production costs.

Why do strikes occur according to the accident model? They are the result of one or both parties misperceiving the shape or position of the other party's concession curve. Incorrect perceptions of the concession curves will result in disagreement about the expected final wage settlement as well as the expected strike length. For example, if the union perceives that employer resistance will be weaker than it actually is (i.e., perceives the EC curve as higher or steeper than the actual one), the union would expect a higher wage than the firm expects to be settled after a strike. This disagreement will cause a strike to occur.

FIGURE 10.8 Accident Model

The employer concession curve EC shows the *maximum* wage that the firm would be willing to pay to avoid a strike of a given length. The union resistance curve UR shows the *minimum* wage that a union would be willing to accept to avoid a strike of a given length. If both the union and firm are well informed about the other party's concession curve, the wage settlement will occur at W^* where the EC and UR curves intersect, and no strike will occur. If either party misperceives the other party's concession curve, a strike will occur.

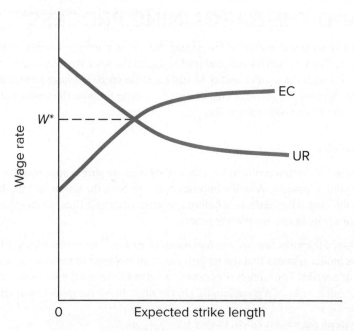

The accident model makes two predictions about when strikes should be more likely. First, they should be more likely when uncertainty is greater about the other party's concession curves.[45] Second, they should be less likely when the *joint* costs of a strike are greater.[46] The distribution of strike costs, which depends on the shape of the concession curves, will determine the wage settlement. However, the distribution of strike costs will not affect the probability of a strike.

Asymmetric Information Models

More recently, two types of strike models based on *asymmetric information* have been developed. The first model type focuses on the information differences between the union leadership and rank-and-file union members.[47] Union leaders are assumed to have a better understanding of the bargaining possibilities than are rank-and-file union members. The union members are assumed to have unrealistic wage demands. Because the union leaders don't want to risk losing their positions by signing a contract with a wage increase less than the rank-and-file members expect, the union leaders may call for a strike. As the strike goes on, the members decrease their wage demands until they match what the firm is willing to offer. The union leadership protects its image of doing all it can to achieve the members' goals. There is some evidence consistent with this conjecture because strikes rose after the passage of the Landrum–Griffin Act, which increased union democracy.[48]

The second type of strike model emphasizes the information differences between the union and the firm.[49] This model assumes that the firm has more information about the current and future profitability of the firm than the union. The firm has an incentive to understate the profitability of the firm because it can reduce the wage settlement by doing so. In this case, the optimal strategy for a union is to make a wage demand that would be accepted if the profits are high but rejected if they are low. The firm's willingness to accept a costly strike reveals to the union that profits are indeed low. The union lowers its wage demand as the strike progresses.

This asymmetric information model has two implications about strike activity. First, it implies that strikes should be more likely and longer when there is more uncertainty about a firm's profitability. Consistent with this hypothesis, Tracy finds that strikes are more likely and longer when a firm's profitability is more variable over time.[50] Second, the model predicts that the wage settlement will be lower if a contract is signed after a strike than if it is agreed to without a strike. The empirical evidence is consistent with this prediction: Both Canadian and U.S. bargaining data reveal that wage settlements were lower when contracts were signed after strikes.[51]

---

[45] The empirical evidence indicates that strikes occur because of mistakes. For example, one study indicates that the length and probability of a strike decline as the experience level of bargainers rises, see Edward Montgomery and Mary Ellen Benedict, "The Impact of Bargainer Experience on Teacher Strikes," *Industrial and Labor Relations Review,* April 1989, pp. 380–392, see also Martin J. Mauro, "Strikes as a Result of Imperfect Information," *Industrial and Labor Relations Review,* July 1982, pp. 522–538; and John F. Schnell and Cynthia L. Gramm, "Learning by Striking: Estimates of the Teetotaler Effect," *Journal of Labor Economics,* April 1987, pp. 221–241.

[46] For evidence showing that strikes are less likely when joint costs of a strike are higher, see Melvin W. Reder and George R. Neumann, "Conflict and Contract: The Case of Strikes," *Journal of Political Economy,* October 1980, pp. 867–886; and Barry Sopher, "Bargaining and the Joint Cost Theory of Strikes: An Experimental Study," *Journal of Labor Economics,* January 1990, pp. 48–74.

[47] For a discussion of this model, see Orley Ashenfelter and George Johnson, "Bargaining Theory, Trade Unions, and Industrial Strike Activity," *American Economic Review,* March 1969, pp. 35–49.

[48] Ashenfelter and Johnson, ibid.

[49] For example, see Beth Hayes, "Unions and Strikes with Asymmetric Information," *Journal of Labor Economics,* January 1984, pp. 57–82; and Oliver D. Hart, "Bargaining and Strikes," *Quarterly Journal of Economics,* February 1989, pp. 25–44.

[50] See Joseph S. Tracy, "An Empirical Test of an Asymmetric Information Model of Strikes," *Journal of Labor Economics,* April 1987, pp. 149–173.

[51] Sheena McConnell, "Strikes, Wages, and Private Information," *American Economic Review,* September 1989, pp. 801–815; and David Card, "Strikes and Wages: A Test of the Asymmetric Information Model," *Quarterly Journal of Economics,* August 1990, pp. 625–659.

10.3 *Quick Review*

- The monopoly union model assumes that the union sets the wage rate and the firm determines the level of union employment based on this wage rate. Compared to the nonunion outcome, the wage rate will be higher and the employment level will be lower.

- The efficient contracts model assumes that the union and firm bargain over the wage rate and employment. In general, the efficient contracts outcome will result in lower wages and more employment than the monopoly union outcome.

- Unions can raise the wage rate by increasing labor demand through actions that *(a)* increase product demand, *(b)* enhance productivity, *(c)* alter the prices of related inputs, and *(d)* increase the number of employees.

- Unions can increase the wage rate by restricting labor supply; actions include *(a)* reducing the number of qualified labor suppliers and *(b)* influencing nonwage income.

- Unions can raise the wage rate by gaining control over a firm's potential labor supply and threatening to withhold labor unless an acceptable negotiated wage rate is obtained.

- In the accident strike model, strikes occur because one or both parties misperceive the willingness of the other party to concede.

- Asymmetric information strike models imply that strikes occur because of information differences either between union leaders and the rank-and-file union members or between the union and the firm.

Your Turn

What is likely to happen to the probability of a strike occurring as the number of years that the firm and union are bargaining with each other rises? Explain. (*Answer:* See page 541.)

Chapter Summary

1. Unions are in part the consequence of industrialization, which changed the economy from one dominated by self-employment to one where labor depends on management for employment and earnings.

2. Approximately 14.7 million workers—about 1 worker in 10—belong to a labor union. Membership is relatively strong in goods-producing industries and weak in service-providing industries. Unionization is also relatively strong in the public sector.

3. Male, older, and African–American workers are more likely to belong to unions than female, young, and white workers. These differences are largely explained by the industrial and occupational affiliations of these demographic groups.

4. Labor unions are strongest in the heavily urbanized, heavily industrialized states and are relatively weak in the South.

5. The structure of the labor movements reveals three basic levels of union organization. The American Federation of Labor and Congress of Industrial Organizations (AFL–CIO) is concerned with formulating and expressing labor's political views and resolving jurisdictional disputes among national unions. The Change to Win federation focuses on organizing unorganized workers. The national unions negotiate collective bargaining agreements as well as organize workers. The task of

administering bargaining agreements falls primarily to the local unions. Bargaining structures are many and diverse.

6. Unionism has been declining relatively in the United States. Some labor economists attribute this to changes in the composition of domestic output and in the demographic structure of the labor force that has been uncongenial to union growth. Others contend that employers, recognizing that unionization lowers profitability, have more aggressively sought by both legal and illegal means to dissuade workers from being union members. Still others feel that government programs and "progressive" labor relations by employers have usurped many of organized labor's traditional functions, lessening workers' perceived need for union membership.

7. The monopoly union model assumes that the union sets the wage rate, and the firm determines the level of union employment based on this wage rate. The model results in a settlement on the firm's labor demand curve. Compared to the nonunion outcome, the wage rate will be higher and the employment level will be lower.

8. The monopoly union model outcome is not efficient for the firm and union because other wage and employment combinations can make at least one party better off without making the other party worse off.

9. The efficient contracts model assumes that the union and firm bargain over the wage rate and employment, rather than just the wage rate. In general, the efficient contract outcome will result in lower wages and more employment than the monopoly union outcome.

10. Unions can increase the wage rate paid to members who are employed by *(a)* increasing the demand for labor, *(b)* restricting the supply of labor, and *(c)* bargaining for an above-equilibrium wage. To increase the demand for labor, unions try to increase product demand, enhance productivity, influence the price of related inputs, and increase the number of employers. To restrict labor supply, unions attempt to affect the number of qualified suppliers, nonwage income, and alternative wages. To control labor supply, unions organize inclusively and bargain for union shops.

11. In the accident strike model, strikes occur because one or both parties misperceive the willingness of the other party to concede.

12. Models of strikes based on asymmetric information imply that strikes result from information differences either between union leaders and the rank-and-file union members or between the union and the firm.

Terms and Concepts

American Federation of Labor and Congress of Industrial Organizations (AFL–CIO)

Change to Win federation

national unions

local unions

bargaining structure

pattern bargaining

structural change hypothesis

managerial opposition hypothesis

substitution hypothesis

monopoly union

efficient contracts

strongly efficient contract

Davis–Bacon Act

exclusive unionism

occupational licensure

inclusive unionism

union shop clause

accident model

asymmetric information

Questions and Study Suggestions

1. Why have unions evolved? To what extent is the civilian labor force unionized? Indicate the *(a)* industrial and *(b)* occupational distribution of union members. Why are relatively fewer white-collar workers organized than blue-collar workers? Briefly explain union membership differences related to gender, race, and age. Evaluate this statement: "Whether an individual worker is a union member depends not so much on the worker's feelings toward membership as on her or his occupational choice."

2. Summarize the organizational structure of the American labor movement, indicating the functions of the AFL–CIO, Change to Win federation, the national unions, and the local unions.

3. Describe the various bargaining structures that exist in the United States. What might be the advantages of multiemployer bargaining to a union? To employers? What is pattern bargaining?

4. Critically evaluate each of these statements:

   a. "The relative decline of the American labor movement can be explained by the shift from goods-producing to service-providing industries and by the closely related shifts from blue- to white-collar occupations and from male to female employees."

   b. "The success of unions in raising their wages relative to nonunion workers has contributed to the decline of unionism."

   c. "Unionized firms have tended to become less profitable and, therefore, employers are more resistant to unionization."

5. Explain the rapid growth of public sector unionism in the 1960s and early 1970s, despite the general deunionization of the economy during this period.

6. Assume that a union's utility depends on only the wage rate and not the level of employment. In this case, what will be the outcome under the efficient contracts model?

7. How can both the union and the firm be better off by bargaining over the wage rate and employment rather than just the wage rate?

8. Explain the difference between efficient contracts and strongly efficient contracts.

9. Under what elasticity of labor demand conditions could a union restrict the supply of labor—that is, shift the supply curve leftward—and thereby increase the collective wage income (wage bill) of the workers still employed?

10. Are strikes inefficient for the union and firm? Explain.

11. What role do information differences play in causing strikes?

Internet Exercise

What Has Happened to Union Membership?

 Go to the Bureau of Labor Statistics Current Population Survey website **(https://www.bls.go v/cps)** and select "Union Members" under "Economic News Releases." What percentage of wage-earning and salaried workers were union members in the most recent year? What was the unionization rate (percent) for men, women, African–Americans, whites, and Hispanics in the latest year? Provide any other two facts relating to union membership from this source.

Internet Links

 The Unionstats website reports unionization rates by industry, occupation, and state **(https://www.unionstats.com)**.

The AFL–CIO website contains information about labor campaigns and strikes as well as policy statements about current political issues **(https://www.aflcio.org)**.

The website of the Institute for Research on Labor and Employment Library provides a directory of links to labor unions, labor union news sources, and many other sites related to the union movement **(http://www.irle.berkeley.edu/library/collections_dig.html)**.

Chapter **11**

The Economic Impact of Unions

After reading this chapter, you should be able to:

1. Explain the issues regarding measuring the pure union wage advantage and summarize the empirical evidence.
2. Explain the ways by which unions may affect productivity and allocative efficiency and summarize the empirical evidence.
3. Describe the effects of unionism on firm profitability.
4. Describe how unions may affect earnings inequality.
5. Assess the impact of unions on inflation, employment, unemployment, and the share of national income paid as wages.

In the previous chapter, we focused on (a) the industrial, occupational, and demographic characteristics of organized labor; (b) the institutional structure of the American labor movement; (c) union objectives; and (d) strikes and the bargaining process.

In this chapter, we direct our attention to the economic effects of unions and collective bargaining. How large a wage advantage are unions able to gain through collective bargaining? What are the implications of unions and collective bargaining for productivity and allocative efficiency? Do unions affect the profitability of firms? What is the impact of unions on the distribution of earnings?

THE UNION WAGE ADVANTAGE

Most people undoubtedly assume that union workers are paid more than nonunion workers. That is, they assume that unions gain a wage differential or *wage advantage* for their constituents. A union, after all, is able to deprive a firm of its workforce by striking and can thus impose associated costs on the firm. Presumably an employer, within limits, will pay the price of higher wage rates to avoid the costs of a strike. And indeed Bureau of Labor Statistics data reveal that average hourly earnings of union members were $29.58 in 2018 compared to $25.58 for nonunion workers.

Preliminary Complications

Closer examination suggests that this issue is not so clear-cut. In the first place, envision a unionized employer in a perfectly (or at least a highly) competitive industry. If rival firms in the industry are nonunion, other things being equal, this firm will not be able to survive if it pays a higher wage to its employees than competitors are paying to their nonunion workers. Despite its potential to impose strike costs on the employer, the union would face the dilemma of "no wage advantage" or "no firm" in these circumstances. A wage advantage would imply a higher average cost of production than the market-determined product price—that is, an economic loss.

The competitive model implies two additional points. On the one hand, the model tells us why unions are anxious to organize not just single firms but entire industries. If *all* firms are unionized and have higher wage costs, then no single firm will be at a competitive disadvantage and, therefore, faced with the prospect of losing market share to rivals. The United Automobile Workers' (UAW) intense desire to organize workers of new automobile plants established by foreign manufacturers in the United States is prompted by much more than the goal of adding thousands of workers to UAW ranks. On the other hand, the model implies that unions may fare better in industries where product markets are imperfect, such as government-regulated industries and the oligopolistic industries dominating much of the manufacturing sector of our economy. Such firms realize economic or surplus profits that in part can be expropriated by unions through higher wages without necessarily reducing output and employment.

This leads us to a second complication. Suppose we find a positive association between the degree of unionization and the average level of wage rates in various industries. That is, we discover that strongly unionized industries do in fact pay higher wage rates than weakly unionized industries. How do we know that unions are responsible for the higher wages? Do unions cause higher wages, *or* are unions prone to organizing industries that already pay high wages? The automobile industry, for example, was renowned for paying relatively high wages long before it was unionized in the late 1930s. In fact, one can cite considerations other than the presence of unions that might explain at least a part of the wage advantage that is enjoyed by highly unionized industries.[1] First, female workers generally constitute a larger proportion of the workforce in weakly unionized industries than they do in strongly unionized industries. We will find in Chapter 14 that women—because of discrimination and other considerations—are paid less than men. One can, therefore, argue that at least some portion of the wage differential found between strongly and weakly unionized industries is due not to the existence of unions but to the differing demographic makeup of the workforces in these industries. Second, strongly unionized industries usually have larger plants *and* are more capital-intensive than weakly unionized industries. The fact that unionized plants tend to be larger raises the possibility that supervision and monitoring may be more costly in such firms, causing employers to seek out and hire "superior" workers who can work effectively with less supervision. Such workers would be paid relatively high wages even if the union were not present. Similarly, capital-intensive production often requires more highly skilled workers who naturally command higher wages.[2] Our basic point is that higher wages in unionized industries might be attributable (at least in part) to factors other than the existence of the union.

Measuring the Wage Advantage

Aside from the complications just discussed, there is also a basic conceptual problem in measuring the *pure* union–nonunion differential. This arises because unionization may affect wage rates in nonunion labor markets, pushing them upward or downward and creating a bias in the measurement of the union wage advantage.

---

[1] The following discussion is based on Daniel J. B. Mitchell, *Unions, Wages, and Inflation* (Washington, DC: Brookings Institution, 1980), pp. 83–85.

[2] Of course, one can push the causal relationship back one step further by arguing that highly unionized industries are capital-intensive *because* of union wage pressure that prompts employers to substitute capital for labor.

To begin, the *pure union wage advantage* is the amount by which the union wage exceeds the nonunion wage that would exist without the union. This difference is expressed as a percentage. In Equation (11.1) the pure union wage advantage is A:

$$A = \frac{W_u - W_n}{W_n} \times 100 \quad (11.1)$$

where W_u is the union wage and W_n is the nonunion wage. The $(W_u - W_n)/W_n$ term is multiplied by 100 to express the union wage advantage as a percentage. For example, if the union wage were \$24 per hour and the nonunion wage were \$20, the union wage advantage would be 20 percent $[(24 - 20)/20 \times 100]$.

Ideally, the union wage advantage should be determined under laboratory conditions in which we compare union and nonunion wages with all other possible influences on wages being constant. Thus, in Figure 11.1 we first would want to observe the level of wages before the presence of the union (W_n) and then compare this with the wage rate after the union was added (W_u). We would then use the relevant numbers in our union wage advantage formula as just described. The problem, of course, is that there is no way of conducting such a controlled experiment. In particular, it is impossible to observe what the earnings of unionized workers would be in a given labor market if the union did not exist. We must, therefore, make real-world comparisons of a more complex and tentative nature.

The best that can be done in this regard is to compare the wages of workers of a specific kind in unionized (or strongly unionized) markets with the wages of workers in nonunion (or weakly unionized) markets. But in making this comparison, our aforementioned conceptual difficulty intrudes. *Unions may influence the wage rates of nonunion workers as well as the wage rates of their own workers.* Furthermore, the potential influence of unions on nonunion wages can take several different forms, so the overall impact is ambiguous. We are theoretically uncertain whether an increase in union wages will cause nonunion wages to rise or fall.

FIGURE 11.1   The Union Wage Advantage Measured under Ideal Conditions

If we could compare wage rates in a given labor market, where all conditions were held constant except for the presence of the union, we could calculate a pure measure of the union's wage advantage. That pure advantage is $(W_u - W_n)/W_n \times 100$.

In addition, the union wage may result in more productive workers in union firms. Let's briefly explore several different effects that describe various ways union wage setting may affect nonunion wages and may influence the quality of the unionized workforce.

1 Spillover Effect

The *spillover effect* refers to the decline in nonunion wages that results from displaced union workers supplying their services in nonunion labor markets. The higher wages achieved in the unionized sector of the labor market will be accompanied by a loss of jobs, and displaced workers will "spill over" into the nonunion sector and depress nonunion wages.

The basics of the spillover effect are portrayed in Figure 11.2. Assume that both sectors are initially nonunion and that movement between the two sectors entails a common equilibrium wage rate of W_n for this labor. Now assume that sector 1 becomes unionized and that the union is successful in increasing the wage rate to W_u. We observe that the higher wage rate in this sector causes unemployment of Q_1Q_2. The spillover effect assumes that some or all of these unemployed workers will seek and find employment in the nonunion sector. This movement of workers from the union to the nonunion sector will reduce the supply of labor in the union sector and increase the supply in the nonunion sector. If we assume downward flexibility of wages, then wages will fall in the nonunion sector to W_s.

To the extent that the spillover effect occurs, our *measured union wage advantage*, which is the amount by which the union wage exceeds the *observed* nonunion wage, will *overstate* the pure union wage advantage. We can grasp this by comparing our hypothetical laboratory experiment of Figure 11.1 with the real-world comparison of Figure 11.2 embodying the spillover effect. Specifically, instead of comparing the union wage

FIGURE 11.2 The Spillover Effect, the Threat Effect, and the Measured Wage Advantage

The spillover effect suggests that as a union is able to raise wage rates from W_n to W_u in sector 1, it will reduce employment by Q_1Q_2. Assuming downward wage flexibility, the reemployment of these workers in sector 2 will reduce wages there from W_n to W_s. The measured union wage advantage will be $(W_u - W_s)/W_s \times 100$, which overstates the pure advantage of $(W_u - W_n)/W_n \times 100$. The threat effect indicates that as the union raises wages from W_n to W_u in sector 1, nonunion employers will grant a wage increase from, say, W_n to W_t in sector 2 to counter the threat of unionization. The measured wage advantage will be $(W_u - W_t)/W_t \times 100$, which understates the pure advantage of $(W_u - W_n)/W_n \times 100$.

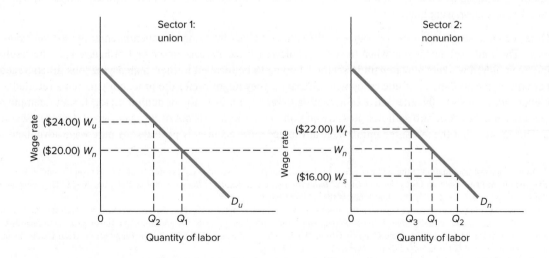

W_u with the nonunion wage W_n in Figure 11.1 to get the pure union wage advantage of 20 percent, we must compare the union wage W_u ($24) with the nonunion wage W_s ($16). Because W_s is less than W_n due to the spillover effect, the measured wage advantage in this case is 50 percent [(24 − 16) / 16 × 100]. The spillover effect depresses observed nonunion wages, so the measured union wage advantage is larger than the pure union wage advantage of 20 percent. To repeat, a spillover effect will cause the union wage advantage to be *overstated.*[3]

2 Threat Effect

In contrast, some labor economists, labeled *institutionalists,* argue that market forces, as described by the spillover effect, are largely subverted or set aside by collective bargaining and that wage rates are determined mainly on the basis of *equitable comparisons.* This implies that wages for any group of workers will be determined on the basis of wages being paid to comparable workers and that union and nonunion wages may be positively linked.

More specifically, the *threat effect* refers to an increase in nonunion wages that a nonunion employer offers as a response to the threat of unionization. The reasoning is that nonunion employers will feel increasingly threatened with unionization when workers in union firms obtain wage increases. An enlarged union–nonunion differential will increase the incentive for the workers in the nonunion firms to organize. To meet this threat, the nonunion employer will grant wage increases. Thus, if we once again start from the W_n equilibrium wage in both sectors (Figure 11.2), the wage increase from $20 to $24 resulting from the unionization of sector 1 might *increase* nonunion wages in sector 2 from W_n ($20) to, say, W_t ($22). Now the measured union wage advantage will be about 9 percent [(24 − 22) / 22 × 100] rather than the pure advantage of 20 percent (Figure 11.1). To recapitulate: If the threat effect causes union wage increases to pull up nonunion wages, then the measured union wage advantage will *understate* the pure union advantage.[4]

3 Other Effects

Our brief discussions of the spillover and threat effects do not exhaust all the possible ways in which union wages may influence nonunion wages. For example, there may be a *product market effect:* an increase in nonunion wages caused by consumer demand shifting away from relatively high-priced union-produced goods and toward relatively low-priced goods produced by nonunion workers. The product market effect works as follows: A "union pay increase, through its effect on costs and prices, shifts demand to firms in the nonunion sector. The added demand for nonunion output is translated into added demand for nonunion labor, which could have a pay-raising influence."[5]

Other economists question the relevance of the spillover effect by citing the phenomenon of *wait unemployment.* The argument here is that when the union achieves a wage increase in sector 1 of Figure 11.2, the resulting unemployed workers may remain in sector 1 hoping to be recalled to their high-paying jobs. Encouraged perhaps by the availability of unemployment insurance, they might prefer the probability of being recalled at higher union wages to the alternative of accepting lower-wage jobs in the nonunion sector. If wait unemployment occurs, the downward spillover pressure on nonunion wages does not occur to any great degree in sector 2. This implies that the measured union wage advantage more accurately portrays the pure wage advantage.

---

[3] For an empirical examination of the spillover effect, see David Neumark and Michael L. Wachter, "Union Effects on Nonunion Wages: Evidence from Panel Data on Industries and Cities," *Industrial and Labor Relations Review,* October 1995, pp. 20–38. They conclude there is mixed evidence regarding the importance of the spillover effect.

[4] For a study finding mixed evidence regarding the magnitude of the threat effect, see Henry S. Farber, "Nonunion Wages and the Threat of Unionization," *Industrial and Labor Relations Review,* April 2005, pp. 335–352. For research finding a threat effect with regards to employer-provided health insurance, see Craig A. Olson, "Union Threat Effects and the Decline in Employer-Provided Health Insurance," *Industrial and Labor Relations Review,* March 2019, pp. 417–445.

[5] Mitchell, Daniel J. B. *Unions, Wages, and Inflation* (Washington, DC: Brookings Institution, 1980).

There is also the notion of the *superior worker effect*. This idea is that the higher wages paid by union firms will cause workers to queue up for these good union jobs. Given the availability of many job seekers, unionized employers will carefully screen these prospective workers for those having the greatest ability, the most motivation, the least need for costly supervision, and other worker traits contributing to high productivity. This means that, in time, high-wage union firms may acquire superior workforces in comparison to nonunion firms;[6] thus, in seeking to measure the union wage advantage accurately, the researcher is confronted with determining how much of an observed union wage advantage is due to the presence of the union as an institution and how much it reflects the presence of more highly productive workers in the unionized firms. To the extent that superior workers acquire the high-wage union jobs, the measured union wage advantage would be *overstated*. Part of the higher wages paid to such workers is attributable to their higher productivity rather than to the union.

Finally, part of the union wage advantage may be a *compensating wage differential* that accounts for the fewer amenities in the workplace encountered by union workers. Alternatively stated, some portion of the wage advantage enjoyed by union members may be compensation for the fact that their working conditions are more structured, their working hours are less flexible, and the work pace is faster.[7]

Table 11.1 lists these various effects and summarizes how each biases the measured wage advantage from the pure wage advantage. Although unanimity does not exist on the issue, most studies indicate that the threat and product market effects dominate the spillover effect, meaning that the overall impact of unions on nonunion wages is positive. Furthermore, this positive impact on nonunion wages is more than sufficient to counter any superior worker effect that might be present. As a result, the measured union wage advantage probably understates the pure union wage advantage.[8]

Empirical Evidence

Now that we have some appreciation of the practical and conceptual difficulties in estimating the union wage advantage, let's turn to the available empirical evidence. Hirsch and Macpherson have examined the union

TABLE 11.1 Difficulties in Measuring the Pure Union Wage Advantage

Effect	Consequence
Spillover	Lowers nonunion wages, causing measured wage advantage to overstate pure advantage.
Threat	Increases nonunion wages, causing measured wage advantage to understate pure advantage.
Product market	Increases nonunion wages, causing measured wage advantage to understate pure advantage.
Superior worker	Results in more productive workers in union firms, causing measured wage advantage to overstate pure wage advantage.

[6] On the other hand, unions may seek higher wages in the future if worker quality improves, see Walter J. Wessels, "Do Unionized Firms Hire Better Workers?" *Economic Inquiry,* October 1994, pp. 616–629. For empirical evidence consistent with Wessels's model, see Barry T. Hirsch and Edward J. Schumacher, "Unions, Wages, and Skills," *Journal of Human Resources,* Winter 1998, pp. 201–219.

[7] Greg J. Duncan and Frank P. Stafford, "Do Union Members Receive Compensating Wage Differentials?" *American Economic Review,* June 1980, pp. 355–371, see also Stanley W. Siebert and X. Wei, "Compensating Wage Differentials for Workplace Accidents: Evidence for Union and Nonunion Workers in the UK," *Journal of Risk and Uncertainty,* July 1994, pp. 61–76.

[8] Barry T. Hirsch and John T. Addison, *The Economic Analysis of Unions* (Boston: Allen & Unwin, 1986), pp. 120, 176. For some recent evidence that questions the strength of the threat effect, however, see David Neumark and Michael L. Wachter, op. cit.; and Farber, op. cit.

wage premium for the 1983-2019 period using a consistent methodology and data source.[9] Their findings are summarized in Figure 11.3. In 2019 the average overall union wage advantage was 15 percent.[10] This estimate is near the top of the 10-15 percent range that Lewis estimated for the 1923-1958 period.[11] Hirsch and Macpherson also examined the union wage advantage in the public sector, as opposed to the overall wage advantage. They estimate that all else being equal, the pay of unionized government workers is 8 percent higher than that of nonunionized government workers. This union wage advantage is 9 percentage points lower than the advantage commanded by union workers in the private sector.

In the 1970s, the union wage advantage was even larger. Lewis found that the union wage advantage peaked at 20 percent in 1976.[12] Other researchers have found an even higher union wage premium in the mid-1970s. Mitchell,[13] using three different data sets, surmised that the union wage premium in the mid-1970s was in the range of 20-30 percent. Also, Freeman and Medoff, using six data sets for individual workers, found union wage advantages ranging from 21 to 32 percent and concluded that "in the 1970s the archetypical union wage advantage was on the order of 20-30 percent."[14]

The period in question was one of *stagflation*—simultaneous inflation and high unemployment—resulting largely from dramatic oil price increases. Through collective bargaining and cost-of-living adjustments (COLAs) in contracts, union workers were better able than nonunion workers to keep their nominal wages rising with inflation. The loose labor markets (high unemployment) apparently slowed the relative pace of nominal wage increases for nonunion workers. Recall from Chapter 10 that the high union wage advantage of the 1970s is cited as a possible cause of the decline in union employment during the 1980s.

FIGURE 11.3   Union Wage Advantage

The union wage advantage averaged 19 percent over the 1983-2019 and is currently about 14 percent.

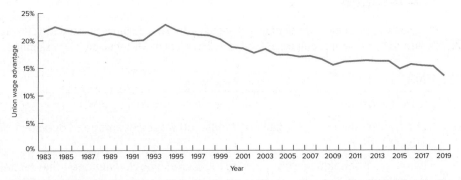

Source: Barry T. Hirsch and David A. Macpherson, *Union Membership and Earnings Data Book: Compilations from the Current Population Survey* (2019 Edition) (Washington, DC: Bureau of National Affairs, 2019); updated by author.

[9] Barry T. Hirsch and David A. Macpherson, *Union Membership and Earnings Data Book: Compilations from the Current Population Survey* (2019 Edition) (Washington, DC: Bureau of National Affairs, 2015). For an analysis over the 1990-2010 period, see P. E. Gabriel and S. Schmitz, "A Longitudinal Analysis of the Union Wage Premium for US workers," *Applied Economics Letters,* Issue 7 2014, pp. 487-489.

[10] Errors in the classification of union and nonunion status of workers as well as other data errors may cause the existing estimates of the union wage differential to be too low, see Barry T. Hirsch, "Reconsidering Union Wage Effects: Surveying New Evidence on an Old Topic," *Journal of Labor Research,* Spring 2004, pp. 233-266. The statistical technique used also affects the estimate of the union wage differential, see Ozkan Eren, "Measuring the Union-Nonunion Wage Gap Using Propensity Score Matching," *Industrial Relations,* October 2007, pp. 766-780.

[11] H. Gregg Lewis, *Unionism and Relative Wages in the United States* (Chicago: University of Chicago Press, 1963).

[12] H. Gregg Lewis, *Union Relative Wage Effects* (Chicago: University of Chicago Press, 1986).

[13] Mitchell, op. cit., p. 95.

[14] Richard B. Freeman and James L. Medoff, *What Do Unions Do?* (New York: Basic Books, 1984), p. 46.

The union wage advantage has fallen from its lofty heights in the 1970s. From 1983 to 1994 there was little change in the union wage advantage. Since 1994 the union wage advantage has drifted downward, reflecting a decline in the union wage premium among both private and public sector workers.

Union wage advantages vary greatly by industry, occupation, race, gender, and state of the economy. Although no unassailable generalizations can be drawn from the studies that try to sort out these differences, the following comments seem to be defensible.[15]

1. The union wage advantage moves countercyclically, increasing during recessions and narrowing during expansions. Union wages are locked in by long-term bargaining contracts that are not readily adjusted. At the same time, nonunion wages are free to rise and fall with changes in the economy and labor market. As a result, nonunion wages rise relative to union wages in economic booms and vice versa during recessions.

2. Craft unions in the construction industry have achieved union wage advantages that are much larger than average. The bargaining power of such unions is great because each craft union represents a small proportion of total building costs, and construction workers can often find employment in other firms during a strike.

3. African–American males, on average, gain more from being union members than do whites and females.

4. Unions achieve higher wage advantages for blue-collar workers (craftspeople, operatives, laborers) than for white-collar workers (clerical workers, salespeople).

5. Less educated workers have higher union wage premiums than better-educated workers.

Total Compensation: Wages plus Fringe Benefits

We would be remiss not to examine the impact of unions on fringe benefits. Recall from Chapter 7 that *fringe benefits* include public (legally mandated) programs such as Social Security, unemployment compensation, and workers' compensation as well as a wide variety of private nonmandatory programs including private pensions, medical and dental insurance, and paid vacations and sick leave. *Total compensation* is simply the sum of wage earnings and the value of fringe benefits. If union workers enjoy more generous fringe benefits than nonunion workers, then the overall economic advantage that union workers have over nonunion workers is greater than the wage advantage suggests. On the other hand, if union wage gains are realized at the expense of fringe benefits and nonunion workers receive larger fringe benefits, then the union wage advantage overstates the economic advantage of union workers.

Evidence

How do union fringe benefits compare with those of nonunion workers? The answer is that union workers enjoy a greater variety and higher overall level of fringe benefits than do nonunion workers. Using 2002 data, Budd reports that union members are 31 percentage points and 25 percentage points more likely than their nonunion counterparts to have pension and health insurance coverage, respectively.[16] Knepper finds, using

---

[15] For example, see H. Gregg Lewis, 1986, op. cit.; David G. Blanchflower and Alex Bryson, "What Effect Do Unions Have on Wages Now and Would 'What Do Unions Do?' Be Surprised?" *Journal of Labor Research,* Summer 2004, pp. 383–414; and McKinley L. Blackburn, "Are Union Wage Differentials in the United States Falling?" *Industrial Relations,* July 2008, pp. 390–418.
[16] John W. Budd, "Non-Wage Forms of Compensation," *Journal of Labor Research,* Fall 2005, pp. 669–676.

11.1   World of Work

The Cost of a Union Member*

In March 1999, workers at the National Linen Service, a large linen supply firm, voted to unionize by a 2 to 1 margin. Because of lower expected profits after unionization, the stock market response was strongly negative. By March 2001, its price had fallen by 15 percent, while the overall stock market had risen 25 percent over the same time period.

David Lee and Alexandre Mas examine whether the stock market response to National Linen Service's unionization was a typical one or not. They examine the effect of new private sector unionization using data on union elections matched to stock market data for the 1961–1999 period. The study restricts the analysis to the 1,436 elections in which at least 5 percent of the firm's workforce voted on unionization. The average percentage of the workforce voting on unionization is 22 percent and unions won 29 percent of the elections.

Consistent with unions lowering firm profits, a firm's stock price declines when the union wins an election. The findings show that an additional union member lowers a firm's market value on average by $40,500. This effect takes 15–18 months to be completely reflected in a firm's value.

The effect of a union victory varies by the strength of the win. Narrow wins by unions have only a small effect on a firm's value. However, wins with a more than 60 percent lead to large decreases in the firm's stock price.

The study also conducts simulations of the impact of policy changes. Lowering the threshold for a union win from 50 percent to 33 percent would approximately double the union win rate and lower the value of firms at risk of unionization by 4.3 percent. If the threshold was lowered to an extreme value of 10 percent, the union win rate would rise to 99 percent and firm value would fall by 11 percent.

* Based on David S. Lee and Alexandre Mas, "Long-Run Impacts of Unions on Firms: New Evidence from Financial Markets, 1961–1999," *Quarterly Journal of Economics,* February 2012, pp. 333–378.

---

firm data, that newly certified unions increase pension contributions more than wages.[17] Freeman and Medoff have shown that unions gain a larger fringe benefit advantage than wage advantage. Finally, Lewis contends that the inclusion of fringe benefits would raise estimates of the union compensation advantage by two or three percentage points. In short, substantial agreement exists that union workers generally achieve not only a wage advantage but also a considerable fringe benefit advantage compared to nonunion workers.

Role of Unions

Why do union members receive more generous fringe benefits than nonunion workers? A number of interrelated reasons may be involved. First, union fringes may be higher for the same reason that union wage rates are higher. The union can deprive management of its workforce, and the employer is willing to pay both higher wages *and* larger fringe benefits to avoid the costs of a strike. Second, union workers, by virtue of their higher earnings, may simply choose to "buy" mor e fringe s than lower-income nonunion workers. Third, as

---

[17] Matthew Knepper, "From the Fringe to the Fore: Labor Unions and Employee Compensation," *Review of Economics and Statistics,* March 2020, pp. 98–112.

11.1 *Quick Review*

- The pure union wage advantage is the percentage by which the union wage exceeds the wage that would exist if there were no union.

- If the spillover and superior worker effects are dominant, the measured union wage advantage will overstate the pure advantage; if the threat and product market effects are dominant, the measured union wage advantage will understate the pure wage advantage.

- Overall, the union wage advantage is an estimated 15 percent. This advantage rises by 2–3 percentage points when fringe benefits are considered.

- The union wage advantage *(a)* moves countercyclically, *(b)* is particularly high for craft unions in the construction industry, *(c)* is higher for African–American males than for other racial or gender groups, and *(d)* is higher for less educated workers than for better-educated workers.

Your Turn

Suppose the union wage is $20 an hour; the current nonunion wage, $18 an hour; and the nonunion wage that would exist without the union, $16 an hour. What is the measured union wage advantage? The pure wage advantage? (*Answers:* See page 541.)

a collective-voice institution, a union may formulate fringe benefit proposals, inform its constituents of the details of such proposals, and crystallize worker preferences; the union then communicates these preferences to management. Fourth, older workers are usually more active in the internal politics of a union and are, therefore, more influential in determining union goals. These older workers are typically more interested in pensions and insurance programs than are younger workers. Fifth, as we will discover momentarily, unionism reduces worker quit rates and thus increases job tenure. Greater tenure, in turn, increases the probability that workers will actually receive benefits from such fringes as nonvested pensions and life insurance. Finally, there is the simple fact that under collective bargaining law, fringe benefits are a mandatory item on the bargaining agenda, which accords them more serious and systematic attention than in nonunion labor markets.

EFFICIENCY AND PRODUCTIVITY

Are unions a positive or a negative force insofar as economic efficiency and productivity are concerned? How do unions affect the allocation of resources? Although much disagreement exists about the efficiency aspects of unionism, it is useful to consider some of the ways unions might affect efficiency both negatively and positively. We will consider the negative view first.

Negative View

Unions might exert a negative impact on efficiency in three basic ways. First, unions may impose work rules that diminish productivity *within* union firms. Second, strikes may entail a loss of output. Finally, the union wage advantage is a distortion of the wage structure, causing a misallocation of labor *between* union and nonunion firms and industries.

1 Restrictive Work Rules

Perhaps the most apparent way unions might impair productivity and efficiency is by imposing various work rules on management. These "make-work" rules can take a variety of interrelated forms. First, the union may obtain a direct limit on hourly, daily, or weekly output per worker. Example: Allegedly to control output quality, the bricklayers have sought to restrict the number of bricks laid per hour or per day. Second, the union may insist on the use of time-consuming production methods. Illustrations: Painters' unions may prohibit the use of spray guns or limit the width of paint brushes. In past years, the typographers' unions resisted the introduction of computers in setting type. Third, a union may require that unnecessary work be done. Example: Craft unions have sometimes promoted the enactment of building codes requiring that prefabricated housing units be broken down and reassembled on the construction site. Fourth, work crews of excessive size may be required. Examples: Historically the musicians' union insisted on oversized orchestras for musical shows and required that a union standby orchestra be paid by employers using nonunion orchestras. For many years, the Brotherhood of Locomotive Firemen and Engineers was able to retain a fireman on train crews, even though the worker's function was eliminated by the shift from steam to diesel engines. Such practices are labeled *featherbedding.*[18] Fifth, unions may impose jurisdictional restrictions on the kinds of jobs workers may perform. Illustration: Sheet metal workers or bricklayers may be prohibited from performing the simple carpentry work often associated with their jobs. Observance of such rules means, in this instance, that unneeded and underutilized carpenters must be available. Finally, unions may restrain management in the assignment of workers to jobs. The most prevalent example is that unions typically insist that workers be promoted in accordance with seniority rather than ability and efficiency.

This recitation of reasons that union work rules might impede intrafirm efficiency merits modification in several respects. To begin, one must not make the mistake of assuming that productivity will necessarily be enhanced by "speeding up the assembly line." A speedup may in fact cause workers to tire and become demoralized and, therefore, be *less* efficient. Similarly, it is also incorrect to associate featherbedding, unnecessarily large work crews, make-work rules, and the like solely with unionized workers. Although unions may be responsible for codifying and enforcing such practices, the practices themselves are quite common in both union and nonunion sectors of the economy. Peer pressure and the threat of social ostracism can be as effective as a clause in a collective bargaining agreement in controlling the pace of production.[19] Finally, the productivity-reducing practices just outlined often come into being against a backdrop of technological change. Labor and management may agree to a crew size that is reasonable and appropriate at the time the agreement is concluded. But labor-saving technology may then emerge that renders the crew "too large." The union is likely to resist the potential loss of jobs.[20]

2 Strikes

A second way unions may adversely affect efficiency is through strikes. If union and management reach an impasse in their negotiations, a strike will result and the firm's production will generally cease for the strike's duration. The firm will forgo sales and profits, and workers will sacrifice income.

GP11.1

Simple statistics on strike activity suggest that strikes are relatively rare and the associated aggregate economic losses are relatively minimal. Figure 11.4 provides data on the number of major work stoppages, defined as those involving 1,000 or more workers and lasting at least one full day or one work shift. Given that about 700 major collective bargaining agreements are

---

[18] For a discussion of methods of featherbedding, see George E. Johnson, "Work Rules, Featherbedding, and Pareto Optimal Union–Management Bargaining," *Journal of Labor Economics,* Part 2, January 1990, pp. S237–259.

[19] See Paul A. Weinstein (ed.), *Featherbedding and Technological Change* (Boston: D. C. Heath and Company, 1965).

[20] For an analysis of when unions are likely to resist labor-saving technology, see Steve Dowrick and Barbara J. Spencer, "Union Attitudes to Labor-Saving Innovation: When Are Unions Luddites?" *Journal of Labor Economics,* April 1994, pp. 316–344.

FIGURE 11.4   **Number of Major Work Stoppages in the United States**

There have been only a few major strikes in the United States in recent years.

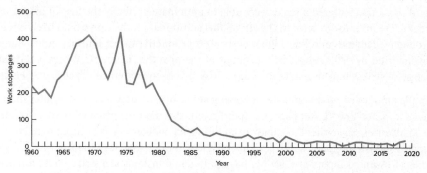

Source: U.S. Department of Labor, Bureau of Labor Statistics, Major Work Stoppages, https://www.bls.gov/wsp

negotiated each year, the number of major work stoppages is surprisingly small. Figure 11.5 presents the percentage of total work time lost due to major strikes in the United States for the 1960–2019 period. Most strikes last only a few days. As a result, the lost work time from major strikes has been consistently far less than one-half of 1 percent of total work time. In fact, over this period the amount of work time lost was typically less than two-tenths of 1 percent of total work time. This loss is the equivalent of four hours per worker per year, which is less than five minutes per worker per week.[21]

But these data on time lost from work stoppages can be misleading as a measure of the costliness of a strike. For example, employers in the struck industry may have anticipated the strike and worked their labor force overtime to accumulate inventories to supply customers during the strike period. This means that the overall loss of work time, production, profits, and wages is less than the work time loss figures suggest. Similarly, other nonstruck producers in an industry may have increased their output to offset the loss of production by

FIGURE 11.5   **Percentage of Total Working Time Lost Due to Major Work Stoppages in the United States**

The amount of work time lost due to major strikes in the United States is typically less than two-tenths of 1 percent of total work time.

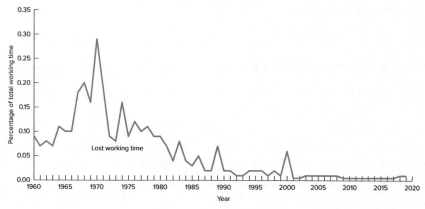

Source: U.S. Department of Labor, Bureau of Labor Statistics, Major Work Stoppages, https://www.bls.gov/wsp

[21] Marten Estey, *The Unions,* 3rd Edition (New York: Harcourt Brace Jovanovich, 1981), p. 140.

firms engaged in a strike. In other words, although a strike may impose significant losses on participants, the total output loss to the industry or to society at large may be minuscule or nonexistent. Note, however, that the production adjustments made in anticipation of, or as a consequence of, a strike may entail some efficiency losses. If firms that suffered a strike were able to anticipate perfectly the loss of output and sales and, therefore, accumulate inventories prior to the strike, this additional production would likely entail the overutilization of productive facilities and thus higher costs (less productivity) per unit of output. Similar efficiency losses may be incurred by firms replacing the output of the firm that is struck. Whereas the data on worker days lost because of strikes may overstate the output loss, a consequent efficiency loss may be concealed.

Furthermore, the amount of production and income lost because of strikes will be greater than suggested by work time loss data when a work stoppage in a specific industry disrupts production in associated industries. These affected industries may either buy inputs from the struck industry or sell output to it. Nonstriking workers in the affected industries may lose work time and the economy may lose their output if a strike depletes these industries of essential inputs or essential buyers. In some instances, a strike could force affected firms to cease or curtail operations.

11.1 Global Perspective

Strike Incidence*

The United States has a low proportion of workers involved in strikes compared to other major industrial countries.

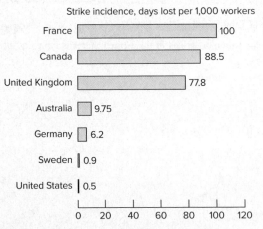

Strike incidence, days lost per 1,000 workers

France	100
Canada	88.5
United Kingdom	77.8
Australia	9.75
Germany	6.2
Sweden	0.9
United States	0.5

Source: ILOSTAT Database, International Labour Organization. www.ilo.org

* The strike incidence rate is the annual average of the number of days lost per 1,000 workers for wage-earning and salaried workers for the 2014–2017 period, except for Germany, which is for the 2005–2008 period.

Alternatively, output in industries linked as purchasers or suppliers to struck industries may decline while paid work time remains steady. If so, labor productivity (output per worker) in the affected industries will fall and the average cost of the output will rise. McHugh[22] finds empirical support for this possible outcome. He suggests that many employers in nonstruck firms affected by strikes retain their workforces during the strike. This "hoarded" labor is redundant; because output falls, these firms experience declines in labor productivity.

As a broad generalization, the adverse effects of a strike on nonstriking firms and customers are likely to be greater when services are involved and less when products are involved. For example, a 10-day strike in 2002 by 10,500 West Coast dockworkers shut down 29 ports from San Diego to Seattle. These ports handle 40 percent of the seaborne cargo in the United States. As a result, the strike costs the U.S. economy an estimated $10 billion. The backlog of cargo created by the strike took weeks to clear up. In contrast, a strike in a durable goods industry is likely to have negligible effects on the public.

Overall it is appropriate to say that, on average, the costs imposed on the immediate parties to a strike and affected firms and consumers are not as great as one might surmise. A study of some 63 manufacturing industries over the 1955–1977 period concluded that strike costs were significant in only 19 of these industries.[23] Furthermore, in these 19 industries the amount of output lost was typically a small fraction of 1 percent of total annual output. The ability of struck firms to draw on inventories and the capacity of nonstruck firms to increase their output apparently make industry output losses minimal.

 Postscript: Strikes are precipitated by the failure of *two* parties—union and management—to reach agreement. In fact, a growing number of work stoppages in recent years have taken the form of lockouts initiated by employers. Popular opinion to the contrary, it is unfair to attribute all of the costs associated with a strike to labor alone.

3 Wage Advantage and Labor Misallocation

A third major way unions may adversely affect efficiency is through the wage advantage itself.

A Simple Model This effect can be seen through reconsideration and extension of the spillover model in Figure 11.2. In Figure 11.6 we have drawn (for simplicity's sake) identical labor demand curves for the unionized and nonunion sectors of the labor market for some particular labor. We assume that the relevant product market is purely competitive so that the labor demand curves reflect not only marginal revenue product (MRP) but also value of marginal product (VMP).[24] If there is no union present, the wage rate that would result from competition in hiring labor is W_n. Now assume that a union establishes itself in sector 1 and increases the wage rate from W_n to W_u. In accordance with our analysis of the spillover effect, the result is that the $Q'_1 Q'_2$ workers who lose their jobs in the union sector move to nonunion sector 2, where we assume they secure employment. These additional workers depress the wage rate from W_n to W_s in nonunion sector 2.

Because we have kept the level of employment unchanged, this simple model allows us to isolate the efficiency or allocative effect of the union wage differential. The area $Q'_2 abQ'_1$ represents the loss of domestic output caused by the $Q'_1 Q'_2$ employment decline in the union sector. This area is the sum of the VMPs—the total contribution to the domestic output—of the workers displaced by the W_n to W_u wage increase achieved by the union. As these workers spill over into nonunion sector 2 and are reemployed, they add to the domestic

---

[22] Richard McHugh, "Productivity Effects of Strikes in Struck and Nonstruck Industries," *Industrial and Labor Relations Review,* July 1991, pp. 722–732.

[23] George R. Neumann and Melvin W. Reder, "Output and Strike Activity in U.S. Manufacturing: How Large Are the Losses?" *Industrial and Labor Relations Review,* January 1984, pp. 197–211. Another study concludes that a strike reduces the stock market value of a struck firm by 3 percent, see John DiNardo and Kevin F. Hallock, "When Unions 'Mattered': Assessing the Impact of Strikes on Financial Markets," *Industrial and Labor Relations Review,* January 2002, pp. 219–233.

[24] Recall from Chapter 5 that MRP measures the amount that an additional worker adds to a firm's total revenue, while VMP indicates the value of a worker's extra output to society. VMP tells us the dollar amount an extra worker contributes to the domestic output.

FIGURE 11.6   The Effect of the Union Wage Advantage on the Allocation of Labor

The higher wage W_u that the union achieves in sector 1 causes the displacement of $Q'_1 Q'_2$ workers. The reemployment of these workers in nonunion sector 2 reduces the wage rate there from W_n to W_s. The associated loss of output in the union sector is the area $Q'_2\, abQ'_1$, whereas the gain in the nonunion sector is only area $Q'_1\, cdQ'_2$. Because the shaded areas are of equal size in each diagram, the net loss of output is area $c'\, abd'$.

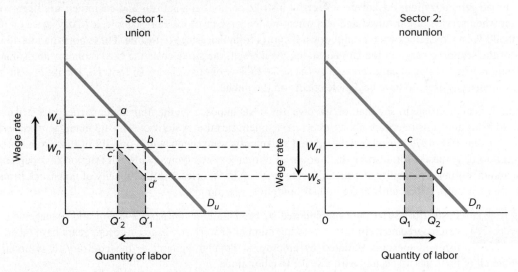

output the amount indicated by the $Q_1 cdQ_2$ area. Because $Q'_2\, abQ'_1$ exceeds $Q_1 cdQ_2$, there is a net loss of domestic output. More precisely, because the shaded areas are equal in each diagram, the net loss of output attributable to the union wage advantage is equal to area $c'abd'$ as shown in the union sector diagram. The same amount of employed labor is now producing a smaller output, so labor is obviously misallocated and inefficiently used. Viewed from a slightly different perspective, *after* the spillover of $Q_1 Q_2$ workers from the union to the nonunion sector has occurred, workers will be paid a wage rate equal to their VMPs in both sectors. But the VMPs of the union workers will be higher than the VMPs of the nonunion workers. The economy will always benefit from a larger domestic output when any given type of labor is reallocated from a relatively low-VMP use to a relatively high-VMP use. But given the union's presence and its ability to maintain the W_u wage rate in its sector, this reallocation from sector 2 to 1 will not occur.

Qualifications Our model of the allocative inefficiency stemming from a union wage advantage is very simplified. Let's briefly call attention to some additional real-world considerations that might cause the efficiency loss to be greater or less than our model suggests.

1. **Unemployment:** Recalling our earlier comments about wait unemployment, what if some workers who lost their jobs because of higher wages in the union sector decided to remain in that sector in the hope of reemployment? The consequence is a net loss of output in excess of $c'abd'$ in Figure 11.6. The reason? While output would decline by area $Q'_2\, abQ'_1$ in the union sector, it would increase by *less than* $Q_1 cdQ_2$ in the nonunion sector. In the extreme, if all $Q'_1 Q'_2$ displaced workers remained unemployed in the union sector, the loss of output to society would be $Q'_2\, abQ'_1$. The same result might stem from downward wage rigidity in sector 2. If for some reason wages would not decline to W_s, it would not be profitable for sector 2 firms to hire additional workers beyond Q_1. Finally, to the extent that the threat and product market effects increase nonunion wages, workers will be displaced in that sector as well as in the union sector.

11.2   World of Work

Labor Strife and Product Quality

In 2000, 14.4 million Bridgestone/Firestone tires were recalled. About 6.5 million of the tires were still being used, mostly on Ford Explorers. The National Highway Traffic and Safety Administration issued a statement claiming that the recalled tires were related to 271 deaths and more than 800 injuries. The most frequent reason for the failure of the tires was the separation of the rubber tread from the steel belts, which causes a tire to blow out.

Some observers suggested at the time that a long and contentious strike at a Bridgestone/Firestone plant in Decatur, Illinois, may have played a role in causing the tire defects. Tires are still mostly handmade; so human error can lower product quality. Krueger and Mas confirm the speculation that the labor strife lowered product quality. They find that the defect rate was greatest when management requested concessions from workers and when striking workers returned and worked alongside replacement workers hired during the strike. This finding suggests that workers provide more careful work and effort when they feel they are being treated well.

The labor strife imposed costs in various ways. Krueger and Mas estimate that more than 40 deaths were caused by the labor dispute. The number of deaths would have been more than twice as high if the tires had not been recalled. The labor strife also hurt the financial health of Bridgestone/Firestone because tires manufactured at the Decatur plant during the labor dispute were 15 times more likely to have resulted in a financial claim against the company than those manufactured at other Bridgestone/Firestone plants. The market value of the firm dropped from $16.7 billion to $7.5 billion in the four months following the recall. This suggests that good labor relations are beneficial for both management and labor.

Source: Alan B. Krueger and Alexandre Mas, "Strikes, Scabs, and Tread Separations: Labor Strife and the Production of Defective Bridgestone/Firestone Tires," *Journal of Political Economy,* April 2004, pp. 253–289.

2. **Job search costs:** A second and related point is that our model understates the loss of output because it implicitly assumes that workers instantly and costlessly shift from the union to the nonunion sector. Job search by unemployed workers takes time and entails both out-of-pocket costs (paying for advertisements and for the service of employment agencies) and opportunity costs (earnings forgone during the search period). And as we discovered in Chapter 9, the geographic movement that may be involved in shifting from the union to the nonunion sector is also costly.

3. **Investment behavior and productivity growth:** The model discussed in the preceding section (Figure 11.6) portrays only the *static* or short-run efficiency effects of the union wage advantage. The union wage differential may also have an adverse *dynamic* or long-run effect on efficiency. Specifically, unions may reduce firm and industry profitability, thereby retarding investment and economic growth. If a powerful union can expropriate a sizable portion of the returns from a firm's investment in either physical capital (machinery and equipment) or in research and development, such investments may diminish. Because the path of labor productivity over time depends heavily on the stock of capital goods per worker and technological progress (Chapters 5 and 17), any significant union encroachment on profits from such investments could be expected to reduce the growth of labor productivity.

Empirical Estimates

Several estimates have been made of the static efficiency loss associated with union wage gains. They are in agreement that the loss is small. In a pioneering study Rees assumed a 15 percent union wage advantage and estimated that approximately 0.14 percent—only about one-seventh of 1 percent—of the domestic output was lost.[25] A more recent estimate by Freeman and Medoff indicates that "union monopoly wage gains cost the economy 0.02–0.04 percent of gross national product, which in 1980 amounted to about $5 to $10 billion or $20.00–$40.00 per person."[26] And in a 1983 study, DeFina estimated that a 15 percent union wage advantage would cause only a 0.08–0.09 percent loss of output.[27]

Positive View

Other economists believe that on balance, unions make a positive contribution to productivity and efficiency.

1 Investment and Technological Progress

One may carry Figure 11.3's discussion of the labor misallocation that stems from the union wage advantage a step further and argue that union wage increases may *accelerate* the substitution of capital for labor and *hasten* the search for cost-reducing (productivity-increasing) technologies. When faced with higher production costs due to the union wage advantage, employers will be prompted to reduce costs by using more machinery and by seeking improved production techniques that use less of both labor and capital per unit of output. In fact, if the product market is reasonably competitive, a unionized firm with labor costs that are, say, 15–20 percent higher than those of nonunion competitors will not survive unless productivity can be raised. In short, union wage pressure may inadvertently generate managerial actions that increase domestic productivity. This is essentially the opposite of the argument made a moment ago that higher union wages will reduce profits, inhibit investment in capital goods and innovation, and reduce labor productivity.

2 Unions as a Collective Voice

Freeman and Medoff have stressed the view that on balance, unions contribute to rising productivity in firms by voicing worker grievances and through their effects on labor turnover, worker security, and managerial efficiency.[28]

The Voice Mechanism The positive impact of unions on productivity occurs in part because unions function as a *collective voice* for their members in resolving disputes, improving working conditions, and so forth. If a group of workers is dissatisfied with its conditions of employment, it has two potential means of response. These are the exit mechanism and the voice mechanism. The *exit mechanism* refers to the use of the labor market—by leaving or exiting the present job in search of a better one—as a means of reacting to unpleasant employers and working conditions. In contrast, the *voice mechanism* entails communication between workers and the employer to improve working conditions and resolve worker grievances. It may well be risky for *individual* workers to express their dissatisfaction to employers because employers may retaliate by firing such workers as "troublemakers." But unions can give workers a *collective* voice to communicate problems and grievances to management and to press for their satisfactory resolution. This enhances worker job satisfaction and morale and, therefore, increases productivity. According to Freeman and Medoff, unions can positively affect productivity not only through the voice mechanism but also in a variety of other ways.

---

[25] Albert Rees, "The Effects of Unions on Resource Allocation," *Journal of Law and Economics,* October 1963, pp. 69–78.

[26] Freeman, Richard B., and James L. Medoff. *What Do Unions Do?* (New York: Basic Books, 1984).

[27] Robert H. DeFina, "Unions, Relative Wages, and Economic Efficiency," *Journal of Labor Economics,* October 1983, pp. 408–429.

[28] Freeman and Medoff, op. cit., Chapter 11. For a critical review of the collective voice role of unions, see John T. Addison and Clive R. Belfield, "Union Voice," *Journal of Labor Research,* Fall 2004, pp. 563–596.

Reduced Turnover Substantial evidence exists that unionization reduces quits and turnovers. On the one hand, the collective voice of the union may be effective in correcting job dissatisfaction that otherwise would be resolved by workers through the exit mechanism of changing jobs. On the other hand, other things being the same, the union wage advantage will tend to reduce the quit rates of union workers.

A variety of studies suggest that the decline in quit rates attributable to unionism is substantial, ranging from 31 to 65 percent.[29] A lower quit rate increases efficiency by producing a more experienced labor force within unionized firms and by reducing the firm's recruitment, screening, and hiring costs. Furthermore, the reduced turnover makes investments in specific training by employers more attractive. Reduced turnover increases the likelihood that the employer will capture a positive return on worker training.

Seniority and Informal Training

Because of union insistence on the primacy of seniority in such matters as promotion and layoff, worker security is enhanced. Given this security, workers are more willing to pass on their job knowledge and skills to new or subordinate workers through informal on-the-job training. Obviously this enhances labor quality and productivity.[30]

Managerial Performance

Union wage pressure may precipitate a *shock effect* that is favorable to productivity. Confronted with a strong union and higher wage demands, firms may be forced to adopt better personnel and production methods to meet the union's wage demands and maintain profitability. For example, in his study of the impact of unionization on productivity in the cement industry, Clark observes that after unionization, plant management was improved.[31] He documents a managerial shift to "a more professional, businesslike approach to labor relations." Furthermore, after unionization, greater stress was placed on production goals and the monitoring of worker performance. "Perhaps the most cogent description of the differences in the management process before and after unionization was given by a plant manager who remarked, '. . . before the union this place was run like a family; now we run it like a business.'[32]" Finally, it is worth noting that collective bargaining provides a potential avenue of communication through which the union can point out to management ways of enhancing productivity.

Recapitulation: Unions may improve efficiency by (*a*) functioning as a collective voice mechanism for resolving worker grievances, (*b*) reducing worker turnover, (*c*) enhancing worker security and thereby creating an environment favorable to on-the-job training, and (*d*) stimulating managerial efficiency through the shock effect.

Empirical Evidence

Many studies have been undertaken to measure the impact of unionization on productivity. These studies attempt to control for labor quality, capital–labor ratios, the newness of capital equipment, and other

---

[29] Freeman and Medoff, op. cit. pp. 95–96.

[30] The "lifetime" job security that some Japanese firms provide for a portion of their labor force is often cited as an important determinant of their rapid productivity growth. However, the contention that unionization increases on-the-job training has been challenged, see John M. Barron, Scott M. Fuess, Jr., and Mark A. Loewenstein, "Further Analysis of the Effects of Unions on Training," *Journal of Political Economy,* July 1987, pp. 632–640. For similar findings using British and Canadian data, see Kim Hoque and Nicolas Bacon, "Trade Unions, Union Learning Representatives, and Employer-Provided Training in Britain," *British Journal of Industrial Relations,* December 2008, pp. 702–731; and David A. Green and Thomas Lemieux, "The Impact of Unionization on the Incidence of and Sources of Payment for Training in Canada," *Empirical Economics* 2–3 (2007), pp. 465–489.

[31] Kim B. Clark, "The Impact of Unionization on Productivity: A Case Study," *Industrial and Labor Relations Review,* July 1980, pp. 451–469.

[32] Clark, Kim B. "The Impact of Unionization on Productivity: A Case Study." *Industrial and Labor Relations Review 33,* no. 4 (July 1980), 451–469.

variables aside from unionization that might contribute to productivity differences. The empirical score on the union–productivity issue is about even. For every study that finds a positive union effect on productivity, another study using different data or techniques concludes that there is a negative effect. In fact, a statistical analysis of existing studies based on U.S. data reveals that the mean effect of unions on productivity is a positive 3 percent.[33] Hirsch in a recent survey concludes that the average union effect on productivity is near zero.[34]

Hirsch argues that two patterns have emerged regarding union productivity effects. First, the impact of unions on productivity tends to be larger in industries where the union wage advantage is largest. This finding is consistent with the shock effect of unions, where firms respond to higher wage costs by operating more efficiently and thus raising productivity. Second, the positive union productivity effects are mostly confined to the private for-profit sector, and the largest productivity effects are in the most competitive industries. For example, positive productivity effects do not appear in public libraries, schools, government agencies, or law enforcement.

 Although there is less evidence regarding the long-run effects of unions on productivity, existing empirical evidence suggests that unionized firms have lower productivity growth. Nearly all of the lower productivity growth for unionized firms seems to be due to these firms being in industries that have slow productivity growth.[35] There is apparently no *direct* effect of unions on productivity growth. However, unions *indirectly* lower productivity growth by reducing the rate of investment in physical capital and research development activity.[36]

FIRM PROFITABILITY

Does unionization raise or lower firm and industry profitability? Do the wage gains of union workers come at the expense of business profits? Or do productivity increases that *may* accompany unionization offset higher wages so that profits are unaffected? Or are unionized firms and industries able to shift their higher wage costs to consumers through higher product prices and thereby preserve profitability?

Virtually all empirical studies associate unionization with diminished profitability. (Indeed, it would be difficult to reconcile employer resistance to unions if the opposite were true.) Freeman and Medoff, for example, report significant (17–37 percent) reductions in profits due to unionization.[37] Two studies using firm-level data report that unionization reduces profitability.[38] Similarly, a statistical analysis of 45 existing studies reveals that the mean effect of unions on profits for U.S. firms is negative 23 percent if a firm is completely unionized and is negative 6 percent for the average unionization rate.[39]

---

[33] Hristos Doucouliagos and Patrice Laroche, "What Do Unions Do to Productivity? A Meta-Analysis," *Industrial Relations,* October 2003, pp. 650–691.

[34] Barry T. Hirsch, "Unions, Dynamism, and Economic Performance," in *Research Handbook on the Economics of Labor and Employment Law,* Michael Wachter and Cynthia Estlund, eds., Edward Elgar Series of Research Handbooks in Law and Economics, 2012.

[35] Ibid.

[36] For evidence that unions reduce innovation activities, see Daniel Bradley, Incheol Kim, and Xuan Tian, "Do Unions Affect Innovation?" *Management Science,* pp. 2251–2271.

[37] Freeman and Medoff, op. cit., Table 12.1, p. 183.

[38] Barry T. Hirsch, "Union Coverage and Profitability among U.S. Firms," *Review of Economics and Statistics,* February 1991, pp. 69–77; Stephen G. Bronars, Donald R. Deere, and Joseph S. Tracy, "The Effects of Unions on Firm Behavior: An Empirical Analysis Using Firm-Level Data," *Industrial Relations,* October 1994, pp. 426–451; and Barry T. Hirsch, "Unionization and Economic Performance: Evidence on Productivity, Profits, Investment, and Growth," in Fazil Mihlar (ed.), *Unions and Right-to-Work Laws,* Vancouver, B. C.: The Fraser Institute, 1997, pp. 35–70.

[39] Hristos Doucouliagos and Patrice Laroche, "Unions and Profits: A Meta-Regression Analysis," *Industrial Relations,* January 2009, pp. 146–184.

Is this redistribution from profits to wages desirable? There are two polar scenarios. Scenario 1: If the unionized industry is less competitive, the effect of a union may simply be to transfer unwarranted "excess" profits from the pockets of capitalists to those of workers, with no negative effects on economic efficiency. Scenario 2: If the unionized industry is highly competitive and profits are, therefore, about normal, higher union wage costs may have adverse effects. Specifically, higher wage costs will mean below-normal profits and the impairment of investment in capital equipment and technological progress; and in the long run, firms will leave the industry. The resulting smaller output will mean higher product prices for consumers and less employment for workers. Declining investment in the industry will mean a lower overall rate of economic growth.

11.3 World of Work

Unions and Investment

Theoretically, the impact of unions on firm investments in physical capital is ambiguous. One possibility is that the union wage advantage may cause firms to substitute relatively cheaper capital and thus increase their investment rate. Alternatively, higher union wages may raise the price of the product and reduce the amount of output sold. This would lower the rate of return on investment and reduce the investment rate. In addition, if unions can extract a large share of the returns to physical capital through higher wages, then firms will reduce their rate of investment.

Fallick and Hassett examine the impact of unions on investment decisions using a sample of more than 2,000 firms listed on the New York Stock Exchange. They find that a successful election certifying a new union lowers investment in capital by 30 percent in the year following the election. They note that unionization has about the same effect as would a doubling of the corporate tax rate of 34 percent. Fallick and Hassett suggest this evidence helps explain why unionized firms tend to merge with other unionized firms, whereas nonunionized firms normally merge with nonunion companies. They argue that these outcomes result from the substantial "tax" that unions place on a firm's investments. If one union firm buys another, this tax will have no effect on the value of the acquired assets. But if a nonunion firm buys a union firm, the assets of the nonunion firm become subject to the tax liability of the union. As a result, nonunion firms are less likely than union firms to merge with a unionized firm.

Source: Bruce C. Fallick and Kevin A. Hassett, "Investment and Union Certification," *Journal of Labor Economics,* July 1999, pp. 570–82.

Which scenario is more relevant? Empirical findings differ. Some research indicates that unions obtain part of the profits that result from a firm's market power. Specifically, unions appear to capture profits resulting from limited import competition as well as entry restrictions.[40] For example, union workers in the airline and trucking industries received large wage premiums prior to the deregulation of these industries. In other words, these findings seem to support the more socially desirable scenario 1 than the less desirable scenario 2. Other empirical results support the opposite conclusion. These findings suggest that unions achieve wage gains by reducing the return on firm investments in research and development and physical capital.[41] This, of course, lends support to scenario 2.

---

[40] See Hirsch, 2012, op. cit.

[41] See Hirsch, 1991, op. cit; and Brian E. Becker and Craig A. Olson, "Unions and Firm Profits," *Industrial Relations,* Fall 1992, pp. 395–415.

11.2 *Quick Review*

- Unions may impair efficiency and productivity through *(a)* restrictive work rules, *(b)* strikes, and *(c)* labor misallocation resulting from the union wage advantage.
- The static efficiency loss from unionism is thought to be relatively small.
- Unions may positively contribute to efficiency and productivity through *(a)* inadvertently accelerating the substitution of capital for labor and hastening the search for cost-reducing technologies and *(b)* serving as a collective voice mechanism that reduces labor turnover, enhances worker security, and induces managerial efficiency.
- Empirical evidence of the union impact on productivity is mixed and inconclusive.
- Studies indicate that unions significantly reduce the profitability of firms.

Your Turn

Explain why the following two statements could be consistent: "Unions enhance productivity"; "unions reduce firm profitability." (*Answer:* See page 541.)

To summarize: There is agreement that, overall, unions reduce firm profitability. But there is no consensus about whether this redistribution reduces economic efficiency.

DISTRIBUTION OF EARNINGS

Some disagreement also arises about the impact of unions on the distribution of earnings. A few economists reason that unions contribute to earnings inequality; most take precisely the opposite view.

Increasing Inequality

Those who argue that unions increase inequality in the distribution of wages contend that unions (*a*) simultaneously increase the wages of union workers and depress the wages of nonunion workers through the spillover effect, (*b*) raise the wages of skilled blue-collar workers relative to those of unskilled blue-collar workers, and (*c*) increase the demand for skilled labor within unionized firms.

Union-Nonunion Wages

Perhaps the simplest argument in support of the position that unions enhance inequality is based on the spillover effect. Recall once again that the higher wage rates realized in the union sector of Figure 11.2 displace workers who then seek reemployment in the nonunion sector. The result of this displacement is that nonunion wage rates are depressed; thus, although we began with equal rates of W_n in both submarkets, the effect of unionism is to generate higher wage rates of W_u for union workers but lower wages of W_s for nonunion workers.

Blue-Collar Wages

The fact that unionization is more extensive among the more highly skilled, higher-paid blue-collar workers than among less skilled, lower-paid blue-collar workers also suggests that the obtaining of a wage advantage by unions increases the dispersion of earnings.

Skilled Labor Demand

Pettengill[42] has argued that when unions force employers to pay above-equilibrium wage rates, the long-run response is to hire higher-quality workers. This constitutes a shift in the structure of labor demand away from low-quality and toward high-quality workers. The net result is a widening of the dispersion of wages or, in short, greater wage inequality.

Pettengill elaborates his reasoning with the following example shown in Table 11.2. Here we assume that *A, B,* and *C* designate various levels of labor quality—say, high school graduates, high school dropouts, and workers with no high school education, respectively—that are available to a nonunion employer. The productivity or output per hour of each quality level is given in column 2, and wage rates are specified in column 3. By dividing productivity into the wage rate, we obtain wage cost per unit of output as shown in column 4. Given these options, the firm will hire *B* labor at $4 per hour because the associated wage costs per unit of output are minimized.

Now suppose the firm is unionized and the wages of *B* labor increase to $30.00. What are the consequences? In the short run, the per-unit cost of production rises to $7.50 and the lifetime earnings prospects of *B* workers are enhanced. In the long run, the normal attrition of *B* workers through retirement, voluntary quits, deaths, and so forth will prompt the firm to replace such workers with *A* workers. That is, if the union forces the employer to pay $30.00 per hour for labor, the firm will seek the best-qualified workers obtainable at that wage rate. Specifically, the firm will now require all of its new employees to have a high school diploma. Note that when all *B* workers are eventually replaced with *A* workers at the $30.00 wage rate, labor costs per unit of output will have fallen from $7.50 to $6.00 because *A* workers are more productive.

If this scenario is repeated on a wide scale, we find that an increase in the demand for high-quality *A* workers and a decline in the demand for lower-quality *B* workers occur. This causes the ratio of the going wage of high school graduates to increase relative to the going wage of high school dropouts, widening the dispersion of wages and increasing earnings inequality. Less obviously, the higher wages for high school graduates will reduce the incremental income received by college graduates in comparison with high school graduates (see Figure 4.2). This decline in the college premium will reduce the rate of return on an investment in a college education and in time reduce the supply of college graduates. As a result, the wages and salaries received by college graduates will tend to rise, further increasing the dispersion of wages and increasing earnings inequality.

TABLE 11.2 Labor Quality, Productivity, and Wage Rates

(1) Type of Labor	(2) Output per Hour	(3) Wage Rate	(4) = (3) ÷ (2) Wage Cost per Unit of Output
A	5	$30.00	$6.00
B	4	20.00	5.00
C	2	12.50	6.25

[42] John S. Pettengill, *Labor Unions and the Inequality of Earned Income* (Amsterdam: North-Holland Publishing Company, 1980).

Promoting Equality

Other aspects of union wage policies, however, suggest that unionism promotes greater, not less, equality in the distribution of earnings. What are these other ways in which unions tend to equalize wages?

1 Uniform Wages within Firms

Without unions, employers are apt to pay different wages to individual workers on the same job. These wage differences are based on perceived differences in job performance, length of job tenure, and perhaps favoritism. Unions, on the other hand, have a tradition of seeking uniform wage rates for all workers performing a particular job. In short, while nonunion firms usually assign wage rates to *individual workers,* unions—in the interest of worker allegiance and solidarity—seek to assign wage rates to *jobs.* To the extent that unions are successful, wage and earnings differentials based on supervisory judgments of individual worker performance are eliminated. An important side effect of this standard-wage policy is that wage discrimination against African–Americans, other minorities, and women is likely to be less when a union is present. Recall from Chapter 10 that African–American male workers tend to benefit more from unionization than any other demographic group.

Wage and earnings inequality within a firm may be reduced by unionism for another reason. Industrial unions—those comprising a variety of workers, ranging from unskilled to highly skilled—frequently follow a wage policy of seeking equal *absolute* wage increases for all of their constituents. This means that larger *percentage* increases are realized by less skilled workers, and the earnings gap between unskilled and skilled workers is reduced. Consider this simple illustration. Assume that skilled workers are initially paid $20 and unskilled workers $10 per hour. Suppose the union negotiates equal $4 increases for both groups so that skilled workers now receive $24 and unskilled $14 per hour. Originally unskilled workers earned 50 percent (= $10/$20) of what skilled workers received. But after the wage increase, unskilled workers get about 58 percent (= $14/$24) of skilled wages. Relative wage inequality has diminished.

Why would an industrial union adopt a policy of equal absolute wage increases for workers of different skills? The answer is twofold. On the one hand, it reflects the union's egalitarian ideology. On the other hand, it allows union leaders to largely sidestep politically awkward and potentially divisive decisions concerning the relative worth of various groups of constituents.

2 Uniform Wages among Firms

In addition to seeking standard wage rates for given occupational classes *within* firms, unions also seek standard wage rates *among* firms. The rationale for this policy is almost self-evident. The existence of substantial wage differences among competing firms in an industry may undermine the ability of unions to sustain and enhance wage advantages. For example, if one firm in a four-firm oligopoly is allowed to pay significantly lower wages to its union workers, the union is likely to find it difficult to maintain the union wage advantage in the other three firms. In particular, during a recession the high-wage firms are likely to put great pressure on the union to lower wages to the level of the low-wage firm. To avoid this problem, unions seek to "take labor (wages) out of competition" by standardizing wage rates among firms, thereby reducing the degree of wage dispersion. You may recall from Chapter 10 that multi-employer bargaining that culminates in an industry-wide contract is an important means of standardizing wage rates.

3 Reducing the White-Collar to Blue-Collar Differential

In examining the empirical evidence on the union wage advantage, we observed that unions achieve larger wage gains for blue-collar workers than for white-collar workers. Because on the average white-collar workers enjoy higher earnings than do blue-collar workers, the larger wage gains that unions achieve for the latter reduce earnings inequalities between blue- and white-collar workers.

Increased Equality?

WW 11.4

What is the *net* effect of unionism on the distribution of earnings? There is a rather strong consensus that unions decrease the degree of wage dispersion. Freeman and Medoff have used empirical analysis to conclude that the spillover effect *increases* earnings inequality by about 1 percent, but the standardization of wage rates within and among firms *decreases* inequality by about 4 percent. The net result is a 3 percent decline in earnings inequality due to unionism. Noting that only a relatively small percentage of the labor force is unionized, the authors contend that this 3 percent reduction in inequality should be regarded as "substantial."[43] This conclusion is reinforced by Card[44] who estimates that unions reduced wage inequality by 7 percent in 1987. He also points to the decline in unionism as a contributor to the recent increase in wage inequality in the United States (Chapter 17). For the 1973–1974 to 1993 period, Card concludes that 15–20 percent of the rise in earnings inequality among male workers and little of the rise in inequality among female workers was due to declining unionism.[45] In a recent study, Farber, Herbst, Kuziemko, and Naidu find that the rise in unionization contributed to the decline in inequality during the 1940–1960 period and the fall in unionization helps explain the rise in inequality in the 1970–2004 period.[46] The estimated change in inequality due to changes in unionism is sensitive to the methodology employed.

OTHER ISSUES: INFLATION, UNEMPLOYMENT, AND INCOME SHARES

Our discussion of the possible economic impact of unions is not complete. Unions could conceivably affect inflation, employment and unemployment, and the share of national income paid as wages. Let's briefly assess each, necessarily leaving detailed discussion to textbooks about macroeconomics.

Inflation

Economists generally agree that union wage determination is *not* a basic cause of inflation. Most of our serious inflationary episodes have been associated with excess aggregate demand or supply shocks rather than wage push considerations. Specifically, recent inflations can be attributed largely to expansionary fiscal or monetary policies or supply shocks, such as the dramatic Organization of Petroleum Exporting Countries oil price increases of the 1970s. On the other hand, wage determination under collective bargaining may perpetuate an ongoing inflation because unions may seek and receive wage gains in anticipation of future inflation. These actions hinder the effectiveness of anti-inflationary policies.

---

[43] Freeman and Medoff, op. cit., pp. 90–93, and additional studies cited therein.

[44] David Card, "The Effect of Unions on the Structure of Wages: A Longitudinal Analysis," *Econometrica,* July 1996, pp. 957–979.

[45] David Card, "The Effect of Unions on Wage Inequality in the U.S. Labor Market," *Industrial and Labor Relations Review,* January 2001, pp. 296–315, see also David Card, Thomas Lemieux, and W. Craig Riddell, "Unions and Wage Inequality," *Journal of Labor Research,* Fall 2004, pp. 519–559.

[46] Henry S. Farber, Daniel Herbst, Ilyana Kuziemko, Suresh Naidu, "Unions and Inequality Over the Twentieth Century: New Evidence from Survey Data," National Bureau of Economic Research Working Paper Number 24587, May 2018.

11.4   World of Work

Unions and Executive Compensation

Executive compensation is an important tool to attract top executive talent, but it has often been criticized as being too high. Chief Executive Officer (CEO) pay has soared relative to average worker pay over the past three decades (see Chapter 7). Critics argue that the high CEO pay is the result of cozy relationships between corporate board members, who set CEO pay, and CEOs. Many members of corporate boards are themselves CEOs of other corporations and often overate CEO's importance and worth.

Huang, Jiang, Lie, and Que examine whether labor unions may pressure corporate boards to curtail the pay of CEOs. Unions argue that CEOs receive a too large share of corporate revenue and the large pay gap between CEO and average worker pay reduces worker morale. Using data from 1993 to 2011, they find that a one-standard-deviation increase in industry unionization lowers CEO compensation by 9.2 percent or about $260,000.

The negative impact of unionization on CEO compensation is larger when unions are in a stronger bargaining position. For example, the union effect is larger for firms in states with no right-to-work laws, lower unemployment rates, and firms with concentrated business operations.

Corporate boards appear to strategically reduce CEO compensation around contract negotiation times to win concessions and cooperation from unions. A one-standard-deviation increase in the share of workers in contract negotiations lowers CEO compensation by 7.5 percent in the year before negotiations. The decline in CEO pay is largest for equity-based compensation likely because the firms can readily alter this compensation component. The reduction in CEO compensation before contract negotiations may be because high, recent increases in CEO compensation before contract negotiations raise the probability of a strike. These compensation reductions are more likely to occur among strong and independent corporate boards.

Source: Based on Qianqian Huang, Feng Jiang, Erik Lie, and Tingting Que, "The Effect of Labor Unions on CEO Compensation," *Journal of Financial and Quantitative Analysis,* April 2017, pp. 553–582.

Unions and Unemployment

The relationship between unionism and unemployment is complex and highly controversial. One view is that unions are a major cause of downward wage inflexibility in our economy.[47] As a result, declines in labor demand affect employment almost exclusively and not wages. Because of the downward inflexibility of wages, wage reduction cannot cushion or ameliorate the impact of recession on unemployment. The counterview is that downward wage rigidity is largely attributable to factors other than unionism. For example, nonunion workers have informal understandings or implicit contracts with employers that obligate employers to maintain wage rates unless economic conditions are so severe as to threaten the firm with bankruptcy. Furthermore, firms may prefer selective layoffs to across-the-board wage reductions during an economic slump. The reason is that the latter might cause higher-skilled, more experienced workers in whom the firm has made large training investments to quit and take other jobs. A fixed-wage-with-layoffs strategy allows employers to hoard these more valuable workers during an economic downturn and to lay off less trained workers who can be more easily and less expensively replaced.

---

[47] See Chapter 18 for a fuller discussion.

Apart from cyclic changes in labor demand, unions may affect employment in at least two other ways. First, unionism is associated with lower worker turnover, which tends to reduce unemployment rates. Second, by raising wages unions may increase unemployment by attracting additional workers into the labor force (see Figure 10.7 and the accompanying discussion).

Overall, the unionism–unemployment picture is mixed, and no consensus exists about the net effect. It is relevant to note, however, that in one study Montgomery examined data for some 42 metropolitan areas in an attempt to assess the impact of union strength (as measured by both the percentage of workers organized and the size of the union–nonunion wage differential) on employment. He found that greater union strength is associated with a lesser likelihood of employment, but the quantitative effects are very small. For example, a 10 percent increase in the percentage of workers unionized reduces the likelihood of being employed by only 0.2 percent. Similarly, a 10 percent increase in the union wage premium reduces the likelihood of being employed by just 0.06 percent.[48]

Labor's Share

There is no significant evidence to suggest that unions have been able to increase labor's share and decrease the capitalist share of national income. The reasons for this are several. In the first place, as our analysis of the spillover effect implies, higher wages for union workers may come largely at the expense of the wages of nonunion workers (Figure 11.2) and not out of the capitalist share. Second, union wage increases may induce the substitution of capital for labor; therefore, the potential positive effect that higher union wages have on labor's share in the unionized sector may be offset by the negative effect associated with fewer union jobs. Finally, management may largely escape a redistribution of national income from capital to labor through productivity and price increases. The potential encroachment on profits stemming from wage increases may partially be absorbed or offset by productivity or price increases. The lack of any significant impact on labor's share is undoubtedly related to the fact that only a relatively small percentage of the labor force is unionized.

Chapter Summary

1. Considerations other than the presence of unions may explain at least in part why strongly unionized industries pay higher wages than weakly organized industries. These factors include relatively fewer female workers, larger-scale plants, and more capital-intensive production methods in the strongly unionized industries.

2. The pure union wage advantage A is equal to $(W_u - W_n) / W_n \times 100$, where W_u is the union wage and W_n the nonunion wage that would exist without unions.

3. The spillover and superior worker effects cause the measured union wage advantage to overstate the pure wage advantage; the threat and product market effects cause the measured union wage advantage to understate the pure wage advantage.

4. Research evidence consistently indicates that unions achieve a wage advantage for their constituents, although the size of the advantage varies substantially by occupation, industry, race, and gender. Estimates by Lewis for the 1923–1958 period suggest that the average union wage advantage was on the order of 10–15 percent, but the advantage widens during depression and diminishes when unexpected inflation occurs. The union wage advantage widened in the mid-1970s. The advantage has fallen since then to 14 percent.

5. Union workers also generally receive a higher level and greater variety of fringe benefits, causing the union total compensation advantage to exceed the wage advantage.

[48] Edward Montgomery, "Employment and Unemployment Effects of Unions," *Journal of Labor Economics,* April 1989, pp. 170–190.

6. Disagreement exists about whether the net effect of unions on allocative efficiency and productivity is positive or negative. The negative view cites *(a)* the inefficiencies associated with union-imposed work rules, *(b)* the loss of output through strikes, and *(c)* the misallocation of labor created by the union wage advantage.

7. The positive view contends that *(a)* union wage pressure spurs technological advance and the mechanization of the production process and *(b)* as collective voice institutions, unions contribute to rising productivity by resolving worker grievances, reducing labor turnover, enhancing worker security, and inducing greater managerial efficiency.

8. Consensus exists that unions reduce firm profitability, but disagreement arises over whether this reduction has undesirable effects on economic efficiency.

9. Those who contend that unions increase earnings inequality argue that *(a)* unionization increases the wages of union workers but lowers the wages of nonunion workers; *(b)* unions are strongest among highly paid, skilled blue-collar workers but are relatively weak among low-paid, unskilled blue-collar workers; and *(c)* union wage increases generate an increase in the demand for high-quality workers and a decline in the demand for low-quality workers. The opposing view is that unions contribute to greater earnings equality because *(a)* unions seek uniform wages for given jobs within firms, *(b)* unions favor uniform wages among firms, and *(c)* unions have achieved higher wage gains for relatively low-paid blue-collar workers than for relatively high-paid white-collar workers. Recent empirical evidence finds that unionism does reduce wage inequality and that the decline of unionism has contributed to growing wage inequality.

Terms and Concepts

pure union wage advantage	superior worker effect
spillover effect	fringe benefits
measured union wage advantage	featherbedding
threat effect	collective voice
product market effect	exit and voice mechanisms
wait unemployment	shock effect

Questions and Study Suggestions

1. What is the commonsense basis for expecting a union wage advantage? Explain how each of the following differences between union and nonunion firms might complicate one's determination of whether unions actually are responsible for an observed wage advantage: *(a)* the demographic makeup of the labor forces, *(b)* plant sizes, and *(c)* the amount of capital equipment used per worker.

2. Evidence suggests that the union wage advantage varies directly with the proportion of a given industry that is organized. Why is this?

3. How is the pure union wage advantage defined? If in a given labor market the wage rate would be $16 without a union and $20 with a union, then what is the pure union wage advantage? Explain how, and in what direction, each of the following might cause the measured union wage advantage to vary from the pure advantage: *(a)* the spillover effect, *(b)* the threat effect, *(c)* the product market effect, and *(d)* the superior worker effect.

4. Indicate the overall size of the measured union wage advantage. Does recent evidence suggest that the advantage has increased or decreased? Comment on and explain cyclic changes in the union wage advantage.

5. Compare the size of the fringe benefits received by union and nonunion workers and indicate why unions might be responsible for any differences.

6. Comment on each of the following statements:

   a. "Unions tie the hands of management and inhibit efficient decision making."

   b. "Unions contribute to economic efficiency in that union wage pressure hastens the weeding out of the high-cost, least efficient producers in each industry."

   c. "Although unions may reduce wage inequality, to the extent that they reduce wage differentials based on individual merit and effort, the outcome may be rightly perceived as both inequitable and inefficient."

   d. "Unions impair the efficiency of our economy indirectly by diminishing profits and thereby reducing investment and economic expansion."

7. Indicate the amount of work time lost each year because of strikes. Cite circumstances under which the amount of work time lost during a specific strike might be a poor indicator of the amount of lost output.

8. "There is an inherent cost to society that accompanies any union wage gain. That cost is the diminished efficiency with which labor resources are allocated." Explain this contention. Do you agree? In your response, distinguish between static and dynamic efficiency.

9. Evidence suggests that firms that sell their products in less competitive product markets are more likely to be unionized than firms selling in highly competitive markets. Recalling from Chapter 5 that the elasticity of product demand is an important determinant of the elasticity of labor demand, how might this affect (a) the elasticities of the union and nonunion demand curves in Figure 11.6 and (b) the net loss of output due to the union wage advantage?

10. In what specific ways might the presence of a union raise productivity within a firm? Use the exit mechanism and voice mechanism concepts in your response.

11. Describe the various avenues through which unions might alter the distribution of earnings. On balance, do unions enhance or mitigate wage dispersion?

12. Would our economy function better if it were union-free? Explain your answer. Provide a counterargument to your position.

13. What has been the impact of deregulation on the relative wages and employment of unionized workers in the airline and trucking industries? What factors help explain the difference in outcomes between the airline and trucking industries?

Internet Exercise

What Is Up (or Down) with Relative Union Earnings?

 Go to the Bureau of Labor Statistics website (http://www.bls.gov) and select "Economic Releases." Find and select "Employment & Unemployment." Under "Quarterly, annual, and other" find "Union Members." What are the median weekly earnings of union members compared with the median for nonunion wage-earning and salaried workers for the most recent year? What is the measured union wage advantage?

Provide *one* other statistic of your choice from the data on union and nonunion wages.

Internet Links

The Bureau of Labor Statistics Work Stoppages website reports statistics regarding strikes involving 1,000 or more workers **(http://www.bls.gov/wsp)**.

Chapter 12

Government and the Labor Market: Employment, Expenditures, and Taxation

After reading this chapter, you should be able to:

1. Compare and contrast public sector compensation and employment growth with that of the private sector.
2. Discuss the differences between the effects of an all-volunteer military versus a conscription military.
3. Explain the effects on labor supply and demand of the government's nonpayroll spending.
4. Discuss the effects on labor supply and demand of publicly provided goods and services.
5. Explain the impact of income taxes on wages and employment for individuals and overall.

In Chapters 10 and 11, we discussed the role of unions in influencing wage rates and employment levels in labor markets. We now turn our attention to another major institution—government—and the various ways it affects wages and employment throughout the economy. Government's participation in the labor market is substantial. For example, in 2020 the number of Americans working for federal, state, and local governments exceeded the number of workers in manufacturing jobs!

This chapter examines public sector employment and the impacts of government spending and selected taxes on wages and employment in the private sector. In the following chapter, we discuss examples of direct government intervention in labor markets via laws and regulations.

PUBLIC SECTOR EMPLOYMENT AND WAGES

Government is a major—or even the sole—employer of specific types of workers in many labor markets. For example, it hires military personnel, antitrust prosecutors, postal workers, air traffic controllers, park rangers, schoolteachers, agency managers, firefighters, and highway maintenance personnel. The demand for these employees is derived from society's demand for the public sector goods and services that these workers help provide. When the government employs workers, it "exhausts" or "absorbs" economic resources. More precisely, government employment makes a direct claim on the nation's productive capabilities. For example, when the government employs postal workers, those laborers are no longer available to produce other goods and services. Likewise, when the military either drafts personnel or persuades them to enlist voluntarily, society forgoes the private sector output that those resources could have produced. Presumably, society values the public sector output or services more highly than the alternative uses for these resources.

Government Employment: Extent and Growth

WW12.1

Figures 12.1 and 12.2 demonstrate the extent and growth of government employment in the United States since 1950. Close examination of the figures reveals several generalizations. First, the absolute number of federal civilian and state and local government employees (Figure 12.1) increased over this period. This is not surprising because total employment in the economy also rose considerably. Second, the growth of federal government employment was much less dramatic than the increase in state and local government employment. Clearly, most employment growth in the public sector since 1950 has occurred at the state and local levels of government. Federal civilian employment as a percentage of total employment fell from 3.2 percent in 1950 to 1.8 percent in 2018 (Figure 12.2). During those same years, state and local employment rose from 7.0 percent to 12.6 percent of total employment (Figure 12.2). Third, in 1950, one out of ten U.S. workers was employed by the government; by 2018, that figure had risen to about one out of seven workers. Finally, the number of active-duty personnel in the armed services (Figure 12.1) varied between 1.3 and 3.6 million during these years.

FIGURE 12.1 Government Employment in the United States

Government employment rose rapidly between 1950 and 2018, with most of the rise occurring at the state and local levels.

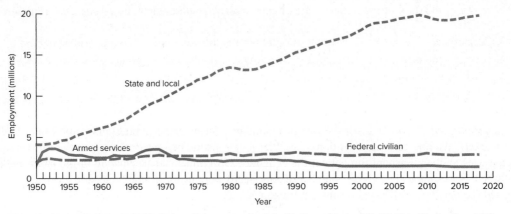

Source: Bureau of Labor Statistics and U.S. Defense Department, Statistical Information Analysis Division, "Active Duty Military Strength by Service by Fiscal Year," www.bls.gov

GP12.1

The relative growth of public sector employment over the past several decades can be envisioned in terms of our familiar labor demand and supply model (Figure 6.2). Although labor supply has increased at roughly the same pace in both the public and private sectors, the labor demand curve has shifted to the right more rapidly in the public sector than in the private sector. The result has been a faster rate of equilibrium employment growth in the public sector.

FIGURE 12.2 **Government Employment as a Percentage of Total U.S. Employment**

Relative to total U.S. employment, state and local government employment increased sharply over the last seven decades while federal civilian employment declined slightly.

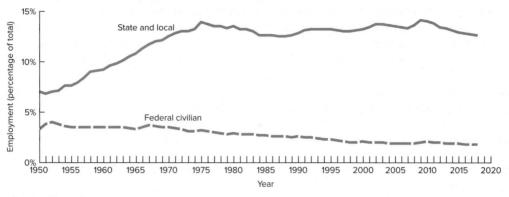

Source: Bureau of Labor Statistics, www.bls.gov

12.1   World of Work

What Do Government Workers Do?

The type of jobs government workers do depends on the level of government. State and local government employment is focused in education: Over half of such workers are in the education sector. The next largest sector is law enforcement, which accounts for about one-ninth of employment. Another large area of employment is hospitals and health, accounting for about one-twelfth of state and local government employment. Smaller sectors such as public welfare and highways together total less than one-tenth of total employment. The "other" category is composed of workers in areas such as parks and recreation, fire protection, transit, and libraries.

Federal government civilian workers are concentrated in different areas than state and local government workers. Nearly one-half of federal government workers are in defense and postal

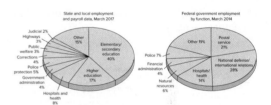

service jobs. One-seventh of workers are in the hospitals and health sector. The natural resources, police, and financial administration sectors each account for 4–7 percent of total employment. The "other" category is composed of workers in areas such as justice and law, corrections, air transportation, and social insurance administration.

Source: U.S. Census Bureau, "State and Local Government Employment and Payroll Data, by State and Function," March 2017, www.census.gov; and "Federal Government Employment by Function," Bureau of Labor Statistics, March 2014, www.bls.gov

Economists cite several reasons for this relative growth of labor demand in the public sector. In the first place, the attendant needs and problems associated with population growth, urbanization, and urban sprawl increased the demand for many state and local government services. Furthermore, the age composition of the population dramatically changed over this period. The post–World War II baby boom caused a considerable increase in school-age children, which in turn raised demand for public schoolteachers. A third factor at work was the growth of real income in society, which increased demand for such income-elastic government services as higher education, health services, parks, and a clean environment. In addition, public sector unions emerged as a more powerful and militant force in the public sector labor market. Some observers contend that public employee unions and professional groups increasingly used their political power—via campaign contributions, organizational support, endorsements, and votes—to elect government officials who favored greater spending for governmentally provided goods and services. This may have increased the derived demand for public employees.[1] Finally, the government's regulatory role in the economy has expanded over the past five decades, and this has also increased the demand for government workers.

12.1 Global Perspective

Public Sector Employment

The percentage of the labor force employed by the government varies substantially among major industrial countries.

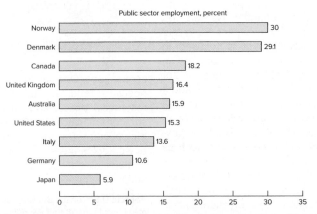

Public sector employment, percent

Country	Percent
Norway	30
Denmark	29.1
Canada	18.2
United Kingdom	16.4
Australia	15.9
United States	15.3
Italy	13.6
Germany	10.6
Japan	5.9

Source: Organization for Economic Cooperation and Development, *Government at a Glance, 2017*, www.oecd.org. The public sector includes those employed by general government and public corporations.

[1] See Paul Courant, Edward Gramlich, and Daniel Rubinfeld, "Public Employee Market Power and the Level of Government Spending," *American Economic Review,* December 1979, pp. 806–817. Marick F. Masters and John Thomas Delaney provide a good review of the scholarly literature on labor's role in U.S. national politics since 1945 in "Union Political Activities: A Review of the Empirical Literature," *Industrial and Labor Relations Review,* April 1987, pp. 336–353. In particular, see Table 1, pp. 339–342, see also John T. Delaney, Jack Fiorito, and Paul Jarley, "Evolutionary Politics? Union Differences and Political Activities in the 1990s," *Journal of Labor Research,* Summer 1999, pp. 277–295.

Public versus Private Sector Pay

The increase in public sector employment over the 1950–2018 period was accompanied by an increase in public sector pay. In theory, most governmental units adhere to a *prevailing wage rule* (or *comparable wage rule*). That is, they attempt to set public employees' wages equal to those earned by comparably trained and employed private sector workers.[2] In 2018 the average hourly pay of public sector workers was $27.77, while the average for private sector workers was $25.70.[3] But these averages fail to adjust for such factors as differences in union status, education and training, and demographic characteristics (gender, race). Smith undertook a comprehensive study in the mid-1970s to test empirically whether public sector employees did in fact achieve wages comparable to private counterparts, once these other factors were accounted for. She found that in 1975 federal employees received wages that were 13–20 percent *higher* than those earned by comparably educated and experienced private sector workers. At the state level, female workers received 6–7 percent more and males 3–11 percent less than similar private sector employees. Local government workers appeared to earn wages nearly equal to their private sector counterparts.[4]

Does the wage differential still exist? The available evidence indicates that the wage premium for public sector workers has declined appreciably since the mid-1970s. Moulton discovered that the federal pay differential had dropped by between 8 and 14 percentage points between 1977–1979 and 1988.[5] Moulton concluded that the federal pay premium is about 3 percent nationally and has disappeared entirely in high-wage urban areas and for administrative and professional occupations.[6] A recent study by Gittleman and Pierce indicates that in 2009 there was no premium for state government workers and about a 5 percent premium for local government workers.[7]

WW12.2 Several additional points are worth noting about public versus private sector pay. First, the percentage of total compensation paid in the form of fringe benefits is higher for public employees than for private workers.[8] Gittleman and Pierce report state government workers earn 3–10 percent more in total compensation than private sector workers. The premium is 10–19 percent for local government workers. Second, the rate at which federal government employees quit their jobs is lower than that of comparable workers in the private sector. Some economists conclude that this is an indication that federal workers are overpaid.[9] But others point out that the portion of federal pay taking the form of pensions is very high, which may encourage federal workers to remain in their jobs. If this is the case, quit rates may be poor indexes for judging the adequacy of pay.[10] Third, the occupational wage structure is more egalitarian within government than in the private sector (Chapter 17). Political considerations apparently cause government to pay lower-skilled workers relatively more, and elected and appointed officials relatively

---

[2] The prevailing wage principle was codified for federal workers in the Federal Pay Comparability Act of 1970. Many state and local governments have similar formal policies.

[3] Barry T. Hirsch and David A. Macpherson, *Union Membership and Earnings Data Book: Compilations from the Current Population Survey* (2019 Edition) (Washington, DC: Bureau of National Affairs, 2019).

[4] Sharon P. Smith, *Equal Pay in the Public Sector: Fact or Fantasy* (Princeton, NJ: Princeton University Press, 1977).

[5] Brent R. Moulton, "A Reexamination of the Federal–Private Wage Differential in the United States," *Journal of Labor Economics,* April 1990, pp. 270–293. For a similar conclusion using data from the 1990s, see Dale Belman and John S. Heywood, "The Structure of Compensation in the Public Sector," in Dale Belman, Morley Gunderson, and Douglas Hyatt (eds.), *Public Sector Employment in a Time of Transition* (Madison, WI: Industrial Relations Research Association, 1996).

[6] For evidence indicating that the actual public sector wage differential is reduced substantially if the analysis uses more detailed definitions of occupations, see Dale Belman and John S. Heywood, "Public Wage Differentials and the Treatment of Occupation Differences," *Journal of Policy Analysis and Management,* Winter 2004, pp. 135–152. Also see Josefa Ramoni-Perazzi and Don Bellante, "Do Truly Comparable Public and Private Sector Workers Show Any Compensation Differential?" *Journal of Labor Research,* Winter 2007, pp. 117–133.

[7] Maury Gittleman and Brooks Pierce, "Compensation for State and Local Government Workers," *Journal of Economic Perspectives,* Winter 2011, pp. 217–242.

[8] Ibid.

[9] James Long, "Are Government Workers Overpaid? Alternative Evidence," *Journal of Human Resources,* Winter 1982, pp. 123–131.

[10] Richard A. Ippolito, "Why Federal Workers Don't Quit," *Journal of Human Resources,* Spring 1987, pp. 281–299.

less, than comparably trained and experienced private sector workers. Finally, studies indicate that female and African–American workers in government receive higher pay than their counterparts in the private sector. Rather than indicating overpayment to workers, however, this higher pay may be the result of a greater relative commitment by government to equal treatment of minorities and women.[11]

12.2 World of Work

Beaches, Sunshine, and Public Sector Pay

There has been an increasing media and political attention in recent years as to whether public sector workers are overpaid relative to their private sector counterparts. This concern arises from the fact that public sector wages are set by the political process and not in a competitive market. Furthermore, unionization is high in the public sector and unions are active politically.

Economists have argued the bargaining power of public sector unions will be constrained by the out-migration of a location's residents. If a public sector union raises wage and thus increases taxes, then citizens may move from such a high tax location to a lower tax location. As a result, unions will be less able to increase wages due to a smaller tax base.

Although there will be some out-migration, Jan Brueckner and David Neumark argue that public sector unions may be able to gain higher wages in areas that are more desirable to live in. Citizens living in desirable locations receive more

utility than people living in less desirable locations. As a result, public sector unions have a greater ability to extract rents from residents of desirable areas and thus increase their wages.

Jan Brueckner and David Neumark test whether public sector workers do receive a higher wage relative to private sector workers in desirable locations. Their results indicate that the public sector workers are paid more relative to private sector workers in locations that are drier, closer to the water, or more densely populated. This pattern exists for both local and state government workers as well as subsets of public sector workers such as teachers and prison guards. The relationship between desirable location characteristics and public sector wages is stronger in states with higher rates of public sector unionization. Jan Brueckner and David Neumark suggest the adoption of weaker collective bargaining laws in desirable areas since that would lower public sector wages and thus costs.

Source: Based on Jan K. Brueckner and David Neumark, "Beaches, Sunshine, and Public Sector Pay: Theory and Evidence on Amenities and Rent Extraction by Government Workers," *American Economic Journal: Economic Policy,* May 2014, pp. 198–230.

THE MILITARY SECTOR: THE DRAFT VERSUS THE VOLUNTARY ARMY

Over the past three decades, the number of active-duty military personnel employed by the United States has varied between a high of 3 million in 1970 to a low of 1.3 million in 2018. Before 1973 the United States used the selective service system—commonly called the *draft*—to compel people to serve in the military. These draftees worked alongside *volunteers,* some of whom offered their labor services to the military rather than waiting to be drafted. Under this system of military conscription, wages were below those that many draftees and enlisted personnel could have earned in civilian sector jobs. In 1973 the federal government abandoned the draft in favor of armed services staffed by people recruited voluntarily through wages and benefits that

---

[11] This point is discussed in Robert G. Gregory and Jeff Borland, "Recent Developments in Public Sector Labor Markets," in Orley Ashenfelter and David Card (eds.), *Handbook of Labor Economics,* Volume 3C (Amsterdam: North-Holland, 1999).

were sufficiently high to attract the required number of employees. In a sense, the military has become a professional, market-based entity, much like the U.S. Postal Service, the Federal Bureau of Investigation, and the National Park Service. In fact, a 2001 study indicated that for most of a male enlistee's military career, his earnings are about the 70th percentile of those for similarly experienced full-time workers who are high school graduates and about the median for full-time workers with some college education.[12] We might add that a part of military earnings may be a compensating wage payment for the added risk and poorer working conditions generally associated with jobs in the military.

The voluntary, wage-based army remains somewhat controversial. Calls for a return to the peacetime draft or for establishment of a new system of universal national service are commonplace. Critics of the modern voluntary army argue that it produces an army drawn mainly from the ranks of low-income citizens, creates a racially imbalanced military force, reduces the overall sense of duty to one's country, and increases the cost of the military to taxpayers.

Defenders of the voluntary approach counter that the professional army is better prepared to achieve its goals, minimizes society's overall cost of allocating labor to the services, promotes the use of a more efficient combination of labor and capital in the military, creates employment opportunities for low-skilled workers, provides on-the-job training that is transferable to the private sector, and maximizes individual freedom. These defenders also argue that it is more equitable to have taxpayers, rather than draftees, bear the costs of the armed services; that the voluntary army reduces the military's training costs by lessening the turnover of personnel; and that shortages of skilled personnel or reservists can be eliminated by raising wages in the areas where more personnel are needed.

A comprehensive examination of these pros and cons is well beyond our present discussion. Because our interest is government's role in the labor market, we limit our analysis here to the *labor market* aspects of the two alternatives.

The Economics of Military Conscription

Figure 12.3 shows labor supply and demand as viewed by the military. For simplicity we assume that the market from which the military drafts personnel is perfectly competitive and that the nation is not at war. Initially disregard the labor demand curve labeled D_v and instead concentrate on curves S and D_d. The curve S is a conventional competitive supply curve as *viewed by an employer.* The perfectly inelastic demand curve D_d is drawn on the assumption that Congress authorizes the armed services to conscript or *draft* $0G$ people and pay each of them wage rate $0A$. Initially suppose that those drafted are the specific individuals who would have voluntarily enlisted had the wage rate been at the equilibrium level $0B$ rather than $0A$.

Let's now address two questions. First, what is the total wage bill that the military (taxpayers) will have to pay under this draft authorization? Second, given our assumptions, what is the overall cost to society of drafting these specific $0G$ workers? The answer to the first question is simple and straightforward. The military's wage bill is the area $0AfG$, which is found by multiplying the authorized wage $0A$ times the authorized employment level $0G$.

Is this wage bill also the total cost to society? The answer is no, and we can understand this by examining the labor supply curve. The vertical height of curve S measures the opportunity cost of using each unit of labor in this employment or, in other words, the forgone civilian earnings for each of the $0G$ workers drafted. For example, suppose these workers would earn $45,000 a year at wage rate $0B$ and only $30,000 at the military wage rate $0A$. The annual income these individuals sacrifice and the output forgone by society from drafting

---

[12] Beth J. Asch, James R. Hosek, and John T. Warner, *On Restructuring Enlisted Pay: Analysis in Support of the 9th Quadrennial Review of Military Compensation* (Santa Monica, CA: Rand, 2001).

them is $35,000 times $0G$ draftees. The fact that the military pays these workers $30,000 does *not* reflect the actual costs either to these individuals or to society. By drafting $0G$ workers, the military imposes an opportunity cost on draftees and society equal to the area under the labor supply curve, $0BcG$. It pays the draftees $0AfG$ and imposes the remainder of the cost—$ABcf$—on those drafted. This cost is the difference between what draftees could earn as civilians and the amount earned in the military. To generalize: The true social cost of drafting any specific group of workers into the military is *independent* of the total wage rate that the military pays them. The actual cost consists of the income (output) sacrificed by draftees. *Military conscription* at low pay reduces the military's (taxpayers') personnel costs, but it does *not* lower the costs of the military to society. Rather, it shifts a portion of the true costs—$15,000 per draftee in this case—from taxpayers to those drafted.[13]

Thus far, we have assumed that draftees are people who have opportunity costs that are reflected by the perfectly elastic supply curve in Figure 12.3. This assumes that government drafts only those from the low-skilled labor market—people who have low civilian earnings. But what if the military imposes a *lottery* to select the $0G$ draftees? Many of those selected will have higher civilian wage opportunities than $0B$. Stated differently,

FIGURE 12.3   The Draft versus the Voluntary Army

If the military drafts the specific group of workers $0G$ and pays each of them $0A$, the wage bill to taxpayers ($0AfG$) will be less than the total opportunity costs to those drafted ($0BcG$). Under a voluntary or market-based system, the relevant demand curve becomes D_v, the cost to taxpayers increases ($0BeH$ as compared to $0AfG$), those who volunteer are fully compensated for their opportunity costs ($0BeH$), and the military is likely to reduce its total workforce ($0G$ to $0H$). The true cost of employing any specific group of workers is *independent* of the wage bill.

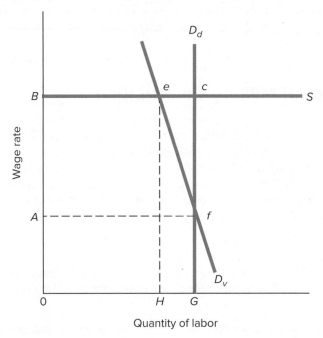

[13] An additional cost to draftees is that military service may lower future civilian earnings. Vietnam-era draftees initially had lower earnings than nondraftees during the 1970s and 1980s, but their earnings rose over time so that by 2000 they achieved parity, see Joshua D. Angrist and Stacey H. Chen, "Long-Term Consequences of Vietnam-Era Conscription: Schooling, Experience, and Earnings," *American Economic Journal: Applied Economics,* April 2011, pp. 1–24. On the other hand, voluntary military service appears to raise earnings for African-Americans and workers at the low end of the earnings distribution, see Francesco Renna and Amanda Weinstein, "The Veteran Wage Differential," *Applied Economics,* Issue 12, pp. 1284–1302.

the collective civilian wage opportunities of the $0G$ draftees selected through a lottery will exceed area $0BcG$. The relevant generalization here is that the true cost to individuals and society of a lottery draft will exceed that of a draft of low-paid civilian workers.

The Voluntary, Market-Based Approach

We can analyze the economic implications of a *voluntary or market-based army* by turning to the demand curve D_v in Figure 12.3. Notice that we have drawn a typical downward-sloping demand curve, as opposed to the perfectly inelastic one used to analyze the draft. This downward-sloping curve reflects a realistic expectation that higher market wages for military personnel will cause the armed services to reduce the number of its employees. As seen by the intersection of D_v and S, the equilibrium military wage and quantity of labor will be $0B$ and $0H$, respectively. The total wage bill to the military will be $0BeH$, which is considerably greater than $0AfG$, the total wage bill under the draft. Assuming that the military's demand for personnel is relatively inelastic, we conclude that a voluntary army will increase the money cost of military personnel to taxpayers. Notice that a voluntary army transfers income from taxpayers to military personnel so that the latter are totally compensated for their opportunity costs $0BeH$.

Figure 12.3 shows that *if* the wage rate were at the draft level of $0A$, the voluntary army would hire the same number of employees that it previously drafted ($0G$). But the existence of the voluntary army with a market-determined wage rate reduces military employment from $0G$ to $0H$. We assume that this occurs for two reasons. First, as the wage rises from $0A$ to $0B$, the military will likely substitute capital for labor. The military can lower its costs by engaging in such activities as purchasing dishwashing machines, procuring more weapons, and computerizing routine paperwork. This will enable the armed services to economize on the use of the higher-priced labor. Second, although the higher-wage bill adds nothing to the true cost of the military, it does raise the price of the armed services *as perceived by Congress and taxpayers.* We would expect this price increase to cause Congress to reduce its "output" of military services or reduce the *scale* of the total military establishment, which then would reduce military employment. The alert reader will recognize that we are here referring to both substitution and output effects of a wage rate increase.

A final point is germane to our discussion. The payment to enlistees of an amount equal to the supply price of labor rather than an artificially low wage can be expected to improve military morale and reduce labor turnover. These factors may join those previously discussed in lowering the costs of the military to society.

> **WW12.3** To summarize: Government's conscription or hiring of personnel for the military is another example of how government influences specific labor markets in the economy. Labor market analysis suggests that (*a*) the true cost of allocating personnel to the military is independent of the wage paid to those workers, (*b*) the methods (a lottery versus a draft of low-wage workers) used to obtain labor may affect the total cost of acquiring a given amount of military personnel, (*c*) the cost of a voluntary army may be less than that of a drafted army because of higher productivity related to reduced turnover and higher morale, (*d*) a voluntary army is likely to increase the price of the military as viewed by taxpayers, and (*e*) society can be expected to allocate fewer labor resources to the military under a higher-pay voluntary system than a lower-pay compulsory one.[14] Finally, while labor market analysis *can* help us understand the costs and benefits of various public policy options, it *cannot* determine which option society should select.

---

[14] For an evaluation of the voluntary army, see John T. Warner and Beth J. Asch, "The Record and Prospects of All-Volunteer Military in the United States," *Journal of Economic Perspectives,* Spring 2001, pp. 169–192.

12.3   World of Work

The Impact of Military Cutbacks on Civilians

Military bases bring jobs and investment to an area, and so military cutbacks are unpopular. The number of military personnel in the United States was relatively unchanged for most of the 1980s. However, at the end of the 1980s, the Cold War was ending, and federal deficits were rising. As a result of these changes, the U.S. government started to shrink the size of the military.

Ben Zou examined the effects of a 30 percent decline in the number of military personnel between 1988 and 2000 on local civilian labor and rental markets. This was one of the largest employment reductions for an industry in modern U.S. history. Zou compared the changes over time in wages, employment, and rents for counties with military bases with those counties which had no military bases. He finds that for every eliminated military position 1.2 civilian jobs were lost in the same county. Mainly through reduced in-migration, the county population fell by 2.4 civilians for every lost civilian job. The large population adjustment resulted in only a small change in local wages but a large decline in rental prices.

Zou finds that the military downsizing caused a negligible welfare loss for workers. A one percentage point drop in military personnel share as a portion of the population, which was the average change, caused the utility of workers to fall by a minuscule 0.02 percent. Due to the drop in rental prices, landowners bore most of the welfare loss.

Source: Based on Ben Zou "The Local Economic Impacts of Military Personnel," *Journal of Labor Economics,* July 2018, pp. 589–621.

NONPAYROLL SPENDING BY GOVERNMENT: IMPACT ON LABOR

We have established that government employment of civilian and military workers is a major factor in the overall labor market. Government's nonpayroll spending also influences wages and employment. This spending is substantial and takes two forms: (*a*) purchases of private sector goods and services and (*b*) transfer payments and subsidies. In 2018 the government purchased $2,843 billion of labor, goods, and services. About half of this amount was for goods produced by private industry. Also, government transfers and subsidies were $3,066 billion in 2018. Let's briefly examine selected labor market impacts of each category of expenditure.

Government Purchases of Private Sector Output

Government purchases include procurement of such items as computers, tanks, medical supplies, textbooks, buses, submarines, paper clips, furniture, and weather satellites. This type of spending by the government creates a derived demand for specific kinds of private sector workers. In some cases, it creates demands for labor that would not exist—or at least not be nearly as great—without government. We could expect such changes in demand to affect equilibrium wage rates and employment levels. For example, *cuts* in government spending on strategic missiles could be expected to eventually reduce the wages and employment levels of aerospace engineers. Similarly, *increases* in federal construction spending would likely increase the demand for—and the collective bargaining position of—a wide range of construction workers.

Transfer Payments and Subsidies

Government payroll expenditures and nonpayroll spending for private sector goods and services have one common feature. Both are *exhaustive* or resource-absorbing expenditures in that they account for the employment of labor and other economic resources. In contrast, transfer payments and subsidies are *nonexhaustive* because, as such, they do not directly absorb resources or account for production. More precisely, as their name implies, *transfer payments*–such as Social Security benefits to the retired, unemployment compensation, welfare payments, and veterans' benefits–transfer income from one group to another group of individuals, depending upon such criteria as age, work status, income, and military service. The recipients perform no current productive activities in return; hence, transfers are nonexhaustive. Similarly, a *subsidy* is a transfer payment to a firm, institution, or household that consumes or produces some specific product or service. Medicare for the elderly, price supports for farmers, and public education for youth are all examples of governmental subsidies.

Demand Effects

Although transfers and subsidies do not directly exhaust or absorb labor or other resources, they alter the structure of total demand in the economy and, therefore, affect the derived demands for specific types of labor. For example, cash and in-kind medical transfers provided to older Americans under provisions of the Social Security program increase the demand for products and services that older Americans tend to purchase. More specifically, the transfers increase the demand for such items as prescription and over-the-counter drugs, nursing home services, hospital care, and retirement property. This demand, in turn, increases the derived demand for workers who help produce, deliver, or sell these goods and services. In a similar sense, the cash transfers provided through welfare programs for low-income families increase the demand for a variety of products, including children's clothing, toys, and foodstuffs. Other things being equal, these increases in product demand boost product prices, which then increase the demand for labor in the affected industries (demand determinant 1, Table 6.1).

Subsidies provided to private firms and nonprofit organizations also increase the demand for specific types of workers. For instance, the U.S. government, through the Export–Import Bank, provides loans at below-market interest rates to some foreign buyers of U.S. exports. This reduces the effective price of U.S. exports while leaving the price charged by the exporters intact, thus increasing foreign purchases and ultimately the derived demand for labor in the U.S. export sector. Similarly, the federal government provides subsidies to such nonprofit organizations as private universities, which then demand more workers to deliver their services.

Supply Effects

In addition to their impact on labor demand, transfer payments and subsidies affect short- and long-run labor supply. Recall from our discussion of individual labor supply in Chapter 2 that transfers (e.g., a guaranteed income program) generate an *income effect* that tends to reduce the optimal number of work hours offered by the recipient. Put simply, transfer income induces the recipient to buy more normal goods and services, including leisure (Figure 2.12). Also, if the amount of the cash transfer is inversely related to work income–that is, if a benefit reduction rate applies to earned income–then the program creates an accompanying *substitution effect* that further reduces work effort. By reducing the opportunity cost–or price–of leisure, the transfer payment encourages the substitution of the lower-priced leisure for the now relatively higher-priced work.

Transfers and subsidies also influence long-run labor supply decisions. For example, the existence of cash and in-kind transfers may reduce incentives to invest in human capital. In essence, the present value of the net returns to the investor is reduced because future gains in earned income that result from the training or education are accompanied by the loss of future transfers. Other things being equal, the higher the benefit reduction rate of a transfer plan, the less the actual net rate of return on any given investment in human capital.

Not all transfers and subsidy programs, however, reduce long-run labor supply. Transfers and subsidies that reduce the private cost of investing in human capital produce just the opposite effect. For example, the government provides subsidized, below-market interest rates on loans to many college students. Recall that the economic rationale for these loans was outlined in Chapter 4. This subsidy reduces the private cost of investing in a college education, which increases the personal rate of return on this form of human capital. As a direct consequence, the long-run labor supply in various skilled and professional labor markets increases. In addition, we know that better-educated people stay in the labor force longer than people who have less education. We, therefore, conclude that government transfers and subsidies may either positively or negatively affect supply in specific labor markets.

LABOR MARKET EFFECTS OF PUBLICLY PROVIDED GOODS AND SERVICES

Thus far, we have established that government employment and public sector purchases of private sector output influence wage rates and employment levels in specific labor markets. We next raise an interesting related question: Do publicly provided goods and services affect labor demand and supply *independently* of the public and private employment necessary to provide these items? Publicly provided goods and services range from *pure public goods,* whose benefits are indivisible and, therefore, impossible to deny to those who have not paid for them, to goods and services provided by the government but also sold in the private sector. An example of the former is national defense; an example of the latter is college education. It is clear that some publicly provided goods *do* affect private sector demand for labor. It is also conceivable that these goods and services reduce the overall labor supply in the economy. Let's examine each possibility.

Effects on Labor Demand

The provision of public sector goods and services influences labor demand in a variety of ways. For example, suppose the government builds a major dam on a river. Assume this project creates multiple benefits such as electricity generation, flood control, irrigation, and recreational opportunities. Government affects the labor market by employing labor and private sector products to construct the dam, power station, irrigation network, and adjacent recreational areas. But the *existence* of the dam also independently affects labor demand. For example, the irrigation system will likely increase the demand for farmworkers; the new recreational opportunities will increase the demand for fishing boats, motors, and water skis, which will increase the derived demand for workers who help produce these products; the availability of cheap electric power may entice manufacturing firms to the area, thereby increasing the demand for specific skilled and unskilled workers; and control of downriver flooding may actually *reduce* the demand for flood insurance agents and claims adjusters. In fact, we may generalize as follows: Other things being equal, the provision of a public good that is a *complement* in either production or consumption to a specific private good will *increase* the derived demand for workers who help produce the private good. Conversely, the provision of a public good that is a *substitute* in production or consumption to a specific private good will *reduce* the derived demand for workers who help produce the private good.

FIGURE 12.4   Impact of Publicly Provided Goods on Individual Labor Supply

If real income is defined as the total quantity of public and private goods and services obtainable from any specific level of work, then the presence of Y_{pu} public sector goods or services shifts the effective budget constraint upward from W' to $W_1W'_1$. Assuming leisure to be a normal good and disregarding the tax consequences of the increased public sector provision, this creates an income effect that reduces the optimal number of hours worked by h_1h_2.

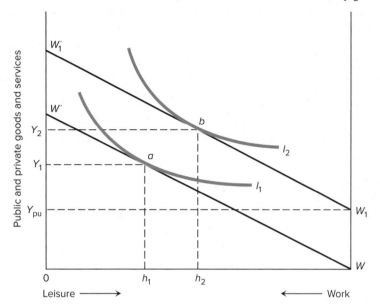

Effects on Labor Supply

A modified version of the basic income–leisure model of short-run individual labor supply suggests that publicly provided goods and services may reduce the quantity of labor supplied. Recall from Chapter 2 that the basic model of income–leisure choice contains a preference map composed of indifference curves, each one showing the various combinations of real income and leisure that yield some specific level of utility. Also recall that the model contains a wage rate, or budget, line indicating the *actual* combination of income and leisure that the individual can obtain given his or her wage.

Figure 12.4 presents a modified version of the basic model. Notice from the vertical axis that we are defining real income as the total amount of private *and* public sector goods and services obtainable from any specific level of work. Suppose that Y_{pu} (= $WW1$) of public sector goods is available to Green regardless of how much he works. The real income available to him will be Y_{pu} plus the level of private goods that his work income will allow him to obtain. Prior to the provision of Y_{pu} public goods, Green's budget constraint was WW', but the existence of the publicly provided output means that his effective budget constraint is $W_1W'_1$. This latter line shows the combinations of leisure and goods (private and public sector) available to Green at each level of work, given his wage rate. The vertical distance between the two budget lines measures the value of the public goods available to Green.

If no public goods were available to this individual, he would maximize his utility at a by working h_1 hours, from which he would earn Y_1 goods (real income). The existence of the public goods, however, creates an income effect that allows Green to "buy" more leisure. The provision of the public sector goods Y_{pu} increases his total utility by moving him from a on indifference curve I_1 to b on curve I_2. But in achieving this gain in utility, Green *reduces* his labor hours from h_1 to h_2.

12.1 *Quick Review*

- Most of the sizable growth of public sector employment occurring since 1950 has been at the state and local levels of government.

- Although a large federal pay advantage existed a decade or two ago, it is thought to have largely evaporated in recent years.

- A conscripted army at below-market pay does not reduce the cost of the military to society; it simply shifts part of the cost to those drafted. A voluntary, market-based army is likely to be less costly to society because it *(a)* reduces turnover, *(b)* creates higher morale, and *(c)* induces the military to use socially optimal combinations of labor and capital.

- Government transfers (and subsidies) and the existence of publicly provided goods have widespread impacts on labor supply and labor demand.

Your Turn

How might Figure 12.4 relate to the lack of work effort observed under the old Communist regimes of Eastern Europe and Russia? (*Answer:* See page 542.)

We thus conclude that the existence of publicly provided goods and services may reduce individual and over-all labor supply in the economy. The more closely the public goods are substitutable for private goods, the greater the reduction in labor supply. For example, free medical care provided by the public sector may reduce the incentive to earn income to pay for medical care. In fact, one study estimated that eligibility for Medicaid reduced the labor supply of childless adults by 5 percentage points or a 12 percent decline.[15] On the other hand, the more complementary the public goods are to leisure, the greater the decline in labor supply. Example: A public golf course conceivably could reduce labor supply by encouraging more leisure. Finally, the more complementary the public goods are to work, the less the reduction in labor supply. Example: By reducing the cost of getting to work, a mass-transit system may augment labor supply.

Our discussion of the labor supply effects of public goods overlooks an important fact: Government must collect taxes from people to provide the public goods in question, and these taxes also have potential labor supply impacts. It is to this topic that we turn next.

INCOME TAXATION AND THE LABOR MARKET

To this point, our emphasis has been on government's influence on labor markets through its spending and hiring decisions. We now examine the effects of selected taxes on the labor market, focusing on the personal *income tax*. Income from wages and salaries constitutes approximately 70 percent of national income in the United States. Because a large portion of this income is subjected to the personal income tax, it is particularly important to ascertain the impact of this tax on labor markets. Specifically, do workers bear the full burden of the tax in the form of lower net, or after-tax, wage rates? Or is it possible that part or all of the tax is borne by employers, who must pay higher market wage rates to attract profit-maximizing quantities of labor? What impact does the income tax have on employment?

---

[15] Laura Dague, Thomas DeLeire, and Lindsey Leininger, "The Effect of Public Insurance Coverage for Childless Adults on Labor Supply," *American Economic Journal: Economic Policy,* May 2017, pp. 124–154.

12.2 Global Perspective

Income Tax Rates*

The average income tax for the average single worker ranges from 28.9 percent in Australia to 49.5 percent in Germany.

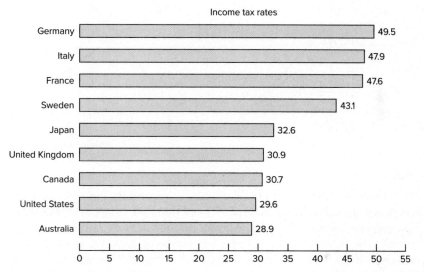

Income tax rates

Germany	49.5
Italy	47.9
France	47.6
Sweden	43.1
Japan	32.6
United Kingdom	30.9
Canada	30.7
United States	29.6
Australia	28.9

Source: Organization for Economic Cooperation and Development, *Taxing Wages, 2019* (Paris: OECD, 2019).

* The income tax rates include personal income taxes, employer Social Security contributions, and employees' Social Security contributions. Data are for 2018.

The Income Tax: Impact on Wages and Employment

We will discover from the following discussion that given the elasticity of labor demand, the effects of the personal income tax on wages and employment depend principally on the elasticity of labor supply. Figure 12.5(a) and (b) demonstrates this proposition. The labor supply curve in graph (a) is perfectly inelastic, indicating that workers do not collectively change the extent of their labor force participation in response to wage rate changes. In graph (b) the labor supply curve displays some elasticity: People collectively increase their labor hour offerings when the wage rises and reduce them when it falls.

The demand curves in the two graphs are identical and reflect the *before-tax* wage rates and corresponding quantities of labor that firms will desire to employ. The curves labeled D_t lie below the conventional demand curves in each graph and show the *after-tax* wages as viewed by workers. The progressive income tax on labor earnings pivots the after-tax wage rate lines downward from D to D_t by the amount of the tax per hour of work.

FIGURE 12.5 Impact of the Personal Income Tax on Wages and Employment

If the aggregate labor supply curve in the economy is perfectly inelastic as in (a), then the personal income tax—measured by the vertical distance between D and D_t—will not affect the market wage ($18) but will reduce the after-tax wage by the amount of the tax per hour. If the labor supply curve displays some elasticity as in (b), the tax reduces the quantity of labor hours supplied and raises the before-tax market wage—in this case from $18 to $20. Given labor demand, the greater the elasticity of labor supply, the greater the increase in the wage rate and the greater the reduction in employment resulting from the tax.

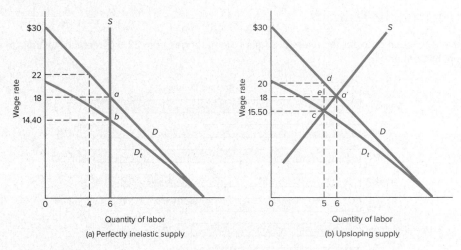

(a) Perfectly inelastic supply

(b) Upsloping supply

Table 12.1 helps us better understand the crucial distinction between the conventional labor demand curve D and the after-tax wage rate line D_t in Figure 12.5(a) and (b). Notice that columns (1) and (2) constitute the before-tax labor demand schedule, which graphically is shown as curve D in each of the figures. Columns (2) and (4) establish the after-tax wage rate lines D_t in the two graphs. Example: If the wage rate is $24 (column 1), firms will employ three workers (column 2). Observe from column (3) that the tax per hour is $6.50 at the $24 wage rate. Hence the *net* or *after-tax wage rate* is $17.50 (= $24 − $6.50), as shown in column (4). When plotted graphically against the quantity of labor, the after-tax wage rates shown in column (4) establish the D_t curves in Figure 12.5(a) and (b). The vertical distances between the demand curves and the after-tax wage rate lines measure the tax per hour of work at each particular market wage rate (and at each particular quantity of labor demanded).

Column 5 of Table 12.1 shows the average hourly tax rate (= T/W) for each wage rate. Notice that the average tax rate rises as earnings per hour increase, indicating that this tax is progressive. In terms of Figure 12.5(a) and (b), this progressivity is reflected in the fact that the distances between D and D_t increase as a percentage of the wage as the wage rises.

Perfectly Inelastic Labor Supply

Let's now focus on graph (a) in Figure 12.5. The before-tax equilibrium market wage and quantity of labor are $18 and 6 units, respectively (point a). Once the tax is introduced, however, workers perceive their net wage to be only $14.40 (= $18 − $3.60), as shown by point b. But because the supply is perfectly inelastic, the income tax will not affect the collective quantity of labor supplied; therefore, workers bear the entire burden of the tax; the before-tax wage rate remains at $18, and the after-tax hourly pay falls by the full amount of the tax, $3.60 (= $18 − $14.40).

To confirm this proposition, suppose workers are angered by their *net* wage decline and try to shift the tax to their employers. If they demand, say, $22 (= $18 + $4), employers will seek only 4 units of labor, while

TABLE 12.1 Before-Tax versus After-Tax Earnings per Unit of Labor (Hypothetical Data)

(1)	(2)	(3)	(4)	(5)
W	*Q*	*T*	*W – T*	*T/W* (%)
$28	1	$8.50	$19.50	30.4
26	2	7.50	18.50	28.8
24	3	6.50	17.50	27.1
22	4	5.50	16.50	25.0
20	5	4.50	15.50	22.5
18	6	3.60	14.40	20.0
16	7	2.80	13.20	17.5
14	8	2.10	11.90	15.0
12	9	1.50	10.50	12.5
10	10	1.00	9.00	10.0
8	11	.60	7.40	7.5
6	12	.30	5.70	5.0
4	13	.10	3.90	2.5

workers will continue to offer 6 units. Assuming competition, the excess supply of workers will drive the before-tax wage down to $18, where the labor market will once again clear. It is evident that if the labor supply curve is perfectly inelastic, employees will be unable to pass the tax forward to their employers, and the tax will have no impact on either the market wage rate or equilibrium employment.[16]

Positively Sloped Labor Supply

We next turn our attention to graph (b) in Figure 12.5, where we discover a labor supply curve that displays a positive slope. This implies that workers collectively will respond to wage or income tax changes by adjusting the amount of labor supplied. In the absence of the income tax, the equilibrium wage rate and quantity of labor are $18 and 6 units (point *a'*). How will these workers react to a newly imposed income tax? As we see from the intersection of D_t and *S,* workers will reduce the amount of labor supplied from 6 to 5 units (point *c*). Employers will encounter a labor shortage of 1 unit (= 6 − 5) *at the $18 market wage.* This excess demand will drive the wage to $20, and the market will again clear at point *d*—this time at 5 units of labor. Those still working following the tax will receive a before-tax wage rate of $20 rather than $18. The workers' after-tax wage will fall by $2.50 (= $18 − $15.50) to $15.50. Notice that this decline is less than the tax per hour of $4.50 (= $20 − $15.50). The reason is that $2 of the tax is borne indirectly by employers as higher wage rates. That is, of the total tax *dc* in Figure 12.5, *ec* is borne by workers as lower after-tax pay while *ed* is borne by employers as higher wage costs.

---

[16] This is true even in the presence of a strong union, assuming that the union has already bargained for its optimal contract package. If it has squeezed all it can extract from the employers, the sudden enactment of an income tax can do nothing to enhance its ability to gain still more.

To summarize: Other things being equal, if the overall labor supply curve slopes upward, a personal income tax will reduce the quantity of labor supplied, cause the wage rate to rise, and decrease employment. Given the elasticity of demand, the greater the elasticity of supply, the greater the portion of the income tax borne by employers in the form of a higher market wage. You might want to rework the analysis for a *perfectly elastic* labor supply curve to demonstrate that under these conditions the *entire* tax will be borne by employers and that the employment effect will be greater.

The Income Tax and Individual Labor Supply

Which of the two graphs in Figure 12.5 best portrays reality? How elastic is the overall supply of labor? Economists have approached this question both theoretically and empirically.

Theoretical Analysis

The income tax is similar in impact to a wage rate decrease: Both reduce the actual return from an hour of work and lower total net income from any specific number of hours of work. The tax generates income and substitution effects that act in opposing directions. By reducing income at any specific level of work, the tax lowers consumption of all normal goods, including leisure; therefore, the incentive to work increases (the income effect). But the tax also reduces the net return from work or, stated alternatively, decreases the opportunity cost (price) of leisure. This creates an incentive to substitute the relatively lower-priced leisure for the now relatively higher-priced work, so work declines (the substitution effect).

Graphical Depiction Figure 12.6 illustrates this graphically. The figure shows the indifference maps and budget constraints for Smith (graph a) and Jones (graph b). Notice that each graph portrays two budget lines: HW, which is linear, and HW_t, which lies below HW and increases at a diminishing rate as work hours increase from 0 to 24. The HW curves shows the *before-tax* income for Smith and Jones at each level of work hours, and the HW_t curves depict the *after-tax* income from that specific work effort. The vertical distances between HW and HW_t measure the income tax paid at each work–income combination. These distances increase as a percentage of income as income rises, again indicating that the tax is progressive.

Without the tax, Smith (graph a) will choose to work h_1 hours, earn income Y_b, and maximize her utility at point a on indifference curve I_2. Once the income tax is imposed, Smith's after-tax wage rate falls as shown by the downward shift of HW to HW_t, and she reacts by *reducing* her work effort to h_2 (point b). At this level of work, she earns a gross income of Y_g, pays a total tax of $Y_g Y_a$, and receives an after-tax income of Y_a. For Smith, the income tax *reduces* the number of labor hours supplied by $h_1 h_2$.

What is the outcome for Jones (graph b)? By employing the same logic, we find that he reacts to the tax by *increasing* his labor hours. Given his subjective preferences for income versus leisure, he discovers it to be in his interest to increase work from h_1 to h_2 (point d rather than c), earn a gross income of Y_g, pay a tax equal to the vertical distance of $Y_g Y_a$, and retain an after-tax income of Y_a. Thus, Figure 12.6 illustrates a basic point: The progressive income tax (and changes in tax rates) causes some workers to work less, others to work more, and still others to maintain their pretax level of work. For Smith (graph a), the substitution effect outweighs the income effect and she works less; but for Jones (graph b), the income effect swamps the substitution effect, leading him to work more. (Remember from Chapter 2 that the income effect increases hours of work, and the substitution effect decreases hours of work when we are considering a reduction in wages.) The basic work–leisure theory of individual labor supply does not permit us to predict whether the aggregate labor supply curve is negatively sloped, perfectly inelastic, or positively sloped. Thus, we are uncertain whether the aggregate amount of labor supplied will increase or decrease in response to, say, an income tax reduction.

Caveat

We must note, however, that this matter is not entirely settled. Recall from our previous analysis that the government's provision of public goods theoretically can produce income effects that reduce labor hour offerings. These goods are financed partially through the personal income tax and are available to people independent of their work effort. Consequently, workers need not work as much to achieve a given level of real goods or total utility. This income effect may reduce labor hours offered and offset any added work effort generated by the income effect from the imposition of the tax. If so, only a substitution effect remains, and the overall outcome may be less labor supplied.[17]

Empirical Analysis

Many economists have tried to measure the relative strengths of the income and substitution effects and thereby estimate the elasticity of aggregate labor supply in the economy. The task of designing these studies to incorporate and control properly the many intercorrelated influences on labor supply behavior is extremely complex and difficult. The success of existing studies in accomplishing this task is subject to some debate, so their findings must be regarded with caution. Recall from Chapter 2 that most such studies reveal that the income effect slightly exceeds the substitution effect for adult males as a group. This implies that the supply

FIGURE 12.6 **The Impact of a Personal Income Tax on Individual Labor Supply**

A personal income tax shifts the after-tax wage rate line downward to W_t and may cause either an increase or a decrease in a person's optimal supply of labor hours. For Smith (a), the substitution effect generated by the tax overpowers the income effect, resulting in a *decrease* in work from h_1 to h_2. Alternatively, for Jones (b), the income effect swamps the substitution effect, leading to an *increase* in work hours from h_1 to h_2. The overall effect of the tax on the quantity of labor supplied is indeterminate.

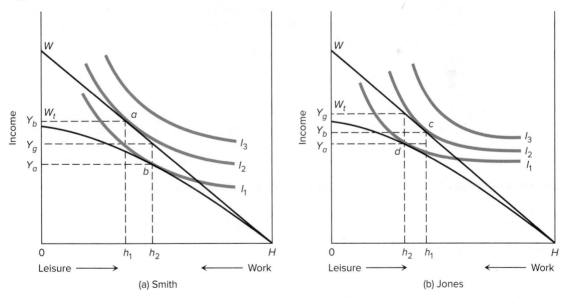

(a) Smith

(b) Jones

[17] The view that a tax change produces only a substitution effect on the economywide labor supply is found in James Gwartney and Richard Stroup, "Labor Supply and Tax Rates: A Correction of the Record," *American Economic Review,* June 1983, pp. 446–451. The Gwartney–Stroup criticism of the traditional model (Figure 12.6), in turn, has been challenged by several economists. For example, see Firouz Gahvari, "Labor Supply and Tax Rates: Comment," *American Economic Review,* March 1986, pp. 280–283; and David M. Betson and David Greenberg, "Labor Supply and Tax Rates: Comment," *American Economic Review,* June 1986, pp. 551–556.

curve for this group is negatively sloped; that is, tax increases (net wage decreases) cause males to increase their work hours slightly. For females, the substitution effect appears to dominate the income effect so that tax increases (wage decreases) create reductions in hours worked. The studies generally find that aggregating various individual labor supply curves yields an overall supply curve that is extremely inelastic. The major portion of U.S. income tax falls squarely on workers; therefore, the tax has a minimal net impact on work effort, the market wage rate, and equilibrium employment, as shown in Figure 12.5(a).

Specific Individuals and Markets

Although the overall impact of the income tax on labor supply may be negligible, impacts on specific individuals and specific labor markets may be considerable. Examples: Variations in income taxes among states may cause some workers to migrate from high- to low-tax geographic areas;[18] high marginal tax rates may entice some salaried workers to switch to "underground" activity to avoid paying income taxes; and exclusions, deductions, and credits—which are part of the tax code—may influence the composition of labor demand by affecting spending patterns of consumers. With regard to this third example, we point out that the tax deductibility of interest paid on mortgages increases the demand for residential construction workers; the tax deduction for charitable contributions enhances the ability of colleges to provide financial aid, which in turn increases the supply of graduates to such occupations as teaching, medicine, and law; and the complexity of the tax code increases the demand for tax accountants, tax lawyers, and Internal Revenue Service agents.

12.2 *Quick Review*

- If labor supply is perfectly inelastic, workers will bear the full burden of the personal income tax; if labor supply is positively sloped, some of the tax will be borne by employers through higher wages.

- The impact of the income tax on individual labor supply is indeterminate in terms of theory because the tax creates income and substitution effects having opposite impacts on desired hours of work.

- Empirical studies suggest that labor supply is highly inelastic, meaning that *(a)* workers bear nearly all of the personal income tax and *(b)* the tax has little impact on market wages and employment levels.

Your Turn

In 2018, the maximum marginal tax rate on income fell from 39.6 to 37.0 percent. Explain why Stone may work more as a result, whereas Smythe may work less. (*Answer:* See page 542.)

---

[18] See Enrico Moretti and Daniel J. Wilson, "The Effect of State Taxes on the Geographical Location of Top Earners: Evidence from Star Scientists," *American Economic Review,* July 2017, pp. 1858–1903.

WW12.4

12.4 World of Work

Who Pays the Social Security Payroll Tax?

The federal government levies a flat-rate payroll tax on all earnings below a set minimum to finance the Social Security program (old age, survivors, disability, and health insurance). In 2020 employers and employees each paid a Social Security tax of 7.65 percent of the first $137,700 of wage and salary earnings. Because these taxes are significant and are levied directly on earnings, labor economists are interested in their impact on wages.

The consensus expert opinion is that workers bear more than half of the Social Security tax. How can this be? We have just said that employers and employees are assessed equal Social Security taxes. The answer is that firms "collect" some or all of these tax proceeds from their workers. They "collect" this money by reducing the employees' wages below levels they would have received without the tax.

The part of the Social Security tax levied on employers reduces the after-tax marginal revenue product of labor, as viewed by firms. Suppose, for example, that the pretax wage rate is $20 an hour and the employer is assessed a 7.65 percent Social Security tax (half of 15.3 percent). From the firm's perspective, the workers' Marginal Revenue Product thus becomes $18.47 [= $20 − $1.53 (= 0.0765 × $10)] . If labor supply is perfectly inelastic [Figure 12.5(a)] and the wage rate equals MRP, the after-tax hourly pay becomes $18.47, not $20. In this case, workers have indirectly paid the employer's $1.53 per hour Social Security tax through a $1.53 per hour pay cut.

Also, employees must pay the 7.65 percent tax directly levied on their earnings. With the $18.47 market wage, this tax is $1.41 per hour (0.0765 × $18.47) . The after-tax hourly wage, therefore, falls to $17.06. The Social Security tax reduces the workers' market wage from $20 to $18.47 per hour and lowers their after-tax wage from $20 to $17.06. Thus, under these circumstances, the workers in effect pay the full Social Security tax.

Empirical studies confirm that employers do not pay their full half of the Social Security tax, although they apparently do pay a small part of it.[*] These findings imply that the overall labor supply curve may be somewhat elastic rather than perfectly inelastic. As the Social Security tax rises, spouses, teenagers, semi-retired workers, and others who do not have strong attachments to the labor force may reduce their labor offerings. If the overall labor supply curve is somewhat elastic [Figure 12.5(b)], employers cannot reduce workers' wages by the full amount of the employers' portion of the Social Security tax. They will have to bear some of the tax themselves to continue to attract a profit-maximizing number of workers.

[*] The classic research is John A. Brittain, *The Payroll Tax for Social Security* (Washington, DC: Brookings Institution, 1972). Other research includes Daniel Hamermesh, "New Estimates of the Incidence of the Payroll Tax," *Southern Economic Journal,* February 1979, pp. 1208–1219; and Patricia M. Anderson and Bruce D. Meyer, "The Effects of the Unemployment Insurance Payroll Tax on Wages, Employment, Claims and Denials," *Journal of Public Economics,* October 2000, pp. 81–106.

Chapter Summary

1. Government employment has increased both absolutely and as a percentage of total employment since 1950. The growth rate of public sector employment has been greatest at the state and local levels of government.

2. Federal workers had higher wage rates in the 1970s than comparably educated and experienced private sector employees, but that pay differential largely eroded during the 1980s and 1990s.

3. The total economic cost of allocating labor to the military consists of the total value of the alternative output (income) that is forgone. A voluntary army requires that economic costs be paid by taxpayers; a drafted army at below-market wage rates imposes some of the costs on those who are conscripted.

4. Taken alone, the government's provision of goods and services may create an income effect that reduces one's optimal supply of hours of work.

5. Government transfer payments and subsidies affect the composition of labor demand in the economy and also influence labor supply decisions.

6. Other things being equal, the more elastic the overall labor supply in the economy, the greater the extent to which a personal income tax will cause *(a)* a decline in the hours of labor supplied, *(b)* an increase in the market wage, and *(c)* lower overall employment. Most economists, however, judge the aggregate labor supply curve to be highly inelastic.

7. The impact of an income tax on an individual's optimal supply of labor is theoretically indeterminate in that the tax generates income and substitution effects that work in opposite directions with respect to the quantity of labor supplied. Government purchases transfer payments subsidy.

Terms and Concepts

prevailing wage rule

military conscription

voluntary or market-based army

government purchases

transfer payments

subsidy

pure public goods

income tax

Questions and Study Suggestions

1. List and discuss factors that help explain why public sector employment rose faster than private sector employment between 1950 and 2018. At what levels of government has public sector employment increased most dramatically?

2. Comment on this statement: "In general, federal government employees are underpaid compared to similar private sector workers. This is due to the monopsony power of government."

3. Speculate about the reason(s) for each of the following facts about public sector pay:

   a. The pay premium received by federal employees declined in the middle and late 1980s.

   b. Local governments tend to pay less skilled workers more, and more skilled workers less, than comparably trained and experienced private sector workers.

   c. Female and African–American workers in government receive higher pay on average than their equally qualified counterparts in the private sector.

4. Explain why a voluntary army may be less expensive to society than an army composed of draftees. Which will likely be less expensive to taxpayers?

5. Explain why a draft system might cause the U.S. military to overemploy labor and underemploy capital (from society's perspective). Speculate about why the army increasingly contracts out construction and maintenance work to private firms now that it is voluntary.

6. Assuming that income includes both private and public goods and that leisure is a normal good, explain how a major reduction in governmentally provided goods might increase a person's optimal number of hours of work.

7. Explain how the existence of national, state, and city parks might affect

    a. Labor demand in the recreational vehicle industry.

    b. The demand for workers who build and maintain equipment for private recreational theme parks.

    c. The overall supply of labor.

8. Use the following labor market data to determine the answers to (a) through (d):

(1) Wage Rate	(2) Quantity Demanded	(3) Quantity Supplied	(3) Tax per Hour
$30	14	22	$10
24	18	22	8
18	22	22	6
12	26	22	4
6	30	22	2

    a. Is this tax progressive? Explain.

    b. What is the before-tax equilibrium wage rate?

    c. What effect does the tax have on the number of hours of work supplied and the market wage rate?

    d. If the labor supply curve were highly elastic, rather than perfectly inelastic, how would your answers to (c) change?

Internet Exercise

What Is Up (or Down) with the State and Local Government Compensation Differential?

Go to the Bureau of Labor Statistics Data website (http://www.bls.gov/data/home.htm) and select "Series Report." Then enter the following ID series numbers: CIU3010000000000I and CIU2010000000000I. Last, click on "All Years." This will retrieve indexes of total compensation of state and local government workers and private industry workers (100 = Quarter 4, 2005).

What is the index value for state and local government workers for the most recent quarter shown? What is the index value for private industry workers for the most recent quarter shown?

What is the percentage change in compensation for state and local government workers since Quarter 1, 2001? What is the percentage change in compensation for private industry workers since Quarter 1, 2001? What do these figures indicate has happened to the state and local government compensation differential since Quarter 1, 2001?

Internet Links

 The website of the Selective Service System provides extensive information about the history of the military draft in the United States as well as a description of what would happen if a draft was reinstituted **(http://www.sss.gov)**.

Chapter 13

Government and the Labor Market: Legislation and Regulation

After reading this chapter, you should be able to:

1. Explain the effects of the major labor laws on union bargaining power and union membership.
2. Explain the likely labor market impacts of the minimum wage and summarize the empirical evidence.
3. Discuss the labor market impacts of job injury and effects of government regulation of job safety.
4. Explain how government regulation can generate economic rent.

Besides directly employing labor, providing public goods, transferring income, and levying taxes, the government engages in the important task of establishing the legal rules for the economy. Many of these laws and regulations directly or indirectly affect wage and employment outcomes. We examine such laws throughout this book; for example, in Chapter 9 we discussed immigration laws. In later chapters, we discuss laws outlawing discrimination and promoting full employment.

Laws affecting labor markets are so numerous that we must be highly selective. We limit our analysis here to four main topics: labor relations law, the federal minimum wage, the Occupational Safety and Health Act of 1970, and laws providing workers with increases in economic rent.

LABOR LAW[1]

Laws governing labor relations in general and collective bargaining, in particular, constitute a significant institutional factor influencing wages, employment, and resource allocation. The major laws in this category are

---

[1] Instructors in colleges that offer a separate course in labor relations may wish to skip this section.

summarized in Table 13.1. A careful reading of this table will complement the discussion that follows. The labor relations laws summarized in the table affect the labor market in diverse ways, two of which are (*a*) by influencing the extent and growth of union membership, which in turn influences the ability of unions to secure wage gains, and (*b*) by establishing the rules under which collective bargaining transpires.

Labor Law and Union Membership

The effect of labor relations laws and regulations, or the absence thereof, on union membership is not always easy to determine. Such factors as changes in industry structure and altered worker attitudes may create conditions that simultaneously foster both new labor laws *and* changes in union membership. That is, observed changes in union membership may not necessarily result from changes in labor laws. Untangling cause and effect, therefore, is not an easy task. Nevertheless, there can be no doubt that labor law per se can be an important determinant of union membership. This relationship between labor law and union membership is observable in both the private and public sectors.

1 Labor Law and Private Sector Union Membership

A glance back at Figure 10.2 reveals that union membership was 7 percent of the labor force in 1900 and only 11 percent of the labor force in 1930. Two decades later, union membership stood at over 30 percent of the labor force. Relative to total employment, union membership peaked in the mid-1950s (or in 1970 if members of professional associations are included) and has since declined. Although the reasons for this pattern of union growth and decline are many and varied, the imprint of labor law on these trends is readily discernible.

Pre-1930 Period   Prior to the 1930s, union organizers and members were legally unprotected against reprisals by employers or even government itself. Stated bluntly, joining a union might involve job loss, fines, or even bodily harm. Attempts to unionize were met with *discriminatory discharge* in many instances. Those dismissed often were placed on *blacklists* and therefore denied opportunities to gain alternative employment. Workers sometimes were required to sign *yellow-dog contracts* that, as a condition of continued employment, legally prohibited them from joining unions. A violation could result not only in discharge but also in a lawsuit initiated by the employer and a court-imposed fine. Firms also used *lockouts* (plant shutdowns) as a way to stop organizing attempts in their infancies. By closing down the plant for a few weeks, employers could impose high costs on those contemplating joining labor unions. Where workers did successfully organize and attempt to force their employers to bargain, firms often countered strikes by employing *strikebreakers,* who sometimes clashed violently with union workers. The Homestead Strike of 1892 and the Pullman Strike of 1894 are cases in point. Often government intervened with police action on the side of employers during these confrontations.

Court hostility toward unionization was a related factor explaining the low union membership during this period. Without labor laws, courts relied on common law interpretations. This placed unions in the weak position of seeking new legal rights for labor at the expense of long-standing property rights of firms. This court hostility manifested itself in several ways, including the courts' interpretation of antitrust laws and the use of *injunctions*. For example, the Supreme Court held that the Sherman Antitrust Act of 1890 applied to unions, even though the intent of the legislation was clearly directed toward prohibiting price fixing and monopolization by firms. Injunctions were readily dispensed as a way of stopping actions such as picketing, striking, and boycotting, which employers claimed would reduce their profits. Lower profits would reduce the capitalized value of the firm's assets and, according to the courts, violate the firm's property rights.

TABLE 13.1 A Summary of Basic Labor Relations Laws

The Norris–LaGuardia Act of 1932

1. Increased the difficulty for employers to obtain injunctions against union activity.
2. Declared that yellow-dog contracts were unenforceable. These contracts required employees to agree as a condition of continued employment that they would not join a union.

The Wagner Act of 1935 (National Labor Relations Act—NLRA)

1. Guaranteed the "twin rights" of labor: the right of self-organization and the right to bargain with employers engaged in interstate commerce.
2. Listed a number of "unfair labor practices" on the part of management. Specifically, it *(a)* forbids employers to interfere with the right of workers to form unions; *(b)* outlaws company unions (i.e., pseudo-unions) established by firms to discourage the establishment of worker-controlled unions; *(c)* prohibits antiunion discrimination by employers in hiring, firing, and promoting; *(d)* outlaws discrimination against any worker who files charges or gives testimony under the Act; and *(e)* obligates employers to bargain in good faith.
3. Established the National Labor Relations Board (NLRB), which was given the authority to investigate unfair labor practices occurring under the Act, to issue cease-and-desist orders, and to conduct elections by workers on whether they desire union representation.
4. Made strikes by federal employees illegal and grounds for dismissal.

The Taft–Hartley Act of 1947 (Amendment to the NLRA of 1935)

1. Established "unfair labor practices" on the part of unions. Specifically, it prohibits *(a)* coercion of employees to become union members, *(b)* jurisdictional strikes (disputes between unions over who is authorized to perform a specific job), *(c)* secondary boycotts (refusing to buy or handle products produced by another union or group of workers), *(d)* sympathy strikes (work stoppages by one union designed to assist some other union in gaining employer recognition or some other objective), *(e)* excessive union dues, and *(f)* featherbedding (forcing payment for work not actually performed).
2. Regulated the internal administration of unions—for example, required detailed financial reports to the NLRB.
3. Outlawed the closed shop but made union shops legal in states that do not expressly prohibit them (state "right-to-work" laws).
4. Set up emergency strike procedures allowing the government to stop for up to 80 days a strike that imperils the nation's health and safety.
5. Created the Federal Mediation and Conciliation Service to provide mediators for labor disputes.

The Landrum–Griffin Act of 1959 (Amendment to the NLRA of 1935)

1. Required regularly scheduled elections of union officers and excluded Communists and people convicted of felonies from holding union office.
2. Held union officers strictly accountable for union funds and property.
3. Prevented union leaders from infringing on individual workers' rights to participate in union meetings, vote in union proceedings, and nominate officers.

To summarize: Prior to the 1930s, the absence of protective labor legislation allowed firms and the courts to repress union activity and growth. Low union membership translated into an inability of unions, in general, to make a significant impact on the overall labor market.

Post-1930 Period   As evidenced in the summary of labor legislation in Table 13.1, Congress enacted significant labor relations laws during the 1930s. The Norris–LaGuardia Act of 1932 and the Wagner Act of 1935 placed a protective umbrella over the union movement and greatly encouraged the growth of union membership. By outlawing yellow-dog contracts, the *Norris–LaGuardia Act* significantly reduced the personal costs of becoming a union member and thus made it easier to organize a firm's workforce. Previously the cost of joining a union might be the loss of one's job. Also, the Act's provision limiting the use of the court-issued injunction to halt normal union activities such as striking increased the ability of unions to impose costs on firms as a way to obtain higher wage offers. Larger union wage gains, in turn, increased the incentive for workers to become union members.

The *Wagner Act* had an even greater impact on union membership. In fact, one of the expressed purposes of this law was to promote the growth of unionism. Table 13.1 informs us that this legislation guaranteed unions (*a*) the right to self-organization, free of interference from employers, and (*b*) the right to bargain as a unit with employers. Furthermore, the Act outlawed several "unfair labor practices" that management had used successfully to thwart unionism. The Wagner Act enabled the American Federation of Labor (AFL) to solidify its power within various crafts and also permitted the rapid growth of industrial unions affiliated with the Congress of Industrial Organizations (CIO). These CIO unions organized millions of less-skilled workers employed in mass-production industries such as steel, rubber, and automobiles. By the time of the merger between the AFL and CIO in 1955, union membership had risen to about 17 million.

The dramatic surge in union membership in the two decades following the pro-union legislation of the mid-1930s strengthened the ability of unions to achieve dominance of many labor markets and thus secure improvements in wage rates and working conditions. That is increases in union membership translated into increased union bargaining power and a greater overall impact of unionism on labor market outcomes.

The growing strength of labor unions produced a political backlash against unions, resulting in the passage of the *Taft–Hartley Act* of 1947 and the *Landrum–Griffin Act* of 1959, both of which are annotated in Table 13.1. Union membership continued to grow, however, until the more recent decline in unionism discussed in detail in Chapter 10. Recall that some observers contend that part of the recent decline in unionism can be traced to increased use of illegal antiunion tactics by management. If this assertion is true, then it might be argued that the *degree of enforcement* of labor laws is also a factor in explaining trends in union membership within the private sector.

2 Labor Law and Public Sector Union Membership

Recall from Chapter 10 that membership in public employee unions spurted during the 1960s and 1970s. The driving force for this growth at the federal level was a set of presidential executive orders that provided for the recognition of unions composed of federal workers. At the state level, the main factors explaining the rapid rise in public employee unionism were (*a*) laws recognizing the rights of state workers to organize and (*b*) laws establishing public employee relations boards to conduct elections to determine whether workers desire union representation.[2]

---

[2] Richard Freeman, "Unionism Comes to the Public Sector," *Journal of Economic Literature,* March 1986, pp. 41–86. Table 4 in this article summarizes empirical work supporting the thesis that changes in the legal environment independently encourage membership in public sector unions. For more information on public sector labor laws, see Richard C. Kearney and Patrice M. Mareschal, *Labor Relations in the Public Sector,* 5th Edition (Boca Ration, FL: CRC Press, 2014), Chapter 4.

Labor Law and Bargaining Power

The overall body of labor law and specific provisions of the law influence bargaining power independently of effects on the level of union membership. Many provisions of labor law enhance the bargaining power of unions, enabling them to secure higher wage gains; other provisions strengthen the negotiating positions of employers. Let's briefly examine an example of each outcome.

1 Limitation on the Use of the Injunction

The Norris–LaGuardia Act of 1932 limited the use of court-issued injunctions to enjoin picketing, striking, and related union activities. This prohibition clearly strengthened union bargaining power. Because firms could no longer gain legal relief from, say, a work stoppage, threats by unions to strike now became more credible. Previously firms knew they could get the courts to enjoin a strike once it began.

2 Prohibition of Secondary Boycotts

Secondary boycotts are actions by one union to refuse to handle, or to get one's employer to refuse to buy, products made by a firm that is a party to a labor dispute. Although the Taft–Hartley Act of 1947 presumably made these secondary pressures illegal, trucking unions continued to demand and obtain "hot-cargo" clauses in their contracts. The courts ruled that such clauses technically did not constitute an illegal secondary boycott. What were these clauses and how did they affect union bargaining power?

Hot-cargo clauses declared that trucking firms would not require unionized truckers to handle or transport products made by an "unfair" employer involved in a labor dispute. For example, suppose a manufacturer of fabricated steel products was being struck by its employees. Unionized transportation firms governed by hot-cargo provisions would refuse to transport these fabricated steel items while the labor dispute was in progress. The union representing the steel fabricators, therefore, had more bargaining power than it might otherwise have possessed. The reason is that, as a result of the hot-cargo provisions, the strike would effectively curtail all revenue to the firm, thus causing it to suffer losses; it could not maintain its sales and profits through such actions as hiring strikebreakers, using supervisory personnel, or selling from its inventory. Once struck by a union, the firm could not get its products transported to its customers.

The Landrum–Griffin Act of 1959 declared hot-cargo contracts illegal. Specifically, the Act stated that it was an unfair labor practice for a union and employer "to enter into any contract or agreement, express or implied, whereby the employer ceases or refrains or agrees to cease or refrain from handling; using; selling; transporting; or otherwise dealing in any products of any other employer, or to cease doing business with any other persons."[3] Once passed and enforced, this prohibition increased management bargaining power by increasing the union's cost of disagreeing in many labor disputes. Many firms now could continue to maintain their profits during strikes by hiring strikebreakers, using supervisory personnel, or selling previously produced goods.

MINIMUM WAGE LAW

The *Fair Labor Standards Act* of 1938, which established a *minimum wage* of $0.25 per hour, is another way government legislation affects the labor market. Before undertaking a detailed analysis of these effects, it will be useful to establish some facts about the minimum wage law and provide a brief synopsis of the alternative positions taken on the wisdom of this government intervention into the labor market.

---

[3] U.S. Government Publishing Office. "U.S.C. United States Code" Title 29 Labor. https://www.govinfo.gov/content/pkg/USCODE-2011-title29/html/USCODE-2011-title29.htm

Facts and Controversy

Congress has amended the Fair Labor Standards Act many times to increase the legal minimum wage in monetary terms. Between 1991 and 1996, the legal minimum wage was $4.25 per hour. Because inflation occurred during this period, the ratio of the minimum wage to the average wage fell from 37.3 percent to 32.4 percent.[4] As a result, in 1996 Congress upped the minimum wage to $5.15 per hour (after September 1997). In mid-2007 Congress raised the minimum wage over two years to $7.25. An increasing number of states and cities have raised their minimum wage above the federal minimum wage. By 2019, 29 states, 41 cities, and the District of Columbia had a minimum wage above the federal minimum wage.

Congress has extended the coverage of the minimum wage law over the years. The original legislation placed about 44 percent of all nonsupervisory workers under its coverage; today about 88 percent of all such workers are included. Recent statistics reveal that 47 percent of workers earning the minimum wage are aged 16–24, 63 percent are women, and 15 percent are African–American. About 95 percent of minimum-wage employees work in private sector industries. Approximately 56 percent of those receiving the minimum wage work part-time.[5]

The minimum wage has been controversial since its inception. Proponents argue that it is needed to ensure that workers receive a "living wage"—one that will provide full-time workers an annual income sufficient to purchase the bare necessities of life. They also contend that this wage floor prevents monopsonistic employers from exploiting low-skilled labor, a disproportionate number of whom are minorities and women.

Opponents of the minimum wage, on the other hand, argue that it increases unemployment, particularly among teenagers, females, and minorities. Second, opponents cite the possibility that the legal wage floor causes a spillover effect that reduces wage rates in sectors of the economy that are not covered by the law. Third, detractors argue that it encourages teenagers to drop out of school. Finally, critics contend that the minimum wage is poorly targeted to reduce poverty; that is, a majority of minimum-wage workers do *not* live in poverty households.

The Competitive Model

The competitive labor supply and demand model is the best starting place for analyzing the possible labor market effects of the minimum wage.[6] Considering Figure 13.1, suppose that all employees in the economy are covered by the minimum wage law and that labor and product markets are perfectly competitive [MRP (marginal revenue product) = VMP (value of the marginal product) = MWC (marginal wage cost) = P_L]. The figure depicts the impact of a specific minimum wage W_m on a labor market in which the equilibrium wage and employment levels are W_0 and Q_0. One point needs to be stressed at the outset. *If* the minimum wage W_m is at or below the equilibrium wage W_0, which is true for higher-wage labor markets, then the law is irrelevant and has *no* direct wage and employment consequence. The actual wage and employment outcome will remain at W_0 and Q_0. This is *not* the situation in Figure 13.1, where W_m exceeds the equilibrium wage W_0.

---

[4] Barry T. Hirsch and David A. Macpherson, *Union Membership and Earnings Data Book: Compilations from the Current Population Survey* (2019 Edition) (Washington, DC: Bureau of National Affairs, 2019).

[5] U.S. Bureau of Labor Statistics, "Characteristics of Minimum Wage Workers, 2018," *BLS Reports,* March 2019.

[6] The effects of the minimum wage have also been examined in other types of models. For a discussion of its effect in a monopsonistic competition model, see V. Bhaskar and Ted To, "Minimum Wages for Ronald McDonald Monopsonies: A Theory of Monopsonistic Competition," *Economic Journal,* April 1999, pp. 190–203. For an analysis of its impact in an efficiency wage model, see James B. Rebitzer and Lowell J. Taylor, "The Consequences of Minimum Wage Laws: Some New Theoretical Ideas," *Journal of Public Economics,* February 1995, pp. 245–255.

FIGURE 13.1   Minimum Wage Effects: Competitive Model

The above-equilibrium minimum wage W_m reduces employment in this low-wage labor market by ab and creates unemployment of ac. The more elastic the labor supply and demand curves, the greater the unemployment consequences of the law.

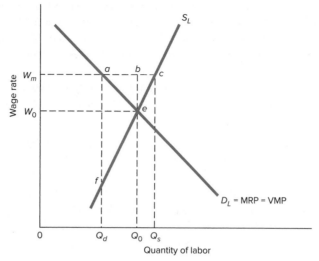

What employment, unemployment, and allocation effects will this government-imposed minimum wage produce? First, observe that at W_m, employers will hire only Q_d workers rather than the original Q_0. Stated differently, the marginal revenue product of the Q_d through Q_0 workers will be less than the minimum wage; therefore, profit-maximizing employers will reduce employment.

Second, the supply curve suggests that the minimum wage will attract Q_s as opposed to Q_0 workers to the market. The minimum wage changes the behavior of employers and labor suppliers so that employment declines by the amount ba and unemployment increases by the larger amount ac.

Third, the minimum wage W_m creates allocative inefficiency. Notice from segment ae of the labor demand curve that the VMP for each of the Q_d to Q_0 workers exceeds the supply price of these individuals (as shown by segment fe of S_L). This implies that society is giving up output of greater value ($Q_d ae Q_0$) than the $Q_d Q_0$ displaced workers can contribute in their next most productive employment ($Q_d fe Q_0$). The *net* loss of domestic output is shown then by area fae (= $Q_d ae Q_0$ - $Q_d fe Q_0$). You should use Figure 13.1 to verify the following generalizations: (*a*) Other things being equal, the higher the minimum wage relative to the equilibrium wage, the greater the negative employment and allocation effects; and (*b*) the more elastic the labor supply and demand curves, the greater the unemployment consequences of the law.

Two factors, of course, might dampen the minimum wage effects just mentioned. One such factor is a failure on the part of some firms to comply with the minimum wage law.[7] The other factor is the possibility that some firms offset the minimum wage by reducing fringe benefits (say, sick leave or health insurance).[8] In either case, hourly labor cost would not rise in Figure 13.1 by the full amount $W_0 W_m$, and therefore the indicated employment and efficiency effects would be lessened.

---

[7] For evidence of this possibility, see Orley Ashenfelter and Robert S. Smith, "Compliance with the Minimum Wage Law," *Journal of Political Economy,* April 1979, pp. 335–350.

[8] Walter J. Wessels, "The Effect of Minimum Wages in the Presence of Fringe Benefits: An Expanded Model," *Economic Inquiry,* April 1980, pp. 293–313. Also relevant are J. Harold McClure, Jr., "Minimum Wages and the Wessels Effect in a Monopsony Model," *Journal of Labor Research,* Summer 1994, pp. 271–282; and Kosali Ilayperuma Simon and Robert Kaestner, "Do Minimum Wages Affect Nonwage Job Attributes? Evidence on Fringe Benefits," *Industrial and Labor Relations Review,* October 2004, pp. 52–70.

Monopsony

Thus far, we have assumed that the low-wage labor market is perfectly competitive. We now dispose of this assumption and analyze the potential employment effects of the minimum wage under conditions of nondiscriminating monopsony. Figure 13.2 portrays a labor market comprising only a single employer of labor services or several employers colluding to set a below-competitive wage. Recall from Figure 6.7 that a monopsonist's MWC exceeds its average wage cost (AWC) at each level of employment. Because it is the only buyer of labor services, the monopsonist faces the typical upward-sloping market supply of labor curve. To hire more workers, it must attract them away from other occupations, and it accomplishes this by raising the wage it pays. But because the nondiscriminating monopsonist must pay *all* its workers the same wage, it discovers that its extra cost of hiring one more worker (MWC) exceeds the higher wage payment to that worker alone (AWC).

The monopsonist depicted in Figure 13.2 will use the profit-maximizing hiring rule (MRP = MWC) and employ Q_0 workers. As we see from point c on the labor supply curve, to attract that number of workers it has to pay a wage of W_0. But now suppose that the government sets a minimum wage somewhere between W_0 and W_2—say W_1. In effect, the labor supply curve becomes perfectly horizontal at W_1 over the $0Q_1$ range of employment. Because the firm can hire up to Q_1 extra workers at the minimum wage, its marginal wage cost equals its AWC over this entire range. Contrast this to the previous situation where it has to raise the wage to attract more workers (MWC > AWC).

FIGURE 13.2 Minimum Wage Effects: Monopsony

Without the minimum wage, this monopsonist will choose to hire Q_0 workers and pay a wage equal to W_0. Any legal minimum wage above W_0 and below W_2 will transform the firm into a wage taker, and the firm will choose to increase its level of employment. For example, if the minimum wage is W_1, this firm will hire the same number of workers as if competition existed in this labor market. Thus, it is possible that a minimum wage might increase employment in some industries.

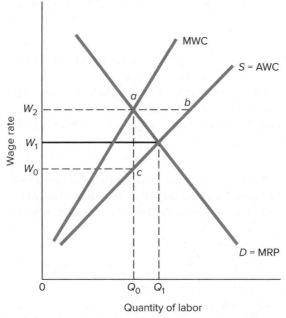

With the legal minimum wage of W_1, the monopsonist becomes a wage taker rather than a wage setter and maximizes its profits by hiring Q_1 workers. The additional Q_0 through Q_1 workers are now hired because their MRPs exceed the minimum wage (MWC). In this case, the minimum wage *increases* employment from Q_0 to Q_1 by perfectly countervailing the monopsony power of the employer. Close scrutiny of Figure 13.2 shows that any legal wage above W_0 and below W_2 will increase employment above Q_0. It, therefore, is possible that a well-chosen and selectively implemented minimum wage might increase employment and improve allocative efficiency.

But much caution is needed here. First, if the government sets the minimum wage above W_2, employment will decline. Second, even though *employment* may be equal to or greater than Q_0 at minimum wage levels above the monopsony wage W_0, *unemployment* could easily be higher. For example, b laborers seek employment in this market at wage rate W_2, whereas firms hire only a workers. At W_2, although *employment* is the same as at the monopsony wage W_0, the excess supply of workers—*unemployment*—rises from zero to ab. Third, being the only employer of a specific type of low-wage labor, a monopsonist might be able to discriminate—that is, pay each worker a wage just sufficient to attract her or his employment. If so, the MWC curve will coincide with the labor supply curve, and the firm's profit-maximizing level of employment (MRP = MWC) will be the competitive one, Q_1, rather than Q_0. This is true because the firm must pay the higher wage that is necessary to attract each extra worker only to that particular worker. Where discriminating monopsony exists, a minimum wage will either be ineffective or reduce employment; it cannot increase employment. Fourth, empirical studies on this subject find little evidence of monopsony in most labor markets.[9]

Empirical Evidence

Economists have devoted much attention to estimating the effects of the minimum wage on employment. In addition, they have used statistical studies to try to determine whether the minimum wage influences human capital investment decisions and achieves the goal of creating more equality in the distribution of earnings and household income. The results of several of these studies are summarized as follows.

1 Employment

Many studies have analyzed the employment effects of the minimum wage. Much of this analysis has been devoted to examining teenagers because this is the age group most likely to be affected by the minimum wage. Until recently, a 10 percent increase in the minimum wage typically caused a 1–3 percent decline in the number of jobs held by teenagers, if all other factors were held constant.[10] This long-standing research finding, however, has been challenged by some recent and controversial studies.

Card and Krueger have examined the impact of the 1992 rise in the New Jersey minimum wage on employment in fast-food restaurants in the state.[11] To conduct their research, the authors surveyed managers of 410 fast-food restaurants in New Jersey and eastern Pennsylvania before and after the rise in the minimum wage. They report employment rose faster in New Jersey restaurants than in Pennsylvania restaurants (where the minimum wage did not change). The results also revealed that restaurants in New Jersey that paid high

---

[9] For a survey of theoretical and empirical studies of monopsony, see William M. Boal and Michael R. Ransom, "Monopsony in the Labor Market," *Journal of Economic Literature,* March 1997, pp. 86–112. Also see, *Journal of Labor Economics,* special issue "Modern Models of Monopsony in Labor Markets: Tests and Estimates," November 2010.

[10] See Charles Brown, "Minimum Wages, Employment, and the Distribution of Income," in Orley Ashenfelter and David Card (eds.), *Handbook of Labor Economics,* Volume 3B (Amsterdam: North-Holland, 1999).

[11] David Card and Alan B. Krueger, "Minimum Wages and Employment: A Case Study of the Fast-Food Industry in New Jersey and Pennsylvania," *American Economic Review,* September 1994, pp. 772–793.

wages before the minimum wage hike did not have faster employment growth than those that paid low wages. Thus, the authors concluded that the minimum wage did not decrease employment.

Although this and other studies by Card and Krueger have generated strong interest from policymakers, they have also produced warnings that these results should be considered tentative.[12] One criticism of the New Jersey study is that the quality of the data collected by Card and Krueger may be poor. A study by Neumark and Wascher, using actual payroll data collected from fast-food restaurants from New Jersey and Pennsylvania, finds a negative effect of the minimum wage on employment.[13] However, a follow-up study by Card and Krueger, also using a payroll data set, confirms their original conclusion.[14] Critics also point out that the employment declines from new minimum wage legislation could occur before the law takes effect because the laws are announced well in advance. Alternatively, declines could lag many years behind hikes in the minimum wage.[15]

These findings have renewed empirical interest in the employment effects of minimum wage hikes. Neumark and Wascher survey over 90 studies since the Card and Krueger analysis and conclude that most studies find a negative effect of the minimum wage on employment and work hours.[16] Some recent research examining the effect of 138 state-level minimum wage changes on the number of jobs close to the new minimum wage finds no effect of the minimum wage.[17] A team of researchers at the University of Washington find negative employment effects for increases in the minimum wage for Seattle.[18] The minimum wage-employment debate is still ongoing.

2 Investment in Human Capital

The effect of the minimum wage on investment in human capital is likely negative. The minimum wage probably *reduces* on-the-job training. Recall from Chapter 4 that firms sometimes hire workers and provide them with general on-the-job training. To cover the expense, they pay a lower wage during the training period. But the minimum wage places a floor on the wage firms can offer. Therefore, some firms may decide against providing general job training under these circumstances, and thus the minimum wage may reduce the formation of this type of human capital.[19] Also, empirical evidence suggests that the minimum wage increases since 2000 have led teenagers to focus more on schooling so as to better compete for jobs with a higher minimum wage.[20]

---

[12] Much of their research on this topic is summarized in David Card and Alan B. Krueger, *Myth and Measurement: The New Economics of the Minimum Wage* (Princeton, NJ: Princeton University Press, 1995). For a critical review, see "Review Symposium on *Myth and Mismeasurement: The New Economics of the Minimum Wage* by David Card and Alan B. Krueger," *Industrial and Labor Relations Review,* July 1995, pp. 842–848.

[13] David Neumark and William Wascher, "Minimum Wages and Employment: A Case Study of the Fast-Food Industry in New Jersey and Pennsylvania: Comment," *American Economic Review,* December 2000, pp. 1362–1396.

[14] David Card and Alan B. Krueger, "Minimum Wages and Employment: A Case Study of the Fast-Food Industry in New Jersey and Pennsylvania: Reply," *American Economic Review,* December 2000, pp. 1397–1420.

[15] For evidence consistent with this criticism, see Michael Baker, Dwayne Benjamin, and Shuchita Stanger, "The Highs and Lows of the Minimum Wage Effect: A Time-Series Cross-Section Study of the Canadian Law," *Journal of Labor Economics,* April 1999, pp. 318–350.

[16] See David Neumark and William Wascher, *Minimum Wages* (Cambridge, MA: MIT Press, 2008).

[17] See Doruk Cengiz, Arindrajit Dube, Attila Lindner, and Ben Zipperer, "The Effect of Minimum Wages on Low-Wage Jobs," *Quarterly Journal of Economics,* August 2019, pp. 1405–1454.

[18] See Ekaterina Jardim, Mark C. Long, Emma van Inwegen, Jacob Vigdor, and Hilary Wething, "Minimum Wage Increases and Individual Employment Trajectories," National Bureau of Economic Research Working Paper Number 25182, October 2018.

[19] For evidence consistent with this hypothesis, see David Neumark and William Wascher, "Minimum Wages and Training," *Journal of Labor Economics,* July 2001, pp. 563–595. For a study finding no effect on training, see David Fairris and Roberto Pedace, "The Impact of Minimum Wages on Job Training: An Empirical Exploration with Establishment Data," *Southern Economic Journal,* January 2004, pp. 566–583.

[20] See David Neumark and Cortnie Shupe, "Declining Teen Employment: Minimum Wages, Returns to Schooling, and Immigration," *Labour Economics,* August 2019, pp. 49–68.

3 Income Inequality and Poverty

The minimum wage does *not* generally alter the overall distribution of family income or appreciably reduce poverty. This somewhat surprising conclusion rests on the empirical evidence that people paid a minimum wage are more likely to be members of middle- or high-income families than low-income families. About 84 percent of minimum-wage workers reside in families that have family income above the poverty line. Thus, the minimum wage appears to be poorly targeted as an antipoverty weapon.[21] Furthermore, wage growth among the average minimum-wage workers is substantial, rising more than 60 percent above the minimum wage within a year.[22]

Final Remarks

The minimum wage *does* increase the annual earnings of some low-income workers. Perhaps this is the reason for the strong public support for the minimum wage and the fact that the debate over it has largely moved away from the question of whether it should exist and toward the issue of how high it should be set. Economists commonly agree that there is some real minimum wage that would be so high that it would severely reduce employment and economic efficiency. But based on the evidence summarized here, it does not appear that this level has yet been reached. In this regard, one knowledgeable reviewer of the minimum wage literature has concluded that "the minimum wage is overrated: by its critics as well as its supporters."[23]

13.1 *Quick Review*

- The Norris–LaGuardia Act of 1932 and the Wagner Act of 1935 encouraged the growth of U.S. unionism; the Taft–Hartley Act of 1947 and the Landrum–Griffin Act of 1959 sought to restrain union power.
- In a competitive labor market, an above-equilibrium minimum wage will reduce employment, increase unemployment, and create an efficiency loss.
- Researchers have estimated that a 10 percent increase in the minimum wage causes a 1–3 percent decline in teenage employment. Some question exists, however, whether the most recent increases in the minimum wage followed this pattern.

Your Turn

Suppose the federal government increases the minimum wage by 25 percent. Based on theory and traditional evidence, predict the impact of this increase on *(a)* the average wage of teenagers, *(b)* teenage employment, and *(c)* teenage unemployment. (*Answer:* See page 542.)

---

[21] Joseph J. Sabia and Richard V. Burkhauser, "Will a $9.50 Federal Minimum Wage Really Help the Working Poor?" *Southern Economic Journal,* January 2010, pp. 592–623; and Brandyn F. Churchill and Joseph F. Sabia, "The Effects of Minimum Wages on Low-Skilled Immigrants' Wages, Employment, and Poverty," *Industrial Relations,* April 2019, pp. 275–314.

[22] See William E. Even and David A. Macpherson, "Wage and Employment Dynamics of Minimum Wage Workers," *Southern Economic Journal,* January 2003, pp. 676–690. Also see, John W. Lopresti and Kevin J. Mumford, "Who Benefits From a Minimum Wage Increase?" *Industrial and Labor Relations Review,* October 2016, pp. 1171–1190.

[23] Charles Brown, "Minimum Wage Laws: Are They Overrated?" *Journal of Economic Perspectives,* Summer 1988, pp. 133–145.

OCCUPATIONAL HEALTH AND SAFETY REGULATION

Another important and controversial area of direct government intervention into the labor market is the regulation of occupational health and safety. This intervention has taken several forms, including state workers' compensation programs and the federal *Occupational Safety and Health Act of 1970*. The former mandated that firms purchase insurance that pays specified benefits to workers injured on the job. The latter, which will be our main focus, requires employers to comply with workplace health and safety standards established under the legislation.

Government regulation of workplace health and safety is worthy of discussion for several reasons. First, statistics show that work is more dangerous than generally perceived. In 2017, 5,147 workers died in job-related accidents in the United States, and roughly 3.3 million people incurred nonfatal injuries. As observed in Table 13.2, these accidents varied greatly by industry. Note, for example, that there were 23.0 deaths per 100,000 workers in agriculture as compared to 2.0 deaths per 100,000 employees in service. Second, job safety—or the lack thereof—is an important nonwage aspect of work, which is an important determinant of labor supply. Therefore, degrees of workplace safety help explain wage differentials among certain occupations. Finally, just as with such labor market interventions as the minimum wage and affirmative action legislation, controversy exists over the appropriateness and effectiveness of regulation of workplace health and safety.

This topic will be approached as follows. First, we will discuss how a profit-maximizing firm determines how much job safety to provide to its workers. Then we will analyze why this level of protection against workplace hazards might be less than society's optimal amount. Finally, we will discuss the controversies surrounding the Occupational Safety and Health Act of 1970.

TABLE 13.2 Occupational Fatalities and Nonfatal Injuries by Industry

Industry	Deaths	Rate per 100,000 Workers	Rate of Nonfatal Occupational Injuries per 100 Workers*
Agriculture	581	23.0	4.7
Mining and extraction	112	12.9	1.5
Construction	971	9.5	3.0
Manufacturing	303	1.9	3.2
Transportation and utilities	910	13.8	4.1
Trade	461	1.8	3.1
Service	1,336	2.0	2.3
Government	473	2.0	4.3
Total	5,147	3.5	2.9

Source: Bureau of Labor Statistics, "National Census of Fatal Occupational Injuries in 2017," http://stats.bls.gov/iif/home.htm; and Bureau of Labor Statistics, "Employer-Reported Workplace Injuries and Illnesses, 2017," *News Release* USDL-18-21788, November 8, 2018. www.bls.gov

Profit-Maximizing Level of Job Safety[24]

Competition in the product market will force a profit-maximizing firm to minimize its internal costs of producing any specific amount of output. One cost of production is the expenditure necessary to make the workplace safe. The production of job safety normally involves diminishing returns, which, translated into cost terms, means that each dollar of additional expenditure yields successively smaller increases in job safety. More concretely, firms will first use such relatively inexpensive techniques as disseminating safety information and issuing protective gear (say, hard hats) to make the job safer; but to make further gains, they may have to resort to such increasingly costly actions as purchasing safer equipment and slowing the work pace. Therefore, most firms experience a rising *marginal cost of job safety:* Successively higher amounts of direct expense, reduced output, or both will be required to gain additional units of job safety. We depict a marginal cost of safety curve MC_S in Figure 13.3. Each additional unit of job safety, measured on the horizontal axis, costs more than previous units.

Knowing that it is costly to provide job safety, why would a firm choose to offer workers *any* protection from workplace hazards? The answer is provided by the marginal benefit of safety curve MB_S (disregard the curve labeled MB_S' for now). An employer benefits from creating a relatively safe workplace; job safety reduces certain costs that the firm might otherwise incur. Notice, however, that as more units of job safety are produced by this firm, the *marginal benefit from job safety* (MB_S) to the firm falls. Just as individuals experience diminishing marginal utility as successive units of a good are consumed, firms find that the extra benefit (cost savings) of job safety diminishes with every increase in the amount of job safety.

FIGURE 13.3   The Optimal Level of Job Safety

A profit-maximizing firm will provide a level of job safety at which its marginal benefit and marginal cost of safety are equal, say at Q_S, which is determined by the intersection of MB_S and MC_S. If workers have full information about possible work hazards and accurately assess job risks, this level of output will optimize society's well-being. If workers are unaware of workplace danger or underestimate it, they will not be paid a proper wage premium, and the firm will not gain the benefit of lower wages as it provides more safety. Thus, the marginal benefit of each unit of job safety will be less (MB_S' rather than MB_S), and the firm will under-provide job safety from society's viewpoint (Q_S' rather than Q_S).

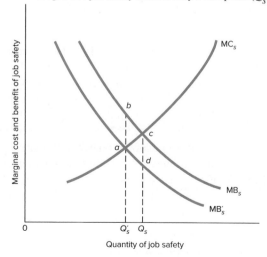

[24] The basic analytical framework for this section and the section that follows was developed by Walter Oi in "An Essay on Workmen's Compensation and Industrial Safety," in *Supplemental Studies for the National Commission on State Workmen's Compensation Laws,* vol. 1, 1974, pp. 41–106.

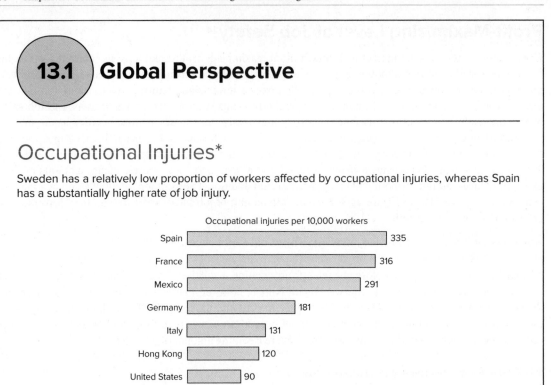

13.1   Global Perspective

Occupational Injuries*

Sweden has a relatively low proportion of workers affected by occupational injuries, whereas Spain has a substantially higher rate of job injury.

Occupational injuries per 10,000 workers

Spain	335
France	316
Mexico	291
Germany	181
Italy	131
Hong Kong	120
United States	90
Sweden	71

Source: International Labour Organization, www.ilo.org

* The injury rate is defined as the average annual percentage of workers losing work time due to a job injury. The statistics are based on 2013 data, except for Germany and United States are based on 2010 data and Italy is based on 2008 data. Germany and Hong Kong statistics include only people losing more than four and three days of work time, respectively.

Just what are these benefits to the firm? First, lower risks of injury or death enable employers to attract workers at lower wage rates. Because workers value job safety, they are willing to accept a lower wage for work performed in a healthful, relatively safe environment. Second, a safer workplace reduces the amount of disruption of the production process that job accidents create. Workplace mishaps and the absence of key employees during rehabilitation often halt or slow the production process. Third, a safer workplace reduces the cost of recruiting, screening, and training workers. The fewer workers injured on the job, the fewer resources will be required to hire and train new employees. Fourth, workplace safety helps maintain the firm's return on its specific investment in human capital. Job fatalities and injuries terminate or reduce the firm's returns on its previously financed specific, formal, and on-the-job training. Finally, fewer job-related accidents translate into lower workers' compensation insurance rates. Such rates are determined by the probability and types of accidents experienced in a given firm.

To determine the profit-maximizing level of workplace safety, the cost-minimizing firm will compare the marginal benefit of safety (MB_s) against the marginal cost (MC_s). In so doing, it will use the following decision rule: Provide additional job safety so long as the marginal benefit exceeds the marginal cost. In Figure 13.3 we see that the profit-maximizing level of job safety is Q_s units, at which $MB_s = MC_s$. Conclusion? Even in the absence of government intervention, this firm will find it cost-effective and profitable to provide some degree of job safety. In this case, our firm will provide Q_s units.

Another observation merits comment here. The perception that some jobs, say coal mining and construction, are *inherently* dangerous while others, say accounting and teaching, are innately safe is slightly misleading. A more accurate statement is that given present technology, it is inherently more costly to provide job safety in some occupations than others. Therefore, firms with similar marginal benefit schedules but different marginal costs of safety will offer differing levels of job safety. A firm with the same marginal benefits curve as that in Figure 13.3 but with significantly higher marginal costs of providing job safety than those shown by MC_s would provide much less job safety than Q_s units.

Society's Optimal Level of Job Safety

A firm's profit-maximizing level of job safety *may or may not* be society's optimal level of job safety. In addressing this topic, let's first assume perfect information about and assessment of job risk, and then examine a situation where these are not the case.

1 Perfect Information and Assessment

If workers have full information about possible work hazards and accurately assess the likelihood of occupational fatality, injury, or disease, then the amount of job safety offered by employers will match the level required to maximize society's well-being. Where workers have full knowledge of job risk, employers providing hazardous work environments will have to pay a wage premium to attract a sufficient number of employees. The existence of the compensating wage differential will ensure that the employer's extra benefit from providing a safer workplace (including a *reduced* wage premium) will match the extra benefit of job safety from society's perspective.

In Figure 13.3 we are saying that given our assumption of perfect information and assessment, curve MB_s depicts both the private *and* social marginal benefits of job safety. The number of units of job safety shown as Q_s will maximize the firm's profits *and* optimize society's well-being.

2 Imperfect Information and Assessment

Where information about job hazards is limited and/or workers underestimate the personal risk of occupational fatality, injury, or disease, employers will provide less job safety than is socially optimal.

To demonstrate this generalization, suppose workers mistakenly judge the job in question to be risk-free, when in reality one of the substances handled by workers is highly hazardous. Because employees are unaware of the long-term danger, the job hazard will *not* reduce labor supply to this occupation and employer. The market wage therefore will *not* contain a wage premium required to compensate workers for the added job risk. Consequently, the firm's marginal benefit from reducing the health hazard—that is, from providing a safer workplace—will be smaller than it would be if workers had full information about the job danger. Extra units of job safety will fail to reduce the wages paid by this firm because the labor market has not dictated payment of a wage premium to compensate workers for their true risk. From the firm's perspective, the marginal benefit from providing job safety is less than it would be if full information about the long-term health consequences of the job were known.

13.1 | World of Work

Climate Change and Occupational Health

The rising amount of greenhouse gases in the earth's atmosphere is forecast to increase global temperatures in the near future. In some cases, individuals can offset the negative effects of rising temperatures through the use of air conditioning and reducing the amount of time spent outside. However, for certain workers, this approach is not possible since their jobs require them to be outside. The impact of rising temperatures on the health of these workers is important since productivity and health are linked, and occupational injuries and illnesses are costly. Thus, knowing the effects of higher temperature on workers' health is important to assess the costs of climate change.

Marcus Dillender investigates the impact of temperature on occupational health by merging information on worker injuries and illness from two sources with daily temperature data. One data set uses workers' compensation claim data from Texas. The other data set uses daily injury data from above ground mining sites across the United States.

The Texas data reveals that both abnormally cool and hot days have higher injury rates. A day with a high temperature between 86 and 88 degrees will have claim rates for the following three days that are 2.1–2.8 percent higher than for a day with a high temperature of 59–61 degrees. The results indicate that the claim rates are 3.5–3.7 percent higher for a day with a high temperature of over 100 degrees. Likewise, days with cold temperatures also have higher claim rates. A day with a high temperature below 35 degrees will have claim rates for the following three days that are 3.4–5.8 percent higher than for a day with a high temperature of 59–61 degrees.

The results from the mining data indicate that high temperatures in hot climates have more harmful effects than the rare high temperatures in cooler climates. This finding may be because there are more limited options to mitigate the effects of high temperatures in already hot locations.

Source: Based on Marcus Dillender, "Climate Change and Occupational Health: Are There Limits to Our Ability to Adapt?" *Journal of Human Resources,* forthcoming.

WW13.1

The marginal benefit schedule of job safety as viewed by the firm in this situation is shown in Figure 13.3 as curve MB_S'. The firm compares MB_S' with its marginal cost of providing safety (MC_S) and settles for Q_S' units of job safety. Result: *Job safety is underprovided from society's viewpoint.* Suppose the true marginal benefits of each added unit of safety are those shown as MB_S rather than MB_S'. Given full information and accurate assessment by workers of the job danger, the firm's relevant marginal benefit curve would be MB_S, and both the profit-maximizing and socially optimal levels of job safety would be Q_S' units. As we can observe by extending a vertical line upward from Q_S' to MB_S and observing the triangle *abc,* the $Q_S'Q_S$ units of job safety generate marginal benefits to society that exceed the marginal costs MC_S. But under conditions of incomplete information or underestimation of risk by workers, and therefore no market wage premium, the firm has no incentive to provide these extra units. From its perspective, the marginal benefit is less than the marginal cost. We conclude that a firm's profit-maximizing level of job safety may not always conform to society's optimal level of job safety. In our example, society's welfare loss from this inefficiency is area *abc.*

The Occupational Safety and Health Act

The Occupational Safety and Health Act of 1970 interjected the federal government directly into regulation of workplace hazards. The Act's purpose was to reduce the incidence of job injury and illness by identifying and eliminating hazards found in the workplace. The Occupational Safety and Health Administration (OSHA) was given the responsibility of developing safety and health standards and enforcing them through workplace inspections and fines for violations.

The Case for OSHA

OSHA was controversial when passed and remains subject to debate today. Those who support the legislation contend that the costs of providing a healthful and safe workplace are legitimate business costs that should not be transferred to workers. According to this view, imperfect information, underestimation of risk, and barriers to occupational mobility prevent the labor market from making the adjustments that would provide adequate wage premiums for hazardous jobs. Thus, for reasons described earlier, government standards are needed to force firms to provide more job safety than is dictated by their own self-interests. Finally, supporters of OSHA regulation point out that much of the criticism has originated in the corporate community, where resistance is predictable and understandable. To see why, note in Figure 13.3 that under conditions of incomplete information and improper assessment of risk, a minimum safety standard, say of Q_s units, would force this firm to provide $Q_s' Q_s$ units of safety, which, from its perspective, cost more to produce than they generate in private benefits. We see this by comparing the *ac* segment of MC_s to the *ad* segment of MB_s'.

Criticisms of OSHA

Critics of OSHA counter that safety standards and inspections represent an unwarranted, costly government intrusion into the private sector. They point out that even though information about job hazards may be imperfect and workers may inaccurately assess personal risk, no reason exists to expect that workers will systematically underestimate the risk of job hazards. Rather, workers could just as well overestimate the likelihood that they will be the unlucky parties affected by occupational death, injury, or illness, just as many purchasers of state lottery tickets or sweepstake entrants overestimate the probability that they will win. According to this line of reasoning, it is possible that wage premiums for hazardous jobs are greater than they would be if there were perfect information and risk assessment. Restated, the perspective that "it will probably happen to me" may dissuade people from hazardous occupations, driving up the wage rate for those who perform such work. Recall that when such wage premiums exist, the firm's marginal benefit from reducing the job hazard is greater than otherwise, and an under-allocation of resources to job safety is not likely.

Critics of OSHA also assert that workplace standards often bear no relationship to reductions in injury and illness. They point to the numerous trivial standards—wall height rules for fire extinguishers, specified shapes of toilet seats, and so forth—to support this assertion. In addition, opponents of OSHA cite the complexity of determining just what the standards are. Wiedenbaum has noted OSHA's original definition of an "exit": "That portion of a means of egress which is separated from all other spaces of the building or structure by construction or equipment as required in this subpart to provide a protected way of travel to the exit discharge." Wiedenbaum contrasts this definition with one from a dictionary: An exit is "a passage or way out."[25] In the face of criticism over trivial rules and bureaucratic language, OSHA revoked over 1,100 standards in 1978 and attempted to rewrite remaining standards in simple terms.

---

[25] Wiedenbaum, Murray L. *Business, Government, and the Public* (Englewood Cliffs, NJ: Prentice-Hall, Inc., 1977).

Findings and Implications

The controversy over OSHA has been heightened by the mixed findings on whether OSHA standards and inspections have reduced occupational accidents and injuries. Since the passage of OSHA, the rate of fatal injury on the job has declined, but the rate of workdays lost per year from nonfatal injuries has risen.

Studies attempting to sort out OSHA's role in the overall workplace fatality and accident trends are fraught with data and interpretation problems. Nevertheless, several noteworthy attempts have been made. Research looking at early years following passage of OSHA found little indication that OSHA reduced industrial injury rates. Specifically, Viscusi[26] found that OSHA had no significant effect on workplace safety for the years 1972–1975, and Smith and McCaffrey[27] found no effects of OSHA inspections during 1974–1976. These scholars warned, however, that caution needed to be exercised in interpreting their findings. The results may be due to lack of enforcement of the law or inadequate penalties for firms failing to meet the safety standards.

Studies of more recent periods are mixed. In a follow-up study to the earlier Smith and McCaffrey research, Ruser and Smith[28] found that OSHA had little impact on workplace injuries in the early 1980s. On the other hand, a 1986 study by Viscusi[29] covering the 1973–1983 period discovered that OSHA inspections modestly reduced the rate of both occupational injury and lost workdays. Gray and Jones[30] found that OSHA inspections within the manufacturing sector have reduced the number of OSHA citations of safety violations by one-half. Using 1998–2005 data, Haviland Burns, Gray, Ruder, and Mendeloff report that an OSHA inspection with penalties reduced injuries by 19–24 percent in the two years following an inspection.[31]

If OSHA becomes increasingly effective in reducing workplace fatalities, injuries, and diseases in hazardous jobs, existing wage differentials between hazardous and safe jobs should decline over time. Recall from Chapter 6 that one determinant of labor supply to an occupation is the nonwage aspects of employment. By making dangerous jobs safer, effective OSHA standards may increase the supply of labor to the formerly hazardous jobs, eventually reducing the wage premiums paid in those lines of work. Wage premiums for risk of workplace death or injury are one of several sources of wage differentials among workers. Thus, over the long run, highly effective OSHA regulations conceivably could reduce some of the wage disparity among jobs in the economy.

Other subtle labor market effects may possibly result from government regulation of occupational health and safety. For example, the high cost of complying with OSHA standards in some industries may result in the demise of smaller nonunion firms, increased product market share for larger unionized producers, and enhanced bargaining power and wages for union workers.[32] As a second example, the amount of money firms

---

[26] W. Kip Viscusi, "The Impact of Occupational Safety and Health Regulation," *Bell Journal of Economics,* Spring 1978, pp. 117–140.

[27] Robert Smith and David McCaffrey, "An Assessment of OSHA's Recent Effect on Injury Rates," *Journal of Human Resources,* Winter 1983, pp. 131–145.

[28] John W. Ruser and Robert S. Smith, "Reestimating OSHA's Effects: Have the Data Changed?" *Journal of Human Resources,* Spring 1991, pp. 212–235.

[29] W. Kip Viscusi, "Reforming OSHA Regulation of Workplace Risks," in Leonard W. Weiss and Michael W. Klass (eds.), *Regulatory Reform: What Actually Happened?* (Boston: Little, Brown, 1986), p. 262.

[30] Wayne B. Gray and Carol Adaire Jones, "Longitudinal Patterns of Compliance with OSHA in the Manufacturing Sector," *Journal of Human Resources,* Fall 1991, pp. 623–653. For evidence that the effect of OSHA enforcement diminished over the 1979–1998 period, see Wayne B. Gray and John M. Mendeloff, "The Declining Effects of OSHA Inspections on Manufacturing Injuries, 1979–1998," *Industrial and Labor Relations Review,* July 2005, pp. 571–587.

[31] Amelia M. Haviland, Rachel M. Burns, Wayne B. Gray, Teague Ruder, and John Mendeloff, "A New Estimate of the Impact of OSHA Inspections on Manufacturing Injury Rates, 1998–2005," *American Journal of Industrial Medicine,* November 2012, pp. 964–975.

[32] For empirical support for this scenario as it relates to the Federal Coal Mine Health and Safety Act of 1969, see Scott Fuess and Mark Lowenstein, "Further Analysis of the Effects of Government Safety Regulation: The Case of the 1969 Coal Mine Health and Safety Act," *Economic Inquiry,* April 1990, pp. 354–389. Also relevant is David Weil, "Are Mandated Health and Safety Committees Substitutes for or Supplements to Labor Unions?" *Industrial and Labor Relations Review,* April 1999, pp. 339–360.

spend to comply with OSHA standards may directly compete with more productive expenditures to improve job safety.[33]

13.2 | World of Work

The Effect of Workers' Compensation on Job Safety

Each of the 50 states has workers' compensation laws requiring employers to pay legally established benefits to workers injured on the job (or to families of workers who die from work-related accidents). Firms are mandated by law to purchase insurance to finance these benefits.* The insurance premiums the firms must pay vary directly with the risk of accidents at their establishments. For example, logging firms, which typically have higher-than-average accident rates, have larger workers' compensation premiums than, say, fast-food establishments, which have better safety records.

What are the effects of workers' compensation laws on workplace safety? These laws produce two opposing effects. First, the insurance premiums required under the laws create an incentive for firms to make their workplaces safer. By reducing accident rates, firms can lower the workers' compensation premium they must pay. Thus the marginal benefit of providing any given level of safety is greater for the firm in the presence of workers' compensation. Firms therefore discover that it is in their profit interest to increase their levels of job safety. (You should use Figure 13.3 to demonstrate this effect.)

But workers' compensation laws also create an opposing effect—a *moral hazard problem.* Generally defined, this problem is the tendency of one party to a contract to alter his or her behavior

in ways that are costly to the other party. As it relates to workers' compensation insurance, the moral hazard problem is that workers may be less careful as they go about their work, knowing they are insured against on-the-job accidents. Taken alone, this change in behavior would lead to higher incidences of job accidents.

In a major study, Moore and Viscusi have found that the workers' compensation laws have had a dramatic effect in reducing job fatalities.[†] This finding implies that the positive incentive effect of the laws swamps the negative moral hazard effect. Specifically, Moore and Viscusi show that fatality risks in American industries would rise by over 40 percent if the workers' compensation program were not in place. They also conclude that the program saves almost 2,000 lives per year. Finally, Moore and Viscusi note that these sizable positive effects stand in contrast to the smaller effects identified in other studies as resulting from direct workplace regulation by the OSHA. This fact suggests that an "injury tax" imposed on employers might be a more efficient way to reduce on-the-job accidents than the present regulatory approach.

* Depending on the state, this insurance may be purchased from a state agency or from private insurance firms. Also, some states allow firms to "self-insure," which means they may establish an insurance plan within their own enterprises.

† Michael J. Moore and W. Kip Viscusi, *Compensating Mechanisms for Job Risks: Wages, Workers' Compensation, and Product Liability* (Princeton, NJ: Princeton University Press, 1990).

---

[33] Ann P. Bartel and Lacy Glenn Thomas, "Direct and Indirect Effects of Regulation: A New Look at OSHA's Impact," *Journal of Law and Economics,* April 1985, pp. 1–25.

13.2 *Quick Review*

- Each year about 5,147 occupational fatalities and about 3.3 million nonfatal occupational injuries occur in the United States.

- A firm's profit-maximizing level of workplace safety occurs where its marginal cost and marginal benefit of providing safety are equal.

- Profit-maximizing levels of job safety may be lower than socially optimal levels where workers lack information about job risk or underestimate the probability of being hurt or killed.

- The Occupational Safety and Health Act of 1970 remains somewhat controversial; only recently has preliminary evidence emerged finding that OSHA standards and inspections are effective in reducing job injuries.

Your Turn

Suppose a firm's marginal cost of an extra unit of job safety is $250,000; the marginal private benefit, $200,000; and the marginal social benefit, $300,000. Will the firm provide this extra unit of job safety? Should the government intervene? If so, what are its policy options? (*Answer:* See page 542.)

WW13.2 Questions about the effectiveness of OSHA in relationship to its costs have led some economists to call for alternative or complementary approaches to promoting job safety. As one option, the government could accumulate and directly provide information to workers about the injury experience of various employers, much as it publishes the on-time performance of airlines. Alternatively, it could mandate that firms develop and disclose information about known workplace hazards. In either case, the availability of information would help workers assess risk. This, in turn, would enable labor markets to establish more appropriate compensating wage differentials.

As a second option, government could impose an "injury tax" on employers based on their incidences of work-related injuries and deaths. By boosting the employers' marginal benefit of job safety, such a tax would provide an incentive for firms to make their workplaces safer.

GOVERNMENT AS A RENT PROVIDER

Government influences wages and employment in labor markets in more subtle ways than establishing labor laws, imposing a legal minimum wage, and setting occupational safety standards. One such method is through providing economic rent to labor market participants. *Economic rent in the labor market is the difference between the wage paid to a particular worker and the wage just sufficient to keep that person in his or her present employment.* Recall from Chapter 6 that a market labor supply curve such as the one shown in Figure 13.4 is essentially a marginal opportunity cost curve. The curve reflects the value of each worker's next best alternative, whether that be another job, household production, or leisure. Given the market wage of $8 in Figure 13.4, all employed workers with the exception of the marginal one, Q_0, receive economic rent, the total of which is area *abc*. To clarify further, suppose Jones is the worker shown by Q_j and that her marginal opportunity cost is $16 an hour. We can see then that Jones is receiving a $2 per hour "rent" (= $18 − $16).

What would happen to Jones's economic rent if the government passed a law that had the effect of increasing the market wage to $20 an hour? She and all other workers who remain employed would receive an *increase* in

FIGURE 13.4 Economic Rent in Labor Markets

At the market wage of $18, employers will hire Q_0 workers. The labor supply curve indicates that these Q_0 workers collectively receive economic rent equal to the area *abc*. The Q_j worker receives a $2 per hour rent ($18 minus the person's opportunity cost of $16).

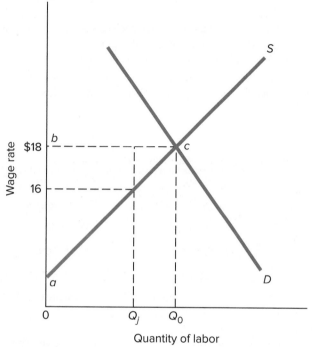

economic rent of $2 (= $20 − $18). But why might the government be interested in providing increases in economic rent to workers? According to some economic and political theorists, the main goal of politicians is to get and stay elected. Consequently, they offer and provide a wide range of publicly provided goods and services that enhance the utility of their constituents. One such service may be the provision or the enhancement of economic rents. According to this controversial theory, groups of workers—for example, professional groups or unions—have a demand for economic rent; that is, they are *rent seekers*. Elected officials respond to this demand by supplying the publicly provided service, economic rent; they are *rent providers*.[34]

Admittedly, care must be taken not to oversimplify here. Higher wages provided by law or regulation may produce lower market-determined wages for other workers, higher product prices for consumers, lower corporate dividends for common stockholders, or some combination of all three. These groups are interested in their own rents and may intervene politically to block the provision of rents to a group of workers. But because the acquisition of information and political lobbying are costly, people have little incentive to try to block rent provision when they perceive their personal losses to be small. Hence elected officials may find it beneficial to dispense economic rent to highly organized groups of workers.

This concept of rent provision is apparent in some instances of occupational licensure and in legislation that establishes tariffs, quotas, and domestic content laws.

---

[34] A political scientist once defined *politics* as "who gets what, when, and how." This view of politics has been formalized into a theory of regulation by several economists, see, for example, George J. Stigler, "The Theory of Economic Regulation," *Bell Journal of Economics and Management Science*, Spring 1971, pp. 3–21, see also Sam Peltzman, "Toward a More General Theory of Regulation," *Journal of Law and Economics*, August 1976, pp. 181–210.

Occupational Licensure

In the United States, 20 percent of all workers are subject to some form of occupational licensing. In fact, over 800 occupations are licensed in at least one state.[35] Table 13.3 provides a partial list of occupations requiring licenses in one state.

In many instances, licensing of occupational groups (pharmacists, surgeons) is held to be necessary to protect consumers against incompetents who might do irreparable damage. In these circumstances, governmental licensing may be the most efficient way to minimize the costs of obtaining information needed by consumers to make optimal buying decisions. In other situations, the occupational groups themselves, not consumers, generate the demand for licensing. These groups may wish to restrict access to licenses as a way to obtain economic rent for licensees.

TABLE 13.3 Selected Licensed Occupations: State of Washington

Accountants	Dentists	Osteopaths
Agricultural brokers	Dispensing opticians	Oyster farmers
Aircraft pilots	Egg dealers	Pesticide applicators
Ambulance drivers	Embalmers	Pharmacists
Architects	Engineers	Physical therapists
Auditors	Fish dealers	Physician assistants
Barbers	Funeral directors	Physicians and surgeons
Beauticians	Harbor pilots	Proprietary school agents
Blasters	Insurance adjusters	Psychologists
Boathouse operators	Insurance agents	Real estate brokers
Boiler workers	Landscape architects	Real estate sales agents
Boxers	Law clerks	Sanitarians
Boxing managers	Lawyers	Security advisers
Chiropodists	Librarians	Security brokers
Chiropractors	Livestock dealers	Surveyors
Commercial fishers	Marine pilots (inland)	Teachers
Commercial guides	Milk vendors	Veterinarians
Dairy technicians	Naturopaths	Weighers and graders
Debt adjusters	Nurses	Well diggers
Dental hygienists	Optometrists	Wrestlers

Source: Employment Security Department, State of Washington.

---

[35] Morris M. Kleiner, *Licensing Occupations: Ensuring Quality or Restricting Competition?* (Kalamazoo, MI: W.E. Upjohn Institute, 2006). For evidence that is very difficult to de-license an occupation, see Robert J. Thornton and Edward J. Timmons, "The De-Licensing of Occupations in the United States," *Monthly Labor Review,* May 2015, pp. 1–19.

FIGURE 13.5 **Rent Provision through Occupational Licensure**

By setting a limit of 7,000 licenses in this labor market, the government indirectly increases the wage from $18 to $21, thereby providing licensees collectively with an increase in economic rent of *abce* and creating an efficiency loss of *gcf*.

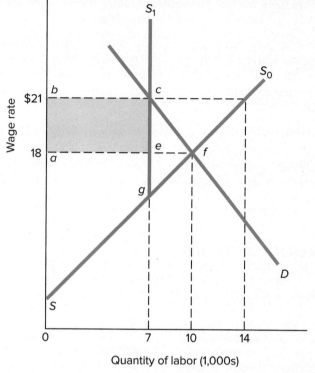

Quantity of labor (1,000s)

Figure 13.5 demonstrates how occupational licensure can confer economic rent. Suppose the prelicensing equilibrium wage and employment level are $18 and 10,000 workers, respectively. Next assume that licensing has the effect of restricting the total number of licensed workers to 7,000. In effect, the postlicensing labor supply curve is S_gS_1, compared to the old curve of SS_0. Notice that licensing increases the market wage to $21 an hour and that total employment falls from 10,000 to 7,000. The $21 wage attracts another 4,000 workers (= 14,000 – 10,000) who would like to work in this occupation. These 14,000 workers see 7,000 licenses, and those who get licensed receive increases in economic rent of $3 for every hour worked. As a consequence, the government's action *raises* the total rent *to those employed* by $21,000. This can be determined by noting that the total rent was area *Saf* prior to the licensing. Following licensing, the total economic rent increases to *Sbcg*. Thus, the *gain* in rent is *abce*—the shaded area in the figure—and the loss of rent to the workers displaced by the licensing is area *gef*.

Close inspection of Figure 13.5 reveals that occupational licensure of a type that restricts labor supply creates an efficiency loss for society—in this case, triangle *gcf*. The 3,000 additional employees who would have been employed in this occupation would contribute more to the value of society's output in this employment (as shown by segment *cf* of the demand curve) than in their most productive alternative uses of time (as shown by segment *gf* of the supply curve). In addition, the true efficiency loss to society may be greater than area *gcf*. To secure the licensing law and thus the added economic rent, this particular occupational group most likely had to spend large amounts for political lobbying, public relations advertising, and other activities. From society's perspective, these expenditures diverted resources away from potentially higher-valued uses, adding to the overall efficiency cost of the occupational licensing.

To summarize: Occupational licensure of the type restricting labor supply increases the market wage, confers economic rent to licensees, and causes economic inefficiency. We might add that it is possible that the competition for the limited number of licenses will cause the new licensees to expend dollars in an amount equal to the expected rents. Thus those who are automatically granted licenses when the law is passed and those who train potential licensees will be the major beneficiaries of the law.

WW13.3 Morris Kleiner and Alan Krueger used the first nationally representative survey to examine the prevalence and effects of occupational licensing.[36] They report that in 2006 about 29 percent of workers were required to hold a federal, state, or local government issued occupational license. This is a sharp increase from the early 1950s, when less than 5 percent of the workforce was covered by state-level licensing laws.

Their analysis reveals several patterns regarding which workers are likely to be required to hold an occupational license. First, more educated workers are more likely to hold an occupational license. More than 40 percent of workers with a postcollege education are required to hold a license. On the other hand, only 11 percent of high school dropouts have a license. Second, occupational licensing is more common among

---

13.3 World of Work

Who Can Whiten Teeth?*

Teeth whitening is usually done by placing disposable strips infused with a whitening agent on a person's teeth. These strips are determined to be safe by the Food and Drug Administration and are classified as a cosmetic. Dentists started to offer teeth whitening services to their patients in the 1990s. As teeth whitening increased in popularity, businesses such as hair salons and day spas started to perform this procedure. Dentists, who charged as much as 10 times the price for the same service, started to complain to state dental regulatory boards.

In 2003, the North Carolina Board of Dental Examiners (NCBDE), which is primarily composed of dentists, sent at least 47 cease and desist letters to nondentists providing teeth whitening services and product manufacturers. These letters tried to prevent them from offering teeth whitening services by warning them that the practice of dentistry without a license is a crime. The Federal Trade Commission (FTC) determined that the NCBDE was motivated by self-interest and not patient safety. As a result, the FTC deemed the cease and desist letters to be anticompetitive and unfair competition and told the NCBDE to stop trying to prevent nondentists from providing teeth whitening services. In response, the NCDBE sued the FTC arguing it was immune from antitrust regulation since it was a state-authorized entity.

By a 6-3 vote, the Supreme Court in 2015 ruled the NCBDE was not immune from antitrust regulation. The Court determined that the NCBDE had not been actively supervised by state government. The majority opinion stated that market participants (in this case dentists) are not allowed to regulate their own markets without antitrust regulation.

* Based on "Tooth and Justice," *Economist,* October 18, 2014, page 32; and Brent Kendall, "Supreme Court Affirms Anti-Trust Authority Over Licensing Boards," *Wall Street Journal,* February 25, 2015.

---

[36] Morris M. Kleiner and Alan B. Krueger, "The Prevalence and Effects of Occupational Licensing," *British Journal of Industrial Relations,* December 2010, pp. 676–687. Also see Maury Gittleman, Mark A. Klee, and Morris M. Kleiner, "Analyzing the Labor Market Outcomes of Occupational Licensing," *Industrial Relations,* January 2018, pp. 57–100.

union members and government workers. Third, minorities are more likely to hold licenses, but there is no difference across genders.

Some studies have examined the effects of licensing. Kleiner and Krueger find having a license raises hourly wages by about 15 percent (about the same effect as labor unions). In contrast to unions, however, licensing does not reduce the dispersion of wages across workers. Kleiner, Marier, Park, and Wing, using data on basic health care services, report that states that gave greater independence for nurse practitioners did not result in worse health ouctomes.[37] However, prices for well-child visits fell 3–16 percent and the wages for physicians fell 3 percent with looser licensing restrictions due to the increased competition.

Tariffs, Quotas, and Domestic Content Rules

Collectively, tariffs, quotas, and domestic content rules provide a second example of governmental provision of economic rent to groups of workers. *Tariffs* are excise duties on imported products, *import quotas* are limits on the quantity or total value of imports, and *domestic content rules* are requirements that a specified portion of imported products contain domestically produced or domestically assembled components. These laws and regulations tend to increase the prices of foreign goods, raise the sales of the competing protected domestic products, and increase the derived demand for the U.S. workers who help produce the domestic

FIGURE 13.6 Rent Provision: Tariffs, Quotas, and Domestic Content Laws

Import restrictions reduce labor demand in foreign nations and increase the demand for specific types of labor in the protected country. These restrictions therefore cause increases in wages in these specific labor markets. In this case, the wage rises from $20 to $22, and economic rent increases by the amount *bcef.*

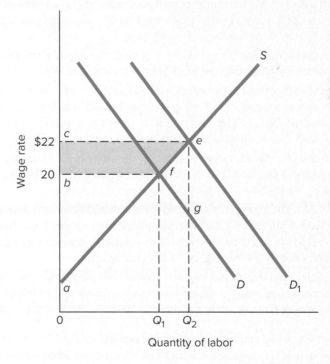

[37] See Morris M. Kleiner, Allison Marier, Kyoung Won Park, and Coady Wing, "Relaxing Occupational Licensing Requirements: Analyzing Wages and Prices for a Medical Service," *Journal of Law and Economics,* May 2016, pp. 261–291.

goods. Assuming a competitive labor market in which there is a normal upward-sloping labor supply curve, the increased domestic demand for labor increases the equilibrium wage and employment. If the labor market is imperfectly competitive, the increase in labor demand enhances the bargaining position of unions and increases the probability that union-negotiated wages will rise. It is therefore perfectly understandable why some U.S. unions—for example, the United Steelworkers and the United Auto Workers—strongly support tariffs, quotas, and domestic content rules. Quite simply, these laws increase economic rent for domestic workers at the expense of foreign producers and domestic consumers.

It is a fairly simple matter to portray this gain in economic rent graphically. Figure 13.6 depicts an initial equilibrium wage of $20 per hour at which firms hire Q_1 workers. The tariff, import quota, or domestic content law increases the derived demand for labor from D to D_1. The increase in labor demand raises the equilibrium wage from $20 to $22 an hour and causes the level of employment to rise to Q_2. Prior to the trade restriction, the total economic rent to workers was *abf*. After the law, it is *ace*. The workers in this market thus collectively gain an increase in economic rent equal to the shaded area *bcef*.

Chapter Summary

1. Labor relations laws and regulations have influenced the growth of both private and public sector unionism in the United States. To the extent that union membership and union bargaining power are positively correlated, labor law influences the determination of wages and employment in labor markets.

2. Labor law in general and specific provisions of labor law in particular influence union bargaining power—and therefore labor market results—independently of impacts on union membership.

3. The basic model of a competitive labor market predicts that an above-equilibrium minimum wage applied to all sections of the economy will reduce employment. The more elastic the supply and demand for labor, the greater the resulting unemployment.

4. The existence of a nondiscriminatory monopsony may cause the negative employment and efficiency consequences predicted by the competitive model to not fully materialize.

5. Empirical evidence indicates that the minimum wage *(a)* reduces employment, particularly for teenagers; *(b)* increases unemployment of teenagers by less than the reduction in employment; *(c)* reduces the amount of on-the-job training offered to low-wage workers; and *(d)* does not greatly alter the degree of family income inequality and extent of poverty.

6. A firm incurs both costs and benefits when it improves the safety of its workplace. A profit-maximizing firm will provide a level of job safety at which its marginal benefit and marginal cost of safety are equal.

7. If workers have full information about possible work hazards and accurately assess job risks, the profit-maximizing level of job safety will tend to be optimal from society's viewpoint. If information is incomplete and job risks are inaccurately assessed, then society's optimal level of job safety may be greater than the level willingly provided by profit-maximizing firms.

8. The Occupational Safety and Health Act imposed a set of workplace safety standards on individual firms. The Act is controversial, and the debate over its provisions and methods of enforcement has been heightened by studies that present mixed findings about its effect on the number of work-related accidents.

9. Government affects wages and employment in specific occupations through its rent provision activities. Two examples are *(a)* occupational licensure that restricts labor supply; and *(b)* tariffs, import quotas, and domestic content laws, which increase labor demand for protected domestic workers.

Terms and Concepts

discriminatory discharge

blacklists

yellow-dog contracts

lockouts

strikebreakers

injunctions

marginal cost of job safety

marginal benefit from job safety

Norris–LaGuardia Act of 1932

Wagner Act of 1935

Taft–Hartley Act of 1947

Landrum–Griffin Act of 1959

economic rent

rent seekers and rent providers

tariffs

secondary boycotts

hot-cargo clauses

Fair Labor Standards Act of 1938

minimum wage

Occupational Safety and Health Act of 1970

import quotas

domestic content rules

Questions and Study Suggestions

1. Explain each of the following statements:

   a. "The Wagner Act of 1935 reduced the costs of providing union services and thereby increased the number of union members."

   b. "The Wagner Act of 1935 increased the demand for union services by increasing the relative bargaining power of unions. This increased union membership."

2. Show graphically how an increase in the minimum wage might affect employment in (a) a competitive labor market and (b) a labor market characterized by monopsony.

3. Explain how an increase in the minimum wage could

   a. Reduce teenage employment but leave the teenage unemployment rate unaffected.

   b. Reduce investment in human capital.

   c. Leave the poverty rate unchanged.

4. Why are most labor unions—whose constituents receive wages substantially above the minimum wage—strong supporters of the minimum wage? Why might unions composed of skilled workers who are *pure complements in production* with raw materials produced by low-skilled workers *oppose* a large increase in the minimum wage?

5. Evaluate this statement: "Profit-maximizing firms lack an incentive to provide job safety, and consequently, the federal government must intervene legislatively to protect workers against the unsafe working conditions that will surely result."

6. Answer these questions on the basis of the information in the accompanying table. The data are for a competitive firm.

   a. What is the profit-maximizing level of job safety as viewed by the firm? Explain.

   b. Assume that information is perfect and that workers accurately assess personal risk. What is the optimal level of job safety from society's perspective? Explain.

   c. Suppose the government imposed a minimum safety standard of 5 units. Why would the firm object? Speculate about why some workers might object.

   d. Suppose new technology reduced this firm's marginal cost data to $1, $2, $3, $4, and $5 for the first through fifth units of safety. How would this firm respond?

Marginal Benefit from Safety	Amount of Safety Provided	Marginal Cost of Safety
$60	1	$1
40	2	3
20	3	6
10	4	9
6	5	15

7. How might each of the following be interpreted as an example of rent provision by the government?

   a. State laws require that out-of-state big-game hunters be accompanied by one of a limited number of licensed in-state hunting guides.

   b. An increase in the minimum wage increases the likelihood that firms will hire skilled unionized labor rather than unskilled labor.

   c. A state law requires that graduates of dental schools pass a stringent examination, established by a panel of dentists, in order to practice dentistry.

Internet Exercise

Who or What Is the NLRB?

Go to the National Labor Relations Board's home page **(http://www.nlrb.gov)**. Where is the NLRB located? What does it do? How many members are on the board? What is common to all board members' educational backgrounds? What is the main message of the board's most recent press release? List the titles of three recent decisions made by the board.

Internet Links

The Occupational Safety and Health Administration website provides detailed information about safety regulations as well as safety inspection statistics **(http://www.osha.gov)**.

The Department of Labor website reports information about the current federal and state minimum wage laws **(http://www.dol.gov/WHD/minimumwage.htm)**.

Chapter 14

Labor Market Discrimination

After reading this chapter, you should be able to:

1. Compare gender and racial differences in key economic variables and summarize nondiscriminatory factors that contribute to gender and racial differences in labor markets.
2. Distinguish between wage, employment, occupational, and human capital discrimination.
3. Use the taste for discrimination model to analyze the effects of discrimination.
4. Discuss the theory of statistical discrimination.
5. Explain the crowding model of discrimination and summarize the empirical evidence.
6. Explain the extent to which observed wage differentials may be the result of rational choices and summarize the empirical evidence regarding discrimination against women and minorities.
7. Describe the major government laws and policies to reduce discrimination and their effectiveness.

Few would seriously question the assertion that discrimination based on race, gender, religion, and ethnic background is a fact of American life. Abundant statistical evidence exists to suggest discrimination: Comparison of African–Americans and whites and women and men reveals substantial differences in earnings, unemployment rates, allocations among various occupations, and accumulations of human capital. Also, anecdotal evidence of discrimination can be found in newspaper headlines almost daily: "Court upholds racial discrimination suit against grocery chain"; "Few jobs for African–American teenagers"; "Minorities excluded from top executive positions"; "Wage gap for women persists"; "Sexual harassment in the workplace." Because of the importance of labor market discrimination as an institutional feature of labor markets, we will devote this chapter to this subject.

Several caveats must be made explicit at the outset. Discrimination is complex, multifaceted, and deeply ingrained in behavior. It is also difficult to measure or quantify. Furthermore, any reasonably complete explanation of discrimination must be interdisciplinary; economic analysis can contribute only insights rather than a full-blown explanation of the phenomenon. In fact, we will find a number of contrasting explanations of discrimination within economics, and these frequently imply different policy prescriptions. Bluntly stated, discrimination constitutes an untidy area of study that is characterized by controversy and

FIGURE 14.1 **Female to Male Hourly Wage Ratio in the United States**

The ratio of female to male hourly earnings in the United States rose substantially between 1979 and the mid-1990s and has risen slightly since then.

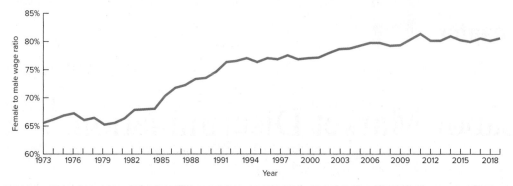

Source: Author calculations from "Current Population Survey." U.S. Bureau of Labour Statistics. www.bls.gov

a lack of consensus. Finally, to achieve a degree of focus in our discussion, discrimination based on gender (sex) and race is emphasized in this chapter. But keep in mind that age, ethnic origin, religious background, physical disability, and sexual orientation are equally important bases for discrimination and are neglected here only for the sake of brevity.

GENDER AND RACIAL DIFFERENCES

It is not difficult to find statistical discrepancies that lead one to suspect the presence of discrimination based on gender and race.

Earnings

Figure 14.1 shows the ratio of female to male hourly wages. We observe that from 1973 to 1978 the hourly earnings of women workers in the United States were about 65 percent of those of men. From 1979 to the mid-1990s the percentage rose significantly, and it has risen slightly since then to about 80 percent.

Several explanations have been given for this narrowing of the gender gap in earnings. First, evidence exists that the skill levels of female workers have increased. Second, labor market discrimination perhaps has declined. Third, the industrial restructuring of the economy away from manufacturing jobs and toward services may have negatively affected the earnings of men more than women. Fourth, the decline in unionism may have reduced male pay more than female pay. Finally, the occupational distribution of men and women workers may have changed positively in favor of women.[1]

---

[1] This list is drawn from Elaine Sorensen, *Exploring the Reasons behind the Narrowing Gender Gap in Earnings* (Washington, DC: Urban Institute Press, 1991), pp. 129–130. For more on recent earnings trends, see Francine D. Blau and Lawrence M. Kahn, "The U.S. Gender Pay Gap in the 1990s: Slowing Convergence," *Industrial and Labor Relations Review,* October 2006, pp. 45–66; and Casey B. Mulligan and Yona Rubinstein, "Selection, Investment, and Women's Relative Wages over Time," *Quarterly Journal of Economics,* August 2008, pp. 1061–110. Sonja C. Kassenboehmer and Mathias G. Sinning, "Distributional Changes in the Gender Wage Gap," *Industrial and Labor Relations Review,* April 2014, pp. 335–361.

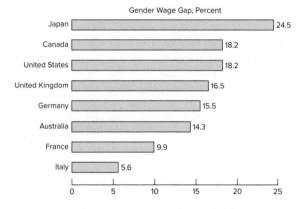

14.1 Global Perspective

Gender Wage Gap

The gender wage gap among major industrial countries ranges from 5.6 percent in Italy to 24.5 percent in Japan.

Gender Wage Gap, Percent

Japan	24.5
Canada	18.2
United States	18.2
United Kingdom	16.5
Germany	15.5
Australia	14.3
France	9.9
Italy	5.6

Source: International Labour Organization. www.ilo.org. Organization for Economic Cooperation and Development, "Gender wage gap." http://www.oecd.org. The statistics are based on 2017 data, except Australia, Germany, and Italy are based on 2015 data and France is based on 2014 data.

Figure 14.2 presents the ratio of African–American to white hourly wages. The ratio has shown little change over the past four decades, and a substantial earnings gap remains.[2] In fact, African–American women have lost some ground relative to white women since the mid-1980s.

Unemployment

Figure 14.3 shows data on unemployment by race and gender over the past three decades in the United States. During the 1970s, white females were at some disadvantage compared with white males. This gap diminished over time, and there is little difference now.

African–Americans, however, have consistently had unemployment rates roughly twice as great as those of whites. Furthermore, the data understate the disadvantage of African–Americans because a larger percentage of African–Americans than whites have been discouraged workers: They have dropped out of the labor force because of poor job prospects and are therefore not counted among the unemployed.

---

[2] Progress was made in the African-American to white earnings ratio prior to the early 1970s. For example, see James P. Smith and Finis Welch, "Black Economic Progress after Myrdal," *Journal of Economic Literature,* June 1989, pp. 519-564, see also James J. Heckman, Thomas M. Lyons, and Petra E. Todd, "Understanding Black-White Wage Differentials, 1960-1990," *American Economic Review,* May 2000, pp. 344-349.

14.1 World of Work

The Gender Wage Gap Among Millennials*

For the first time, young women are starting their careers at pay levels close to that of their male counterparts. In 2012, the median hourly earnings for women aged 25–34 were 93 percent of men's earnings. The corresponding figure, for all workers aged 16 and older, was 84 percent.

Part of the relative wage gain for young women is due to their greater education levels. Among older millennials (aged 25–32), women are more likely to have a college degree than men (38 percent versus 31 percent). For younger millennials (aged 18–24), women are more likely to be attending college than men (45 percent versus 38 percent).

Although these young women are well positioned at the start of their careers, it is unclear whether their wages will remain close to that of men. In the past, the wage gap between men and women has expanded as they aged. Women tended to devote less time to market work with the addition of parental and family responsibilities, while men did the opposite.

To gain some insight with regard to the career and family expectations of millennials as well as other generations of men and women, Pew

Research conducted a survey in late 2013. With regard to career expectations, the survey revealed that a majority, across all age groups, believe men and women are equally focused on careers. Among those expressing a gender difference, only millennials believe that women are more focused on their careers than men. For all age groups, fewer women state they want to be a manager but the gap is smallest among millennials.

Balancing work and family issues is difficult, and the survey reflects that dilemma, particularly for women. Among all parents with children younger than 18, women (51 percent) are three times as likely to say that being a parent made it more difficult to advance in their career than do men (16 percent). Consistent with that belief, 39 percent of women who have worked have taken significant time off to care for a child or family member. The corresponding figure for men is 24 percent. Almost two-thirds of millennial women, aged 18–32, indicate having children hurts their career.

* Based on Pew Research Center, "On Pay Gap, Millennial Women Near Parity—For Now Despite Gains: Many See Roadblocks Ahead," December 11, 2013.

Occupational Distribution

Substantial differences in the occupational distribution of workers by gender and race are revealed in Table 14.1. Women, who constitute about 47 percent of the employed labor force, have been disproportionately concentrated in the following occupations: nursing, public school teaching, clerical work, cashiers, services, secretarial work, and private household employment. All these occupations rank low in relative earnings. It must be added, however, that women have recently made significant gains in the professions.

African–Americans constitute about 11 percent of the total labor force and have also been concentrated in a limited number of low-paying jobs as laundry workers, cleaners, nursing aides, and other manual workers. Conversely, note that women and African–Americans have both been underrepresented among such highly paid professionals as dentists and physicians.

FIGURE 14.2 **African–American to White Hourly Wage Ratio in the United States**

The African–American to white hourly wage ratio in the United States has changed little in the past four decades. Not shown, the ratio increased significantly in the 1960s.

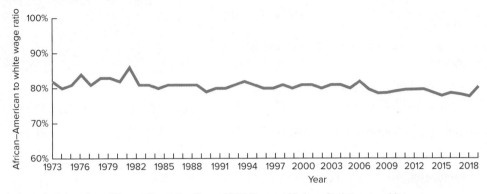

Source: Author calculations from "Current Population Survey." U.S. Bureau of Labour Statistics. www.bls.gov

Education

Figure 14.4 provides some basic insights into differentials in human capital accumulation, although the data provide no information about apprenticeship programs and on-the-job training. We found in Chapter 4 that individuals who acquire the most formal education also tend to receive the most on-the-job training. The advantages that whites have enjoyed compared with African–Americans in obtaining college education have been magnified through the greater access these whites have had to postmarket job training that has increased their productivity and earnings. Furthermore, studies indicate that the quality of education received by African–Americans has been generally inferior to that acquired by whites.

FIGURE 14.3 **Unemployment Rates by Race and Gender in the United States**

The unemployment rates of African–Americans are about twice those of whites; the unemployment rates of men and women of each race are quite similar.

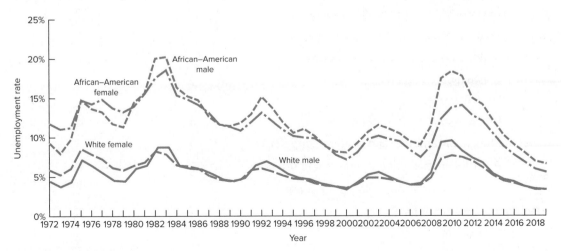

Source: U.S. Bureau of Labor Statistics. www.bls.gov

TABLE 14.1 Occupational Distribution of Employed Workers by Gender and Race

Occupation	Percent Female	Percent African–American
Management, business, and financial operations occupations	44	8
Construction managers	8	3
Insurance underwriters	60	13
Professional and related occupations	57	11
Physicians and surgeons	40	8
Dentists	36	2
Registered nurses	89	13
Elementary and middle schoolteachers	80	11
Service occupations	58	17
Waiters and waitresses	70	11
Nursing, psychiatric, and home health aides	89	36
Janitors and building cleaners	34	19
Child care workers	94	16
Sales occupations	49	11
Cashiers	72	18
Office and administrative support occupations	72	14
Word processors and typists	85	22
Secretaries and administrative assistants	94	9
Receptionists and information clerks	91	13
Construction and extraction occupations	3	7
Brickmasons, blockmasons, and stonemasons	2	9
Helpers, construction traders	6	13
Installation, maintenance, and repair occupations	4	9
Precision instrument and equipment repairers	13	13
Automotive body and related repairers	2	5
Production occupations	29	14
Tool and die makers	6	2
Laundry and dry-cleaning workers	72	20

Occupation	Percent Female	Percent African–American
Transportation and material moving occupations	18	19
Crane and tower operators	6	12
Taxi drivers and chauffeurs	18	18

Source: U.S. Department of Labor, *Employment and Earnings,* January 2019, Table 11.

Average Earnings by Educational Attainment

Although Figure 14.4 clearly indicates differences in educational levels by gender and race, it is important to note that these differences do not fully explain the earnings differences observed in Figures 14.1 and 14.2. As shown in Table 14.2, full-time women workers and African-American workers have significantly lower average earnings levels than white male workers at each level of educational attainment. The pattern is clear:

FIGURE 14.4 Selected Measures of the Educational Attainment of the U.S. Population by Race and Gender

In the United States, white males and females have more education on average than African-Americans.

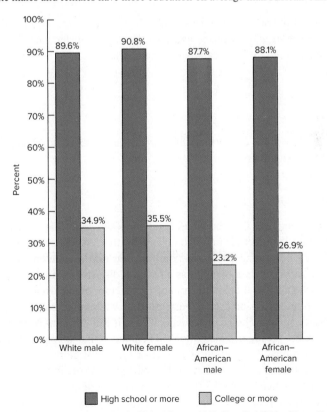

Source: U.S. Census Bureau, "Educational Attainment in the United States: 2018 - Detailed Tables," htttp://www.census.gov. The data are based on persons aged 25 and older.

TABLE 14.2 Average Earnings of Full-Time Workers (18 Years of Age or Older) by Educational Attainment

	White Male	White Female	African–American Male	African–American Female
No High School Degree	$ 39,345	$ 27,097	$ 35,425	$ 27,436
High School	$ 53,128	$ 38,395	$ 43,607	$32,408
Associate	$ 65,029	$ 47,807	$ 57,447	$42,962
Bachelor's	$ 92,812	$ 65,709	$ 68,603	$54,432
Master's Degree	$122,392	$ 83,160	$ 88,609	$ 71,394
Doctorate	$156,770	$ 111,183	$115,560	$ 85,571
Professional Degree	$ 177,112	$125,910	n/a	$ 95,601
Total	$ 75,041	$ 56,244	$ 55,178	$ 45,477

Source: Derived from "2017 Personal Income Tables." U.S. Census Bureau. www.census.gov
u = Data unavailable.

On average, white males who work full-time earn more than African–American males. African–American males, in turn, earn more than white females and African–American females. These data mean that the age-earnings profiles for women and African–Americans lie significantly below those displayed earlier in Figure 4.1 (all males).

Related Points

Two additional points must be made concerning this survey of empirical data, each point clarifying potential misinterpretations of the raw numbers.

Nondiscriminatory Factors

Although it is tempting to conclude that the tables and figures shown in this chapter prove the existence of discrimination, the situation is in fact far more complex than this. As will soon become clear from our discussion, a variety of factors other than discrimination may bear on the differences shown in the tables. For example, perhaps women earn less than men not as a result of discrimination, but rather because they freely choose academic programs and jobs that are less valued in the labor market than those chosen by men. Similarly, if African–American professors on average earn less than white professors, is this the result of discrimination or some other factor such as choice of academic discipline or African–Americans having gotten their training and degrees from less prestigious institutions? The point is that simple raw data comparing incomes, unemployment, and occupational distribution by gender or race must be regarded with caution as evidence of discrimination. *Nondiscriminatory factors* may explain part or all of the indicated differentials. Conversely, in some instances raw data indicating workforce integration and comparable *average* salaries can disguise underlying discrimination, once productivity differences are introduced.

14.1 *Quick Review*

- The ratio of hourly earnings of women to men has risen substantially over the past four decades. However, the African–American to white hourly earnings ratio has changed little during this period.

- Unemployment rates of African–Americans are roughly twice those of whites; unemployment rates of women and men are similar.

- About 35 percent of white males and females have completed four or more years of college compared to 27 percent of African–American females and 23 percent of African–American males.

- Compared with white men, women and African–Americans who work full-time have lower average earnings at each level of educational attainment.

- Not all differences in earnings by race and gender result from discrimination. Nondiscriminatory factors such as differences in preferences also are at work.

Your Turn

Compare the average earnings of African–American males to those of white males in Table 14.2. Explain how this difference might be responsible for the difference in the percentage of African–American males and white males attending college (Figure 14.4). (*Answers:* See page 542.)

Interrelated Data

The second point is that the various gender and racial differences in the earlier tables and figures are interrelated. For example, differences in human capital accumulation shown in Figure 14.4 are undoubtedly an important causal factor in explaining the earnings, unemployment, and occupational differences observed in Figures 14.1 and 14.2 and Table 14.1. Also, the occupational differences shown in Table 14.1 help explain the differences in earnings by education shown in Table 14.2.

DISCRIMINATION AND ITS DIMENSIONS

Discrimination is easier to define than to discern. *Economic discrimination exists when female or minority workers—who have the same abilities, education, training, and experience as white male workers—are accorded inferior treatment with respect to hiring, occupational access, promotion, wage rates, or working conditions.* Note that discrimination may also take the form of unequal access to formal education, apprenticeships, or on-the-job training programs, each of which enhances one's stock of human capital.

Types of Discrimination

This definition is sufficiently important to merit elaboration. Implicit in our definition, labor market discrimination can be classified into four general types.[3]

---

[3] We are concerned here only with those kinds of discrimination that are relevant to the labor market. Although discrimination in access to housing or consumer credit is important, it is less germane to the subject matter of labor economics.

1. *Wage discrimination* means that female (African–American) workers are paid less than male (white) workers for doing the same work. More technically, wage discrimination exists when wage differentials are based on considerations other than productivity differentials.

2. *Employment discrimination* occurs when, other things being equal, African–Americans and women bear a disproportionate share of the burden of unemployment. African–Americans, in particular, have long faced the problem of being the last hired and the first fired.

3. *Occupational* or *job discrimination* means that females (African–Americans) have been arbitrarily restricted or prohibited from entering certain occupations, even though they are as capable as male (white) workers of performing those jobs, and are conversely crowded into other occupations for which they are frequently overqualified.

4. *Human capital discrimination* is in evidence when females (African–Americans) have less access to productivity-increasing opportunities such as formal schooling or on-the-job training. African–Americans in particular often obtain less education and education of inferior quality compared to whites.

The first three categories of discrimination are frequently designated as *postmarket* (also *current* or *direct*) *discrimination* because they are encountered *after* the individual has entered the labor market. Similarly, the fourth category is called *premarket* (also *past* or *indirect*) *discrimination* because it occurs *before* the individual seeks employment.[4]

These distinctions among the various kinds of discrimination are useful for at least two reasons. First, the significance of the various kinds of discrimination varies among African–Americans and women. Generally speaking, African–Americans are subject to a much greater degree of employment discrimination than women. And although African–Americans and women are both subject to occupational segregation, this form of discrimination is especially relevant with respect to women. Second, awareness of the various forms of discrimination helps one understand how discrimination may be self-reinforcing and therefore perpetuate itself. For example, if African–Americans and women anticipate that occupational discrimination will confine them to low-wage, dead-end jobs or that they will be exposed to frequent and prolonged periods of unemployment, they will rationally choose to invest less than otherwise in schooling. That is, the expectation of postmarket discrimination will reduce the rate of return expected on investments in education and training, which will aggravate the premarket condition of inadequate preparation for many jobs.

Theories of Labor Market Discrimination

As indicated earlier, there is no generally accepted economic theory of discrimination. There are undoubtedly a variety of reasons for this. First, the interest of economists in explaining the phenomenon of discrimination is relatively recent. The pioneering book in the field, Gary Becker's *The Economics of Discrimination,*[5] was published in 1957. Second, discrimination may assume a variety of guises and take different forms for different groups. For example, African–Americans traditionally have been at a substantial disadvantage in obtaining employment, whereas women have had access to jobs but only in a restricted number of occupations. Finally, we noted at the outset that the roots of discrimination are diverse and complex, ranging beyond the boundaries of economics. A discipline such as economics, which predicates its analysis on rational behavior,

---

[4] On-the-job training poses a bit of a problem for our pre- and postmarket classification. Although such training is a human capital investment, people do not have access to it until they have entered the labor market. A useful and more detailed taxonomy of discrimination is presented by Brian Chiplin and Peter J. Sloane, "Sexual Discrimination in the Labor Market," in Alice H. Amsden (ed.), *The Economics of Women and Work* (New York: St. Martin's Press, 1980), p. 285.

[5] Chicago: University of Chicago Press, 1957.

may be at a severe disadvantage in explaining a phenomenon that many regard as irrational. Nevertheless, economists have contributed important analytic and empirical work on the problem of discrimination, and our immediate goal is to summarize several of the more prominent theories: (*a*) the taste for discrimination model, (*b*) statistical discrimination, and (*c*) the crowding model. You should be aware that, for the most part, the models to be discussed apply to all types of discrimination. For example, although we will present the taste for discrimination model in terms of racial discrimination, the model is also useful in explaining discrimination by gender, ethnicity, age, and sexual orientation.

TASTE FOR DISCRIMINATION MODEL

Becker's *taste for discrimination model* envisions discrimination as a preference or "taste" for which the discriminator is willing to pay. Becker uses an analogy based on the theory of international trade. It is well known that a nation can maximize its total output by engaging in free trade based on the principle of comparative advantage. But in fact nations obstruct trade through the use of tariffs, quotas, and a variety of other techniques. Nations are apparently willing to sacrifice economic efficiency to have certain goods produced domestically rather than imported. Society seems to have a preference or taste for domestically produced goods, even though it must pay the price of a diminished national income in exercising that taste. Similarly, Becker argues that unfortunately society also has a taste for discrimination and is willing to forgo productive efficiency—and therefore maximum output and profits—to exercise its prejudices. The reduction in discrimination against women and minorities between 1960 and 2010 and resulting convergence in occupational distribution may account for 20-40 percent of the growth in output per person over the period.[6]

Becker's theory is general because it can be applied to, say, white (male) workers who discriminate against African-American (female) workers, *or* white consumers who discriminate against firms that employ African-American workers or salespeople, *or* white employers who discriminate against African-American workers. The latter aspect of this theory—white employers who exercise their taste for discrimination against African-American workers—is the most relevant to our discussion, so we will concentrate on it. Why do employers discriminate? Employers' tastes for discrimination are based on the idea that they and their employees want to maintain a physical or social distance from certain groups; for example, white employers and their workers may not want to associate with African-American workers. These employers may then choose not to hire African-American workers because they and their employees do not want to work alongside them.

The Discrimination Coefficient

Assuming that African-American and white (male and female) workers are equally productive, a nondiscriminating employer will regard them as perfect substitutes and will hire them at random if their wages are the same. But if a white employer is prejudiced against African-Americans, then the situation is significantly altered. According to Becker, prejudiced white employers have "tastes for discrimination" and behave as if employing African-American workers imposed subjective or psychic costs on the employer. The strength of this psychic cost is reflected in a *discrimination coefficient d,* which can be measured in monetary terms. Given that the employer is *not* prejudiced against other whites, the cost of employing a white worker will simply be the wage rate W_w. However, the cost of employing an African-American worker to a prejudiced employer will be regarded as the African-American worker's wage W_{aa} plus the monetary value of the discrimination coefficient—in other words, $W_{aa} + d$. The prejudiced white employer will be indifferent

---

[6] Chang-Tai Hsieh, Erik Hurst, Charles I. Jones, and Peter J. Klenow, "The Allocation of Talent and U.S. Economic Growth," *Econometrica,* forthcoming. For an analysis indicating a large effect on per capita income of gender discrimination, see Tiago Cavalcanti and Jose Tavares, "The Output Cost f Gender Discrimination: A Model-Based Macroeconomics Estimate," *Economic Journal,* February 2016, pp. 109-134.

about hiring African-American and white workers when the total cost per worker is the same—that is, when $W_q = W_{aa} + d$. It follows that our prejudiced white employer will hire African-Americans only if their wage rate is *below* that of whites. More precisely, for the prejudiced employer to employ African-Americans, their wage must be less than the wages of whites by the amount of the discrimination coefficient—in other words, $W_{aa} = W_w - d$. For example, if we suppose that the going wage rate for whites is $20 and that the monetary value of the psychic costs the employer attaches to hiring African-Americans is $4 (i.e., $d = \$4$), then that employer will be indifferent about hiring African-Americans or whites only when the African-American wage is $16 ($W_{aa} = W_w - d$ or $16 = \$20 - \$4$).

It is apparent that the larger a white employer's taste for discrimination as reflected in the value of d, the larger the disparity between white wages and the wages at which African-Americans will be hired. As noted earlier, for a nondiscriminating or "colorblind" employer ($d = 0$), equally productive African-Americans and whites will be hired randomly if their wage rates are the same. At the other extreme, the white employer whose d was infinity would refuse to hire African-Americans at any wage rate, no matter how low that wage was in comparison to white wages. But note carefully that we are *not* saying prejudiced employers will refuse to hire African-Americans under all conditions. Thus in our initial example where the monetary value of d was $4, the white employer would prefer to hire African-Americans if the actual white to African-American wage gap exceeded $4. For example, if in fact whites could be hired at $20 and equally productive African-Americans at only $15 per hour, the employer would choose to hire African-Americans. The prejudiced employer would be willing to pay a wage premium of up to $4 per hour for whites in order to satisfy his or her taste for discrimination, but no more than that. At the $5 differential, the employer would choose to hire African-Americans. Conversely, if whites could be hired at $20 and African-Americans at $17, whites would be hired. The employer would be willing to pay a wage premium of up to $4 for whites; having to pay only a $3 premium means that hiring whites is a "bargain."

Demand and Supply Interpretation

Modified demand and supply analysis is useful in deepening our understanding of Becker's model and, more specifically, in explaining the prevailing wage differential between African-American and white workers. In Figure 14.5 we assume a competitive labor market for some particular occupation. The vertical axis differs from the usual labor market representation in that it measures the ratio of African-American to white wages W_{aa} / W_w, and the horizontal axis shows the quantity of *African-American* workers. The quantity of white workers and their wage rate are assumed to be given. The kinked demand curve for African-American workers D_{aa} is constructed by arraying white employers left to right from lowest to highest discrimination coefficients. Thus, we find that the horizontal portion (ab) of the demand curve where W_{aa} / W_w equals 1.00 reflects nondiscriminating white employers—those whose d's are zero. These employers do not discriminate between equally productive African-American and white workers so long as the wage rates of the two groups are equal. The downward-sloping portion of the demand curve (bD_b) reflects discriminating employers, whose d's increase as we move down that segment. On this segment of the curve, W_{aa} / W_w is less than 1.00 and diminishes as we move to the southeast.

To this demand curve, we now add the supply of African-American labor. Not surprisingly, this curve is upward-sloping; the quantity of African-American labor supplied increases as W_{aa} / W_w increases. The intersection of the two curves establishes the actual W_{aa} / W_w ratio—that is, the extent of wage discrimination—and the number of African-American workers who will be employed in this occupation. Using the numbers from our initial illustration, let's assume that the actual wage rates being paid to African-Americans and whites are $16 and $20, respectively, so that W_{aa} / W_w is 16/20 or .8. This model suggests that nondiscriminating white employers (segment ab of the demand curve) and those whose d's are less than $4 (segment bc) will hire all African-American workers in this occupation; those shown by the cD_{aa} range of the demand curve have d's greater than $4 and will hire only whites.

FIGURE 14.5 Wage Discrimination in the Labor Market

The D_{aa} and S_{aa} curves show the demand for and the supply of African-American labor. Their intersection determines the African-American to white wage ratio and the number of African-American workers employed.

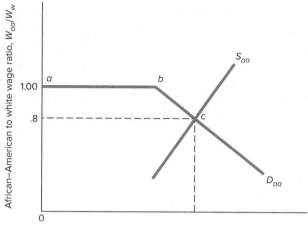

Two Generalizations

Two generalizations concerning the size of the African-American to white wage differential emerge from the taste for discrimination model:

1. A change in the shape or location of the demand curve will alter the W_{aa}/W_w ratio. For example, suppose that a change in societal attitudes or antidiscrimination legislation has the effect of reducing the discrimination coefficient of employers. This will extend the horizontal portion of the demand curve farther to the right *and* reduce the slope of the remaining downward-sloping segment. Given the supply of African-American labor, the effect will be to raise the equilibrium W_{aa}/W_w ratio—that is, to reduce the discriminatory wage differential and increase the employment of African-American workers. For example, the equilibrium W_{aa}/W_w ratio in Figure 14.5 may rise from .8 to, say, .85.

2. The size of the discriminatory wage differential varies directly with the supply of minority (African-American) workers. If the supply of African-American labor in Figure 14.5 were so small as to intersect the horizontal segment of the demand curve, there would be no discriminatory wage differential. If the supply of African-American labor increased to the position shown on the diagram, the differential would be .8 or 8/10. A further increase in supply will lower the W_{aa}/W_w ratio, indicating a widening of the wage differential.

These two generalizations raise an interesting question: Is the greater observed wage differential between African-American and white workers in the South as compared with the North the consequence of a stronger taste for discrimination in the South—that is, a demand curve farther to the left? Or, alternatively, is it the result of a greater relative supply of African-American workers in the South? In either case, of course, the *source* of the discrimination is white prejudice, not the size of the African-American labor force.

Gainers, Losers, and the Persistence of Discrimination

Becker's taste for discrimination model indicates that white workers will gain from discrimination because their wage rates will be higher than otherwise. Just as import restrictions reduce foreign competition to the

14.2   World of Work

Competition and Discrimination

The Becker taste for discrimination model has clear predictions about the relationship between competition and discrimination. Employers who discriminate against women will hire relatively fewer of the less highly paid but equally skilled women than nondiscriminating employers. As a result, discriminators will have higher production costs and thus lower profits. This indicates that employer discrimination can exist only in less competitive markets. Therefore, a rise in product market competition in less competitive industries should reduce discrimination as discriminating employers are driven out of business.

Black and Brainerd examine the impact of international trade, which is one source of heightened competitive pressures, on gender discrimination. They find that a 10 percentage point increase in import share lowers the gender wage gap by 6.6 percent in less competitive industries. They conclude that increased international trade accounted for about one-quarter of the decline in gender discrimination in manufacturing during the 1976–1993 period.

In another test of the impact of increased competition, Black and Strahan examine the effect of deregulation in the banking industry on discrimination. They report that after deregulation male wages fell by 12 percent, whereas women's wages declined by only 3 percent. The relative

rise in the wages of women appears to be partly the result of a movement into higher-skilled occupations. For example, the proportion of women in managerial positions in the banking industry rose by about 4 percentage points to more than 40 percent female.

Hellerstein, Neumark, and Troske directly test the Becker model's predictions regarding profits and discrimination. Consistent with the model, they find that among plants with high levels of market power, those that hire more women have greater profits. Specifically, a 10 percent increase in the proportion female raises the profit rate by 1.6 percentage points among plants with high market power. Consistent with the prediction that discrimination cannot exist in competitive industries, this relationship does not hold for plants with low levels of market power.

Sources: Sandra E. Black and Elizabeth Brainerd, "Importing Equality? The Impact of Globalization on Gender Discrimination," *Industrial and Labor Relations Review,* July 2004; Sandra E. Black and Philip E. Strahan, "The Division of Spoils: Rent-Sharing and Discrimination in a Regulated Industry," *American Economic Review,* September 2001, pp. 814–831; and Judith K. Hellerstein, David Neumark, and Kenneth R. Troske, "Market Forces and Sex Discrimination," *Journal of Human Resources,* Spring 2002, pp. 353–380. For a study showing reduced racial wage gaps after privatization of public transit systems and deregulation of the trucking industry, see James Peoples, Jr., and Wayne K. Talley, "Black–White Earnings Differentials: Privatization versus Deregulation," *American Economic Review,* May 2001, pp. 164–168.

benefit of domestic producers, discrimination by employers protects white workers from the competition of African-American workers. African-Americans, of course, receive lower wages because of discrimination. Finally, employers who discriminate may injure themselves because they will experience higher costs than necessary. Let's explain why this is so.

Returning to Figure 14.5, let's further assume that all of the employers arrayed on the demand curve are producing the same product. All of the nondiscriminating or less discriminating employers on the demand curve to the left of the intersection point will find themselves with a competitive cost advantage relative to the more discriminating employers on the segment of the demand curve to the right of the intersection. To illustrate: In equilibrium, the W_{aa}/W_w ratio is .8—that is, whites are paid \$20 and African-Americans only \$16. Remembering the assumption that African-Americans and whites are equally productive workers, a nondiscriminating employer on the horizontal segment would hire an African–American labor force at $16 per hour, whereas a discriminator far down the demand curve would hire all white workers at $20 per hour. The discriminating employer will incur higher wage costs than the nondiscriminating employer. Therefore, nondiscriminating firms will have lower average total costs and product prices than discriminating producers.

An important implication of Becker's model is that competitive market forces will cause discrimination to diminish and disappear over time because the lower-cost nondiscriminating firms can gain a larger share of the market at the expense of less efficient discriminating firms. In fact, in a highly competitive product market, only nondiscriminating firms (least-cost producers) will survive; discriminators will have average total costs that will exceed product price. Thus, Becker's theory is consistent with a "conservative" or laissez-faire position toward discrimination; that is, in the long run, the operation of the competitive market will resolve the problem of discrimination, and therefore the only governmental action required is that which promotes free occupational choice.[7] Discriminating employers will either have to become nondiscriminators or be driven out of business.

WW14.2   A fundamental criticism of this perspective is that, in fact, progress in eliminating discrimination has been modest. The functioning of the market has *not* eliminated employers' prejudices. Discrimination based on both race and gender has persisted decade after decade. Thus, alternative models have been proposed to explain why discrimination has continued.

14.2 *Quick Review*

- Labor market discrimination occurs when workers who have the same abilities, education, training, and experience as other workers receive inferior treatment with respect to hiring, occupational access, promotion, or wages.

- Labor market discrimination can be classified as *(a)* wage discrimination, *(b)* employment discrimination, *(c)* occupational or job discrimination, or *(d)* human capital discrimination.

- Becker's taste for discrimination model views discrimination as a preference or "taste" for which the discriminator is willing to pay; the greater this preference, the larger is Becker's discrimination coefficient.

- Employers with high discrimination coefficients will incur higher labor costs than nondiscriminating employers; thus, the nondiscriminators will have a cost advantage in competing with discriminators in the marketplace.

Your Turn

Suppose the hourly market wage for specific white workers is $16, while the wage for equally productive African–American workers is $12. What can be inferred about the dollar value of the discrimination coefficient for an employer that hires all white workers under these circumstances? All African–American workers? (*Answers:* See page 542.)

---

[7] That government will be unsuccessful in eliminating discrimination is the major theme of Thomas Sowell, *Markets and Minorities* (New York: Basic Books, Inc., 1981), see also William A. Darity, Jr., and Rhonda M. Williams, "Peddlers Forever? Culture, Competition, and Discrimination," *American Economic Review,* May 1985, pp. 256–261.

THEORY OF STATISTICAL DISCRIMINATION

Another theory centers on the concept of *statistical discrimination*.[8] By way of definition, we can say that statistical discrimination

> occurs whenever an individual is judged on the basis of the average characteristics of the group, or groups, to which he or she belongs rather than upon his or her own personal characteristics. The judgments are correct, factual, and objective in the sense that the group actually has the characteristics that are ascribed to it, but the judgments are incorrect with respect to many individuals within the group.[9]

A commonplace non-labor market example of statistical discrimination involves automobile insurance. Insurance rates for teenage males are higher than those for teenage females. This rate differential is based on accumulated factual evidence indicating that, on the average, young males are more likely than females to be involved in accidents. However, many young male drivers are equally or less accident prone than the average of young females, and these males are discriminated against by having to pay higher insurance rates.

It is easy to understand how statistical discrimination would function in labor markets. Employers with job vacancies want to hire the most productive workers available to fill open positions. Thus, their personnel departments collect a variety of information concerning each job applicant: for example, an individual's age, education, and prior work experience. Employers supplement this information with scores on preemployment tests that they feel are helpful indicators of potential job performance. But two interrelated considerations pertain to this employee screening process. First, because it is expensive to collect detailed information about each job applicant, only limited data are collected. Second, the limited information available to the employer from job application forms and test scores will *not* permit the employer to predict perfectly which job applicants will be the most productive employees. As a consequence of these two considerations, it is common for employers to use subjective considerations such as race, gender, or age in determining who is hired. In practicing statistical discrimination, the employer is not satisfying a taste for discrimination, but rather is using gender, race, or age as a proxy for production-related attributes of workers that are not easily discernible. Gender, for example, may be used as a proxy for physical strength or job commitment.

To illustrate: An employer may assume that *on the average,* young married women are more likely than males to quit their jobs within, say, two years after hire because they may become pregnant or their husbands may take jobs in different locations. All other things being equal, when choosing between a married female and a male job applicant, the employer may hire the male. Similarly, when considering whether to employ an African-American or a white high school graduate whose age, work experience, and test scores are identical, the employer may hire the white youth because the employer knows that *on the average* African-Americans receive schooling that is qualitatively inferior to that obtained by whites. Note what is happening here: Characteristics that apply to a group are being applied to individuals. *Each* married woman is assumed to behave with respect to employment tenure as the "average" married woman. Similarly, *every* African-American youth is assumed to have the same quality of education as the "average" African-American youth. It is assumed that group or average differences apply in each individual case. As a result, married women who do not plan to have children (or do not plan to quit work if they do) and African-American youths who receive quality education will be discriminated against.

Three further aspects of statistical discrimination merit comment. In the first place, unlike in the taste for discrimination model, the employer is *not* harmed by practicing discrimination. On the contrary, the employer

---

[8] See Edmund S. Phelps, "The Statistical Theory of Racism and Sexism," *American Economic Review,* September 1972, pp. 659-661; and Dennis J. Aigner and Glen G. Cain, "Statistical Theories of Discrimination in Labor Markets," *Industrial and Labor Relations Review,* January 1977, pp. 175-187. For empirical investigations of statistical discrimination, see Julian Lange, "The Speed of Employer Learning," *Journal of Labor Economics,* January 2007, pp. 1-35; and JonasJessen, RobinJessen, and Jochen Kluvec, "Punishing Potential Mothers? Evidence for Statistical Employer Discrimination from a Natural Experiment," *Labour Economics,* August 2019, pp. 164-172.

[9] Thurow, Lester C. *Generating Inequality* (New York: Basic Books, 1975).

is a beneficiary. An employer will enhance profits by minimizing hiring costs. Given that gathering detailed information about each job applicant is costly, applying perceived group characteristics to job seekers is an inexpensive means of screening employees. Some economists feel that the statistical discrimination theory, which envisions employers as "gainers," is more plausible than the taste for discrimination model, which conceives of them as "losers."

Second, as suggested earlier, the statistical discrimination model does not necessarily indicate that an employer is being malicious in his or her hiring behavior. The decisions made may well be correct, rational, and, as noted, profitable *on the average.* The problem is that many workers who differ from the group average will be discriminated against.

Finally, as noted at the outset, there is no compelling reason that statistical discrimination needs to diminish over time. In contrast to the taste for discrimination model, statistical discrimination may persist because those who practice it are beneficiaries.

Our first and third points merit qualification in one important sense. If the average characteristics of any two groups converge over time–perhaps because of a decline in other aspects of discrimination–statistical discrimination may become increasingly costly to employers. For example, suppose human capital discrimination diminishes and African–American youths now obtain high school education equal in quality to that acquired by white youths. By applying statistical discrimination to employ only whites, the employer will now be making more hiring mistakes. These mistakes will be of two types: hiring more whites who are not qualified and failing to hire African–Americans who are qualified.

WW 14.3 Similarly, the increasing availability of child care facilities, higher female pay, and changing female preferences have meant that having children no longer seriously interrupts the work careers of many women. Also, studies reveal that the difference in turnover rates of men and women in similar jobs is small.[10] Thus, employers who base hiring decisions on the average turnover rate of females may make costly hiring mistakes. The cost to the employer of such mistakes is that the most productive workers available are not selected. Employers who make fewer mistakes will have lower production costs and will increase their market share at the expense of rivals.

THE CROWDING MODEL: OCCUPATIONAL SEGREGATION

A glance back at Table 14.1 will reveal that occupational distributions of whites and African–Americans *and* of males and females are substantially different. We have also noted in Chapter 8 that wages differ substantially by occupation, so the occupational structure is an important factor in explaining wages differences across workers. Thus, it is no surprise to find that an entire theory of discrimination has been based on the concept of occupational segregation. This *crowding model* uses simple supply and demand concepts to explore the consequences of confining women and African–Americans to a limited number of occupations.[11]

Why does crowding occur? Why do employers practice job segregation based on gender or race? One important reason is that worker productivity is the result of a group or "team" effort. If social interactions on the job are unfavorable, productivity will suffer. Some male (white) workers may become disgruntled when obligated to work along with or to take orders from women (African–Americans). Thus in the interest of

---

[10] Anders Frederiksen, "Gender Differences in Job Separation Rates and Employment Stability: New Evidence from Employer-Employee Data," *Labour Economics,* October 2008, pp. 915–937.

[11] For a detailed discussion of the crowding hypothesis by one of its leading exponents, see Barbara R. Bergmann, *The Economic Emergence of Women,* 2nd Edition (New York: Palgrave Macmillan, 2005), Chapters 4–6, and more specifically, pp. 85–90. Also see Elaine Sorensen, "The Crowding Hypothesis and Comparable Worth," *Journal of Human Resources,* Winter 1990, pp. 55–89.

productivity and profits, employers decide to segregate men and women (African–Americans and whites) on the job. Furthermore, many employers have preconceived notions concerning the job capabilities of women and minorities. As a result, few women, for example, have jobs driving trucks or selling electronics equipment or automobiles.

Assumptions and Predictions

The following simplifying assumptions will facilitate our discussion of the crowding model:

1. The labor force is equally divided between male and female (or white and African–American) workers. Let's say there are 6 million male and 6 million female workers.

2. The total labor market is composed of three occupations—X, Y, and Z—each having identical labor demand curves as shown in Figure 14.6.

3. Men and women have homogeneous labor force characteristics; males and females are equally productive in each of the three occupations.

14.3 World of Work

Does Ban the Box Cause Discrimination?

Ban the Box (BTB) laws prohibit employers from asking for information about the criminal history of job applicants on initial job applications or interviews. The "box" in BTB refers to a question on a job application asking whether the applicant has been convicted of a crime, which is typically answered by checking a yes or no checkbox. BTB laws are often promoted as a measure to increase the employment of African–American men since they are more likely to have a criminal record. However, BTB could increase statistical discrimination against them since employers might use an applicant's race to infer who has a criminal background.

Amanda Agan and Sonja Starr investigate the impact of BTB by using about 15,000 online job applications for entry-level positions by fictitious young males to employers in New Jersey and New York City before and after BTB became effective there in 2015. The applications consisted of matched pairs (African–American and white) of applicants who were randomly assigned whether the job candidate had a felony conviction. This approach enabled the researchers to investigate whether employers changed their response to race after BTB was adopted.

Consistent with the motivation for BTB, their results indicate that felony convictions are a significant impediment to employment when employers ask about them. The callback (positive response to an application) rate was 63 percent higher for those without a conviction relative to those without one.

BTB does appear to increase racial discrimination. Before BTB, white job applications to employers with the box received 7 percent more callbacks than comparable African–American job applicants. After the box was removed under BTB, the racial gap in callbacks rose to 43 percent. The rise in the racial gap is greater than would be expected under statistical discrimination based on empirical racial differences in felony convictions. Instead, Amanda Agan and Sonja Starr suggest that the increase in the racial gap in callbacks is due to stereotyping or bias.

Source: Based on Amanda Agan and Sonja Starr, "Ban the Box, Criminal Records, and Racial Discrimination: A Field Experiment," *Quarterly Journal of Economics,* February 2018, pp. 191–235.

FIGURE 14.6 Occupational Segregation: The Crowding Model

By crowding women into occupation Z, men will receive high wage rates of W_m in occupations X and Y, while women will receive low wage rates of W_f in occupation Z. The abandonment of discrimination will equalize wage rates at W_e and result in a net increase in the domestic output [$(abcd + efgh) - ijkl$].

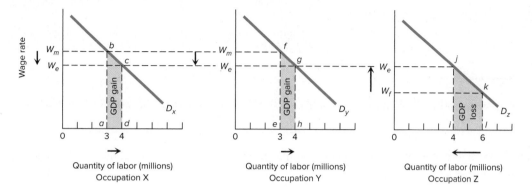

4. Product markets are competitive so that the demand curves reflect not only marginal revenue product (MRP) but also value of marginal product (VMP) (Chapter 5).

5. We assume that as a result of occupational segregation, occupations X and Y are "men's jobs" and occupation Z is a "woman's job." Women are confined to occupation Z and systematically excluded from occupations X and Y.

Men will distribute themselves equally among occupations X and Y so that there are 3 million male workers in each and the resulting common wage rate for men is W_m. Assuming no barriers to mobility, any initially different distribution of males between X and Y would result in a wage differential that would prompt labor shifts from low- to high-wage occupations until wage equality was realized. Note that all 6 million women, on the other hand, are crowded into occupation Z and, as a consequence of this occupational segregation, receive a much lower wage rate W_f. Given the reality of discrimination, this is an "equilibrium" situation. Women *cannot,* because of discrimination, reallocate themselves to occupations X and Y in the pursuit of higher wage rates. Although men could presumably enter occupation Z if they so chose, they would not want to do so in the face of Z's lower wage rates.

The net result of occupational segregation is obvious: Men realize higher wage rates and incomes at the expense of women. Note, however, that women are not being disadvantaged as the result of exploitation: They are *not* being paid a wage rate less than their MRP. In occupation Z women *are* being paid a wage rate equal to their MRP *and* to their contribution to society's output (VMP). Their problem is that by being restricted to only occupation Z, their supply is great relative to demand and their wage rate is therefore low compared to that of males.

Ending Discrimination

Suppose that through legislation or sweeping changes in social attitudes, discrimination disappears. What are the results? Women, attracted by higher wage rates, will shift from Z to X and Y. Specifically, if we assume occupational shifts are costless, 1 million women will shift into X and another 1 million into Y, leaving 4 million workers in Z. At this point, 4 million workers will be in each occupation and wage rates will be equal to W_e in all three occupations, so there is no incentive for further reallocation. This new, nondiscriminatory

14.3 *Quick Review*

- The theory of statistical discrimination holds that employers often wrongly judge individuals on the basis of the average characteristics of the group to which they belong rather than on their own personal characteristics.

- The crowding model of discrimination suggests that women and minorities are systematically excluded from high-paying occupations and crowded into low-paying ones.

Your Turn

How might statistical discrimination reinforce occupational segregation? (*Answer:* See page 542.)

equilibrium is to the advantage of women, who now receive higher wages, and to the disadvantage of men, who now receive lower wages.

If the elimination of occupational segregation results in both winners (women) and losers (men), it is pertinent to ask whether the gains exceed the losses. That is, does society reap an economic gain by ending occupational segregation? Figure 14.6 reveals that there *is* a net gain to society. Our labor demand curves reflect value of marginal product, the contribution of each successive worker to the domestic output. Hence the movement of 2 million women out of occupation Z yields a *decrease* in domestic output shown by area *ijkl*. But the areas *abcd* and *efgh* for occupations X and Y show the *increases* in domestic output—the market values of the marginal products—realized by adding 1 million women to each of these occupations. We observe that the sum of the additions to domestic output in occupations X and Y exceeds the decline in domestic output that occurs when women leave occupation Z. The conclusion that society gains from the termination of occupational segregation is not unexpected. Women reallocate themselves from occupation Z, where their VMP is relatively low, to occupations X and Y, where their VMPs are relatively high. This reallocation continues until the VMPs of labor in each alternative use are equal—a condition that defines the efficient allocation of labor. Thus, our analysis underscores that discrimination has both equity and efficiency connotations. Discrimination influences not only the distribution but also the size of the domestic income.

Index of Segregation

How extensive is crowding or occupational segregation? An ***index of segregation*** has been devised to quantify occupational segregation. As applied to sex discrimination, *this index is designed to show the percentage of women (or men) who would have to change occupations for women to be distributed among occupations in the same proportions as men.* The hypothetical figures of Table 14.3 are instructive. Suppose the occupational distributions of male and female workers are as shown in columns 2 and 3. To make the distributions identical, *either* 30 percent of the total of *female* workers would have to move *from* occupation C (20 percent going to A and 10 percent to B) *or* 30 percent of the total of *male* workers would have to move *to* occupation C (20 percent coming from A and 10 percent coming from B). Because 30 percent of either female or male workers would have to change occupations for males and females to be distributed in the same proportions among occupations, the index of segregation is 30 percent, or simply 0.30. For more numerous occupational categories, the index can be calculated by determining the absolute value of the percentage differences for each occupation (without regard to sign) and summing these differences as shown in column 4. To obtain

TABLE 14.3 Determining the Index of Segregation (Hypothetical Data)

(1) Occupation	(2) Male	(3) Female	(4) = (2) − (3) Absolute Differences
A	50%	30%	20%
B	30	20	10
C	20	50	30
	100%	100%	60%

Index of segregation $= \frac{60\%}{2} = 30\%$ or 0.30.

the index of segregation, the resulting 60 percent is then divided by 2 because any movement of workers is counted twice: as a movement *out of* one occupation and as a movement *into* another occupation.

The conclusion from our simple hypothetical illustration is that 30 percent of the female (or male) labor force must change occupations for the proportions of men and women in each occupation to be the same. Note that this new distribution would result in an index of segregation of zero. The other extreme where, say, occupations A and B are each populated 50 percent by men and occupation C 100 percent by women yields an index of 100 percent or 1.00. Hence the index of segregation may take on any value ranging from 0 to 1.00, and the higher the value, the greater the extent of occupational segregation.

Evidence

WW14.4

What are the magnitudes of the indexes of occupational segregation based on gender and race for the United States? And what, if anything, has happened to these indexes over time? Figure 14.7 presents the index of occupational segregation between men and women. The index of occupational segregation by gender was 68.1 percent in 1973 and declined to 48.3 percent by 2019.[12] Slightly more than half the women (or men) in the United States would have to change occupations for women to be distributed among occupations in the same proportions as men. This considerable change in the index is consistent with growing evidence that women have made substantial occupational gains in professions such as dentistry, medicine, pharmacy, and law.[13]

Occupational segregation based on race is less pronounced than that based on gender and has declined noticeably over time. Figure 14.8 presents data for the index of racial occupational segregation by gender. Comparing white women and African–American women, the index of segregation was 37.1 percent in 1973 and fell to 21.9% percent in 2019.[14] This is consistent with a general integration of African–American women into occupations traditionally held by white women. When white men and African–American men are analyzed, the change was slightly more modest: The index fell from 37.0 percent in 1973 to 25.6% percent in 2019.

---

[12] For more about gender occupational segregation, see David A. Macpherson and Barry T. Hirsch, "Wages and Gender Composition: Why Do Women's Jobs Pay Less?" *Journal of Labor Economics,* July 1995, pp. 426–471; Francine D. Blau, Peter Brummund, and Albert Yung-Hsu Liu, "Trends in Occupational Segregation by Gender 1970–2009: Adjusting for the Impact of Changes in the Occupational Coding System," *Demography,* April 2013, pp. 471–492; and John T. Addison, Orgul D. Ozturk, and Si Wang, "The Occupational Feminization of Wages," *Industrial and Labor Relations Review,* January 2018, pp. 208–241.

[13] See Francine D. Blau and Anne E. Winkler, *The Economics of Women, Men, and Work,* 8th Edition (Englewood Cliffs, NJ: Prentice-Hall, 2018).

[14] For more about racial occupational segregation, see Barry T. Hirsch and David A. Macpherson, "Wages, Sorting on Skill, and Racial Composition of Jobs," *Journal of Labor Economics,* January 2004, pp. 189–210; and Olga Alonso-Villar, Coral Del Rio, and Carlos Gradin, "The Extent of Occupational Segregation in the United States: Differences by Race, Ethnicity, and Gender," *Industrial Relations,* April 2012, pp. 179–212.

FIGURE 14.7   Index of Occupational Segregation by Gender, United States

The index of occupational segregation between men and women fell considerably between 1973 and 2019.

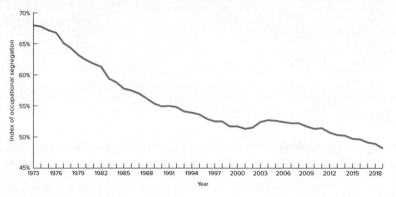

Source: Author calculations from "Current Population Survey." Bureau of Labor Statistics. www.bls.gov

14.4   World of Work

Evolution of a Family Friendly Occupation

Pharmacy now is a majority female occupation that is both well-paid and has a small gender earnings gap. Pharmacists can work part-time with little or no reduction in their wage rate. Over time, the pharmacist occupation has undergone significant changes and has evolved into a family-friendly profession.

Claudia Goldin and Lawrence Katz examine the changes for pharmacists over the past five decades. Between 1970 and 2010, the median full-time full-year earnings of pharmacists rose relative to other professions such as physicians, attorneys, and veterinarians. Over the same period, the female–male median earnings ratio among full-time-full-year workers rose from .66 to .92. The gender gap for pharmacists is now smaller than for nearly all other high-wage professions.

Earnings of pharmacists vary mostly due to differences in the number of hours of work. The hourly wage of female pharmacists is only 4–7 percent less than men. The hourly wage penalty for working part-time has nearly disappeared over the past decades for pharmacists but not for other college graduates. Managers earn only about 7 percent more per hour than employees, and owners earn 12 percent more per hour than employees. Higher earnings for owners and managers are mainly because they work more hours than employees.

Goldin and Katz conclude that increased substitutability among pharmacists is the major factor behind the changes for pharmacists. The expansion of employment of pharmacists in large pharmacy chains, hospitals, and mail-order pharmacies and a decline in owner-operated pharmacies in the share of employment in independent pharmacies have made pharmacists better substitutes for each other and to handoff clients. Pharmacies are now more able to switch pharmacists due to the increased standardization of training and products as well as the heavy use of information technology and prescription drug insurance.

Source: Based on Claudia Goldin and Lawrence F. Katz, "A Most Egalitarian Profession: Pharmacy and the Evolution of a Family-Friendly Occupation," *Journal of Labor Economics,* July 2016, pp. 705–746.

FIGURE 14.8 **Index of Racial Occupational Segregation by Gender, United States**

The index of racial occupational segregation fell noticeably for men and women between 1973 and 2019.

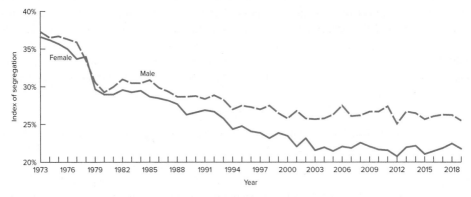

Source: Author calculations from "Current Population Survey." Bureau of Labor Statistics. www.bls.gov

CAUSE AND EFFECT: NONDISCRIMINATORY FACTORS

As we have indicated, economists know that many factors other than discrimination may bear on female to male and African–American to white earnings differentials. Finding that Ms. Anderson earns $40,000 a year while Mr. Alvarez earns $50,000 annually is not necessarily evidence of gender discrimination. This is true even where Ms. Anderson and Mr. Alvarez have equal levels of education or work for the same employer. A variety of considerations that have nothing to do with prejudice may simply cause Alvarez to be more productive than Anderson. More generally, cause-and-effect considerations are difficult to unravel in attempting to isolate the role of discrimination in explaining differences in socioeconomic status. Let's consider this issue in terms of gender discrimination.

Rational Choice versus Discrimination as a Cause

Some economists argue that the inferior economic position of women is basically the result of rational and freely rendered decisions by women. The essence of this view is that most women anticipate marriage and childbearing, and this generates for women a conflict between labor market careers and marriage that explains much of women's economic disadvantage. More specifically, the proponents of this position argue that in attempting to make their traditional homemaking role more compatible with labor market work, women make decisions concerning human capital investments, hours of work, and other job characteristics that result in incomes lower than those earned by men.

The traditional childbearing and family roles of women mean that their participation in the labor market will be discontinuous and truncated. This fact has a variety of implications. First, because women will work fewer lifetime hours, their expected rate of return on human capital investments (education and training) will be lower than that of men. As a result, women as well as their employers may be less willing to invest in education and on-the-job training, causing the productivity and earnings of women to be less than for men. Second, the stock of human capital that women possess may deteriorate when they are out of the labor force, thus lowering their productivity and earnings. Third, it can be argued that occupational segregation is the result of rational choice. Knowing they will not be in the labor force continuously, women may prefer occupations such as nursing or elementary school teaching, which will have the greatest carryover value for productive activity within the home.

Some portion of the male–female earnings differential may be the result of differences in the type of jobs women desire to hold. If women put a high value on, say, shorter hours, job safety, and the location of jobs close to their homes, then the exercise of these preferences may result in lower wages and earnings for women. Stated differently, some portion of the higher earnings of males *may* be a wage differential that compensates them for longer hours and for performing more hazardous and inconveniently located jobs and thus may be unrelated to sex discrimination. In fact, women—particularly married women—are much more likely than men to hold part-time jobs. In addition, full-time male workers on average work more hours per week than do full-time female workers. Some economists contend that the desire of women to work part-time or shorter hours contributes to occupational segregation—and consequently to lower female earnings—because occupations differ in the opportunities for part-time work and relatively shorter workweeks.

The "rational choice" view suggests that voluntary decisions by women concerning the amounts and types of education and training they receive and the kinds of jobs they choose *cause* them to realize lower earnings than men. Skeptics argue that it is more plausible to reverse the implied cause–effect sequence and thereby assign a primary role to discrimination in explaining female–male earnings differentials. To facilitate our discussion, we will concentrate on the rational choice contention that women freely choose to truncate their labor market careers with the result that it is rational for employers and women themselves to invest less in human capital.

One can argue that women invest in less education and training or invest in types of training that have the greatest carryover value for household production *because* of labor market discrimination and manifest income disparities. For example, the decision of many women to withdraw from the labor force for extended periods may be the consequence of the low opportunity cost of nonparticipation, the latter being the result of low market pay due to discrimination. Poor labor market opportunities for women lower their earnings and increase the relative attractiveness of work in the home. In this interpretation, labor market discrimination *causes* women to choose the amounts and kinds of human capital investment that they do and to withdraw from the labor market for extended periods.

It is also possible that many women who experience sexual harassment and discrimination in the workplace respond by changing careers or having children and working in the home. Thus, the truncated careers of women and their resulting lower earnings may be an outcome of discrimination, not the consequence of truly free choice.[15]

Which position is correct? Both views are right. Discrimination entails a complex intermingling of cause and effect. Differences in supply decisions with respect to human capital investment and occupational choice of males and females may *result* from labor market discrimination and existing earnings disparities and simultaneously be a *cause* of these earnings differentials.

Evidence

Despite the difficult cause–effect interrelationships involved, many empirical studies have attempted to disaggregate female to male and African–American to white earnings differentials in the hope of determining what portion of them is due to productivity differences as opposed to discrimination per se. These studies attempt to control for such factors as education, age, training, industry and occupation, union membership, location and continuity of workforce experience, health, and so forth. The reasoning is that these are allegedly nondiscriminatory considerations that cause productivity differences and therefore earnings differences. A comprehensive study by Blau and Kahn found that approximately three-fifths of the female–male earnings

---

[15] For evidence of this effect, see David Neumark and Michele McLennon, "Sex Discrimination and Women's Labor Market Interruptions," *Journal of Human Resources,* Fall 1995, pp. 713–740.

differential is attributable to such factors as differences in years of work experience (14 percent), industry (18 percent), and occupation (33 percent).[16] That is, males have more work experience, and work in higher-paying industries and occupations. Consequently, their productivity was higher, and this justified three-fifths of the earnings advantage they enjoyed. The remaining two-fifths of the earnings gap was unexplained and presumably due, wholly or in part, to discrimination. As Figure 14.1 shows, the female–male hourly earnings ratio rose from 64.6 percent in 1973 to 80.2 percent in 2018. Blau and Kahn found that about two-fifths of the decline in the earnings differential between 1980 and 2010 was due to an increase in the relative productivity characteristics of women. The remaining three-fifths was due to a decline in the unexplained gap. The gender wage gap has been shrinking faster at the low end of the wage distribution than at the upper end. Kassenboehmer and Sinning report that between 1993–1995 and 2004–2008 the gender wage gap decreased by 16 percent at the lowest wage decile and by less than 5 percent at the highest decile of the wage distribution.[17] They find the decline in the gender wage gap is mainly due to increases in educational attainment by women at the upper part of the wage distribution and increases in work experience by women at the lower part of the wage distribution.

Regarding the African–American to white gap, productivity differences account for a large portion of the pay differential between African–American and white men. A study by Neal and Johnson found that racial differences in cognitive achievement as measured by the Armed Forces Qualifying Test (AFQT) score alone appear to "explain" about two-thirds of the pay gap between young African–American and white men.[18] They found that African–American men have lower AFQT scores due to lower-quality schooling and other environmental factors. In contrast to the gender pay gap, the African–American to white male pay differential has not narrowed in recent years.[19] The stall in progress for African–American men appears to be partly the result of offsetting factors. On one hand, African–American men have, on average, less education than white men, so the increased payoff to education starting in the 1980s caused the African–American to white pay gap to expand. On the other hand, the African–American to white gap in education has shrunk, which has tended to diminish the African–American to white earnings differential. The net result has been little change in the African–American to white male earnings differential.[20]

Controversy

The interpretation of such studies has been controversial. Some economists feel that the unexplained earnings differential overstates the role of discrimination; others contend that it is an underestimation. Those who feel that the discrimination estimate is too high argue that other productivity-influencing considerations (such as worker motivation, quantitative skills, or course of study in school) have not been taken into account.

---

[16] Francine D. Blau and Lawrence M. Kahn, "The Gender Wage Gap: Extent, Trends, and Explanations" *Journal of Economic Literature,* September 2017, pp. 789–865. They also report that the higher education levels for women result in -6 percent of the gap.

[17] Sonja C. Kassenboehmer and Mathias G. Sinning, "Distributional Changes in the Gender Wage Gap," *Industrial and Labor Relations Review,* April 2014, pp. 335–361.

[18] Derek Neal and William Johnson, "The Role of Premarket Factors in Black–White Wage Differences," *Journal of Political Economy,* October 1996, pp. 869–895. Also see Donal O'Neill, Olive Sweetman, and Dirk Van de Gaer, "The Impact of Cognitive Skills on the Distribution of the Black–White Wage Gap," *Labour Economics,* June 2006, pp. 343–356; Sergio Urzua, "Racial Labor Market Gaps: The Role of Abilities and Schooling Choices," *Journal of Human Resources,* Fall 2008, pp. 919–971; and C. Simon Fan, Xiangdong Wei, and Junsen Zhang, "Soft Skills, Hard Skills, and the Black/White Wage Gap," *Economic Inquiry,* April 2017, pp. 1032–1053.

[19] See Barry T. Hirsch and John V. Winters. "An Anatomy of Racial and Ethnic Trends in Male Earnings in the U.S.," *Review of Income and Wealth,* December 2014, pp. 930–947.

[20] For an analysis of the African-American to white male wage gap since 1940, see Patrick Bayer and Kerwin Kofi Charles, "Divergent Paths: A New Perspective on Earnings Differences Between Black and White Men Since 1940," *Quarterly Journal of Economics,* August 2018, pp. 1459–1501. For evidence that the African-American to white pay gap has expanded over time among women, see Jonathan D. Fisher and Christina A. Houseworth, "The Widening Black-White Wage Gap among Women," *Labour,* September 2017, pp. 288–308.

These factors allegedly increase the productivity of males relative to females and, if included, would reduce the unexplained (discriminatory) portion of the wage differential.[21]

Others, however, take the opposite view and contend that certain omitted variables (e.g., men are more likely to smoke and abuse alcohol and drugs, have criminal records, and have bad driving records) suggest that the job performance and productivity of men should be lower than that of females. Taking such variables into account would increase the size of the unexplained female–male earnings gap. A second argument is that in fact many of the control variables—such as formal education, on-the-job training, and occupational placement—reflect discriminatory decisions. Although male productivity may exceed that of females, that higher productivity reflects discriminatory decisions with respect to (*a*) the quantity and type of education and job training provided men and women and (*b*) occupational segregation.

14.5   World of Work

The Gender Gap in the Gig Economy

The gig economy has become an increasingly important source of earnings for individuals. For example, nearly 4 million drivers were working for Uber by the end of 2018. The gig economy involves splitting work into small chunks and hiring independent workers to do the work in real-time. This division of labor increases the substitutability across workers and potentially reduces the gender wage (see World of Work 14.4, Evolution of a Family Friendly Occupation).

Cody Cook, Rebecca Diamond, Jonathan Hall, John A. List, and Paul Oyer use data from 1.9 million U.S. Uber drivers between January 2015 and March 2017 to examine the gender wage gap at Uber. The average male driver earned $21.28 per hour, while the average female driver earned $20.04 per hour. Thus, the average driver hourly wage is about 7 percent higher for men than women.

Their analysis states that the gender wage gap among Uber drivers can be explained entirely with three factors. First, male drivers tend to live near more profitable locations and because men earn a compensating wage differential for their willingness to drive in areas with higher crime rates and more bars. This factor explains about one-sixth of the gender wage gap.

Second, male drivers have more driving experience with Uber and earnings rise with additional trips. For example, a driver with more than 2,500 trips has hourly earnings that are 14 percent higher than a driver with less than 100 trips. The wages rise with additional experience since the drivers learn when to cancel and accept trips as well as where to drive. About one-third of the wage gap is due to gender differences in Uber driving experience.

Third, men earn more per hour because they drive at faster speeds. Uber driver earnings depend on both the distance driven and the time spent driving on a trip. However, in nearly all cases, a faster speed increases Uber earnings. Gender differences in speed explain nearly one-half of the gender wage gap.

Source: Based on Cody Cook, Rebecca Diamond, Jonathan Hall, John A. List, and Paul Oyer, "The Gender Earnings Gap in the Gig Economy: Evidence from over a Million Rideshare Drivers," Stanford University Working Paper, March 8, 2019.

---

[21] As much as 95 percent of the gender gap in starting salary offers for college graduates can be explained by differences in college major selected, see Judith A. McDonald and Robert J. Thornton, "Do New Male and Female College Graduates Receive Unequal Pay?" *Journal of Human Resources,* Winter 2007, pp. 32–48. For analysis indicating that gender differences in college majors are mostly due to gender differences in preferences, see Basit Zafar, "College Major Choice and the Gender Gap," *Journal of Human Resources,* Summer 2013, pp. 545–595.

WW 14.5

Conclusion? When all is said and done, we cannot make a precise estimate of the proportion of the wage gap that is due to discrimination, but we can say with considerable confidence that the statistical evidence points strongly to discrimination as an important factor in the labor market.[22]

14.4 *Quick Review*

- Some economists contend that the inferior economic position of women has resulted mainly from educational decisions, occupational choices, interrupted careers, and other voluntary choices made by women.

- Other economists stress discrimination as the root cause of the inferior economic position of women; discriminatory outcomes help explain the economic choices made by women.

- After sorting out nondiscriminatory sources, empirical studies typically find a large, unexplained residual difference in pay by gender and race; many researchers attribute most of this residual to discrimination.

- Controversy remains on the question of how successfully empirical studies have isolated true discriminatory outcomes.

Your Turn

On average, women have less mathematical and quantitative training than do men. Jobs demanding high levels of such training often pay exceptionally high salaries. Relate these factors to each of the arguments made in the first two review points here. (*Answers:* See page 542.)

ANTIDISCRIMINATION POLICIES AND ISSUES

There are several avenues through which government might attack the problem of discrimination.[23] One very general policy is to achieve a tight labor market through the use of appropriate monetary and fiscal policies. On one hand, an expanding economy makes it increasingly expensive for employers to indulge their tastes for discrimination. On the other hand, tight labor markets help to overcome stereotyping. For example, the over-full employment of World War II simultaneously created new labor market opportunities for minorities and women and made it clear that females and African–Americans could effectively perform jobs that heretofore had been closed to them.

A second general policy is to improve the education and training opportunities of those who have been discriminated against. For example, upgrading the quantity and quality of schooling received by African–Americans will enable them to become more competitive with white workers.

The third and most obvious means of dealing with discrimination is through direct governmental intervention. We will focus on this aspect of policy.

---

[22] Barbara R. Bergmann, *The Economic Emergence of Women,* 2nd Edition (New York: Palgrave Macmillan, 2005), p. 54.

[23] For a more detailed discussion of antidiscrimination policies, see Barbara Bergmann, *The Economic Emergence of Women,* 2nd Edition Chapters 7 and 8, op. cit., and her *In Defense of Affirmative Action* (New York: Basic Books, 1996).

TABLE 14.4 A Summary of Antidiscrimination Laws and Policies Relating to Gender and Race

Equal Pay Act of 1963
Mandates equal pay for women and men who perform the same, or highly similar, jobs.
Civil Rights Act of 1964, Title VII
Seeks to eliminate discrimination based on race, gender, color, religion, or national origin in hiring, promoting, firing, and compensating workers.
Executive Orders (1965–1968)
Prohibit federal contractors from discriminating among workers on the basis of race, gender, color, religion, or national origin; require affirmative action programs for firms that underuse women and minorities.

Direct governmental intervention has stressed equal employment opportunities for minorities and for women. The purpose has been to deal directly with labor market inequalities by prohibiting certain practices in hiring, promotion, and compensation. Table 14.4 provides a summary of the salient legislation and policies that are the focal point for our discussion.

Equal Pay Act of 1963

This was the first major federal act to deal with sex discrimination. The Act makes it illegal for employers to pay men and women different wage rates if they "do equal work on jobs, the performance of which requires equal skill, effort and responsibility, and which are performed under similar working conditions."[24] Although the *Equal Pay Act of 1963* was clearly a landmark piece of legislation, it did not comprehensively deal with all forms of gender discrimination. In particular, we have seen that women workers are plagued with the problem of occupational segregation as indicated by the crowding model. A discriminating employer could simply dodge the provisions of the Act by practicing strict occupational segregation—that is, by *not* employing women and men in the same jobs. In fact, an employer with an all-male labor force would be in compliance with the law.

Civil Rights Act of 1964

Title VII of the *Civil Rights Act of 1964* is the centerpiece of U.S. antidiscrimination policy. This law applies to not only discriminatory wages but also discrimination in hiring and promotions. Specifically, the Act made it illegal for any employer "to refuse to hire or to discharge any individual, or otherwise to discriminate against any individual with respect to his compensation, terms, conditions, or privileges or employment, because of such individual's race, color, religion, sex, or national origin."[25] By requiring equal treatment in hiring, firing, promotion, and compensation (including fringe benefits), the law virtually eliminated the ability of employers to practice overt discrimination legally. As amended, the Act applies to all employers in interstate commerce with 15 or more workers, to all labor unions with 15 or more members, and to workers employed by educational institutions, state and local governments, and federal agencies. Enforcement rests primarily with the Equal Employment Opportunity Commission (EEOC).

---

[24] U.S. Equal Employment Opportunity Commission. "The Equal Pay Act of 1963". Approved May 14, 1947. https://www.eeoc.gov/laws/statutes/epa.cfm

[25] U.S. Equal Employment Opportunity Commission. "Title VII of the Civil Rights Act of 1964". https://www.eeoc.gov/laws/statutes/titlevii.cfm

Executive Orders and Federal Contracts

Executive orders issued in 1965 and 1968 attempted to eliminate all discriminatory policies that might be practiced by businesses or other institutions holding government contracts. Thus, the executive order of 1968 specifies,

> The contractor will not discriminate against any employee or applicant for employment because of race, color, religion or national origin. The contractor will take *affirmative action* to ensure that applicants are employed, and that employees are treated during employment, without regard to their race, color, religion, sex or national origin. Such action shall include, but not be limited to the following: employment, upgrading, demotion, or transfer; recruitment or recruitment advertising; layoff or termination; rates of pay or other forms of compensation; and selection for training, including apprenticeship.[26]

As revised, the executive orders require firms with contracts totaling $50,000 or more to develop *affirmative action programs*. If on examination it is found that a firm underuses women and minorities compared to their proportions in the available labor force, the firm must establish a program embodying numerical goals and timetables for increasing its employment of women and minorities. In a series of important decisions in 1986 and 1987 involving, among others, sheet metal workers in New York City, firefighters in Cleveland, and the Alabama state police, the Supreme Court upheld the constitutionality of affirmative action programs. More recently, however, the Court's decisions have upheld the constitutionality of affirmative action plans but have limited their scope. For example, in 2003 the Court ruled that the University of Michigan's policy of assigning 20 points to every minority undergraduate applicant out of a possible 150 points necessary to guarantee admission was unconstitutional. However, in another case, the Court ruled that the University of Michigan law school, which reviewed applications individually, was permitted to ensure that a "critical mass" of minority students was accepted for admission. In June 2016, the Supreme Court ruled a race-conscious admissions policy at the University of Texas was permissible. On the political scene, in the 1990s voters in the states of California and Washington passed constitutional amendments that ended all state programs giving racial and gender preferences in government hiring and contracting as well as public education. The states of Florida and Michigan instituted similar bans in 2000 and 2006, respectively. It is fair to say that affirmative action is under legal and political attack.

Have Antidiscrimination Policies Worked?

Over the past four decades, there have been increases in the African–American to white and female to male earnings ratios.[27] How much of these increases are explained by antidiscrimination policy? Before an assessment can be made, it is important to isolate the effect of antidiscrimination policies from other factors and policies that might have impacted the relative economic status of women, African–Americans, and whites.

WW14.6 Three factors other than antidiscrimination policies may have caused the observed rise in the African–American white earnings ratio.[28] First, there was an increase in the quality of education of African–Americans relative to whites during this period. One study estimates that 5–20 percent of the increase in the earnings ratio is due to the improvements in quality of education.[29] Second, the average level of schooling rose relatively more among African–Americans than whites. This rise in

---

[26] U.S. Equal Employment Opportunity Commission. "Executive Order 10925". https://www.eeoc.gov/eeoc/history/35th/thelaw/eo-10925.html

[27] Note that nearly all of the rise in the African-American to white earnings ratio occurred in the 1960s and early 1970s, and most of the increase in the female to male earnings ratio took place in the 1980s and early 1990s.

[28] For more about these factors, see John J. Donohue III and James J. Heckman, "Continuous versus Episodic Change: The Impact of Civil Rights Policy on the Economic Status," *Journal of Economic Literature,* December 1991, pp. 1603–1643.

[29] David Card and Alan B. Kreuger, "School Quality and Black–White Earnings: A Direct Assessment," *Quarterly Journal of Economics,* February 1992, pp. 151–200.

14.6   World of Work

Orchestrating Impartiality

Until recently, members of the major symphony orchestras in the United States were mostly handpicked by the music director. Although the hiring process involved an audition before the conductor and the section leader, most of the applicants were male students of a small group of instructors. As a result, the typical symphony orchestra was less than 10 percent female.

During the 1970s and 1980s, orchestras changed their hiring procedures to make the process more open and systematic. Job openings became widely advertised, and audition committees were expanded to include orchestra members. To increase impartiality, they adopted use of heavy cloth screens descending from the ceiling to hide the identity of the person auditioning. Some orchestras even use a carpet on the stage to muffle footsteps that could reveal the gender of the applicant.

After the change in hiring procedures, there was a substantial increase in the female proportion of major orchestras. At the five highest-ranked orchestras, the female percentage now ranges from 20 to 35 percent. The fraction of new hires that are female is even higher. The empirical evidence indicates that one-quarter to one-third of the rise in the female proportion is due to the use of screens in the audition process.

Source: Claudia Goldin and Cecilia Rouse, "Orchestrating Impartiality: The Impact of 'Blind' Auditions on Female Musicians," *American Economic Review*, September 2000, pp. 715–741.

schooling has been estimated to account for 20–25 percent of the increase in the earnings ratio.[30] Third, there was a large decline in the labor force participation of low-income African–Americans, which caused the earnings ratio of the remaining workers to rise. This factor has been estimated to account for 10–20 percent of the rise in the earnings ratio.[31]

The unexplained portion of the rise in the African–American to white earnings ratio ranges from 35 to 65 percent. It is difficult to directly attribute the unexplained portion of the increase in the earnings ratio to antidiscrimination policies. However, a couple of factors indicate that antidiscrimination policies played an important role. First, most of the increase in the earnings ratio occurred between 1960 and 1975, when antidiscrimination policies were instituted. Second, the largest increase in the earnings ratio occurred in the South. This is where antidiscrimination enforcement was initially concentrated and the earnings gap was largest.[32]

The picture painted by the empirical literature on the impact of affirmative action is a bit clearer.[33] Leonard[34] has concluded from a series of studies that affirmative action led to improvements in the employment opportunities of both minorities and females between 1974 and 1980 but that this progress largely ended in the 1980s. Specifically, he statistically compared the changes in the demographic

---

[30] James P. Smith and Finis Welch, "Black Economic Progress after Myrdal," *Journal of Economic Literature,* June 1989, pp. 519–564.

[31] Donohue and Heckman, op. cit. For a study finding an even larger impact of selective withdrawal from the labor force, see Amitabh Chandra, "Labor-Market Dropouts and the Racial Wage Gap: 1940-1990," *American Economic Review,* May 2000, pp. 333–338.

[32] Donohue and Heckman, op. cit. For additional evidence that federal antidiscrimination efforts improved the economic situation of African-Americans, see Kenneth Y. Chay, "The Impact of Federal Civil Rights Policy on Black Economic Progress: Evidence from the Equal Employment Opportunity Act of 1972," *Industrial and Labor Relations Review,* July 1998, pp. 608–632.

[33] For a survey of the effects of affirmative action, see Harry J. Holzer and David Neumark, "Affirmative Action: What Do We Know?" *Journal of Policy Analysis and Management,* Spring 2006, pp. 463–490.

[34] Jonathan S. Leonard, "The Impact of Affirmative Action on Employment," *Journal of Labor Economics,* October 1984, pp. 439–463; and Leonard, "Women and Affirmative Action," *Journal of Economic Perspectives,* Winter 1989, pp. 61–75.

composition of the workforce in more than 68,000 firms, isolating the role of affirmative action by controlling for other factors that might have brought about these changes in demographic composition. Between 1974 and 1980, female and minority shares of employment grew faster in firms obligated to undertake affirmative action than in establishments not subject to this requirement. In this period, affirmative action increased the demand for African–American males by 6.5 percent, for other minority males by 11.9 percent, and for white females by 3.5 percent.

But the positive effects of affirmative action apparently ended during the 1980s, when the government's enforcement slackened under the Reagan administration. Leonard reports that, after accounting for other factors, the employment shares of African–Americans actually grew less rapidly over the 1980–1984 period in companies required to practice affirmative action than in firms not covered by the law.

A final comment: We can be quite certain that controversy will continue to surround not only the scope and techniques of antidiscrimination policies but also the question of their actual effectiveness.[35] But these debates should not obfuscate the clear reality that discrimination in America continues to influence labor supply and demand—and therefore wage rates and the allocation of labor. An understanding of discrimination and antidiscrimination policies is essential to a realistic conception of how labor markets work.

Chapter Summary

1. Empirical data suggest that *(a)* the earnings of full-time female and African–American workers are substantially less than those of white male workers, *(b)* African–Americans have higher unemployment rates than whites, *(c)* occupational distributions differ significantly by gender and race, *(d)* there are gender and racial differences in human capital acquisition, and *(e)* women and African–Americans have lower total earnings than white men at each level of educational attainment.

2. Discrimination occurs when female or African–American workers—who have the same abilities, education, training, and experience as male or white workers—are accorded inferior treatment with respect to hiring, occupational access, promotion, or wage rates.

3. Forms of labor market discrimination include wage, employment, occupational, and human capital discrimination.

4. According to Becker, some white employers have a "taste for discrimination" that can be measured by the discrimination coefficient *d*. Prejudiced white employers will be indifferent to hiring African–Americans only when the wage rate of African–Americans is less than that of whites by the monetary value of *d*. In supply and demand form, the model indicates *(a)* that a decline in the discrimination coefficient will increase the ratio of African–American to white wages and increase African–American employment, and *(b)* that the size of the African–American to white wage differential will vary directly with the supply of African–American workers.

5. The theory of statistical discrimination indicates that because detailed information concerning the potential productivity of job applicants is costly to obtain, profit-seeking employers base employment decisions on the perceived characteristics of groups of workers. The imputation of group characteristics to individuals discriminates against many individuals within those groups.

6. The crowding model focuses on occupational segregation. Using supply and demand analysis, it demonstrates that occupational crowding results in lower wages for women (African–Americans), higher wages for men (whites), and a net loss of domestic output. The index of occupational segregation measures the percentage of women or men who would have to change occupations for the

---

[35] For a discussion of seven misperceptions regarding affirmative action, see Roland G. Fryer Jr. and Glenn C. Loury, "Affirmative Action and Its Mythology," *Journal of Economic Perspectives,* Summer 2005, pp. 147–162.

occupational distribution of women to be the same as for men. The index for the United States has declined significantly since 1973.

7. Much disagreement exists about the extent to which earnings differentials based on gender or race are rooted in discrimination per se as opposed to rational decision making by women and African-Americans.

8. Economists have found several nondiscriminatory factors that help explain gender and racial pay differentials. Nevertheless, even after these factors are accounted for, large unexplained pay disadvantages for African-Americans and women remain. Many economists attribute these unexplained pay differences to discrimination.

9. Governmental antidiscrimination legislation, policies, and proposals involving direct labor market intervention include the Equal Pay Act of 1963, the Civil Rights Act of 1964, and executive orders applicable to federal contractors.

10. Statistical evidence suggests that antidiscrimination policy has reduced the racial pay gap. There is also evidence indicating that affirmative action programs have increased African-American employment and earnings in affected industries.

Terms and Concepts

nondiscriminatory factors	discrimination coefficient
discrimination	statistical discrimination
wage discrimination	crowding model
employment discrimination	index of segregation
occupational or job discrimination	Equal Pay Act of 1963
human capital discrimination	Civil Rights Act of 1964
taste for discrimination model	affirmative action programs

Questions and Study Suggestions

1. What has been the general secular trend of the weekly earnings of full-time female workers compared with male workers? What factors help explain this trend?

2. Women have increased the amount of education they have achieved relative to men, and average years of schooling completed are now approximately the same for males and females. Human capital theory predicts that this would close the male-female earnings gap. In fact, this has not happened. How can you explain it?

3. In Becker's taste for discrimination model, what is the meaning of the discrimination coefficient d? If the monetary value of d is, say, $6 for a given white employer, will that employer hire African-American or white workers if their actual wage rates are $16 and $20, respectively? Explain. In Becker's model, what effect would a decrease in the supply of African-American labor have on the African-American to white wage ratio and the employment of African-American workers? Use the model to explain the economic effects of an increase in employer prejudice. What are the basic public policy implications of this model?

4. What is statistical discrimination and why does it occur? The theory of statistical discrimination implies that discrimination can persist indefinitely, whereas the taste for discrimination model suggests that discrimination will tend to disappear. Explain the difference.

5. Use simple supply and demand analysis to explain the impact of occupational segregation or "crowding" on the relative wage rates of men and women. Who gains and who loses as a consequence of eliminating occupational segregation? Explain the following statement: "A gender-blind labor market would allocate labor more efficiently throughout the economy, and productivity would be higher on average."

6. Explain the following statement: "In the taste for discrimination model, discrimination is practiced even though it is costly to do so. But in the statistical discrimination model, it is clear that discrimination pays."

7. Assume that the occupational distribution of males and females is as follows:

Occupation	Male	Female
E	60%	5%
F	20	5
G	10	40
H	10	50

Calculate the index of segregation and explain its meaning. Compare the meaning of an index of 0.40 with indexes of 1.00 and 0. As applied to gender, has the index changed significantly over time?

8. Is the following statement true or false? If it's false, explain why. "The unemployment rates for white females and African–American men are considerably higher than the rate for white men."

9. Table 14.2 reveals significant earnings differences by gender and race at each level of education. What nondiscriminatory factors might explain part of the earnings differences between females and males? Between African–Americans and whites? Do you think that nondiscriminatory factors explain all the earnings differences in the table?

10. In what way does discrimination redistribute national income? How does it reduce national income?

11. There has been considerable controversy over the fact that certain pension plans into which males and females make equal contributions pay smaller monthly benefits to women than to men on the grounds that women live longer on average than men. Is this practice discriminatory? Explain. The use of female military personnel in most forms of ground combat is currently prohibited. Do you favor this ban?

12. It has been argued that to correct the inequalities of past discrimination, African–Americans and females should be given preference in employment and promotion. Do you agree? In the famous *Bakke* case, the plaintiff argued that he had been unjustly denied admission to medical school because less qualified African–American applicants were given preference under a quota system. Evaluate the plaintiff's argument: "To discriminate in favor of one individual or group is necessarily to discriminate against some other individual or group." Do you agree?

13. "Wage differences between men and women reflect not discrimination but rather differences in job continuity and rational decisions with respect to education and on-the-job training." Explain why you agree or disagree.

14. Some economists have argued that the unemployment effects associated with the minimum wage have been greater for African–Americans than for whites. Explain why this might be the case.

15. Critically evaluate each of the following statements:

    a. "Affirmative action plans have not worked; there is no evidence that they have increased African–American or female employment and wages."

    b. "The greatest barriers to economic equality between men and women are marriage and children."

16. Although the labor market opportunities for women have improved greatly over the past 30 years, poverty has become increasingly concentrated among women. How can you reconcile these two developments?

Internet Exercise

What Has Happened to the Female–Male Earnings Ratio?

 Go to the Census Bureau Historical Income Tables: People website (**http://www.census.go v/data/tables/time-series/demo/income-poverty/historical-income-people.html**). Click on "Full-Time, Year-Round Workers by Mean Earnings and Sex" This will retrieve a historical series of the female and male mean earnings.

What are the earnings ratios (female earnings/male earnings) for 1979, 1995, and the most recent year shown? What was the change in the ratio between 1979 and 1995? What might explain this change? What is the change in the ratio between 1995 and the most recent year?

Internet Links

 Harvard University's Project Implicit website offers a quiz to test one's conscious and unconscious preferences on over 90 different topics ranging from pets to ethnic groups (**https://implicit.harvard.edu/implicit/takeatest.html**).

The U.S. Equal Employment Opportunity Commission website provides detailed information about laws prohibiting discrimination (**http://www.eeoc.gov**).

Nonprofit organizations set up to fight discrimination include the Anti-Defamation League (**http://www.adl.o rg**), National Organization for Women (**http://www.now.org**), and the National Association for the Advancement of Colored People (**http://www.naacp.org**).

Chapter 15

Job Search: External and Internal

After reading this chapter, you should be able to:

1. **Explain the external job search model and summarize the empirical evidence.**
2. **Describe internal labor markets and discuss the effects of internal labor markets.**

A large amount of job switching occurs in the labor market. Nearly two-thirds of young people will work for three or more different employers in their first five years of work experience.[1] About 22 percent of all workers have been with their current employers for less than one year.[2] Individuals also switch jobs without changing employers.

Individuals search for jobs for a variety of reasons. Firms may suffer a decrease in demand and lay off workers who then search for new employment. New high school and college graduates will search for their first permanent employment. Individuals who dropped out of the labor force to raise children may reenter the job market. Workers may search for jobs that are a better match with their abilities.[3] For a given occupation, earnings and other working conditions differ widely within a city or even a firm.[4] As a result, workers search for jobs that offer them better combinations of wages and job characteristics.

Our discussion of the job search process will proceed as follows: We first analyze how workers attempt to find jobs at a new employer (external job search). Then we address the issue of job search within a firm (internal job search) and develop the notion of internal labor markets in some detail.

EXTERNAL JOB SEARCH

Two major characteristics of the labor market contribute to the need for people to search for the best job offer and for firms to search for employees to fill job vacancies. First, as we indicated in our earlier discussion of

---

[1] Henry S. Farber, "The Analysis of Interfirm Worker Mobility," *Journal of Labor Economics,* October 1994, pp. 554–593.

[2] U.S. Department of Labor, Bureau of Labor Statistics, "Employee Tenure in 2018," USDL-18-1500 News Release, September 20, 2018.

[3] For an analysis of the job matching process, see Boyan Jovanovic, "Job Matching and the Theory of Turnover," *Journal of Political Economy,* October 1979, pp. 972–990; Derek Neal, "The Complexity of Job Mobility among Young Men," *Journal of Human Resources,* April 1999, pp. 237–261; and Shintaro Yamaguchi, "The Effect of Match Quality and Specific Experience on Career Decisions and Wage Growth," *Labour Economics,* April 2010, pp. 407–423.

[4] For evidence on the variation in wages, see Stephen G. Bronars and Melissa Famulari, "Wage, Tenure, and Wage Growth Variation within and across Establishments," *Journal of Labor Economics,* April 1997, pp. 285–317.

the wage structure workers and jobs are highly heterogeneous. Personalities, levels of motivation, capabilities, and places of residence differ greatly even though individuals may possess similar levels of education, training, and experience. Jobs also are often unique: Employers pay differing wages, offer varying opportunities for advancement, and provide various working conditions, even for similar workers.

Second, market information about such differences in individuals and jobs is imperfect and takes time to obtain. Therefore, job seekers—many of whom are not working elsewhere—and prospective employers find it is in their respective interests to search for information about each other as a way to improve the terms of the transaction. People who are not employed and who are actively seeking work or "job shopping" are officially unemployed. Because there are continuous *flows* to and from the labor force and between jobs, the *stock* of unemployed people is simultaneously being diminished and replenished.[5]

Both expected gains and costs are associated with acquiring job information. Let's examine each in terms of a *job search model*.[6] Let's assume the job searcher is unemployed and seeking work.[7] Also suppose the person recognizes that the heterogeneous nature of jobs and employers, together with imperfect market information, generates a wide variance of likely wage offers for his or her occupation. Further assume that this person faces the distribution of wage offers shown in Figure 15.1. This frequency distribution is interpreted as follows: The horizontal axis measures the various wage offers, higher offers being farther to the right; and the vertical axis shows the relative frequency of offers at each wage level. For example, the frequency with which wage offers occur in the lowest *a* to *b* range will be 0.05. Stated differently, 5 percent of wage offers will be in this range; similarly, 15 percent of the wage offers will fall within the slightly higher *b* to *c* range, 30 percent in the still higher *c* to *d* range, and so on.

Next we assume that this person can roughly estimate the mean and variance of the frequency distribution of wage offers but has no way of knowing which employer has a job opening or which employer is offering which wage. In other words, the worker knows the cards in the deck but recognizes that they have been thoroughly shuffled.[8]

How will job search benefit this worker? Because this person is unemployed, he or she does not have an immediately available wage opportunity. A job search allows people to obtain wage offers and increases the likelihood of discovering wage opportunities in the rightward areas of the distribution shown in Figure 15.1.

And what are the costs of gaining job information? They include costs of such things as "for hire" notices in newspapers and other publications, fees paid to employment agencies, and transportation to and from interviews. But job search also includes significant opportunity costs. For instance, suppose this person searches for one job offer at a time, either getting an offer or not, and if the former, either accepting it or rejecting it before continuing to search for other offers. If this person receives and rejects an offer, that wage opportunity is lost; most wage offers cannot be "stored." Therefore, *a major cost of continued job search is the forgone earnings of the best known opportunity.* As higher wage offers are received, the *marginal* cost (MC) of continued search rises.

What decision rule might this person employ in accepting or rejecting a particular wage offer? One approach is to establish a reservation wage or, in this context, an *acceptance wage* and reject any wage offer that falls below it. But how would one rationally select such a wage? Theoretically, if a person knows the frequency

---

[5] See Chapter 18 for a more complete discussion of the definition of unemployment and the stock–flow model of the labor market.

[6] For a nontechnical discussion of a job search model and the empirical estimation of such a model, see Adam M. Zaretsky and Cletus C. Coughlin, "An Introduction to the Theory and Estimation of a Job Search Model," *Federal Reserve Bank of St. Louis Review*, January–February 1995, pp. 53–65.

[7] Only about 20 percent of new hires come directly from another job. For an analysis of job search by employed workers, see Joseph R. Meisenheimer II and Randy E. Ilg, "Looking for a 'Better' Job: Job Search Activity of the Employed," *Monthly Labor Review*, September 2000, pp. 3–14.

[8] Arthur M. Okun, *Prices and Quantities: A Macroeconomic Analysis* (Washington, DC: Brookings Institution, 1981), p. 27.

FIGURE 15.1 **Wage Offers, the Acceptance Wage, and Unemployment**

Given this frequency distribution of nominal wage offers and the person's acceptance wage W_a, she or he will reject all offers lower than c and accept any offer between c and g. The probability that a specific offer will exceed the acceptance wage is 80 percent (.30 + .30 + .15 + .05). During the period of search for an acceptable wage offer, this person is unemployed.

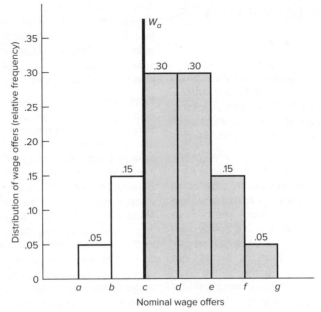

distribution in Figure 15.1 and can estimate the cost of generating new job offers, she or he can find the wage that equates the expected marginal benefit (MB) and expected MC from search. If the job seeker is offered an hourly wage above this acceptance wage, that person will conclude that it is not worthwhile to continue searching (MB < MC); if offered a wage below this amount, the person will reject the offer and continue to look for new offers because the expected MB of the activity exceeds the expected extra cost (MB > MC).

This optimal acceptance wage is shown as the vertical line W_a in Figure 15.1. The shaded area of the frequency distribution indicates the probability that any single offer will be above the acceptance wage. In this case, the probability is 80 percent (= .30 + .30 + .15 + .05). The probability that this person will accept any wage offer in the c to g range is 100 percent, and the probability that she or he will accept offers in the 0 to c range is zero. During the period of searching for a wage offer that exceeds the acceptance wage, this person is actively seeking work and, therefore, is officially unemployed. Because of the continuous nature of the labor force flows in the economy, this type of unemployment is always present.

Several important implications arise from our search model. We will examine two in detail and then briefly list several others.

Inflation and Job Search

Will inflation change how long people search for jobs? To answer this question, we assume initially that the rate of inflation is zero and that the economy is operating at its natural levels of output and employment. Now suppose expansionary fiscal and monetary policies increase aggregate demand so that the general price

15.1 World of Work

Thinking of Quitting? The Boss Knows[*]

Worker turnover is expensive for firms. If a worker quits, then a business will incur hiring costs to replace the worker and it will suffer a loss of its investment in firm-specific training. Credit Suisse indicates that a 1 percentage point reduction in unwanted turnover saves the firm $75–$100 million per year.

Firms such as Credit Suisse and Box Inc. are trying to reduce their turnover costs by developing models to predict who is likely to quit and then using those predictions to reduce the number of unwanted quits. The models use a wide variety of data, including information on job tenure, location, performance evaluations, worker surveys, and personality tests. Some models even use anonymized employee e-mail messages and calendars to measure the degree of social interactions among firm employees.

Work relationships have emerged as an important determinant of whether a worker quits. Box Inc. finds the quit rate is higher among workers who don't feel connected to their team. Credit Suisse reports that quits are more likely for large teams and low-rated managers. A data analytic firm discovered it could predict quits up to one year in advance for those who interacted less with colleagues and did not attend meetings other than required ones.

Firms have been utilizing the results of their models to reduce their quit rates. After Credit Suisse learned that workers who changed jobs at the bank were more likely to stay, it changed from policy of not posting a majority of its open jobs and hiring many outsiders to posting 80 percent of jobs and allowing internal workers to apply. Credit Suisse also used turnover models to offer new jobs to those internal workers who are most likely to leave. Box Inc. is trying to make workers more connected to their team by holding social events. It is also pointing out career opportunities for individuals and "stretch assignments." Micron found turnover was higher if job was not accurately described and so it is attempting to provide more accurate job descriptions to potential workers.

[*] Based on Rachel Emma Silverman and Nikki Waller, "Thinking of Quitting: The Boss Knows," *Wall Street Journal,* March 14, 2015, pp. A1.

---

level rises by 5 percent. Also assume that increases in nominal wage offers match this increase in the price level so that real wage offers remain unchanged.

Figure 15.2(a) repeats the frequency distribution of wage offers discussed previously, indicating again that, given the acceptance wage W_a, the probability that the job searcher will accept any specific offer is 80 percent. But now observe from graph (b) that the entire frequency distribution has shifted rightward because nominal wage offers are now 5 percent higher than previously. What impact will this shift have on a person's length of job search? Let's examine two distinct circumstances.

1 Expected Inflation

If the job searcher represented by Figure 15.2(a) and (b) fully anticipates the 5 percent rate of inflation, she or he will simply raise the acceptance wage by 5 percent to keep it constant in real terms. This is shown in graph (b) as the rightward shift of line W_a to W'_a. In this case, the worker's expectation that inflation will rise by 5 percent offsets the 5 percent increase in the nominal wage distribution and leaves the probability that any specific wage offer will be accepted at 80 percent (= .30 + .30 + .15 + .05).

Generalization: When the actual rate of inflation matches the expected rate, job searchers will *not* be influenced by the inflation. Their average length of job search will remain constant and, therefore, the unemployment level will stay at the natural rate.

2 Unexpected Inflation

Suppose the present rate of inflation is zero and our job searcher expects this price stability to continue. Also suppose that in the short run, this person does not adjust her expectation to the reality of higher inflation. Under these circumstances, the 5 percent inflation will lead our unemployed job seeker to reduce her search time. As a result, unemployment will decline temporarily below its natural rate.

This is easily demonstrated in Figure 15.2. Expecting inflation to be zero, this individual holds the acceptance wage rate at W_a. But the 5 percent inflation shifts the wage distribution rightward as shown in Figure 15.2(b). We observe that the probability that a new wage offer will be accepted increases from 80 percent to 95 percent (= .15 + .30 + .30 + .15 + .05). This person's duration of job search, therefore, falls; and if this pattern is widespread, unemployment declines. But according to this *adaptive expectations theory,* the unemployment decline will be short-lived. In the long run, unemployed job searchers will adjust their expectations of future inflation to the actual 5 percent rate. Consequently, they will increase their acceptance wages and lengthen their job searches, causing the unemployment rate to return to its natural level.

Generalization: Actual rates of inflation that exceed expected rates may temporarily reduce unemployment below its natural rate.

FIGURE 15.2 The Impact of Unexpected Inflation on Job Search

Unexpected inflation results in higher nominal wage offers, and the frequency distribution shifts from that shown in (a) to that seen in (b). Because this person's acceptance wage initially remains at W_a, he or she is more likely to accept the next wage offer—a probability of 95 percent versus 80 percent—and, hence, the length of job search falls. But once people recognize that the nominal wage offers are no higher in real terms than previously, they adjust their acceptance wages (e.g., W_a to W'_a), and the job search length returns to normal.

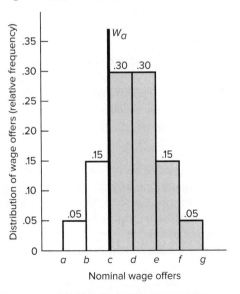

(a) Initial distribution of wage offers

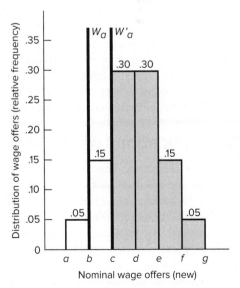

(b) Higher distribution of nominal wage offers

FIGURE 15.3 **The Impact of Unemployment Benefits on Unemployment**

Unemployment benefits reduce the net opportunity cost of rejecting wage offers and continuing to search for higher-paying employment and thus allow people to increase their acceptance wages. For the person shown, the increase in the acceptance wage from W_a to W'_a means that the probability of receiving an acceptable wage offer in the next attempt falls from 80 to 20 percent (.15 + .05). The length of job search and the amount of unemployment, therefore, rise.

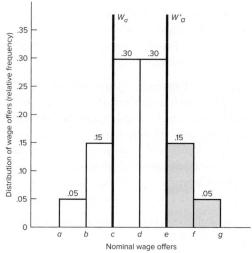

Unemployment Compensation and Job Search

A second major implication of our search model is that unemployment benefits provided by the government, past employers, or both will increase the extent of unemployment by enabling unemployed people to search for higher wage offers at less *net* cost.[9] Recall that a person's acceptance wage is established at the level where the expected gain from more search just equals the expected cost. Quite understandably, the presence of unemployment compensation increases one's acceptance wage because it *reduces* the expected *net* cost of searching for a higher wage offer. The opportunity cost of the continued search is reduced to the existing highest offer minus the unemployment benefits. As portrayed in Figure 15.3, an individual who qualifies for unemployment benefits may have an acceptance wage W'_a rather than W_a, and given the distribution of wage offers, the probability that this person will accept the next job offer falls to 20 percent (= .15 + .05) compared to the previous probability of 80 percent (= .30 + .30 + .15 + .05). This person's optimal length of job search, therefore, increases, and the overall rate of unemployment in the economy rises.

Other Implications of the Search Model

Let's briefly consider several other important implications of the job search theory. First, a prospective worker may not accept the initial job offer or even seek available jobs that pay below the acceptance wage. This fact helps explain the presence of numerous unfilled job vacancies in the presence of considerable overall unemployment. Second, the longer the expected length of tenure on the job, the higher a person's acceptance wage, all else being equal. For instance, suppose a person expects to be employed in a new job for 20 years. The anticipated gain from searching for a high wage offer is greater in this case, and the acceptance wage higher,

---

[9] This is *not* to suggest that such programs are undesirable; in fact, one expressed purpose of these payments is to allow workers to search for positions commensurate with their skills and experience, rather than being forced through economic necessity to take jobs in which they are underemployed. Also, much unemployment occurs in the form of layoffs, and unemployment compensation cushions the decline in earnings while workers wait to be called back.

than if the job searcher expects to work only a month or two for the new employer. Third, random luck will play a part in the wage and earnings distribution in the economy. One person may receive the highest wage offer in the frequency distribution on the first try; another may get a lower offer, continue to search, and finally accept an offer above the acceptance wage but below the highest wage in the distribution. Fourth, the level of unemployment is partly a function of the overall demand for labor. During recessions, the length of time required to discover each wage offer rises because so few firms are hiring workers. Also, if job searchers perceive a recession to be temporary, they may retain their acceptance wages, thereby prolonging their job search and contributing to a rise in unemployment.

Empirical Evidence

There have been two major strands in studies of the job search process. One line has focused on determinants of the acceptance wage and the other on the length of the job search. Several patterns have emerged regarding the acceptance wage. The acceptance wage falls with time unemployed as individuals become more realistic about the available wage offers.[10] The acceptance wage rates also fall—one estimate is by 15 percent—when people exhaust their unemployment benefits.[11] More highly educated and union workers have a higher acceptance wage.[12] African–American male youth have similar acceptances wages to white male youth, but they are higher relative to what is available in the market.[13] Wealthy people have a somewhat higher acceptance wage.[14]

In a summary of the available evidence, Devine and Kiefer conclude that most studies find that the average acceptance rate of offers is between 80 and 100 percent.[15] Thus, most of the variation in the rate of exiting from unemployment results from variations in the rate at which workers receive offers, not from variations in acceptance rates.

Numerous empirical studies indicate that unemployment insurance lengthens the job search process. The consensus estimate is that a 10 percent increase in real monthly unemployment benefits on average lengthens a person's unemployment duration by one-half to one week.[16] Other research is consistent with this finding. Studies using data from other countries show that higher unemployment benefits increase unemployment duration.[17] Lengthening the period for which recipients may collect unemployment benefits raises

---

[10] Nicholas M. Kiefer and George R. Neumann, "An Empirical Job Search Model with a Test of the Empirical Reservation Wage Hypothesis," *Journal of Political Economy,* February 1979, pp. 89–107. Also see Alan B. Krueger and Andreas I. Mueller, "A Contribution to the Empirics of Reservation Wages," *American Economic Journal: Economic Policy,* February 2016, pp. 142–179.

[11] Raymond Fishe, "Unemployment Insurance and the Reservation Wage of the Unemployed," *Review of Economics and Statistics,* February 1982, pp. 12–17. Also see Rafael Lalive, "How Do Extended Benefits Affect Unemployment Duration? A Regression Discontinuity Approach," *Journal of Econometrics,* February 2008, pp. 785–806.

[12] Keifer and Neumann, op. cit.

[13] Harry J. Holzer, "Reservation Wages and Their Labor Markets Effects for Black and White Male Youth," *Journal of Human Resources,* Spring 1986, pp. 157–177. Although black male youth have higher acceptance wages, that does not explain their longer duration of unemployment, see Stephen M. Petterson, "Black–White Differences in Reservation Wages and Joblessness: A Replication," *Journal of Human Resources,* Summer 1998, pp. 758–770.

[14] Hans G. Bloemen and Elena G. F. Stancanelli, "Individual Wealth, Reservation Wages, and Transitions into Employment," *Journal of Labor Economics,* April 2001, pp. 400–439.

[15] Theresa J. Devine and Nicholas M. Kiefer, "The Empirical Status of Job Search Theory," *Labour Economics,* June 1993, pp. 3–24.

[16] For reviews of some of these studies, see Bruce D. Meyer, "Lessons from U.S. Unemployment Insurance Experiments," *Journal of Economic Literature,* March 1995, pp. 99–131; and Peter Fredriksson and Bertil Holmlund, "Improving Incentives in Unemployment Insurance: A Review of Recent Research," *Journal of Economic Surveys,* July 2006, pp. 357–386. Also seeAndrew C. Johnston and Alexandre Mas, "Potential Unemployment Insurance Duration and Labor Supply: The Individual and Market-Level Response to a Benefit Cut," *Journal of Political Economy,* December 2018, pp. 2480–2522.

[17] For evidence of the impact of unemployment insurance in Norway and Sweden, see Knut Roed, Peter Jensen, and Anna Thoursie, "Unemployment Duration and Unemployment Insurance: A Comparative Analysis Based on Scandinavian Micro Data," *Oxford Economic Papers,* April 2008, pp. 254–274. Also see Peter Kuhn and Chris Ridell, "The Long-Term Effects of a Generous Income Support Program: Unemployment Insurance in New Brunswick and Maine, 1940–1991," *Industrial and Labor Relations Review,* January 2010, pp. 183–204.

unemployment duration.[18] Finally, the probability of finding work rises sharply after unemployment benefits have ended.[19]

15.1 *Quick Review*

- The unemployed worker looking for work determines an acceptance wage based on the expected MCs and MBs of longer searches. If a given wage offer exceeds the acceptance wage, the person takes the job; if the wage offer is less than the acceptance wage, the individual rejects the offer.

Your Turn

How do unexpected inflation, anticipated inflation, and unemployment insurance each affect the optimal length of a person's job search? (*Answer:* See page 542.)

Other factors also influence the duration of job search. African–Americans tend to have a longer job search than whites. Although union workers have a higher acceptance wage, there is only weak evidence that they have a longer job search than nonunion workers.[20] Older workers tend to have longer job searches than younger workers. This likely occurs because they face a wider range in wage offers than younger workers and thus the return to job search is greater.[21] Impatient individuals search less intensively and have a longer job search.[22]

INTERNAL LABOR MARKETS

A strict interpretation of neoclassical theory evokes the notion of an auction market in which workers are openly and continuously competing for jobs *and,* conversely, firms persistently bid to attract and retain labor services. Orthodox theory assumes that the firm, as an institution, poses no obstacle or barrier to the competitive pressures of the labor market. It is assumed that the wage rates of every type of labor employed by the firm are determined by market forces; therefore, the wage structures of all firms employing the same types of workers would be identical. Workers would have access to jobs at all skill levels for which they are qualified, and mobility between firms would be unimpeded and extensive.

But critics of orthodox theory contend, and many mainstream economists increasingly agree, that this portrayal is sorely at odds with the real world. The public schoolteacher, the skilled machinist, and the government bureaucrat, to cite but a few, are *not* faced with the daily prospect of being displaced from their jobs by someone who is equally capable and who is willing to work for a slightly lower salary. Workers enjoy "job rights," and employers seek to

---

[18] Stepan Jurajda and Frederick J. Tannery, "Unemployment Durations and Extended Unemployment Benefits in Local Labor Markets," *Industrial and Labor Relations Review,* January 2003, pp. 324–348. Also see Jan C. van Ours and Milan Vodopivec, "How Shortening the Potential Duration of Unemployment Benefits Affects the Duration of Unemployment: Evidence from a Natural Experiment," *Journal of Labor Economics,* April 2006, pp. 351–378.

[19] Lawrence Katz and Bruce Meyer, "Unemployment Insurance, Recall Expectations, and Unemployment Outcomes," *Quarterly Journal of Economics,* November 1990, pp. 993–1002.

[20] Devine and Kiefer, op. cit.

[21] Solomon W. Polachek and W. Stanley Siebert, *The Economics of Earnings* (Cambridge, England: Cambridge University Press, 1993), pp. 235–236. Also see, HilaAxelrad,IsraelLuski, and MikiMalul, "Reservation Wages and the Unemployment of Older Workers," *Journal of Labor Research,* June 2017, pp. 206–227.

[22] Stefano DellaVigna and M. Daniele Paserman, "Job Search and Impatience," *Journal of Labor Economics,* July 2005, pp. 527–588.

maintain stable workforces. Although there is considerable occupational and geographic mobility in our economy, the average worker's employment is in fact quite stable. Farber has calculated that among workers aged 35–64, 35 percent have been with their current employers 10 or more years.[23] Even for women—who sometimes have problems achieving access to more desirable jobs—some 30 percent have been working for the same employers for more than a decade. Indeed, perhaps as much as 50 percent of the workforce participates in "internal labor markets" in which they are substantially shielded from the competitive pressures of the "external labor market."[24]

15.1 Global Perspective

Job Tenure

Job tenure—the number of years with the current employer—varies widely across countries, ranging from 7.5 years in Denmark to 13.2 years in Italy.

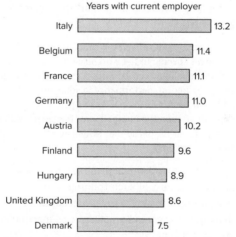

Years with current employer

Italy	13.2
Belgium	11.4
France	11.1
Germany	11.0
Austria	10.2
Finland	9.6
Hungary	8.9
United Kingdom	8.6
Denmark	7.5

Source: Organization for Economic Cooperation and Development, OECD Stat, http://www.oecd.org/. Data are for 2018.

Characteristics of Internal Labor Markets

What is an internal labor market? How and why do such markets evolve? What are their implications? An *internal labor market* is "an administrative unit, such as a manufacturing plant, within which the pricing and

---

[23] Farber, 1999, op. cit.

[24] W. Stanley Siebert and John T. Addison, "Internal Labour Markets: Causes and Consequences," *Oxford Review of Economic Policy,* Spring 1991, pp. 76–92.

allocation of labor is governed by a set of administrative rules and procedures"[25] rather than by economic variables.[26] Within many firms we find more or less elaborate hierarchies of jobs, each of which centers on a certain skill (machinist), a common function (building maintenance), or a single focus of work (the computer). Furthermore, each job hierarchy entails a sequence or progression of jobs that forms what is called a mobility chain or *job ladder*. As suggested by Figure 15.4, a new worker will typically enter this job ladder as a trainee in the least skilled job at the bottom of the ladder. The position at which workers gain access to the job ladder is called, for obvious reasons, a *port of entry*. It is through the port of entry that the sequence of jobs that constitutes the job ladder makes contact with the *external labor market*. This external labor market is the "auction market" of orthodox theory. That is, in recruiting workers to fill vacancies for the least skilled position in a job ladder, the firm must compete with other firms that are hiring the same kind of labor. Whereas the market forces of supply and demand may be paramount in determining the wage rate paid for the port-of-entry position, market forces are held to be superseded by administrative rules and procedures in explaining the wages paid for other jobs constituting the job ladder of the internal labor market. The point to be stressed is that within the internal labor market, institutionalized rules and procedures, along with custom and tradition, are foremost in determining how workers are allocated in the job hierarchy and what wage rates they are paid.

Reasons for Internal Labor Markets

Why do internal labor markets exist? The basic answer to this question is that firms typically encounter significant costs in recruiting and training workers, and these costs can be minimized by reducing labor turnover. Let's first consider the matter of training. Internal labor market theorists contend that many job skills are unique and specific to individual enterprises:

> Almost every job involves some specific skills. Even the simplest custodial tasks are facilitated by familiarity with the physical environment specific to the workplace in which they are performed. The apparent routine operation of standard machines can be importantly aided by familiarity with a particular piece of operating equipment. . . . Moreover, performance in some production and most managerial jobs involves a team element, and a critical skill is the ability to operate effectively with the given members of the team. This ability is dependent upon the interaction of the personalities of the members, and the individual's work "skills" are specific in the sense that skills necessary to work on one team are never quite the same as those required on another.[27]

The specificity of job skills and technology to individual firms means that workers require *specific training* that is most efficiently acquired on the job. The cost of such training, you will recall from Chapter 4, is borne by the employer. But to obtain a return on this investment in human capital, the employer must *retain* specifically trained workers *over time*. The job ladder—the core characteristic of internal labor markets—is the mechanism by which the desired workforce stability is achieved.

Advantages to Employers

The mutual advantageousness of the internal labor market to both the firm and the workers merits further comment. As just noted, the reduction of worker turnover increases the return the firm receives on its

[25] "The Measurement and Interpretation of Job Vacancies; a Conference Report of the National Bureau of Economic Research," Columbia University Press, 1966.

[26] Peter B. Doeringer and Michael P. Piore, *Internal Labor markets and Manpower Analysis* (Lexington, MA: D. C. Heath and Company, 1971). The Doeringer and Piore book is a comprehensive discussion of the evolution and character of internal labor markets. For a series of papers analyzing various aspects of internal labor markets, see Isao Ohashi and Toshiaki Tachibanaki (eds.), *Internal Labour Markets, Incentives, and Employment* (New York: St. Martin's Press, 1998). For a critical assessment of internal labor market theory, see George Baker and Bengt Holmstrom, "Internal Labor Markets: Too Many Theories, Too Few Facts," *American Economic Review,* May 1995, pp. 255–259; and "The Measurement and Interpretation of Job Vacancies; a Conference Report of the National Bureau of Economic Research," Columbia University Press, 1966.

[27] Doeringer and Piore, pp. 15–16.

investments in specific training. Furthermore, the amount of training a firm needs to provide will be reduced by the presence of the internal labor market. If the firm fills a vacancy from the external labor market, it will have to finance *all* of the specific training the worker requires. It can avoid much of this cost by simply promoting an internal applicant who, by virtue of having worked for the firm for some time, has already acquired a portion of the specific training that is prerequisite to the job opening. Similarly, recruitment costs will be larger if a position is filled from the external labor market. The firm—even after interviewing and screening—will have only limited knowledge about the quality of workers in the external labor market. But it will have accumulated a great deal of information about members of its present workforce. Thus, promoting from within will greatly reduce recruitment and screening costs and lessen the chances of making an error in filling the job. Another advantage of the internal labor market to the firm is that the existence of a clearly defined job ladder will provide an incentive for its existing workforce to be disciplined, productive, and continuously motivated to seek new skills. That is, the internal labor market will help solve the principal–agent problem discussed in Chapter 7. Finally, and related, internal labor market configurations may induce greater employee identification with the goals of the organization. Osterman asserts that "this heightened commitment may in

FIGURE 15.4 An Internal Labor Market

A worker typically enters an internal labor market at the least skilled port-of-entry job in the job ladder or mobility chain. Whereas the wage rate of the port-of-entry job will be strongly influenced by the forces of demand and supply in the local external labor market, wage rates and the allocation of workers within the internal labor market are governed primarily by administrative rules and procedures.

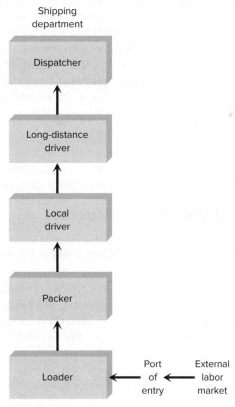

Source: Adapted from Robert M. Fearn, *Labor Economics: The Emerging Synthesis* (Cambridge, MA: Winthrop Publishers, Inc., 1981), p. 142.

turn lead to more effort, more attention to quality, lower turnover rates, and other behaviors which enhance productivity."[28]

Advantages to Workers

Internal labor markets also confer advantages on workers who are accepted into them. Workers who are admitted receive benefits in the form of enhanced job security and built-in opportunities for job training and promotion. Workers need not leave the firm to secure better jobs but rather may ascend a well-defined sequence of jobs that constitute the job ladder. Furthermore, those in the internal labor market are shielded from the competition of workers in the external labor market. In addition, the formalization and codification of the rules and procedures governing both worker allocation and wage rates within the internal labor market protect workers from favoritism and capricious managerial decisions. Workers in internal labor markets are more likely to enjoy due process and equitable treatment with respect to layoffs, promotion, and access to training opportunities.[29]

The Role of Unions

Although the presence of a labor union can accelerate the development of internal labor markets, the cause–effect relationship is rather complicated. Internal labor markets tend to invite unionization; conversely, unions promote or accelerate the evolution of internal labor markets.

On the one hand, several reasons make an internal labor market conducive to unionization. First, the enhanced stability of the labor force resulting from an internal labor market promotes unionization. A fluid, unstable workforce is an obstacle to organization, but a stable group of workers develops a community spirit and perhaps a common set of grievances that lead to formalization through a union. Second, workers in internal labor markets possess specific training that endows them with considerable bargaining power. Remember: Employers must retain specifically trained workers to realize a return on their human capital investments. It is only natural that workers might want to express this bargaining power collectively through a union. Finally, the administrative rules and procedures that prevail in the internal labor market define quite clearly the scope and character of managerial decisions. Unionization is a logical response to instances where managerial actions are at odds with customary rules and procedures.

On the other hand, the presence of a union can be important in reinforcing the development of an internal labor market. A written collective bargaining agreement codifies, formalizes, and makes more rigid the rules and procedures that prevail in the functioning of an existing internal labor market.

Labor Allocation and the Wage Structure

Let's consider in more detail the promotion process—the allocation of labor—*and* the determination of wages within the internal labor market. The critical point to recall is that in the internal labor market, the pricing and allocation of labor are determined not by the forces of supply and demand but rather by administrative rules and procedures. Thus in the case of promotions, the typical administrative rule is that, other things being roughly equal, the worker who has been on a particular rung of a job ladder for the longest time will be promoted to the next rung when an opening occurs. That is, promotions are generally determined on the basis of *seniority*. Seniority is typically tempered, however, by the presumed ability of the individual to perform the job satisfactorily after a trial period. In short, the rules indicate that the "right" to the promotion resides with

---

[28] Lewin, David, Mitchell, Olivia S., and Peter D. Sherer, *Research Frontiers in Industrial Relations and Human Resources* (Cornell University Press, 1992).

[29] For more about the potential benefits of internal labor markets to both employers and employees, see Peter B. Doeringer, "Internal Labor Markets and Noncompeting Groups," *American Economic Review,* May 1986, pp. 48–56. Michael J. Carter and Susan B. Carter detail two interesting case studies of the evolution of internal labor markets in their "Internal Labor Markets in Retailing: The Early Years," *Industrial and Labor Relations Review,* July 1985, pp. 586–598.

the most experienced worker, not necessarily the most able worker available from either the internal or the external labor market. Similarly, layoffs are allocated on the basis of reverse seniority: The newest workers are laid off first (Chapter 18).

The wage structure within an internal labor market is also determined by administrative procedures, through custom and tradition, and by the pattern of mobility that is sought. In terms of Figure 15.4, how should the wage rate of a packer in the shipping department, for example, compare with that of a local driver? Frequently a system of job evaluation is used to establish the wage rate attached to each job in a job ladder. *Job evaluation* is a procedure by which jobs are ranked and wage rates assigned in terms of a set of job characteristics and worker traits. Table 15.1 shows an illustrative job evaluation scheme where points have been assigned, undoubtedly with some degree of arbitrariness, to various job characteristics and traits. Thus, using this system, the actual points assigned to a packer's job and a driver's job might be 50 and 75, respectively. This ranking implies that the wage rate of a driver should be 50 percent higher than that of a packer. For example, if packers receive $12 per hour, then drivers should be paid $18. Note in particular that in the internal labor market, wage rates frequently are attached to jobs rather than individuals. Internal labor market theorists are suggesting in effect that productivity often resides in jobs rather than in workers. Also observe that administrative procedure has supplanted the forces of demand and supply.

Once established, custom and tradition intervene to make the internal wage structure rigid: "Any wage rate, set of wage relationships, or wage setting procedure which prevails over a period of time tends to become customary; changes are then viewed as unjust or inequitable, and the work group will exert economic pressure in opposition to them."[30] Recalling the notion of equitable comparisons, we should note that custom and rigidity evolve around wage *relationships* as opposed to specific wage *rates.*

The wage structure is not determined in isolation from the allocative function of the internal labor market. One important constraint is that the wage structure must foster and facilitate the internal allocation of labor

TABLE 15.1 Model Job Evaluation System

Factor		Maximum Points
Working conditions		15
Noise	5	
Dirt	5	
Smell	5	
Responsibility for equipment		25
Responsibility for other workers		20
Skill		20
Manual dexterity	10	
Experience	10	
Education		35
Physical effort		10
Total		125

Source: Peter B. Doeringer and Michael J. Piore, *Internal Labor Markets and Manpower Analysis* (Lexington, MA: D. C. Heath and Company), p. 67; and M.E. Sharpe, "Internal Labor Markets and Manpower Analysis." www.routledge.com

[30] Doeringer, Peter B. and Michael J. Piore. *Internal Labor Markets and Manpower Analysis* (M.E. Sharpe, 1985).

that the employer seeks. "The wage on every job must be high enough relative to the job or jobs from which it is supposed to draw its labor and low enough relative to the jobs to which it is supposed to supply labor to induce the desired pattern of internal mobility."[31] In Figure 15.4, the wage of the packer must be sufficiently higher than that of a loader so that the latter will aspire to become the former.

The Efficiency Issue

The question of whether internal labor markets are efficient is intriguing and important. The basic premise of orthodox economics is that competitive pressures result in the efficient use of labor and other inputs. When competition prevails, any given firm must combine labor and other productive resources in the most efficient way, or it will be driven out of business by other firms that are efficient. But the critical feature of the internal labor market is that aside from port-of-entry jobs, workers are shielded from competition. Wages in internal labor markets are determined not by market forces but by rather arbitrary administrative procedures embodied in job evaluation, through custom and tradition, and so forth. Thus, say orthodox economists, it would be only by chance that the various kinds of workers would be paid in accordance with their productivities. Furthermore, workers are promoted (allocated) largely on the basis of seniority, rather than in terms of worker ability (productivity). More senior workers may or may not be more productive than some junior workers. These characteristics imply that the existence of internal labor markets conflicts with society's interest in allocative efficiency.

But for several reasons, most internal labor market theorists and some mainstream economists rebut this line of reasoning. Internal labor markets and the wage structures embodied in them may exist precisely because they efficiently allocate labor.

In the first place, recall that the internal labor market decreases labor turnover, reducing the costs of training, recruitment, screening, and hiring. Of particular significance, the job ladders of internal labor markets give the employer abundant information about the quality of its workers; therefore, the firm is less likely to promote a nonproductive worker if it selects that worker from within the internal labor market. In comparison, hiring from the external labor market is based on more limited information, which may increase the risk of obtaining an unproductive worker. It is also noteworthy that the use of seniority in the allocation of labor is *not* necessarily at odds with efficiency. The worker who has been on the job the longest is probably a suitable candidate for promotion. Also, only in a very few instances is internal labor market promotion based *solely* on seniority. The senior worker with the requisite ability and an acceptable performance record typically gets promoted, rather than simply the most senior employee.[32]

A second reason that internal labor markets may be efficient centers on the distinction between static and dynamic efficiency. *Static efficiency* refers to the combining of labor and other resources *of given quality* in the most efficient (least costly) way. *Dynamic efficiency,* on the other hand, has to do with increases in productive efficiency that arise from *improvements in the quality* of labor and other resources. For present purposes, the relevant contention is that internal labor markets promote dynamic efficiency, which is held to be of greater consequence than realizing static efficiency. The gain from using *existing* skills of workers more efficiently is a "one-shot" gain, whereas the gains from *improving* worker knowledge and skills can go on indefinitely.[33] Furthermore, internal labor markets are conducive to dynamic efficiency because providing a greater amount of security to more skilled senior workers makes those workers willing to pass along their knowledge and skills to less skilled colleagues. Highly skilled senior workers will want to conceal their knowledge from less skilled junior workers *if* the latter can become competitors for the formers' jobs. But seniority rules and

---

[31] Doeringer, Peter B. and Michael J. Piore. *Internal Labor Markets and Manpower Analysis* (M.E. Sharpe, 1985).

[32] Noted, however, that length of service frequently takes priority over ability and performance in promotion, see D. Quinn Mills, "Seniority versus Ability in Promotion Decisions," *Industrial and Labor Relations Review,* April 1985, pp. 421–425.

[33] Lester Thurow, *Investment in Human Capital* (Belmont, CA: Wadsworth Publishing Company, 1970), pp. 194–195.

other security provisions embodied in internal labor markets guarantee that this will not happen. If senior workers are assured that they have priority in promotions, that their wages will not be reduced as more workers acquire knowledge of their jobs, and that they will be the last to be laid off, then senior workers will be amenable to sharing their skills with fellow workers. Internal labor markets may provide these assurances.

15.2 *Quick Review*

- Evidence indicates that many people work for the same employers for numerous years and, in effect, "search" for improved pay and job characteristics through promotions and reassignments within their existing firms.

- Internal labor markets are characterized by hierarchies of jobs called job ladders, which workers enter via ports of entry. Only the wages at the ports of entry are truly market-based.

- Some economists think that internal labor markets contribute to inefficiency because wages are determined by rigid administrative procedures and rules.

- Other economists argue that internal labor markets enhance productivity by *(a)* reducing recruitment, screening, and training costs; *(b)* inducing senior workers to share their skills and knowledge with junior workers; and *(c)* providing younger workers with greater incentives to work productively.

Your Turn

Have you worked in a firm that has a clearly defined job ladder? If so, how much upward mobility did you observe along the ladder? (*Answer:* See page 542.)

Finally, some economists point out that the pay structures within typical internal labor markets may be effective incentive-generating devices, particularly in large firms where it is difficult to monitor the work effort of employees. The wage structure of the internal labor market may be such that not only are senior workers paid more than junior workers, but also senior workers are paid more than their marginal revenue products (MRPs), while junior workers are paid less than their MRPs.[34] The "premium" paid to senior workers is an inducement for younger employees to work hard. By being productive, young workers demonstrate to employers that they deserve to be retained and to progress up the job ladder to higher-paying jobs in which they, too, will enjoy the premium of a wage rate in excess of their MRPs. Young workers presumably accept wages that are initially less than their MRPs for the privilege of participating in a labor market where in time the reverse will be true. This wage structure is also appealing to young workers in that it offers the prospect of higher lifetime earnings. The greater work effort and higher average worker productivity that result from this wage structure increase the firm's profits, in which workers may share through wage bargaining.[35]

---

[34] This implies a relationship between wage rate and MRPs that is just the opposite of that shown in Figure 4.8(b).

[35] Edward P. Lazear, "Agency, Earnings Profiles, Productivity, and Hours Restriction," *American Economic Review,* September 1981, pp. 606–620; Lazear, "Why Is There Mandatory Retirement?" *Journal of Political Economy,* December 1979, pp. 1261–1284; and Lazear and Sherwin Rosen, "Rank-Order Tournaments as Optimum Labor Contracts," *Journal of Political Economy,* October 1981, pp. 841–864, see also Michael L. Wachter and Randall D. Wright, "The Economics of Internal Labor Markets," *Industrial Relations,* Spring 1990, pp. 240–262.

Chapter Summary

1. Job search is a natural and often constructive occurrence in a dynamic economy characterized by heterogeneous workers and jobs and by imperfect information.

2. The rational job seeker forms an acceptance wage at a level where the expected marginal costs and benefits of continued search are equal and then compares this wage to actual wage offers.

3. Fully anticipated inflation has no impact on the optimal length of job search because job seekers will adjust their acceptance wages upward at the same rate that nominal wage offers rise. But if job searchers mistakenly view inflation-caused rises in nominal wage offers as real wage increases, they will shorten their job search, and unemployment will temporarily fall.

4. Unemployment benefits extend the optimal length of job search by reducing the net opportunity cost of continuing to seek still higher wage offers.

5. Most firms and plants embody internal labor markets in which wages and the allocation of labor are determined by administrative rules and procedures rather than strictly by supply and demand.

6. Internal labor markets entail hierarchies of jobs called job ladders, which focus on a certain job skill, function, or technology. Having entered the job ladder through a port of entry, internal labor market workers are largely shielded from the competitive pressure of external labor markets.

7. Internal labor markets exist because they generate advantages for both employers and workers. For employers, internal labor markets reduce worker turnover and thereby increase the return on specific training and reduce recruitment and training costs. For workers, internal labor markets provide job security, opportunities for training and promotion, and protection from arbitrary managerial decisions.

8. By providing labor force stability, internal labor markets attract unions; conversely, unions promote and accelerate the development of internal labor markets.

9. It is unclear whether internal labor markets diminish or enhance productive efficiency.

Terms and Concepts

job search model	port of entry
acceptance wage	external labor market
adaptive expectations theory	seniority
internal labor market	job evaluation
job ladder	static and dynamic efficiency

Questions and Study Suggestions

1. What are the benefits and costs of job search? Why don't job seekers endlessly search for a higher wage offer?

2. What is meant by the term *acceptance wage?* How does a job seeker determine his or her acceptance wage? Why might the acceptance wage for one new college graduate differ from that of another new college graduate?

3. Explain how each of the following would affect the probability that a job searcher will accept the next wage offer and thus affect the expected length of his or her unemployment: *(a)* a decline in the rate of inflation below the expected one and *(b)* a decrease in unemployment benefits.

4. How do you explain the existence of internal labor markets? What are their advantages to employers? To workers?

5. How does a worker search for a better job in an internal labor market? What is the employer's search process within internal labor markets?

6. Explain the following statement: "Unions are both a consequence and a cause of internal labor markets." Why might the presence of internal labor markets in a firm encourage unionization?

7. Do you think internal labor markets enhance or detract from efficiency? How might one argue that the realization of dynamic efficiency is more important than achieving static efficiency? Do you agree?

Internet Exercise

What Is Happening to Long-Term Job Tenure?

Go to the Bureau of Labor Statistics Current Population Survey website (**http://www.bls.gov/ cps/home.htm**). Click on "Employee Tenure" under the heading "CPS News Releases."

Go to the table that presents the percentage of workers with 10 years or more of tenure. What are the percentages of all workers with 10 years or more of tenure in 2004 and the most recent year shown? How has job stability changed based on this measure? Replicate the same analysis for men and women. What might explain the gender difference in the change in job stability?

Internet Links

Indeed.com is the world's largest job search website (**http://www.indeed.com**).

Chapter 16

The Distribution of Personal Earnings

After reading this chapter, you should be able to:

1. Discuss the alternative methods for describing the distribution of earnings.
2. Discuss the human capital and multifactor approach to explaining the earnings distribution.
3. Explain the basic types of mobility within the earnings distribution.
4. Specify and evaluate the reasons for the recent increase in earnings inequality.

Thus far, our focus has been mainly on microeconomic aspects of labor markets. Specifically, we have discussed in some detail the labor market decisions of individuals, families, and firms. As illustrated in Figure 1.1, the next three chapters examine the *macroeconomics* of labor markets. Recall that macroeconomics deals with broad aggregates or collections of specific economic units treated as if they were one. The topics in these three chapters include the personal distribution of earnings, aggregate labor productivity, and employment and unemployment.

The micro–macro distinction is clearly evident in the present chapter, where our attention turns away from an analysis of specific wages and toward an examination of the *distribution of personal earnings*. This distribution is the national pattern of the shares of individual wage earnings. How unequal is the distribution of wages and salaries? What general factors explain the observed pattern? How much mobility is there within the overall distribution? Why has this distribution become more unequal over the past three decades?

In pursuing these questions, we first will discuss alternative ways of describing the earnings distribution and measuring the degree of observed inequality. Second, we will examine theories that help explain the distribution pattern of U.S. earnings. Our focus then shifts to personal earnings mobility, or movements within the aggregate earnings distribution. The chapter concludes with a discussion of the trend toward greater inequality in the earnings distribution over the past four decades.

DESCRIBING THE DISTRIBUTION OF EARNINGS

The degree of inequality in the distribution of earnings can be described in several ways. Let's examine two graphic portrayals: the frequency distribution and the Lorenz curve.

Frequency Distribution

The distribution of annual earnings received by full-time U.S. workers in 2017 is shown in Figure 16.1. This *absolute frequency distribution*—or *histogram*—shows the number of full-time wage and salary workers (measured on the vertical axis) whose annual earnings fell within each $5,000 earnings range shown on the horizontal axis. For example, the fourth bar from the left represents earnings within the $15,000–$19,999 range. We know from the height of this bar that about 4.4 million people had annual earnings in this category in 2017. Or as a second example, the bar representing the $55,000–$59,999 earnings range tells us that 4.4 million people received work income between $55,000 and $59,999 in 2017.

It is equally common to represent the distribution of income in terms of *relative* frequencies, in which case the vertical axis is converted to the percentage of total earners rather than being the *absolute* number of such workers, as shown here.

FIGURE 16.1   **The Distribution of Annual Earnings for Full-Time Wage and Salary Workers**

The personal distribution of annual earnings is highly unequal and is skewed to the right. The histogram (absolute frequency distribution) of earnings is characterized by (*a*) much bunching around the mode, (*b*) an extended rightward tail, and (*c*) a mean (arithmetic average) that exceeds the median (half above, half below).

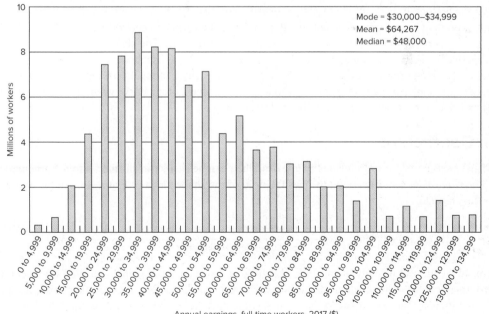

Source: Author calculations from March 2018 *Current Population Survey*

Three measures of location, or central tendency, are commonly used to summarize histograms or absolute frequency distributions such as that in Figure 16.1. The *mode* is the income category occurring with the greatest frequency. The *mean* is the arithmetic average, obtained by dividing the total earnings by the number of workers. Finally, the *median* is the amount of annual work income received by the individual who stands at the midpoint of the array of earnings. Half of those earning wages and salaries receive more than the median, while the other half receives less. With these definitions in mind, note from Figure 16.1 that the distribution of annual earnings for full-time U.S. workers is concentrated around a single leftward mode ($30,000–$34,999 in 2017); has a median level of earnings ($48,000 in 2017) that is to the right of the mode; and possesses a mean, or average ($64,267 in 2017), that is greater than both the mode and median. The mean exceeds the median because the average is pulled upward by the extremely high earnings of the relatively few workers who have earnings in the long rightward tail of the histogram. This tail is so long that our truncated diagram prevents it from reaching the horizontal axis. These characteristics correctly suggest that most U.S. workers receive earnings in the leftward two-thirds of the overall distribution, while some people receive extraordinarily large annual earnings relative to the median and mean.

Lorenz Curve

The degree of earnings inequality can also be shown by a *Lorenz curve*, such as the one portrayed in Figure 16.2. This curve indicates the *cumulative* percentage of all full-time wage and salary earners from left to right on the horizontal axis and the corresponding *cumulative* percentage of the total earnings accruing to that percentage of earners on the vertical axis. If each full-time worker received the average earnings, the Lorenz curve would be the diagonal (45°) line that bisects the graph. Twenty percent of all full-time earners would receive 20 percent of all earnings, 40 percent of the workers would get 40 percent, and so forth. All these points would fall on the diagonal line that we appropriately label *perfect equality*.

The actual Lorenz curve in Figure 16.2 is derived by plotting the data for 2017 from Figure 16.3. This figure shows the percentages of total earnings accruing to five numerically equal groups, or *quintiles*. For 2017 we see that the bottom 20 percent of all full-time workers received 6.5 percent of the total earnings, which plots as point *b* on the Lorenz curve. The bottom 40 percent of the earners received 18.0 percent (= 6.5 + 11.5) of the total earnings, which yields point *c* on the curve, and so forth. The shaded area between the diagonal line of perfect equality of earnings and the Lorenz curve provides a visual measure of the extent of earnings inequality. The larger this area, the greater the degree of disparity in annual earnings. If there were complete inequality—if one person had 100 percent of total earnings—the Lorenz curve would coincide with the horizontal and right vertical axis, forming a 90° angle at point *g*.

Gini Coefficient

The visual measure of earnings inequality just described can be easily transformed into a mathematical measure. The *Gini coefficient*, Equation (16.1), is the ratio of the shaded area of Figure 16.2 to the entire triangle below the diagonal:

$$\text{Gini coefficient} = \frac{\text{area between Lorenz curve and diagonal}}{\text{total area below diagonal}} = \frac{A}{A+B} \quad \textbf{(16.1)}$$

If there were complete equality of earnings, the distance between the diagonal and the Lorenz curve would be zero; therefore, the Gini coefficient also would be zero [= 0/(A + B)]. On the other hand, if one person had all the income, the area between the Lorenz curve and the diagonal would be equal to A + B, and the Gini coefficient would be 1 [= (A + B)/(A + B)]. The larger the Gini coefficient, the greater the degree of earnings inequality. The Gini coefficient for the 2017 data shown in Figure 16.3 and the Lorenz curve in Figure 16.2 is 0.40.

Cautions

Great care must be exercised in interpreting frequency distributions, Lorenz curves, and Gini coefficients.

FIGURE 16.2 The Lorenz Curve for Annual Earnings

The Lorenz curve is a useful way of summarizing the distribution of earnings. Line *af* represents perfect equality in the distribution, while the Lorenz curve *abcdef* illustrates the actual earnings distribution for 2017. The greater the area between the line of perfect equality and the Lorenz curve, the more unequal the distribution of earnings.

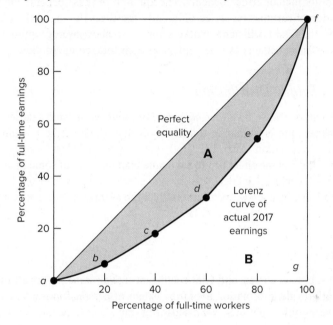

FIGURE 16.3 The Distribution of Annual Wage and Salary Earnings for Full-Time U.S. Workers

Over 40 percent of total earnings among full-time workers are received by the top 20 percent of earners.

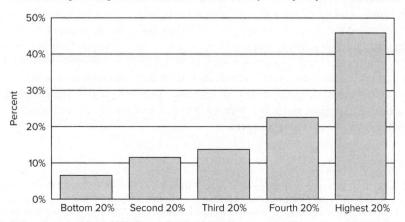

Source: Author calculations from the March 2018 *Current Population Survey*

1 Full- versus Part-Time Workers

Annual earnings are a product of both wages per hour *and* the number of hours worked in a year. A distribution that includes part-time workers and people who work full-time only portions of the year will display greater variability than distributions that include only full-time workers. The histogram in Figure 16.1 and the Lorenz curve in Figure 16.2 include only *full-time* wage and salary earners.

2 Fringe Benefits

Most earnings data do not include fringe benefits. The addition of these benefits increases the skewness of the frequency distribution of earnings or, stated differently, increases the sag of the Lorenz curve away from the diagonal and raises the Gini coefficient. Workers who have above-average annual earnings also tend to have higher-than-average fringe benefits as a percentage of their total compensation.[1]

3 Individual versus Family Distributions

Earnings distributions can be shown by either *individual* or *family* wages and salaries. Although the general shape of the family distribution is similar to that for individual workers, the median and average incomes are higher in the family formulation. Also, the family distribution is tighter; that is, the Gini coefficient is lower. The reason is that the income effect produced by the high incomes of some men reduces the likelihood that their wives are labor force participants. This income effect is offset somewhat by the tendency for men with higher earnings to marry women who earn more than the average female salary when they do choose to work.[2]

4 Static Portrayals

Frequency distributions, Lorenz curves, and Gini coefficients are all *static* portrayals or measures of earnings inequality. They do not provide information about the extent of personal movement within the distribution from year to year or over people's lifetimes. We discuss this important topic later in the chapter.

5 Other Income Sources

A final important caution is that annual earnings are only one of several possible sources of individual or family income. People who have high earnings from salaries tend to have disproportionately higher rental, interest, and dividend income than lower-wage workers. Taken alone, the inclusion of these nonwage incomes would make the distribution of individual or family income even more unequal than the distribution of wages and salaries. But government transfer payments such as Social Security benefits, welfare payments, and veterans' benefits offset this added inequality. Individuals and families who have zero or very low-wage earnings receive proportionately more transfer income than higher-earnings individuals. The outcome is a slightly less unequal distribution of individual and family income than that based solely on individual or family wage and salary earnings (full-time and part-time workers).

---

[1] For an empirical analysis of the impact of fringe benefits on the distribution of income, see Daniel Slottje, Stephen Woodbury, and Rod Anderson, "Employee Benefits and the Distribution of Income and Wealth," in William T. Alpert and Stephen A. Woodbury (eds.), *Employee Benefits and Labor Markets in Canada and the United States* (Kalamazoo, MI: W. E. Upjohn Institute, 2000).

[2] See Maria Cancian and Deborah Reed, "The Impact of Wives' Earnings on Income Inequality: Issues and Estimates," *Demography,* May 1999, pp. 173–184. Also see Peter Gottschalk and Sheldon Danziger, "Inequality of Wage Rates, Earnings, and Family Income in the United States, 1975–2002," *Review of Income and Wealth,* June 2005, pp. 231–254.

16.1 *Quick Review*

- The absolute frequency distribution (histogram) of earnings is a graphical depiction showing the number of employees whose earnings fall within various earnings ranges.

- The Lorenz curve graphically displays the cumulative percentage of all wage and salary earners on the horizontal axis and the corresponding cumulative percentage of total earnings accruing to that group; the farther the curve from the diagonal line of perfect equality, the greater the earnings inequality.

- The Gini coefficient is an arithmetic measure of earnings inequality; it is the area between the Lorenz curve and the diagonal line, divided by the total area beneath the diagonal line. The higher the Gini coefficient, the greater the earnings inequality.

- As measured by the histogram, Lorenz curve, and Gini coefficient, the degree of earnings inequality in the United States is high.

Your Turn

Suppose the Lorenz curve of earnings moves closer to the diagonal line. What has likely happened to the histogram of earnings and the Gini coefficient? (*Answer:* See page 542.)

EXPLAINING THE DISTRIBUTION OF EARNINGS

Human characteristics that we might associate with earnings—intelligence, physical strength, motivation, determination—are thought to be distributed according to the familiar bell-shaped normal curve. So why aren't earnings also distributed in this manner? Numerous theories attempt to explain this paradox.[3] Rather than describing each of these theories, we will approach this topic by first discussing the basic human capital explanation for earnings inequality and then exploring the diversity of alternative explanations by synthesizing several of them into a modified, multifactor model.

Human Capital Theory

The *human capital model* provides valuable insights into why the personal distribution of earnings is unequal and has a long rightward tail. Recall that human capital investments take various forms, the two most critical for present purposes being formal education and on-the-job training. Each relates to the earnings distribution.

1 Formal Education: Amount and Quality

Formal education has an investment component in that it requires present sacrifice to enhance future productivity and, therefore, lifetime earnings. A review of Figure 4.2 reminds us that a given investment will be undertaken only if the present value of the expected stream of enhanced earnings (area 3) equals or exceeds the present value of the sum of the direct and indirect costs (areas 1 + 2). Other things being equal, the greater the amount of formal schooling and the better its quality, the higher the investment costs (areas 1 + 2) and thus

---

[3] For a review of these theories, see Derek Neal and Sherwin Rosen, "Theories of the Distribution of Earnings," in A. B. Atkinson and F. Bourguignon (eds.), *Handbook of Income Distribution* (Amsterdam: North-Holland, 2000).

the greater the enhancement of productivity and the future earnings stream needed to justify the investment. Thus we have a rudimentary theory of earnings inequality. If other things such as ability, nonwage aspects of jobs, uncertainty of earnings, and life expectancies are held constant, earnings will be systematically and positively related to the amount and quality of a person's formal education. An unequal distribution of educational attainment will produce an unequal distribution of personal earnings.

A glance back at Table 14.2 offers casual evidence of the link between the amount of education undertaken and average annual earnings. It reveals that men and women—both African–Americans and whites—who have high school diplomas earn more than people who have obtained less than 12 years of education. Observe that workers with doctorates and professional degrees earn more than those with master's degrees; those with master's degrees earn more than those with bachelor's degrees; and those with bachelor's degrees earn more than those with associate degrees.

Econometric studies that account for other factors confirm the positive relationship between education and earnings shown in Table 14.2. Also, a few studies have found a direct relationship between the quality of formal education and subsequent earnings. For example, Card and Krueger[4] have discovered that, all else being equal, men who were educated in states with higher-quality public schools and who had better-educated teachers experienced a higher average rate of return on their investments in education. Care must be taken, however, not to overstate the importance of the link between education and earnings. Formal schooling explains only about 7–12 percent of the observed differences in individual earnings.

2 On-the-Job Training

The explanatory power of the basic human capital model rises appreciably once on-the-job training is added to the analysis. On-the-job training varies from simple "learning by doing" to formal apprenticeships and training programs and may be either general or specific to the firm. In the case of *general training*, the worker usually bears the investment cost through a reduced wage. The worker's expected gain in future wages, therefore, must be sufficient to produce a rate of return on the investment cost (reduced present wage) equal to what the worker could obtain through alternative investments. With nontransferable *specific training*, the firm will be forced to pay the investment expense. The employer will undertake this investment only if the expected increase in the worker's productivity justifies it. Training is undertaken in both cases in expectation of an increase in productivity and enhanced future earnings; therefore, we would expect to observe a direct relationship between the amount and quality of on-the-job training and a person's annual earnings.

Mincer has shown that about one-half to two-thirds of the variation of personal earnings is explained once postschooling on-the-job training investment is included in the definition of human capital.[5] This inclusion adds so much explanatory power for two reasons. First, taken alone, formal schooling does little to explain why people's earnings typically *rise* with age. That is, education explains why postschooling earnings exceed preschooling pay, but it alone does not explain why earnings rise more rapidly for educated people over their work lives. After all, most people conclude their formal education relatively early in their lives. On-the-job training, on the other hand, provides a basic explanation for the age variations in earnings that are so apparent in the distribution. As a person accumulates more training on the job, productivity and earnings rise. Furthermore, evidence shows that people who possess greater amounts of formal education also receive more on-the-job training from employers. People with the most formal education have demonstrated their ability

[4] David Card and Alan B. Krueger, "Does School Quality Matter? Returns to Education and the Characteristics of Public Schools in the United States," *Journal of Political Economy,* February 1992, pp. 31–39. Most other studies also find a positive relationship between school quality and earnings. For a survey of such studies, and other school quality research by David Card and Alan Krueger, see Randall K. Q. Akee and Klaus F. Zimmermann (eds.), *Wages, School Quality, and Employment Demand: David Card and Alan B. Krueger* (Oxford: Oxford University Press, 2011).
[5] Jacob Mincer, *Schooling, Experience, and Earnings* (New York: Columbia University Press, 1974).

to absorb training and are the workers firms choose for on-the-job training. Those who have more education, therefore, have disproportionately greater earnings than less-educated workers.

A second reason postschooling investment helps explain the observed inequality in the distribution of earnings is its impact on hours of work. Assuming that in the aggregate the substitution effect dominates the income effect, people who have more schooling and on-the-job training not only will have higher hourly wage rates but also will choose to work more hours annually than less educated and less trained workers. This will mean that the annual earnings—wage rate × hours worked—will be *disproportionately* greater than the differences in schooling and on-the-job training, implying that the earnings distribution will be skewed to the right.

A Modified Human Capital Model: A Multifactor Approach

The basic human capital explanation of earnings disparities is not without its critics. Of particular interest to our topic is the criticism that schooling and on-the-job training do not sufficiently explain the long, extended rightward tail of the earnings distribution. Many economists believe that we can better understand why the earnings distribution is skewed rightward by modifying the human capital model to include elements beyond the traditional ones of education and on-the-job training. In this *multifactor approach to the earnings distribution,* we specifically consider (*a*) ability, (*b*) family background, (*c*) discrimination, and (*d*) chance and risk taking, as well as education and training.

1 Ability

Ability is broadly defined as "the power to do" and, as used here, consists of something separate and distinct from the skills gained through formal education or on-the-job training. Ability is difficult to isolate and measure but is thought to be normally distributed. In addition, ability is multidimensional; that is, it takes several forms, including intelligence (IQ), physical dexterity, and motivation. It may be either genetic or environmental in origin. Our interest in this discussion is not the source of observed differences in ability but rather the consequences of these differences for the distribution of earnings. Ability can influence earnings directly—in other words, independently of human capital investments—and indirectly, through its impact on the optimal amount and quality of human capital acquired.

Direct Impact   Those who envision a direct effect of ability on earnings argue that in a market economy, people are rewarded in a general way according to their ability to contribute to a firm's output. Other things being equal, the greater one's ability, the greater one's productivity and, therefore, earnings. Recall from the discussion of the "ability problem" in Chapter 4 that some critics of the human capital theory contend that the observed positive relationship between formal education and earnings largely reflects *self-selection,* which is based on differences in ability. People who possess more intelligence are more likely to choose to attend college than those with less intelligence. Even if these highly intelligent people did not go to college, they could be expected to have higher earnings than less intelligent people who did not attend college. In other words, if we could somehow control for the skills and knowledge gained during college, this high-quality group still would have substantially higher earnings than their less able counterparts. Consequently, much of the inequality of earnings normally attributed to differences in education and training could be the result of differences in ability.

Complementary Elements   A related possibility is that *elements* of differences in ability are complements to one another in the production of earnings. This implies that the addition of one factor will increase the productivity of other elements of ability. In other words, ability differences may act *multiplicatively* to generate the exceptionally high earnings that some people receive. To illustrate, let's suppose that ability consists of several normally distributed complementary elements, two of which are intelligence and the *D-factor,* where *D* represents drive, dynamism, doggedness, or determination.[6]

With these assumptions, a person who is fortunate enough to be located in the rightward tail of both the normal distribution of intelligence *and* the normal distribution of the *D*-factor will have earnings that are disproportionately greater than her or his relative position in either of the two distributions. This idea can be illustrated by a simple example. Suppose we could place a cardinal value on intelligence and the *D*-factor. Next suppose Assad's intelligence is 4 on a scale of 1–5 (where 5 is high and 1 is low) while Bates' is 1. Also assume that Assad's *D*-factor is 4 compared to a rating of 1 for Bates. If intelligence and the *D*-factor interacted in an *additive* way to determine earnings, we would add 4 + 4 for Assad (= 8) and 1 + 1 for Bates (= 2) and note that Assad could be expected to earn four times as much as Bates (= 8/2). But we have speculated that the two factors might interact *multiplicatively* to determine earnings; that is, Assad's score will be 16 (= 4 × 4) while Bates' will be 1 (= 1 × 1). In this case, Assad's earnings will be 16 times those of Bates (= 16/1). The point is that if elements of ability are positively correlated and interact in a complementary fashion, a skewed distribution of earnings is entirely consistent with normal distributions of the elements.

Effect on Human Capital Decisions   Perhaps of greater significance is the notion that ability can influence earnings through its effect on the human capital investment decision. You may recall from Figure 4.6 that greater ability enables some people to translate any given investment in human capital, say a year of college or a year of on-the-job training, into a larger increase in labor market productivity and earnings than others. Therefore, the rate of return on each year of schooling or training will be higher for those who possess greater ability.[7] Consequently, these people will have a greater demand for formal education, and their employers will possess a stronger desire to train them on the job than will be the case for less able people. The result? People possessing greater ability will tend to have disproportionately greater stocks of human capital and earnings than simple differences in abilities would suggest. Stated simply, people who do well in school because of ability tend to get more schooling, and people who get more education, in turn, tend to receive more on-the-job training than others. These tendencies skew the overall distribution of earnings to the right.

2 Family Background

Differences in family background—indicated by such variables as family income, father's and mother's years of education, father's and mother's occupations, number of children, and so forth—also influence earnings both directly and indirectly.

Direct Effect   The direct effect of family background on earnings often comes through employment of family members in family-owned businesses. A youth born into a family owning a prosperous Mercedes dealership stands a good chance of earning a sizable income later in life. Also, family connections may enable sons and daughters of the wealthy to gain high-paying positions in firms that are owned or managed by their parents' close friends or business associates. Sometimes these networks simply increase a job seeker's access to information about job openings, but in other instances they generate jobs for adult children through intricate reciprocity arrangements among those who interact both socially and commercially with one another.

Effect on Human Capital Decisions   Of perhaps greater significance, however, is the role of family background in influencing the decision of how much formal education to obtain. This influence affects both the demand for human capital and the supply price of investment funds. High-income families tend to provide more

---

[6] Howard F. Lydall, "Theories of the Distribution of Earnings," in A. B. Atkinson (ed.), *The Personal Distribution of Income* (Boulder, CO: Westview Press, 1976), p. 35.

[7] This conclusion must be viewed cautiously. Greater ability also may imply larger forgone earnings during the investment period, in which case the observed greater postinvestment earnings may *not* yield higher rates of return, see John Hause, "Ability and Schooling as Determinants of Lifetime Earnings, or If You're So Smart, Why Ain't You Rich?" in F. Thomas Juster (ed.), *Education, Income and Human Behavior* (New York: McGraw-Hill Book Company, 1975), pp. 123–149.

preschool education for children, are more likely to live in areas that have better schools, and often stress the importance of higher education as a route toward a professional career. Their children also may be socialized to think in terms of attending higher-quality educational institutions. Consequently, high-income parents on average have a greater *demand* for human capital for their children; therefore these offspring obtain more formal education.

Family background may also provide easier financial access to higher education. Wealthier families may be able to finance their children's education from annual earnings or personal savings, incurring only the opportunity cost of forgone goods or interest. Lower-income families most probably will need to borrow funds from imperfect financial markets at high interest rates. Because of these differing supply costs of human capital, the children of wealthier parents will find it optimal to obtain more formal education than children of poorer families (Figure 4.7).[8]

These differences in education will combine with *direct* family influences to produce an unequal, rightwardly skewed distribution of earnings.[9]

3 Discrimination

In Chapter 14 we saw that discrimination explains part of the wage inequality between males and females and between whites and minorities in the United States. Discrimination adds to earnings inequality in a number of ways. First, overt pay discrimination and discrimination in promotion directly reduce the pay of those discriminated against. Second, occupational crowding or segregation not only reduces the pay of females and minorities but also increases the pay of males and whites. Both outcomes contribute to greater earnings inequality. Finally, poorer African–American and other minority families are often segregated into city neighborhoods where there is low-cost or public housing. These areas often have lower-quality schools and contain few adult role models with college degrees. Thus children from these areas are much less likely to obtain higher education than are children growing up in higher-income neighborhoods. Adding to this problem is the sheer expense of attending college. This expense deters many African–Americans and Hispanics from obtaining college degrees.

In short, wage and occupational discrimination contribute directly to earnings inequality while human capital discrimination, by reducing the quantity and quality of education and training, further contributes to this inequality.

4 Chance and Risk Taking

Some economists have incorporated the role of random elements such as chance or luck into theories of the distribution of earnings and income. These *stochastic theories* demonstrate how the cumulative impacts of

---

[8] Care must be taken not to overstate this effect, however. Financial aid–low-interest loans, scholarships, and so forth–received by students from lower-income families reduces the cost of investment funds for this group. Also, the *implicit* borrowing costs to the rich may not be that much lower than the *actual* borrowing costs to the poor. The empirical evidence is mixed. For a study showing that family income has little impact on the acquisition of human capital, see John Shea, "Does Parents' Money Matter?" *Journal of Public Economics,* August 2000, pp. 155–184. In contrast, a study examining the effect of transfer payments finds a large family income impact, see Randall K. Q. Akee, William E. Copeland, Gordon Keeler, Adrian Angold, and E. Jane Costello, "Parents' Incomes and Children's Outcomes: A Quasi-Experiment Using Transfer Payments from Casino Profits," *American Economic Journal: Applied Economics,* January 2010, pp. 86–115.

[9] For a survey of studies examining the relationship between family background and earnings, see Gary Solon, "Intergenerational Mobility in the Labor Market," in Orley Ashenfelter and David Card (eds.), *Handbook of Labor Economics,* Volume 3A (Amsterdam: North-Holland, 1999); Sandra E. Black and Paul J. Devereux, "Recent Developments in Intergenerational Mobility," in David Card and Orley Ashenfelter (eds.), *Handbook of Labor Economics,* Volume 4, Part B (Amsterdam: Elsevier, 2011); and Markus Jantti and Stephen Jenkins, "Income Mobility," in Anthony Atkinson and Francois Bourguignon (eds.), *Handbook of Income Distribution,* Volume 2, Part A (Amsterdam: Elsevier, 2015).

random fortune tend to produce a long rightward tail in the distribution of such nonwage income as profits, rents, and capital gains. Because this is a text about labor economics, our interest, of course, is strictly in the distribution of earnings, and thus many of the stochastic theories have little relevance.

Nevertheless, according to some economists, stochastic elements offer important insights into why earnings are unequal and why the earnings distribution is skewed to the right. Three examples of ways in which risk and luck might enter into the earnings determination process are as follows. First, suppose that at a specific instant, all people possess a given level of normally distributed earnings plus an opportunity to participate in a lottery. Further suppose that the lottery winnings consist of opportunities to be a premier professional athlete, a rock star, a motion picture celebrity, a major corporate executive, or a best-selling author. These positions are few in number but pay considerably more than the average salaries in society. But there is a catch: You must incur *risk* if you wish to play the lottery; that is, you must buy a lottery ticket. The ticket price may be, say, the cost associated with advocating bold business ventures to your employer only to have one of them fail; the direct and indirect costs of refining your acting, musical, or athletic skills only to discover that the investment does not result in stardom; or the cost of forgoing present job security to become a writer whose uncertain earnings derive from book royalties.

Will all workers of equal ability participate in this lottery? Obviously not. Some people simply are much too averse to risk. Only those who are less averse to risk will decide that the chance of winning the few big prizes is worth the price of the ticket. How then might the distribution of earnings be affected by the lottery? Three distributions, each individually symmetrical, would be observable. First, there would be a distribution of earnings for the many nonparticipants in the lottery. Second, we would observe a distribution, possibly lying to the left of the one for nonparticipants, indicating the earnings of lottery losers. Finally, there would be a distribution lying to the right of that for nonparticipants displaying the very large average earnings of the relatively few lottery winners. Even though each of these three distributions might be normally distributed, the composite distribution of earnings would be skewed to the right.[10]

In Chapter 8, we implied a second way that chance may account for differences in personal earnings. In Figure 8.5 it was observed that differences in pay for the same type of work can exist under circumstances of imperfect wage information and costly job search. Who receives which wage in the frequency distribution shown in the figure is in part determined randomly. For example, suppose that Gomez and Green are equally qualified job seekers who both have the same reservation wage (minimum acceptable wage). Also, assume that each is searching in a random fashion for job openings in the frequency distribution shown in Figure 8.5. Through good luck, Gomez may receive the highest wage offer in the distribution on her first try, while the less fortunate Green may get an offer above her reservation wage but well below the pay received by Gomez.

A final example of the role of chance in theories of personal earnings is provided by Thurow. He contends that "marginal products are inherent in jobs and not individuals. The individual will be trained into the marginal productivity of the job he is slated to hold, but he does not have this marginal productivity independent of the job in question."[11] The implication of this thesis is that workers possessing a particular set of general background characteristics—that is, being equally trainable—will make up a labor pool from which employers will draw randomly. Those who are fortunate will get selected for jobs with high marginal productivity and annual earnings; but because such jobs are few, other equally qualified people will end up in lower-paying occupations. Thus, according to Thurow, "similar individuals will be distributed across a range of job opportunities and earnings. In effect, they will participate in a lottery."[12]

---

[10] This example is based on a more complex model presented by Milton Friedman, "Choice, Chance, and the Personal Distribution of Income," *Journal of Political Economy,* August 1953, pp. 273-290. For a highly technical criticism of Friedman's article, see S. M. Kanbur, "Of Risk Taking and the Personal Distribution of Income," *Journal of Political Economy,* August 1979, pp. 769-797.

[11] Lester C. Thurow, *Generating Inequality: Mechanisms of Distribution in the U.S. Economy* (New York: Basic Books, Inc., 1975), p. 85.

[12] Lester C. Thurow, *Generating Inequality: Mechanisms of Distribution in the U.S. Economy* (New York: Basic Books, Inc., 1975).

FIGURE 16.4 **Factors Affecting Personal Annual Earnings**

The basic human capital explanation of the personal distribution of annual earnings is shown by the heavy solid arrow that connects education and training to annual earnings. The multifactor approach adds ability, family background, and discrimination as variables that can directly influence earnings (heavy lines) or indirectly affect earnings by having an impact on the amount and quality of education and training that a person receives (thin lines). Luck, or chance, also plays a role in affecting annual earnings (broken line).

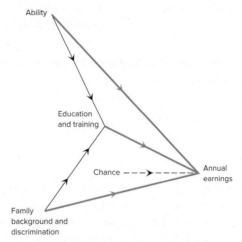

Source: Adapted from A. B. Atkinson, *The Economics of Inequality,* 2nd Edition (Oxford: Oxford University Press, 1983), p. 122.

Schematic Summary

Figure 16.4 summarizes the major determinants of earnings just discussed.[13] The basic human capital explanation of earnings is represented by the thick solid line connecting education and training with earnings. The more comprehensive multifactor explanation is portrayed by the entire figure. Ability (independent of education) affects earnings directly, as shown by the thick line connecting the two, and indirectly via its impact on the optimal amount and quality of education and training (thin line). Likewise, family background and discrimination have direct and indirect effects on personal earnings. The solid arrow between these factors and earnings represents the roles of family firms, family connections, and wage and occupational discrimination. The thin line from family background and discrimination to education and training illustrates the impact of family education and wealth on the demand for, and the supply price of, human capital. It also captures the effect of racial and gender discrimination on human capital and, therefore, indirectly on earnings. Finally, the role of chance is portrayed by the broken line leading directly to earnings.

We could easily add more complexity to Figure 16.4; for example, we could connect chance with family background and ability, for in a sense both are partly products of luck. Also, we could add a feedback loop from earnings to education and training, inasmuch as present earnings may help determine how much subsequent education one might find optimal. Then, too, we could recognize the role of compensating wage premiums in causing earnings differences. Finally, as pointed out by Lydall, Rosen, and others, hierarchical structures of organizations may create large earnings disparities.[14] But these important considerations aside, Figure 16.4 adequately summarizes the major determinants of the personal distribution of earnings.

---

[13] For a fuller discussion of this representation, see A. B. Atkinson, *The Economics of Inequality,* 2nd Edition (Oxford: Clarendon Press, 1983), p. 122.
[14] Howard Lydall, *The Structure of Earnings* (London: Oxford University Press, 1968); and Sherwin Rosen, "Authority, Control, and the Distribution of Earnings," *Bell Journal of Economics,* Autumn 1982, pp. 311–323.

MOBILITY WITHIN THE EARNINGS DISTRIBUTION

The aggregate personal distribution of earnings is quite rigid from one year to the next and changes only slightly from one decade to the next. But this fact masks the degree of individual movement within that fixed distribution. As Schiller colorfully points out, on the one hand, individuals may be highly mobile from year to year and over their lifetimes within the static aggregate distribution, suggesting a game of musical chairs in which the positions of the chairs remain the same but the occupants regularly change. On the other hand, "the rigid shape of the aggregate distribution is equally compatible with a total lack of personal mobility—a game, as it were, that individuals play by remaining in their chairs until the music . . . is over."[15]

Which of these two possibilities best describes reality? The answer appears to be the musical chairs scenario. The evidence suggests that considerable movement or mobility occurs within the rather rigid static distribution. This *earnings mobility* is of two main types: life-cycle mobility and a "churning" that is independent of age.

Life-Cycle Mobility

We know from our previous discussions of age–earnings profiles (Figure 4.1) that people's earnings typically vary systematically with age over the life cycle. Most people have relatively low earnings when they are young; later, during their prime earning years, their earnings rise substantially; and finally, their earnings fall near the time of retirement. Thus, even if everyone had an identical stream of earnings over her or his lifetime, we still would observe age-related inequality in the distribution of earnings. In any specific year, the static annual distribution of earnings would include, say, young (low-earnings) workers just beginning their labor force participation, middle-aged (high-earnings) employees in the prime of their careers, and older workers who were phasing into retirement. This inequality of *annual* earnings for a specific year would be present despite complete equality of *lifetime* earnings.

Because of *life-cycle mobility* of earnings, there will be more equality in lifetime earnings than is observed using static cross-sectional annual data.

"Churning" within the Distribution

There is also movement within the earnings distribution that is independent of age itself. Because of *"churning" within the earnings distribution,* people's relative age-adjusted earnings positions change during their lifetimes. For example, a salesperson may have relatively small commissions and earnings in the first year of a new job but receive considerably larger annual compensation in subsequent years. Or a manager may get promoted to a new job that pays considerably more than the job previously held. Or as an example of churning in the downward direction, a performer who is highly paid in one year may earn much less during following years.

Evidence

How much movement is there within the earnings distribution? To answer this question, Diaz-Gimenez, Glover, and Rios-Rull used a sample of household heads aged 35–45 in 2011.[16] They divided the sample into

---

[15] R. Schiller, Breadley, "Relative Earning s Mobility in the United States," *American Economic Review,* 67, No. 5 (December, 1977), p. 926.

[16] Javier Diaz-Gimenez, Andy Glover, and Jose-Victor Rios-Rull, "Facts on the Distributions of Earnings, Income, and Wealth in the United States: 2007 Update," Federal Reserve Bank of Minneapolis *Quarterly Review,* February 2011, pp. 2–31.

five earnings categories (quintiles), each containing 20 percent of the workers, and then observed the movements of individuals between 2001 and 2007. Diaz-Gimenez, Glover, and Rios-Rull found that 43 percent of workers changed at least one earnings quintile or one-fifth of the way from one of the ends of the earnings distribution to the other. Some workers had even greater earnings mobility: 9 percent changed two or more quintiles over the six-year period.

One must not overstate the extent of earnings mobility, however. Diaz-Gimenez, Glover, and Rios-Rull found that earnings mobility in and out of the *lowest* and *highest* quintiles was lower than to and from other categories. In addition, Gittleman and Joyce report that women and African–Americans are more likely to stay

---

16.1 World of Work

Cross-Country Differences in Earnings Mobility across Generations

Another measure of earnings mobility in a society is the degree to which earnings are transferred from one generation to the next. A large body of literature for the United States indicates that the intergenerational earnings elasticity between a father's earnings and his son's earnings is about 0.4. This elasticity implies that if a father has earnings 10 percent greater than average, his son will earn about 4 percent more than average.

How does U.S. intergenerational earnings elasticity compare to that of other countries? The United States has similar or more intergenerational mobility than the United Kingdom but less than that of several other countries. The estimates for the intergenerational earnings elasticity in the United Kingdom range from 0.42 to 0.57. Suggestive evidence indicates that less developed countries also tend to have lower intergenerational mobility. For example, the intergenerational earnings elasticity for South Africa is about 0.44. In contrast, Canada, Finland, and Sweden are relatively more mobile, by this measure. Their elasticities range from 0.1 to 0.3.

Solon points to several factors that explain these cross-country differences. First, countries with greater earnings inequality at points in time tend

to have lower intergenerational earnings mobility. For example, the United States and the United Kingdom have greater income inequality and, therefore, lower intergenerational earnings mobility than do Sweden and Finland. Second, countries that have greater inheritability of income-producing traits—due to selective mating between individuals with those traits—tend to have less intergenerational earnings mobility. Third, higher returns to investments in education and other forms of human capital increase earnings differentials across generations and thus tend to reduce the intergenerational mobility rate. The United States, in particular, has higher returns to postsecondary education than many other nations. Finally, countries that invest relatively more in the human capital of children from high-earnings households have less intergenerational earnings mobility.

Source: Gary Solon, "Cross-Country Differences in Intergenerational Earnings Mobility," *Journal of Economic Perspectives,* Summer 2002, pp. 59–66. For evidence there is slightly more intergenerational earnings mobility among daughters than sons in Sweden, see Lalaina H. Hirvonen, "Intergenerational Earnings Mobility among Daughters and Sons: Evidence from Sweden and a Comparison with the United States," *American Journal of Economics and Sociology,* November 2008, pp. 777–826. For similar evidence for Norway, see Espen Bratberg, Oivind Anti Nilsen, and Kjell Vaage, "Trends in Intergenerational Mobility across Offspring's Earnings Distribution in Norway," *Industrial Relations,* January 2007, pp. 112–129.

in the bottom quintile and less likely to stay in the top quintile.[17] Although there is much movement in the earnings distribution, the extent of this mobility is neither uniform throughout the distribution nor equal for all groups of workers.[18]

> WW16.1   Nevertheless, earnings mobility does reduce the amount of inequality in lifetime earnings. Gottschalk found that averaging earnings over a 17-year period reduces inequality by about one-third relative to using data for a single year.[19] Buchinsky and Hunt report that earnings mobility reduces inequality by 12–26 percent over a four-year period.[20]

16.2   World of Work

Government Employment and the Earnings Distribution

One out of six U.S. workers is employed by the government. How do the wages paid to these employees affect the distribution of earnings? The answer is that government employment and remuneration reduce overall earnings inequality.

Government agencies and government contractors usually adhere to a prevailing wage rule under which the wages paid to public employees are comparable to the earnings of similar workers in the private sector. But this rule tends to be modified at both the bottom and the top ends of the government pay structure. Blue-collar public employees are paid more than their private sector counterparts, whereas white-collar workers in government—particularly executives—are paid much less. As a consequence, the personal distribution of earnings in the public sector is more egalitarian than in the private sector, causing the overall distribution in society to also be less unequal.

The reasons for the compression of earnings in the public sector are many. For example, elected officials may pay low-wage workers more than their private sector counterparts to avoid the potentially politically embarrassing circumstance of having full-time government workers qualify for government cash and in-kind welfare benefits. Also, it seems probable that low- to middle-wage-earning employees, who are large in number and strong politically, are more likely to secure wage increases than higher-paid managers and professionals, who are few in number. Furthermore, it may be that the large salaries paid to executives in corporations (Table 7.1) simply are not politically feasible when paid to top governmental administrators and elected officials. In this regard, we might note that in a typical year, the total of the combined salaries and bonuses of the 10 highest-paid corporate executives in the United States exceeds the combined salaries of the following government officials: the president of the United States, the vice president, the 100 U.S. senators, the 50 state governors, the 9 Supreme Court justices, and the 50 heads of major regulatory agencies.

---

[17] Maury Gittleman and Mary Joyce, "Earnings Mobility and Long-Run Inequality: An Analysis Using Matched CPS Data," *Industrial Relations,* April 1996, pp. 180–196.

[18] For more evidence on this point, see John Geweke and Michael Keane, "An Empirical Analysis of Earnings Dynamics among Men in the PSID: 1968–1989," *Journal of Econometrics,* June 2000, pp. 293–356. Also see Brett Theodos and Robert Bednarzik, "Earnings Mobility and Low-Wage Workers in the United States," *Monthly Labor Review,* July 2006, pp. 36–47.

[19] Peter Gottschalk, "Inequality, Income Growth, and Mobility: The Basic Facts," *Journal of Economic Perspectives,* Spring 1997, pp. 21–40.

[20] Moshe Buchinsky and Jennifer Hunt, "Wage Mobility in the United States," *Review of Economics and Statistics,* August 1999, pp. 351–368, see also Richard V. Burkhauser and John G. Poupore, "A Cross-National Comparison of Permanent Inequality in the United States and Germany," *Review of Economics and Statistics,* February 1997, pp. 10–17; and Richard V. Burkhauser, Douglas Holtz-Eakin, and Stephen E. Rhody, "Labor Earnings Mobility and Inequality in the United States and Germany during the Growth Years of the 1980s," *International Economic Review,* November 1997, pp. 775–794.

16.2 *Quick Review*

- The human capital theory looks at differences in the amount and quality of education and the extent of on-the-job training as the major reasons for earnings inequality.

- The multifactor approach to earnings distribution takes into account ability, family background, discrimination, chance, and risk taking, in addition to education and training.

- Workers exhibit considerable earnings mobility over their work lives; earnings typically are low in earlier years, rise in prime working years, and then decline.

- There is much year-to-year movement of workers across earnings categories, independent of life-cycle aspects of earnings. This mobility is less in the lowest and highest earnings categories.

Your Turn

Of all the factors explaining earnings inequality, which one do you think is the most significant? (*Answer:* See page 542.)

WW16.2

RISING EARNINGS INEQUALITY

During the past three decades, labor economists have devoted much research to tracking and explaining changes in the distribution of earnings in the United States. The initial motivation for this research was the controversial hypothesis expressed in the early 1980s that the middle class in America is shrinking. In its extreme form, this view holds that American employment is being polarized between high-paying positions requiring considerable education and low-paying jobs in the service sector.[21]

Although most labor economists reject the extreme polarization view, a consensus has arisen that the distribution of work and salary earnings has indeed become more unequal.[22] Evidence indicates that earnings inequality has increased over the past four decades and that this trend has accelerated since 1980.[23]

Trends in Wage Inequality

A useful measure of wage inequality is the ratio of wages at different parts of the wage distribution. For example, a commonly used differential is the 90–10 ratio, which is the wage at the 90th percentile divided by the wage at the 10th percentile. Figure 16.5 shows the ratio of the hourly wage for wage and salary workers by

---

[21] Barry Bluestone and Bennett Harrison, *The Deindustrialization of America* (New York: Basic Books, Inc., 1982). Also see Bennett Harrison and Barry Bluestone, *The Great U-Turn: Corporate Restructuring and Polarization of America* (New York: Basic Books, Inc., 1988); and Barry Bluestone, *The Polarization of American Society: Victims, Suspects, and Mysteries to Unravel* (New York: Twentieth Century Fund Press, 1995).

[22] Evidence indicates that inequality among workplace disamenities such as job injuries and shift work is also rising, see Daniel S. Hamermesh, "Changing Inequality in Markets for Workplace Amenities," *Quarterly Journal of Economics,* November 1999, pp. 1085–1123. Also see Nicole Maestas, Kathleen J. Mullen, David Powell, Till von Wachter, and Jeffrey Wenger, "The Value of Working Conditions in the United States," National Bureau of Working Paper Number 25204, October 2018.

[23] For a survey of research on the rise in wage inequality since 1980, see Wiemer Salverda and Daniele Checchi, "Labour-Market Institutions and the Dispersion of Wage Earnings," in Anthony Atkinson and Francois Bourguignon (eds.), *Handbook of Income Distribution*, Volume 2, Part B (Amsterdam: Elsevier, 2015).

gender. For men, in 1973 the 90–10 ratio was 3.75. This indicates that men at the 90th percentile earned 3.75 times as much as men at the 10th percentile. The ratio rose to 5.25 in 2019 indicating that inequality increased.[24]

The rate of increase, however, was not steady over this period. It rose at a modest pace of 0.013 points per year between 1973 and 1979. It increased by a rapid 0.076 points per year between 1979 and 1994. Between 1994 and 1999, the ratio fell modestly; and it has since risen above its 1994 value. A further breakdown of the distribution of earnings indicates that the recent relative stability in inequality is due to offsetting factors.[25] On the one hand, the wages for males at the low end of the wage distribution have risen relative to those in the middle, which has tended to reduce inequality. On the other hand, the wages of men near the top of the wage distribution have continued to rise relative to those in the middle, which has tended to increase inequality.

Wage inequality has also risen among women. The 90–10 ratio rose from 3.07 in 1973 to 4.38 in 2019. The change in inequality across time was different for women: The 90–10 ratio fell between 1973 and 1979, in contrast to the slight rise for men. On the other hand, the ratio rose one-fifth faster for women than for men between 1979 and 1994.

Why the Increase in Earnings Inequality?

Economists have advanced several explanations for why earnings inequality has grown over the past three decades. Let's briefly assess four potential explanations.

FIGURE 16.5   **Wage Inequality, 90–10 Ratio**

Earnings inequality for both men and women has increased in recent decades.

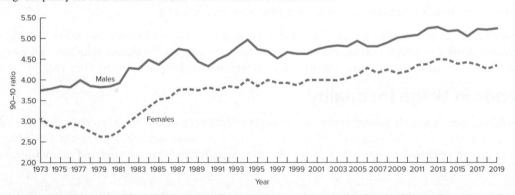

Source: Author calculations from 1973–1978 *May Current Population Survey* and the monthly *Outgoing Rotation Group Current Population Survey* files from 1979 to 2018; "Current Population Survey (CPS) Data at the NBER," www.data.nber.org

---

[24] There is evidence that inequality measures are sensitive to the sample of workers examined and the earnings measure. Mark S. Handcock, Martina Morris, and Annette Bernhardt, "Comparing Earnings Inequality Using Two Major Surveys," *Monthly Labor Review,* March 2000, pp. 48–61; and Thomas Lemieux, "Increasing Residual Wage Inequality: Composition Effects, Noisy Data, or Rising Demand for Skill?" *American Economic Review,* June 2006, pp. 461–498.

[25] The source of the statistics in this section is author calculations from 1973–1978 *May Current Population Survey* and the monthly *Outgoing Rotation Group Current Population Survey* files from 1979 to 2018.

1 Deindustrialization

Since the mid-1970s employment in the service sector has increased dramatically relative to employment in manufacturing. Because the service sector has a lower average wage and a higher variance of earnings than the manufacturing sector, this tilt toward services has undoubtedly increased earnings inequality.[26]

But economists warn that this is an incomplete explanation. The change in the mix of employment toward services accounts for only a small portion of the overall rise in wage inequality. The vast majority of the rise in earnings inequality is explained by increased wage and salary dispersion *within* industries.[27] This intraindustry increase in earnings inequality is not easily explained by the shift from manufacturing to service employment. Moreover, it is important to remember that several high-growth service industries—for example, law, consulting, accounting, medicine, and education—are high-pay sectors, not low-pay ones.

16.1 **Global Perspective**

Earnings Inequality*

The United States has a higher degree of earnings inequality, as measured by the 90–10 wage ratio, than major European countries.

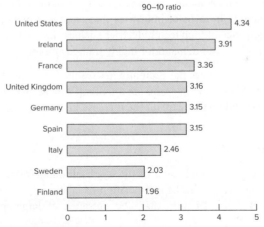

90–10 ratio

United States	4.34
Ireland	3.91
France	3.36
United Kingdom	3.16
Germany	3.15
Spain	3.15
Italy	2.46
Sweden	2.03
Finland	1.96

Source: Hipólito Simón, "International Differences in Wage Inequality: A New Glance with European Matched Employer–Employee Data," *British Journal of Industrial Relations,* June 10, pp. 310–346, Table A2; and Lawrence Mishel, Jared Bernstein, and Heidi Shierholz, *State of Working America, 2008/2009* (Ithaca, NY: ILR Press, 2009), Table 3.5.

* Data are for 2002.

[26] Lawrence F. Katz and David H. Autor, "Changes in the Wage Structure and Earnings Inequality," in Orley C. Ashenfelter and David Card (eds.), *Handbook of Labor Economics,* Volume 3A (Amsterdam: Elsevier, 1999), pp. 1463-1555.
[27] Robert G. Valletta, "The Effects of Industry Employment Shifts on the U.S. Wage Structure, 1979-1995," Federal Reserve Bank of San Francisco *Economic Review,* no. 1 (1997), pp. 16-32.

2 Decline of Unionism

In theory, unions have ambiguous effects on wage inequality. Unions increase wage inequality because they raise the wages of union workers relative to their nonunion counterparts and because they are made up largely of higher-paid blue-collar workers. Unions lower wage inequality because they equalize wages within and across firms with unionized workers. In addition, unions tend to lower the wage gap between white-collar and blue-collar workers because they raise the relative wages of their mainly blue-collar members. Although unions have uncertain effects in theory on wage inequality, the evidence generally indicates they tend to reduce wage inequality.

Research evidence supports the view that the decline of unionism has contributed to the rise in earnings inequality.[28]

3 Increased Demand for Skilled Workers

Recall that the college wage premium rose substantially starting in the 1980s implying a growing wage gap between more skilled workers and less skilled workers. One potential explanation for the rising rate of return to higher education and, therefore, for increased earnings inequality is that the demand for more skilled workers may have sharply increased relative to the demand for less skilled workers. Other things being equal, a relative increase in the demand for more skilled, higher-paid workers will widen the earnings distribution.

Increased demand for more skilled workers may have evidenced itself in two ways. First, the demand for more skilled workers may have occurred *within* industries.[29] Responding to new technologies, industries in general may have changed their production techniques in ways that require more college-educated workers. For example, manufacturing and service industries alike have expanded their use of computer-aided technologies.[30] Second, a shift in product demand may have occurred *among* industries. Specifically, the derived demand for labor may have shifted in favor of industries that employ a higher proportion of more skilled workers. For instance, the emergence of high-tech industries such as the computer software and biomedicine industries may have increased the overall demand for highly trained workers.

It is also possible that the rise in the college pay premium has resulted from a relative slowdown in the historical increase in the proportion of young people who are attending college. Together with a rising demand for college-educated workers, this would further explain the increase in earnings inequality.[31]

4 Demographic Changes

Some economists have looked to the supply side of the aggregate labor market to explain rising earnings inequality. Specifically, they cite changes in the composition of labor supply between more skilled and less skilled workers as an important factor. In particular, the entrance of large numbers of less skilled baby

---

[28] For evidence that the decline in unionism has contributed to rising earnings inequality, see Bruce Western and Jake Rosenfeld, "Unions, Norms, and the Rise in U.S. Wage Inequality," *American Sociological Review,* August 2011, pp. 513–537. For evidence that unions have a larger effect on inequality in the public sector than the private sector, see David Card, Thomas Lemieux, and W. Craig Riddell, "Unions and Wage Inequality: The Roles of Gender, Skill, and Public Sector Employment," National Bureau of Economic Research Working Paper Number 25313, November 2018.

[29] One-third of the increase in earnings inequality between 1978 and 2013 occurred *within* firms, see Jae Song, David J. Price, Fatih Guveen, Nicholas Bloom, and Till Von Wachter, "Firming Up Inequality," *Quarterly Journal of Economics,* February 2019, pp. 1–50.

[30] For evidence regarding the mechanisms by which computer technology increases the demand for skilled workers, see David H. Autor, Frank Levy, and Richard J. Murnane, "The Skill Content of Recent Technological Change: An Empirical Exploration," *Quarterly Journal of Economics,* November 2003, pp. 1279–1333.

[31] See Daron Acemoglu and David Autor, "Skills, Tasks, and Technologies: Implications for Employment and Earnings," in Orley Ashenfelter and David Card (eds.), *Handbook of Labor Economics,* Volume 4B (Amsterdam: Elsevier, 2011), pp. 1043–1166. Some economists have downplayed the role of increased demand for skilled workers; see Lemieux, op. cit.

16.3 | World of Work

Rising Leisure Time Inequality

In the United States, the average male spends 53 hours per week doing market work or chores at home. The corresponding figure for females is 47 hours per week. The rest of their time is spent on leisure activities.

The amount of leisure time has risen significantly over the past four decades. Mark Aguiar and Erik Hurst report that between 1965 and 2003, leisure time rose by 6.2 hours per week for men and 4.9 hours per week for women. This increase in leisure time amounts to about 320 hours per year for men and 255 hours per year for women.

The amount of leisure time increase differed by education level. In 1965 men and women had similar amounts of leisure time across education groups. By 2003 a significant gap in leisure time had emerged between highly educated and less educated individuals. Among male high school dropouts, leisure time increased by 12 hours per week between 1965 and 2003. In contrast, leisure time was virtually unchanged over this period for male college graduates. Among women, leisure time increased by eight hours per week for high school dropouts but by only one hour per week for college graduates.

Most of the divergence in leisure time across education levels was due to changes in time devoted to market work rather than housework. Among men, market work hours fell much more for the less educated than the highly educated. For women, market hours rose by four hours per week for college graduates and fell by two hours per week for high school dropouts. Time devoted to housework increased by a similar amount across education levels for men and fell by a like amount across education groups for women.

Changes have also occurred with leisure time activities. All education groups have experienced large increases in time spent watching television. Time spent watching television rose by five hours per week for college graduates and nine hours per week for high school dropouts. The increase in time watching television for college graduates was offset by a decline in time devoted to reading and socializing. Time spent sleeping rose three hours per week for high school dropouts but decreased one hour per week for college graduates.

The rise in leisure time inequality is the mirror image of the rise in earnings inequality in recent decades. Highly educated workers have received larger increases in earnings than less educated workers. However, they have had a smaller increase in leisure time than less educated workers.

Source: Mark Aguiar and Erik Hurst, "Measuring Trends in Leisure: The Allocation of Time over Five Decades," *Quarterly Journal of Economics,* August 2007, pp. 969–1006.

boomers and female workers into the labor market during the 1970s and 1980s may have contributed to increased earnings inequality.

The link between the surge in the number of inexperienced, less skilled workers and earnings inequality has two dimensions. First, this surge may have raised the proportion of low-wage workers to high-wage workers in *all industries,* creating greater wage disparity. Second, the increased supply of young workers and inexperienced female workers in various *lower-wage labor markets* may have depressed the relative earnings of workers in those markets. In either case, the predicted impact would be a rise in the pay differential between less skilled (less experienced) and more skilled workers.

The demographic explanation for rising earnings inequality is logically appealing and often cited. But it is difficult to reconcile this explanation with evidence that increases in aggregate inequality largely result from growing earnings inequality *within* each age group. The research consensus is that the baby boom, the surge of female labor force entrants, and immigration have only modestly contributed to the growing earnings inequality.[32]

Conclusions and Future Prospects

What can we conclude from our discussion of possible sources of growing wage inequality? The main conclusion is that there appears to be no single cause of this phenomenon. The evidence on this matter points to demand-side, supply-side, and institutional factors being at work. The demand for college-trained workers appears to have risen relative to the supply of these workers. The supply of less skilled workers appears to have increased relative to the demand for less skilled workers. Meanwhile, trade deficits and the decline of unionism have reduced traditional mid-paying jobs and channeled workers into lower-paying employment. The result has been a widening distribution of earnings for both women and men.

WW16.3   Will the distribution of earnings continue to widen during the next decade? The tentative answer provided by experts in this area is probably not. Declining labor force growth should tighten the aggregate labor market in the future and increase wages for less skilled workers. Also, the rising rate of return to investment in education and training should entice more people to enroll in colleges and encourage firms to invest more in training their employees. Eventually, we would expect the increased supply of more skilled workers to reduce the earnings premium paid to this group. But keep in mind that the factors affecting earnings inequality are manifold and complex; therefore, predicting the future course of earnings inequality is highly speculative.

Chapter Summary

1. The degree of inequality in personal earnings can be shown by a histogram (absolute frequency distribution), a relative frequency distribution, or a Lorenz curve. A frequency distribution shows either the absolute or the relative number of employed individuals whose annual earnings fall within various ranges of annual earnings. The Lorenz curve portrays the cumulative percentage of all wage and salary earners and their corresponding cumulative percentage of total earnings.

2. The frequency distribution for U.S. earnings evidences considerable bunching around a single mode that is to the left of the median and mean and displays a long rightwardly skewed tail, indicating wide disparities in personal earnings.

3. The Gini coefficient measures the degree of earnings inequality on a scale of zero (complete equality) to 1 (complete inequality). It can be found graphically by comparing the area between the diagonal line and the Lorenz curve to the entire area below the diagonal.

4. Frequency distributions, Lorenz curves, and Gini coefficients of *personal* earnings must be interpreted cautiously because they *(a)* differ depending on whether part-time workers are included or excluded, *(b)* fail to include fringe benefits, *(c)* do not provide information about *family* earnings, and *(d)* display more inequality than when based on income after transfers.

5. According to human capital theorists, approximately one-half to two-thirds of earnings inequality is explained by the interactive differences in people's formal education and on-the-job training.

6. Ability *(a)* is thought by some economists to influence earnings *directly* through enhancement of productivity, *(b)* may take several forms that interact multiplicatively to produce the observed skewed distribution of earnings, and *(c)* may *indirectly* have an impact on earnings by determining the return from—and hence the optimal amount of—investment in human capital.

---

[32] See David Card, "Immigration and Inequality," *American Economic Review,* May 2009, pp. 1–21.

7. Family background, discrimination, extent of risk taking, and degree of luck also are variables that help explain earnings inequality and the rightwardly skewed tail of the earnings distribution.

8. There is considerable movement by individuals within the overall distribution of earnings. This mobility is related to the life cycle, reflecting the generally positive relationship between age and earnings. It can also be of a "churning" nature, in which people with more education, training, ability, or luck rise from lower to higher levels of age-adjusted earnings.

9. The distribution of earnings in the United States has become more unequal over the past 40 years. Potential causes that have been cited include *(a)* deindustrialization, *(b)* import competition and the decline of unionism, *(c)* increased demand for skilled workers, and *(d)* demographic changes. None of these factors alone can explain the increase in wage and salary inequality. It would appear that demand-side, supply-side, and institutional factors all are involved.

Terms and Concepts

distribution of personal earnings

absolute frequency distribution

histogram

Lorenz curve

Gini coefficient

human capital model

multifactor approach to the earnings distribution

self-selection

D-factor

stochastic theories

earnings mobility

life-cycle mobility

"churning" within the earnings distribution

Questions and Study Suggestions

1. Suppose a hypothetical economy consists of 20 nonunionized private sector workers who have the following annual earnings: $18,000, $9,000, $82,000, $12,000, $13,000, $76,000, $61,000, $14,000, $22,000, $23,000, $21,000, $46,000, $59,000, $26,000, $27,000, $37,000, $6,000, $41,000, $3,000, and $24,000.

   a. Using annual earnings ranges of $10,000 (i.e., 0–$10,000, $10,000–$20,000, and so forth), construct a histogram (absolute frequency distribution) of this economy's distribution of personal earnings. What is the mode of the histogram? What is the average (mean) level of earnings? What is the median level of earnings? Characterize the distribution as being normal, skewed leftward, or skewed rightward. Explain.

   b. Construct a Lorenz curve showing the quintile distribution of earnings for this economy.

   c. What would be the likely impact of unionization of this entire workforce on the Lorenz curve? Explain.

2. Speculate about why a given Gini coefficient is compatible with more than one particular Lorenz curve. Illustrate graphically.

3. Why do people who have more formal education than others also in general tend to receive more on-the-job training during their careers? What is the implication of this fact for the distribution of earnings?

4. Critically evaluate this statement: "Lifetime earnings are less equally distributed than annual earnings."

5. Speculate about how successful attempts by government to tighten the distribution of family *income* through transfers might inadvertently make the distribution of annual *earnings* more unequal.

6. Explain how both ability and family background can *directly* influence earnings, independently of education and training. How do ability and family background *indirectly* determine earnings through the human capital investment decision? How does discrimination contribute to earnings inequality?

7. What has happened to the location of the Lorenz curve of annual earnings over the past 35 years? Make a case that the Lorenz curve will shift leftward over the next 35 years. Make a case that it will shift farther to the right than its present location. Which of your two scenarios do you think is most realistic?

8. Which two of the text's possible explanations for increasing wage and salary inequality seem least consistent with the following fact? The distribution of earnings has become more unequal *within* industries (both goods and service industries) and *within* age groups. Explain.

9. In light of the information presented in this chapter, answer Question 11 at the end of Chapter 4.

Internet Exercise

Is Income Inequality Rising or Falling?

Go to the Census Bureau Historical Income Inequality website (**http://www.census.gov/data/tables/time-series/demo/income-poverty/historical-income-inequality.html**). Click on "Gini Ratios for Households, by Race and Hispanic Origin of Householder." This will retrieve historical Gini data for households.

What are the Gini indexes for all races in 1973, 1979, 1999, and the most recent year shown? What happened to income inequality in the following periods: 1973–1979, 1979–1999, and 1999 to the most recent year? Repeat the same analysis for one race.

Internet Link

The United Nations University and United Nations Development Programme have a large database of measures of income inequality for many countries (**http://www.wider.unu.edu/research/WIID3-0B/en_GB/database/**).

Chapter 17

Labor Productivity: Wages, Prices, and Employment

After reading this chapter, you should be able to:

1. Explain the concept of productivity and how it is measured.
2. Explain the impact of productivity growth on real wages and inflation.
3. List and discuss the basic causes of long-term productivity growth.
4. Explain why labor productivity displays a procyclic pattern.
5. Analyze the relationship between productivity growth and employment growth in a specific industry.
6. Discuss the factors that may have contributed to the resurgence and recent slowdown of productivity growth.

Previous chapters emphasized the determination of wage rates for specific types of workers, explained the complex cluster of individual wages that constitute the wage structure, and examined the distribution of personal earnings. The spotlight now shifts to the long-term trend of the average level of real wages. What propelled the increase in average real wages during the last century? Why did real wage growth in America slow so dramatically between 1979 and 1995? Why did real wage growth rebound between 1995 and 2008 and slow down since 2008?

In answering these questions, we will find that the secular expansion of the level of real wages is intimately linked to the growth of labor productivity. Much of the present chapter is thus devoted to productivity growth and its various ramifications.

THE PRODUCTIVITY CONCEPT

In essence, productivity is a simple concept. It is merely a relationship between real output—the quantity of goods and services produced—and the quantity of input used to produce that output. Productivity, in other words, is a measure of resource or input efficiency expressed in terms of a ratio:

$$\text{Productivity} = \frac{\text{output}}{\text{input}} \quad (17.1)$$

Productivity tells us how many units of output we can obtain from a unit of input. If output per unit of input increases, productivity has risen.

As you might sense from this definition, there is a whole family of productivity measures that vary depending on the specific data chosen for insertion in the numerator and denominator of the productivity equation. The output in the numerator might be the real gross domestic product (GDP), the real output of the private sector, or the real output of a particular industry or plant. Whatever output measure is used in the numerator, it must be stated in *real* rather than nominal terms. The production of more goods and services per unit of input constitutes an increase in productivity; higher prices on a fixed or even declining quantity of output clearly do not. As for the denominator, some productivity analysts combine inputs of both labor and capital to derive a measure of *total factor productivity*. Because labor is the focal point of our discussion, we will be concerned with *labor productivity*, in which worker-hours are related to total product, or real GDP.[1]

Measurement

Figure 17.1 provides information enabling us to calculate labor productivity for each of two specific years for a hypothetical economy. The figure shows two aggregate production functions, TP_1 and TP_2, each of which represents a specific year and relates quantities of worker-hours to total annual real GDP for that period. We will initially focus on the aggregate production function labeled TP_1. This curve reflects two assumptions: first, that the quality of labor, amount of capital, and methods of production are fixed; and second, that production is subject to diminishing marginal returns. To simplify, we assume diminishing returns over the entire range of output. Thus, TP_1 indicates the relationship between worker-hours and total product, *other things being equal*, and shows that total product rises at a diminishing rate as added units of labor are used in conjunction with the fixed capital stock.

FIGURE 17.1   **The Aggregate Production Function and Labor Productivity**

The aggregate production functions TP_1 and TP_2 portray the relationship between worker-hour inputs and total product, or real GDP, for two time periods and differing capital stocks. Assuming no change in labor hours, the upward shift of the production function portrays a 50 percent increase in labor productivity.

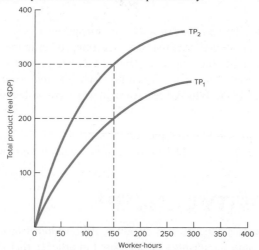

[1] For a survey of available productivity measures, see Charles Steindel and Kevin Stiroh, "Productivity: What Is It, and Why Do We Care About It?" *Business Economics,* October 2001, pp. 13–31. See also Bureau of Labor Statistics, *BLS Handbook of Methods* (Washington, DC: Government Printing Office, 1997), Chapter 10.

The input–output information provided by curve TP$_1$ allows us to measure labor productivity for this hypothetical economy for this particular year. Specifically,

$$\text{Labor Productivity} = \frac{\text{total product (real GDP)}}{\text{number of worker} - \text{hours}} \quad (17.2)$$

Equation (17.2) confirms that labor productivity is simply the average productivity of labor inputs for the economy as a whole. For illustrative purposes, we assume that the number of worker-hours–the denominator in Equation (17.2)–is 150. The aggregate production function of Figure 17.1 reveals that the corresponding total product is 200. Dividing 200 by 150, we conclude that labor productivity is 1.33. Equation (17.3) allows us to convert this labor productivity figure to an index number, using this specific year as the base year:

$$\text{Productivity index}_{\text{base year}} = \frac{\text{productivity}_{\text{year 1}}}{\text{productivity}_{\text{base year}}} \times 100 \quad (17.3)$$

Equation (17.3) simply sets labor productivity equal to 100 for the base year. That is, $100 = (1.33/1.33) \times 100$.

We now can turn our attention to the upward shift of the aggregate production function from TP$_1$ to TP$_2$ in Figure 17.1. In the long run, other things are *not* equal; that is, labor quality can improve, the capital stock can increase, and more efficient methods for combining resources may be discovered. For example, suppose this economy enlarged its stock of capital goods, which in turn enabled workers to use more machinery and tools in the production process. As illustrated by the upward shift of the aggregate production function from TP$_1$ to TP$_2$, this would increase output per unit of labor input. Assuming that the number of worker-hours remains constant at 150, total product would rise to 300, and labor productivity would increase to 2 (= 300/150). By comparing this new productivity level, 2, to productivity for the base year, 1.33, we can determine the productivity index in year 2:

$$\text{Productivity index}_{\text{year 2}} = \frac{\text{productivity}_{\text{year 2}}}{\text{productivity}_{\text{base year}}} \times 100 \quad (17.4)$$

The new index is 150 [= $(2/1.33) \times 100$], which represents a 50 percent increase relative to the base year index of 100.

The BLS Index

The Bureau of Labor Statistics (BLS) publishes an official index of labor productivity for the U.S. economy. Figure 17.2 shows the course of the BLS index of output per worker-hour since 1960. Note that 2012 is the base year for the index. Because this *BLS productivity index* is widely used and cited, it is important to be familiar with its characteristics.

First, the index is calculated by dividing constant dollar (real) GDP originating in the private sector by the number of worker-hours employed in the private sector. The public sector is excluded from the BLS index for a very practical reason: The public goods and services provided by government–such things as national defense, flood control, and police and fire protection–are not sold in a market to individual buyers. Therefore, it is extremely difficult to estimate the economic value of the public sector output. Most productivity experts believe that productivity has grown less rapidly in the public sector than in the private sector. For this reason, the BLS data tend to overstate the entire economy's productivity growth.

FIGURE 17.2 **Index of U.S. Labor Productivity***

Labor productivity has more than tripled over the past 59 years.

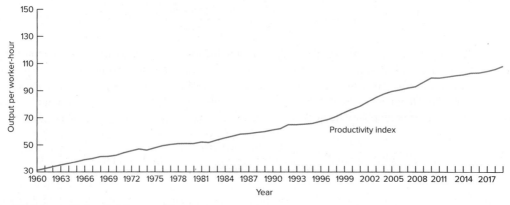

Source: U.S. Bureau of Labor Statistics, www.bls.gov
*Business sector.

Second, the index understates productivity growth because improvements in the *quality* of output are not taken into account. This, of course, is merely a reflection of a shortcoming involved in calculating real output or GDP for the private sector; GDP measures changes in the quantity, but not the quality, of output.

Third, the use of output per worker-hour subtly implies that labor alone is responsible for rising productivity. This is not true. As we already indicated in our discussion of Figure 17.1, the factors affecting labor productivity are manifold and diverse. They include improvements in the quality of labor, the use of more capital equipment, improvements in production technologies and managerial organizational techniques, increased specialization as the result of expanding markets, shifts in the structure of the economy, public policies, and societal attitudes. While the BLS index of labor productivity provides information about changes in labor productivity, it does not explain the *causes* of these changes.

Despite its limitations and biases, the BLS index of labor productivity provides a reasonable approximation of how private sector efficiency has changed through time. Indeed, the official BLS measure has certain notable virtues. First, the index is conceptually simple and can quite easily be calculated from available data. Second, because it is calculated on a per worker-*hour* basis, the index automatically takes into account changes in the length of the workweek. In contrast, an index of output per worker per year would understate the growth of labor productivity if the length of the average workweek decreased through time. Finally, as a measure of hourly output, the index can be directly compared with hourly wage rates.[2]

IMPORTANCE OF PRODUCTIVITY INCREASES

The growth of labor productivity is important for at least two reasons:

1. Productivity growth is the basic source of improvements in real wages and living standards.
2. Productivity growth is an antiinflationary force in that it offsets or absorbs increases in nominal wages.

Let's consider these two points in the order stated.

---

[2] For a discussion of the problems involved in measuring productivity, see Edwin R. Dean, "The Accuracy of the BLS Productivity Measures," *Monthly Labor Review,* February 1999, pp. 22–34.

FIGURE 17.3 Real Wage Increases: Labor Supply and Demand Explanation

Increases in real wages occur when the demand for labor rises more rapidly than the labor supply.

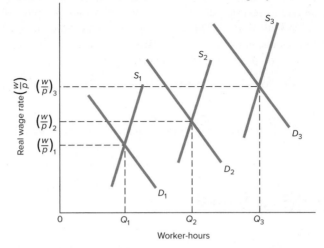

Productivity and Real Wages

Real wage rates have increased in the United States over the past century at an average annual rate of 2–3 percent. Figure 17.3 provides an accurate but somewhat superficial explanation for that secular trend. The figure shows that increases in real wages—for example, from $(w/p)_1$ to $(w/p)_2$ to $(w/p)_3$—occur when the demand for labor rises more rapidly than labor supply. As shown in the figure, these rising real wages are fully compatible with increases in the number of worker-hours (Q_1 to Q_3).

This simple supply and demand explanation for rising real wages naturally raises a more penetrating question: Why has labor demand increased over the decades? Figure 17.4 identifies the primary source of this increase: rising labor productivity. Notice the extremely close relationship between the increase in output per worker-hour and the growth of average real hourly compensation. Increases in labor productivity have increased the

FIGURE 17.4 Labor Productivity and the Average Level of Real Compensation

Because real output is real income, the growth of real output per worker-hour and the growth of real compensation per hour are closely related.

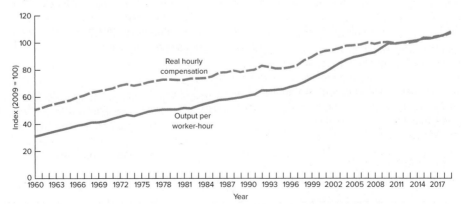

demand for labor relative to labor supply and, therefore, have boosted the average real wage rate. When one recognizes that society's real output *is* its real income, the close relationship between productivity and real compensation is no surprise. Generally, for the economy as a whole, real income per worker per hour can increase at only the same rate as real output per worker per hour; more output per hour means more real income to distribute for each hour worked. The simplest case is the classic one of Robinson Crusoe on his deserted island. The number of coconuts he can pick or fish he can catch per hour *is* his real income or wage per hour. Crudely stated, what you produce is what you get.

The importance of the contribution that the growth of labor productivity has made to the overall growth of our economy can hardly be overstated. We can rearrange the labor productivity Equation (17.2) as follows:

$$\text{Real GDP} = \text{worker} - \text{hours} \times \text{labor productivity} \quad (17.5)$$

17.1   World of Work

Growing Gap Between Productivity and Compensation*

Historically, there has been a tight link between productivity and real hourly compensation. An increase in productivity led to a very similar rise in compensation. In recent decades, however, productivity has been rising at a faster rate than hourly compensation. For example, between 1980 and 2014, productivity rose 98 percent but real hourly compensation rose only 39 percent. The gap between productivity and real hourly compensation got particularly large after 2000.

There are two factors behind the widening gap between productivity and real hourly compensation. First, real hourly compensation and productivity are calculated using the two different measures of inflation. Hourly compensation is converted into real terms using the **consumer price index (CPI)**, which is based on a bundle of goods purchased by a typical consumer. Productivity is computed using the implicit price deflator, which is based on all output. An analysis by Susan Fleck, John Glaser, and Shawn Sprague indicates that the CPI grew more rapidly than the implicit price deflator during the 1980s and 1990s and was the main cause of the wedge between productivity and real hourly compensation during that period.

Second, the share of national income received by labor has drifted downward since 1980 and particularly rapidly since 2000. In other words, income for workers has grown more slowly than the value of the output they are producing. Michael Elsby, Bart Hobijn, and Aysegül Sahin have examined the causes behind the fall in labor's share of income and reached four conclusions. First, they found that about one-third of the decline in labor's share of income since the late 1980s is a spurious artifact of the method used to impute the labor income for self-employed individuals. Second, part of the decline is due to the substitution of capital for unskilled labor. Third, the decline in the strength of labor unions did not play a significant role in the decline in labor's share. Fourth, offshoring of the labor-intensive portion of production did appear to play an important role in the decline. According to the analysis by Fleck, Glaser, and Sprague, the gap between productivity and compensation since 2000 is due to the decline in labor's share of income.

*Based on Susan Fleck, John Glaser, and Shawn Sprague, "The Compensation-Productivity Gap: A Visual Essay," *Monthly Labor Review,* January 2011, pp. 57–91; and Michael W. L. Elsby, Bart Hobijn, and Aysegül Sahin, "The Decline of the U.S. Labor Share," *Brookings Papers on Economic Activity,* Fall 2013, pp. 1–61.

WW17.1

Equation (17.5) implies that real output can increase because of an increase in inputs of worker-hours *or* because each of those hours of work generates more output. In other words, total product as shown in Figure 17.1 can rise because of a rightward movement along an existing aggregate production function (more inputs of labor hours) or as a result of an upward shift of the function (rising labor productivity). Data indicate that rising productivity has been the more important of the two contributors to the growth of real GDP in the United States. Over the 1960–2019 period, for example, real output increased by 592 percent. During this same period, labor productivity rose by 249 percent, while worker-hours of labor increased by 98 percent.

Inflation and Productivity

Although the causes of inflation are complex and controversial, economists acknowledge a link between the rate of productivity growth and the rate of inflation. Other things being equal, rapid productivity growth helps limit the rate of inflation, and slow productivity growth causes the inflation rate to be higher than would otherwise be the case. More specifically, productivity gains offset increases in nominal wages and thereby help restrain increases in unit labor costs and ultimately product prices.

Let's employ several simple numerical examples to grasp the relationship between changes in nominal wages, productivity, and unit labor costs. If, for example, hourly nominal wages are $10.00 and a worker produces 10 units per hour, then unit labor costs—that is, labor cost per unit of output—will be $1.00. If nominal wages increase by 10 percent to $11.00 per hour and productivity also increases by 10 percent to 11 units per hour, then unit labor costs will be unchanged. That is, $10.00/10 = $11.00/11 = $1.00. Generalization: *Equal percentage increases in nominal wages and productivity leave unit labor costs unchanged.*

Similarly, if nominal wages rise by 10 percent and labor productivity does not rise at all, unit labor costs will rise by 10 percent. That is, if the wage is $10.00 initially and output per hour is 10 units, unit labor costs will be $1.00. But with wages now at $11.00 and output still at 10 units per hour, unit labor costs will be $1.10, which is a 10 percent increase. Generalization: *If nominal wage increases exceed the increase in labor productivity, unit labor costs will rise.*

Finally, suppose the nominal wage rate does not rise, but productivity increases by 10 percent. Specifically, if wages remain at $10.00 and productivity increases from 10 to 11 units per hour, then unit labor costs will decline from $1.00 to about $0.91. Generalization: *If productivity increases exceed the increase in nominal wages, unit labor costs will fall.*

Columns 2 through 5 of Table 17.1 show the indicated relationships between changes in the hourly compensation of workers, productivity, and unit labor costs for the 1960–2018 period.

Because labor costs on the average constitute 70–75 percent of total production costs and higher production costs eventually cause higher product prices, the link between productivity increases and the rate of inflation is clear. Other things being equal, the 10 percent increase in unit labor costs in our example would translate into a 7.0–7.5 percent increase in total costs. As the data in Table 17.1 suggest, with important exceptions, changes in unit labor costs (column 4) and the rate of inflation (column 5) do track closely. As a rough rule of thumb, in most years changes in unit labor costs are associated with roughly similar changes in the rate of inflation.

TABLE 17.1 The Relationship between Changes in Wages, Productivity, Unit Labor Costs, and the Price Level (Annual Percentage Changes)

Year	Change in Compensation per Hour	Change in Output per Hour	Change in Unit Labor Costs	Change in Price Level*
1960	4.2	1.8	2.4	1.2
1962	4.4	4.6	−0.2	0.9
1964	3.7	3.3	0.4	1.3
1966	6.7	4.1	2.5	2.3
1968	7.8	3.5	4.2	3.9
1970	7.5	2.0	5.4	4.4
1972	6.3	3.4	2.9	3.1
1974	9.3	−1.7	11.2	10.4
1976	8.0	3.3	4.5	5.4
1978	8.4	1.2	7.1	6.5
1980	10.7	0.0	10.7	9.5
1982	7.5	−0.5	8.0	6.2
1984	4.4	2.9	1.5	2.8
1986	5.7	2.8	2.8	1.4
1988	5.3	1.5	3.7	3.1
1990	6.3	2.0	4.2	3.4
1992	6.1	4.7	1.4	1.7
1994	0.7	0.6	0.1	1.9
1996	3.6	2.5	1.1	1.4
1998	5.9	3.1	2.7	0.7
2000	6.9	3.4	3.4	1.6
2002	2.2	4.3	−1.9	0.8
2004	4.7	3.0	1.6	2.3
2006	3.9	1.1	2.7	2.8
2008	2.7	1.0	1.6	1.6
2010	1.8	3.3	−1.5	1.0
2012	2.8	0.8	2.0	1.9
2014	2.6	0.7	1.9	1.8
2016	1.1	0.2	0.9	1.1
2018	2.9	1.4	1.5	2.2

Source: U.S. Bureau of Labor Statistics, "Monthly Labor Report," www.bls.gov
*Implicit price deflator.

We must be careful not to infer from Table 17.1 that the relationship between the growth of nominal wages and the increase in labor productivity is necessarily a primary cause of inflation. Many other factors—the money supply, inappropriate fiscal policy, expectations, supply shocks—are all held by various economists to be of greater significance. Indeed, some economists would argue that the relationship between the growth of real output and increases in the money supply is the primary determinant of changes in the price level. They contend that excessive growth of the money supply causes all prices to rise, including the price of labor: the nominal wage. The great majority of economists believe that both demand and supply (cost) factors can cause inflation, at least in the short term. They believe that the relationship between nominal wages and productivity is an important determinant of the price level. In fact, the U.S. government has at times implemented wage–price policies designed to restrict nominal wage increases to the average labor productivity increase as a means of controlling inflation.

The question of whether increases in unit labor costs cause inflation or are simply a symptom of inflation is subject to debate. Suffice it to say that given the rate of increase in nominal wage rates, the higher the rate of labor productivity, the smaller the rate of inflation.

LONG–RUN TREND OF LABOR PRODUCTIVITY[3]

Data suggest that in the long run—say, over the past century—average annual increases in output per worker-hour have been on the order of 2–3 percent. Although these figures may not seem particularly impressive, the "miracle" of compounding translates this annual increase into very large increases in hourly output and income over time. Specifically, a 2.5 percent annual increase in hourly output will double output per worker-hour in about 28 years. As we will soon see, the productivity growth between 1995 and 2007 was substantially higher than that experienced in the prior two decades.

What causes productivity growth? Generally speaking, the critical determinants of productivity growth can be classified under three headings: (*a*) the average quality of the labor force; (*b*) the amount of capital goods employed with each worker-hour of labor; and (*c*) the efficiency with which labor, capital, and other inputs are combined. Figure 17.5 presents Jorgenson, Ho, and Stiroh's estimates of the contributors to the growth of labor productivity for the period 1959–2006. These factors are the focal point of the following discussion.

Improved Labor Quality

The quality of labor depends on its education and training, its health and vitality, and its age–gender composition. Other things being the same, a better-educated, better-trained workforce can produce more output per hour than a less educated, inadequately trained one. Indeed, Chapter 4's discussion of education and training as investments in human capital that increase labor productivity and earnings is highly relevant. Figure 17.6 provides a general overview of the increases in formal educational attainment of the population (25 years of age and older) since 1950. For the 1959–2006 period, Jorgenson, Ho, and Stiroh estimate that approximately 12 percent of the growth of labor productivity was due to enhanced worker education and training (see Figure 17.5).

Investments in human capital that enhance the health and vitality of workers also improve the average quality of labor. Improved nutrition, more and better medical care, and better general living conditions improve the physical vigor and morale of the labor force. These same factors enhance worker longevity and contribute to a workforce that is more productive because it is more experienced.

---

[3] For more about productivity growth, see Charles R. Hulten, Edwin R. Dean, and Michael J. Harper (eds.), *New Developments in Productivity Analysis* (Chicago: University of Chicago Press, 2001); and Kevin J. Stiroh, "What Drives Productivity Growth?" Federal Reserve Bank of New York, *Economic Policy Review,* March 2001, pp. 37–59.

FIGURE 17.5   Relative Importance of the Causes of U.S. Productivity Growth

Increases in the quantity of capital account for about half of the growth of productivity. Increased efficiency and improvements in labor quality account for the other half.

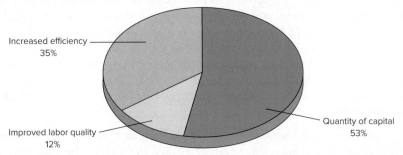

Source: Dale W. Jorgenson, Mun S. Ho, and Kevin J. Stiroh, "A Retrospective Look at the U.S. Productivity Growth Resurgence," *Journal of Economic Perspectives,* Winter 2008, pp. 3–24.

Finally, changes in the age–gender composition of the labor force may also affect average labor force quality and, therefore, productivity. For example, historically, increasingly stringent child labor and school attendance legislation has kept potential young workers—workers who would be unskilled and relatively unproductive by virtue of their lack of education and work experience—out of the labor force. This exclusion has increased the *average* quality of the labor force. As a second example, changes in the age–gender composition of labor may have lowered productivity growth in the 1970s and 1980s.

A benevolent circle of feedback and self-reinforcement may evolve historically with respect to labor quality. If the productivity of labor rises, real wages also rise. These enhanced earnings permit workers to improve their health and education, which further improves labor quality and productivity. And so the cycle repeats itself. This circular interaction may be strengthened because the demands for education and health care are both elastic with respect to income. This means that rising national income generates more than proportional percentage increases in expenditures on these items.

FIGURE 17.6   Educational Attainment Completed by the U.S. Population (25 years of age or older)

The percentage of individuals with a high school or college degree has risen over time.

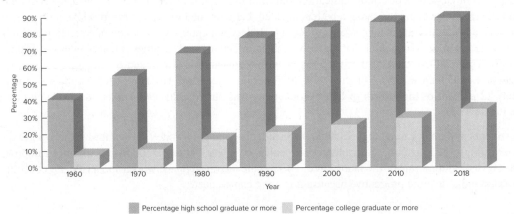

Source: U.S. Census Bureau, "Educational Attainment in the United States: 2018," www.census.gov

17.2 World of Work

Is Public Capital Productive?

The impact of spending on public sector capital, such as highways and airports, on productivity growth is controversial. The results from empirical investigations range from public capital having no effect on productivity to it having triple the productivity effect of private capital.

The wide range of productivity estimates arises from several factors. The largest estimates derive from studies based on national data. We should be skeptical of these findings because the studies use broad definitions of public capital goods, and the results vary by estimation technique. Investigations using state–regional data and narrower definitions of public capital yield substantially smaller productivity estimates, but they ignore the positive impact of infrastructure on other states. In summary, it is likely that

public capital does increase productivity, but the exact magnitude is unclear.

A recent study by Born and Ligthart attempts to reconcile the diverse public capital productivity findings by statistically examining 578 estimates from 68 studies over the 1983–2008 period. They conclude that public capital is more productive when it is installed by regional/local governments or invested in core infrastructure (i.e., roads, railways, airports, and utilities). It is about three times as productive when a long-run horizon is taken. The study indicates the marginal benefits of additional public capital are exceeded by the marginal costs only when the investment is undertaken by regional/local governments or it is spent on core infrastructure.

Source: Pedro R.D. Bom and Jenny E. Ligthart, "What Have We Learned from Three Decades of Research on the Productivity of Public Capital?" *Journal of Economic Surveys,* December 2014, pp. 889–916.

Quantity of Physical Capital

WW17.2

The productivity of any given worker will depend on the amount of capital equipment with which he or she is equipped. A construction worker can dig a basement in a much shorter period with a bulldozer than with a hand shovel! A critical relationship with respect to labor productivity is the amount of capital available per unit of labor or, more technically, the capital–labor ratio. This ratio has increased historically. For example, in the 1959-2006 period, the stock of capital goods is estimated to have approximately quadrupled; and over the same period, labor hours are estimated to have roughly doubled. Thus, the quantity of capital goods per labor hour was about 100 percent larger in 2006 than in 1959. Stated differently, the capital–labor ratio increased by half over this 47-year period.[4] Jorgenson, Ho, and Stiroh's estimates for 1959-2006 indicate that approximately 53 percent of the growth of labor productivity was the result of increases in the stock of physical capital (see Figure 17.5).

Increased Efficiency

The third source of rising productivity is greater efficiency in the use of labor and capital. In the present context, *increased efficiency* is a comprehensive term that includes a variety of both obvious and subtle factors that enhance labor productivity. At a minimum, increased efficiency encompasses (*a*) technological progress, including that embodied within both improved capital and improved business organization and managerial techniques; (*b*) greater specialization as the result of scale economies; (*c*) the reallocation of labor from less

---

[4] Dale W. Jorgenson, "Information Technology and the U.S. Economy," *American Economic Review,* March 2001, pp. 1-32. Updated tables are available at **www.economics.harvard.edu/faculty/jorgenson/recent_work_jorgenson**

to more productive uses; and (*d*) changes in a society's institutional, cultural, and environmental setting and in its public policies. Note in Figure 17.5 that increased efficiency accounts for about one-third of the productivity gains that occurred over the 1959–2006 period.

Let's comment briefly on each of these factors. First, technological advance involves the development of more efficient techniques of production. The evolution of mass-production assembly-line techniques immediately comes to mind, as do computers, biotechnical developments, xerography, robotics, and containerized shipping. The switch from the old open-hearth process of steelmaking to the oxygen method enhanced productivity in that industry, as did the supplanting of the distillation process by the newer cracking process in petroleum refining. Improved managerial techniques—time-and-motion studies and the creation of new systems of managerial control of production—have similarly enhanced productive efficiency. A variety of worker participation, job enrichment, and profit-sharing plans are being experimented with in the hope that they will enhance worker productivity.

Second, production efficiencies called *economies of scale* are typically derived from growing market and firm size. Market growth allows firms to become mass producers, which in turn permits greater specialization in the use of labor and, therefore, greater output per worker. Market expansion also enables firms to avail themselves of the most efficient production techniques. For example, a large manufacturer of automobiles can use elaborate assembly lines, featuring computerization and robotics, whereas small producers have to settle for less advanced technologies.

Third, productivity has also been stimulated by the reallocation of labor from less productive to more productive employments. Thus, for example, productivity gains have been realized historically by the reallocation of labor from agriculture, where the average productivity of labor is relatively low, to manufacturing, where the average productivity of labor is relatively high.

17.1 *Quick Review*

- Labor productivity is a measure of output per unit of labor input (worker-hours).
- Productivity growth is important for two reasons: It is the basic source of improvements in real wages and living standards, and it helps offset inflationary forces by holding down unit labor costs when nominal wages are rising.
- Productivity growth has averaged between 2 and 3 percent annually since the turn of the century.
- The critical determinants of productivity growth include the average quality of the labor force; the amount of capital goods per worker-hour; and the efficiency with which labor, capital, and other inputs are combined. This last category includes technology, economies of scale, improved resource organization, and the legal–human environment.
- Figure 17.5 summarizes the relative weights of the various factors that have contributed to U.S. productivity growth.

Your Turn

Suppose real output in a hypothetical economy is 10 units, 5 units of labor are needed to produce this output, and the price of labor is $2 per unit. What is the economy's labor productivity? What is its unit or average labor cost? (*Answer:* See page 542.)

17.1 Global Perspective

Manufacturing Productivity Growth

Between 2007 and 2017, France had the highest rate of productivity growth in manufacturing among industrial nations.

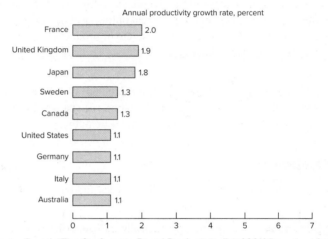

Source: The Conference Board, "The Conference Board Productivity Brief 2019," www.conference-board.org

Finally, the cultural values of a society, the nature of its institutions, and the character of its public policies affect labor productivity in myriad ways. The facts that American values condone material advance and that the successful inventor, innovator, and business executive are accorded high levels of respect and prestige have been important historically for productivity growth. Similarly, the work ethic is generally held in high esteem. Equally critical is the existence of a complex array of financial institutions that marshal the funds of savers and make them available to investors. On the other hand, recall from Chapter 11 that the impact of unions on productivity is unclear.

Public policies and social attitudes provide a mixed picture with respect to their implications for productivity. For example, while the long-run trend toward freer international trade and the general policy of promoting domestic competition bode well for productivity growth, the many exceptions to both free trade and procompetition policies do not. Tariffs and import quotas shelter American producers from competition and can have the effect of retaining labor and other inputs in relatively inefficient industries. Similarly, we know from Chapter 14 that discrimination based on race, gender, or age is an artificial impediment to allocative efficiency and, therefore, a barrier to productivity growth.

Two final comments are in order. First, although Jorgenson, Ho, and Stiroh conclude that about half of the increase in labor productivity is due to the use of more capital goods and the other half is the result of increased labor quality and greater efficiency, other experts offer somewhat different estimates. For example, Dean and Harper attribute approximately half of the productivity increase to enhanced efficiency, with labor quality and capital goods accounting for the other half.[5] The second point is that the factors in productivity growth are interrelated. For example, investment in capital equipment is stimulated by technological advance. Similarly, highly educated and well-trained workers cannot be used productively in the absence of sophisticated capital goods.

CYCLIC CHANGES IN PRODUCTIVITY

Emphasis thus far has been on the long-term trend of labor productivity. Because of the close relationship between productivity growth and real wages, this attention is entirely appropriate; however, productivity also exhibits a rather systematic short-run or cyclic pattern around the long-term trend.

Labor productivity generally displays a procyclic pattern; that is, productivity growth falls below the long-term trend during a cyclic downturn or recession and rises above the trend during an economic upturn or recovery. For example, over the 1948–2018 period, total real output declined in 10 years and increased in the remaining 61 years. In the 10 years of declining output, the rate of productivity growth was low, averaging 1.5 percent per year; in the 61 years of expanding aggregate output, labor productivity rose by 2.5 percent per year.[6]

The reasons for these cyclic changes in productivity are quite detailed. We will simplify the discussion by considering just three factors: (*a*) changes in the utilization of labor, (*b*) changes in the utilization of plant and capital equipment, and (*c*) changes in the composition of aggregate output.[7]

Utilization of Labor

As the economy moves into a downturn or recession, a firm's sales and output will decline more rapidly than its inputs of labor:

> Specifically, during cyclica contractions, employers normally are loath to fire workers—preferring instead to shunt labor into maintenance and other less essential tasks rather than the production of goods—until they are convinced that the downturn is not a temporary aberration. As a consequence, *measured* productivity (the ratio of output to *employed* labor) declines. Analogously, once a recovery starts, employers put these underutilized labor resources back on the production line. So output can expand briskly with little need for new hiring, and measured productivity registers dramatic gains.[8]

Why the reluctance to fire workers during a downswing? Why is labor a quasi-fixed, rather than a completely variable, input? Some employees, of course, are salaried workers or "overhead" labor. Few firms will dispense with top or mid-level executives during a downturn. An internal auditor, a marketing manager, and a personnel director will all be needed, even though output is currently down. Also, the typical firm will have invested in the specific training of its skilled and semiskilled workers. Remember from Chapter 4 that such workers must be retained for the firm to realize a return on its human capital investment. If these workers are furloughed, the firm runs the risk of losing them to other employers. Finally, there are layoff and rehiring costs

---

[5] Edwin R. Dean and Michael J. Harper, "The BLS Measurement Program," in Charles R. Hulten, Edwin R. Dean, and Michael J. Harper (eds.), *New Developments in Productivity Analysis* (Chicago: University of Chicago Press, 2001), The Dean and Harper estimates cover the period 1948–1997.

[6] Author calculations are based on Bureau of Labor Statistics (**www.bls.gov**) output data and productivity data.

[7] Researchers have also suggested two other explanations for the observed procyclic variations in productivity. First, technological innovations may be procyclic. Second, imperfect competition and increasing returns to scale may lead to rises in productivity when inputs rise. Empirical evidence indicates that the use of inputs rises and falls with the business cycle; however, a study indicates that these factors do not play a major role in explaining procyclic productivity. See Susanto Basu and John Fernald, "Why Is Productivity Procyclical? Why Do We Care?" in Charles R. Hulten, Edwin R. Dean, and Michael J. Harper (eds.), *New Developments in Productivity Analysis* (Chicago: University of Chicago Press, 2001).

[8] Alan S. Blinder, Economic Policy and the Great Stagflation, New York: Academic Press, 1981.

to contend with, and within limits, it may be less expensive to retain and underutilize workers if layoff and rehiring costs can be avoided by so doing. Thus firms find it to be in their long-run profit-maximizing interest to hoard labor during recession and, from a social perspective, use labor less productively than previously.

DeLong and Waldmann find evidence of *labor hoarding* during cyclic downturns in the United States.[9] Such hoarding diminishes, however, as the unemployment rate rises. Laid-off workers are less likely to find employment at other firms and are more likely to be available when the firm wants to rehire them. Thus firms have less incentive to practice labor hoarding when the unemployment rate is high. Consistent with this conjecture, they find that productivity is less procyclic when the unemployment rate is high.

But during the upswing or recovery phase of the cycle, output can be increased substantially by simply correcting this underutilization. Within limits, firms can increase output by taking up the slack in their currently employed labor forces. More output can be obtained from the number of worker-hours now being employed so that productivity will rise sharply. It has also been observed that workers are generally more productive when there is more work to be done. For example, checkout personnel at supermarkets work faster when shopper queues are long.[10]

Utilization of Plant and Equipment

A similar point can be made with respect to capital equipment. Competition forces firms to design their plants so that they operate with maximum efficiency during normal times. This means that during a recession, falling output causes the plant and equipment to be used at less than the optimal level, and productivity consequently falls. Conversely, during recovery, plant utilization moves back in the direction of the most efficient level of output, and productivity tends to rise.

Composition of Output

Cyclic fluctuations affect the various sectors of the economy with differing degrees of severity. Specifically, the demand for durable manufactured goods—machinery and equipment and such consumer goods as automobiles, refrigerators, and microwave ovens—is very sensitive to cyclic changes. By way of contrast, the demand for most services is much less responsive to cyclic changes. Thus, the *relative* share of manufactured goods in domestic output declines during cyclic downswings and increases during upswings. Because the level of productivity in manufacturing is among the highest of all sectors of the economy, it follows that the relative decline in manufacturing during a recession will reduce overall labor productivity.

Conversely, the relative expansion of manufacturing as a proportion of total output during recovery causes average labor productivity to rise. Note that this effect is independent of other cyclic influences on productivity. Even if no individual firm or industry experienced a productivity change due to a change in the use of labor and capital, the indicated relative shift in the composition of output would cause average labor productivity to vary procyclically.

Implications

Of what consequences are these cyclic changes in productivity? In the first place, they are not merely the result of cyclic fluctuations but rather an integral part of the business cycle. When the economy lapses into

---

[9] J. Bradford DeLong and Robert J. Waldmann, "Interpreting Procyclical Productivity: Evidence from a Cross-Nation Cross-Industry Panel," Federal Reserve Bank of San Francisco *Economic Review,* no. 1, 1997, pp. 33–52. Other studies finding evidence of labor hoarding include Argia M. Sbordone, "Interpreting the Procyclical Productivity of Manufacturing Sectors: External Effects or Labor Hoarding?" *Journal of Money, Credit, and Banking,* February 1997, pp. 26–45; and Basu and Fernald, op. cit.

[10] George A. Akerlof and Janet L. Yellen, "Introduction," in Akerlof and Yellen (eds.), *Efficiency Wage Models of the Labor Market* (Cambridge, England: Cambridge University Press, 1986), p. 5.

a recession, productivity falls sharply, and this tends to increase unit labor costs. If nominal wage rates continue to rise during the recession, unit labor costs will rise by an even larger amount. Rising costs typically squeeze business profits. This profit decline deters investment spending in two ways: It diminishes the financial resources (undistributed profits) that firms have for investing, *and* it generates pessimistic business expectations. Falling investments, of course, intensify the cyclic downswing. Conversely, rising productivity during recovery stimulates the upturn. Rapidly increasing productivity keeps unit labor costs down and contributes to rising profits. Profit growth is conducive to expanded investment spending, which accelerates the economic expansion.

A second related point is that cyclic changes in productivity have important implications for economic policy. For example, some economists are more or less resigned to the view that to arrest rapid inflation, it is necessary to create a recession through the application of restrictive monetary and fiscal policies. But an understanding of cyclic changes in productivity suggests that any such recession may have to be deep and long to produce its intended effects. Specifically, the decline in productivity that accompanies recession may contribute to rising unit costs, which in turn may contribute to supply, or cost-push, inflation. On the other hand, if the economy is already in a recession and unemployment is high, then the rapid labor productivity increase that occurs in the early stages of recovery may permit policymakers to increase output and employment through expansionary monetary and fiscal measures with less fear of generating added inflation. The reason is that high productivity growth tends to limit cost and price increases.

PRODUCTIVITY AND EMPLOYMENT

Let's now consider the impact of productivity growth on the level of employment. Do employees "work themselves out of their jobs" as they become more productive?

Superficial consideration of the relationship between productivity and employment often leads people to conclude erroneously that productivity growth causes unemployment. The reasoning normally is that an increase in labor productivity means that fewer workers are needed to produce any given level of real output. For example, if a firm employs 50 workers whose average productivity is $10 worth of real output per hour, then $500 worth of output can be produced. If the productivity of the 50 employees were to increase by 25 percent to $12.50 worth of output per hour, the same output could now be produced with only 40 workers (= 40 × $12.50). Thus, 10 of the 50 workers would seem to be redundant.

But this illustration is too simple because it ignores society's desire for additional output and the fact that rising productivity increases aggregate demand. Society's wants tend to exceed its available resources. Productivity increases allow society to achieve higher levels of output—that is, to fulfill more wants—given these limited resources. In terms of the previous example, the 25 percent productivity increase enables society to gain $125 worth of output. The 50 workers now can produce $625 worth of output (= 50 × $12.50) compared to $500 (= 50 × $10 = $500). But will there be sufficient aggregate spending to take this additional output off the market? We know that productivity and real wages are closely correlated. Thus the 25 percent increase in productivity can be expected to increase real incomes, which would increase aggregate spending and generate additional jobs. Although our economy has been characterized by cyclic fluctuations in output and employment, the long-term historical trend of productivity growth in the United States has *not* given rise to a growing stockpile of unemployed workers. Rather, increases in labor productivity have been associated in the aggregate with both higher real wages *and* higher levels of employment.

Does this positive relationship between productivity and employment also apply on an industry-by-industry basis? In answering this question, it will be useful to (*a*) ascertain the relationship between productivity growth and changes in employment in an industry, given the locations and elasticity of the product demand curves; (*b*) indicate the complexities that arise once these demand assumptions are relaxed; and (*c*) present actual data on the relationship between industrial productivity and employment growth in the United States.

Demand Factors Constant

Let's analyze how productivity growth and employment changes in an industry would be related without shifts in, and varying elasticities of, product demand. We must first establish that wage rates in various U.S. industries move more in accord with *national* productivity than with *industry* productivity. As indicated in the right column of Figure 17.7, compensation per hour rises more or less evenly in all industries, even though output per worker-hour varies greatly by industry (left column). Why is this the case? If wages began to diverge—rising rapidly in high-productivity-growth industries and increasing slowly in low-productivity-growth industries—the wage structure would be pulled apart. But this doesn't occur because workers respond to the growing wage differentials by leaving the low-growth, low-wage industries to seek the higher wages in the high-growth industries. Similarly, new labor force entrants would choose employment in the high-growth industries and shun the low-growth industries. The increased labor supply would tend to reduce wages in the

FIGURE 17.7 **Output per Worker-Hour and Compensation per Worker-Hour, Selected Industries**

Changes in labor productivity vary considerably by industry on an annual basis, but compensation increases per hour of work tend to be closely matched across industries. Hourly increases in pay per year are more closely related to the average increase in labor productivity for the entire economy than to the change in productivity within specific industries.

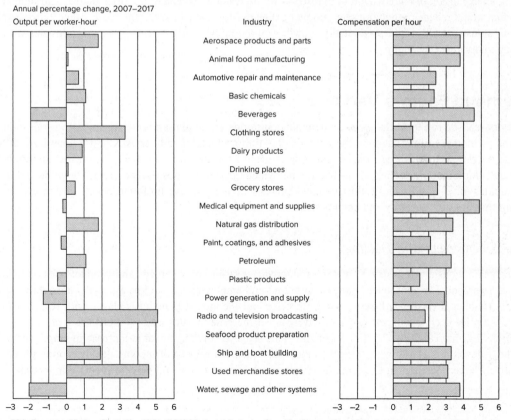

Source: U.S. Bureau of Labor Statistics, "May 2018 National Industry-Specific Occupational Employment and Wage Estimates," www.bls.gov

high-productivity industries, and the diminished labor supply would increase wages in the low-productivity industries. In short, labor supply responses would prevent wages from diverging in the various industries. To repeat: The trend of wages paid by specific industries is dominated by the nationwide trend of productivity primarily because workers respond to wage differentials.

With this fact in mind, let's now reconsider the productivity–unit labor cost relationship in the context of a simple numerical example designed to illustrate the relationship between productivity growth and employment changes in an industry, *all else being constant*. Assume that (*a*) the annual rate of productivity growth for the economy as a whole is 3 percent; (*b*) industry X realizes a 6 percent annual productivity increase, while productivity growth in industry Y is 0 percent; and (*c*) nominal wage rates and earnings in both industries increase by 3 percent in accordance with the economy's overall rate of productivity growth. We find that unit labor costs would *decrease* in industry X and *increase* in industry Y. Further assuming that changes in unit labor costs result in roughly equivalent price changes, we can expect prices to *fall* by about 3 percent in industry X and to *rise* by approximately 3 percent in industry Y. Specifically, a 3 percent increase in nominal wages in industry X coupled with its 6 percent productivity increase would cause its unit labor costs and product price to fall by about 3 percent. Similarly, the 3 percent increase in nominal wages in industry Y combined with its zero rate of productivity growth would cause unit labor costs and product price to increase by approximately 3 percent. Given the locations and elasticities of the product demand curves for the two industries, output and sales would rise in industry X and decline in Y. Provided that the increase in sales more than compensates for the fact that each unit of output can now be produced with a smaller quantity of labor, an expansion of employment in industry X would result. Conversely, the price increase for industry Y's product would reduce output and sales, implying the need for fewer workers; therefore, other things being the same, industries with rapid productivity growth would employ more workers, whereas industries with slow productivity growth would provide less employment.

Demand Factors Variable

It is not realistic to expect that product demand conditions are similar and unchanging for various industries in the economy. In our example, the demands for the products of industries X and Y may have different elasticity characteristics *and* may be changing (shifting) through time in such a way as to undermine the generalization that productivity growth and employment growth are positively related. The price and income elasticities of, and shifts in, product demand curves can and do have profound effects on the cause–effect chain that links productivity and employment.

Industry Growth and Decline

Once again, consider industry X, where productivity is rising by 6 percent and product price is falling by about 3 percent. The consequent increase in output and employment would be especially large *if* the demand for its product is elastic with respect to both price and income. If demand is elastic with respect to price, then the price decline will generate a relatively larger increase in sales. For example, the 3 percent decrease in price may increase sales by 8 or 9 percent. This suggests a relatively large increase in employment. Similarly, if demand is elastic with respect to income,[11] then the growth of income in this economy will cause relatively larger increases in the demand for product X. For example, a 3 percent increase in income—which

---

[11] Income elasticity is measured as the percentage change in quantity demanded relative to a given percentage change in income. If the percentage increase in the quantity demanded is greater than the percentage increase in the income that triggered the increase in the amount demanded, we say that demand is *income-elastic* or *income-sensitive*. If the percentage increase in quantity demanded is less than the percentage increase in income, then demand is *income-inelastic* or *income-insensitive*. In the special case of an *inferior good*, an *increase* in income *decreases* the demand for the product.

is the amount by which real income is increasing in our hypothetical two-industry economy—might shift the demand curve to the right so that perhaps 9 or 10 percent more of the product would be purchased at any given price. Of course, industry X's demand curve may shift rightward for reasons other than rising incomes. For example, consumer preferences for the product may become stronger, or the imposition of tariffs or quotas on competing foreign products may have deflected consumer purchases from imports toward domestic production. The point is that increases (rightward shifts) in product demand will enhance output and, therefore, employment in the industry so as to offset any declines in employment due to the fact that less labor is needed per unit of output.

In contrast, if the demand for industry X's product is inelastic with respect to both price and income, the increases in output would tend to be small. If sufficiently small, the increase occasioned by the enhancement in sales may fail to offset the fact that rising productivity has reduced labor requirements per unit of output. In this case, employment in industry X will decline, despite the high rate of productivity growth.

The worst scenario in terms of adverse employment effects would occur if product X were an *inferior good*—a product of which people buy *less* as their incomes rise—because the resulting decrease (leftward shift) of the product demand curve would reduce employment even though product price is falling. Enhanced foreign competition or declines in the prices of substitute goods are other developments that could also decrease demand and diminish output and employment. To recapitulate: The conditions most conducive to employment growth in an industry experiencing rapid productivity growth are (*a*) a price- and income-elastic product demand curve and (*b*) fortuitous circumstances that increase product demand.

Conversely, recall that industry Y, achieving no productivity growth, would find that the price of its product is *rising* by about 3 percent. The adverse effect of this price increase on output and employment will be minimized, or perhaps completely offset, if product demand is inelastic with respect to price and elastic with respect to income. The employment-diminishing effect would be aggravated, however, if demand is price-elastic and income-inelastic. Once again, changes in product demand stemming from a variety of causes other than rising real income may intensify or alleviate the impact on output and employment.

Illustrations

Our analysis can give us insight into the waxing and waning—particularly the waning—of various industries in our economy. For example, productivity in higher education—particularly in teaching—has been relatively constant. The result has been rising educational costs and rising tuition. But the demand for higher education is inelastic with respect to price and elastic with respect to income. As a consequence, higher education has absorbed an expanding proportion of per capita income. As another example, the production of certain highly crafted goods—fine pottery, glassware, and furniture—has also experienced little or no productivity growth. This has resulted in sharply rising prices for such products. But the demand for these products is price-elastic, and the result has been a decline in the total production of high-quality products. A similar analysis applies to the performing arts. (Given the size of the audience, how does one increase the productivity of a string quartet?) The symphonies and community theaters of most cities and towns depend on public and private subsidization. Furthermore, the financial problems of many large cities may be intimately tied to the fact that they provide services—of police, hospital workers, social workers—for which it is difficult to raise productivity. As the wages of public employees rise in accordance with the (higher) productivity growth of the national economy, the cost of government services will necessarily increase. The source of soaring government budgets may lie much more in the low productivity growth associated with public services than with bureaucratic mismanagement or malfeasance.[12]

---

[12] These examples are from William J. Baumol, "Macro-Economics of Unbalanced Growth: The Anatomy of Urban Crisis," *American Economic Review,* June 1967, pp. 415–426.

Observed Productivity–Employment Relationship

Figure 17.8 compares for an 11-year period the average annual percentage changes in employment with the average annual percentage changes in productivity for 162 industries. You will observe that the scattering of industry data points is random; we simply cannot generalize about the relationship between productivity growth and employment growth by industry.

Although productivity increased for 104 of the 162 industries over the 2007–2017 period, employment increased in 47 industries and declined in 115. In some industries, rapid productivity growth was associated with declines in employment (wireless communications carriers, cable and other subscription programming), whereas other industries experienced both rapid productivity growth and employment growth (electronic shopping and mail-order houses). Similarly, some industries that have been comparatively stagnant with respect to productivity growth have experienced large employment increases (warehousing and storage) while employment has decreased in others (book stores and news dealers).

It is challenging to speculate about the productivity and employment changes shown for specific industries in Figure 17.8. For example, the large fall in employment in the tobacco industry, where productivity growth has been positive, might reflect the increased awareness of the negative health effects of smoking that occurred in recent decades. Similarly, we note that in the manufacture of fabrics, productivity growth has been quite rapid. The accompanying decline in employment undoubtedly reflects the rise in the import share of the fabric industry that started in the 1990s and has continued. You are urged to use your general knowledge of the economy to ponder the production and employment changes of various other industries shown in Figure 17.8.

FIGURE 17.8 **Output per Worker-Hour and Employment, Selected Industries**

Average annual percentage changes in employment within industries are not systematically related to industry average annual productivity changes.

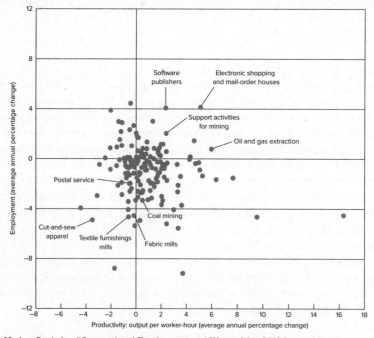

Source: U.S. Bureau of Labor Statistics, "Occupational Employment and Wages, May 2018," www.bls.gov

17.2 *Quick Review*

- The rate of productivity growth fluctuates with the business cycle, falling as the economy recedes and rising as the economy expands.

- Although productivity growth means that society can produce its existing output with fewer workers, it also permits society to obtain more total output. Overall, productivity growth has been associated with growing employment, not rising unemployment.

- Compensation per hour rises more or less evenly in all industries, even though output per worker-hour varies greatly by industry. Other things being equal, this fact implies rising per-unit costs and reduced output and employment in industries with slow productivity growth, and falling per-unit costs and increased output and employment in industries with high productivity growth.

- Variable demand factors confound the actual relationship between productivity and employment growth within industries; data reveal no systematic relationship between industry productivity growth and industry employment growth.

Your Turn

Productivity growth in 2008 was 0.8 percent; in both 2009 and 2010, it was 3.3 percent. Can you think of a possible explanation for this abrupt change? (*Hint:* The economy was in recession in 2008.) (*Answer:* See page 542.)

A "NEW ECONOMY" OR NOT?

Between the mid-1990s and the Great Recession, the United States experienced a resurgence of productivity growth. This rekindled productivity growth rate has led some to suggest that the United States is at the beginning of a "new economy." The new economy perspective proponents argue that innovations in information technology are spreading throughout the economy and have altered the structure of the economy.[13] Others are more skeptical and believe it is only a temporary resurgence of productivity growth.

Figure 17.9 shows the rate of productivity growth for the 1948–2018 period. Between 1948 and 1973, the United States had a vigorous annual productivity growth rate of 3.2 percent. Productivity grew at less than half that rate during the 1974–1995 period; however, productivity growth rebounded to a rapid 2.8 percent per year between 1996 and 2008. Between 2008 and 2018, the productivity growth rate dropped back to a rate similar to that of the 1974–1995 period.

The effects of this resurgence and slowdown are those discussed earlier. The standard of living in the United States rose more rapidly between 1996 and 2007 than it had in the prior 20 years and more rapidly than in other nations. For example, real compensation per hour rose at an annual rate of 1.8 percent between 1996 and 2007 compared to the sluggish annual rate of only 0.4 percent between 2008 and 2018. Also, according to many economists, the revival in productivity growth contributed to the low inflation experienced in the last half of the 1990s and 2000s.

---

[13] For more about these different new economy perspectives, see Kevin J. Stiroh, "Is There a New Economy?" *Challenge,* July–August 1999, pp. 82–101.

FIGURE 17.9 **Labor Productivity Growth Rates in the United States**

Productivity growth surged in the 1996–2008 period after being relatively low for two decades. Since 2008, productivity has increased at a lower rate.

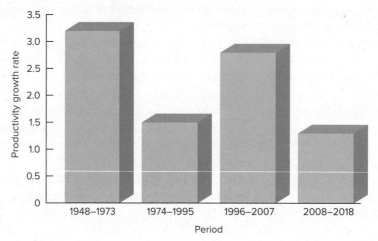

Source: U.S. Bureau of Labor Statistics, "Net Multifactor Productivity and Cost, 1948 - 2018," www.bls.gov

Causes of Resurgence

No consensus exists among experts as to whether the increase in the U.S. productivity growth rate is a part of a new long-run trend or simply a temporary aberration. Nevertheless, it is enlightening to survey some possible causes of the productivity resurgence. The following are the primary explanations for the acceleration of productivity.

Increased Use of Information Capital

One possibility is that faster increases in the quantity of capital relating to information technology may have increased productivity growth. In the last half of the 1990s, firms invested heavily in information capital such as computer hardware, software, and communications equipment. In 1999 spending on information capital was responsible for 11 percentage points of the 14 percent real growth in business spending on capital.[14]

Empirical studies indicate that higher spending on information technology played an important role in the increased productivity growth. Jorgenson, Ho, and Stiroh's analysis indicates that 37 percent of the productivity growth for the 1995–2000 period was due to increases in the use of information technology.[15] The corresponding figure for the 2000–2006 period was a somewhat lower, 23 percent. Increases in spending on other types of capital contributed 18 and 28 percent of the productivity growth for the 1995–2000 and 2000–2006 periods, respectively.

Increased Technological Progress and Efficiency

Another potential explanation is that greater technological progress and efficiency, particularly in information technology (as distinct from simply more capital goods), have increased the productivity growth rate. As measured by prices, the pace of innovations in computer technology has clearly quickened in recent years.

[14] Council of Economic Advisers, *Economic Report of the President, 2001* (Washington, DC: Government Printing Office, 2001), Chapter 1.
[15] Dale W. Jorgenson, Mun S. Ho, and Kevin J. Stiroh, "A Retrospective Look at the U.S. Productivity Growth Resurgence," *Journal of Economic Perspectives,* Winter 2008, pp. 3-24.

Prices for computer equipment fell at a rate of 27 percent per year for 1996–2001 as compared to 18 percent in 1991–1995,[16] reflecting innovation and improved efficiency.

Empirical studies confirm that faster technological progress in high-technology industries played an important role in the speedup of the productivity growth rate. Jorgenson, Ho, and Stiroh find that 22 percent of the productivity growth between 1995 and 2000 was caused by increased efficiency in the production of information technology products.[17] The comparable figure for the 2000–2006 period was 15 percent. They estimate that another 16 percent and 22 percent resulted from technological progress and efficiency gains in the rest of the economy for the 1995–2000 and 2000–2006 periods, respectively.

Causes of Productivity Slowdown

Three possible explanations exist for the slowdown in the rate of productivity growth since 2008. First, the rate of growth of worker skills could have declined. Second, investment in capital may have increased at a slower rate. Third, technological progress may have slowed.

The empirical evidence finds that the slowdown is not the result of declining growth in worker skills or investment in capital. Fernald and Wang point out the educational attainment of workers has continued to increase.[18] They also note that capital per worker hour has risen modestly since 2008. Fernald finds that most of the decline in productivity growth is due to a decline in technological progress and efficiency.[19] In particular, he reports that the slowdown has been concentrated in industries that either produce information technology or intensively use information technology.

The future for productivity growth depends critically on the rate of technological progress. Fernald, using a model that puts some weight on the information technology sector induced fast-growth period, estimates the long-term annual rate of productivity growth will be 1.9 percent or slightly more than the average over the 2008–2018 period.[20] It remains to be seen what the future rate of innovation will be in the information technology industries.

Chapter Summary

1. Productivity is the relationship between real output and inputs. The "official" Bureau of Labor Statistics (BLS) index of labor productivity is the ratio of real GDP originating in the private sector to the number of worker-hours employed in the private sector.

2. The BLS index overstates productivity growth because it excludes the public sector. On the other hand, it understates productivity growth in that quality improvements in output are ignored. The BLS index measures, but does not reveal the causes of, productivity growth.

3. The advantages of the BLS index are that *(a)* it is conceptually simple, *(b)* it automatically takes changes in the length of the workweek into account, and *(c)* it is directly comparable to hourly wage rates.

4. Economists are interested in labor productivity primarily because changes in productivity correlate with changes in real wage rates.

[16] Stephen D. Oliner and Daniel E. Sichel, "Information Technology and Productivity: Where We Are Now and Where We Are Going," *Journal of Policy Modeling,* July 2003, pp. 477–503.

[17] Jorgenson, Ho, and Stiroh, op. cit.

[18] John Fernald and Bing Wang, "The Recent Rise and Fall of Rapid Productivity Growth," *Federal Reserve Bank of San Francisco Economic Letter,* February 9, 2015.

[19] John Fernald. "Productivity and Potential Output Before, During, and After the Great Recession," in Jonathan Parker and Michael Woodford (eds.), *NBER Macroeconomics Annual 2014* (Chicago: University of Chicago Press, 2015).

[20] For a more optimistic view, see Martin Baily, James Manyika, and Shalabh Gupta, "U.S. Productivity Growth: An Optimistic Perspective," *International Productivity Monitor,* Spring 2013, pp. 3–12; and Chad Syverson, "Will History Repeat Itself Comments on 'Is the Information Technology Revolution Over?'" *International Productivity Monitor,* Spring 2013, pp. 37–40.

5. Other things being equal, productivity growth offsets increases in nominal wages and thereby restrains increases in unit labor costs and product prices.

6. The basic factors that determine productivity growth are *(a)* improvements in the quality of labor, *(b)* increases in the capital–labor ratio, and *(c)* increased efficiency in the use of labor and capital inputs. Increased efficiency is quantitatively the most important factor.

7. Labor productivity falls below the long-term rate of growth during recession and rises above that rate during recovery. Causal factors include cyclic changes in the use of labor and capital and changes in the relative importance of the manufacturing sector.

8. There is no easily discernible relationship between productivity growth and employment changes in various industries. Price and income elasticities of product demand, coupled with demand shifts from changes in such factors as consumer tastes or public policy, make it virtually impossible to predict whether a productivity increase will be associated with increasing or declining employment in any given industry.

9. The rate of productivity growth accelerated dramatically starting in the second half of the 1990s. Possible structural factors in the rise include *(a)* increased use of capital relating to information technology and *(b)* increased technological progress and efficiency. Recently, the rate of productivity growth has slowed possibly due to decreased technical progress in information technology industries.

Terms and Concepts

labor productivity   labor hoarding
BLS productivity index

Questions and Study Suggestions

1. How is *labor productivity* defined? Comment on the shortcomings and advantages of the Bureau of Labor Statistics index of labor productivity.

2. Suppose that in an economy 100 worker-hours produce 160 units of output in year 1. In years 2 and 3, worker-hours are 120 and 130 and units of output are 216 and 260, respectively. Using year 2 as the base year, calculate *(a)* the productivity index for all three years and *(b)* the rates of productivity growth.

3. How do you account for the close correlation between changes in the rate of productivity growth and changes in real wage rates for the economy as a whole? Does this relationship also hold true on an industry-by-industry basis? Explain.

4. Explain this statement: "High wage rates are both an effect and a cause of high labor productivity."

5. Discuss the relationship between aggregate productivity growth and price inflation. Draw a diagram (similar to Figure 17.8), putting average annual productivity growth on the horizontal axis and average annual price changes on the vertical axis. If you were to plot relevant data for, say, 60 or 70 major industries, what general relationship would you expect? Explain.

6. Suppose in a given year a firm's productivity increases by 2 percent and its nominal wages rise by 5 percent. What would you expect to happen to the firm's unit labor costs and product price?

7. Briefly comment in quantitative terms on the long-term trend of labor productivity in the United States; cite the three primary factors that contributed to that growth, and indicate the relative quantitative importance of each. Discuss the specific factors that have contributed to increased efficiency in the use of labor and capital.

8. Describe and explain the cyclic changes that occur in labor productivity. Of what significance are these changes?

9. Explain the relationship between changes in *(a)* nominal wage rates, *(b)* productivity, *(c)* unit labor costs, and *(d)* product price. What does this relationship suggest about the expected impact of productivity growth on employment in a particular industry? Can you reconcile your generalization with Figure 17.8?

10. Assume that labor productivity is rising by 6 percent in the economy as a whole but by only 1 percent in industry X. Also assume that nominal wages for all industries rise in accordance with the economy's overall rate of productivity increase. Labor costs are 90 percent of total costs in industry X. The demand for industry X's product is highly elastic with respect to price and inelastic with respect to income. Assuming no shifts in demand curves for products in the economy other than those associated with changes in income, forecast the future growth or decline of industry X, specifying all of the steps in your reasoning.

11. Comment on each of the following statements:

    a. "Although most highly productive companies are profitable, not all profitable companies are highly productive."

    b. "Increased public demand for such amenities as clean air and safer work-places has complicated the comparison of productivity rates over time."

    c. "Rising productivity means that it takes fewer workers to produce a given level of output. Productivity increases are, therefore, a source of unemployment."

12. U.S. productivity growth accelerated in the second half of the 1990s. How do you account for this speedup? Why is it still impossible to know if this speedup is the start of a long-term trend or simply a transitory change?

Internet Exercise

Has the Resurgence of Productivity Growth Continued?

 Go to the Bureau of Labor Statistics website (**http://www.bls.gov**) and in sequence select "Databases and Tables" and "Series Report." Then enter the following ID series number: PRS84006091. Last, click on "All Years." This will retrieve the percentage change in output per hour since a year ago (growth in labor productivity).

What was the average rate of increase in labor productivity between 1991 and 1995? Between 1996 and 2006? Between 2006 and the most recent year shown? On the basis of these figures, do proponents of the new economy perspective or their critics have the upper hand in the debate? Explain your answer.

Internet Link

 The Bureau of Labor Statistics Labor Productivity website has a large amount of information regarding productivity (**http://www.bls.gov/lpc/home.htm**).

Chapter **18**

Employment and Unemployment

After reading this chapter, you should be able to:

1. Discuss the measurement of unemployment and employment statistics.
2. Use aggregate supply-aggregate demand analysis to show graphically how real output, the price level, and employment are jointly determined.
3. Analyze the factors that give rise to frictional unemployment.
4. Explain structural unemployment.
5. Discuss demand-deficient unemployment.
6. Describe the distribution of unemployment across demographic groups.
7. Analyze public policies that may be used to combat unemployment.

Facts: In the 1990s, the U.S. economy created 18 million new jobs; an additional 3 million jobs came into existence in the 2000s; and 20 million more jobs were created between 2010 and 2018. In 2018, 3.9 percent of the U.S. labor force was unemployed, down 2.3 percentage points from 4 years earlier. Unemployment rates in 2018 fell to 5.7 percent in Canada and 2.4 percent in Japan. Meanwhile, 15.3 percent of the Spanish labor force was unemployed in 2018, which has made more than a decade of unemployment rates above 10 percent.

Questions! What explains the growth of employment over time? How much unemployment is natural for an economy? What causes higher-than-usual unemployment rates? Who are the unemployed? How long do they remain unemployed? What policies does government use to try to reduce unemployment?

In earlier chapters we analyzed how individuals make short- and long-term labor supply decisions and how firms determine their profit-maximizing levels of employment under varying conditions in labor and product markets. We also examined how unemployment might arise in specific labor markets where a union wage, a legal minimum wage, or an efficiency wage exceeded the market-clearing wage. We now turn our attention to the *aggregate* labor market and to the determinants of the *total* levels of employment and unemployment in the economy.

EMPLOYMENT AND UNEMPLOYMENT STATISTICS

Employment and unemployment statistics are widely used to assess the macroeconomic health of the economy. It is important to know how total employment and unemployment are measured, to be aware of the recent employment and unemployment record, and to understand the limitations of the data as guides to public policy.

Measurement

Each month the Bureau of the Census conducts a current population survey (CPS) commonly referred to as the *Household Survey*. About 60,000 households are selected to represent the U.S. population 16 years of age or older and are interviewed to determine the proportions of the population employed, unemployed, or not in the labor force. The Bureau of Labor Statistics (BLS) of the U.S. Labor Department then uses the sample data to estimate the number of people in each category in the survey week.

Employed People

Those officially *employed* include people who, during the survey week, were 16 years of age or older and (*a*) were employed by a private firm or government unit; (*b*) were self-employed; or (*c*) had jobs but were not working because of illness, bad weather, labor disputes, or vacations.

Once the total employment for the survey week is known, the *employment-population ratio* is easily computed. As shown by Equation (18.1), this ratio is total employment as a percentage of the total noninstitutional population:

$$\text{Employment} - \text{population} = \frac{\text{employmet}}{\text{noninstitutional population}} \times 100 \quad (18.1)$$

Recall from the discussion of the labor force participation rate in Chapter 3 that the noninstitutional population comprises all people 16 years of age and older who are not in institutions such as prisons, mental hospitals, or homes for the aged.

Unemployed People

People are considered officially *unemployed* if during the survey week they were 16 years of age or older, were not institutionalized, and did not work, *but* were available for work *and* (*a*) had engaged in some specific job-seeking activity during the past four weeks, (*b*) were waiting to be called back to a job from which they were temporarily laid off, (*c*) would have been looking for a job but were temporarily ill, or (*d*) were waiting to report to a new job within 30 days.

Those who are 16 years of age or older and not institutionalized but officially neither employed nor unemployed are classified as "not in the labor force." The labor force itself, therefore, consists of those employed and unemployed:

$$\text{Labor force} = \text{employment} + \text{unemployment} \quad (18.2)$$

The *unemployment rate*, then, is the percentage of the labor force that is unemployed:

$$\text{Unemployment rate (\%)} = \frac{\text{unemployment}}{\text{labor force}} \times 100 \quad (18.3)$$

FIGURE 18.1   **Total Population, Labor Force, Employment, and Unemployment, in Millions**

Of the total population of 327.2 million people in the United States in 2018, 162.1 million were in the labor force. Of this latter group, 155.8 million workers were employed and 6.3 million people were unemployed. The unemployment rate for 2018 was 3.9 percent, and the employment-population ratio was 60.4 percent.

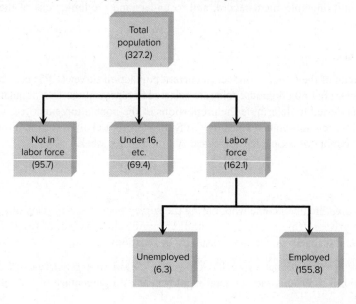

Recap

Figure 18.1 helps clarify how the BLS breaks down the total population into various components; it also provides a basis for computing values for Equations (18.1) through (18.3). The *employment-population ratio* [Equation (18.1)] for 2018 was 60.4 percent. This number is found by dividing the number of people employed (= 155.8 million) by the noninstitutional population of 257.8 million (= 327.2 million - 69.4 million) and multiplying by 100. Consistent with Equation (18.2), we observe that the size of the *labor force* in 2018 was 162.1 million. It is found by adding the number of those employed (= 155.8 million) and the number unemployed (= 6.3 million). The *unemployment rate* [Equation (18.3)] in 2018 was 3.9 percent, calculated by dividing the number of people unemployed (= 6.3 million) by the size of the labor force (= 162.1 million) and multiplying by 100.

Historical Record

Figure 18.2 presents the employment-population ratio since 1960. We see that the ratio rose from 1960 to 2000, but has fallen since then. The ratio was 60.8 percent in 2019, which is 3.6 percentage points below its 2000 peak. Figure 18.3 shows the unemployment rate for the last five decades. The unemployment rate has been highly variable during these years: Its low was 3.5 percent in 1968 and its high was 9.7 percent in 1982. Observe that the unemployment rate fell steadily between 1992 and 2000. The 2000 rate of 4.0 percent was the lowest unemployment rate since the early 1970s. After 2000, the unemployment rate rose and reached 6.0 percent by 2003. It fell after 2003 and dropped to 4.6 percent in 2006 and 2007. It rose between 2008 and 2010 to reach 9.6 percent in 2010. The unemployment rate dropped after 2010 and fell to 3.7 percent by 2019.

FIGURE 18.2 Employment–Population Ratio in the United States

The U.S. employment–population ratio rose until 2000 and has fallen since then.

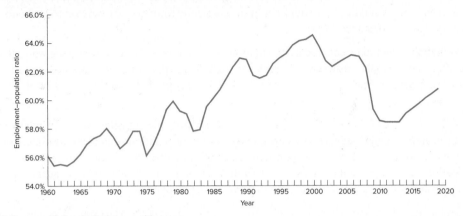

Source: U.S. Bureau of Labor Statistics, www.bls.gov

FIGURE 18.3 U.S. Unemployment Rate

The U.S. unemployment rate has been highly variable over the past 59 years.

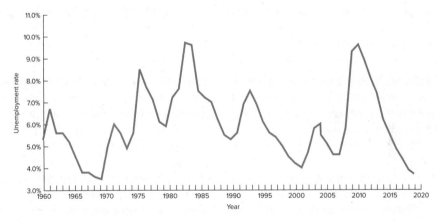

Source: U.S. Bureau of Labor Statistics, www.bls.gov

A Critique of the Household Data

The official employment-related statistics based on the CPS household interviews and reported by the BLS possess several notable virtues that make them useful to economists. First, the sampling technique is uniform throughout the nation and, with the exception of minor changes, has remained consistent over the years; therefore, economists can compare employment and unemployment rates between periods and track cyclic and secular trends. Second, the time lag between the survey and the reporting of the data is short, and the information is highly accessible through government publications. Third, the data are reported in disaggregated as well as overall forms; for example, unemployment rates are provided by race, age, gender, marital status, occupation, reasons for unemployment, and duration of unemployment. This aids in analyzing the distribution of the burden of unemployment. Finally, the data provide useful clues about the direction of the overall economy during a business cycle.

Unfortunately, however, these official statistics also have limitations. In the first place, the official data include all *part-time workers as fully employed,* when in reality some of these people desire to work full-time. In 2018, about 21.3 million people worked part-time because of personal choice. Another 4.8 million part-time workers either wanted to work full-time but could not find suitable full-time work or were on short hours because of a temporary slack in consumer demand.[1]

A second limitation is that to be counted as unemployed, a person must be actively seeking work. But studies show that after many people unsuccessfully look for work for a time, they become discouraged and then abandon their job search. Specifically, an estimated 423,000 people fell into this category in 2018. These *discouraged workers* constitute hidden unemployment.

A third problem is that the data do not measure the *subemployed;* the statistics fail to include people who are forced by economic circumstances to accept employment in occupations that pay lower wages than those they would qualify for in periods of full employment. Each of these three limitations causes the official unemployment statistics to *understate* the extent of underutilization of labor resources and the degree of economic hardship associated with a particular official overall rate of unemployment.

But other problems with the data cause some observers to conclude that the true extent of economic hardship in the nation may be *overstated* by the official unemployment rate. First, it is likely that some respondents to the monthly Household Survey provide false information that increases the official unemployment rate. To present a good image of themselves and family members, interviewees may indicate that household members are actively seeking work when in fact they are not in the labor force.

A second problem is that each unemployed person is counted equally whether he or she is, say, normally a full-time worker who has a strong attachment to the labor force, a semiretired person who wishes to work part-time, or a teenager seeking an after-school job. To the extent that the unemployment statistics include people in the latter two categories, the official unemployment rate may be misleading.[2]

Moreover, the household data do not contain information about the *minimum acceptable* wages (reservation wages) for those unemployed, some of whom may have recently been discharged from high-paying jobs in declining sectors of the economy. These people may remain unemployed until they accept the reality that they no longer can command their initial reservation wages. Unemployment insurance benefits, supplemental unemployment benefits (SUBs) provided by firms, and severance pay may increase the length of this adjustment period. A closely related criticism of using the official data as an indicator of the social impact of unemployment is that the increase in the number of multiearner families over the past few decades has reduced the amount of poverty corresponding to any specific level of unemployment. The loss of a job by one family member greatly lessens the standard of living of most families, but it does not push as many families into poverty as it once did.[3]

The Stock–Flow Model

One final limitation of the overall unemployment rate requires comment. This rate does not distinguish between people who are experiencing short—perhaps less serious—unemployment spells and those who are going through long periods of unemployment. Suppose, as a simple illustration, that an economy has only 12 members in the labor force. In situation A, each person is unemployed for one separate month during a year;

---

[1] For research indicating that the Bureau of Labor Statistics classification of these workers as "involuntarily" part-time is correct, see Leslie S. Stratton, "Are 'Involuntary' Part-Time Workers Indeed Involuntary?" *Industrial and Labor Relations Review,* April 1996, pp. 522–536.

[2] Well over half of all teenagers who are unemployed are enrolled in school and seeking only part-time work.

[3] S. L. Terry, "Unemployment and Its Effects on Family Income," *Monthly Labor Review,* April 1982, pp. 35–43. See also Adam D. Seitchik, "When Married Men Lose Jobs: Income Replacement within the Family," *Industrial and Labor Relations Review,* July 1991, pp. 692–707.

FIGURE 18.4   The Stock-Flow Model of Unemployment

At any point in time, there is a measurable *stock* of people in each of the three boxes that represent categories of labor force status. But these stocks are simultaneously being depleted and replenished by numerous *flows* into and out of each category. Changes in the rates of these flows can significantly affect the unemployment rate.

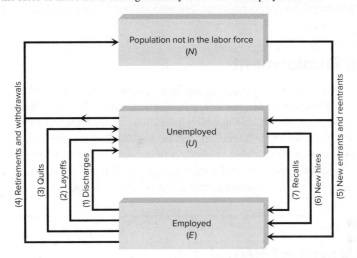

in situation B, one person is unemployed and the rest employed for the entire year. The Household Survey would discover that in each case, 1 out of 12 workers is unemployed *in each month* and, therefore, the annual employment rate is 8.3 percent (1/12). Yet most observers would judge situation B to be of greater social concern: It leaves one person without any wage income for a full year.

This example demonstrates an important fact: The household data measure *stocks* of people in each of the three important labor force categories—employed, unemployed, and not in the labor force—but do not reveal the continuous movement—or *flows*—of people between the various categories. This movement is captured in the *stock-flow model* of unemployment shown in Figure 18.4. Two things to note from this diagram are that (*a*) the unemployment rate [= $U/(E + U)$] can remain constant even though the specific people in the unemployment "pool" change and (*b*) several distinct flow factors can act independently or interact with one another to change the unemployment rate. As one example of the latter, suppose that the rate of inflow to the unemployment category U by way of layoffs, flow 2, increased, while all other flow rates remained constant. Obviously this would increase the absolute number of people who are unemployed while leaving the size of the labor force ($E + U$) unchanged, thereby causing the unemployment rate to rise.

As a second and more complex example, suppose that the rate of exit from the employed category E via retirements and withdrawals, flow 4, increased while all other flow rates remained unchanged. Once again the unemployment *rate* would rise, but in this case the *absolute* number of unemployed people would remain at its previous level. The size of the labor force ($E + U$) would shrink; and because unemployment (U) would remain constant, the unemployment rate [= $U/(E + U)$] would rise.

WW18.1   An analysis of the flows between the categories of labor force status helps us understand the length of unemployment spells of individuals and the reasons why unemployment rates rise and fall. The following are examples of insights gleaned from the stock-flow analysis of unemployment rates: (*a*) Empirical evidence suggests that a considerable amount of unemployment is due to prolonged spells of unemployment for relatively few people.[4] (*b*) During recessions, the rates of layoffs and

---

[4] Kim B. Clark and Lawrence H. Summers, "Labor-Market Dynamics and Unemployment: A Reconsideration," *Brookings Papers on Economic Activity*, no. 1, 1979, pp. 13–60.

discharges rise and the rates of new hires and recalls fall, more than compensating for the decline in voluntary job quits. Consequently, the overall unemployment rate rises. (*c*) First-time labor force entrants and people reentering the labor force from the "not in the labor force" category typically constitute over one-third of the unemployed. (*d*) Unemployment rates stay higher than expected during earlier phases of an economic recovery because improved job prospects entice people who are out of the labor force to seek work; that is, to become officially unemployed.

Defining Full Employment

Not only is a zero rate of unemployment unachievable in a dynamic economy where information is imperfect and workers and firms are heterogeneous, but it may in fact be undesirable. Later in this chapter we will find that some *voluntary* unemployment is a way in which individuals increase their personal earnings and is part of the process through which society enhances its real output and income. We also will observe that some *involuntary* unemployment is an unavoidable by-product of changes in tastes, population shifts, and technological advance. These changes create structural mismatches between labor demand and supply and require adjustments in the allocation of labor resources from some occupations and regions to others.

18.1   World of Work

Effects of Graduating from College in a Bad Economy*

It is not surprising that graduating from college during a recession initially leads to worse labor market outcomes. Due to higher unemployment rates, graduates will be less likely to be employed. Those graduates who do obtain employment are more likely to suffer from job mismatch and be underemployed.

An important question is how does graduating in a recession affect workers later in their careers? They may be able to offset the adverse effects of job mismatching if they can easily switch into career paths they would have otherwise been in. However, the negative effects may persist if early labor market experience has a larger effect than the later beneficial effects of a better economy, such as promotions and additional training.

The long-run effects of recessions have been examined using both U.S. and Canadian data. Lisa Kahn, using data on U.S. white males who graduated from college between 1979 and 1989, examined their earnings for at least 17 years since graduation. She finds large initial earnings losses associated with graduating in a recession, as earnings drop 6–7 percent for each one percentage point rise in the unemployment rate. The earnings loss steadily falls over time, but is at 2.5 percent 15 years after graduation.

Oreopoulos, von Wachter, and Heisz, using data on Canadian males, find that graduating from college during a typical recession lowers earnings initially by 9 percent. This negative earning effect drops in half five years after graduation and fades to 0 percent after 10 years. They also find that those who graduate with a lower-paying major or graduate from a lower-quality school suffer a larger initial earnings decline and take longer to recover.

* Based on Lisa B. Kahn, "The Long-Term Labor Market Consequences of Graduating from College in a Bad Economy," *Labour Economics,* April 2010, pp. 303–316; and Philip Oreopoulos, Till von Wachter, and Andrew Heisz, "The Short- and Long-Term Career Effects of Graduating in a Recession," *American Economic Journal: Applied Economics,* January 2012, pp. 1–29.

18.1 Global Perspective

Comparative Unemployment Rates

Unemployment rates vary greatly among nations of the world over specific periods. The major reasons for these differences are that nations have different natural rates of unemployment and may be in different phases of their business cycles.

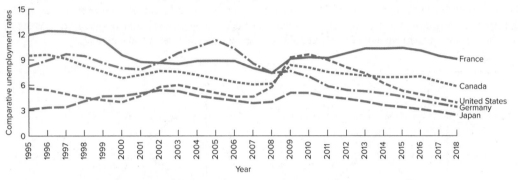

Source: Organization for Economic Co-operation and Development, "Unemployment rate," www.data.oecd.org/
The unemployment rate measure used is the harmonized unemployment rate.

How much voluntary and unavoidable involuntary unemployment is there in the U.S. economy? What rate of unemployment constitutes *full employment?* In the 1960s economists concluded that a 4 percent unemployment rate was an achievable full-employment policy goal. But in the 1970s and 1980s, numerous factors led economists to boost this figure to 5.5 or even 6 percent. Two of the more important factors were (*a*) a changed composition of the labor force such that groups having high unemployment rates—teenagers, for example—constituted a larger fraction of the overall labor force and (*b*) evidence that rates of unemployment in the 4 percent range were associated with accelerating rates of inflation.

In the 1990s demographic changes tended to lower the unemployment rate associated with full employment. Of greatest importance, youthful workers declined as a share of the labor force as baby boomers entered middle age. The growth of temporary help agencies and the improved information resulting from the Internet also lowered the unemployment rate. So, too, did the work requirements under the new welfare rules, which moved many people from the ranks of the unemployed to the ranks of the employed. Finally, some economists point out that the doubling of the U.S. prison population since 1985 removed relatively high-unemployment individuals from the labor force and thus lowered the overall unemployment rate.

Today the consensus appears to be that an unemployment rate of about 4.0–5.0 percent constitutes "practical" full employment and that attempts to reduce the rate through policies that increase aggregate demand will cause the existing rate of inflation to rise. This "practical" rate is sometimes called the *equilibrium* or *natural rate of unemployment* and is defined as (*a*) *the unemployment rate at which there is neither excess demand nor excess supply in the overall labor*

market or (*b*) *the unemployment rate that will occur in the long run if expected and actual rates of inflation are equal.*[5] We will defer explanations of the economic rationales for these two definitions to later in this chapter.

MACROECONOMIC OUTPUT AND EMPLOYMENT DETERMINATION

The macroeconomic models shown as graphs (a) and (b) in Figure 18.5 are central to much of the discussion in this chapter; therefore, a close look at their components is imperative.

FIGURE 18.5   **Real Output and Total Employment Determination**

The intersection of the aggregate demand and supply curves D and S_kAS_c in graph (a) produces equilibrium price and real output levels P_0 and Q_n. In the aggregate labor market (b), the equilibrium wage rate and level of total employment are determined at the intersection of the aggregate labor demand and supply curves. Employment level E_n is the natural level of employment; it is the amount of labor needed to produce the natural level of real output Q_n.

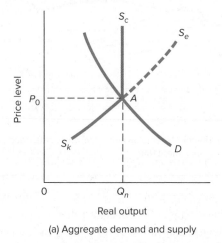
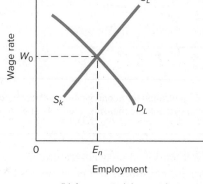

(a) Aggregate demand and supply

(b) Aggregate labor market

Aggregate Demand and Supply

Graph (a) depicts the familiar aggregate demand and supply curves introduced in principles of macroeconomics textbooks to discuss price level and real output determination. The vertical axis shows the *price level* for a hypothetical economy, and the horizontal axis measures *real output*. Conceptually, real output always equals real income; $1 of output generates $1 of income as wages, rent, interest, and profits. The horizontal axis, therefore, also measures real income.

Aggregate Demand

Aggregate demand for goods and services is shown as curve D in Figure 18.5(a) and indicates the total quantity of real output that domestic consumers, businesses, government, and foreign buyers will collectively desire to purchase at each price level. As the price level falls (rises), the quantity of goods and services demanded rises (falls).

---

[5] For more about the natural rate of unemployment, see "Symposium: The Natural Rate of Unemployment," *Journal of Economic Perspectives,* Winter 1997, pp. 3–108; and "Symposium: Friedman's Natural Rate Hypothesis After 50 Years" *Journal of Economic Perspectives,* Winter 2018, pp. 81–134.

The negative slope of the aggregate demand curve results from three interacting effects, the first being the *interest rate effect.* As the price level declines, the demand for money drops because fewer dollars are needed to purchase any given quantity of goods and services. If the money supply is fixed, this decrease in money demand will reduce interest rates, which then will increase spending on such interest-sensitive commodities as new autos, homes, and plants and equipment. Thus, other things being equal, the lower the price level, the greater the quantity of output demanded.

The second effect that helps explain the downward slope of the aggregate demand curve is the *wealth* or *real balances effect.* Lower price levels increase the *real value* of such assets as currency, checking deposits, and savings deposits, whose values are fixed in money terms. As the price level falls, the purchasing power of dollar-denominated wealth held by consumers rises, and people increase their spending on normal goods and services.

The final effect at work is the *foreign purchases effect.* As the domestic price level falls relative to prices of products produced abroad, foreign consumers will shift their spending toward U.S. goods. Hence, the lower price level will be associated with a greater amount of U.S. real output and income.

Aggregate Supply

Aggregate Supply of goods and services is the relationship between the price level and the total quantity of real output that firms are willing to produce and offer for sale. The curve in Figure 18.5(a) is a synthesis of varying interpretations of aggregate supply. The solid curve labeled S_kAS_c incorporates traditional Keynesian (S_kA) and classical (AS_c) assumptions about the working of the economy. The curve's segment S_kA is explained as follows: As aggregate demand falls (D shifts leftward), firms experience declines in sales and increases in inventories of unsold goods. Because wages are relatively inflexible downward, firms respond by laying off or discharging workers and reducing production. Consequently, output falls.

On the other hand, the AS_c segment of the aggregate supply curve shows that when labor and capital resources are being fully used, as is assumed to be true at the full-employment output level Q_n, increases in aggregate demand boost only the price level. The greater demand and higher prices cannot generate greater output. The *monetary* value of the Q_n output rises because of the higher price level, but *real* output remains constant at Q_n.

Other economists envision a short-run aggregate supply curve as shown by S_kAS_e. They assume that in the long run, the economy generates a natural level of output Q_n, but that in the short run, output can be less or greater than that amount depending on the relationship between the actual and expected price levels. We must defer a full discussion of this interpretation to later, but the following constitutes its essence. Suppose the price level is P_0 and workers expect it to remain there. Now suppose unanticipated inflation occurs so that the price level rises above P_0. As a result, the prices firms receive for their products will rise, while nominal wage rates, at least temporarily, will remain fixed at their previously contracted levels. This will mean that real wages will fall and profits will rise, causing firms collectively to increase their employment and output.

Meanwhile, unemployed workers who are searching for jobs will begin to receive inflation-induced higher nominal wage offers and mistakenly think that they are being offered higher real wages. Consequently, they will begin to accept job offers more quickly; the level of employment will rise, unemployment will fall, and real output temporarily will rise above Q_n. Thus, the aggregate supply curve will extend upward as shown by the broken line AS_e.

Equilibrium Price Level and Real Output

The equilibrium levels of price and real output occur where the quantities of total output demanded and supplied are equal–that is, where D and S_kS_c in Figure 18.5(a) intersect. Real output and income level Q_n is the full-employment level of real output or, rephrased, the natural level of real output and income.

The Aggregate Labor Market

Graph (b) in Figure 18.5 shows the aggregate labor market. This graph is our familiar labor market diagram "writ large." The labor demand curve D_L in the figure can be thought of as the aggregate marginal revenue product curve for the economy. This curve is found by multiplying the aggregate marginal product of labor by the price level, in this case P_0. This curve tells us the profit-maximizing level of employment associated with each wage rate. The aggregate labor supply curve S_L indicates the amount of labor services people collectively are willing to offer at each nominal wage rate, given the price level. We assume that in the short run, workers expect the existing price level to remain. We observe that the equilibrium wage rate is W_0 and the equilibrium level of employment is E_n. This level of employment is the natural level of employment–or "full employment"–and is just sufficient to produce the Q_n level of real output shown in graph (a). As noted earlier, most economists feel that the natural rate of unemployment associated with E_n and Q_n is 4.0–5.0 percent.

Why is this natural rate of unemployment so high? Why has the actual rate of unemployment in the United States greatly exceeded the natural rate in some years? To answer these questions we must next consider the three major types of unemployment and their causes. Throughout the discussion, bear in mind that the boundaries between unemployment categories are not absolute and that the extent of one type of unemployment may be a function of the amount of one or both of the other types.

FRICTIONAL UNEMPLOYMENT

Even when aggregate demand is sufficient to employ all the labor force and when those who are unemployed possess skills matching those required by firms with job openings, the nation's unemployment rate will remain positive. As implied in our stock–flow model (Figure 18.4), people continuously (*a*) quit present jobs to shop for new ones, (*b*) look for new jobs after losing previous ones, (*c*) enter the labor force to seek work for the first time, (*d*) reenter the labor force after periods of absence, and (*e*) move from one job to take another within the next 30 days. Likewise, employers continuously (*a*) search for replacements for workers who quit or retire, (*b*) discharge some employees in hopes of finding better ones, and (*c*) seek new workers to fill jobs created by expansion of their firms. Thus unlike "auction" markets such as stock and wheat exchanges, the overall labor market never fully "clears." At any moment there is considerable *frictional unemployment*; that is, not all active job searchers will have yet found or accepted employment, and not all employers will have yet filled their job vacancies.

Search unemployment is an important source of frictional unemployment. This type of unemployment is created by individuals searching for the best job offer and firms searching for workers to fill job openings. The job search process and its relationship to unemployment compensation and inflation are discussed in Chapter 15.

Not all frictional unemployment is of the search variety. In some instances, unemployed workers willingly wait to be recalled from temporary layoffs or willingly wait in job queues to obtain union jobs. In addition, efficiency wages may attract workers into the labor force who are forced to wait for such jobs to open. These types of frictional unemployment collectively might best be described as *wait unemployment*, rather than search unemployment. Let's briefly examine each of these potential sources of frictional unemployment.

1 Temporary Layoffs

Although large layoffs are normally associated with recessions, temporary layoffs by firms occur throughout the economy even during periods of robust overall aggregate demand. Such layoffs may account for as much as 1–1.5 percentage points of the natural rate of unemployment.[6] Workers on temporary layoff normally do not search for new employment; rather, they wait to be recalled to their former jobs. We know from our discussion of the Household Survey that these workers are counted as unemployed.

Seasonal unemployment might also be thought of as temporary layoff and, therefore, a type of wait unemployment. Examples: Construction workers often are unemployed during the winter, farmworkers occasionally are unemployed between planting and harvesting seasons, and professional athletes may be unemployed during parts of the year. In each case, these workers are waiting to resume their jobs.

2 Union Job Queues

Unions also contribute to frictional unemployment. Analysis in Chapter 10 demonstrated that union wage scales may contribute to wait unemployment by reducing the number of workers demanded by firms and increasing the number of willing suppliers of labor. In brief, some workers may be willing to wait in the employment queue for union jobs rather than take nonunion jobs available at lower pay.

3 Efficiency Wages

Finally, efficiency wages may contribute to the relatively high rate of frictional unemployment. Recall that efficiency wages are those that firms set above the market-clearing levels as a way to elicit hard work, reduce costly labor turnover, or achieve some other desirable end that adds to worker productivity. We observed earlier in Figure 7.8 that efficiency wage payments and permanent frictional unemployment go hand in hand. As concisely stated by DeFina,

---

18.1 *Quick Review*

- The employment–population ratio measures total employment as a percentage of the total noninstitutional population; the unemployment rate is the percentage of the labor force that is unemployed.
- The total level of employment is largely determined by aggregate demand and aggregate supply. Full employment exists when the rate of unemployment is 4.0–5.0 percent.
- Frictional unemployment is the unemployment resulting mainly from voluntary job quits, job switches, and new entrants and reentrants into the labor force.

Your Turn

What factors cause the "official" unemployment rate to overstate the true extent of economic hardship in the United States? What factors cause it to understate economic hardship? (*Answers:* See page 543.)

---

[6] D. M. Lilien, "The Cyclical Pattern of Temporary Layoffs in United States Manufacturing," *Review of Economics and Statistics,* February 1980, pp. 24–31.

Unemployed individuals, whether they have quit, have been fired, or have entered the labor force for the first time, might try to get jobs by bidding down the wages of current workers. But in contrast to the simple competitive market situation, firms will not accept those offers. Firms have already weighed the benefits and costs of lower wages and decided that keeping wages high yields them their greatest profit. And because the unemployed cannot bid their way into jobs, they must instead wait until new openings arise from quits, firings, or increases in firms' demands for workers. They must then hope to be chosen over other jobless persons. On the whole, unemployed persons might remain jobless for quite some time.[7]

STRUCTURAL UNEMPLOYMENT

Another type of unemployment that is part of a nation's natural rate of unemployment is *structural unemployment*. This unemployment shares many of the same features as frictional unemployment but is differentiated by being long-lived. It, therefore, can involve considerable costs to those unemployed and substantial loss of forgone output to society.

Structural unemployment is caused by changes in the *composition* of labor supply and demand; it is a "square pegs, round holes" phenomenon. This unemployment generally has one or both of the following dimensions. First, it may result from a mismatch between the skills needed for available jobs and the skills possessed by those seeking work. Second, structural unemployment may occur because of a geographic mismatch between the locations of job openings and job seekers. Examples of structural unemployment abound: Robotics technology and the increase in the market share of imports greatly reduced employment in the U.S. textile industry over the past three decades. Many of the workers who were displaced did not have the skills required for positions that were open, such as in accounting and computer programming. Similarly, improvements in agricultural technology over the past 100 years caused job losses for many farm operators and laborers who did not possess readily transferable job skills in expanding areas of employment and who were not geographically mobile. Unemployment resulting from job losses associated with the spate of mergers in the United States during the 1990s is another example of structural unemployment, as is unemployment resulting from the deregulation of the trucking and airline industries.

Displaced Workers

In recent decades many of the people who were structurally unemployed were *displaced workers*—individuals who had lost their jobs specifically because of permanent plant closings or job cutbacks. A total of 3.0 million workers 20 years of age and older who had been at their jobs at least three years were displaced between January 2015 and December 2017. By January 2018, 66.4 percent of these workers were reemployed in new jobs. Another 19.3 percent of them had left the labor force. Finally, 14.4 percent of the displaced workers were still unemployed and looking for work. This 14.4 percent figure was more than triple the overall unemployment rate in 2018. Of the full-time workers who were back at work, 41.0 percent were earning less than before they were displaced. About quarter were earning 0–19 percent more than before, and about one-fifth were earning at least 20 percent more.[8]

Not all plant closures and job cutbacks occur where we would most expect them: in declining industries or industries hurt by import competition. The level of employment within firms is surprisingly volatile from one

---

[7] DeFina, Robert H., "Explaining Long-Term Unemployment," *Business Review,* Federal Reserve Bank of Philadelphia (May–June 1987), 19.

[8] "Worker Displacement: 2015-2017," United States Department of Labor, News Release 18-1370, August 28, 2018. These statistics are summarized for the past three and half decades in Henry S. Farber, "Employment, Hours, and Earnings Consequences of Job Loss: US Evidence from the Displaced Workers Survey," *Journal of Labor Economics,* July 2017, pp. S235–S272.

year to the next, *independent* of the business cycle or major industry trends. Jobs themselves are more unstable than generally thought, implying that much structural unemployment results from workers being in the wrong place at the wrong time. Changes in labor demand within firms alone may account for as much as one-fourth of the natural rate of unemployment.[9]

The extent of structural unemployment depends on the *degree* of the compositional changes in labor demand and supply and the *speed* of the adjustments of the imbalances and mismatches. Training and retraining play a key role in this adjustment process, and efforts to shorten the duration of structural unemployment normally involve retooling of skills to match job vacancies.

Additional Observations

Several additional observations about structural unemployment deserve mention. In the first place, higher levels of general education are associated with lower levels of structural unemployment. For instance, college graduates who are displaced from their employment because of changes in demand or technology have a wider range of job options and usually find retraining to be easier than do people who have little formal education.[10]

A second observation is that structural and cyclic unemployment overlap. When the economy is at full employment and rapidly expanding, firms experiencing shortages of skilled workers often find it profitable to hire people who do not possess the required job skills but who can be trained while on the job. This training reduces the amount of structural unemployment. But when a recession occurs and the overall rate of unemployment rises, firms hiring new or replacement workers can draw skilled workers from the large unemployment pool. Workers who do not possess the required job skills will stay unemployed longer, and structural unemployment will rise.

A final observation is that futurists in nearly every historical period have warned of impending massive increases in technological unemployment. To date, however, the historical record indicates that on the average, technological change creates more jobs than it destroys and does not greatly alter the overall rate of structural unemployment. More generally, recall the discussion surrounding Figure 17.8, which suggested that no systematic relationship exists between productivity changes and employment changes on an industry-by-industry basis.

But might not the high-technology revolution change this pattern? Most economists doubt that it will. They point out that although specific workers will lose their jobs—and many firms, communities, and perhaps even regions will suffer negative consequences—the new technologies will spur capital investment, spawn secondary industries, and generate output effects that will increase overall labor demand. To fill available positions in the expanding sectors, firms there may need to engage in more concerted on-the-job training. Most economists view the current explosion of new technology as presenting a major challenge to society but not one that is fundamentally different from previous challenges posed by other new technologies.

DEMAND–DEFICIENT UNEMPLOYMENT

In many years, the unemployment rate greatly exceeds the 4.0–5.0 percent natural rate. For example, unemployment was 8.5 percent in 1975, 9.7 percent in 1982, and 9.6 percent in 2010. In the depth of the Great

---

[9] Jonathan S. Leonard, "In the Wrong Place at the Wrong Time: The Extent of Frictional and Structural Unemployment," in Kevin Lang and Jonathan S. Leonard (eds.), *Unemployment and the Structure of Labor Markets* (New York: Basil Blackwell, 1987), pp. 141–163.

[10] W. R. Johnson, "The Demand for General and Specific Education with Occupational Mobility," *Review of Economic Studies,* October 1979, pp. 695–705; and Farber, 2005, op. cit.

Depression (1933), 24.9 percent of the labor force was unemployed. These high unemployment rates are by-products of recessions and depressions and result from deficiencies in aggregate demand that force firms to lay off and discharge workers. The evidence strongly suggests that declines in aggregate demand—rather than, say, differences between expected and actual inflation rates—are the *primary* cause of cyclic unemployment.[11]

Graphic Analysis

The analytic framework we developed earlier helps clarify *demand-deficient* or *cyclic unemployment*. In Figure 18.6(a) we depict a sharp, unexpected decline in aggregate demand, shown as the movement from D to D_1. Keynesians view a decline in investment or consumption spending as the usual cause of such a shift, whereas monetarists look to a reduction in the money supply as the underlying culprit. Irrespective of the cause, the fall in aggregate demand decreases real output from the full-employment level Q_n by the amount Q_nQ_1.

As shown in graph (b) of Figure 18.6, the decline in aggregate demand in graph (a) reduces the derived aggregate demand for labor from D_L to D_{L1}. In technical terms, this decline in labor demand occurs because the lower price level P_1 in graph (a) reduces revenue to producers; that is, marginal revenue product in the aggregate falls. More generally, firms experience rapid rises in their inventories because they are unable to sell their existing output. They, therefore, curtail their production and reduce their demand for labor. Put simply, they no longer wish to hire as many workers at each wage rate as previously.

Let's assume, for reasons we will explore shortly, that the wage rate in graph (b) remains at W_0. We note that employment declines from the natural level E_n to the smaller amount E_1. At wage W_0, a individuals desire work—and previously were working—but firms employ only b workers. Thus, ab workers are cyclically unemployed.

FIGURE 18.6 Demand-Deficient Unemployment

A decline in the aggregate demand for output [D to D_1 in (a)] reduces the demand for labor [D_L to D_{L1} in (b)]. Assuming a rigid nominal wage W_0, the decline in labor demand results in involuntary demand-deficient unemployment by the amount ab in graph (b).

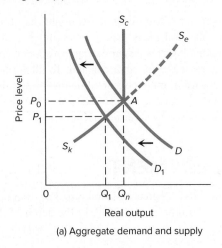

(a) Aggregate demand and supply

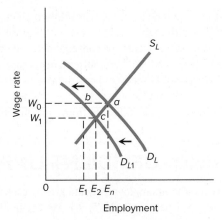

(b) Aggregate labor market

[11] Ronald S. Warren, Jr., "Labor Market Contracts, Unanticipated Wages, and Employment Growth," *American Economic Review*, June 1983, pp. 389–397.

The full decline in employment and emergence of unemployment rest on the crucial assumption that the wage rate in our model does not fall. If it were to decline to W_1, firms would adjust their employment to E_2 (point c). We note that employment is only E_2 at W_1, compared to E_n at the original W_0 equilibrium. The E_2 E_n decline in employment, however, would be voluntary on the part of these workers. As shown by segment ca of the labor supply curve, these workers have reservation wages that exceed the new lower wage W_1. Because the E_2E_n workers voluntarily withdraw from the labor force, they are not officially unemployed.

Just how flexible downward are nominal wages in the U.S. economy? Although nominal wages eventually do fall under pressure of slack aggregate demand, they are relatively rigid downward in the short run. Declines in aggregate demand, therefore, produce demand-deficient or cyclic unemployment.[12]

Wage Rigidity

Why are nominal wages relatively inflexible downward? Several diverse explanations have been cited.

1 Unions

Unions are one reason why nominal wages are rigid downward. Unions view wage cuts as "givebacks" of previous hard-earned collective bargaining gains and thus vigorously resist wage reductions. Reductions in nominal wages do occur in unionized industries, but normally only *after* severe cutbacks in employment have occurred. Unions appear to prefer layoffs to temporary wage reductions. The latter affect all workers, whereas layoffs usually affect only a small percentage of the firm's workforce and normally involve people with little seniority. Thus, a *majority* of workers benefit by a layoff policy as contrasted to wage cuts, and elected union leaders are likely to be responsive to this majority when negotiating wage and layoff provisions.

2 Bias toward Layoffs by Firms

Another reason that nominal wages are inflexible downward is that firms themselves may favor temporary selective layoffs to across-the-board temporary wage reductions. The latter might cause higher-skilled, more experienced workers in whom a firm has invested large amounts of training to quit and take jobs elsewhere. The layoff strategy allows the firm to "inventory" or "hoard" this skilled labor and instead lay off workers who are more easily replaced if they happen to take alternative employment rather than wait for a callback. Furthermore, the existence of unemployment compensation and the way it is financed bias the decision toward layoffs. Those laid off experience a *net* loss of income that is much less than the full decline in wages; therefore, they will be less likely to accept other permanent jobs during this period. Also, because the taxes paid by firms to the unemployment compensation program are not perfectly related to layoff experience, firms that dismiss substantial numbers of workers are subsidized by the tax payments of other firms. Stated technically, the unemployment benefits received by workers who are temporarily unemployed exceed the *incremental* tax cost to the firms that lay them off.[13]

3 Implicit Contracts

A closely related reason that wages appear to be inflexible downward during recessions is that implicit contracts govern many employment relationships. *Implicit contracts* are informal, often unstated, understandings

---

[12] According to Keynes, even if nominal wages did fall, so too would product costs and prices; therefore, the *real* wage—the nominal wage divided by the price level—would remain constant, and employment would not increase.

[13] See Martin Feldstein, "The Importance of Temporary Layoffs: An Empirical Analysis," *Brookings Papers on Economic Activity,* no. 3, 1975, pp. 725-744; and Robert H. Topel, "On Layoffs and Unemployment Insurance," *American Economic Review,* September 1983, pp. 541-559. See also Donald R. Deere, "Unemployment Insurance and Employment," *Journal of Labor Economics,* October 1991, pp. 307-324.

that are "invisible handshakes."[14] One common feature of many implicit contracts is an understanding that the firm will maintain existing nominal wages and pay cost-of-living wage increases except under severe economic conditions, such as impending bankruptcy. In return for this guarantee, employers obtain the right to lay off workers in response to cyclic declines in the demand for their products. By providing "insurance" against wage declines during recessions, employers can attract workers at a lower average wage. In addition, the "fixed wage–variable employment" contract provides firms with certainty in the reduction of the wage bill (wage × number of worker-hours) compared to the uncertainty associated with a wage reduction, which might cause some highly valued workers to quit. Finally, these contracts may produce positive "reputation effects" that may allow firms to attract better-quality workers who require less supervision.

18.2 World of Work

Why Bad Unemployment News Is Usually Good for Stocks

Stock prices are clearly affected by unexpected news. For example, when the U.S. Treasury unexpectedly announced on March 23, 2009, a plan to help troubled banks, the average stock price rose by 7.1 percent. Alternatively, when Standard and Poor's unexpectedly downgraded the U.S. government from AAA to AA+ on August 8, 2011, the average stock price fell by 7.2 percent.

Another source of unexpected news is the monthly unemployment report produced by the U.S. Bureau of Labor Statistics. Unemployment news supplies information that can affect stock prices in three ways: It provides information about future interest rates, corporate profits and dividends, and the riskiness of investing in stocks.

The three information components contained in the unemployment rate have conflicting effects on stock prices. On the one hand, a higher unemployment rate tends to lead to lower expected future interest rates on bonds. The lower rates make bonds a less attractive investment and thus raise stock prices. On the other

hand, a higher unemployment rate lowers future expected corporate profits and stock dividends and makes stocks a riskier investment. These changes make investing in stocks less appealing and lead to lower stock prices.

John H. Boyd, Jian Hu, and Ravi Jagannathan examine the effects of unemployment news on stock prices using data from February 1957 to December 2000. They examine the effects of unexpected changes in the unemployment rate on the average stock price on the day before and the day when the monthly unemployment rate information is released to the public.

Boyd, Hu, and Jagannathan find that unanticipated increases in the unemployment rate reduce stock prices during contractions. This implies that the corporate profits and riskiness effects are larger than the interest rate effect. Conversely, they report that unexpected rises in unemployment during expansions raise stock prices. This indicates that the interest rate effect dominates the corporate profits and riskiness effects. Stock prices usually rise with bad unemployment news because the economy is usually expanding.

Source: John H. Boyd, Jian Hu, Ravi Jagannathan, "The Stock Market's Reaction to Unemployment News: Why Bad News Is Usually Good for Stocks," *Journal of Finance,* March 2005, pp. 649–672.

---

[14] A voluminous, but difficult, literature on implicit contracts has developed. The major contributions are surveyed in Costas Azariadis and Joseph E. Stiglitz, "Implicit Contracts and Fixed-Price Equilibria," *Quarterly Journal of Economics,* vol. 98, suppl. 1983, pp. 1–22.

4 Insider-Outsider Theories

Recently a set of so-called *insider-outsider theories* has emerged that purports to explain downward wage rigidity on the basis of "insiders" and "outsiders."[15] *Insiders* are employed people who have some degree of market power; *outsiders* are unemployed people who are unable or unwilling to underbid the existing wage rate to gain employment. In terms of Figure 18.6(b), outsiders are represented by distance ab at wage W_0.

> **WW18.2**
>
> Why are outsiders unable or unwilling to secure jobs for themselves by bidding down the wage rate to, say, W_1 in Figure 18.6(b)? They may be *unable* to do this because firms may view the cost of hiring them as being prohibitive. Firms may expect that if they hire outsiders at less

than the existing wage rate, the remaining incumbent workers will withhold cooperation from those who "stole" jobs. Where workplace cooperation is important in the production process, the firms' output and profits will surely suffer. Moreover, even if firms were willing to hire outsiders, this group may be *unwilling* to offer their services for less than the present wage rate for fear of being harassed by remaining incumbent workers. Outsiders may thus opt to wait for an increase in aggregate demand to obtain or regain employment. Meanwhile, the cyclic unemployment described in Figure 18.6(b) will persist.

THE DISTRIBUTION OF UNEMPLOYMENT

The distribution of unemployment is uneven over the labor force and changes as demand-deficient unemployment rises and falls. In Table 18.1 we present disaggregated civilian unemployment rates by race, age, gender, and duration of unemployment for two different years. These years were selected for contrast: In 2018 the economy reached full employment, experiencing a 3.9 percent unemployment rate; and in 2010 a major recession ended the year before, raising the overall unemployment rate to 9.6 percent.

Observation of the large variance in the disaggregated rates of unemployment *within each year* and comparison of the rates *between* the two years support several generalizations drawn from more extensive studies of unemployment data. First, the unemployment rates for people in occupations requiring less human capital tend to be higher than those for people in positions requiring more skills. For example, in 2018 the unemployment rate for managers and professionals was 2.1 percent compared with 5.2 percent for blue-collar workers.

As a corollary, the unemployment rate usually is disproportionately higher for lower-skilled workers during a recession. Observe in Table 18.1 that the unemployment rate in 2010 for blue-collar workers was 14.3 percent compared with the 4.7 percent for managerial and professional workers. This 14.3: 4.7 ratio is greater than the 4.8: 2.1 ratio occurring in the full-employment year 2018.

The reasons for the different rates between workers of various skills and the normally rising relative rates for lower-skilled workers during recessions include: (*a*) lower-skilled workers are often subject to more technologically caused unemployment and longer spells of structural unemployment; (*b*) higher-skilled workers are more likely to be self-employed; and (*c*) during periods of falling product demand, firms lay off or discharge workers in whom they have invested the least amount of human capital over the years and retain more skilled workers, managers, and professionals.

---

[15] Assar Lindbeck and Dennis Snower, "Wage Setting, Unemployment, and Insider–Outsider Relations," *American Economic Review,* May 1986, pp. 235-239; and Lindbeck and Snower, "Cooperation, Harassment, and Involuntary Unemployment: An Insider–Outsider Approach," *American Economic Review,* March 1988, pp. 167-188. For empirical evidence against the insider–outsider model, see Denise J. Doiron, "A Test of the Insider–Outsider Hypothesis in Union Preferences," *Economica,* August 1995, pp. 281-290.

TABLE 18.1 Unemployment Rates for Labor Force Subclassifications, 2018 (Full Employment) versus 2010 (Recession)

Category	Unemployment Rate, 2018 (%)	Unemployment Rate, 2010 (%)
Occupation		
Managerial and professional	2.1	4.7
Blue-collar	4.8	14.3
Age		
16–19	12.9	25.9
African–American, 16–19	21.9	43.0
White, 16–19	11.3	23.2
Males, 20+	3.3	9.8
Females, 20+	3.6	8.0
Race		
African–American	6.5	16.0
White	3.5	8.7
Gender		
Female	3.5	8.6
Male	3.6	10.5
Duration		
15+ weeks	1.4	5.7
Overall	3.9	9.6

Source: U.S. Bureau of Labor Statistics, "Employment & Earnings, January 2011, 2019, Vol. 58 No. 1." www.bls.gov

A second generalization concerning the disaggregated unemployment data shown in Table 18.1 is that the rate of unemployment for 16- to 19-year-olds is considerably higher than that for adults. In addition, the African–American teenage unemployment rate greatly exceeds that for white teenagers. The overall teenage unemployment rate was 25.9 percent in 2010 and 12.9 percent in 2018, but the African–American teenage rates for the two years were 43.0 and 21.9 percent, respectively. Teenagers have low skill levels, high rates of job quits and discharges, little geographic mobility, and frequent transitions to and from the labor force. They, therefore, have numerous spells of frictional and structural unemployment. Also, some teenage unemployment is attributable to the minimum wage.[16]

A third broad generalization based on Table 18.1 is that over the years, the unemployment rate for all African–Americans—teenage and adult—has been about two times that for whites. For example, in 2010 the African–American unemployment rate was 16.0 percent compared with the white rate of 8.7 percent.

---

[16] The causes and consequences of unemployment among African-American youths are analyzed in Richard B. Freeman and Harry J. Holzer, *The Black Youth Employment Crisis* (Chicago: University of Chicago Press, 1986). Also of interest are Harry J. Holzer, "Can We Solve Black Youth Unemployment?" *Challenge,* November–December 1988, pp. 43–49; and John Bound and Richard B. Freeman, "What Went Wrong? The Erosion of Relative Earnings and Employment among Young Black Men in the 1980s," *Quarterly Journal of Economics,* February 1992, pp. 201–232.

The reasons for the higher rates of African-American unemployment are difficult to sort out, but one factor is that African-Americans are more heavily represented in lower-skilled occupations. Recall from our prior discussion that such occupations have high rates of frictional and structural unemployment. Also, African-Americans live disproportionately in declining inner cities, where the demand for labor is often insufficient to employ all those seeking work. Finally, discrimination undoubtedly plays an important role in explaining the African-American to white unemployment rate gap. Only 20-40 percent of the unemployment rate differential between African-American and white men can be explained by observable characteristics such as education and job experience.[17]

A fourth generalization from the disaggregated unemployment data is that female unemployment rates are very similar to those of males. This has occurred over the past decade as females have moved into positions that are career-oriented and characterized by lower unemployment rates. We see in Table 18.1 that in 2018 the overall unemployment rate was 3.6 for males and 3.5 for females. In 2010, the female unemployment rate actually was lower than that for males. This is explained by the impact of the recession on unemployment rates in such specific industries as wood products, autos, construction, and steel, which have high male-female employment ratios.

A final generalization concerning the disaggregated data illustrated in Table 18.1 is that the number of people unemployed for long periods—say 15 weeks or more—as a percentage of the labor force is much less than the overall unemployment rate but rises during recessions. The unemployment rate for people without work for 15 weeks or longer was only 1.4 percent in 2018, compared to the overall rate of 2.9 percent. But this rate was 5.7 percent in 2010, indicating that recessions tend to create longer periods of idleness of labor resources and much more social hardship than does the unemployment we associate with the natural rate of unemployment.

18.2 *Quick Review*

- Structural unemployment results from the mismatch between the skills required for available job openings and the skills possessed by those seeking work; it also results from a geographical mismatch between jobs and job seekers.

- Many displaced workers—those who lose their jobs because of permanent plant closings or job cutbacks—become structurally unemployed.

- Demand-deficient unemployment (also called cyclic unemployment) results from declines in aggregate demand and thus is associated with recessions and depressions.

- Unemployment rates vary by race, age, and occupation; specifically, African–Americans, youth, and lower-skilled workers have disproportionately high unemployment rates.

Your Turn

True or false? The unemployment rate of women typically has been twice that of men in recent years. (*Answer:* See page 543.)

---

[17] See Leslie S. Stratton, "Racial Differences in Men's Unemployment," *Industrial and Labor Relations Review,* April 1993, pp. 451–463.

REDUCING UNEMPLOYMENT: PUBLIC POLICIES

The U.S. government is officially committed to the goal of full employment. The Employment Act of 1946 proclaimed among other things that "it is the continuing policy of the Federal Government to use all practical means consistent with its needs and obligations and other essential considerations of national policy . . . to promote maximum employment, production, and purchasing power."[18] The Full Employment and Balanced Growth Act of 1978 reaffirmed this goal and required that government (a) establish five-year employment and inflation goals and (b) formulate programs to achieve them.

Table 18.2 deserves careful examination because it summarizes the wide variety of government programs that in full or in part are designed to reduce frictional, structural, and cyclic unemployment. Analysis of each of these approaches is impossible in a single chapter; therefore, we will confine our attention in the remainder of this chapter to a single topic: stabilization (fiscal and monetary) policy.

Fiscal and Monetary Policy

As defined in Table 18.2, *fiscal policy* is the deliberate manipulation of expenditures and taxes by the federal government for purposes of promoting full employment, price stability, and economic growth. Alternatively, *monetary policy* consists of the deliberate actions taken by the Federal Reserve authorities to adjust the nation's money supply and interest rates to promote these same goals.

The impact of expansionary fiscal and monetary policy on domestic output and unemployment is shown in Figure 18.7. Suppose initially that aggregate demand has fallen from D_1 to D, reducing real output to Q_0 (graph a). This decline in aggregate demand is accompanied by a decline in the demand for labor from D_{L1} to D_L (graph b). For the moment, suppose that labor supply is shown by curve S_L. Because the nominal wage is assumed to be inflexible downward at W_0, the decline in the demand for labor to D_L produces demand-deficient unemployment of ab. If the full-employment level of output in graph (a) is Q_n and the natural rate of employment in graph (b) is E_n, then E_0E_n represents cyclic unemployment.

Successful fiscal and monetary policy would increase aggregate demand to D_1, which would raise domestic output to its natural level Q_n and, as seen by the intersection of D_{L1} and S_L in graph (b), restore total employment to its natural level E_n.

The increase in aggregate demand to D_1 and the corresponding rise in labor demand to D_{L1} can be accomplished through some combination of (a) tax cuts for individuals to increase personal consumption spending, (b) expansion of the money supply to reduce interest rates and promote investment spending, (c) tax reductions or direct subsidies to firms to increase investment spending, and (d) increases in government expenditures.

TABLE 18.2 Government Policies and Programs to Reduce Unemployment*

Frictional Unemployment

Job information and matching: government programs that increase the availability of information concerning job vacancies and skills of those seeking work and help match job applicants and employers. Examples: U.S. Job Service (state employment agencies).

---

[18] The Employment Act of 1946. U.S. Government Publishing Office, 1946.

Structural Unemployment

1. *Educational subsidies:* government programs and expenditures that reduce the investment costs of obtaining human capital and thereby enhance people's ability to obtain jobs that are less likely to become obsolete as new technology emerges. Examples: Pell Grants and guaranteed student loans for college students; subsidies under the Vocational Educational Act; funding of primary and secondary schools, community colleges, and state universities.

2. *Equal employment opportunity laws:* laws making it illegal to discriminate in hiring and promotion on the basis of race or gender, thus removing an institutional barrier that creates structural unemployment. Examples: Title VII of the Civil Rights Act of 1964; Executive Order 11246.

3. *Job training and retraining:* programs designed to provide skills and work experience for those structurally unemployed. Examples: Manpower Development and Training Act (MDTA), occupational training at skill centers; MDTA on-the-job training programs; Job Corps; Comprehensive Employment and Training Act (CETA) programs aimed at youth, Native Americans, and displaced homemakers; Job Training Partnership Act; Trade Adjustment Assistance.

4. *Public service employment:* direct government hiring and on-the-job training of the long-term structurally unemployed. Examples: CETA, Title II as amended in 1978.

5. *Directed wage subsidies or employment tax credits:* direct payments or tax credits to firms that hire members of specific disadvantaged groups that experience high rates of structural unemployment. Examples: Targeted Employment Tax Credit program of 1979; AFDC–WIN program.

6. *Layoff warning:* requirement that firms anticipating plant closures or major layoffs provide advance notice, thus enabling workers to immediately search for new jobs or enroll in retraining programs. Example: Worker Adjustment and Retraining Notification Act of 1988.

Demand-Deficient Unemployment

1. *Fiscal policy:* deliberate manipulations of expenditures and taxes by government for the purposes of increasing aggregate demand and thereby increasing domestic output and employment. Examples: tax cuts in 1964, 1970, 1974, and 2001; and American Recovery and Reinvestment Act of 2009.

2. *Monetary policy:* deliberate actions taken by the Federal Reserve to increase the nation's supply of money to reduce interest rates and increase aggregate demand for products and services. Examples: monetary expansions in 1982, 1991–1993, 2001, and 2008–2014.

3. *Supply-side policies:* deliberate actions taken by the government to increase labor supply, savings, and investment and to reduce the costs of goods and services so that the aggregate supply curve shifts rightward. Examples: Reagan administration 1981 tax cuts; Individual Retirement Accounts; deregulation; Bush 2001 tax cuts, Trump 2018 tax cuts.

4. *Public service employment:* direct government hiring of people unable to find jobs. Examples: Works Progress Administration in the 1930s; CETA; Title VII; Public Service Employment in the 1970s.

5. *Wage subsidies or employment tax credits:* direct payments or tax credits to firms that expand their employment. Example: New Jobs Tax Credit program of 1977.

*Not all of the programs cited as specific examples are currently operating; some examples are historical.

FIGURE 18.7   Fiscal and Monetary Policy to Reduce Unemployment

Expansionary fiscal and monetary policy that increases aggregate demand from D to D_1 in graph (a) increases real output from Q_0 to Q_n. In the labor market, the corresponding rise in labor demand from D_L to D_{L1} eliminates cyclic unemployment and raises employment to E_n. But if policymakers mistakenly increase aggregate demand to D_2, labor demand will rise to D_{L2}. Eventually labor suppliers will adjust their behavior to the higher expected price level, their labor supply will decline from S_L to S'_L, and unemployment will then move to its natural level E_n.

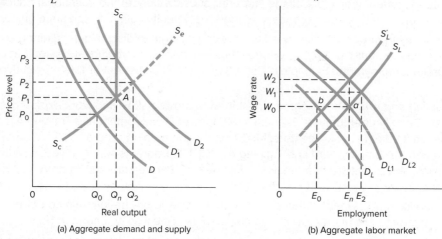

(a) Aggregate demand and supply

(b) Aggregate labor market

Complications

What appears simple in theory—shifting the aggregate demand curve rightward precisely to D_1—is difficult in reality. Timing is crucial, and several time lags make precise management of aggregate demand difficult. Once the administration has recognized that aggregate demand has declined, it must formulate a fiscal policy and submit it to Congress. Next Congress must hold hearings on the proposed policy and pass it as law. Once in place, the policy itself takes time to have full impact on the economy. During these lags, factors independent of the fiscal policy can shift the aggregate demand curve further inward or rightward. Thus, a specific dose of fiscal policy may turn out to be either inappropriately large or small.

Careful coordination of fiscal and monetary policy is needed to avoid another potential complication of stabilization policy: the *crowding-out effect*. This is a problem arising from the federal government's need to borrow funds from the money market to finance the deficits accompanying expansionary fiscal policy. Government borrowing may compete with private borrowing, increasing interest rates and reducing private investment spending. Thus, the stimulus of the fiscal policy may be weakened or canceled. To keep this crowding out from occurring, the monetary authorities need to increase the money supply by just enough to offset the deficit-caused rise in the equilibrium interest rate.

Another complication of stabilization policy is that government may overshoot its mark. Because this overshooting has happened in the past, it is worthwhile to examine the implications in aggregate product and labor markets. Let's suppose that expansionary fiscal and monetary policies shift the aggregate demand curve further to the right than expected, say to D_2 rather than D_1, thus causing a higher than expected price level (P_2 rather than P_1). In the short run, this unexpectedly high inflation temporarily may increase real output above its natural level; the economy may move upward along the broken-line segment of AS_e. In the long run, however, real output will return to its natural level Q_n. In the meantime, with aggregate demand at D_2, the price level will continue to rise to its equilibrium level at P_3.

We need to examine closely what is happening in the labor market to understand why real output temporarily rises to Q_2, only to eventually fall back to Q_n. The expansion of aggregate demand to D_2 (graph a) increases the demand for labor to D_{L2} (graph b). Employment temporarily rises above its natural level as firms, which have contracted for existing labor at W_0, expand their hiring. Also, job searchers, who now are being offered nominal wages at W_1, reduce their search time. To repeat: The reason for the rise in employment is that the actual rate of inflation has exceeded the expected rate, reducing frictional unemployment (recall our previous discussion of this topic). But once suppliers of labor recognize that the new price level is higher than previously expected, they readjust their behavior so that labor supply shifts from S_L to S_L'. Why is this so? The answer is that workers will no longer supply as much labor *at each nominal wage* now that the price level is P_2 rather than the expected level of P_1. The *real wage* (nominal wage/price level) associated with *each* nominal wage is now *lower*, and this fact translates into a leftward shift of the labor supply curve.

Observe from the intersection of D_{L2} and S_L' that the nominal wage, which *is* flexible upward, has increased to W_2. At this higher nominal wage, employment returns to its natural level E_n. This employment decline corresponds to the return of real output from Q_2 to Q_n in graph (a). Observe also that both the price level *and* the nominal wage are now higher. The inappropriately expansionary fiscal and monetary policy eliminated cyclic unemployment but also produced price and wage inflation.

Chapter Summary

1. A person is officially unemployed if she or he is 16 years of age or older, is not institutionalized, and is actively seeking work, waiting to be called back to a job after being laid off, or waiting to report to a new job within 30 days.

2. The official unemployment data have several limitations as measures of economic hardship and as guides to public policy. The stock–flow model sorts out causes of changes in the unemployment rate and provides information about the duration of employment spells for individuals.

3. An unemployment rate of about 4.0–5.0 percent represents a "full" or natural rate of unemployment. At this rate, neither an excess demand nor an excess supply of labor occurs, and the actual and expected rates of inflation are equal.

4. Frictional unemployment is a natural and often constructive occurrence in a dynamic economy characterized by heterogeneous workers and jobs, imperfect information, and continuous movements of people among the various categories of labor force status. It can take two basic forms: search unemployment, which is associated with the time required to find a job, and wait unemployment, where workers either wait to be recalled to former jobs or remain in job queues resulting from above-market-clearing wages.

5. Structural unemployment results from a mismatch between the skills needed for available jobs and the skills possessed by those seeking employment. Many of those structurally unemployed are displaced workers who lose their jobs because of permanent plant closings or job cutbacks.

6. Declines in the aggregate demand for goods and services cause a deficiency in the aggregate demand for labor. Wage rates tend to be inflexible downward for a variety of reasons, including the presence of unions, a bias toward layoffs by firms, implicit contracts, and insider–outsider relationships. As a result, involuntary demand-deficient unemployment arises when aggregate demand declines.

7. Unemployment is distributed unevenly in the labor force. For example, the unemployment rate for African–Americans is about twice that for whites.

8. Fiscal policy is a major tool used to combat demand-deficient unemployment, but it is fraught with several complications, including *(a)* time lags, *(b)* the need to coordinate fiscal and monetary policies to avoid the crowding-out effect, and *(c)* tendencies to create inflation.

Terms and Concepts

Household Survey (CPS)

employment–population ratio

unemployment rate

discouraged workers

subemployed

stock–flow model

full employment

equilibrium

natural rate of unemployment

aggregate demand

aggregate supply

frictional unemployment

search unemployment

wait unemployment

structural unemployment

displaced workers

demand-deficient (cyclic) unemployment

implicit contracts

insider–outsider theories

fiscal policy

monetary policy

crowding-out effect

Questions and Study Suggestions

1. Use the following data to calculate *(a)* the size of the labor force, *(b)* the official unemployment rate, and *(c)* the labor force participation rate (Chapter 3) for a hypothetical economy: population = 500; population 16 years or older and noninstitutionalized = 400; people employed full- or part-time = 200; people unemployed and actively seeking work = 20; people who have quit seeking work due to lack of success = 10; part-time workers seeking full-time jobs = 30.

2. What factors tend to *understate* the extent to which the official unemployment rate accurately measures the degree of economic hardship in the nation? What factors lead some observers to conclude that the official unemployment rate *overstates* economic hardship?

3. Use the basic model shown in Figure 18.5 to illustrate graphically each of the following: *(a)* demand-deficient unemployment and *(b)* temporary increases in output and employment beyond their natural, or full-employment, levels.

4. Define the term *structural unemployment* and distinguish it from frictional and demand-deficient unemployment. Why might structural unemployment fall when demand-deficient unemployment declines?

5. Suppose you are an economic adviser to the president, who has asked you to design a program to reduce the amount of unemployment associated with displaced workers. What major elements would your plan include?

6. Why are nominal wages inflexible downward? What is the implication of this characteristic for the ability of involuntary demand-deficient unemployment to persist for a considerable length of time?

7. Assume that the official national unemployment rate rises from 4 percent to 8 percent because of a major recession. What impact do you predict this would have on *(a)* the African–American to white unemployment rate ratio, *(b)* the labor force participation rate, and *(c)* the teenage–adult unemployment rate ratio? Explain.

8. Do you expect the natural rate of unemployment to *(a)* increase, *(b)* decrease, or *(c)* remain at the present level over the next decade? Explain your reasoning.

9. Examine critically this statement: "Unemployment in the United States can be resolved quickly and efficiently. The government should simply provide jobs for everyone who wants to work who cannot find suitable employment in the private sector."

Internet Exercise

The Unemployment Rate

Go to the Bureau of Labor Statistics website (**http://www.bls.gov**). Click on "Unemployment Rate." This will retrieve the latest Bureau of Labor Statistics news release regarding the labor force in the United States.

Use this news release to answer the following questions: What is the unemployment rate for the last two months? How many people were unemployed in each of the last two months? Did the unemployment rate change between the two months because of a change in the size of the labor force or a change in the number of unemployed people? Explain your answers.

Internet Links

The U.S. Department of Labor Unemployment Insurance website includes many details about the unemployment benefits program (**http://www.oui.doleta.gov/unemploy**).

The Bureau of Labor Statistics Local Unemployment Statistics website reports employment, unemployment, and labor force data for census regions and divisions, states, counties, metropolitan areas, and many cities (**http://www.bls.gov/lau/home.htm**).

Appendix

Information Sources in Labor Economics

The purpose of this appendix is to survey significant sources of information about labor economics. This information should prove useful to individuals preparing term papers in this or subsequent courses. In this regard, note the list of potential term paper topics in Appendix Table 1. Also, this appendix provides valuable information about how you might keep your personal and professional knowledge of labor economics current in the years ahead. If you are a business or economics major, we urge you to keep this book (or at least a copy of this appendix) in your personal library.

An overview of the appendix will point our way. First, we identify and briefly describe key Internet sites relating to labor economics and labor statistics. Then we annotate print sources of labor statistics. Third, we call your attention to various publications containing articles about labor economics and policy. There we annotate bibliographic indexes, professional journals, compendiums of essays, and nontechnical publications. Next several advanced textbooks in labor economics are briefly described. Finally, mention is made of textbooks that cover closely related fields such as labor law, collective bargaining, labor relations, and labor history.

SOURCES OF LABOR STATISTICS

Statistical sources can be classified as being either primary or secondary and as providing either time-series or cross-sectional data. A *primary statistical source* is an original source of data such as that generated from the U.S. Census Bureau's *Current Population Survey* (CPS) and reported by the U.S. Bureau of Labor Statistics (BLS). You may recall from Chapter 18 that this particular survey samples about 60,000 households nationwide each month to obtain information about labor force participation, employment, and unemployment. The CPS data are replicated or summarized in numerous *secondary statistical sources* such as handbooks of statistics, business periodicals, and textbooks. Secondary sources are normally reliable, but you should be aware that they usually present truncated versions of the data; therefore, you can often obtain more information by going to the primary source.

APPENDIX TABLE 1 A Selected List of Term Paper Topics

Worker Absenteeism

Multiple Job Holding (Moonlighting)

The Retirement Decision

Female Labor Force Participation Rates

Discouraged- versus Added-Worker Effects

Cyclic and Secular Changes in the Average Workweek

Racial Differences in Labor Force Participation

Educational Attainment and Earnings, Hours of Work, and Unemployment

Trends in Labor Force Participation of Older Males

The Economics of Student Loans

Criticisms of Human Capital Theory

The Economic Value of Life

The Firm's Investment in Human Capital: On-the-Job Training

Corporate Sponsorship of Education

The Economics of Pensions

CEO Pay

Effectiveness of Public Sector Training Programs

Monopsony in Labor Markets

The Market for Nurses

Occupational Licensing

Efficiency Wage Theories

Should Fringe Benefits Be Taxed?

The Decline of Unionism

Determinants of Union Membership

Deregulation and the Labor Market

Theories of Collective Bargaining

Collective Bargaining in

Professional Sports

The Economics of Seniority

Labor-Owned Enterprises

Incentive Pay Systems

Employee Stock Option Plans (ESOPs)

Compulsory Arbitration

Effects of Right-to-Work Laws

The Economics of Fringe Benefits

Pay, Performance, and Productivity

Unions and Job Turnover

Economic Impacts of Strikes

Trends in Government Employment

Public versus Private Pay

The Impact of Taxes on Labor Supply

The North American Free Trade Agreement and American Labor

Lifetime Employment in Japan

Unemployment and Underemployment in the Developing Countries

The Americans with Disabilities Act and the Labor Market

National Service Plans

Effects of the Minimum Wage

Labor Market Impacts of OSHA

Sexual Harassment in the Workplace

Earnings Disparities by Race

Trends in the Female–Male Earnings Ratio

Occupational Discrimination

Effectiveness of Antidiscrimination Laws

Compensating Wage Differentials

Firm Size and Pay Levels

The Earnings of "Superstars"

Family Background and Human Capital Investment in Children	Implicit Contracts: Theory and Implications
Trends in the Distribution of Earnings	Teenage Unemployment
Unions and the Distribution of Earnings	African–American Unemployment
Occupational Mobility	Wage Subsidies: The Earned Income Tax Credit
Earnings of Recent Immigrants	Rational Expectations and Labor Markets
Immigration Reform: Labor Market Issues	Profit Sharing
Plant Closures and Displaced Workers	Labor Market Effects of Unemployment Insurance Benefits
Are Internal Labor Markets Efficient?	International Differences in Unemployment Rates
Trends in Real Wage Rates	Alternative Work Arrangements: Compressed Work, Flextime, and Work Sharing
International Comparisons of Real Wages	
Productivity Growth and the New Economy	Occupational Employment Trends in the United States
International Trends in Productivity Growth	Trends in Manufacturing versus Service Employment
Trends in Self-Employment	Trends in the Natural Rate of Unemployment
What Is "Full" Employment?	
Theories of Job Search	Does Competition Reduce Discrimination?
Technological Unemployment	

Labor statistics are reported as time-series data, cross-sectional data, or some combination of the two. *Time-series data* are ordered chronologically; that is, by some period of time such as month or year. Examples are Figure 3.2, which graphs population and the labor force since 1950; Figure 11.4, which shows the number of work stoppages in the United States since 1960; and Figure 17.2, which chronicles the BLS's annual labor productivity index since 1960.

Cross-sectional data, on the other hand, are measurements of a particular variable at a specific time, but for different economic units or groups; for example, Table 13.2 reports occupational fatalities and injuries in 2017 *by industry.* Similarly, Table 8.3 presents data on the average hourly wages of private workers in manufacturing industries in 2018 *by selected state,* and Table 18.1 summarizes unemployment rates for specific years *by occupation, race, gender, age, and duration.*

What are the major (primary and secondary) sources of time-series and cross-sectional labor statistics? We will approach this topic by annotating each of the following: Internet sites, bibliographies of statistical sources, print sources of general U.S. statistics, print sources of statistics specific to labor economics, and data sets available from research institutes. Where possible, we paraphrase the descriptions supplied by the sources themselves.[1]

---

[1] Our organization in this section roughly follows that used by Charles Helppie, James Gibbons, and Donald Pearson, *Research Guide in Economics* (Morristown, NJ: General Learning Press, 1974), pp. 69–91.

Internet Sites

The Internet contains several excellent sources that provide information and statistics relating to labor economics. We list and annotate these sites in Appendix Table 2. We urge you to try out several of the sites listed in the table. (Some of these Internet sites contain full copies of the print sources described here.)

APPENDIX TABLE 2 Internet Sites Relating to Labor Economics

Bureau of Economic Analysis
[http://www.bea.gov]

Provides data on GDP and selected tables in the *Survey of Current Business.*

Bureau of Labor Statistics
[http://www.bls.gov]

Includes detailed data on employment, unemployment, prices, productivity, and foreign labor statistics.

Economic Journals on the Web
[http://www.oswego.edu/~economic/journals.htm]

Provides an index to Web locations of numerous economics journals.

Economic Report of the President
[http://www.gpo.gov/erp]

The entire reports for years 1996 and beyond are online. This site also includes statistical tables summarizing important economic data series.

FRED
[https://fred.stlouisfed.org/]

This St Louis Federal Reserve Bank website supplies easy to access economic data from many sources.

Health and Retirement Survey (HRS)
[http://hrsonline.isr.umich.edu/]

Provides survey data on the economic, demographic, and health characteristics of individuals.

Department of Homeland Security
[http://www.dhs.gov/immigration-statistics]

Provides comprehensive annual immigration statistics for recent years.

International Labour Organization
[http://www.ilo.org]

The ILO provides data, for more than 230 countries, on over 100 measures.

Minnesota Population Center
[http://www.ipums.umn.edu]

Contains Census data from 1850 to 2010 as well as Current Population Survey data until the present.

National Labor Relations Board
[http://www.nlrb.gov/]

Contains information about the NLRB and its decisions relating to alleged unfair labor practices of firms and unions.

Organization for Economic Cooperation and Development
[http://www.oecd.org]

Includes data on selected economic measures for OECD countries.

Panel Study of Income Dynamics
[http://psidonline.isr.umich.edu/]

Consists of longitudinal data on the characteristics and labor market behavior of the survey respondents.

Resources for Economists on the Internet
[http://www.aeaweb.org/rfe]

Provides links to more than 700 economics-related Internet sites.

Social Security Administration
[http://www.ssa.gov]

Provides statistical information on Social Security programs (benefit formulas, number of beneficiaries, trust funds, average benefits, etc.).

W. E. Upjohn Institute
[http://www.upjohninst.org]

Provides an online catalog of publications as well as working papers.

U.S. Census Bureau
[http://www.census.gov]

Comprehensive site with extensive data on topics such as population,

earnings, and demographic characteristics. It also provides all Census Bureau Publications data since January 1996. Finally, it includes links to data extraction from sources such as the Current Population Survey (CPS), American Housing Survey (AHS), and Public Use of Microdata Samples (PUMS) of the census.

Bibliographies of Statistical Sources

Bibliographies of statistical publications index sources of statistical series by topical heading, much as the familiar *Reader's Guide to Periodical Literature* lists magazine articles. Just as the *Reader's Guide* contains no articles itself, bibliographies of statistical sources contain no statistical series themselves. These bibliographies or indexes complement the Internet as a good place to begin a search for statistical series. For labor economics, you might fruitfully seek listings under such topics as unions, employment, labor, and productivity. Of the several bibliographic guides, the following are particularly useful:

American Statistics Index (Washington, DC: Congressional Information Service). Annual with monthly supplements.

This index provides the most comprehensive print access to U.S. government statistical publications available. It indexes and abstracts all of the statistical publications issued by federal agencies and therefore provides a starting point in searching for specific statistical series.

U.S. Bureau of the Census: *Directory of Federal Statistics for Local Areas: A Guide to Sources* (Washington, DC: U.S. Government Printing Office).

This directory lists sources of federal statistics for metropolitan statistical areas (MSAs). An MSA is a geographic area containing either (*a*) one city having 50,000 or more inhabitants or (*b*) an urbanized area of at least 50,000 people *and* a total MSA population of at least 100,000.

General Summary Statistics

Several excellent volumes contain summaries of statistical series on a full range of political, economic, social, and demographic variables. These "data books," "statistical abstracts," or "statistical handbooks" contain numerous tables of interest to students of labor economics. A few of the more significant works are the following:

U.S. Bureau of the Census: *Historical Statistics of the United States, Colonial Times to 1970* (Washington, DC: U.S. Government Printing Office). Issued 1976.

This book contains more than 12,500 statistical time series, largely annual, on American social, economic, political, and geographic developments covering periods from 1610 to 1970.

U.S. Office of the President: *Economic Report of the President* (Washington, DC: U.S. Government Printing Office). Annual.

This annual report has an extensive appendix containing statistical data relating to income, the labor force, employment, and production. A section of the appendix that is particularly useful to labor economists is "Population, Employment, Wages, and Productivity." Furthermore, the text of the report usually contains sections or chapters pertaining to recent labor market developments. For example, the 2007 report contains an entire chapter on the recent growth in labor productivity.

Labor-Specific Statistical Sources

Considerable overlap of tables occurs in the various statistical sources. For example, the *Statistical Abstract of the United States* contains many labor-related series also found in the more specialized sources that we are about to annotate. But in general, labor-specific sources contain a wider range of data and statistical series that relate directly to labor economics. Awareness of these specialized sources is therefore critical for finding data that may not be presented elsewhere. Let's examine several excellent publications:

Eva E. Jacobs (ed.): *Handbook of U.S. Labor Statistics* (Lanham, MD: Bernan Press). Periodic.

This publication presents the major series of statistics generated annually by the Bureau of Labor Statistics. The most recent edition (2019) contained tables grouped into the following categories: (*a*) population, labor force, and employment status; (*b*) employment, hours, and earnings; (*c*) occupational employment and wages; (*d*) labor force and employment projections by industry and occupation; (*e*) productivity and costs; (*f*) compensation of employees; (*g*) recent trends in the labor market; (*h*) labor–management relations; (*i*) prices; (*j*) foreign labor force statistics; (*k*) consumer expenditures; (*l*) American Time Use Survey; (*m*) income in the United States; and (*n*) occupational safety and health.

Barry T. Hirsch and David A. Macpherson: *Union Membership and Earnings Data Book: Compilations from the Current Population Survey (2019 Edition)* (Washington, DC: Bureau of National Affairs). Annual.

This annual report presents current and historical data on union membership as well as earnings for union and nonunion workers. Breakdowns of these and related measures are provided by state, industry, occupation, and demographic group.

Directory of U.S. Labor Organizations (Washington, DC: Bureau of National Affairs, Inc.). Periodic.

In addition to providing aggregate union membership data for American labor, this publication presents detailed statistics concerning the membership of individual unions and the demographic, occupational, industrial, and geographic characteristics of union members.

U.S. Department of Labor, Bureau of Labor Statistics: *Monthly Labor Review* (Washington, DC: U.S. Government Printing Office). Monthly.

This periodical is a source of current statistics on labor force participation, productivity, employment, unemployment, and consumer prices. An appendix reports the results of the (*a*) Current Population Survey, (*b*) Establishment Payroll Survey, and (*c*) Consumer Price Survey, all of which are conducted monthly.

U.S. Department of Labor, Bureau of Labor Statistics: *Employment and Earnings* (Washington, DC: U.S. Government Printing Office). Monthly.

Employment and Earnings is a monthly publication that provides current information about employment status, characteristics of the employed and unemployed, hours and earnings, productivity, and state and area labor force data. It is worth noting that in 1985 this publication introduced a valuable series—reported in January issues—showing union membership by age, race, gender, occupation, and industry.

U.S. Department of Labor, Bureau of Labor Statistics: *Compensation and Working Conditions* (Washington, DC: U.S. Government Printing Office). Monthly.

This publication, previously titled *Current Wage Developments,* includes data and brief articles on the total compensation package and other aspects of the work environment, such as major collective bargaining settlements, employer costs for employee compensation, union membership, employee benefits, and area wages.

U.S. Department of Commerce, Bureau of the Census: *Money Income of Households, Families, and Persons in the United States* (Current Population Report P–60). Annual.

This publication, found in libraries that are depositories for federal government publications, reports detailed statistics on the functional and personal distribution of income in the United States. The tables summarize data from the Census Bureau's annual *Current Population Survey.*

International Labour Office: *Yearbook of Labour Statistics* (Geneva, Switzerland: ILO Publications). Annual.

This international yearbook contains time series of labor-related data classified by 190 countries or territories.

Research Institute Survey Data

Several sets of primary data from surveys conducted by research institutes are available to scholars wishing to do original research. Three such sources are the following:

Survey Research Center, Institute for Social Research, University of Michigan: *Health and Retirement Survey.*

This survey, conducted biannually, provides information about aspects of work such as working conditions and earnings for people who were age 51–62 in 1992.

Survey Research Center, Institute for Social Research, University of Michigan: *Panel Study on Income Dynamics (PSID).*

This survey provides information about employment, earnings, unemployment, fringe benefits, and so forth. Nearly 5,000 families were first surveyed in 1968 and were interviewed annually each year thereafter. When family members leave home and set up new families, the latter also become part of the annual surveys.

U.S. Department of Labor, Employment and Training Administration: *National Longitudinal Survey (NLS).* Conducted by the Center for Human Resource Research, Ohio State University.

The *NLS* collects information from the same group of people periodically over an extended time. It provides information about union status, wages, fringe benefits, job separations, and job satisfaction. The availability of extensive personal information allows researchers to control for such factors as education, age, and parents' income.

Updating and Augmenting Tables

Most of the statistical tables found in *Contemporary Labor Economics* are drawn from the general abstracts or labor-specific statistical sources just discussed. These tables can be updated by noting the source cited for each and then finding the most recent edition of that particular publication. Normally, series found in earlier editions are included somewhere within the new ones. Alternatively, you can update many of these tables via the Internet.

For such purposes as writing term papers, tables in the text may not be sufficiently detailed to meet your needs. But keep in mind that the source cited in the table likely contains many more data than those summarized in the table; for example, Table 8.2 provides statistics of wages by industry for 2018. By referring to the source, *Union Membership and Earnings Data Book: Compilations from the Current Population Survey,* you would discover a wealth of information about unions and earnings, such as (*a*) average union and nonunion wages and (*b*) rates of unionization by industry. Furthermore, you would discover there that a *primary* source of unionization and earnings information is the *Current Population Survey.*

APPLICATIONS, NEW THEORIES, EMERGING EVIDENCE

Our attention now turns to sources in which new developments in labor economics are reported. We will annotate numerous professional journals, compendiums of essays, and nontechnical publications in the discussion that follows. But first let's highlight works that provide indexes or bibliographies of labor-related publications.

Indexes and Bibliographies

Several publications help direct interested people toward specific books and journal articles that treat labor economics. Two useful sources are the following:

American Economic Association: *Index of Economic Articles* (Homewood, IL: Richard D. Irwin). Updated via new volumes.

This series contains bibliographic citations to articles from over 250 economics journals, with each volume covering a particular period. For example, Volume I covers the 1886–1924 period while Volume XIX indexes articles published in 1977. This index is not current, however, and thus those interested in recently published articles should consult the source that follows.

American Economic Association: *Journal of Economic Literature (JEL).* Quarterly.

This publication contains (*a*) review articles of research on particular topics, (*b*) reviews of selected books, (*c*) an annotated listing of new books in economics, and (*d*) the *Journal of Economic Literature classification system.* The "J" listing in the classification system, shown in Appendix Table 3, defines subtopics in labor and demographic economics.

APPENDIX TABLE 3 *Journal of Economic Literature* Classification System: "J" Listings

J Labor and Demographic Economics

J00 General

J1 Demographic Economics

J10 General	J14 Economics of the Elderly
J11 Demographic Trends and Forecasts	J15 Economics of Minorities and Races
J12 Marriage; Marital Dissolution; Family Structure	J16 Economics of Gender
	J17 Value of Life; Forgone Income
J13 Fertility; Family Planning; Child Care; Children; Youth	J18 Public Policy
	J19 Other

J2 Time Allocation, Work Behavior, and Employment Determination and Creation

J20 General*

J21 Labor Force and Employment, Size, and Structure

J22 Time Allocation and Labor Supply

J23 Employment Determination; Job Creation; Demand for Labor; Self-Employment

J24 Human Capital; Skills;

Occupational Choice; Labor Productivity

J26 Retirement; Retirement Policies

J28 Safety; Accidents; Industrial Health; Job Satisfaction; Related Public Policy

J29 Other

J3 Wages, Compensation, and Labor Costs

J30 General

J31 Wage Level and Structure: Wage Differentials by Skill, Training, Occupation, etc.

J32 Nonwage Labor Costs and Benefits; Private Pensions

J33 Compensation Packages; Payment Methods

J38 Public Policy

J39 Other

J4 Particular Labor Markets

J40 General

J41 Contracts: Specific Human Capital, Matching Models, Efficiency Wage Models, and Internal Labor Markets

J42 Monopsony; Segmented Labor Markets

J43 Agricultural Labor Markets

J44 Professional Labor Markets and Occupations

J45 Public Sector Labor Markets

J48 Public Policy

J49 Other

J5 Labor–Management Relations, Trade Unions, and Collective Bargaining

J50 General

J51 Trade Unions: Objectives, Structure, and Effects

J52 Dispute Resolution: Strikes, Arbitration; and Mediation

J53 Labor–Management Relations;

Industrial Jurisprudence

J54 Producer Cooperatives; Labor-Managed Firms

J58 Public Policy

J59 Other

J6 Mobility, Unemployment, and Vacancies

J60 General

J61 Geographic Labor Mobility;

Immigrant Workers

J62 Occupational and

Intergenerational Mobility

J63 Turnover; Vacancies; Layoffs

J64 Unemployment: Models, Duration, Incidence, and Job Search

J7 Discrimination

J70 General

J71 Discrimination

J8 Labor Standards: National and International

J80 General

J81 Working Conditions

J82 Labor Force Composition

J65 Unemployment Insurance; Severance Pay; Plant Closings

J68 Public Policy

J69 Other

J78 Public Policy

J79 Other

J83 Workers' Rights

J88 Public Policy

J89 Other

Professional Journals

Scholarly journals contain articles in which economists report new theories, new evidence, new techniques for testing established theories, and the like. The main audiences for these articles are other specialists in economics; therefore, most undergraduates will find the mathematical models and econometric techniques employed to be formidable. However, the basic conclusions of the articles can be gleaned through careful reading.

Articles about labor economics are found in *general* economics journals and labor-specific journals. Examples of the former include *The American Economic Review, Journal of Political Economy, Review of Economics and Statistics, Quarterly Journal of Economics, Brookings Papers on Economic Activity, Economic Inquiry, Journal of Economic Issues, Southern Economic Journal, Canadian Journal of Economics,* and *Oxford Economic Papers.*[2]

The following are important *labor-specific* journals:

New York State School of Industrial and Labor Relations, Cornell University: *Industrial and Labor Relations Review.* Quarterly.

For example, the May 2019 issue presented research on pensions, labor standards, worker cooperatives, employment law, employee well-being, unions, workers safety, and employee motivation.

University of Chicago: *Journal of Labor Economics.* Quarterly.

This journal publishes theoretical and applied research on the supply and demand for labor services, compensation, labor markets, the distribution of earnings, labor demographics, unions and collective bargaining, and policy issues in labor economics.

Basil Blackwell: *Industrial Relations.* Triannual.

---

[2] For a listing of 130 economics journals, see David N. Laband and Michael J. Piette, "The Relative Impacts of Economics Journals," *Journal of Economic Literature,* June 1994, pp. 640–666.

This cross-disciplinary international journal is a publication of the Institute of Industrial Relations, University of California at Berkeley. It contains papers and original articles, as well as research notes and "current topic" articles, on the employment relationship.

University of Wisconsin: *Journal of Human Resources.* Quarterly.

This excellent journal publishes articles about the role of education and training in enhancing production skills, employment opportunities, and income, as well as human resource development, health, and welfare policies as they relate to the labor market.

International Labour Office, Geneva, Switzerland: *International Labour Review.* Monthly.

This journal contains articles, comparative studies, and research reports about such topics as employment and unemployment, wages and conditions of work, industrial relations, and workers' participation. Authors are international scholars.

George Mason University: *Journal of Labor Research.* Quarterly.

Articles about labor unions, labor economics, labor relations, and related topics appear in this quarterly. Interdisciplinary studies are common, and many papers have a public policy orientation. Occasionally it includes papers from symposia, conferences, and seminars sponsored by the journal.

North-Holland: *Labour Economics: An International Journal.* Quarterly.

This new international journal publishes research in micro and macro labor economics in a balanced mix of theory, empirical testing, and policy applications. Of particular interest are articles that explain the origin of institutional arrangements of national labor markets and the impacts of these institutions on labor market outcomes.

Basil Blackwell: *British Journal of Industrial Relations.* Triannual.

Articles on labor economics, labor relations, and collective bargaining are published in this British journal. For example, a typical issue contained articles titled "Collective Bargaining and the Evolution of Wage Inequality in Italy"; "Long-Run Patterns of Labour Market Polarization: Evidence from German Micro Data"; "Gender Pay Gap, Voluntary Interventions and Recession: The Case of the British Financial Services Sector"; "Shades of Authoritarianism and State–Labour Relations in China"; and "A Tale of Two Deltas: Labour Politics in Jiangsu and Guangdong."

New York University: *Labor History.* Quarterly.

This journal is concerned with research in labor history, the impact of labor problems on ethnic and minority groups, theories of the labor movement, comparative analysis of foreign labor movements, studies of specific unions, and biographical portraits of important labor leaders.

Industrial Relations Research Association: *Proceedings of the Industrial Relations Research Association.* Annual.

These proceedings consist of addresses by distinguished labor experts, contributed papers, and invited papers on topics of interest to industrial and labor relations specialists and practitioners.

Commerce Clearing House: *Labor Law Journal.* Monthly.

This journal contains a survey of important legislative, administrative, and judicial developments in labor law. Articles about subjects pertaining to legal problems in the labor relations field are featured.

Our annotated listing of labor-specific journals is far from exhaustive. Other English-language journals that relate to labor include *Labor Studies Journal, Human Resource Planning, Economic and Industrial Democracy, Women at Work, Journal of Collective Negotiations in the Public Sector, International Journal of Manpower, Journal of Productivity Analysis, Government Union Review, Labour and Society, Japan Labor Bulletin, Journal of Industrial Relations, Work and Occupations,* and *Journal of Population Economics.*

Compendiums of Essays

Several organizations and publishers regularly release edited books that contain papers or chapters on current aspects of labor economics. Three examples follow:

> *Research in Labor Economics* (Bingley, United Kingdom: Emerald). Annual. Solomon Polachek and Konstantinos Tatsiramos, series co-editors.

> Contributions to this series consist of original papers that are longer than normal journal articles but shorter than traditional monographs. The series began in 1977. Contributors include many prominent researchers in labor economics.

> Labor and Employment Relations Association Series. Annual.

> The Labor and Employment Relations Association (LERA) annually publishes a book made up of papers on a specific topic. Examples include *The Gloves Off Economy: Workplace Standards at the Bottom of America's Labor Market,* edited by Howard R. Stanger, Paul F. Clark, and Ann C. Frost; *Disunited States of America: Employment Relations Systems in Conflict,* edited by David Jacobs and Peggy Kahn; and *Inequality, Uncertainty, and Opportunity: The Varied and Growing Role of Finance in Labor Relations,* edited by Christian E. Weller.

> Kluwer Law: *Proceedings of New York University Conference on Labor.* Annual. Samuel Estreicher, editor.

> This annual publication, which began in 1948, stresses collective bargaining and the labor relations field. Thus, recent volumes contain chapters about developments in labor law, arbitration, worker absenteeism and incompetence, age and gender discrimination, public sector bargaining, comparable worth, two-tier wage systems, and so forth.

Nontechnical Publications

Although articles in professional journals are useful, their specialized language and esoteric statistical techniques often diminish their accessibility to undergraduate students. Sometimes of greater usefulness are nontechnical books, journals, magazines, and even newspapers that report and summarize recent theory and research.

1 *Nontechnical Books*

Many important books in labor economics are directed to wide audiences, not just labor specialists. Some publishing houses specialize in publishing analytic books that are accessible to nonspecialists. The W. E. Upjohn Institute of Employment Research (Kalamazoo, MI), in particular, is noted for books about timely employment topics. Recent examples are H. Allan Hunt and Marcus Dillender, *Workers' Compensation: Analysis for Its Second Century*; Stephen A. Wandner, Editor, *Unemployment Insurance Reform: Fixing a Broken System*; and Susan Pozo, Editor, T*he Human and Economic Implications of Twenty First Century Immigration Policy.* Also, the Brookings Institution occasionally publishes books of interest to students of labor economics. An example is Darrell M. West *The Future of Work: Robots, AI, and Automation.*

2 *Hearings Testimony*

Testimony before congressional committees is a valuable source of information about important research in labor economics. These volumes, published by the U. S. Government Printing Office, are located in libraries that are depositories of federal government publications. Although numerous committees hold hearings on legislation relating to labor, two of the more relevant ones are the Senate Human Resources Committee and the House Education and Labor Committee (and subcommittees of each).

3 *Nontechnical Journals*

A few nontechnical journals are also of interest to students of labor economics. The *Monthly Labor Review* mentioned earlier is of particular importance in this regard. It contains informative and readable articles about such topics as labor markets, wages and earnings, fringe benefits, mobility, unionism, and collective bargaining. Also, the AFL–CIO *Federationist* is a good source of information about organized labor's position on policy issues. Third, the May issue of the *American Economic Review* (previously cited) contains papers delivered at the annual meeting of the American Economics Association. Usually, one or two sessions of the conference pertain to labor economics; and because presenters are instructed to keep their papers noneconometric, these discussions usually are accessible to undergraduates. Finally, two journals that contain articles about current economic policy issues are worth checking for discussions of labor topics: *Contemporary Economic Policy* and *Journal of Economic Perspectives.*

4 *Magazines and Newspapers*

The economics or labor sections of popular magazines such as *BusinessWeek, Newsweek, Time,* and *U.S. News and World Report* occasionally contain stories about current labor economics issues. By mentioning economists who have done research on a particular topic, these articles serve as helpful starting points for identifying academic sources. This is also true of newspaper articles, particularly those found in financial papers such as *The Wall Street Journal.* Listed next are a nontechnical magazine devoted exclusively to economics and two important indexes through which one can identify specific nontechnical magazine and newspaper articles:

> *Challenge: A Magazine of Economic Affairs.* Six issues yearly.
>
> Among other things, *Challenge* contains invited articles about economic policy issues, interviews with leading economists, and a comment section called "The Growlery." It is not uncommon for an issue to contain one or two articles pertinent to labor economics. The articles are written by economics experts but are directed toward all people interested in the topics, not just specialists in the field.
>
> *Reader's Guide to Periodical Literature,* 1900–present.
>
> This familiar reference source provides a cumulative topic index for articles in over 230 U.S. nontechnical, general, and popular magazines.
>
> *The Wall Street Journal Index.*
>
> *The Wall Street Journal* articles are listed by topic and corporation in this index.

TEXTBOOKS AND RESEARCH SURVEYS

There are several advanced textbooks in the "new" labor economics and numerous undergraduate texts in closely related fields. The former strengthen one's *depth* of understanding of labor economics, whereas the latter add *breadth* beyond the topics included in this textbook.

Advanced Texts and Surveys

Advanced textbooks presume more knowledge of mathematics, econometrics, and economic theory than this text. Nevertheless, the diligent reader whose preparation in those areas is modest can gain much from them. The following books are particularly useful in this regard:

Solomon W. Polachek and W. Stanley Seibert: *The Economics of Earnings* (Cambridge, UK: Cambridge University Press, 1993).

This book covers many of the topics in *Contemporary Labor Economics* but treats them with considerably greater analytic rigor. The topics covered include discrimination, training, minimum wage laws, unionism, human capital, and health and safety regulations.

Robert F. Elliott: *Labor Economics: A Comparative Text* (London: McGraw-Hill, 1991).

Using extensive graphical analysis and some calculus, this British publication treats the economics of labor markets at a slightly higher level than traditional American undergraduate texts. It also contains many tables comparing labor market data among the industrialized nations.

Pierre Cahuc, Stéphane Carcillo, and André Zylberberg: *Labor Economics,* 2nd edition (Cambridge, MA: MIT Press, 2014).

This advanced textbook assumes that readers have substantial training in microeconomics and are familiar with quantitative research techniques. The text discusses topics related to labor supply and demand, wage determination, unemployment, inequality, and labor market policies.

Orley Ashenfelter and Richard Layard (eds.); and Orley Ashenfelter and David Card (eds.): *Handbook of Labor Economics,* 4 vols. (Amsterdam: North-Holland, 1986, 1999, 2011).

The 73 chapters of this four-volume advanced survey of labor economics are written by prominent labor economists. In volume 1, the supply of labor, the demand for labor, and the wage structure are examined. Volume 2 looks at labor market equilibrium and friction and discusses institutional structures of labor markets. Volume 3 examines topics related to labor supply, labor demand, emerging labor markets, labor markets and the macroeconomy, and government policy. Volume 4 examines new research methods and specific labor markets, including those defined by age, race, and gender.

Alison L. Booth: *The Economics of the Trade Union* (Cambridge, England: Cambridge University Press, 1995).

This book surveys, synthesizes, and critically analyzes theoretical and econometric work on the economic effects of unions in the United States and Great Britain.

Texts in Related Fields

High-quality textbooks abound for courses of study related to labor economics. One good way to discover them is to browse in your college bookstore for textbooks required for courses in such fields as collective bargaining, labor law, labor history, labor relations, human resource economics, and social insurance. Appendix Table 4 lists several such books by topic. Numerous other texts are available in each of these subject areas and can be identified by visiting a professor who specializes in the particular field. These textbooks typically are revised on three- to five-year cycles.

APPENDIX TABLE 4 Representative Textbooks in Subjects Related to Contemporary Labor Economics

Labor Relations

J. W. Budd, *Labor Relations: Striking a Balance,* 5th Edition (New York: McGraw-Hill, 2018).

Human Resource Management

W. Cascio. *Managing Human Resources,* 11th Edition (McGraw-Hill, 2019).

E. P. Lazear and M. Gibbs, *Personnel Economics in Practice,* 3rd Edition (Hoboken, NJ: Wiley, 2014).

Labor Law

P. J. Cihon and J. O. Castagnera, *Employment and Labor Law,* 9th Edition (Cengage, 2017).

J. F. Beatty, S. S. Samuelson, and P. S. Abril, *Essentials of Business Law,* 6th Edition (Cengage, 2019).

Social Insurance

G. E. Rejda: *Social Insurance and Economic Security,* 6th Edition (Prentice-Hall, 1999).

Labor History

F. R. Dulles and M. Dubofsky: *Labor in America,* 6th Edition (Harlan Davidson, 1999).

Glossary

A

ability problem   The tendency to overestimate rates of return to education if those with more ability tend to obtain more schooling. Earnings differences may reflect differences in ability rather than in education.

absence rate   The ratio of full-time workers with absences from work in a typical week to total full employment. It is usually expressed as a percentage.

absolute frequency distribution   A graphic portrayal (histogram) of the earnings distribution. The horizontal axis shows the various earnings classes, while the heights of the bars indicate the actual numbers of earnings recipients who have earnings in the particular class. *Compare with* relative frequency distribution.

acceptance wage   The lowest wage required to induce an individual to accept an employment offer.

accident model   A model of strikes that assumes they are the result of accidents or errors in the negotiating process.

actual labor force   Those who are either employed or unemployed but actively seeking work.

actual subsidy payment   The subsidy received by a participant in an income maintenance plan. It is calculated by multiplying the benefit reduction rate times the person's earned income and subtracting the product from the plan's basic benefit.

adaptive expectations theory   Theory that assumes individuals form their expectations about the future based on the recent past.

added-worker effect   The change in the labor force that results from other family members entering the labor force when the primary worker loses his or her job.

administered price   A price or wage rate that is established institutionally rather than through the market forces of supply and demand.

affirmative action programs   Policies that establish targets of employment for women and minorities and a timetable for meeting them.

American Federation of Labor and Congress of Industrial Organizations (AFL–CIO)   The American Federation of Labor and Congress of Industrial Organizations. It is the largest U.S. federation of autonomous national unions.

age–earnings profile   A graph showing the earnings levels of a specific worker or group of workers at various ages over the life span.

agents   Parties who are hired to help advance the objectives of others. *Compare with* principals.

aggregate demand curve   The curve indicating the total quantity of goods and services that consumers, businesses, government, and foreigners are willing and able to purchase at each price level.

aggregate supply curve   The curve indicating the total real output that producers are willing and able to provide at each price level.

asymmetric information   One party in the bargaining process has more information than the other.

average product (AP)   Output per unit of labor. It is found by dividing total product by the number of labor units or may be measured as the slope of a straight line drawn from the origin to a particular point on the total product curve.

average wage cost   The firm's total wage cost divided by the number of units of labor employed. If all workers are paid the same, it is simply the wage rate.

B

backward-bending labor supply curve   The hours of work supplied as a function of the wage, where the substitution effect dominates at relatively low wages and the income effect dominates at high wages. In the latter region, the supply curve will be negatively sloped.

bargaining power   A measure of the ability of one side to secure, on its own terms, its opponent's agreement to a labor contract.

bargaining structure   The scope of the employees and employers covered by a collective bargaining agreement; the structure determines who bargains with whom.

basic benefit   The amount of subsidy a household receives from an income maintenance plan if it has no earned income.

beaten paths   Migration routes of previous job changers. The information provided by these movers typically reduces the costs of migration and explains why various racial and ethnic groups may cluster in a given area.

Becker's model of the allocation of time   This model assumes households are economic units deciding how best to allocate their time among work, household production, and household consumption to obtain utility-yielding commodities.

benefit reduction rate   The rate at which the household's basic income maintenance benefit is reduced as earned income increases.

blacklist   A directory of individuals known to be union members or sympathizers. Individuals on the list were often denied employment.

bonus   Payment in addition to the annual salary based on some factor such as personal, team, or firm performance.

break-even income   The level of income at which the household's subsidy from an income maintenance plan is reduced to zero. It is calculated by dividing the basic benefit by the benefit reduction rate.

budget constraint   A line plotted on a graph that shows all the combinations of market goods (real income) and leisure that the consumer can obtain at any given wage rate.

Bureau of Labor Statistics productivity index   The measure of productivity reported by the Bureau of Labor Statistics. It is found by dividing real gross domestic product for the private sector by private sector worker-hours; it is scaled to have a value of 100 in the base year.

C

cafeteria plan   A fringe benefit package that lets workers choose among a wide range of particular benefits.

capital market imperfections   The bias against lending money for investments in human capital that occurs largely because human beings cannot be used as collateral for loans.

capital mobility   The movement of capital (plant and equipment) from one region or nation to another in response to higher rates of return on investment.

Change to Win federation   A loose federation of seven independent national unions, which focuses on organizing new union members.

churning   Mobility of individuals within a static earnings distribution independent of life-cycle effects. *Compare with* life-cycle mobility.

Civil Rights Act of 1964   An Act of Congress that, among other things, made it illegal to hire, fire, or discriminate on the basis of race, color, religion, gender, or national origin.

cobweb model   A labor market characterized by labor supply adjustments that lag behind changes in demand because of the lengthy training periods required. The path of wages and employment in such models traces out a cobweb pattern when plotted on a supply and demand diagram.

collective voice   The role of unions as representatives or agents that speak on behalf of their members in negotiating contracts and resolving disputes.

college wage premium   The average earnings differential enjoyed by college graduates compared with high school graduates.

commissions   Compensation paid to an agent in proportion to the value of sales.

commodity   As defined by Becker, a combination of goods and time that yields utility to the consumer.

comparable worth doctrine   The idea that females in one occupation should receive the same salaries as males in another if the levels of skill, effort, and responsibility and the working conditions in the two occupations are comparable.

compensating wage differential   The extra amount an employer must pay to reimburse a worker for an undesirable job characteristic that does not exist in alternative employment; also called *wage premium* or *equalizing difference*.

Consumer Price Index (CPI)   An index number that measures a weighted average of the prices of goods and services consumed by representative consumer families. The percentage change in its level is the most commonly used measure of the rate of inflation.

cost-of-living adjustment (COLA)   A labor contract clause that provides automatic increases in nominal wages when the price level rises.

cross-sectional data   A collection of observations of a group of variables at a specific time but for different economic units or groups.

crowding   The segregation of women and minorities into low-paying jobs.

crowding model   A supply and demand model that suggests that if women (minorities) are crowded into "female" ("minority") occupations, their wages will be driven down by the relatively greater supply of labor to such occupations.

crowding-out effect   The reduction in private investment spending due to the upward pressure on interest rates when the government increases its borrowing.

D

D-factor   A combination of several personal traits thought to influence an individual's earnings potential. It represents drive, dynamism, doggedness, or determination.

Davis–Bacon Act   A law passed in 1931 that requires contractors engaged in federally financed projects to pay prevailing wages, which have primarily been union scale.

deadline   The date of termination of a union contract; the probable starting time of a work stoppage if no agreement is reached.

demand-deficient unemployment   Unemployment caused by a decline in aggregate demand. Also called *cyclic unemployment.*

demand for human capital curve   A curve displaying a negative relationship between the marginal rate of return on investment in human capital and the optimal amount of such investment undertaken.

derived demand   The idea that demand curves for labor and other productive inputs are derived from the demand for the product they are used to produce. For example, the demand for autoworkers is derived from the demand for automobiles.

determinants of labor demand   Factors that cause shifts in the labor demand curve, as opposed to a movement along the curve. These include product demand, productivity, number of employers, and the prices of other resources.

determinants of labor supply   Factors that cause shifts in the labor supply curve, as opposed to a movement along the curve. These include other wage rates, nonwage income, preferences for work versus leisure, nonwage aspects of jobs, and the number of qualified labor suppliers.

determinants of migration   Personal and geographic characteristics, such as age, education, wages, and distance, that affect the decision to migrate.

discount formula   The mathematical relationship that defines net present value (V_p) in terms of future values (E_t) and the rate of interest (i):

$$V_p = E_0 + E_1/(1 + i) + E_2/(1 + i)^2$$
$$+ ... + E_n/(1 + i)^n$$

discouraged-worker effect   The change in the labor force due to job seekers who drop out of the labor force after becoming pessimistic about their chances of finding suitable employment.

discouraged workers   Individuals who have searched unsuccessfully for work, become discouraged, and then abandoned their job search. They are not officially counted as unemployed because they are not in the labor force.

discrimination   According inferior treatment with respect to hiring, occupational access, training, promotion, or wages to the members of one group having the same abilities, education, training, and experience as others.

discrimination coefficient   The amount by which an African-American's (or female's) wage rate is perceived to exceed that of an equally productive white's (or male's). If an employer acts as though the African-American's (female's) wage is equal to W + d, d is the discrimination coefficient.

discriminatory discharge   Dismissal of an employee for participation in union activity.

displaced workers   People who lose their jobs specifically because of permanent plant closings or job cutbacks.

domestic content rules   Requirements that imported products contain a specified portion of domestically produced or domestically assembled components.

dynamic efficiency   The combination of resources that produces goods and services at their lowest possible costs over a long time. *Compare with* static efficiency.

E

earnings mobility   Year-to-year movement by individuals from one portion of the earnings distribution to another.

economic perspective   An analytic approach that assumes that resources are scarce relative to wants, individuals make choices by comparing benefits and costs, and people respond to incentives and disincentives.

economic rent   The return to a factor of production in excess of its opportunity cost. Specifically, the difference between a worker's wage and the wage that would be just suffi-cient to keep that person in his or her present employment. *Compare with* rent.

efficiency gains from migration   The net increase in total output that accrues to society when labor relocates from regions or nations in which its value of marginal product is rela-tively low to regions or nations in which it is higher.

efficiency wage   A wage rate that minimizes the employer's cost per effective unit of labor employed.

efficient allocation of labor   The state of the economy achieved when the value of goods and services produced is the highest possible given the amount of labor available. This state occurs when the value of marginal product of a given type of labor is the same in all its potential uses and is equal to its opportunity cost (the price of this type of labor).

efficient contracts   The combinations of wage and employment where at least one party can be made better off without the other party being made worse off.

elasticity of labor demand   The responsive-ness of the quantity of labor demanded to a change in the wage rate.

employed   An individual who is 16 years of age or older, not institutionalized, and at any time during the survey week *(a)* is employed by a firm or government, *(b)* is self-employed, or *(c)* has a job but is not working due to ill-ness, inclement weather, vacation, or a labor dispute.

employee compensation   The national income account comprising wages and salaries, plus payments into social insurance, and worker pension, health, and welfare funds.

Employment Act of 1946   An Act of Congress proclaiming the federal government's goal of

promoting "maximum employment, produc-tion, and purchasing power."

employment discrimination   Higher-than-average unemployment rates for a particular group after adjusting for differences in educa-tion and experience.

employment–population ratio   Total employ-ment as a percentage of the total noninstitu-tional population.

Equal Pay Act of 1963   A law that made illegal the payment of unequal wages to women and men for equal work.

equilibrium wage differential   A wage differ-ential that does not cause workers to shift their labor supplies to alternative employments.

equity compensation   A pay scheme where part of the worker's compensation is given or invested in the firm's stock.

excess demand   The excess of quantity demanded over quantity supplied at a given wage rate or price.

excess supply   The excess of quantity sup-plied over quantity demanded at a given wage rate or price.

exclusive unionism   A union structure wherein the members seek to restrict labor supply by excluding potential workers from participating in the trade or profession.

exit mechanism   The process of leaving one's job as a response to dissatisfaction with pre-sent working conditions. *Compare with* voice mechanism.

external benefit   A benefit that accrues to a party other than the buyer or seller; also called *social benefit.*

external labor market   The labor market of orthodox economic theory in which wages and employment are determined by the forces of supply and demand.

F

Fair Labor Standards Act of 1938　A law that established the legal minimum wage and maximum hours and mandated time-and-a-half pay for overtime work.

Family and Medical Leave Act of 1993　Legislation that permits workers in firms employing more than 75 workers to take up to 12 weeks a year of unpaid leave to care for a spouse, a child, or their own health. Upon return, those having taken these leaves are guaranteed their original or equivalent positions.

featherbedding　Employment of workers in unnecessary or redundant jobs.

fiscal policy　Deliberate manipulation of federal expenditures and taxes to promote full employment, price stability, and economic growth.

foreign purchases effect　As the domestic price level falls relative to prices abroad, both domestic and foreign consumers will shift their spending toward U.S. goods, thereby increasing the aggregate quantity demanded.

free-rider problem　The incentive for each worker to shirk when individual compensation is based on team performance. As team size grows, each worker's contribution to the team has an increasingly negligible effect on team performance.

frictional unemployment　Unemployment that is due to voluntary quits, job switches, and new entrants or reentrants into the labor force. It is composed of search unemployment and wait unemployment.

fringe benefits　That part of employee compensation other than wages or salary. This includes pensions, insurance benefits, paid vacations, and sick leave.

full employment　The amount of employment consistent with the natural rate of unemployment.

Full Employment and Balanced Growth Act of 1978　A reaffirmation of the Employment Act of 1946, this Act also required the federal government to set five-year employment and price level goals and design programs to achieve them.

G

general training　The creation of worker skills that are equally valuable in a number of firms or industries.

geographic mobility　Movement of workers from a job in one city, state, or nation to another. This may or may not also involve a change in occupation.

Gini coefficient　An arithmetic measure of earnings inequality. It is the area between the Lorenz curve and the diagonal line of perfect equality, divided by the total area beneath the diagonal.

golden parachute　A contract provision that provides a large lump-sum payoff to executives who lose their jobs as a result of a corporate takeover.

goods-intensive commodities　Commodities that require a relatively large amount of goods and a small amount of time. *Compare with* time-intensive commodities.

government purchases　Expenditures by federal, state, and local governments on goods, services, and resources.

gross complements　Inputs such that when the price of one changes, the demand for the other changes in the opposite direction because the output effect exceeds the substitution effect.

gross substitutes　Inputs such that when the price of one changes, the demand for the other changes in the same direction because the substitution effect exceeds the output effect.

H

hedonic theory of wages A model of equilibrium wage differentials that hypothesizes that workers maximize the net utility of their employment by trading changes in wages for changes in nonwage job attributes.

heterogeneous workers and jobs An assumption that not all workers and not all jobs are identical. As a result, wages will differ to compensate for job and worker differences.

histogram A graphic portrayal (histogram) of the earnings distribution. The horizontal axis shows the various earnings classes, while the heights of the bars indicate the actual numbers of earnings recipients who have earnings in the particular class. *Compare with* relative frequency distribution.

homogeneous workers and jobs An assumption that all workers and all jobs have identical characteristics. If information were perfect and mobility costless, all workers would receive the same real wage.

hot-cargo clause A labor contract provision that states that trucking firms will not require unionized truckers to handle or transport products made by an employer involved in a labor dispute. Such clauses were made illegal by the Landrum–Griffin Act of 1959.

Household Survey A monthly survey conducted by the Bureau of Labor Statistics to determine the number of people who are employed, unemployed, or not in the labor force; also called *Current Population Survey*.

human capital The accumulation of prior investments in education, on-the-job training, health, and other factors that increase productivity.

human capital discrimination Unequal access to productivity-increasing opportunities such as formal schooling or on-the-job training.

human capital investment demand curve The relationship between human capital investment and the marginal rate of return on that investment. It reflects the (individual) optimal amount invested at any given opportunity cost of funds.

human capital investment supply curve The relationship between human capital investment and the marginal opportunity cost of funds required to finance that investment.

I

immediate-market-period labor supply curve A vertical line at the number of workers attracted into a given market by the current wage rate. This number is derived from the long-run supply curve.

Immigration Reform and Control Act of 1986 A sweeping immigration reform bill that granted amnesty to certain undocumented persons, provided sanctions on employers who knowingly hire undocumented persons, and allowed temporary farmworkers into the country to harvest perishable crops.

implicit contracts Informal, often unstated, understandings about the employment relationship.

in-kind benefits Benefits that take the form of a specific good or service rather than money—insurance benefits, for example, or a company car.

incentive pay plan A compensation scheme that ties workers' pay directly to performance. Such plans may include piece rates, commissions and royalties, raises and promotions, bonuses, profit sharing, and tournament pay.

inclusive unionism A union structure wherein the members seek to include all workers employed in a specific industry.

income effect The change in the desired hours of work resulting from a change in income, holding the wage rate constant.

income elasticity   The percentage change in quantity demanded divided by the percentage change in income.

income guarantee or basic benefit   The amount of public subsidy an individual or family would be paid if no earned income were received.

income maintenance program   Program whose purpose is to provide some minimum level of income to all families and individuals.

income tax   A broad-based tax on income received from many sources, not just wages and salaries.

indeterminacy problem   The idea that if a change in the wage rate changes labor productivity, the position of the labor demand curve becomes indeterminate.

Index of Compensation per Hour (ICH)   An index number that measures average hourly compensation of workers, including employer contributions to Social Security and private fringe benefits. The percentage change in its level is a measure of wage inflation.

index of segregation   The percentage of women (minorities) who would have to change occupations in order for them to be distributed across occupations in the same proportion as men (whites).

indifference curve   A curve that shows the various combinations of two goods (real income and leisure or cash wages and fringe benefits) that will yield some given level of utility or satisfaction to the individual.

indifference map   A set of indifference curves that collectively specify an individual's preferences for two goods such as income and leisure or cash wages and fringe benefits.

inferior good   A product for which the quantity demanded falls when income rises.

inflation   A rising general level of prices in the economy.

injunction   A court order to stop a particular activity, such as a strike, boycott, or picketing.

insider–outsider theories   Theories that purport to explain downward wage rigidity and thus cyclic unemployment on the basis of the relationships between incumbent workers ("insiders") and unemployed workers ("outsiders") who might be expected to bid down the wage rate to obtain employment.

interest rate effect   As the price level falls, the demand for money falls, which in turn reduces interest rates. The subsequent rise in spending on interest-sensitive goods and services increases the aggregate amount of output demanded.

internal labor market   A firm or other administrative unit characterized by job ladders. Except for those at the port of entry, jobs are shielded from competitive market pressures in that wages and employment are determined by administrative rules and procedures rather than by the forces of supply and demand.

internal rate of return (r)   The rate of discount that equates the present value of future costs and benefits. An investment is profitable if its internal rate of return exceeds the marginal opportunity cost of the funds as measured by the interest rate (i).

investment in human capital   Any action taken to increase the productivity (by improving the skills and abilities) of workers; expenditures made to improve the education, health, or mobility of workers.

isocost curve   A curve showing the various combinations of capital and labor that can be purchased with a given outlay, given the prices of capital and labor.

isoprofit curve   A curve portraying the various combinations of wages and fringe benefits (or some other nonwage amenity) that yield a specific level of profits.

isoquant   A curve showing the various combinations of capital and labor that are capable of producing a specific quantity of total output.

J

job evaluation   The procedure by which jobs are ranked and wage rates assigned in terms of a set of job characteristics and worker traits.

job ladder   A sequence of jobs within an internal labor market, beginning at a port of entry and progressing through higher levels of skill, responsibility, and wages.

job search model   A theory of how workers and firms acquire information concerning employment prospects.

joint monopsony   A labor market in which a single firm is the sole employer of a particular type of labor (pure monopsony), or when two or more firms, through collusion, act as the sole employer of a particular type of labor (joint monopsony).

Journal of Economic Literature classification system   The system used to classify subfields within economics. The "J" classification identifies labor economics.

L

labor economics   The field of economics that examines the organization, functioning, and outcomes of labor markets; the decisions of prospective and present labor market participants; and the public policies relating to the employment and payment of labor resources.

labor force participation rate   The percentage of the potential force that is either employed or unemployed.

labor hoarding   The practice by which firms retain more workers during recessions than would be technically necessary, specifically "overhead" workers such as executives, managers, and skilled laborers on whom the firms have spent large sums to recruit and train.

labor immobilities   Geographic, institutional, or sociological barriers to labor mobility. These barriers are a major reason why wage differentials occur and persist.

labor mobility   The movement of workers across employers, occupations, or job locations.

labor productivity   Total product (real GDP) divided by the number of worker-hours.

labor turnover   The rate at which workers quit their jobs, necessitating their replacement by new workers.

Landrum–Griffin Act of 1959   An amendment to the Wagner Act that declared hot-cargo clauses illegal, required regularly scheduled elections of union officers, excluded communists and convicted felons from holding union office, held union officers accountable for union funds and property, and prevented union leaders from infringing on individual workers' rights to participate in the governance of the union.

law of diminishing marginal returns   The principle that if technology is unchanged, as more units of a variable resource are combined with one or more fixed resources, the marginal product of the variable resource must eventually decline.

least-cost combination of capital and labor   The point of tangency of an isocost line to a given isoquant. At this point, the marginal rate of technical substitution equals the ratio of the price of labor to the price of capital.

life-cycle mobility   The movement of specific individuals within the income distribution over their lifetimes. *Compare with* churning.

line of perfect equality   The Lorenz curve that would result if all individuals in the economy had the same earnings. It is a diagonal line through the origin.

local union   The basic unit of organized labor. Its main functions are administering the labor contract and resolving worker grievances.

lockout   A plant shutdown used as a means of imposing costs on workers who are engaged in union-organizing activity or any other union activity such as a strike.

long run   A period of time sufficient for the firm to vary the levels of all of its factors of production.

long-run demand for labor   The schedule or curve indicating the amount of labor that firms will employ at each possible wage rate when all factors of production are variable.

long-run supply curve   In the cobweb model, this curve indicates the eventual response of labor suppliers to changes in the wage rate.

Lorenz curve   A graphical depiction of the earnings distribution. It indicates the cumulative percentage of all wage and salary earners (ranked from lowest to highest earnings) on the horizontal axis; the vertical axis measures the corresponding cumulative percentage of earnings accruing to that group.

M

macroeconomics   The subfield of economics concerned with the economy as a whole or with the interrelations of basic aggregates of the economy.

managerial opposition hypothesis   The notion that increased managerial opposition to unions has led to the decline in union membership and growth.

marginal cost (benefit) of safety   The cost (benefit) to the firm of increasing job safety by one unit.

marginal internal rate of return   The internal rate of return on additional human capital. Optimal investment occurs where the marginal internal rate of return equals the marginal opportunity cost of the funds.

marginal product (MP)   The change in total product that results from changing labor input by one unit.

marginal rate of substitution of leisure for income (MRS L,Y)   The amount of income one must give up to compensate for the gain of one more unit (hour) of leisure.

marginal rate of technical substitution of labor for capital (MRTS L, K)   The amount by which capital must decline when labor is increased by one unit along an isoquant (equal output curve); the absolute value of the slope of an isoquant.

marginal resource cost (MRC)   The change in the firm's total cost that results from changing its employment of a particular resource by one unit. It is equal to the per-unit cost of the resource in competitive input markets.

marginal revenue product (MRP)   The change in total revenue that results from changing labor input by one unit.

marginal wage cost (MWC)   The change in the firm's total wage cost that results from changing labor input by one unit. It is equal to the wage rate in competitive labor markets.

market demand for labor   The relationship between the quantity of labor demanded by all firms employing a given type of labor and the wage rate for this labor. It is assumed that the amount of labor employed at various wages may have an impact on product price, which is held constant in the derivation of the individual firm's demand for labor.

market sector   That part of the private sector consisting of the millions of small businesses. Firms in this sector are subject to strong competitive forces and have few economies of scale. This sector is associated primarily with the secondary labor market. *Compare with* planning sector.

master agreement   A contract struck between management and one or more local unions that then applies to workers in all of the firm's plants.

mean   The arithmetic average of a distribution. With respect to earnings, it is found by dividing total earnings by the number of earnings recipients.

measured union wage advantage   The percentage amount by which the union wage exceeds the nonunion wage. The *measured union wage advantage* is $(W_u - W_n)/W_n \times 100$, where W_u is the observed union wage and W_n is the observed nonunion wage. The *pure union wage advantage* is computed in the same manner, but W_n is the nonunion wage that would be observed in the absence of the union.

median   The midpoint of a distribution. With respect to earnings, half earn less and half earn more.

microeconomics   The subfield of economics concerned with the decisions of individual economic units and the functioning of specific markets.

midpoints formula   A method employed to calculate the elasticity coefficient:

$$E_d = \frac{(Q_2 - Q_1) / (\text{average } Q)}{(W_2 - W_1) / (\text{average } W)}$$

military conscription   A method of obtaining labor resources for military service that relies on the ability of government to compel people to serve. The alternative is a volunteer or market-based military.

minimum wage   A legally specified minimum rate of pay for labor employed in covered occupations.

mode   The class of a distribution with the greatest frequency.

monetary policy   Deliberate manipulation of the money supply by the Federal Reserve authorities, intended to promote full employment, price stability, and economic growth.

monitoring   Employing supervisors and using other methods to determine which workers, if any, are shirking.

monopoly power   The ability of a firm to set its price, rather than being forced to accept a market-determined price.

monopoly union model   A model that assumes the union sets the wage rate, and the firm determines the level of union employment based on this wage rate.

monopsony   A labor market in which a single firm is the sole employer of a particular type of labor (pure monopsony), or when two or more firms, through collusion, act as the sole employer of a particular type of labor (joint monopsony).

moral-hazard problem   As it relates to workers' compensation insurance, the tendency of workers to be less careful in their jobs, knowing they are insured against workplace accidents.

MRP 5 MWC rule   A rule specifying the profit-maximizing level of labor employment. With capital fixed, profits are maximized when labor is employed to the point where MRP = MWC.

multiemployer bargaining   A bargaining structure in which employers in a particular industry organize as a group to bargain with the union.

multifactor approach   A method of explaining the earnings distribution that accounts for innate ability, family background, risk taking, chance, and many other factors in addition to schooling and on-the-job training.

N

National Labor Relations Board   A group of individuals empowered by the Wagner Act to ensure that its provisions are carried out.

national union   A federation of local unions that typically are in either the same industry or the same skilled occupation.

natural rate of unemployment   *(a)* The unemployment rate at which there is neither excess demand nor excess supply in the aggregate labor market; *(b)* the unemployment rate that will occur in the long run if expected and actual rates of inflation are equal. Currently this is estimated to be about 4.0 to 5.0 percent.

net present value   The dollar difference between streams of future costs and benefits of an investment that have been discounted to the present at some appropriate rate of interest. The mathematical relationship that defines net present value (V_p) in terms of future values (E_t) and the rate of interest (i):

$$V_p = E_0 + E_1/(1 + i) + E_2/(1 + i)^2$$
$$+ \ldots + E_n/(1 + i)^n$$

noncompeting groups   Categories of labor market participants whose members, because of differences in education, training, and skill, are imperfect labor market substitutes for members of other groups.

nondiscriminatory factors   Factors other than discrimination that cause differences in earnings by race and gender.

normal-profit isoprofit curve   The isoprofit curve consistent with zero economic profits.

Norris–LaGuardia Act of 1932   A law that severely limited the use of injunctions to enjoin labor union activity and outlawed yellow-dog contracts.

O

occupational discrimination   Arbitrarily restricting or prohibiting the members of a group from entering certain occupations even though the group members have the requisite skills; also called *job discrimination*.

occupational licensure   Laws or regulations by a governmental unit that workers meet certain requirements to practice a specific trade or profession. Tests, standards, and other requirements are established that often have the effect of restricting labor supply to the licensed occupation.

occupational mobility   Movement of workers to a different occupation.

Occupational Safety and Health Act of 1970   Legislation that created the Occupational Safety and Health Administration (OSHA), an agency that establishes and enforces workplace health and safety standards.

Old Age, Survivors, Disability, and Health Insurance (OASDHI)   A government transfer program. Commonly referred to as the Social Security system, it is financed through a payroll tax on employers and employees.

on-the-job training   The accumulation of skills acquired while working at a job.

optimal wage rate–job safety combination   The point of tangency between the worker's highest attainable indifference curve and an employer's normal-profit isoprofit curve.

optimal work–leisure position   The point on the worker's budget constraint at which the marginal rate of substitution of leisure for income is equal to the wage rate. At this point, the budget constraint is tangent to the individual's highest attainable indifference curve.

output effect   The change in labor input resulting from the effect of a change in the wage rate on the firm's cost of production and the subsequent change in the desired level of output.

overemployment   A situation in which the worker could increase utility by taking more leisure and less income; a level of work where the marginal rate of substitution of leisure for income exceeds the wage rate.

P

pattern bargaining   A bargaining structure in which a union negotiates a contract with a particular firm in an industry and then seeks to impose similar terms on all other employers in that industry.

payroll tax   A tax on the amount of wages and salaries received.

pecuniary externality   Effects of private actions that impose monetary costs or benefits on third parties. Such externalities do not affect economic efficiency but rather redistribute a constant real income.

perfectly competitive labor market   A labor market characterized by a large pool of similarly qualified workers independently offering their labor services to a large number of firms, none of which has the power to influence the wage rate. Workers and firms have perfect information, and mobility is costless.

personal distribution of earnings   The division of earnings among individuals.

piece rates   Compensation paid in proportion to the number of units of personal output.

planning sector   That part of the private sector consisting of the largest major corporations that carry on the bulk of economic activity. This sector is associated with the primary labor market. *Compare with* market sector.

port of entry   The link between the external market and a job ladder within the internal labor market. The market forces of supply and demand determine wages at this lowest level of a job ladder, and those who obtain jobs here are allowed future access to the higher job levels in the internal labor market.

potential labor force   All noninstitutionalized persons age 16 and over; also called the *age-eligible population*.

prevailing wage rule   The practice by governments of setting public employee wage rates

equal to those received by comparably trained and employed private sector workers; also called the *comparable-wage rule*.

price of labor (P_L)   The marginal value of alternative work, non–labor market production, or leisure for a given type of labor. P_L measures the opportunity cost of labor.

primary statistical source   An original source of data, such as the *Current Population Survey*.

principal–agent problem   A conflict of interest that occurs when agents pursue their own objectives to the detriment of meeting the principal's objectives.

principals   Parties who hire others to help them advance their objectives. *Compare with* agents.

private perspective   Viewing the benefits and costs strictly from the standpoint of an individual who is considering a human capital investment.

product market effect   The increase in nonunion wages that is caused by consumer demand shifting away from relatively higher-priced union-produced goods and toward relatively lower-priced goods produced by non-union workers.

production function   The relationship between the various quantities of inputs and the corresponding output, assuming the resources are combined in a technically efficient manner.

productivity   Output per unit of input; it is a measure of efficiency of resource use.

profit sharing   A compensation scheme that allocates a specified portion of a firm's profits to employees.

progressive tax   A tax for which the rate increases with the size of the tax base (particularly if income is the base).

proprietor's income   The national income account comprising income received by owners of unincorporated businesses (sole proprietorships and partnerships).

pure complements in production   A pair of resources, such as capital and labor, that must be used in direct proportion to one another in producing output. Pure complements in production are always gross complements.

pure monopsony   A labor market in which a single firm is the sole employer of a particular type of labor (pure monopsony), or when two or more firms, through collusion, act as the sole employer of a particular type of labor (joint monopsony).

pure public goods   Collectively consumed goods or services. For these products, use by one person does not diminish the amount available for another's consumption. An example is national defense.

pure union wage advantage   The percentage amount by which the union wage exceeds the nonunion wage. The *measured union wage advantage* is $(W_u - W_n)/W_n \times 100$, where W_u is the observed union wage and W_n is the observed nonunion wage. The *pure union wage advantage* is computed in the same manner, but W_n is the nonunion wage that would be observed in the absence of the union.

Q

quality circles   Joint labor–management committees on productivity.

quasi-fixed resource   A productive resource that has some of the characteristics of both fixed and variable factors. Once made, specific training investments are fixed costs to the firm; thus, workers with such training constitute quasi-fixed resources.

quota   Limits on the quantity or total value of specific imported goods.

R

real balance effect   As the price level falls, the real value of dollar-denominated assets increases. This increase in wealth increases consumption spending and the aggregate amount of output demanded.

real externality   Effects of private actions that spill over to third parties, either adding to (external benefits) or detracting from (external costs) economic efficiency.

real wage   Worker earnings expressed in terms of purchasing power. It is found by dividing the money or nominal wage by the average price level.

relative frequency distribution   A graphic portrayal (histogram) of the earnings distribution. The horizontal axis shows the various earnings classes, while the heights of the bars indicate the percentages of the total number of earnings recipients who have earnings in the particular class. *Compare with* absolute frequency distribution.

relative share   The proportion of national income accruing to a particular productive factor.

rent   The return to nonreproducible resources (land) that are provided in fixed quantities in nature. *Compare with* economic rent.

rent provision   Practices, particularly by government, that yield economic rent to a specific group or individual. Examples include the minimum wage and occupational licensure.

rent-seeking activity   Actions by individuals or specific groups that have the effect of increasing their economic rent.

reservation wage   The highest wage rate at which an individual chooses not to work; the lowest wage rate at which an individual chooses to enter the labor market.

right-to-work laws   State laws (protected by Section 14b of the National Labor Relations Act) that make union shop and agency shop agreements illegal.

royalties   An amount, proportional to sales, paid in compensation for allowing an agent to market the principal's product.

S

screening hypothesis   The view that education only identifies individuals who are trainable or of high ability rather than increasing productivity per se.

search unemployment   Unemployment that is caused by individuals searching for the best job offer and firms searching for workers to fill job openings.

secondary boycott   Actions by a union to refuse to handle or to get an employer to refuse to buy products made by a firm that is party to a labor dispute. A labor contract provision that states that trucking firms will not require unionized truckers to handle or transport products made by an employer involved in a labor dispute. Such clauses were made illegal by the Landrum–Griffin Act of 1959.

secondary statistical source   A source that contains data from original sources in an abridged or truncated form, such as the *Statistical Abstract of the United States.*

self-selection   A type of statistical bias encountered when the effects of individual choices are improperly measured or unaccounted for. For example, if people with more ability are more likely to obtain high earnings, independently of education, and also are more likely to obtain education, failing to account for differences in ability will tend to overstate the effects of education on earnings. With respect to immigration, the idea that those who choose to move tend to have greater motivation for economic gain or greater willingness to sacrifice current for future consumption than

those of similar skills who choose not to migrate.

seniority   A system of granting economic amenities (higher wage rates, better jobs, protection from layoff) based on length of service (job tenure).

shift work   Work done at night, as opposed to during usual daytime work hours.

shirking   Attempts by workers to increase utility by taking unauthorized breaks or by giving less than agreed-upon effort during work hours; the act of neglecting or evading work.

shock effect   The upward shift in the marginal product schedule that results from managerial responses to an increase in the wage rate.

short run   A period of time sufficiently short that the quantity of capital employed by the firm cannot be varied.

short-run labor demand curve   The schedule or curve indicating the amount of labor that firms will employ at each possible wage rate assuming a fixed capital stock. It is the part of the marginal revenue product curve that is positive and lies below the average revenue product curve.

skill differential   The difference in wages between skilled and unskilled workers.

skill transferability   The ability of skills that are appropriate for one job or location to apply in another job or location.

social perspective   Viewing the benefits and costs of human capital investment from the standpoint of society.

specific training   The creation of worker skills that are of value only to the particular firm providing the training.

spillover effect   The decline in nonunion wages that results from displaced union workers supplying their services in nonunion labor markets.

static efficiency   The combination of resources of a fixed quality that produces output at the lowest possible cost at a given point in time. *Compare with* dynamic efficiency.

statistical discrimination   Judging an individual on the basis of the average characteristics of the group to which he or she belongs rather than on his or her personal characteristics.

stochastic theories   Theories of income distribution that are based on change rather than individual choice or institutional structure.

stock–flow model   A model of labor flows into and out of various categories of labor force status. It is used to analyze changes in the unemployment rate.

stock options   A form of compensation that gives an employee the right to purchase a fixed number of shares of stock at a set price for a given period.

straight-time equivalent wage   The wage that would yield the same income at the same number of hours as the income and hour combination actually chosen by an individual paid an overtime premium.

strikebreaker   A nonunion worker hired by the firm to continue operations during a strike.

strongly efficient contract   A contract where the union and firm agree to set the employment at the level that would occur without a union.

structural change hypothesis   The notion that changes in the composition of the labor force and the industrial mix have led to the decline in union growth and membership.

structural unemployment   Unemployment due to a mismatch between the skills required for available job openings and the skills possessed by those seeking work; a geographical mismatch between jobs and job seekers; displaced workers.

subemployed   Those who are forced by economic circumstances to work in occupations that pay lower wages than those for which they would qualify in periods of full employment.

subminimum training wage   A legally specified minimum rate of pay for teenagers established below the minimum rate for older workers.

subsidy   A transfer payment provided to consumers or producers of a specific good or service.

substitutes in production   A pair of inputs, such as capital and labor, such that a given amount of output can be produced with many different combinations of the two. Substitutes in production will be gross substitutes if the substitution effect outweighs the output effect; the inputs will be gross complements if the output effect outweighs the substitution effect.

substitution effect   As it relates to labor supply, the change in the desired hours of work resulting from a change in the wage rate, keeping income constant. As it relates to production, the change in employment resulting solely from a change in the relative price of labor, output being held constant.

substitution hypothesis   The notion that benefits provided by the government and some employers have substituted for their provision by unions, leading to the decline in union growth and membership.

superior worker effect   The increase in average union wages that arises when union employers carefully screen prospective employees and hire only the most productive workers. This practice is made possible by the queuing of employees for the higher-paying union jobs.

supply of investment funds   A schedule or curve showing the relationship between the marginal opportunity cost of investment funds (the interest rate) and the amount of such funds made available for financing various levels of human capital.

T

Taft–Hartley Act of 1947 An amendment to the Wagner Act, it established unfair labor practices on the part of unions, regulated the internal administration of unions, outlawed the closed shop while upholding state right-to-work laws, and established emergency strike provisions.

tariff An excise duty on an imported good.

taste for discrimination model A theory of discrimination developed by Gary Becker that views discrimination as a preference for which employers are willing to pay.

tax incidence The economic location of the burden of a tax, or the determination of who ultimately pays a tax. The redistributive effects of a tax.

Temporary Assistance for Needy Families (TANF) Welfare program that requires recipients to return to work after two years of receiving assistance with few exceptions.

threat effect The increase in nonunion wage rates that a nonunion employer offers as a response to the threat of unionization.

time-intensive commodities Commodities that require a relatively large amount of time and a small amount of goods. *Compare with* goods-intensive commodities.

time preference The notion that most people prefer present consumption to future consumption.

time rates Compensation paid in proportion to time worked such as hours, months, or years.

time-series data A collection of observations of a group of variables ordered sequentially with respect to time.

total compensation The sum of wage earnings and the value of fringe benefits.

total factor productivity Output per standardized unit of combined labor and capital input.

total product (TP) The total output of the firm, expressed as a function of labor input.

total wage bill The total wage cost to the firm; the wage rate multiplied by the quantity of labor hours employed.

total wage bill rules Rules for determining the elasticity of labor demand. Labor demand is elastic (inelastic) if a change in the wage rate causes the total wage bill to move in the opposite (same) direction. If labor demand is unit elastic, then the total wage bill remains constant when the wage rate changes.

tournament pay A compensation scheme that bases payments on relative performance. Typically first prize is very high, with subsequent prizes sinking rapidly for ranks below the top. If everyone aspires to the top, productivity in the lower ranks is enhanced.

transfer payment A government expenditure that merely reflects a transfer of income from government to households. Recipients perform no productive activities in exchange.

transitional wage differential Short-run wage differences that arise from imperfect and costly information as labor markets move toward final equilibrium.

U

underemployment A situation in which the worker could increase utility by taking less leisure and more income; a level of work wherein the wage rate exceeds the marginal rate of substitution of leisure for income. This term may also refer to a situation in which the worker is employed in a position for which he or she is overqualified.

undocumented persons　Individuals who unlawfully immigrate into the United States, usually to work; also called *undocumented workers*.

unemployed　An individual who is 16 years of age or older, is not institutionalized, did not work during the previous week but was available for work, and *(a)* has engaged in some specific job-seeking activity within the previous four weeks, *(b)* is waiting to be called back to a job from which she or he has been laid off, *(c)* would have been looking for a job but was temporarily ill, or *(d)* is waiting to report to a new job within 30 days.

unemployment rate　The percentage of the labor force that is unemployed. It is the ratio of total unemployment to the total labor force, where the latter is the sum of employment and unemployment.

union shop clause　A bargaining agreement that specifies that nonunion workers may be hired but requires that all employees must join the union or pay union dues following a probationary period, usually 60 days.

union wage advantage　The percentage amount by which the union wage exceeds the nonunion wage. The *measured union wage advantage* is $(W_u - W_n)/W_n \times 100$, where W_u is the observed union wage and W_n is the observed nonunion wage. The *pure union wage advantage* is computed in the same manner, but W_n is the nonunion wage that would be observed in the absence of the union.

unit labor cost　Total labor cost divided by the quantity of output. It is alternatively computed as the wage rate divided by labor productivity.

utility　The ability of goods or leisure to satisfy wants: want-satisfying power.

V

value of marginal product (VMP)　The change in the total value of output that results to society from changing labor input by one unit. VMP equals the price of the product times the marginal product $(P \times MP)$.

voice mechanism　The process of using communication channels between the employer and employees to express dissatisfaction with present working conditions. Typically these channels are institutionalized through collective bargaining and union grievance procedures. *Compare with* exit mechanism.

voluntary or market-based army　An army in which the requisite number of military personnel is attracted through payment of wage rates that are sufficiently high to cover the opportunity costs of those taking the jobs.

W

wage bill　The total amount of wages paid by the firm; the wage rate times the number of worker-hours.

wage discrimination　Basing wage rate differentials on considerations other than productivity differentials.

wage elasticity coefficient (E_d)　A measure of the responsiveness of the quantity of labor demanded to a change in the wage rate. *Ed* equals the percentage change in the quantity of labor demanded divided by the percentage change in the wage rate.

wage elasticity of labor supply (E_s)　A measure of the responsiveness of the quantity of labor supplied to a change in the wage rate. E_s equals the percentage change in the quantity of labor supplied divided by the percentage change in the wage rate.

wage–fringe optimum　The composition of total compensation that provides maximum attainable utility to the worker.

wage narrowing The overall impact on wages in both the area of origin and area of destination as a result of migration. Wages tend to rise in the (initially low-wage) origin and fall in the (initially high-wage) destination area.

wage-push inflation An increase in the general level of prices due primarily to decreases in aggregate supply, specifically when total worker compensation rises faster than productivity.

wage structure The observed wage differentials of the economy, broken down by industry, occupation, geographical location, or other job or worker differences.

wage subsidy A direct payment or a reduction in taxes from the government to a firm that expands its employment of low-wage or structurally unemployed workers.

Wagner Act of 1935 (National Labor Relations Act) A law that guaranteed the rights of self-organization and collective bargaining, outlined unfair labor practices on the part of management, established the National Labor Relations Board, and made strikes by federal employees illegal.

wait unemployment The excess supply of workers that results from non–market-clearing wage rates. Workers displaced by union wage gains may prefer unemployment with the likelihood of regaining union employment to employment at the lower nonunion wage rate. Also, the unemployed workers who are forced by efficiency wage payments to wait for jobs to open.

work–leisure optimum The combination of leisure and income that provides the maximum attainable total utility. The point at which the worker is on the highest possible indifference curve given the budget constraint.

Y

yellow-dog contract A labor contract clause that, as a condition of continued employment, prohibited workers from joining a union. Yellow-dog contracts were declared unenforceable by the Norris–LaGuardia Act of 1932.

Z

zone of production Stage II of the production function; quantities of labor input beyond the point of maximum average product but prior to a negative marginal product. In this stage, changes in labor input contribute to increased efficiency by either labor or capital.

Answers to "Your Turn" Questions

Your Turn 1.1: The second statement reflects the economic perspective. Those retiring at age 65 are comparing costs and benefits; that is, responding to incentives and disincentives. Although retirees sacrifice their work earnings, they gain private pension benefits, Social Security benefits, and added leisure, which more than compensate for these forgone earnings.

Your Turn 2.1: If the slope of the budget line is steeper than the slope of the indifference curve that it intersects, the worker should work more hours than those identified by the intersection. Working more hours will allow the person to achieve greater total utility (attain a higher indifference curve). The worker will maximize total utility where the slopes of the budget line and the highest attainable indifference curve are equal.

Your Turn 2.2: When a worker's wage rate declines and the income effect dominates the substitution effect, the person will work more hours. The backward-bending portion of the labor supply curve is the relevant segment here.

Your Turn 2.3: Other things being equal, we would prefer jobs where we can select our work hours. That way we can choose to work the precise number of hours that will maximize our total utility. This optimal number of work hours may differ from that prescribed by an employer. Employer-required hours can lead to either underemployment or overemployment; worker-determined hours cannot.

Your Turn 3.1: The fact that women's real wages and rates of labor force participation have simultaneously increased implies that the Becker substitution effect has exceeded the Becker income effect.

Your Turn 3.2: The labor force size in this hypothetical nation is 60 million (= 53 million employed *plus* 7 million unemployed who are actively seeking work). The potential labor force is 85 million (= 60 million in the labor force *plus* 25 million eligible people who are not in the labor force). The LFPR is 70.6 percent [= (60 million/85 million) × 100].

Your Turn 4.1: If the net present value of an investment is highly positive, then the internal rate of return on the investment typically exceeds the interest cost of borrowing funds to finance the investment.

Your Turn 4.2: The marginal rate of return, r, is indeed the same for each person at the optimal level of education. Both r's equal the cost of borrowing, i. But the person with more ability has a greater r at any particular level of education, leading that person to obtain more education than the individual with less ability.

Your Turn 4.3: MBA education is mainly general training that is applicable to numerous employers. The firm's employees probably indirectly pay for this training through lower dollar salaries than would be paid without this fringe benefit.

Your Turn 5.1: In the competitive situation, MRP is $32 (= 8 units × the price of $4). Where there is monopoly, MRP will be less than $32. The firm's marginal revenue from each of the extra 8 units sold will be less than $4.

Your Turn 5.2: The high wages paid autoworkers may have accelerated the substitution of industrial robots for workers (substitution effect). Also, these high wages may have contributed to the cost advantage experienced by Japanese auto producers. Partly because of this cost advantage, imports of autos from Japan surged and employment in the American auto industry declined (output effect).

Your Turn 5.3: Capital and labor are gross complements in this scenario. The decline in the price of capital increased the amount of capital purchased, which increased the demand for labor. The output effect of the decline in the price of capital exceeded the substitution effect.

Your Turn 6.1: The increase in labor supply will reduce the market wage rate [the perfectly competitive firms' marginal wage cost (MWC)]. This decline in MWC will entice firms to employ more units of labor. They will stop adding new workers when MRP declines sufficiently to equal the new lower wage rate (= MWC). Equilibrium will be restored where MRP = MWC.

Your Turn 6.2: The monopsonist's MWC curve lies above the market labor supply curve because the monopsonist must pay a higher wage to attract an extra worker and must pay this higher wage to all workers, including those who otherwise could have been paid less. Monopsony is *not* a disadvantage to an employer; it is an advantage because it allows the monopsonist to reduce its wage rate by restricting the number of workers employed.

Your Turn 7.1: The slopes of the typical worker's indifference curves would become flatter. Workers would be less willing to trade off wage earnings for fringe benefits. Thus, the optimal amount of fringe benefits would decline.

Your Turn 7.2: The major difficulty of profit sharing as a means of overcoming the principal–agent problem is that it can give rise to free riders who know that they will share in any profits even though they shirk. Seeing free riders, other workers may abandon their efforts to increase productivity, thus undermining the objective of the profit-sharing plan.

Your Turn 8.1: State governors receive compensating wage differentials such as fame, prestige, and power not available to most executives in the private sector. There is a ready supply of qualified, willing candidates for governor, even though the pay is far below that of otherwise similar private sector positions.

Your Turn 8.2: Because most people do not like to work outdoors in freezing temperatures, a compensating wage premium will arise for this type of work. A person who enjoys working in cold temperatures will receive this higher wage without suffering the utility loss experienced by the marginal worker enticed to this occupation by the compensating wage.

Your Turn 9.1: The V_p in the net present value equation will fall, reducing the likelihood that V_p will be positive and that migration will occur.

Your Turn 10.1: Based on personal characteristics, occupation, and location of employment, Isaiah is clearly more likely than Susan to be a union member.

Your Turn 10.2: The correct answer is *(b)*. A decline in imports would probably boost output and sales by domestic, unionized manufacturers. Consequently, domestic employment and union membership would rise.

Your Turn 10.3: The probability of a strike should fall because the likelihood of the firm or the union misperceiving the other party's concession curve will decline.

Your Turn 11.1: The measured union wage advantage is $1 an hour, or 11.1 percent [= ($10 − $9/$9) × 100]; the pure union wage advantage is $2 an hour, or 25 percent [= ($10 − $8/$8) × 100].

Your Turn 11.2: Unions could simultaneously increase the firm's productivity (output per worker) while extracting wage rate increases beyond the productivity gains. If so, the firm's profitability would decline.

Your Turn 12.1: People's incentives to work hard were reduced because the state provided many goods at no charge or at low, highly subsidized prices.

Your Turn 12.2: Stone may work more hours if the substitution effect exceeds the income effect of the tax increase (after-tax wage increase). That is, he may work more hours, responding to the fact that the opportunity cost of leisure is now higher. In contrast, for Smythe the income effect of the tax decrease may exceed the substitution effect.

Your Turn 13.1: The average wage of teenagers would increase, teenage employment would fall, and teenage unemployment would rise. It is unlikely that adult employment would change.

Your Turn 13.2: The firm will not provide this extra unit of job safety; the marginal benefit of $250,000 is less than the marginal cost of $300,000. But the marginal cost of $250,000 is less than the marginal social benefit of $300,000. Thus, a strong case can be made for government intervention. Government could simply require the firm to provide this extra job safety; or alternatively, government could provide workers with information about the safety hazards in their workplaces. Greater awareness by workers of job risks creates compensating wage differences that increase the firm's private benefits of providing job safety.

Your Turn 14.1: Because African–American males earn less than white males at higher levels of education, African–Americans may have a reduced incentive to obtain more education.

Your Turn 14.2: The dollar value of the discrimination coefficient for an employer hiring all white workers must be greater than $4. The coefficient for an employer hiring all African–American workers must be less than $4.

Your Turn 14.3: Statistical differences in group averages might lead employers to reject qualified women and minorities for some jobs, confining those discriminated against to lower-paying, stereotypical jobs. For example, women might be excluded from career tracks in management based on the assumption that family responsibilities will interfere with transfers to new locations and other aspects of job performance. Instead women may be segregated into administrative assistant positions.

Your Turn 14.4: The inferior economic position of women may spring partly from their relative lack of mathematical and quantitative interest and training. Perhaps women have freely chosen to avoid preparing for higher-paying professions requiring these skills. On the other hand, women may possibly have less mathematical training than men because of discrimination. That is, socialization, advising in education, and stereotypical hiring may have pushed them away from this type of training and toward training for "women's jobs."

Your Turn 15.1: Unexpected inflation reduces the length of job search, anticipated inflation has no effect on the length of job search, and unemployment insurance increases the length of job search.

Your Turn 15.2: The job ladder in academia involves only three rungs: assistant professor, associate professor, and full professor. There is considerable upward mobility along the ladder.

Your Turn 16.1: A shift of the Lorenz curve toward the diagonal line represents a decline in earnings inequality. Most likely the histogram of earnings will be compressed, and the Gini coefficient of earnings will decline.

Your Turn 16.2: Although all the factors shown in Figure 16.4 are important, if forced to select one set of factors, we would pick differences in education and training.

Your Turn 17.1: Productivity is 2 (= 10 units of output/5 units of labor). Average labor cost is $1 (= $10 of labor cost/10 units of output).

Your Turn 17.2: As the economy emerged from the recession, firms collectively increased their output more rapidly than their employment; therefore, output per worker increased.

Your Turn 18.1: The unemployment rate overstates economic hardship because some survey respondents may falsely claim they are searching for work; it counts people with weak labor market attachment the same as their strongly attached counterparts; and many families have more than one earner. The unemployment rate understates economic hardship because it counts involuntarily part-time workers as fully employed and does not measure either discouraged or subemployed workers.

Your Turn 18.2: False. Recently men and women in the United States have had similar unemployment rates.

Name Index

Note: Page numbers followed by "n" indicate notes.

A

Abowd, John M., 286n
Acemoglu, Daron, 450n
Addison, John T., 106n, 267n, 305n, 316n, 423n
Aguiar, Mark, 452n
Aigner, Dennis J., 396n
Akee, Randall K. Q., 438n
Akerlof, George A., 204n, 469n
Allen, Steven G., 244n
Alonso-Villar, Olga, 401n
Alpert, William T., 436n
Altonji, Joseph G., 113n
Amsden, Alice H., 390n
Anderson, Patricia M., 349n
Anderson, Rod, 436n
Andrews, Emily S., 191n
Angrist, Joshua D., 336n
Aronsson, Thomas, 286n
Asch, Beth J., 335n, 337n
Ashack, Elizabeth A., 281n
Ashenfelter, Orley C., 91n, 141n, 223n, 249n,
    286n, 291n, 395n, 334n, 359n, 361n, 441n
Atkinson, A. B., 440n, 443n
Autor, David H., 166, 450n
Azar, Ofer H., 198
Azariadis, Costas, 496n

B

Bacon, Nicolas, 317n
Bailey, Martha J., 63
Baily, Martin, 477n
Baker, George, 424n
Baker, Michael, 362n
Bansak, Cynthia, 258n

Barrett, Alan, 109n
Barron, John M., 317n
Bartel, Ann P., 371n
Baumol, William J., 473n
Beaudry, Paul, 91n
Becker, Brian E., 320n
Becker, Gary, 5, 49n, 88n
Bednarzik, Robert, 446n
Belasen, Ariel R., 165
Belfield, Clive R., 316n
Bellante, Don, 333n
Belman, Dale, 278n, 333n
Benati, Luca, 70n
Bender, Keith A., 194n, 218n
Benedict, Mary Ellen, 295n
Benjamin, Dwayne, 362n
Bergmann, Barbara, 59n, 397n, 397n, 407n
Bernhardt, Annette, 448n
Betson, David M., 347n
Bhaskar, V., 358n
Bikker, Jacob A., 191n
Bishop, Kelly, 27n
Blachflower, David, 223n, 307n
Black, Dan A., 109n
Black, Sandra E., 394, 441n
Blackburn, McKinley L., 112n, 307n
Blank, Rebecca M., 40n, 41n
Blasi, Joseph, 199n
Blau, David M., 57n
Blau, Francine D., 27n, 52n, 59n, 66, 66n, 255n,
    401n, 405n
Blinder, Alan S., 199n
Bloemen, Hans G., 421n
Bluestone, Barry, 447n,
Boal, William M., 174n, 361n
Bognanno, Michael L., 200n
Bollinger, Christopher R., 255n
Bom, Pedro R. D., 465n

Bonars, Stephen G., 249n
Booth, Alison, 285n
Borghans, Lex, 110n
Borjas, George J., 247n, 249n, 260n
Borland, Jeff, 334n
Bound, John, 68n, 178n, 498n
Bourguignon, F., 437n
Boyd, John H., 497
Brack, John, 72n
Bragal, Breno, 178n
Brainerd, Elizabeth, 394
Bratberg, Espen, 445n
Briggs, Vernon M., 236n
Brittain, John A., 349
Bronars, Stephen G., 318, 415n
Brown, Charles, 194n, 223, 361n, 363
Brown, James N., 286n
Brown, Jeffrey R., 87n
Brueckner, Jan K., 334
Brummund, Peter, 401n
Bryson, Alex, 307n
Buchinsky, Moshe, 446n
Budd, John W., 272n, 307n
Burkhauser, Richard V., 363n, 446n
Burns, Rachel M., 370n
Burtless, Gary, 92n

C

Cadena, Brian C., 254n
Cain, Glen G., 396n
Cancian, Maria, 436n
Card, David, 89n, 91n, 92n, 99n, 223n, 249n,
    261n, 286n, 295n, 323n, 334n, 361n, 438n,
    438n, 441n, 451n
Carmichael, H. Lorne, 2n
Carniero, Pedro, 110n
Carter, Michael J., 426n
Carter, Susan B., 426n
Carter, William H., 278n
Cebula, Richard J., 247n
Chaison Gary N., 280n, 281n
Chandra, Amitabh, 410n
Chatterji, Monojit, 113n
Chay, Kenneth Y., 410n
Chen, Stacey H., 336n
Chen, Susan, 57n

Chen, Yong, 247n
Chetty, Raj, 195
Chingos, Matthew M., 195
Chiplin, Brian, 390n
Chiswick, Barry R., 248n, 249n
Christofides, Louis N., 89n
Clark, Andrew, 285n
Clark, Kim B., 141n, 317n, 485n
Clark, Mike, 289n
Clark, Robert, 244n
Coates, Edward M., III, 199n
Colvin, Alexander J. S., 275n
Compton, Janice, 245n
Cooke, Thomas J., 249n
Coombs, Christopher K., 279n
Costa, Dora L., 56n, 245n
Coughlin, Cletus C., 416n
Courant, Paul N., 219, 331n
Cowling, Keith, 72

D

Dahvale, Dileep G., 280n
Danziger, Sheldon, 436n
Darity, William A., Jr., 395n
DaVanzo, Julie, 246n
Davies, Paul S., 246n
Dean, Edwin R., 458n, 463n, 468n
Deere, Donald R., 318, 495n
DeFina, Robert H., 316n, 492n
De Franco, Gus, 203n
Defreitas, Gregory, 271n
De Freu, Jan, 191n
Delaney, John T., 331n
Della Vigna, Stefano, 422n
DeLong, J. Bradford, 469n
Del Rio, Coral, 401n
DeVaro, Jed, 200n
Devereux, Paul J., 441n
Devine, Theresa J., 421n
Diaz-Gimenez, Javier, 444n
DiNardo, John E., 313n
Doeringer Peter B., 424n
Doiron, Denise J., 406n
Donohue, John J., III, 409n
Dorn, David, 167
Doucouliagos, Hristos, 318n

Dowrick, Steve, 310n
Dube, Arindrajit, 362n
Duncan, Greg J., 305n
Duru, G., 178n
Dustmann, Christian, 109n

E

Edwards, Linda N., 271n
Ehrenberg, Ronald G., 141n, 187n, 249n
Ellwood, David T., 40n
Eren, Ozkan, 306n
Estey, Marten, 311n
Estlund, Cynthia, 318n
Even, William E., 131, 191n, 271n, 363n

F

Fairris, David, 362n
Fallick, Bruce C., 319
Famulari, Melissa, 415n
Farber, Henry S., 277n, 280n, 304n, 415n, 492n
Feldstein, Martin, 495n
Ferber, Marianne A., 52n
Fernald, John, 477n
Fernandez, Raquel, 62n
Ferrer, Ana, 223n
Filer, Randall K., 231n
Fiorito, Jack, 331n
Fishback, Price V., 218n
Fishelson, Gideon, 204n
Fleck, Susan, 460n
Fleisher Belton M., 235n
Frankel, Jeffrey A., 40n
Frazis, Harley, 109n, 113n, 191n
Frederiksen, Anders, 397n
Fredriksson, Peter, 421n
Freeman, Richard B., 87n, 88n, 141n, 178n,
    270n, 272n, 277n, 278n, 279n, 281n, 306n,
    316n, 318n, 323n, 356n, 498n
Freidman, John N., 195
French, Michael T., 100
Friedman, Milton, 442n
Fuchs, Victor R., 64n
Fuess, Scott M., Jr., 317n, 371n

G

Gabriel, P. E., 306n
Garrett, Mario, 223n
Ge, Suqin, 87n
Gebreselassie, Tesfayi, 35n
Gendell, Murray, 56n
Geweke, John, 446n
Gibson, John, 253n
Gittleman, Maury, 333n, 446n
Glaser, John, 460
Glover, Andy, 444n
Gobillon, Laurent, 67n
Golden, Joseph M., 178n
Golden, Lonnie, 35n
Goldin, Claudia, 59n, 63, 277n, 410n
Goodstein, Ryan M., 57n
Gottschalk, Peter, 436n
Gradin, Carlos, 401n
Gramlich, Edward, 331n
Gramm, Cynthia L., 295n
Grant, E. Kenneth, 89n
Grant, Randy R., 6n
Gray, Wayne B., 370n
Green, Colin P., 194n
Green, David A., 91n, 317n
Greenberg, David, 347n
Greenwood, Michael J., 246n
Gregory, Robert G., 334n
Grogger, Jeffrey, 41n
Grossberg, Adam J., 110n
Gunderson, Morley, 333n
Gupta, Shalabh, 477n
Gwartney, James, 347n

H

Haelermans, Carla, 110n
Hagstrom, Paul, 255n
Haider, Steven J., 57n
Hakkinen, Iida, 92n
Hallock, Kevin F., 313n
Hamermesh, Daniel S., 141n, 220n, 349, 447n
Handcock, Mark S., 448n
Hansen, Karsten T., 110n
Hanson, Gordon H., 167, 261n, 262n

Hanushek, Eric. A., 89, 91n, 92n, 95n, 114
Harper, Michael J., 463n, 463n, 468n
Harrison, Bennett, 447n
Hart, Oliver D., 295n
Hassett, Kevin A., 319
Hause, John, 440n
Haviland, Amelia M., 370n
Hay, Joel W., 178n
Hayes, Beth, 295n
Heckman, James J., 26n, 89, 89n, 92n, 110n, 383n, 409n
Heim, Bradley, 27n, 188n
Hellerstein, Judith K., 394
Helwege, Jean, 235n
Herzog, Henry, Jr., 246n
Heywood, John S., 194n, 333n
Hicks, John R., 139n, 293n
Hirsch, Barry T., 173n, 219, 305n, 333n, 277n, 305n, 306n, 318n, 333n, 333n, 401n, 401n, 405n
Hirvonen, Lalaina H., 445
Ho, Mun S., 476n
Holmlund, Bertil, 421n
Holmstrom, Bengt, 424n
Holtz-Eakin, Douglas, 446n
Holzer, Harry J., 410n, 421n, 498n
Homer, Jenny F., 100
Hoque, Kim, 317n
Horvath, Francis, 249n
Hosek, James R., 335n
Hoxby, Caroline M., 86n, 87n
Hu, Jian, 497
Hulten, Charles R., 463n, 468n
Humphries, John Eric, 89
Hunt, Jennifer, 446n
Hurd, Richard, 173n
Hurst, Erik, 451n
Hyatt, Douglas, 333n

I

Ian Salas, J. M., 362n
Idson, Todd L., 223n
Ilg, Randy E., 416n
Ippolito, Richard A., 57n, 333n

J

Jagannathan, Ravi, 497
Jarley, Paul, 331n
Jensen, Peter, 421n
Johnson, George E., 285n, 295n, 310n
Johnson, William R., 35n, 245n, 405n, 493n
Jones, Carol Adaire, 370n
Jones, Ethel B., 74n
Jones, Stephen, 194n
Jorgenson, Dale W., 465n, 476n, 477n
Jovanovic, Boyan, 244n, 415n
Joyce, Mary, 446n
Juhn, Chinhui, 63n
Jurajda, Stepan, 422n
Juster, F. Thomas, 440n

K

Kaestner, Robert, 359n
Kahn, Lawrence M., 27n, 66n, 175, 254n, 382n, 405n
Kahn, Lisa B., 113n, 486n
Kahn, Matthew E., 245n
Kanbur, S. M., 442n
Kane, Thomas J., 86n, 89n
Kantor, Shawn Everett, 218n
Karoly, Lynn A., 41n
Kassenboehmer, Sonja C., 382n, 405n
Katz, Harry C., 275n
Katz, Lawrence F., 63, 102, 289n, 402, 422n, 449n
Kaufman, Bruce E., 277n, 280n, 282n
Keane, Michael P., 32n
Kearney, Melissa S., 68n
Kearney, Richard C., 356n
Keith, Kristen, 248n
Kendall, Brent, 376n
Kessler, Daniel P., 289n
Kevok, Viem, 253n
Khors, Lay B., 263n
Kiefer, Nicholas M., 421n
King, Allan, 236n
Kirjavainen, Tanja, 92n

Klass, Michael W., 370n
Kleiner, Morris M., 277n, 280n, 291n, 374n, 376n, 377n
Knez, Marc, 199n
Kniesner, Thomas J., 74n, 235n
Kochan, Thomas A., 275n, 280n, 281n
Kodrzycki, Yolanda K., 70n
Koeller, C. Timothy, 280n
Kosteas, Vasilios D., 227
Kostiuk, P. F., 231
Krashinsky, Harry A., 147n
Krueger, Alan B., 57n, 68n, 69, 92n, 93n, 147n, 277, 280n, 315, 361n, 362n, 376n, 321n, 338n
Kruse, Douglas L., 199n
Kugler, Adriana D., 207n
Kuhn, Peter J., 421n
Kuziemko, Ilyana, 102, 323n

L

LaFontaine, Paul A., 89
Lalive, Rafael, 421n
Lallemand, Thierry, 223n
Lance, Lochner, 95n
Lang, Kevin, 493n
Lange, Fabian, 95n, 113n
Laroche, Patrice, 318n
Larson, Simeon, 266n
Lawson, Nicholas P., 282n
Layne-Farrar, Anne, 92n
Lazear, Edward, 200n, 429n
Lee, David S., 308
Leibenstein, Harvey, 204n
Lemieux, Thomas, 317n, 448n
Leonard, Jonathan S., 410n, 493n
Levy, Frank, 450n
Lewin, David, 426n
Lewis, H. Gregg, 306n, 307n
Li, Haizheng, 246n
Ligthart, Jenny E., 465n
Lilien, D. M., 491n
Lindbeck, Assar, 496n
Linneman, Peter D., 278n
Lluis, Stephanie, 223n
Lochner, Lance J., 89n
Loewenstein, Mark A., 317n, 371n
Lofgren, Karl-Gustaf, 286n

Logan, John, 279n
Long, James, 249n, 333n
Long, Larry H., 245n
Loughran, David S., 57n
Lowenstein, Mark, 109n, 191n
Lumsdaine, Robin L., 56n
Lurie, Ithai Z., 188n
Lydall, Howard F., 440n, 443n
Lyons, Thomas M., 383n

M

Machin, Stephen, 89, 91n, 95n, 114
Macpherson, David A., 131, 191n, 207n, 272n, 306n, 272n, 306n, 333, 358n, 358n, 363n, 401n
Macunovich, Diane J., 66n
MaCurdy, Thomas E., 286n
Mader, Nicholas S., 89
Madrian, Brigette C., 188
Magnani, Elizabetta, 220n
Manning, Alan, 174n
Manyika, James, 477n
Manzella, Julia, 219
Mareschal, Patrice M., 356n
Marshal, Ray, 266n
Marshall, Alfred, 2, 2n
Marshall, F. Ray, 236n
Mas, Alexandre, 91n, 308, 315
Massey, Douglas S., 258n
Masters, Marick F., 331n
Maurizi, Alex, 291n
Mauro, Martin J., 295n
Mazumder, Bhashkar, 103n
McCaffrey, David, 370n
McCelland, Robert, 25n
McClure, J. Harold, Jr., 359n
McConnell, Sheena, 295n
McCrackin, Bobbie, 115n
McDermed, Ann, 244n
McDonald, Judith A., 406n
McGrattan, Ellen R., 73n
McHugh, Richard, 313n
McKenzie, David, 253n
McKinnish, Terra, 249n
McLennon, Michele, 404n
McWilliams, Abagail, 248n

Mechoulan, Stéphane, 67n
Medoff, James, 223n, 272n, 278n, 306n, 316n, 318n, 323n
Meisenheimer, Joseph R., II, 416n
Mendeloff, John M., 370n
Meyer, Bruce D., 349, 421n, 422n
Mihaly, Kata, 27n
Mihlar, Fazil, 318n
Miller, Paul R., 248n
Mills, D. Quinn, 428n
Mincer, Jacob, 244n, 245n, 438n
Mishel, Lawrence, 202n, 449n
Mitchell, Daniel J. B., 301n
Mitchell, Olivia S., 426n
Mittelhauser, Mark, 146n
Moffitt, Robert, 425n
Moffitt, Robert A., 36n, 42n
Molloy, Raven, 243, 247n
Mom, Shannon, 25n
Montgomery, Edward, 295n, 325n
Moore, Michael J., 371
Moretti, Enrich, 220n
Morris, Martina, 448n
Moulton, Brent R., 333n
Mridha, Hosne, 218n
Mueller, Andreas, 421n
Mulligan, Casey B., 382n
Murnane, Richard J., 450n
Murphy, Kevin M., 63n, 90n, 204n

N

Neal, Derek, 405n, 415n, 437n
Neumann, George R., 279n, 295n, 313n, 421n
Neumark, David, 63, 112n, 304n, 305n, 334, 362n, 394, 404n, 410n
Neyapti, Bilin, 262n
Nicholson, Sean, 179
Nickell, Stephen, 223n
Nilsen, Oivind Anti, 445n
Nissen, Bruce, 266n
Noel, Brett J., 109n

O

O'Connell, Philip J., 109n
Ohashi, Isao, 424n

Oi, Walter Y., 108n, 223
Okun, Arthur M., 416n
Oliner, Stephen D., 477n
Olson, Craig A., 218n, 304n
O'Neill, Donal, 405n
Orrenius, Pia M., 258n
Orszag, Peter R., 40n
Oswald, Andrew, 223n, 285n

P

Paelinck, J. H. P., 178n
Parker, Jonathan, 477n
Parsons, Donald O., 57n
Paserman, M. Daniele, 422n
Patrinos, Anthony, 88n
Pedace, Roberto, 362n
Pencavel, John H., 286n
Peoples, James, Jr., 394
Pettengill, John S., 321n
Petterson, Stephen M., 421n
Phelps, Edmund S., 396n
Phillips, Julie A., 258n
Pierce, Brooks, 333n
Pierret, Charles R., 113n
Piore, Michael J., 248n
Piore, Michael P., 424n
Pischke, Jorn-Steffen, 57n
Plasman, Robert, 223
Pleeter, Saul, 110n, 226n
Polachek, Solomon W., 165, 249n, 422n
Pollak, Robert A., 245n
Popovicic, Ioana, 100
Postlewaite, Andrew, 63n
Poupore, John G., 446n
Prasad, Kislaya, 207n
Psacharopoulos, George, 88n

Q

Quinn, Michael A., 245n

R

Raff, Daniel M. G., 206
Ramoni-Perazzi, Josefa, 333n
Ransom, Michael R., 174n, 361n

Raphael, Steven, 258n
Rebitzer, James B., 358n
Reder, Melvin W., 295n, 313n
Reed, Deborah, 436n
Rees, Albert, 291n, 316n
Rhody, Stephen E., 446n
Riddell, W. Craig, 323n
Ridell, Chris, 421n
Rios-Rull, Jose-Victor, 444n
Rissman, Ellen R., 279n
Rivlin, Alice M., 112n
Roback, Jennifer, 219n
Robbins, Lionel, 22n
Roberston, Raymond, 262n
Robins, Philip K., 100
Rockoff, Jonah E., 195
Roed, Knut, 421n
Rogerson, Richard, 73n
Rose, Nancy L., 203n
Rosen, Sherwin, 200n, 226n, 429n, 437n, 443n
Rosenfeld, Jake, 450n
Rosenthal, Stuart S., 247n
Rouse, Cecilia Elena, 86n, 89n, 410n
Rubb, Stephen, 245n
Rubinfeld, Daniel, 331n
Rubinstein, Yona, 382n
Ruder, Teague, 370n
Rungeling, Brian, 266n
Ruser, John W., 370n
Rycx, Francois, 223n

S

Sabia, Joseph J., 363n
Saks, Raven E., 246n
Salmon, Timothy C., 207n
Sand, Benjamin M., 91n
Sbordone, Argia M., 469n
Schiller, Bradley R., 444n
Schirle, Tammy, 58, 58n
Schlottmann, Alan M., 246n
Schmidt, Lucie, 41n, 219n
Schmitz, S., 306n
Schnell, John F., 295n
Schoenbaum, Michael, 68n
Schönberg, Uta, 109n
Schumacher, Edward J., 173n, 305n

Scully, Gerald W., 175
Seaman, Paul T., 113n
Seitchik, Adam D., 484n
Selden, Thomas L., 190n
Selod, Harris, 67n
Sevak, Purvi, 41n
Shea, John, 441n
Shearer, Bruce, 194n
Sherer, Peter D., 426n
Sichel, Daniel E., 477n
Sicilian, Paul, 110n
Siebert, W. Stanley, 106n, 305n, 422n, 423n
Simester, Duncan, 199n
Simon, Julian L., 255n
Simon, Kosali Ilayperuma, 359n
Sinclair, Diane S., 271n
Singell, Larry D., Jr., 113n, 291n
Sinning, Mathias G., 382n, 405n
Sjaastad, Larry A., 242n
Sloane, Peter J., 390n
Slottje, Daniel, 436n
Smith, Christopher L., 243, 247n
Smith, James P., 59n, 383n, 410n
Smith, Sharon P., 333n
Smith, Robert S., 187n, 359n, 370n
Snower, Dennis, 496n
Solon, Gary, 441n, 445n
Sorensen, Elaine, 297n
Sowell, Thomas, 395n
Spence, Michael, 112n
Spencer, Barbara J., 310n
Spilimbergo, Antonio, 261n, 262n
Spletzer, James R., 109n
Sprague, Shawn, 460
Stafford, Frank P., 305n
Stancanelli, Elena G. F., 421n
Stanger, Shuchita, 362n
Starr, Martha A., 70n
Steindel, Charles, 456n
Stephens, J. Melvin, 70n
Stigler, George J., 236n, 373n
Stiglitz, Joseph E., 496n
Stiroh, Kevin, 456n, 463n, 475n, 476n, 477n
Stock, James H., 56n
Strahan, Philip E., 394
Stratton, Leslie S., 484n, 499n
Strauss, John, 204n
Strayer, Wayne, 94n
Stroup, Richard, 347n

Summers, Lawrence H., 6, 192n, 206, 485n
Sweetman, Olive, 405n
Swindisky, Robert, 89n
Syverson, Chad, 477n

T

Tachibanaki, Toshiaki, 424n
Talley, Wayne K., 394
Tannery, Frederick J., 422n
Taubman, Paul, 102n, 220n
Taylor, Jason E., 206
Taylor, Lowell J., 65, 66, 358n
Terry, S. L., 484n
Theodos, Brett, 446n
Thomas, Duncan, 204n
Thomas, Lacy Glenn, 371n
Thornton, Robert J., 374n, 406n
Thoursie, Anna, 421n
Thurow, Lester C., 252n, 396n, 428n, 442n
Timmons, Edward J., 374n
To, Ted, 358n
Todd, Petra E., 89n, 92n, 383n
Topel, Robert H., 95n, 204n, 220n, 495n
Tracy, Joseph S., 295n, 318n
Trejo, Stephen J., 74n, 249n, 254n
Troske, Kenneth R., 394
Turner, Sarah, 178n

U

Urzua, Sergio, 405n
Uusitalo, Roope, 92n

V

Vaage, Kjell, 445
Vainiomaki, J., 223n
Valletta, Robert G., 449n
Van de Gaer, Dirk, 405n
Van Der Klaauw, Wilbert, 57n
Van Ours, Jan C., 422n
Viscusi, W. Kip, 218n, 370n, 371
Vodopivec, Milan, 422n
Voos, Paula B., 278n

W

Wachter, Michael L., 278n, 304n, 305n, 429n
Wadhwani, Sushil, 223n
Waidmann, Timothy, 68n
Waldmann, Robert J., 469n
Wallace, Geoffrey, 41n
Wang, Bing, 477n
Wang, Zheng, 109n
Ward, Michael P., 59n
Warner, John T., 101n, 226n, 335n, 337n
Warren, Ronald S., Jr., 494n
Wascher, William, 68n, 362n
Wei, Xiangdong, 405n
Weinstein, Paul A., 310n
Weiss, Andrew, 112n, 204n
Weiss, Leonard W., 170n, 370n
Weiss, Yoram, 204n
Weitzman, Martin L., 199n
Welch, Finis, 67n, 90n, 92n, 95n, 383n, 410n
Weltmann, Dan, 199n
Wessels, Walter J., 305n, 359n
Western, Bruce, 280n, 450n
White, Eugene, 277n
Wiatrowski, William J.,200n
Wiedenbaum, Murray L., 369n
Wikstrom, Magnus, 286n
Williams, Rhonda M., 395n
Winegarden, C. R., 263n
Winkler, Anne E., 52, 59n, 64n, 401n
Winters. John V., 405n
Wise, David A., 56n, 113n
Woessmann, Ludger, 89, 91n, 95n, 114
Wolfe, John R., 220n
Wolfram, Catherine, 203n
Wolpin, Kenneth, 113n
Wong, Joyce, 62n
Woodbury, Stephen A., 192n, 436n
Woodford, Michael, 477n
Wozniak, Abigail, 243, 245n, 246n, 247n
Wright, Randall D., 429n

Y

Yamaguchi, Shintaro, 415n
Yang, Fang, 87n
Yellen, Janet L., 204n, 469n

Z

Zafar, Basit, 406n
Zaretsky, Adam M., 416n

Zavodny, Madeline, 258n, 262n
Zenou, Yves, 67n
Zimbalist, Andrew, 175
Zimmermann, Klaus F., 438

Subject Index

Note: Page numbers followed by "n" indicate notes.

A

Ability differences
  complementary elements, 439
  direct impact, 439
  in human capital investment, 98, 99–100
  in multifactor approach to the earnings
    distribution, 439–440
Ability problem, 111–112
Absolute frequency distributions, 433–434
Acceptance wage, 417–418
Access to funds, 100–101
Accident model, strikes, 293–295
Actual labor force, 54
Actual subsidy payment, 37–39
Adaptability, in economic perspective, 4
Adaptive expectations theory, 419
Added-worker effect, 70
Adverse selection problem, 191
Affirmative action programs, 409
AFL-CIO, 272, 274
African-Americans. See also Labor market
    discrimination; Racial differences
  labor force participation rate, 66–68
  population trends, 47, 50
Age differences
  as determinant of migration, 244–245
  labor participation rates, 56–58
  life-cycle mobility of earnings, 444
  in union membership, 271–272
Age-earnings profiles, 78, 79n
Agents
  defined, 193–194
  principal-agent problem, 193–194
Aggregate demand, 488–489
Aggregate labor market, 490

Aid to Families with Dependent Children
    (AFDC) program, 40
Allocative efficiency, 167–168, 191–192, 428–429
  perfect competition and, 168
Alternative pay schemes, 184–207
  efficiency wage payments, 203–207
  fringe benefits. See Fringe benefits
  labor market efficiency, 207
  pay for performance, 194–203
  principal-agent problem, 193–194
American Federation of Labor (AFL), 282, 356
American Federation of Labor and Congress of
    Industrial Organizations (AFL-CIO),
    272, 274
Annual salary, 196
Antidiscriminatory policies, 407–411
  Civil Rights Act of 1964, 408
  Equal Pay Act of 1963, 408
  Executive Orders (1965–1968), 408, 409
  working of, 409–411
Apparel industry, 146
Armed Forces Qualifying Test (AFQT), 405
Asians, population trends, 50
Average product (AP) of labor, 121–124
Average wage cost (AWC), 167
  monopoly, 169
  monopsony, 172–175, 360–361

B

Baby boom, 47, 61
Baby bust, 47
Backflows in migration patterns, 248
Backward-bending labor supply curve, 21, 25
Bargaining power, 357

Bargaining structure, 375–376

Basic benefit, 37

Beaten paths, 246

Becker's model of the allocation of time, 49–53
  household perspective, 49, 50–51, 51–52
  income effect in, 52
  substitution effect in, 52–253

Benefit reduction rate, 37–38, 40n

Birth control pill, 62

Birthrate trends, 61

Blacklists, 354

BLS productivity index, 457–458

Blue-collar wages
  unionization and, 321, 323

Bonuses, 197–199
  personal performance, 197–198
  team performance, 198–199

Box Inc., 417

Break-even level of income, 37

Bridgestone/Firestone tires, 315

Budget (wage) constraint line, 17–18

Bureau of Labor Statistics (BLS), 54n, 185,
    481–482
  BLS productivity index, 457–458
  composition of total compensation, 186

C

Capital market imperfections
  defined, 103
  in human capital investment, 103–104

Capital mobility, 256

Caring jobs, 219

Change to Win federation, 273

Chief executive officer (CEO) compensation,
    200–203

Child care
  commuting time and, 65
  trends, 61

China syndrome, 166

Choice, in economic perspective, 3

"Churning" within the earnings distribution, 444

Civil Rights Act of 1964, 408

Cobweb model, 176–177

Codetermination, 289

Collective voice, 316–317

College students

advantages of college education, 114
  labor force participation rate, 57
  nonparticipation in labor force, 29–30
  recessions and, 87
  reversal of college gender gap, 102

College wage premium, 89–91

Commissions, 195, 196

Commodities
  characteristics, 51

Commuting time, 65

Compensating wage differentials, 217–220, 305
  fringe benefits, 218
  job location, 219–220
  job security, 220
  job status, 218
  prospect of wage advancement, 220
  risk of job injury/death, 218
  for shift work, 230–231
  union wage advantage, 313–315

Compensation
  chief executive officer (CEO), 200–203
  efficiency wage payments, 203–207
  equity, 200
  fringe benefits. See Fringe benefits
  pay for performance, 194–203
  principal-agent problem, 193–194

Congress of Industrial Organizations (CIO), 356

Consumption, in Becker's model, 52, 53

Consumption, investment vs., 110

Contingent workers, 149

Contraception, 62

Contract (bargaining) curve, 285

Cost-of-living adjustments (COLAs), 306

Costs, in human capital model, 86, 86n

Credit Suisse, 417–418

Crowding model of occupational segregation,
    397–402
  assumptions and predictions, 398–399
  defined, 398–399
  ending discrimination, 399–400
  evidence, 401–402
  index of segregation, 400–401

Crowding-out effect, 202

Current discrimination, 390

Current population survey (CPS), 481

Cyclic changes, in productivity, 468–470
  composition of output, 469
  implications, 469–470

utilization of labor, 468–469
utilization of plant and equipment, 469
Cyclic unemployment. *See* Demand-deficient
    unemployment

D

Davis–Bacon Act (1931), 289
Deindustrialization, increase inearnings
    inequality and, 449
Demand, for labor. *See* Labor demand
Demand-deficient unemployment, 493–497, 501
    graphic analysis, 494–495
    wage rigidity, 495–497
Demand for human capital curve, 98–99
Derived demand
    defined, 119
    for labor, 119–121
Determinants of labor demand, 142–146,
    162–165
    number of employers, 142, 163, 289
    prices of other resources, 142–146, 163
    product demand, 142, 163
    productivity, 142, 163
Determinants of labor supply, 162–164
Determinants of migration, 244–247
    age, 244–245
    defined, 244
    distance, 246
    education, 245–246
    family factors, 245
    unemployment rates, 246–247
D-factor, 440
Direct (out-of-pocket) costs of human capital, 80
Direct discrimination, 390
Disability benefits, 57
Discount formula, 83
Discounting, in human capital model, 81–85
Discouraged-worker effect, 70
Discouraged workers, 484
Discrimination. *See also* Labor market
    discrimination
    defined, 389
    in human capital investment, 101
    rational choice *vs.,* 403–407
    types of, 389–390
    uncertainty of earnings and, 100

wage differentials and, 223
Discrimination coefficient, 391–392
Discriminatory discharge, 354
Displaced workers, 492–493
Distance, as determinant of migration, 246
Distribution of personal earnings, 320–323,
    432–452
    absolute frequency distributions, 433–434
    "churning" within distribution, 444
    defined, 432
    earnings inequality, 447–452
    Gini coefficient, 434–436
    government employment, 446
    human capital model, 437–443
    inequality in, 320–321
    Lorenz curve, 434
    mobility within, 444–447
    multifactor approach, 439–443
    schematic summary, 443
Divorce, 47, 62, 62
Domestic content rules, 377–378
Dual-worker families, 47
Dynamic efficiency, internal labor markets, 428

E

Earned income tax credit (EITC) program,
    40–42
Earnings. *See also* Distribution of personal
    earnings
    career, 92
    distribution of. *See* Distribution, of earnings
    estimating, 178
    labor market discrimination in, 382–388
    migration and personal gains, 248–249
    regularity of, 220
    trends, 56
Earnings differentials, 87–88
Earnings mobility, 444–447
    "churning" within the earnings
        distribution, 444
    evidence, 444–446
    intergenerational earnings, 445
    international comparisons, 445
    life-cycle mobility, 444
Economic perspective, 3–4
Economic rent, 372–378

Economies of scale, 466
  fringe benefits, 190
Education levels. *See also* Human capital theory
  age-earnings profiles, 78, 79n
  as determinant of migration, 245–246
  distribution of personal earnings, 437–438
  international comparisons, 81
  labor market discrimination, 384
  male, 79
  rising leisure time inequality, 451–452
Efficiency, and labor unions, 309
  negative view, 309–315
  positive view, 316–318
Efficiency gains from migration, 250–251
Efficiency of labor, 465–466
Efficiency wage
  defined, 204
  shirking model of, 204
Efficiency wage payments, 203–207
  criticism, 206–207
  nonclearing labor markets, 205–206
  wage differentials, 222
  wage-productivity dependence, 203–205
Efficiency wages, 491–492
Efficient allocation of labor, 167–168, 191–192,
    207–208, 428–429
Efficient contracts model, 283–285
Elasticity of labor demand, 137–141
  determinants of wage elasticity, 139–141
  estimates of wage elasticity, 141
  significance of wage elasticity, 141
  total wage bill rules, 137–138
  wage elasticity coefficient, 137
Empirical evidence, 285–286, 305–307, 317–318
Employee stock ownership plan (ESOP), 199n
Employer
  heterogeneities, 222–223
  internal labor market and, 424–426
  isoprofit curve, 188, 190, 228–229
  multiemployer bargaining, 275
  number of, as determinant of labor demand,
    142, 163, 289
Employment, 480–503. *See also* Job search
    model; Unemployment
  aggregate demand, 488–489
  aggregate labor market, 490
  aggregate supply, 489–490
  critique of household data, 483–484

effects of graduating from college in bad
    economy, 486
  employment-population ratio, 481–482
  full, 487–488
  labor productivity and, 470–474
  statistics, 481–488
Employment Act of 1946, 500
Employment discrimination, 390
Employment effects
  of illegal aliens, 259–261
  income tax, 343–346
  of minimum wage, 361–362
Employment-population ratio, 481–482
Entry-level pay, 220
Equal Employment Opportunity
    Commission, 408
Equal Pay Act of 1963, 408
Equilibrium wage differentials, 212
Equitable comparisons, 304
Equity compensation, 200
Excess demand, 161
Excess supply, 161
Exclusive unionism, 291
Executive Orders (1965–1968), 408
Exercise, benefits of, 227
Exit mechanism, 316
Export–Import Bank, 339
External job search, 415–422
  empirical evidence, 421–422
  implications, 420–421
  inflation and, 418–419
  unemployment compensation and, 420
External labor market, 424

F

Fair Labor Standards Act of 1938 (FLSA), 35,
    74, 357
Family background, 440–441
Family factors, as determinants of migration, 245
Featherbedding, 310
Females. *See also* Gender differences
  age-earnings profiles, 79
  college gender gap, 102
  international comparisons, 59
  in labor force participation rate, 55, 56, 58–59
  labor supply of, 66
  wages, 59

Feminist movement, 60
Firm profitability
    profit-maximizing level of job safety, 365–367
    profit sharing, 199
    unions and, 318–320
Firm size, wage differentials and, 223
Fiscal effects, of illegal aliens, 263
Fiscal policy, 500
Florida lobster fishermen, labor supply of, 33
Foreign purchases effect, 489
Free-rider problem, 198
Frequency distributions, 433–434
Frictional unemployment, 490–491, 500
    defined, 490
    efficiency wages, 491–492
    temporary layoffs, 491
    union job queues, 491
Fringe benefits, 184–193
    compensating wage differentials and, 218
    defined, 184–185
    growth, 186, 189–190
    theory of optimal. See Theory of optimal
        fringe benefits
    union wage advantage, 307
Full employment, 487–488
Full Employment and Balanced Growth Act of
    1978, 500

G

Gender differences, 382–389. See also Females;
    Males
    in earnings, 382–388
    in education, 385
    in labor force participation rate, 55, 56
    in nondiscriminatory factors, 403–407
    in occupational distribution, 384–385
    rising leisure time inequality, 451–452
    in unemployment, 383
    in union membership, 271–272
General Education Development (GED), 89
General training, 105, 106–107, 438
Geographic immobilities, 235
Geographic mobility, 242, 243, 245
Gini coefficient, 434–437
Global perspective. See International
    comparisons

Goods-intensive commodities, 51
Government, and labor market, 329–349,
    353–378
    extent and growth, 330–332
    income taxation, 342–348
    international comparisons, 332, 366
    labor law, 353–357
    labor market effects of publicly provided
        goods and services, 340–342
    military sector, 334–337
    minimum wage law, 357–363
    nonpayroll spending by government, 338–340
    occupational health and safety regulation. See
        Occupational health and safety regulation
    public sector unions, 267–271
    public sector vs. private sector pay, 333–334
    as rent provider, 372–378
    role of government workers, 331–332
Government purchases, 338
Great Depression, 494–495
Gross complements, 144–146
Gross domestic product (GDP), 455–457
Gross substitutes, 142–143

H

Health insurance, 192
Hedonic theory of wages, 226–232
    labor market implications, 231–232
    matching workers with jobs, 229–230
    worker's indifference map, 227–228
Heterogeneous workers and jobs, 217–226
    compensating differentials, 217–220
    differing individual preferences, 225–226
    employer heterogeneities, 222–223
    noncompeting groups, 224–225
    skill differentials, 221–222
Hiring decision, by individual firm, 165–167
Hispanics, population trends, 47, 50
Histogram, 433–434
"Hoarded" labor, 313, 469–470
Homestead Strike of 1892, 354
Homogeneous workers and jobs
    defined, 213
    perfect competition, 213–214
Hot-cargo clauses, 357–358
Hourly pay, 196

Hours of work
  standard workday, 33–35
  workweek trends, 72–74
Household productivity trends, 61
Households
  in Becker's model of the allocation of time,
    49, 50, 51–52
Household Survey, 481
Human capital discrimination, 390
Human capital theory, 78–115
  ability differences and, 98–99, 100, 439–440
  capital market imperfections, 103
  criticisms, 110–115
  demand for human capital curve, 97–98
  diminishing rates of return, 96–97
  discounting and net present value, 81–85
  distribution of personal earnings, 437–443
  empirical data, 88–95
  generalizations and implications, 85–87
  internal rate of return, 85
  international comparisons, 81
  investment in human capital, 362. *See also*
    Investment in human capital
  investment *vs.* consumption, 110
  migration as investment in human capital,
    242–255
  multifactor approach to earnings distribution,
    439–443
  noncompeting groups and, 224
  on-the-job training. *See* On-the-job training
  supply of investment funds curve, 97
Hurricanes, local labor markets and, 165

I

Illegal immigration, 259–263
  employment effects, 259–261
  fiscal effects, 263
  international comparisons, 259
  wage effects, 262
Immediate-market-period labor supply curve, 177
Immigration, 47, 48, 157–263
  history and scope, 257–259
  illegal, 259–263
Immigration Act of 1921, 257
Immigration Act of 1924, 257
Immigration and Nationality Act of 1952, 257

Immigration Reform and Control Act of 1986,
    258–259
Imperfectly competitive seller, short-run demand
    for labor, 127–128
Implicit contracts, 495–496
Import quotas, 377
Incentive pay plans, 194
Inclusive unionism, 292
Income effect, 339–340
  in Becker's model, 52
  defined, 21
  graphic portrayal, 23–25
  wage rates and, 21
Income-elastic/income-sensitive demand, 472n
Income elasticity, 472n
Income guarantee, 37
Income-inelastic/income-insensitive
    demand, 472n
Income inequality, 447–452
  international comparisons, 449
  leisure time inequality, 451–452
  minimum wage and, 362
  trends in wage inequality, 477–478
Income maintenance programs, 36–40
  controversy, 39–40
  defined, 36
  earned income tax (EITC) program,
    40–41, 42
  features of, 37
  illustration, 37–39
  social insurance programs *vs.*, 36n
  welfare as entitlement, 40–41
Income tax, 342–348
  defined, 342
  impact on wages and employment, 343–346
  international comparisons, 343
  and labor supply, 344–348
Index of segregation, 400–401
Indifference curves, 13–17
Indifference maps
  income-leisure, 15
  of workers in hedonic wage theory, 227–228
Indirect (opportunity) costs of human capital,
    79–80
Indirect discrimination, 390
Industrial unions, 292
Industry
  productivity, 471–473
  union membership, 268–271

Inferior goods, 52n, 472n

Inflation
    and job search, 418–420
    and labor productivity, 461–463
    labor unions and, 306, 323

Information on labor markets, 233–235
    imperfect information/assessment of job
        safety, 367–368
    lengthy adjustment periods, 235
    migration and personal gains, 247–248
    perfect information/assessment of job
        safety, 367
    wage rate distributions, 234

Injunctions, 356, 357

In-kind benefits, 187

Insider–outsider theories, 496–497

Institutional immobilities, 235–236

Institutionalists, 304

Interactions, in human capital investment,
        101–103

Interest rate effect, 489

Internal labor markets, 422–429
    characteristics of, 423–424
    defined, 422–423
    efficiency issue, 428–429
    job tenure, 423
    labor allocation and wage structure, 426–428
    reasons for, 424–426
    role of unions, 426

Internal rate of return, in human capital
        model, 85

International comparisons
    annual hours of work per employee, 13
    annual net employment range as percentage of
        total employment, 120
    chief executive officer compensation, 202
    college graduates worldwide, 81
    earnings inequality, 449
    earnings mobility across generations, 445
    employer-provided education and training, 107
    hourly pay around the world, 216
    illegal immigration, 259
    income tax rates, 343
    job tenure, 423
    labor force participation for women, 60
    manufacturing productivity growth, 467
    occupational injuries, 366
        occupational segregation, 402
        percentage of union wage differential, 287
        public sector employment, 333
        self-employment as percentage of total
            employment, 144
        strike incidence, 312
        temporary employment as percentage of total
            employment, 145
        time stress, 73
        unemployment rates, 487
        union membership as percentage of wage and
            salary workers, 268

Investment
    consumption vs., 110
    impact of unions on, 319
    union wage advantage and, 316

Investment in human capital, 103
    differences in, 98–103

Isocost curves, 154

Isoprofit curve, 188, 228–229

Isoquant curves, 152–154

J

Job accessibility, 63

Job change, 241

Job discrimination, 390

Job evaluation, 427

Job injury/death, compensating wage
        differentials, 218

Job ladder, 424

Job location, 219–220

Job search costs, 315

Job search model, 415–429
    acceptance wage, 416–418
    defined, 415–416
    external, 415–422
    inflation and, 418
    internal labor markets, 422–429

Job security, 220

Job status, 218

Job tenure
    academic, 195
    international comparisons, 423

Joint monopsony, 171

L

Labor costs, total costs and, 150
Labor demand, 119–156
  comparative advantage and, 136
  derived demand, 120–121d
  determinants, 162–165
  determinants of. *See* Determinants of labor
    demand
  distribution of personal earnings, 450
  effects of publicly provided goods and
    services, 340
  efficiency allocation of labor, 167–168,
    191–192
  elasticity of. *See* Elasticity of labor demand
  hurricanes and, 165
  impact on firm investment, 319
  international comparisons, 120, 144–145
  isocost curves, 154
  isoquant curves, 152–154
  labor unions and wage determination,
    286–293
  least-cost combination of resources, 154–155
  long-run. *See* Long-run demand for labor
  market demand for labor, 133–135
  perfectly competitive labor market, 160–162
  real-world applications, 146–149
  short-run, 124–129
  short-run production function. *See* Short-run
    production function
Labor economics
  defined, 1
  as discipline, 1–9
  economic perspective and, 3–4
  macroeconomics, 6, 488–490
  microeconomics, 6
  "old" and "new" in, 3
  overview, 6–9
Labor force participation rate (LFPR), 54–71.
  See also Labor market participation
  actual labor force, 54
  cyclic changes, 70–71
  female in, 55, 56, 58–64
  males in, 55, 56–58, 66–68
  potential labor force, 54
  racial differences, 66–68
  secular trend, 55–69
Labor hoarding, 313, 468–469

Labor immobilities, 235–237
Labor law, 353–357
  and bargaining power, 357
  basic labor relations laws, 355
  and union membership, 354–356
Labor market discrimination, 381–411
  crowding model of occupational segregation.
    See Crowding model of occupational
    segregation
  earnings, 382–387
  education, 385
  gender and racial differences, 382–389
  international comparisons, 402
  occupational distribution, 384–385
  statistical discrimination, 396–397
  taste for discrimination model. *See* Taste for
    discrimination model
  theories, 390–391
  unemployment, 427
Labor market imperfections, 233–237
  imperfect information, 233–235, 410–411
Labor market participation
  of college students, 29–30
  impact of pollution, 26
  income maintenance programs and, 37–39
  population trends and, 47–49, 50
Labor mobility, 240–263
  capital flows, 256
  defined, 240
  migration, 242–255
  product flows, 257
  types of, 241–242
  U.S. immigration policy, 257–263
Labor productivity, 455–477
  BLS productivity index, 457–458
  and compensation, 460
  concept of, 455–458
  cyclic changes, 468–470
  defined, 455–456
  as determinants of labor demand, 142, 163
  and employment, 470–389
  growth of, 458–463
  inflation and, 461–463
  international comparisons, 468
  long-run trend, 463–468
  measurement, 456–457
  "new economy," 475–477
  wage-productivity dependence, 203–205
Labor quality, 463–464

Labor supply, 12–42
  budget constraint, 17–18
  determinants, 162–164
  distribution of personal earnings, 449
  earned income tax (EITC) program, 41, 42
  effects of publicly provided goods and
      services, 340–342
  efficiency allocation of labor, 167–168,
      207–208
  elasticity *vs.* changes in, 27–28
  empirical evidence, 25–26
  Florida lobster fishermen, 33
  hurricanes and, 165
  income maintenance programs, 36–39
  income taxes and, 344–347
  indifference curves, 13–17
  international comparisons, 12
  male, 55, 56–57, 66–68
  of married women, 66
  nonparticipants, 29–32
  perfectly competitive labor market, 160–161
  pollution and, 26
  premium pay *vs.* straight time, 35–36
  reservation wage, 30–32
  restricting, 289–291
  standard workday, 33–35
  utility maximization, 18–19
  wage rate changes. *See* Wage rates
  of women, 66–67
Labor turnover, 204
  wage differentials and, 316–317
Labor unions, 266–295, 300–323
  as collective voice, 316–317
  college athletes, 269
  decline, 276–282, 450–451
  efficiency and, 309–315
  and firm profitability, 318–320
  and inflation, 306, 323
  and internal labor markets, 425–426
  international comparisons, 267, 287, 313
  labor's share, 325
  membership, 266–272, 276–282
  objectives, 282–286
  productivity and, 309–315
  public sector, 267, 333
  purpose, 267
  responses, 281–282
  strikes, 310–313
  and unemployment, 323–324

  union job queues, 491–492
  union wage advantage. *See* Union wage
      advantage
  wage determination, 356–393
Landrum–Griffin Act of 1959, 295, 355,
    356–357
Law of diminishing marginal returns, 123
Layoffs, temporary, 490
Least-cost combination of resources, 154–155
Leisure time. *See* Work–leisure model
Length of income stream, in human capital
    model, 86
Life-cycle mobility of earnings, 444–445
Lifetime earnings streams, 178
Living standards, maintaining, 63
Local unions, 274–275
Location, union membership, 271
Lockouts, 354
Long-run demand for labor, 129–133
  combined effects, 131–132
  defined, 137
  output effect, 130
  substitution effect, 130–131
Long-run demand for labor curve, 155–156
Long-run supply curve, 177
Lorenz curve, 434

M

Macroeconomics, 6, 488–490
Make-work rules, 310–311
Males. *See also* Gender differences
  age-earnings profiles, 79
  college gender gap, 102
  education levels, 79
  labor force participation rate, 55, 56–58,
      66–68
  wages/earnings, 56
Managerial opposition hypothesis, 278–279
Managerial performance, union wage advantage
    and, 317
Manufacturing. *See* Labor unions
  China syndrome, 166
  deindustrialization and increase in earnings
      inequality, 449
Manufacturing employment, decrease in, 134
Marginal benefit (MB), from job safety, 365–366

Marginal cost (MC), of job safety, 365–367

Marginal internal rate of return, 96

Marginal product (MP) of labor, 121–123

Marginal rate of substitution of leisure for
    income (MRS L, Y), 15, 19

Marginal rate of technical substitution (MRTS),
    153–154

Marginal revenue (MR), monopoly, 169–170

Marginal revenue product (MRP)
    of labor demand, 162–163
    long-run demand for labor, 132–133
    market demand for labor, 133–135
    monopoly, 169–170
    monopsony, 172
    on-the-job training, 106–108
    perfect competition, 168
    short-run demand for labor, 124–128

Marginal wage cost (MWC), 125, 167–168
    monopoly, 169
    monopsony, 172–175, 360–361
    perfect competition, 168

Market demand for labor, 133–135

Marriage
    divorce, 47, 62
    spouse earnings, 249–250

Master agreement, 275

McDonald's, 176

Mean, 433–434

Measured union wage advantage, 303

Median, 433–434

Mergers, of labor unions, 281

Microeconomics, 6

Midpoints formula, 137

Migration, 242–255
    capital flows, 256
    consequences, 247–255
    determinants. See Determinants of migration
    product flows, 257
    U.S. immigration policy and issues, 257–263

Migration externalities, 252–254
    pecuniary, 253–255
    real negative, 252

Military conscription, 335–336

Military sector, 334–337
    military conscription, 335–337
    voluntary/market-based army, 337–338

Minimum wage, 149, 357–363, 484
    competitive model, 358–359

    empirical evidence, 361–362
    facts and controversy, 358
    Fair Labor Standards Act of 1938, 74, 357
    monopsony, 360

Mode, 433–434

Model of the allocation of time (Becker). See
    Becker's model of the allocation of time

Monetary policy, 500–502

Monopoly, 169–170

Monopoly union model, 282–283

Monopsony, 171–174, 360–361

Motor Carrier Act of 1980, 306

MRP = MWC rule, 167, 360–361

MRS L, Y (marginal rate of substitution of
    leisure for income), 15, 19

Multiemployer bargaining, 275

Multifactor approach to earnings distribution,
    439–442
    ability differences, 439–442
    family background, 440–442

Muslims, labor market discrimination, 393

N

National Highway Traffic and Safety
    Administration, 315

National Labor Relations Board (NLRB), 278,
    280, 281

National Linen Service, 307

National unions, 272–273

Natural rate of unemployment, 487

Net effect, wage rates and, 22

Net present value
    defined, 81–82
    formula, 83–84
    in human capital model, 81–84

"New economy," 475
    causes of resurgence, 476–477

Nonclearing labor markets, 205–206

Noncompeting groups, 224–225

Nondiscriminatory factors, 388, 403–407

Nonparticipants in labor force, 29–31

Nonwage benefits, 111

Nonwage income
    as determinant of labor supply, 162
    restricting supply of labor, 291

Normal-profit isoprofit curve, 228

Norris–LaGuardia Act of 1932, 355, 356, 357
North Carolina Board of Dental Examiners
    (NCBDE), 376
Nutritional model, 204

O

Obesity, 226
Occupation, union membership, 267–271
Occupational discrimination, 390
Occupational distribution, labor market
    discrimination, 384–385
Occupational employment trends, 148
Occupational health and safety regulation,
    364–372
    Occupational Safety and Health Act of 1970,
        353, 364, 369–372
    profit-maximizing level of job safety, 365–366
    society's optimal level of job safety, 367–368
    workers' compensation and job safety,
        370–371
Occupational licensure, 291, 373–376
Occupational mobility, 241, 245
Occupational Safety and Health Act of 1970,
    353, 368–372
Occupational Safety and Health Administration
    (OSHA), 368–371
    criticisms of, 368–370
    findings and implications, 370–371
On-the-job training, 104–110
    costs and benefits, 104–105
    distributing training costs, 105–107
    distribution of personal earnings, 438–490
    empirical evidence, 109–110
    general training, 105, 106–107, 438
    international comparisons, 108
    modifications, 108–109
    specific training, 105, 107, 438
    union wage advantage and, 317
Opportunity cost
    defined, 4
    of human capital, 81
Optimal work–leisure position, 19
Organization of Petroleum Exporting
    Countries, 323
Output/scale effect, 130, 155–156
Overemployment, 33–34

P

Parental leave, 64
Past discrimination, 389
Patient Protection and Affordable Care Act
    (PPACA), 130, 192
Pattern bargaining, 275–276
Pay for performance, 194–203
    bonuses, 197–199
    commissions, 195, 196
    piece rates, 208–209
    profit sharing, 199–200
    promotions, 196–197
    raises, 196–197
    royalties, 195, 196
    salaries and wage incentives, 196–197
    tournament pay, 200–203
Payoffs
    personal perspective, 9
    social perspective, 9
Payroll taxes, 190, 349
Pecuniary externalities, 253–254
Perfect equality, 434
Perfectly competitive labor market, 160–168
    allocative efficiency, 167–168
    equilibrium, 161
    hiring decision by individual firm, 165–167
    homogeneous workers and jobs, 213–214
    labor demand and supply, 160–161
Personal appearance
    income benefits of exercise, 226
Personal computers, 147, 149. *See also*
    Technology
Personal distribution of earnings. *See*
    Distribution of personal earnings
Personal gains, as consequence of migration,
    247–248
Personal performance bonuses, 197–198
Personal Responsibility and Work Opportunity
    Reconciliation Act (PRWORA), 1996,
    40, 255
Physical capital quality, 465
Piece rates, 194–195, 197
Pollution, impact on work hours, 26
Population trends, 47–48, 50
Port of entry, 424
Postmarket discrimination, 390
Potential labor force, 54

Poverty
    minimum wage and, 362
Premarket discrimination, 390
Premium pay *vs.* straight time, 35–36
Prevailing wage rule (comparable wage rule), 333
Price of labor, 168–169
Prices, as determinant of labor demand,
        142–144, 162
Principal-agent problem, 193–194
Principals, defined, 193
Private pensions, 57
Private perspective, on human capital
        investment, 94–95
Procyclic labor force changes, 70–71
Product demand
    demand factors constant, 471–472
    demand factors variable, 471–473
    as determinant of labor demand, 142, 162
    elasticity, 139–140
    in long-run demand for labor, 132
Product flows, 257
Production function
    defined, 121
    short-run. *See* Short-run production function
Productivity, and labor unions, 309–318
    negative view, 309–315
    positive view, 316–318
Product market effect, 304
Product quality, labor strife and, 315
Professional baseball, 175
Profit. *See* Firm profitability
Profit sharing, 199
Promotions, 196–197
Public assistance. *See* Income maintenance
        programs
Public capital, and productivity, 465
Pullman Strike of 1894, 354
Pure monopsony, 171
Pure public goods, 340–342
    defined, 341
    and labor demand, 340
    and labor supply, 341–342
Pure union wage advantage, 301
Purposeful behavior, in economic perspective, 4

Q

Quantitative importance, 2
Quasi-fixed resources, 196

Quintiles, 434
Quotas, 377–378

R

Racial differences, 382–388
    in earnings, 382–387
    in education, 385
    in labor force participation rate, 66–70
    in nondiscriminatory factors, 403–407
    in occupational distribution, 384–385
    in unemployment, 383
    in union membership, 271–272
Raises, 196–197
Rate-of-return, in human capital model, 88–89
    diminishing, 96–97
Rational choice *vs.* discrimination, 403–408
Rational expectations, 178
Real balances effect, 489
Real GDP, 461
Real wages, labor productivity and, 458–461
Recessions
    discouraged-worker effect, 70
    impact on college students, 87
Relative scarcity, in economic perspective, 4–5
Relative share, 280–281
Rent providers
    defined, 373
    government as, 372–377
Rent seekers, 373
Reservation wage, 30–32
Restaurant workers, 198
Restrictive work rules, 310–311
Royalties, 195

S

Safety. *See* Occupational health and safety
        regulation
Scale effect. *See* Output/scale effect
Screening hypothesis, 112–113, 114
Search unemployment, 490
Secondary boycotts, 357
Self-employment, 145
Self-selection, 248, 439
Seniority, 426
    union wage advantage and, 317
September 11, 2001 terrorist attacks, 394

Sherman Antitrust Act of 1890, 354
Shift work, compensating wage differentials
    for, 230
Shirking, 193
Shirking model, of efficiency wage, 203–204, 222
Shock effect, 317
Short-run demand for labor, 124–129
    imperfectly competitive seller, 127–129
    perfectly competitive seller, 124–127
Short-run labor demand curve, 125–129
Short-run production function, 121–124
    law of diminishing marginal returns, 123
    stages of production, 121–123
    total/marginal/average product of labor,
        121–124
    zone of production, 123–124
Signaling hypothesis, 112–113
Single-company bargaining, 276
Skilled labor demand, 321
Skill transferability, 248
Social insurance programs, 30n
Socialization, 52
Social perspective
    on human capital investment, 94–95
    payoffs and, 9
Social Security, 57–58
Socioeconomic issues, 2
Sociological immobilities, 236
Specific training, 105, 107, 438
Spillover effect, 303–304
Sports
    pay for performance, 175
Stagflation, 306
Standard workday
    overemployment, 33–34
    underemployment, 34–35
Static efficiency, internal labor markets, 428
Statistical discrimination, 396–397
Stochastic theories, 441
Stock–flow model, 484–485
Stock options, 200
Straight-time equivalent wage, 35–36
Strikebreakers, 279, 281, 354
Strikes
    accident model, 293–295
    asymmetric information model, 295
    and bargaining, 293–295
    effect on efficiency, 309–313
    international comparisons, 312

strikebreakers, 281
Strongly efficient contract curve, 285
Structural change hypothesis, 277–278
Structural unemployment, 492–493, 500–501
    defined, 492
    displaced workers, 492–493
Subemployed, 484
Subsidies, 339
    demand effects, 339–340
    supply effects, 339–340
Substitutability, of other inputs for labor,
        140–141
Substitution effect, 339–340
    in Becker's model, 52–53
    defined, 22, 156
    graphic portrayal, 23–24
    and long-run demand for labor, 130–131
    wage rates and, 22–23
Substitution hypothesis, 279–280
Superior worker effect, 305–306
Supply and demand, in labor markets, 2
Supply elasticity, of other inputs for labor, 140
Supply of investment funds curve, 97
Supply of labor. *See* Labor supply

T

Taft–Hartley Act of 1947, 355, 356–357
Tariffs, 377–378
Taste for discrimination model, 300–305
    competition and discrimination, 395
    defined, 391
    demand and supply interpretation, 392–393
    discrimination coefficient, 391–392
    gainers/losers, and persistence of
        discrimination, 393–395
Taxes
    income, and labor market, 342–348
    payroll, 190, 349
Team performance bonuses, 198–199
Technology
    long-run demand for labor, 133
Telecommuting, 243
Temporary Assistance for Needy Families
    (TANF) program, 40
Temporary employment, 145
Temporary layoffs, 490

Tenure
  academic, 195
Textile industry, 146
Theory of optimal fringe benefits, 186–193
  cause of fringe benefit growth, 189–193
  employer's isoprofit curve, 188, 189
  wage-fringe optimum, 189
  worker's indifference map, 187–188
Threat effect, 304–305
Time
  Becker's model of the allocation of time,
    49–53
  time stress, 73
Time-intensive commodities, 51
Time preference, in human capital model, 82,
    101n, 225–226
Time rates, 194
Tips, 197
Total compensation
  components, 185–186
  union wage advantage, 307
Total costs, labor costs and, 139
Total factor productivity, 456
Total product (TP) of labor, 121–124
Total wage bill rules, 137–138
Total wage cost (TWC), monopsony, 172
Tournament pay, 200–203
Trade liberalization, 288
Trade unions. See Labor unions
Trafficking Victims Protection Act of 2000, 258
Training
  on-the-job. See On-the-job training
Transfer payments, 339
  demand effects, 339–340
  supply effects, 339–340
Transitional wage differentials, 212
Trucking industry, 306
Turnover model, and wage differentials, 222

U

Underemployment, 34–35
Undocumented persons, 259–260, 293

Unemployment, 480–503. See also Employment
  demand-deficient, 493–497
  distribution of, 497–499
  employment-population ratio, 481–482
  equilibrium rate of unemployment, 487
  frictional. See Frictional unemployment
  reducing, 500–503
  search, 490
  statistics, 481–488
  stock–flow model, 484–485
  structural, 492–493
  unemployment rate, 581
  wait, 490
Unemployment rates
  college student, 107
  as determinant of migration, 246–247
  international comparisons, 487
  labor market discrimination, 383
  unions and, 324–325
Uniform wages
  among firms, 322
  within firms, 322–323
Union-nonunion wages, 320
Unions. See Labor unions
Union security, 392
Union shop clause, 292
Union status, wage differentials and, 222
Union wage advantage, 300–301
  evidence, 305–307, 307
  and labor misallocation, 313–315
  measuring, 301–305
  preliminary complications, 301
  role of unions, 308–309
  total compensation, 307
Unique characteristics, 2–3
United Automobile Workers, 276, 301
United States
  government employment, 329–331
  income maintenance programs, 36–39
  occupational licensure, 374–377
United Steelworkers of America (USWA), 288
U.S. Census Bureau, 50, 258
U.S. Postal Service, 144
Utility maximization, income-leisure
    decision, 18–19

V

Value of marginal product (VMP), 126
    of labor, 167–168
Value of total product (VTP) of labor, 250–251
Voice mechanism, 316
Voluntary/market-based army, 337–338

W

Wage bill, 137–138
Wage determination, 159–182
    cobweb model, 176–179
    delayed supply responses, 176–179
    evidence and controversy, 178–179
    monopoly in product market, 169–170
    monopsony, 171–175
    perfectly competitive labor market theory,
        160–168
    unions and, 286–293, 320–323
Wage differentials. *See also* Distribution of
        personal earnings
    capital flows and, 256
    compensating, 217–220, 305
    efficiency wage payments, 222
    employer heterogeneities, 222–223
    hedonic theory of wages, 226–231
    heterogeneous workers and jobs. *See* Hetero-
        geneous workers and jobs
    labor market imperfections, 233–238
    noncompeting groups, 224
    observed differentials, 214–215
    product flows and, 257
    shirking model and, 222
    skills, 221–222
    turnover model and, 222
    unions and, 282–293
Wage discrimination, 389–390. *See also* Labor
        market discrimination
Wage effects, of illegal immigration, 261
Wage elasticity
    of labor demand, 140–141
    significance of, 141
Wage elasticity coefficient, 137
Wage elasticity of labor supply, 27

Wage-fringe optimum, 189
Wage narrowing, 250–251
Wage-productivity dependence, 203–204
Wage rates
    backward-bending labor supply curve, 21,
        25–26
    changes in, 20–22
    imperfect labor market information and,
        233–235
    and income effect, 21–24
    and net effect, 22
    and substitution effect, 22–25
Wage rigidity, 495–497
Wages. *See also* Union wage advantage
    female, 59
    impact of income tax on, 342–345
    male, 56
    trends, 56, 447–448
Wage structure, 212–236. *See also* Distribution
        of personal earnings
    defined, 213
    heterogeneous workers and jobs. *See* Hetero-
        geneous workers and jobs
    homogeneous workers and jobs, 213–214
    international comparisons, 216
    labor allocation and, 426–427
    labor market imperfections, 233–237
    observed differentials, 214–217
    unions and, 286–293, 319–323
Wagner Act of 1935, 355, 356
Wait unemployment, 304, 490
Wealth balances effect, 489
Weather, hurricanes and local labor markets, 165
Welfare. *See* Income maintenance programs
Welfare reform, 40–41
White-collar wages, 446
Worker democracy, 289
Work–leisure model, 12–42. *See also* Labor force
        participation rate (LFPR); Labor market
        participation
    application and extension of, 29–41, 49–53
    basic model, 12–27
    budget constraint, 17–18
    elasticity *vs.* changes in, 27–28
    indifference curves, 13–17, 187–188

inheritance and, 32
standard workday, 33–35
utility maximization, 18–19
wage rate changes, 20–22

Work rules, 309–310
Workweek trends, 72–74
World Trade Organization (WTO), 288

Y

Yellow-dog contracts, 354

Z

Zone of production, 123–124

LABOR STATISTICS FOR SELECTED YEARS, 1952–2018

		1952	1954	1956	1958	1960	1962
1.	Noninstitutional population, 16 years or older (millions)[a]	105.2	108.3	111.0	113.7	117.2	120.2
2.	Labor force (millions)[a]	62.1	63.6	66.6	67.6	69.6	70.6
3.	Labor force participation rate (%)[a]	59.0	58.8	60.0	59.5	59.4	58.8
	3a. Male (%)[a]	86.3	85.5	85.5	84.2	83.3	82.0
	3b. Female (%)[a]	34.7	34.6	36.9	37.1	37.7	37.9
	3c. White (%)[a]	na	58.2	59.4	58.9	58.8	58.3
	3d. African-American (%)[a]	na	na	na	na	na	na
4.	Employment (millions)[a]	60.3	60.1	63.8	63.0	65.8	66.7
5.	Unemployment (millions)[a]	1.9	3.5	2.8	4.6	3.9	3.9
6.	Unemployment rate (%)[a]	3.0	5.5	4.1	6.8	5.5	5.5
	6a. Male (%)[a]	2.8	5.3	3.8	6.8	5.4	5.2
	6b. Female (%)[a]	3.6	6.0	4.8	6.8	5.9	6.2
	6c. White (%)[a]	na	5.0	3.6	6.1	5.0	4.9
	6d. African-American (%)[a]	na	na	na	na	na	na
	6e. 16–19-year-olds[a]	8.5	12.6	11.1	15.9	14.7	14.7
7.	Average hourly earnings (current $)[b]	na	na	na	na	na	na
8.	Average hours worked per week[b]	na	na	na	na	na	na
9.	Average earnings per week ($1,982)[b]	na	na	na	na	na	na
10.	Change in earnings (% in $1,982)[b]	na	na	na	na	na	na
11.	Federal minimum wage rate (current $)	0.75	0.75	1.00	1.00	1.00	1.15
12.	Change in productivity from year earlier[c]	3.0	2.2	0.3	2.9	1.8	4.6
13.	Change in real hourly compensation[c]	4.2	2.5	5.0	1.6	2.4	3.4
14.	Change in unit labor cost from year earlier[c]	3.1	1.0	6.3	1.5	2.4	−0.2
15.	Labor union membership (millions)[d]	15.9	17.0	17.5	17.0	17.0	16.6
16.	Union membership as percentage of nonagricultural workers	31.4	33.5	32.2	32.0	30.4	28.9
17.	Work stoppages	470	265	287	332	222	211
18.	Strike time as percentage of total work time[e]	0.38	0.13	0.20	0.13	0.09	0.08
19.	Employee compensation as a percent of national income	61.7	62.3	62.3	62.9	62.9	62.2

[a]Civilian.   [b]Total private, nonagricultural industries.   [c]Business sector.   [d]Includes members of professional associations, 1970-2018.   [e]Days idle in strikes involving 1,000 or more workers divided by total estimated working time.
na = not available.

1964	1966	1968	1970	1972	1974	1976	1978	1980	1982	1984	1986	1988
124.5	128.1	132.0	137.1	144.1	150.1	156.2	161.9	167.7	172.3	176.4	180.6	184.6
73.1	75.8	78.7	82.8	87.0	91.9	96.2	102.3	106.9	110.2	113.5	117.8	121.7
58.7	59.2	59.6	60.4	60.4	61.3	61.6	63.2	63.8	64.0	64.4	65.3	65.9
81.0	80.4	80.1	79.7	78.9	78.7	77.5	77.9	77.4	76.6	76.4	76.3	76.2
38.7	40.3	41.6	43.3	43.9	45.7	47.3	50.0	51.5	52.6	53.6	55.3	56.6
58.2	58.7	59.3	60.2	60.4	61.4	61.8	63.3	64.1	64.3	64.6	65.5	66.2
na	na	na	na	59.9	59.8	59.0	61.5	61.0	61.0	62.2	63.3	63.8
69.3	72.9	75.9	78.7	82.2	86.8	88.8	96.0	99.3	99.5	105.0	109.6	115.0
3.8	2.9	2.8	4.1	4.9	5.2	7.4	6.2	7.6	10.7	8.5	8.2	6.7
5.2	3.8	3.6	4.9	5.6	5.6	7.7	6.1	7.1	9.7	7.5	7.0	5.5
4.6	3.2	2.9	4.4	5.0	4.9	7.1	5.3	6.9	9.9	7.4	6.9	5.5
6.2	4.8	4.8	5.9	6.6	6.7	8.6	7.2	7.4	9.4	7.6	7.1	5.6
4.6	3.4	3.2	4.5	5.1	5.0	7.0	5.2	6.3	8.6	6.5	6.0	4.7
na	na	na	na	10.4	10.5	14.0	12.8	14.3	18.9	15.9	14.5	11.7
16.2	12.8	12.7	15.3	16.2	16.0	19.0	16.4	17.8	23.2	18.9	18.3	15.3
2.53	2.73	3.03	3.41	3.91	4.44	5.06	5.88	6.84	7.86	8.49	8.92	9.44
38.5	38.5	37.7	37	36.9	36.4	36.1	35.8	35.2	34.7	35.1	34.7	34.6
313	323	326	323	342	326	319	320	291	282	289	285	279
na	0.8%	1.2%	−1.4%	4.4%	−4.5%	1.2%	−0.1%	−5.8%	−1.5%	0.6%	0.2%	−1.1%
1.25	1.25	1.60	1.60	1.60	2.00	2.30	2.65	3.10	3.35	3.35	3.35	3.35
3.3	4.1	3.5	2.0	3.4	−1.7	3.3	1.2	0.0	−0.5	2.9	2.8	1.5
2.4	3.8	3.5	1.7	3.0	−1.5	2.1	1.3	−0.4	1.4	0.2	3.8	1.6
0.4	2.5	4.2	5.4	2.9	11.2	4.5	7.1	10.7	8.0	1.5	2.8	3.7
16.8	17.9	18.9	21.2	21.7	22.8	22.7	22.8	22.4	19.8	17.3	17.0	17.0
28.0	27.1	26.9	26.1	25.5	24.9	23.9	22.6	22.2	20.7	18.4	17.1	16.2
246	321	392	381	250	424	231	219	187	96	62	69	40
0.11	0.10	0.20	0.29	0.09	0.16	0.12	0.11	0.09	0.04	0.04	0.05	0.02
61.9	62.6	63.9	66.5	65.3	65.9	65.1	65.1	67.1	66.8	64.5	66.4	65.9

LABOR STATISTICS FOR SELECTED YEARS, 1952–2018

		1990	1992	1994	1996	1998	1999	2000	2001	2002
1.	Noninstitutional population, 16 years or older (millions)[a]	188.0	191.6	196.8	200.6	205.2	207.8	209.7	215.1	217.6
2.	Labor force (millions)[a]	124.8	127.0	131.1	133.9	137.7	139.4	140.9	143.7	144.9
3.	Labor force participation rate (%)[a]	66.4	66.3	66.6	66.8	67.1	67.1	67.2	66.8	66.6
3a.	Male (%)[a]	76.1	75.6	75.1	74.9	74.9	74.7	74.7	74.4	74.1
3b.	Female (%)[a]	57.5	57.8	58.8	59.3	59.8	60	60.2	59.8	59.6
3c.	White (%)[a]	66.9	66.8	67.1	67.2	67.3	67.3	67.3	67.0	66.8
3d.	African-American (%)[a]	64.0	63.9	63.4	64.1	65.6	65.8	65.8	65.3	64.8
4.	Employment (millions)[a]	117.9	117.6	123.1	126.8	131.5	133.5	135.2	136.9	136.5
5.	Unemployment (millions)[a]	6.9	9.4	8.0	7.2	6.2	5.9	5.7	6.8	8.4
6.	Unemployment rate (%)[a]	5.5	7.4	6.1	5.4	4.5	4.2	4	4.7	5.8
6a.	Male (%)[a]	5.6	7.8	6.2	5.4	4.4	4.1	3.9	4.8	5.9
6b.	Female (%)[a]	5.4	6.9	6.0	5.4	4.6	4.3	4.1	4.7	5.6
6c.	White (%)[a]	4.8	6.6	5.3	4.7	3.9	3.7	3.5	4.2	5.1
6d.	African-American (%)[a]	11.4	14.2	11.5	10.5	8.9	8.0	7.6	8.6	10.2
6e.	16–19-year-olds[a]	15.5	20.0	17.6	16.7	14.6	13.9	13.1	14.7	16.5
7.	Average hourly earnings (current $)[b]	10.20	10.77	11.34	12.04	13.01	13.49	14.02	14.54	14.96
8.	Average hours worked per week[b]	34.3	34.2	34.5	34.3	34.5	34.3	34.3	34	33.9
9.	Average Earnings per week ($1,982)[b]	271	266	269	268	281	284	285	285	288
10.	Change in earnings (% in $1,982)[b]	−1.8%	−0.2%	0.8%	0.4%	2.5%	1.0%	0.3%	−0.1%	1.2%
11.	Federal minimum wage rate (current $)	3.80	4.25	4.25	4.75	5.15	5.15	5.15	5.15	5.15
12.	Change in productivity from year earlier[c]	2.0	4.7	0.6	2.5	3.1	4.0	3.4	2.8	4.3
13.	Change in real hourly compensation[c]	1.3	3.6	−1.3	0.9	4.5	2.7	3.4	1.7	0.6
14.	Change in unit labor cost from year earlier[c]	4.2	1.4	0.1	1.1	2.7	0.8	3.4	1.7	−1.9
15.	Labor union membership (millions)[d]	16.7	16.4	16.7	16.3	16.2	16.5	16.3	16.3	16
16.	Union membership as percentage of nonagricultural workers	15.3	15.1	14.7	13.7	12.9	12.8	12.3	12.1	11.9
17.	Work stoppages	44	35	45	37	34	17	39	29	19
18.	Strike time as percentage of total work time[e]	0.02	0.01	0.02	0.02	0.02	0.01	0.06	0.005	0.005
19.	Employee compensation as a percent of national income	66.6	67.0	65.5	64.3	64.8	65.2	65.9	66.0	65.3

[a]Civilian. [b]Total private, nonagricultural industries. [c]Business sector. [d]Includes members of professional associations, 1970–2008. [e]Days idle in strikes involving 1,000 or more workers divided by total estimated working time.
na = not available.

2003	2004	2005	2006	2007	2008	2009	2010	2011	2012	2013	2014	2015	2016	2017	2018
221.2	223.4	226.1	228.8	231.9	233.8	235.8	237.8	239.6	243.3	245.7	247.9	250.8	253.5	255.1	257.8
146.5	147.4	149.3	151.4	153.1	154.3	154.1	153.9	153.6	155.0	155.4	155.9	157.1	159.2	160.3	162.1
66.2	66.0	66.0	66.2	66.0	66.0	65.4	64.7	64.1	63.7	63.2	62.9	62.7	62.8	62.9	62.9
73.5	73.3	73.3	73.5	73.2	73.0	72	71.2	70.5	70.2	69.7	69.2	69.1	69.2	69.1	69.1
59.5	59.2	59.3	59.4	59.3	59.5	59.2	58.6	58.1	57.7	57.2	57.0	56.7	56.8	57	57.1
66.5	66.3	66.3	66.5	66.4	66.3	65.8	65.1	64.5	64.0	63.5	63.1	62.8	62.9	62.8	62.8
64.3	63.8	64.2	64.1	63.7	63.7	62.4	62.2	61.4	61.5	61.2	6.1	61.5	61.6	62.3	62.3
137.7	139.3	141.7	144.4	146.0	145.4	139.9	139.1	139.9	142.5	143.9	146.3	148.8	151.4	153.3	155.8
8.8	8.1	7.6	7.0	7.1	8.9	14.3	14.8	13.7	12.5	11.5	9.6	8.3	7.8	7.0	6.3
6.0	5.5	5.1	4.6	4.6	5.8	9.3	9.6	8.9	8.1	7.4	6.2	5.3	4.9	4.4	3.9
6.3	5.6	5.1	4.6	4.7	6.1	10.3	10.5	9.4	8.2	7.6	6.3	5.4	4.9	4.4	3.9
5.7	5.4	5.1	4.6	4.5	5.4	8.1	8.6	8.5	7.9	7.1	6.1	5.2	4.8	4.3	3.8
5.2	4.8	4.4	4.0	4.1	5.2	8.5	8.7	7.9	7.2	6.5	5.3	4.6	4.3	3.8	3.5
10.8	10.4	10.0	8.9	8.3	10.1	14.8	16	15.8	13.8	13.1	11.3	9.6	8.4	7.5	6.5
17.5	17.0	16.6	15.4	15.7	18.7	24.3	25.9	24.4	24.0	22.9	19.6	16.9	15.7	14.0	12.9
15.37	15.68	16.12	16.75	17.42	18.06	18.61	19.05	19.44	19.74	20.13	20.61	21.03	21.54	22.06	22.71
33.7	33.7	33.8	33.9	33.9	33.6	33.1	33.4	33.6	33.7	33.7	33.7	33.7	33.6	33.7	33.8
288	287	285	288	291	288	294	297	295	294	296	299	306	309	311	313
0.0%	−0.5%	−0.6%	1.0%	1.0%	−1.0%	2.1%	1.2%	−0.9%	−0.1%	0.4%	1.0%	2.4%	1.0%	0.5%	0.7%
5.15	5.15	5.15	5.15	5.85	6.55	7.25	7.25	7.25	7.25	7.25	7.25	7.25	7.25	7.25	7.25
3.9	3.0	2.2	1.1	1.6	1.0	3.6	3.3	−0.1	0.8	0.9	0.7	1.2	0.2	1.1	1.4
1.5	1.9	0.2	0.6	1.6	−1.1	1.2	0.1	−1.0	0.6	0.0	0.9	2.7	−0.2	1.3	0.3
−0.2	1.6	1.4	2.7	2.8	1.6	−2.7	−1.5	2.2	2.0	0.6	1.9	1.7	0.9	2.3	1.3
15.8	15.5	15.7	15.4	15.7	16.1	15.3	14.7	14.8	14.4	14.5	14.6	14.8	14.5	14.8	14.7
11.6	11.3	11.2	10.8	10.9	11.2	11.1	10.7	10.8	10.2	10.2	10.1	10.1	9.8	9.8	9.6
14	17	22	20	21	15	5	11	19	19	15	11	12	15	7	20
0.005	0.005	0.005	0.005	0.005	0.005	0.005	0.005	0.005	0.005	0.005	0.005	0.005	0.005	0.005	0.010
64.8	64.0	63.1	62.6	64.1	65.4	64.5	62.2	61.6	60.8	60.9	60.7	61.4	62.0	62.3	62.3